CQ's State Fact Finder

CQ's State Fact Finder 2007
Rankings Across America

Kendra A. Hovey

Harold A. Hovey

CQ PRESS

A Division of Congressional Quarterly Inc.
Washington, D.C.

To the memory of Harold A. Hovey

CQ Press
1255 22nd Street, NW, Suite 400
Washington, DC 20037

Phone: 202-729-1900; toll-free, 1-866-427-7737 (1-866-4CQ-PRESS)

Web: www.cqpress.com

Cover design: Vincent Hughes Visualization

⊗ The paper used in this publication exceeds the requirements of the American National Standard for Information Sciences—Permanence of Paper for Printed Library Materials, ANSI Z39.48-1992.

Printed and bound in the United States of America

11 10 09 08 07   1 2 3 4 5

ISBN 978-0-87289-495-2 (cloth)
ISBN 978-0-87289-496-9 (paper)
ISSN 1079-7149

Contents

Detailed Contents of Subject Rankings

Health

Crime and Law Enforcement

Transportation

Welfare

Technology

Introduction

CQ's State Fact Finder is an important source and analytical tool for anyone interested in developments and trends in the fifty U.S. states and the District of Columbia. It is an invaluable reference for researchers, whether policy specialists seeking detailed data or individuals wishing to learn more about today's social, political, and economic currents.

The U.S. economy, population, and governmental policy are constantly changing. Because these changes affect states differently, it is important that information be as up to date as possible. To meet that need, CQ Press publishes *State Fact Finder* annually. The 2007 volume is the thirteenth edition.

Many readers will want to reference previous volumes to identify long- and short-term trends. The tables and statistical concepts in this edition remain similar or comparable to those found in the first edition, published in 1993. They are so closely comparable in the 1996 through 2007 editions that readers can use them for statistical analyses of changes at the state level.

Readers and libraries can receive the next edition of *State Fact Finder* as soon as it is published by establishing a standing order with CQ Press. The data in this and previous editions are also available for purchase in electronic form directly from the authors (614-262-9229, sprhov@gmail.com).

About This Book

State Fact Finder is prepared by experts who analyze state policy and trends and compare states in ways important to policymakers, such as measuring the success of their efforts to promote economic development and the costs and apparent results of their decisions. This book differs considerably from ordinary compilations of statistics in several important ways.

First, *State Fact Finder* includes numerous statistics that are omitted from standard statistical reports of govern-ment agencies and therefore do not appear in compilations of statistics that rely solely on such published reports. For example, many of the tables in the Health and Welfare sections comparing state programs for low-income residents are based on unpublished statistics maintained by the agencies that administer these programs. Also, some tables, such as B-28, the Index of State Economic Momentum, and G-21, a comparison of state spending "needs," reflect original research by the authors.

Second, information from other sources has been converted to a basis that makes comparisons meaningful. For example, information on the headquarters of the largest companies in the United States, in Table B-17, includes the number of companies in each state in relation to population as well as the total number of companies.

Third, each table includes a ranking of the states. This makes it easy for readers to see how the state or states that interest them relate to neighboring states and to other states throughout the nation.

Fourth, the volume begins with an essay—"Finding Information Users Want to Know"—that guides researchers in the use of the data and helps them understand the scope of information available to them.

Fifth, each of the thirteen subject rankings sections begins with national and regional statistics relevant to the subject of that chapter. For instance, in this edition, the contents page of the Population section also includes graphical representations of estimated recent and projected population figures by race and ethnicity, as well as projections regarding the population aged sixty-five and older. Another table on this page reveals that the fastest-growing states are concentrated in the West and the South.

Sixth, *State Fact Finder* offers carefully documented source notes after the tables in each section. These notes cite the origins of the statistics in each table and guide researchers to sources where they can obtain additional information on the subject.

About the Publisher

State Fact Finder was first published in 1993 by Congressional Quarterly Inc., which provides comprehensive, reliable, and focused information on national public policy and political issues in the United States. *State Fact Finder* and *Governing*, a magazine covering all aspects of state government, were part of CQ's effort to offer expanded coverage of developments and trends in the states. CQ Press, a division of Congressional Quarterly, has published *State Fact Finder* since 2000.

About the Authors

Harold A. Hovey was the founder and president of State Policy Research and Kendra A. Hovey is the current president of the company, which government experts nationwide know as one of the most reliable and knowledgeable organizations dealing with state-level information. For more than fifteen years, the authors, through State Policy Research, published the periodicals *State Policy Reports* and *State Budget & Tax News*. For a decade they published *States in Profile*, which merged into *State Fact Finder*.

Information Development

Any data book is by definition a work in progress. What is useful one year may be less relevant the next year, as information needs change. For this reason, the authors of *State Fact Finder* welcome reactions from readers, suggestions for additional information or changes in presentation, and of course any corrections or clarifications that come to readers' attention. Please direct these to Kendra Hovey at State Policy Research (sprhov@gmail.com).

"State Fiscal Snapshot 2007"

Midway through fiscal year 2007, state officials are no longer worrying about the type of shortfalls and overruns that plagued states earlier in the decade. Just as in fiscal year 2006, revenues are on target, and expenditures are, for the most part, in line with appropriations. The budget situation is stable. Yet recent robust growth is showing signs of tapering, and regional differences in economic vitality continue to persist. For officials in most states, it appears to be another year of cautious optimism.

"State Fiscal Snapshot 2007" provides a glimpse into the immediate budget situation in the states by presenting the best information as of January 2007 on state tax revenues and spending appropriations.

"Finding Information Users Want to Know"

Readers differ in their preferences on many things—from what they value in a place to live to the amount of state government spending they consider appropriate. They might also disagree on such subjects as where they should move or which state is governed best.

In this section, rather than imposing personal values as though they were facts by ranking some states as the "best places" to live or do business and so on, the authors provide guideposts on how to use the tables so that readers can obtain the information they need. Using a question-and-answer format, this section leads readers to groups of tables that can be consulted together to deal with broad issues, such as school quality or business opportunities.

This section is divided into three parts, each based on particular types of decisions that people might make. The first covers personal and family decisions, such as those concerning job opportunities. The second focuses on business decisions, such as where to locate a new plant. The third provides information about the government to assist residents in voting and in influencing public policy.

Subject Rankings

The subject rankings section forms the heart of the book. It is organized into thirteen subject areas that are challenging policymakers throughout the country: population, economies, geography, government, federal impacts, taxes, revenues and finances, education, health, crime and law enforcement, transportation, welfare, and technology. States are listed alphabetically in each table. The information also is presented in rankings that allow readers to see how each state compares with the others.

Source Notes

The source notes that follow each section are designed for use in tandem with the subject rankings to understand the specific usefulness of, and any caveats about, the data. The sources for all statistics are documented so that the calculations can be replicated or expanded upon by those who need more detail than space allows here. These source notes also help readers locate other information and sources that may be useful.

State Rankings

The state rankings section presents a composite view of each state, bringing together rankings on most of the data in the volume. This compilation provides brief summaries of states' positions in each subject area.

The Data

Rankings: There is nothing magical about rankings, although *State Fact Finder* generally follows the statistical convention of ranking from highest to lowest. Most rankings can be interpreted similarly by reversing them. For example, a table showing tax burdens from highest to lowest provides the same information when reversed to show tax burdens from lowest to highest by ranking the fiftieth state first, the forty-ninth state second, and so on.

Data Accuracy: The statistics in this volume vary greatly in their accuracy. Some, such as the land area of states or the number of state legislators, can be measured precisely. Other data, such as birth rates or finances of local governments, are estimates. The source notes generally explain how the data were developed or direct readers to the statistical providers, who usually make available detailed technical papers on their methods.

Ranking Positions and Ties: In preparing this book, the authors worked with data as presented by the statistical source. In presenting the data in tables, figures were rounded to a manageable number of digits, for example $24.5 million rather than $24,515,078. As a result, the rankings based on detailed data may show one state ranked above another even though they are apparently tied in the data published in the table.

In some tables, adding the fifty-state total to the total for the District of Columbia will not yield the U.S. total that appears in the last row. In such cases, the original source included figures for U.S. territories in the U.S. total. *State Fact Finder* cites these U.S. totals as originally recorded, without the subtraction of the territories' figures.

Junk Data: Many special interest groups have strong opinions about appropriate policies for governments. They sometimes translate these opinions into rankings of which states are "best" in their areas of interest, such as protecting the environment, providing mental health services, or maintaining a favorable climate for business. The resulting statistics are not always reliable. Sometimes they combine individually reliable statistics into measures that simply reflect the policy preferences of those who rank the composite results. *State Fact Finder* generally avoids inclusion of such reports.

Time Periods: Each table covers a specific time period, which is indicated in the heading and is normally a calendar year or span of years. In the case of fiscal data, the time periods are fiscal years that end in the year shown.

District of Columbia: The District of Columbia has a unique status in statistical compilations. It is not a state in the sense of having voting representatives in Congress—its citizens have none—and it is counted as a city, not a state, in all U.S. Census Bureau statistics on government finances. Federal agencies and private data-gathering organizations differ in how they treat the District, as well as Puerto Rico, the Virgin Islands, and other territories, in their statistics.

State Fact Finder presents information for the District of Columbia in each table but does not include it in the state rankings. The reasons are twofold. First, users of rankings find its inclusion cumbersome to explain, often having to resort to complicated explanations of rankings (such as a state being ranked fifth, fourth among states and also behind the District of Columbia). Second, the District is economically and demographically a central city with fiscal and other attributes of most central cities (such as high taxes, high crime rates, large percentages of the population in poverty and receiving government benefits, and so forth). When ranked alongside states, the District often ranks first or last in the tables, distorting other rankings.

State Fiscal Snapshot 2007

Midway into fiscal year 2007, the states are on solid fiscal ground. Overall, collections are in line with expectations and tax revenues continue to grow. Compared to fiscal year 2006, the pace of growth has slowed. During that year, all but six states reported revenues *above* the budgeted target, and sales, personal income, and corporate income taxes brought in more robust returns. Even so, while the rate has slowed this year, growth is still growth—and is always good news for state finances.

Regional disparites persist. Although new jobs are being created in the United States, job growth varies by region. According to the Fiscal Studies Program at the Nelson A. Rockefeller Institute of Government, the states in the Far West, Southwest, and Rocky Mountain regions of the country "accounted for nearly 50 percent of the nation's job growth in the third quarter [of calendar year 2006] compared to the same period one year ago, while having about 30 percent of the total jobs." Over the same period, two states—Michigan and Louisi-ana—lost jobs, while job growth was slight in the Great Lakes (0.5%) and New England (0.6%) states.

The next three pages offer a snapshot of the immediate fiscal situation in the fifty states. The data are useful and timely but differ from the rest of the statistics in *State Fact Finder* in that they are best read as a measure of the situation in individual states rather than as a measure for comparing states. In addition, the data collected here cover state—not state and local—taxes and spending. The data come from the Fiscal Studies Program at the Nelson A. Rockefeller Institute of Government and the National Association of State Budget Officers.

Annual State General Fund Spending Increase, FY 2006–2007		
Spending Growth	**Number of States**	
	FY 2006 (preliminary actual)	**FY 2007 (appropriated)**
Negative Growth	3	4
0.0% to 4.9%	8	15
5.0% to 9.9%	26	17
10% or more	13	14

Source: National Association of State Budget Officers

Revenue Outlook for the Remainder of the Fiscal Year		
Outlook	**Number of States**	
	FY 2006 as of Nov. 05	**FY 2007 as of Nov. 06**
Optimistic	22	16
Stable	26	28
Concerned	1	6
Pessimistic	1	0

Source: National Conference of State Legislatures

Year-over-Year Change in Quarterly Personal Income Tax Revenue, July to September 2005 to 2006	
Region	**Percent**
New England	6.0
Mid-Atlantic	5.5
Great Lakes	4.6
Plains	6.3
Southeast	6.0
Southwest	4.5
Rocky Mountain	11.5
Far West	9.4

Source: The Nelson A. Rockefeller Institute of Government

Year-over-Year Change in Quarterly Non-Farm Employment, July to September 2005 to 2006	
Region	**Percent**
New England	0.6
Mid-Atlantic	0.9
Great Lakes	0.5
Plains	1.6
Southeast	1.6
Southwest	2.7
Rocky Mountain	3.2
Far West	1.9
United States	1.3

Source: The Nelson A. Rockefeller Institute of Government

State Tax Revenues

The Nelson A. Rockefeller Institute of Government's Fiscal Studies Program collects these numbers from state taxation agencies and analyzes the data as consistently as possible. It then publishes the data in State Revenue Report, which it updates quarterly, usually in March, June, September, and December.

Percent Change in Quarterly Tax Revenue by State, July to September 2005 to 2006	
	%
Alabama	10.5
Alaska	23.9
Arizona	8.2 ***
Arkansas	7.1
California	5.5
Colorado	7.4
Connecticut	0.3 ***
Delaware	-1.2
Florida	0.5
Georgia	5.4
Hawaii	-2.1
Idaho	6.7
Illinois	6.3
Indiana	5.4
Iowa	5.9
Kansas	9.7
Kentucky	2.6
Louisiana	No Data
Maine	3.9
Maryland	2.0
Massachusetts	3.9
Michigan	-3.3
Minnesota	-1.9
Mississippi	18.1
Missouri	2.1
Montana	No Data
Nebraska	0.2 ***
Nevada	3.2
New Hampshire	1.9
New Jersey	1.7 *
New Mexico	19.5
New York	3.9 ***
North Carolina	9.7
North Dakota	No Data
Ohio	-1.8 ***
Oklahoma	8.8
Oregon	8.2
Pennsylvania	4.9
Rhode Island	4.5
South Carolina	7.4 *
South Dakota	6.1
Tennessee	3.9
Texas	5.9 ***
Utah	11.5 ***
Vermont	-2.4 *
Virginia	6.3
Washington	10.7 *
West Virginia	-1.7
Wisconsin	3.4
Wyoming	11.6 ***
United States	4.6

Percent Change in Quarterly Tax Revenue by State, Adjusted for Legislation and Inflation, July to September 2005 to 2006	
	%
Alabama	5.9
Alaska	18.7
Arizona	8.0
Arkansas	2.6
California	1.1
Colorado	3.1
Connecticut	-3.0
Delaware	-5.1
Florida	-3.1
Georgia	1.5
Hawaii	-6.2
Idaho	2.2
Illinois	1.6
Indiana	0.3
Iowa	1.4
Kansas	5.5
Kentucky	-1.9
Louisiana	No Data
Maine	-0.4
Maryland	-2.0
Massachusetts	-0.5
Michigan	-7.4
Minnesota	-5.6
Mississippi	13.1
Missouri	-2.2
Montana	No Data
Nebraska	-3.1
Nevada	-1.1
New Hampshire	-2.4
New Jersey	-10.9
New Mexico	No Data
New York	5.9
North Carolina	5.1
North Dakota	No Data
Ohio	-1.6
Oklahoma	4.2
Oregon	3.6
Pennsylvania	0.8
Rhode Island	0.4
South Carolina	-0.7
South Dakota	1.6
Tennessee	-0.6
Texas	4.8
Utah	9.5
Vermont	-7.6
Virginia	2.0
Washington	4.9
West Virginia	-5.8
Wisconsin	-1.0
Wyoming	7.9
United States	1.1

*   Indicates legislation and/or accounting changes significantly increased tax receipts.
*** Indicates legislation/accounting changes significantly decreased tax receipts.

Percent Change in Quarterly Tax Revenue by State, July to September 2005 to 2006		
	Personal Income Tax	**Corporate Income Tax**	**Sales Tax**
	%	%	%
Alabama	8.7	30.2	9.1
Alaska	n/a	34.2	n/a
Arizona	7.6 ***	14.4 ***	9.6
Arkansas	8.9	10.3	6.4
California	10.2	4.7	0.8
Colorado	9.9	1.9	5.3
Connecticut	6.3 ***	43.1 ***	-16.0
Delaware	8.3	-9.6 ***	n/a
Florida	n/a	7.6	4.1
Georgia	8.9	-18.0	3.9 ***
Hawaii	-0.1	-66.0	4.5
Idaho	12.5	16.1	3.2
Illinois	8.0	24.5	2.6
Indiana	7.5	10.1	3.5
Iowa	3.8	50.6	2.8
Kansas	10.5	50.6	3.8
Kentucky	-3.8	43.8	1.2
Louisiana	No Data	No Data	No Data
Maine	0.5	21.8	3.4
Maryland	0.0	-9.2	2.3
Massachusetts	6.1	17.9	-0.8
Michigan	3.4	-4.3	-6.6
Minnesota	4.2 ***	6.7	0.3
Mississippi	17.7	37.4	21.4
Missouri	7.2	-0.2	1.7
Montana	No Data	No Data	No Data
Nebraska	10.7	15.2	27.8 ***
Nevada	n/a	n/a	3.0
New Hampshire	n/a	59.3	n/a
New Jersey	-1.6	8.8 *	12.2 *
New Mexico	-4.7	7.9	34.1
New York	7.2 ***	14.9 ***	-4.7 ***
North Carolina	8.9	15.7	6.0
North Dakota	No Data	No Data	No Data
Ohio	0.7 ***	5,540.0	-5.3 ***
Oklahoma	4.9	51.5	8.9
Oregon	5.5	7.5	n/a
Pennsylvania	8.2	10.8 ***	1.9
Rhode Island	9.1	31.0 ***	-0.3
South Carolina	8.8	22.5	13.7
South Dakota	n/a	n/a	5.1
Tennessee	n/a	3.3	5.0
Texas	n/a	n/a	10.6
Utah	14.4 ***	42.7	6.5 ***
Vermont	7.4	-31.9	3.5
Virginia	1.6	20.5 ***	23.6
Washington	n/a	n/a	8.7
West Virginia	-4.8	20.1	-3.6
Wisconsin	4.4	9.0	3.2
Wyoming	n/a	n/a	15.8 ***
United States	6.6	10.9	4.0

Overall, revenues slowed in the first quarter of the 2007 fiscal year. Compared to the previous quarter, growth weakened in all three of the major taxes. However, for now, tax collections are meeting expectations in most states. Data are from the Nelson A. Rockefeller Institute of Government's Fiscal Studies Program.

*   Indicates legislation/accounting changes significantly increased tax receipts.
*** Indicates legislation/accounting changes significantly decreased tax receipts.

State Budgets

Forty-seven states maintain budget stabilization funds, also called "rainy-day" funds. More than half of them limit the upper amount of such funds to a certain percentage of appropriations. These reserves, together with year-ending balances, help states weather unforeseen difficulties and economic downturns. In late 2006, the National Association of State Budget Officers (NASBO) reported that "healthy state revenues, even amid substantial spending pressure, have allowed states to begin to rebuild their budget reserves." The stabilization fund and appropriations data, which reflect the budget situation at the end of 2006, are from NASBO's Fiscal Survey of the States, December 2006.

Appropriated Budget Stabilization Fund, FY 2007	$ (in millions)	Percentage Change in Spending, Actual 2005–Appropriated 2006	%
Alabama	658	Alabama	15.0
Alaska	2,597	Alaska	6.3
Arizona	663	Arizona	18.6
Arkansas	0	Arkansas	5.4
California	2,102	California	16.2
Colorado	0	Colorado	16.1
Connecticut	1,273	Connecticut	6.2
Delaware	176	Delaware	12.7
Florida	1,226	Florida	11.0
Georgia	904	Georgia	9.4
Hawaii	61	Hawaii	11.8
Idaho	109	Idaho	5.1
Illinois	276	Illinois	9.1
Indiana	443	Indiana	3.4
Iowa	535	Iowa	9.1
Kansas	0	Kansas	9.6
Kentucky	231	Kentucky	9.6
Louisiana	683	Louisiana	8.6
Maine	110	Maine	3.1
Maryland	1,407	Maryland	9.6
Massachusetts	2,160	Massachusetts	7.6
Michigan	2	Michigan	4.5
Minnesota	1,095	Minnesota	8.8
Mississippi	207	Mississippi	9.8
Missouri	247	Missouri	0.1
Montana	0	Montana	15.9
Nebraska	516	Nebraska	7.2
Nevada	218	Nevada	-6.0
New Hampshire	69	New Hampshire	0.7
New Jersey	449	New Jersey	-2.6
New Mexico	1,132	New Mexico	14.6
New York	944	New York	6.6
North Carolina	629	North Carolina	8.0
North Dakota	100	North Dakota	6.9
Ohio	1,012	Ohio	0.1
Oklahoma	n/a	Oklahoma	11.9
Oregon	0	Oregon	35.6
Pennsylvania	513	Pennsylvania	7.1
Rhode Island	99	Rhode Island	5.9
South Carolina	168	South Carolina	11.2
South Dakota	137	South Dakota	6.7
Tennessee	497	Tennessee	8.3
Texas	1,214	Texas	8.7
Utah	255	Utah	6.2
Vermont	55	Vermont	7.3
Virginia	1,388	Virginia	9.7
Washington	0	Washington	11.5
West Virginia	213	West Virginia	4.4
Wisconsin	0	Wisconsin	4.4
Wyoming	536	Wyoming	-4.4
United States	27,306	United States	8.7

Finding Information Users
Want to Know

Most people look to state statistics to answer questions related to a decision they need to make, but they often discover in the process that the statistics they seek do not appear in the reference books they consult. Or, they may find some comparisons that seem to be relevant but then wonder whether they really are.

"Finding Information Users Want to Know"—a list of frequently asked questions—is a feature not found in other compilations of state data. The answer to each question includes information about which tables in *State Fact Finder* should be helpful and provides road maps to other statistics that might be of use. Readers are also made aware when the statistics they seek are not available or not reliable and why that is so.

This section is divided into three parts, each based on particular ways people might use state statistics: to make personal and family decisions, such as finding the states with the best job opportunities, the best health care, and even the best chances for finding a spouse; to make business decisions, such as where to locate a new business or where to find the most productive workers; and to gather information about government to assist them in their roles as voters and in influencing public policy.

About Personal Decisions on Where to Live or Visit

1. Where is the best place to find a job?

As a general rule, it is easier to get a job, better pay, and increased opportunities for advancement and building professional practices in a state with a rapidly expanding economy. Places in economic decline have fewer job opportunities, and stiff competition exists for the few positions available.

To find states with rapidly expanding economies, look at measures of recent economic growth, particularly the Index of State Economic Momentum (B-28), population growth (A-3), job growth (B-29, B-30), projections of future population growth (A-5), and new companies (B-34). The Index of State Economic Momentum (B-28) is especially useful because it summarizes the three elements of economic growth important to job seekers: population growth, income growth, and increasing numbers of jobs. For positions in high-tech industries, consult the tables in the Technology section (M). High-tech jobs (M-4) and changes in high-tech jobs (M-5) help pinpoint recent hot spots in the industry.

Growth rates are particularly important to note when seeking jobs that are inherently related to growth, such as those in the construction industry. Because the need for construction correlates with changes in the demand for homes and other buildings, there are vast differences in the availability of such jobs in fast- versus slow-growing states. For example, in 2005 there were twenty new homes being built for every 1,000 residents of Nevada but only three new homes for every 1,000 residents of Rhode Island (B-20).

When a state is classified as growing rapidly, it does not necessarily mean that all areas in the state are growing at a fast pace. For example, rapid growth in Nevada is concentrated in the Las Vegas area. To determine which areas are growing and in what types of industries and jobs, consult local sources, such as state economic development departments, local chambers of commerce, or even friends familiar with the area. For nationwide statistics on growth in metropolitan areas, obtain information on recent job growth from the Bureau of Labor Statistics (www.stats.bls.gov). The Department of Commerce (www.commerce.gov) supplies somewhat less current statistics on income and other economic factors, including *County Business Patterns*, an annual series of detailed reports on major counties (www.census.gov/prod/www/abs/cbptotal. html). More general statistics can be found at "State and County QuickFacts" (http://quickfacts.census.gov/qfd) on the U.S. Census Bureau's Web site.

2. Where will tax burdens be least for me and my family?

The tables in the Taxes section (F) are good guides for averaging tax burdens. Table F-1 shows what share of personal income goes toward state and local taxes. Tables F-6, F-9, and F-13 do this for each of the major taxes: property, sales, and personal income. The range among states is great. For example, New York governments take 14.6 percent of income in state and local taxes, while governments in Alabama take 8.9 percent.

The taxes actually paid will depend on individual circumstances, such as property owned in relation to income. Note the differences in Tables F-16 and F-24. For example, wealthy retirees might prefer to live in Florida and Texas, which have no income, inheritance, or estate taxes. A young couple without much income, however, might consider it a burden to pay those states' heavy sales taxes. If they rent their home, they will not share in special property tax breaks for homeowners. For them, a state like Oregon, which has no sales tax but steep income taxes, might be a better deal.

While state government taxes are uniform throughout a state, local taxes vary greatly from place to place within the state. The fifty states each have on average some 1,000 different local governments, which means that there are approximately 50,000 local governments with the power to set tax rates.

Depending on the locality, property taxes may be the sum of any number of individual taxes that may be levied by the following authorities: a county; a municipality or township; a school district; perhaps a second school district, such as a community college or vocational district; and hosts of special districts, such as road districts, transit districts, mosquito control districts, and levee districts. Local governments in many states also levy sales taxes, and a few local governments—for example, those of Philadelphia and New York—have significant local income taxes. The state averages cited in this volume reflect all these taxes.

As a general rule, it is easier to get a job, better pay, and increased opportunities for advancement and building professional practices in a state with a rapidly expanding economy.

To find local areas with low taxes within a state, look for places that take in large amounts of tax revenues from businesses but have a small population to serve. Also, most metropolitan areas have suburbs with concentrations of office buildings, shopping centers, and businesses; their property taxes are often much lower than those of surrounding areas. Realtors in metropolitan regions can identify such areas. The county officials responsible for collecting property taxes can provide rate information for that locality. Most state tax departments, with offices in state capitals and major cities, publish free booklets outlining all state taxes and tax rates.

3. Which state has the best public schools?

To compare student achievement across states, consider the first five tables in the Education section (H). Use Tables H-1 and H-2 for overall comparisons, H-3 for high school students who are not going immediately to college, and H-4 and H-5 for how well schools are preparing students to meet standards for college admission. Also use the tables to compare state per-student spending (H-15), teacher salaries (H-16), class sizes (H-9), and more.

Except in Hawaii, all public schools are locally administrated. Great variation is found within areas in the same state; it is as important as the variation from state to state. All state education departments, located in state capitals, keep statistics on spending and the number of teachers and pupils in each school district. Because of the No Child Left Behind Act of 2001, all states issue "report cards" comparing district performance measures, such as how students do on standardized tests. State departments of education usually make these available on their Web sites. Use these or research locally such indicators as percentage of graduates attending college, percentage of students winning National Merit Scholarships and other awards, and reputation for being a good (or not so good) school.

Student achievement depends heavily on how much help and motivation students get at home as well as on what happens at school. Much of the difference among states results from differences among the students rather than variation in the schools. This is true for districts within a state as well.

One key to accessing a good education is getting a child into the right school, not just the right school district. Some of the best specialized programs and some of the worst schools are both found in central cities.

Parents and guardians who want to send children to private schools should not expect much help from governments. Many states are considering "voucher" plans that help with tuition, but thus far only Florida, Ohio, Rhode Island, Utah, Wisconsin, and the District of Columbia make these available. Their programs mostly serve poor, inner-city children; Utah's program serves special education students. Arizona, Florida, Illinois, Iowa, Minnesota, and Pennsylvania provide limited income tax breaks for private school tuition. The voucher programs in Maine and Vermont serve only students in rural areas without public schools.

4. Which state is best for children?

Many tables throughout *State Fact Finder* compare states on aspects of life important to children and people raising children, including health, education, crime, and economic opportunity. The Children's Defense Fund (www.childrensdefense.org) and the Annie E. Casey Foundation (www.aecf.org) in its annual *Kids Count Data Book* provide even more detailed comparisons than the ones available here.

Children grow up in small worlds, such as school buildings and neighborhoods, so one should not rely completely on facts about states, metropolitan areas, or even individual cities and counties when researching information important to a child's life. A child's community is often much more important than the larger geographical area.

5. Which is the best state for retirement?

Most people retire within twenty miles of where they lived when they stopped working. Thus, finding the right place is often more a matter of finding the right house or apartment in the right community than finding the right state. *State Fact Finder* can be helpful in finding a home in a different state, but additional research is necessary to make an informed decision.

In looking for a new state, it is best to start with personal preference, rather than statistical comparisons (unless the overriding concern is minimizing tax payments). Decide first what is an acceptable distance from family and friends. Next, think about climate issues, such as dealing with ice or not having a change in seasons at all. Making such decisions initially considerably narrows the range of choices. Taking a "preference inventory," such as that found in *Frommer's Retirement Places Rated*, by David Savageau, requires one to consider such issues as whether being able to get a part-time job, attend a symphony orchestra, follow a professional sports team, and take advantage of other opportunities are important issues in terms of where one lives.

The tables in *State Fact Finder* reveal systematic differences among states in such characteristics as income and education levels of residents, living costs, crime, and taxes. Table F-25 in the Taxes section, for instance, contains information on how different state tax systems treat retirement income.

Many other books can help with retirement location decisions. A library or good bookstore should be able to recommend useful references. Some describe places to live and provide information on investments, Medicare, and estate planning. Others deal only with places to retire, often with different emphases, such as culture and lifetime learning. Still others focus on specialized retirement areas, like Florida and Hilton Head, South Carolina, but typically not New York City or any place in Ohio.

AARP is a good source for a variety of publications on retirement. The organization also posts an online retirement checklist that allows comparison of states using twenty different lifestyle factors, including housing prices, sense of community, and even cell phone coverage (www.aarpmagazine.org/bestplaces).

6. Which state universities are best?

State Fact Finder contains important statistics for selecting among state university systems. (See Tables H-19 to H-27.) State statistics alone cannot help determine which university to attend, because state systems include everything from community colleges to medical schools. California even has systems within systems. Its schools vary from the University of California (with campuses at Berkeley and elsewhere and featuring some of the finest institutions in the country) to California State University (which enjoys less of a national reputation but has outstanding specialized programs) to community colleges with diverse and varying strengths and weaknesses.

Students attend schools, not states. Consult guides and ratings of individual schools that provide information on the numbers of students, type of curriculum, costs, and attempted assessments of the quality of students and faculty.

7. Which state has the best cultural attractions and recreation?

Statistics cannot adequately measure recreational opportunities. Attempts to do so often are misleading. For example, Alaska has by far the best ratio of parkland to people, but much of the state is covered by glaciers unfit for hiking or camping by the average recreational user. Some fine experiences—the "big sky" of Montana, the bustle of the streets of New York, and the beauty of fall foliage in New England—cannot be quantified.

Fairly good statistics document how many people participate in various sports in each state. See, for example, Table C-6 on hunting. The table's notes at the end of the chapter provide information on how to obtain information on other sports. Most sports have specialized equipment stores, magazines, and guidebooks that offer information superior to state statistics for making personal recreational choices. For example, the existence of more golfers and courses per capita in a high-ranking state does not mean there would be trouble finding more than enough courses or players to make foursomes in lower-ranked states.

Guidebooks and specialized magazines often track and rate cultural opportunities. Government spending on the arts, shown in Table C-8, is not a useful indicator of the extent or the quality of arts in each state. On average, annual per capita state funding of the arts is about $1, an amount dwarfed by sales revenues, admissions, and donations.

8. Where is the best place to invest in property?

It is hard to pick a winner in a field of losers, and hard to pick a loser in a field of winners. Everybody wants to pick the right state (and area in that state) for their investment.

The old saw about the three keys to real estate investment—location, location, location—applies to states and metropolitan areas within states. For example, statistics in Table B-21, from the Office of Federal Housing Enterprise Oversight, show that in the five years from 2001 to 2006, the average house in Florida appreciated by 113 percent while the average home in Indiana increased in value by 17 percent. Of course, how much an investment will lose or appreciate depends on the property bought, whether the price was right, and local market conditions.

Supply and demand drive real estate prices. Supply does not decrease much in poor markets; who would tear down a house or office building because of decreasing values? Supply responds to increased demand in good markets. Prices still rise because new construction often costs more than established buildings, and prices of lots and construction labor tend to rise. The most desirable locations generally already have buildings on them, so their value will tend to increase regardless of competition from new construction.

The best strategy for real estate investment is to pick an area with an expanding economy, where large numbers of new jobs are being created. See the answer to Question 1 above concerning where to find a job for tips on using *State Fact Finder* to identify such places.

9. Can picking the right states help pick winners in stocks and bonds?

Few economists or investment professionals would suggest purchasing a company's stock based on the state or states in which its headquarters or plants are found. Rather, what matters are product quality and marketing. Some successful companies operate from unlikely places. For example, rural Maine hosts retailer L. L. Bean, and Bentonville, Arkansas, continues to be the base for Wal-Mart, one of the world's largest companies.

For making things, a fast-growing economy represents bad news, not good news. Fast-growing economies make it harder to get and keep good labor, workers' pay is often higher than pay in slow-growing economies, and congestion often plagues transportation facilities. Look for strong state and regional economies only when looking for regionally oriented companies that sell products, such as new homes and fast food, directly to consumers.

Most people who buy tax-exempt bonds do so through mutual funds or rely on bond-rating agencies, such as Standard & Poor's and Moody's. These professional investors rely heavily on the kinds of economic, population, and government statistics found in *State Fact Finder* and analyses of recent fiscal developments in publications like *State Policy Reports*. People who buy individual bonds or buy mutual funds of tax-exempt bonds issued by a single state can use these same statistics.

10. Which state government will interfere least with my freedom?

People occasionally say they would like to live where government interferes little in their daily lives. It is difficult to compare levels of government intrusiveness, because governments often restrict the freedom of some citizens in order to enhance that of others. The ultimate example is capital punishment—the most intrusive of acts carried out against one person in the name of providing freedom from fear and crime for everyone else. State policies are not necessarily consistent on intrusiveness issues. For example, the states most likely to allow residents to own weapons without restriction usually prove least likely to allow residents to grow marijuana on their own property for personal consumption.

Some elements of government intrusiveness can be measured. One is taxes, measured by the many comparisons in the Taxes section (F).

Another way to look at intrusiveness involves the ratio of state and local government employees to population (D-13). For those who find local governments more accessible and less intrusive than state government, a useful measure would be the differences in state and local roles as indicated by public employees (D-15) and revenue raising (D-16).

11. Where are taxes likely to go up/down in the future?

Tax rates are set by state legislatures and local bodies (such as school boards, city councils, county commissions, etc.). Predicting where taxes will be raised or lowered would appear to be a matter of forecasting the views of those who now serve on or will subsequently be elected to these bodies. The economic and population statistics in *State Fact Finder* provide some excellent clues to future tax rates, as does commonsense thinking about why some states have higher taxes than others.

Right now, the states with the lowest taxes on residents are those that raise substantial sums of money from other sources—tourists, oil and gas, and gaming casinos, for example. Alaska, Nevada, Texas, and Wyoming are amply endowed with one or more of these sources. As a result, these four states have succeeded in maintaining low taxes while still offering extensive government services. Some states have managed to keep taxes on their residents relatively low because they attract new residents who pay substantial taxes but do not have children in public schools, which constitute a large portion of state and local spending. Fast-growing states of the Southwest and Florida are the best such examples.

These same states will, however, be under the strongest pressure to raise tax levels in the future. Mathematics

People occasionally say they would like to live where government interferes little in their daily lives. It is difficult to compare levels of government intrusiveness, because governments often restrict the freedom of some citizens in order to enhance that of others.

dictates that as more people move to a state, the amount that its unique resource—be it oil, casinos, or something else—contributes to revenues per resident drops. Furthermore, as time passes, state populations become more like the national average. For example, the childless young people who flocked to Florida in large numbers to work at tourist attractions and to provide health care and other services to retirees are having children in large numbers, which, in turn, is putting more pressure on the public education system.

12. Which states have the least/most pollution?

State Fact Finder presents summary statistics on air and water pollution and hazardous waste (Tables C-10 to C-14). More important, the notes to the tables provide leads for finding more information on local areas. State averages are misleading if used to determine where to live or visit. For example, western cities, like Denver and Salt Lake City, have some of the nation's worst air pollution problems, but outside these urban areas the air is about as pure as it can get. An average for California that lumps downtown Los Angeles with the forests of northern California and the state's deserts presents a misleading overall picture as well.

13. Where do I find the best health care?

Because much more money is spent in gathering state-by-state statistics on health and health care (section I), these figures tend to be quite comprehensive compared with statistics in other fields. The statistics in *State Fact Finder* cover (1) the health of average people in a state's population, (2) apparent availability of care, (3) cost of care, and (4) government programs, which are generally oriented toward poor people. These statistics suggest strong concentrations of health professionals in northeastern states.

People seeking adequate health care for themselves and their family need not be guided by these statistics. For most people health care decisions are limited by health insurers. Because insurers will not pay for long-distance travel and hotel bills except in rare cases, doctors capable of performing all types of procedures and operations have been locating in areas wherever patients are found. One result is the development of top-flight facilities across the country, such as the University of Iowa hospital, which serves as a specialized facility for patients throughout that state, and the medical complex around Birmingham, Alabama. There is no reason to avoid an entire state because of concerns about health care, unless someone has a very specialized medical problem. Where people decide to locate within a state poses the primary limits on access to health care. People who seek near-wilderness isolation by buying ranches in Colorado or residing on small islands in the Atlantic Ocean must accept the consequences of their isolation in terms of the availability of health care services.

Those utilizing public health care services, such as Medicaid, will find differences in the generosity of state programs. Despite federal minimum requirements, states retain some leeway regarding eligibility requirements, promotion of the program, and additional services offered, such as vision and dental programs. Tables I-12, I-13, I-16, I-17, I-18, and I-22 are good sources of information on state Medicaid programs. Keep in mind that recent adjustments to these programs have been rapid and numerous, and that in response to burgeoning health care costs and federal actions, states have been making cuts in public health care programs.

14. Where will I be safest from crime?

State statistics, and even city statistics, on crime are not much help in looking for a safe place to live. In every state, crime is most prevalent in the low-income areas of central cities. Violent crimes are most prevalent in these areas after dark. Thus, reported crime statistics overstate the risk of crime for people who do not spend evenings in low-income central city areas. A high crime rate for an entire state says more about the percentage of a state's population living in such areas than about safety in that state's suburban, small town, and rural areas as compared with similar areas in other states.

City and state crime rates are also misleading when used to consider which places are safe to visit on business or for recreation. All crime statistics that relate a crime category to population use nighttime population figures, that is, the number of people who have regular beds in a city or state. But cities also have daytime commuters and business and vacation travelers. Florida, Hawaii, and Nevada, for instance, have lots of vacationers and conference attendees. Adding these temporary inhabitants to the denominator would certainly decrease crime rates in cities and in these states.

15. Where is the best place to look for a mate?

People looking for a partner of the opposite sex can reasonably expect better opportunities in locations where they are outnumbered by persons of the opposite sex (A-18). Aggregate statistics can, however, be misleading for people under fifty-five looking for a partner around their own age. Because women live longer than men, the states with predominately older populations (A-7) also tend to have high ratios of women to men. Careful work by several women on the Federal Reserve Bank of Boston's research staff found the worst sex ratios—from the standpoint of women seeking men—in older northeastern cities and the states with a high percentage of jobs in health care, government, and financial services, which are disproportionately filled by women. The best ratios from the perspective of women seeking men were in booming western states, where economic growth has drawn large numbers of young men to such occupations as mining and construction.

16. Where can I find the lowest living costs?

State Fact Finder presents the best information available for use in comparative living costs (B-8), but the data must be used with care. For reasons cited in the table notes, these measures are not appropriate for what they try to measure—average living costs—but they represent the best data to be found. Also, substantial variation exists within states. All costs, except state and local taxes, run about the same in all midsize cities and rural areas throughout the nation. Taxes (see section F) and costs related to economic growth (section B) make for the biggest differences.

In booming communities and states, housing prices soar, wage rates tend to be higher, and ample and growing sales discourage everyone, from doctors to owners of corner stores, from engaging in price wars. In depressed communities and slow-growth states—for example, older industrial communities, such as Syracuse, New York, and states like West Virginia—stagnation tends to reduce housing costs, wages, and prices.

Different people buy different things, so the costs experienced by certain types of individuals will differ from averages, often by wide margins. Business travelers have a higher cost of living because of what they buy—downtown hotel rooms, rental cars, and meals at restaurants catering to expense-account crowds. The same is true for highly paid executives with downtown jobs, particularly if they desire a short commute. The largest differentials are associated with the size of metropolitan areas, not with states. Chicago, Los Angeles, and New York City are expensive places, but Joliet, Fresno, and Rochester are not.

The price of consumer goods shows little variation between states. Much of what people buy—cars, furniture, alcoholic beverages and soft drinks, packaged foods, DVDs, books, sports equipment, clothing, and more—is produced at distances far from them. Prices generally reflect minor differences in shipping costs among states, except in Alaska and Hawaii, where shipping increases prices more than on the mainland.

About Business Decisions on Where to Locate and Expand

1. Where is the best place to locate a business?

State Fact Finder provides useful statistics for some kinds of business but not all. Businesses that depend on local customers—from doctors' offices to fast-food franchises—will usually do better in rapidly growing areas. To use *State Fact Finder* to identify these areas, see Question 1 in the previous section. Some local businesses have specialized markets that appeal primarily to clearly defined groups, such as children or retirees. To identify areas of specific large and growing populations, review the tables in the Population (A) and Economies (B) sections.

Sophisticated investors in consumer-oriented businesses, such as franchises, often do extensive market research before committing their money. The same is true of companies deciding how and where to market consumer products, from cars to shampoo. Serious researchers generally look at areas in more geographic detail—such as on the level of zip codes, streets, and census tracts. They also rely on their own publications, most notably *American Demographics*. Many private companies specialize in providing such information and the computer software to use it. These companies advertise in related publications.

Some businesses, such as manufacturing companies, can produce products in locations at distances far from their consumers. Sometimes the nature of a business limits the choice of location. For example, mining and oil production companies need to be on top of their raw materials. Manufacturers need an ample supply of labor

and may have special transportation requirements, such as access to a rail line or deep-water port.

Within these parameters, the factors that help determine the best location for a business relate to labor and transportation costs, state and local taxes, and energy prices. Every firm, indeed every plant, differs in where it gets supplies, where its customers are located, how much and what kind of energy it uses, and the relative use of labor and machinery. Thus the best place to locate depends on the fit between the needs of the firm and the attractions of a potential site.

State Fact Finder contains much useful information for comparing business locations. The Population (A) and Economies (B) sections provide information about potential markets for selling products and hiring workers. The Government (D) section covers how states are governed. The Taxes (F) and Revenues and Finances (G) sections look at factors associated with each state's tax burden. The Education (H) and Transportation (K) sections examine the elements of government-provided services important to business.

In establishing a business oriented toward local economic growth, the predominant issue is what growth will be, not what growth was. Most statistics show what it was. The standard warning about investing in the stock market also applies to state economic growth: past performance is no guarantee of future results.

In establishing a business oriented toward local economic growth, the predominant issue is what growth will be, not what growth was. Most statistics show what it was.

Future growth depends on many factors, including fluctuations in oil prices, federal spending (particularly on defense and homeland security), and how well particular firms and industries (and thus the places where they are located) do in the marketplace. To make predictions on future growth, review trend statistics (A-3, B-29, and E-2) or the composite Index of State Economic Momentum (B-28). Forecasts can be purchased from firms specializing in forecasting, or they can be obtained inexpensively from the Department of Commerce.

2. Where is the best place to locate a high-tech business?

Some businesses require employees with specialized skill sets. For those wanting to attract high-tech or so-called creative workers, location can be essential. Tables M-4 and M-5 provide a breakdown of high-tech employment in the states. Consult the AeA (formerly the American Electronics Association) for more information on state and metropolitan levels.

High-tech industries often locate close to academic institutions and, in some cases, research facilities. For instance, Silicon Valley largely grew out of Stanford University, and two Florida universities spearheaded that state's High-Tech Corridor. Tables H-19 through H-27 in *State Fact Finder* provide information on higher education. Table H-29, which shows how the federal government spreads research and development money among the states, is particularly useful.

Richard Florida, a Carnegie Mellon economic development professor, pioneered what he calls a Creativity Index to attract "creative workers." In it he ranks cities using a variety of measures, including diversity. More information can be found at www.creative-class.org.

3. Which state has the most productive workers?

Through industrial development ads in business magazines, some states try to convince firms to locate within their borders because their workers are more productive. Productivity in this context proves to be an elusive concept. Many experts doubt the accuracy of national figures about changes in worker productivity and question even more state-by-state numbers on the matter.

Employers' ideas of a productive worker vary by sector and situation. For example, software design and advertising place a premium on creativity and originality, so employees who work irregular hours can be considered highly productive. An assembly line, however, cannot work unless all workers report at the same time. Formal schooling may be necessary in the development of productive engineers, but experience may be the best education for training plumbers or people who fish for a living.

State Fact Finder has numerous statistics, particularly in the Education (H) and Health (I) sections, on factors employers may consider in determining productivity. *State Fact Finder* also includes the statistics traditionally used to calculate productivity in the states (B-7), but such data are misleading for the reasons explained in the notes to the table.

> *Employers' ideas of a productive worker vary by sector and situation. For example, software design and advertising place a premium on creativity and originality, so employees who work irregular hours can be considered highly productive. An assembly line, however, cannot work unless all workers report at the same time.*

4. Which states have the lowest labor costs?

Most comparisons among states regarding labor costs are based on average annual pay (B-5), as well as annual averages in retailing (B-10) and manufacturing (B-9). These statistics will not necessarily be useful in researching the hiring of new workers in a particular occupation in a particular location within a state. The wages that must be paid to attract competent workers in such a situation will depend upon the supply of labor and the demand for it in the local labor market. Firms looking for low-wage workers should do just the opposite of workers looking for high-paying firms, as discussed in Question 1 of the personal decisions section.

The most relevant statistic involves how much work an employer gets from a worker in relation to a dollar paid. That figure is elusive because productivity per worker is hard to calculate accurately (see Question 3 in this section). For a sophisticated attempt at calculating unit labor cost in relation to productivity, see the research of Moody's Economy.com, including its *Regional Financial Review*, which routinely analyzes the cost of doing business.

5. Where will my business pay the least taxes?

State taxes on business are a complex web of interlocking provisions made even more complex because many local governments also have separate taxes on business. These combinations affect businesses differently, depending on such factors as how profitable they are; how capital intensive they are; whether they qualify for state and local economic development incentives; and whether they are organized as proprietorships, partnerships, S (small business) corporations, or C (regular) corporations.

For entrepreneurs and businesses looking to move to a new area, there is no substitute for knowing the tax rules of the state and locality and how they will ultimately affect business plans. Such calculations are so complicated that a major consulting industry has developed to produce them.

State Fact Finder provides some good indicators of the possible results of these calculations. Start with the overall levels of taxes (F-1 to F-3). If these are high, the business will pay them somewhere—if not in taxes on the firm, then in taxes on salaries, facilities, and utility services. Next, look at the burdens of the specific taxes relevant to the business's operations. If considerable investments in property are required, such as on a plant and equipment, see Tables F-6 to F-8. If concern revolves around payroll taxes, see Tables F-13 to F-16. For taxes on sales, see Tables F-9 to F-12.

A local service business, such as a bakery or retail store, will not have to worry much about state taxes. Unless the business is situated near a border with another state, its competitors will be paying the same taxes. This may not be true concerning local taxes, so additional checking is necessary. Small businesses need not be as worried as large firms about some taxes, particularly corporate income and franchise taxes. If the concern is about taxes on individuals, such as income and estate taxes, see Tables F-16 and F-24.

Owners of nationally oriented businesses, such as manufacturing interests, may be in for some pleasant as well as unpleasant surprises about business taxes. Some states, including New York, have high overall tax levels but are quite competitive in taxes on manufacturing. Some states with low taxes on households, particularly those with no taxes on personal incomes, impose relatively high taxes on firms. The apportionment of corporate income among states for tax purposes dictates that for multistate firms, opening a plant in one state affects the corporate income taxes it pays in all the other states in which it has operations.

6. Which states provide businesses with the best incentives to locate in them?

The amounts and types of assistance available from state and local governments in tax breaks, grants, and loans for locating in their jurisdiction depend on the type of business. New businesses that inherently serve local customers—a car dealership, restaurant, retail store, or repair business, for example—should expect no significant help from government. This is because the business will not increase the wealth or income of the area it serves; rather it will siphon business from those companies already there and with which it competes. Some technical assistance, and even loans, may be available, but these are mostly from state and local agencies administering federal small business money. Some tax breaks may exist in the right state and right locality within it, because local communities compete with each other to increase their tax base.

If a business draws money from out of state, it will likely be offered major incentives from just about any state. There are so many incentives, and their numbers are growing so quickly, that directories of them are obsolete the day of their release. Avoid trying to use national directories of this type or risk missing out on deals that states might be willing to tailor to fit a business. All states and nearly every community of any size employ "developers"—economic development professionals whose mission is to draw employers to their community or state by providing information and administering incentives. These people are eager to provide details about sites, taxes, worker availability, and state and local incentives. Look for state agencies with development in their titles, and find local agencies through county or city governments or chambers of commerce.

7. Which states have the lowest utility rates?

Statistics comparing state averages of electricity rates for various consumers appear in Table B-33. They are indicative of rate differentials for other fuels as well. Deregulation and restructuring have changed the energy picture, and proximity to energy sources is not necessarily the primary determinant in the price one will pay for energy. Taxes make a big difference, as do policies that determine how to charge households versus industry, as Table B-33 dramatically illustrates.

Prices vary within states among users of differing quantities of energy and among types of industrial service; for example, plants that close on high-use days may be charged cheaper rates. Concessions may also be made to firms newly locating in an area or that demonstrate that they can also obtain service from a competing utility. There is no substitute for checking the prices local utilities charge.

8. Which states regulate business the least?

There is no statistical method for comparing state and local regulation of business across the board, because government regulation touches business operations in so many different ways. The great variation in policies among states and local areas further hinders such comparison. Many of these regulatory differences are not systematic. For example, some southern states have relatively less stringent regulation of workplace conditions but impose more stringent regulation on how corporations are governed.

9. Where is the transportation system best?

Interstate transportation systems—road, rail, air, and water lanes—form an interconnected network that allows access to every state in one way or another. Once a product or raw material embarks on this network, service is close to uniform until it leaves it. For a business with considerable shipping requirements, the key component is how easily it can connect with the national networks it needs. This varies with geography rather than state lines and is critically dependent on where the business is sited relative to transportation access points.

There are, however, systemic differences in quality among states. These appear most dramatically in measures of maintenance and construction, the condition of bridges (K-3), and highway pavement (K-2). The quality of an individual state or region's transportation system may be an important consideration for businesses. Commuting times and transportation options are key concerns for many workers in larger metropolitan areas. Tables K-7 and K-10 illustrate the numbers of workers using public transportation and how many employees support such systems.

10. Which states have pro-business attitudes?

Like most people, business owners and managers have differing needs and differing views of appropriate public policies. For example, a businessperson owning a company engaged in a low-tech, labor-intensive activity, such as poultry processing, is not much concerned with the education of the company's workers but is highly concerned with pollution control costs, state labor regulations, and taxes. A businessperson who owns a company engaged in high-tech competition for improved designs of computer chips or software is not as concerned about such state regulations or even taxes; instead, he or she is highly sensitive to how well educated employees are and whether governments maintain strong university systems and promote cultural and recreational opportunities. Thus, a state with relatively high taxes that is accustomed to paying for top-flight schools and state universities will appear anti-business to some business leaders and pro-business to others.

The phrase *business climate* was widely used in the 1980s in discussions of state policies for economic development, regulation, labor laws, and taxes. Based on characteristics found to be important to manufacturing firms that participated in state manufacturing associations, the Grant Thornton accounting firm developed statistics to rank business climate. The state rankings much favored southeastern states with low taxes, low wages, and little business regulation. The influence of these ratings on state policies encouraged the development of counter statistics,

particularly the annual *Development Report Card for the States*, published by the Corporation for Enterprise Development (CFED), whose sponsors include many unions. As the name implies, the *Development Report Card* gives letter grades, not aggregate rankings, to reflect the complexity and controversy associated with deciding which state policies are pro-business and which are successful in promoting state economic development. The state grades are the opposite of those of the business climate rankings. In the CFED's 2006 evaluation, Massachusetts and Minnesota made the honor roll, while most southeastern states tended to get the lowest grades.

The availability of these more sophisticated measures discouraged use of the old business climate rankings, which are no longer published. The term *business climate* has since been appropriated by the publishers of the business-oriented quarterly *Site Selection*. Its ranking procedure, associated with the number of new jobs (primarily in manufacturing), inherently favors large states over less populous ones. Table B-30 uses the test of which states produce the most new work and shows growth in manufacturing jobs. Table B-17 uses the test of where large firms locate their headquarters.

11. Which states are the best places to sell business-to-business?

Many companies sell goods and services to other businesses rather than to individual consumers. Finding firms that might want to buy office supplies, parts, maintenance services, and other business-to-business offerings is different from finding individual consumers (which is discussed in Question 1 in this section). The statistics needed for finding business customers are too specialized for *State Fact Finder*, but government sources provide them in abundance. The Bureau of Labor Statistics at the Department of Labor maintains up-to-date statistics on the number of jobs in each state, with breakdowns by major industry. The Department of Commerce compiles detailed data and publishes county-level statistics in *County Business Patterns*. The department also conducts major surveys, such as the Economic Census, which includes reports on manufacturing and retail trade.

State governments collect and disseminate even more detailed information, although some do a better job than others in keeping it current and making it available in usable forms. The state agencies that administer unemployment compensation (UC)—typically called the Department of Labor or Employment Services Administration—compile details on all private firms, because they collect UC payroll taxes from them every quarter. Mom-and-pop stores and General Motors both are chartered by states and often need some kind of permit to operate in those states where they are not chartered. Secretaries of state keep such records. Many state economic development departments have detailed statistics on businesses operating in the state, and some publish directories.

About Government and Public Policy

1. Which state is the best managed?

No one has yet found a way to use statistics to determine which states, or for that matter which private companies, are managed the best. Bottom-line results—low taxes, high and growing business profits, etc.—count for something, but some states and companies face greater challenges than others in achieving them because of circumstances beyond the control of their managers and leaders. There are awards for well-managed governments and companies, but these are like civic awards: who gets them depends on who sits on the selection committee, the criteria those particular people apply, and their personal knowledge of the candidates.

Somewhat more objective criteria can be considered in measuring state financial management. Bond rating agencies, such as Moody's, assess credit risks (G-15) much as a bank determines how much to loan a family seeking a mortgage. Like personal credit ratings, these concern only the likelihood that loans will be repaid, not whether the borrower is competent, efficient, or conducting business as he or she should.

States' financial management practices can also be compared, such as whether they conform to generally accepted accounting principles and whether they use performance-oriented budgeting. Most experts believe these practices improve the quality of state decisions. Comparisons can be found in Table G-20. For detailed comparisons of such state practices as balanced budget requirements, governors' use of the line-item veto, and the status of stabilization or "rainy-day" funds, see the National Association of State Budget Officers' *Budget Processes in the States* (available at www.nasbo.org/publications/pdfs/budpro2002.pdf).

2. Which state has the fairest tax system?

Fairness in taxes depends on who one thinks should bear what share of the tax burden, or to quote the old maxim, "Where you stand depends on where you sit."

The data on who pays what, where, and how are found in Tables F-6 through F-23 in the Taxes section. Also included in that section are tables on the progressivity of taxes; relative reliance on sales, income, and other tax bases; and tax burdens on high- and low-income households.

3. Which states keep the share of taxes paid by business low?

Economists argue that all taxes, including business taxes, reduce some person's income in order to make money available for government. Part of their reasoning is that legal abstractions, such as corporations and partnerships, do not bear the burden of taxes. Instead, these entities' tax burdens find their way into prices paid by customers, lower wages paid to workers, lower prices paid to suppliers, and lower profits credited to stockholders.

Many people do not agree with this perspective. Public opinion polls usually show that voters would rather see taxes on corporations than taxes they know they pay, such as sales taxes and personal income taxes. While many business leaders do not agree with the economists' outlook, others share it but want to protect everyone involved—stockholders, suppliers, workers, and customers—by avoiding taxes on their businesses. As a result, comparing how states distribute tax burdens between businesses and people piques a lot of interest.

Good data to make such comparisons will never exist, because the people who might gather the information—the tax collectors—do not care about it. Most collect the same property tax on houses and stores whether they are owned by occupants, individual landlords, or a corporate landlord. When someone buys a pad of paper and pays sales tax, no one asks whether he or she is buying it to do grocery lists or for a business project. The family farm is a business as well as a home, but most states do not divide the value between the two or make the tax lower or higher if the family is organized as a sole proprietorship, partnership, or corporation. Comparisons of states on the share of taxes paid by businesses thus inherently involve guesswork and arbitrary distinctions, such as calling all severance taxes business taxes and all farm taxes people taxes. These comparisons deliberately are not included in *State Fact Finder*.

4. Which state has the highest taxes?

Tables F-1, F-2, and F-3 of the Taxes section present the three standard measures of tax burdens. While these offer general information, other tables in the Taxes section are more useful for considering what taxes are likely to be owed by an individual household or business. For that issue, see the answers to Question 2 in the personal decisions section and Question 5 in the business decisions section.

5. Which state has the best education policies?

As they do in other public policy fields, people disagree on the best education policies. To address this question, sporadic publications rank states by evaluating aggregate policies, but the results simply reflect the policy preferences of the interest group issuing them. The scores and rankings might be useful to those who share whatever the bias but misleading to those who do not. *State Fact Finder* provides statistics on education (section H) and lets the reader decide which are of most importance.

6. Which states help the poor the most?

Much disagreement surrounds what is truly helpful to poor people. For example, some people believe providing cash through welfare helps, whereas others argue that it hurts poor people in the long run because it discourages them from working and hinders their opportunities to rise out of poverty.

State Fact Finder has numerous tables on programs for poor people, including food stamps (L-4), Temporary Assistance to Needy Families (L-2, L-3, L-10, L-11, and L-19), Supplemental Security Income (L-5 and L-12), Women, Infants, and Children Program (L-6), National School Lunch Program (L-7), Medicaid (I-12, I-13, I-16, I-17, and I-18), and Head Start (H-31), as well as on tax policies affecting low-income households (L-13).

For additional information, consult the Center on Budget and Policy Priorities (www.cbpp.org), which analyzes which states are most generous toward poor people in their spending and how regressive state and local tax policies are—that is, whether they take away in taxes a larger percentage of the purchasing power of poor people than of wealthy people.

7. Which states have the best roads?

Comparing state policies on a topic such as education does not work well because different people have different ideas about what constitutes good or bad policy. Even when people can agree on desirable results (for example, how children should perform on standard reading tests), it is difficult to judge states by them because so much of the result is determined by factors governments do not control. However, when it comes to providing well-maintained roads, people generally agree on what is good and

bad, and because state and local governments maintain their own roads, few extraneous factors interfere in making determinations. Highways provide a good example of how services can be compared. See Tables K-2 and K-3. Also, truckers run their own surveys, which can be found in the special-interest magazine *Overdrive*.

8. Overall, which states use tax dollars in the most cost-effective manner?

This question cannot be answered for conceptual reasons: People do not agree on what governments should do and how they should do it. For example, most people would agree that administrative costs for welfare should be kept at a minimum so that all available money can be devoted to actually assisting recipients. Most people would agree that it is bad for society if large numbers of people are allowed to cheat their governments, and most would also agree that welfare recipients should be encouraged to find jobs. These beliefs can produce contradictory results. Consider, for instance, the costs per case of administering welfare (L-19) and collecting child support (L-15). These costs are lowest if a state does little counseling and does not spend much money checking for fraud. Most people would agree that these consequences are not those desired.

Another example of a conceptual problem involves the size of elementary school classes (H-9). Some people think small classes are ideal for all schools, while others believe that small classes result in unnecessary spending.

Conceptual problems are not unique to governments. How can a company effectively measure whether its public relations or shareholder relations departments are cost-effective?

Even if conceptual problems could be solved, enormous difficulties remain in collecting the relevant data. For many functions, good measures of effectiveness do not exist. What makes an effective police officer or an effective university professor or an effective state legislator? How could an effectiveness test be uniformly applied to every police officer, university professor, or legislator in the nation?

Often, good measures of costs are not available either, at least not ones related closely to particular services or outputs of government. Again, this problem is not unique to government. What percentage of the cost of a steer attaches to the beef and what percentage to the leather?

Most attempts to measure the cost-effectiveness of government are experimental and usually confined to activities that can be measured fairly easily, such as gathering refuse, maintaining highways, and collecting bills. For more information, see the many useful books written by Harry Hatry and published by the Urban Institute (www.urban.org).

9. Which states have the best government institutions?

Personal preference rules when it comes to deciding how governments ought to be organized, their policies established, and their leaders selected. Some people have strong opinions on these matters, which are from time to time reflected in comparisons attempting to identify states with the "best practices."

For the past thirty years, experts have advocated and states have moved toward organizing the executive branches of state government in ways that strengthen the power of governors. These moves include (1) strengthening the veto power, including allowing line-item vetoes; (2) reducing the number of executive officials— such as comptrollers, education superintendents, and insurance commissioners—selected by elections rather than appointment; (3) increasing the governor's role in preparing and administering budgets; and (4) extending governors' terms by converting two-year terms into four-year terms and allowing governors to run for reelection. Information on these developments and classifications of which states follow which practices appear in the Government section (D).

For decades state legislatures were criticized as citadels of corrupt power removed from popular control and unresponsive to the needs of citizens. One major change came with a Supreme Court decision on reapportionment, requiring "one man, one vote." Now the U.S. Senate is the only governing body in the nation where voting power is not proportional to population. The National Conference of State Legislatures, business groups, and foundations have sponsored research on "modern" legislatures emphasizing (1) longer annual sessions, (2) more staff, and (3) higher legislative pay and expenses. Three such measures of their results appear in Tables D-5, D-8, and D-9.

These ideas have come under considerable criticism recently. Some people view increases in staffing and full-time legislators as a move toward professionalizing the legislature. Others see it as a recipe for making bureau-

crats out of legislators, creating "full-time politicians," and putting legislators out of touch with the people they represent. One result has been movement toward limiting the number of terms legislators can serve (D-8), in effect encouraging turnover (D-7).

Surveys show that large numbers of Americans consider corruption a common occurrence among elected officials at the state and federal levels. One cannot statistically compare ethics, but laws on conflict of interest and disclosure of personal financial information can be compared. The National Conference of State Legislatures does this, and the organization Common Cause also acts as a watchdog on this issue.

No doctrine consistently prevails on whether bigger is better for business and government. Sometimes consolidation is in fashion, forming conglomerates for business and merging regional governments to reduce the roughly 87,500 different state and local governments. Sometimes decentralization and local control come into vogue, with spin-offs for business and other special districts (for example, downtown revitalization areas, police service districts) and decentralized control of neighborhood schools within large school systems.

One way to look at differing state policies involves comparing the ratio of governments to people (D-4). Another approach examines the percentage of local government spending that local officials do not have to finance with their own taxes (D-16).

One thing is clear: State officials must play the hand they are dealt, balancing the needs of their population and the tax base available for revenue to meet those needs.

10. Overall, which states have the best policies?

For some people, picking the state with the best policy is simple: the one with the lowest taxes, the one that spends the most on schools or taking care of the poor, or the one that is active in some other area of interest to the person making the judgment. For most people, this question is too general to be answered meaningfully, because opinions differ so markedly on what is "best." In one person's eyes, the same state may produce "good" policies on one issue but "bad" policies on another.

One thing is clear: State officials must play the hand they are dealt, balancing the needs of their population and the tax base available for revenue to meet those needs. These needs present themselves in the form of children to be educated (H-10), poor people potentially eligible for services (A-16), and more. Tax bases are apparent from economic differences, as shown in the Economies section (B). State differences in spending needs and tax bases are summarized in Tables G-21 and F-3, respectively.

When comparing these statistics, some conclusions become fairly obvious. For example, compared with most states, Connecticut looks pretty good, as a state with low taxes as well as high ratings on such things as spending per school pupil. Connecticut, however, has a rich tax base and a comparatively small percentage of people needing services. Mississippi faces the opposite situation.

11. All things considered, which state is run the best?

Readers are advised to ignore magazine rankings purporting to show which state governments are best or which states are governed best by the combination of state and local officials responsible for their policies. The slippery nature of such rankings becomes evident by comparing results. For example, in the mid-1990s, two financial magazines, *Worth* and *Financial World*, published a set of rankings. One held that Wyoming was the best governed, with Alaska coming in second. The other ranked Wyoming forty-third and had Alaska next to last.

For a ranking of states to be useful, pick an area where they compete for the same prize, such as jobs (B-29); where residents are judged by the same test (H-3); or where the same objective criteria are applied, such as tax levels (F-1). There is widespread agreement on what constitutes a valuable football player or an outstanding actor. This is not true for governments. Many people think those that govern best govern least, but others think good governance produces good schools, nice roads, and quick responses from police and fire departments.

Subject Rankings

Population

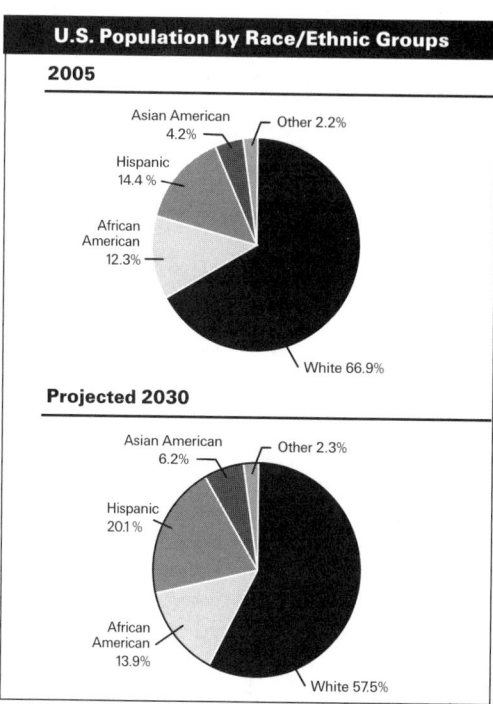

Source: U.S. Census Bureau

Top 10 Fastest-Growing U.S. States July 2005–July 2006		
	State	**Percent**
1	Arizona	3.6
2	Nevada	3.5
3	Idaho	2.6
4	Georgia	2.5
5	Texas	2.5
6	Utah	2.4
7	North Carolina	2.1
8	Colorado	1.9
9	Florida	1.8
10	South Carolina	1.7

Source: U.S. Census Bureau

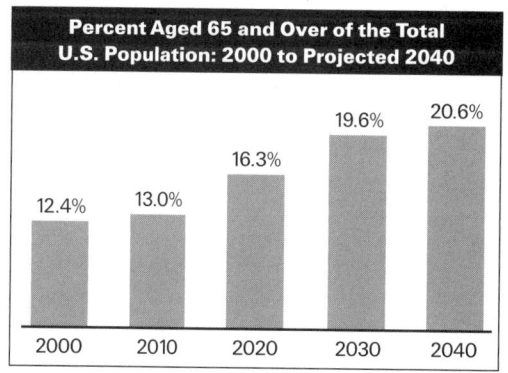

Source: U.S. Census Bureau

A-1 Population and Percentage Distribution, 2006

State	Population 2006 (in thousands)	Percentage of national total 2006	Rank by percentage
Alabama	4,599	1.5	23
Alaska	670	0.2	47
Arizona	6,166	2.1	16
Arkansas	2,811	0.9	32
California	36,458	12.2	1
Colorado	4,753	1.6	22
Connecticut	3,505	1.2	29
Delaware	853	0.3	45
Florida	18,090	6.0	4
Georgia	9,364	3.1	9
Hawaii	1,285	0.4	42
Idaho	1,466	0.5	39
Illinois	12,832	4.3	5
Indiana	6,314	2.1	15
Iowa	2,982	1.0	30
Kansas	2,764	0.9	33
Kentucky	4,206	1.4	26
Louisiana	4,288	1.4	25
Maine	1,322	0.4	40
Maryland	5,616	1.9	19
Massachusetts	6,437	2.2	13
Michigan	10,096	3.4	8
Minnesota	5,167	1.7	21
Mississippi	2,911	1.0	31
Missouri	5,843	2.0	18
Montana	945	0.3	44
Nebraska	1,768	0.6	38
Nevada	2,496	0.8	35
New Hampshire	1,315	0.4	41
New Jersey	8,725	2.9	11
New Mexico	1,955	0.7	36
New York	19,306	6.4	3
North Carolina	8,857	3.0	10
North Dakota	636	0.2	48
Ohio	11,478	3.8	7
Oklahoma	3,579	1.2	28
Oregon	3,701	1.2	27
Pennsylvania	12,441	4.2	6
Rhode Island	1,068	0.4	43
South Carolina	4,321	1.4	24
South Dakota	782	0.3	46
Tennessee	6,039	2.0	17
Texas	23,508	7.9	2
Utah	2,550	0.9	34
Vermont	624	0.2	49
Virginia	7,643	2.6	12
Washington	6,396	2.1	14
West Virginia	1,818	0.6	37
Wisconsin	5,557	1.9	20
Wyoming	515	0.2	50
50 States	298,817	99.8	
DC	582	0.2	
United States	299,398	100.0	

Rank in order by percentage

1 California
2 Texas
3 New York
4 Florida
5 Illinois
6 Pennsylvania
7 Ohio
8 Michigan
9 Georgia
10 North Carolina
11 New Jersey
12 Virginia
13 Massachusetts
14 Washington
15 Indiana
16 Arizona
17 Tennessee
18 Missouri
19 Maryland
20 Wisconsin
21 Minnesota
22 Colorado
23 Alabama
24 South Carolina
25 Louisiana
26 Kentucky
27 Oregon
28 Oklahoma
29 Connecticut
30 Iowa
31 Mississippi
32 Arkansas
33 Kansas
34 Utah
35 Nevada
36 New Mexico
37 West Virginia
38 Nebraska
39 Idaho
40 Maine
41 New Hampshire
42 Hawaii
43 Rhode Island
44 Montana
45 Delaware
46 South Dakota
47 Alaska
48 North Dakota
49 Vermont
50 Wyoming

Note: Numbers that appear to be identical are rounded and vary slightly in actual value. The rankings reflect the actual values before rounding. See the introduction for more details.

A-2 Population and Percentage Distribution, 2005

State	Population 2005 (in thousands)	Percentage of national total 2005	Rank by percentage
Alabama	4,558	1.5	23
Alaska	664	0.2	47
Arizona	5,939	2.0	17
Arkansas	2,779	0.9	32
California	36,132	12.2	1
Colorado	4,665	1.6	22
Connecticut	3,510	1.2	29
Delaware	844	0.3	45
Florida	17,790	6.0	4
Georgia	9,073	3.1	9
Hawaii	1,275	0.4	42
Idaho	1,429	0.5	39
Illinois	12,763	4.3	5
Indiana	6,272	2.1	15
Iowa	2,966	1.0	30
Kansas	2,745	0.9	33
Kentucky	4,173	1.4	26
Louisiana	4,524	1.5	24
Maine	1,322	0.4	40
Maryland	5,600	1.9	19
Massachusetts	6,399	2.2	13
Michigan	10,121	3.4	8
Minnesota	5,133	1.7	21
Mississippi	2,921	1.0	31
Missouri	5,800	2.0	18
Montana	936	0.3	44
Nebraska	1,759	0.6	38
Nevada	2,415	0.8	35
New Hampshire	1,310	0.4	41
New Jersey	8,718	2.9	10
New Mexico	1,928	0.7	36
New York	19,255	6.5	3
North Carolina	8,683	2.9	11
North Dakota	637	0.2	48
Ohio	11,464	3.9	7
Oklahoma	3,548	1.2	28
Oregon	3,641	1.2	27
Pennsylvania	12,430	4.2	6
Rhode Island	1,076	0.4	43
South Carolina	4,255	1.4	25
South Dakota	776	0.3	46
Tennessee	5,963	2.0	16
Texas	22,860	7.7	2
Utah	2,470	0.8	34
Vermont	623	0.2	49
Virginia	7,567	2.6	12
Washington	6,288	2.1	14
West Virginia	1,817	0.6	37
Wisconsin	5,536	1.9	20
Wyoming	509	0.2	50
50 States	295,859	99.8	
DC	551	0.2	
United States	296,410	100.0	

Rank in order by percentage

1 California
2 Texas
3 New York
4 Florida
5 Illinois
6 Pennsylvania
7 Ohio
8 Michigan
9 Georgia
10 New Jersey
11 North Carolina
12 Virginia
13 Massachusetts
14 Washington
15 Indiana
16 Tennessee
17 Arizona
18 Missouri
19 Maryland
20 Wisconsin
21 Minnesota
22 Colorado
23 Alabama
24 Louisiana
25 South Carolina
26 Kentucky
27 Oregon
28 Oklahoma
29 Connecticut
30 Iowa
31 Mississippi
32 Arkansas
33 Kansas
34 Utah
35 Nevada
36 New Mexico
37 West Virginia
38 Nebraska
39 Idaho
40 Maine
41 New Hampshire
42 Hawaii
43 Rhode Island
44 Montana
45 Delaware
46 South Dakota
47 Alaska
48 North Dakota
49 Vermont
50 Wyoming

Note: Numbers that appear to be identical are rounded and vary slightly in actual value. The rankings reflect the actual values before rounding. See the introduction for more details.

A-3   Percentage Change in Population, 2004–2005

State	Population 2004 (in thousands)	Percentage change in population 2004–2005	Rank by percentage change
Alabama	4,525	0.72	25
Alaska	658	0.90	20
Arizona	5,740	3.47	2
Arkansas	2,750	1.06	17
California	35,842	0.81	22
Colorado	4,602	1.38	11
Connecticut	3,499	0.32	41
Delaware	830	1.62	9
Florida	17,385	2.33	4
Georgia	8,918	1.73	6
Hawaii	1,262	1.04	18
Idaho	1,395	2.43	3
Illinois	12,712	0.40	37
Indiana	6,227	0.73	24
Iowa	2,953	0.45	36
Kansas	2,734	0.40	38
Kentucky	4,142	0.76	23
Louisiana	4,507	0.38	40
Maine	1,315	0.50	35
Maryland	5,561	0.70	28
Massachusetts	6,407	-0.13	48
Michigan	10,104	0.16	45
Minnesota	5,097	0.71	26
Mississippi	2,901	0.70	29
Missouri	5,760	0.71	27
Montana	927	0.94	19
Nebraska	1,748	0.63	33
Nevada	2,333	3.51	1
New Hampshire	1,299	0.83	21
New Jersey	8,685	0.38	39
New Mexico	1,903	1.33	13
New York	19,281	-0.14	49
North Carolina	8,540	1.67	8
North Dakota	636	0.06	47
Ohio	11,450	0.12	46
Oklahoma	3,524	0.69	30
Oregon	3,591	1.38	10
Pennsylvania	12,394	0.28	43
Rhode Island	1,080	-0.35	50
South Carolina	4,198	1.36	12
South Dakota	771	0.69	31
Tennessee	5,893	1.18	15
Texas	22,472	1.73	7
Utah	2,421	2.02	5
Vermont	621	0.29	42
Virginia	7,481	1.15	16
Washington	6,207	1.30	14
West Virginia	1,813	0.24	44
Wisconsin	5,504	0.59	34
Wyoming	506	0.67	32
50 States	293,103	0.94	
DC	554	-0.67	
United States	293,657	0.94	

Rank in order by percentage change	
1	Nevada
2	Arizona
3	Idaho
4	Florida
5	Utah
6	Georgia
7	Texas
8	North Carolina
9	Delaware
10	Oregon
11	Colorado
12	South Carolina
13	New Mexico
14	Washington
15	Tennessee
16	Virginia
17	Arkansas
18	Hawaii
19	Montana
20	Alaska
21	New Hampshire
22	California
23	Kentucky
24	Indiana
25	Alabama
26	Minnesota
27	Missouri
28	Maryland
29	Mississippi
30	Oklahoma
31	South Dakota
32	Wyoming
33	Nebraska
34	Wisconsin
35	Maine
36	Iowa
37	Illinois
38	Kansas
39	New Jersey
40	Louisiana
41	Connecticut
42	Vermont
43	Pennsylvania
44	West Virginia
45	Michigan
46	Ohio
47	North Dakota
48	Massachusetts
49	New York
50	Rhode Island

Note: Numbers that appear to be identical are rounded and vary slightly in actual value. The rankings reflect the actual values before rounding. See the introduction for more details.

A-4 Percentage Change in Population, 1995–2005

State	Population 1995 (in thousands)	Percentage change in population 1995–2005	Rank by percentage change
Alabama	4,297	6.1	35
Alaska	604	9.8	21
Arizona	4,432	34.0	2
Arkansas	2,535	9.6	22
California	31,697	14.0	13
Colorado	3,827	21.9	6
Connecticut	3,324	5.6	38
Delaware	730	15.6	10
Florida	14,538	22.4	5
Georgia	7,328	23.8	3
Hawaii	1,197	6.5	31
Idaho	1,177	21.4	7
Illinois	12,008	6.3	32
Indiana	5,851	7.2	28
Iowa	2,867	3.5	45
Kansas	2,601	5.5	39
Kentucky	3,887	7.4	25
Louisiana	4,379	3.3	46
Maine	1,243	6.3	33
Maryland	5,070	10.5	19
Massachusetts	6,141	4.2	43
Michigan	9,676	4.6	42
Minnesota	4,660	10.1	20
Mississippi	2,723	7.3	26
Missouri	5,378	7.8	24
Montana	877	6.7	30
Nebraska	1,657	6.1	34
Nevada	1,582	52.7	1
New Hampshire	1,158	13.2	16
New Jersey	8,083	7.9	23
New Mexico	1,720	12.1	17
New York	18,524	3.9	44
North Carolina	7,345	18.2	9
North Dakota	648	-1.7	50
Ohio	11,203	2.3	47
Oklahoma	3,308	7.2	27
Oregon	3,184	14.3	12
Pennsylvania	12,198	1.9	48
Rhode Island	1,017	5.8	36
South Carolina	3,749	13.5	14
South Dakota	738	5.2	40
Tennessee	5,327	11.9	18
Texas	18,959	20.6	8
Utah	2,014	22.6	4
Vermont	589	5.8	37
Virginia	6,671	13.4	15
Washington	5,481	14.7	11
West Virginia	1,824	-0.4	49
Wisconsin	5,185	6.8	29
Wyoming	485	5.0	41
50 States	265,698	11.4	
DC	581	-5.2	
United States *	266,278	11.3	

Rank in order by percentage change	
1	Nevada
2	Arizona
3	Georgia
4	Utah
5	Florida
6	Colorado
7	Idaho
8	Texas
9	North Carolina
10	Delaware
11	Washington
12	Oregon
13	California
14	South Carolina
15	Virginia
16	New Hampshire
17	New Mexico
18	Tennessee
19	Maryland
20	Minnesota
21	Alaska
22	Arkansas
23	New Jersey
24	Missouri
25	Kentucky
26	Mississippi
27	Oklahoma
28	Indiana
29	Wisconsin
30	Montana
31	Hawaii
32	Illinois
33	Maine
34	Nebraska
35	Alabama
36	Rhode Island
37	Vermont
38	Connecticut
39	Kansas
40	South Dakota
41	Wyoming
42	Michigan
43	Massachusetts
44	New York
45	Iowa
46	Louisiana
47	Ohio
48	Pennsylvania
49	West Virginia
50	North Dakota

Note: Numbers that appear to be identical are rounded and vary slightly in actual value. The rankings reflect the actual values before rounding. See the introduction for more details.

Due to rounding or data sources, the 50-state total plus D.C. may not equal the U.S. total. Please see introduction.

A-5   Projected Population, 2015, and Population Change, 2005–2015

State	Projected population 2015 (in thousands)	Percentage change in population 2005–2015	Rank by percentage change
Alabama	4,663	2.3	43
Alaska	733	10.4	15
Arizona	7,495	26.2	2
Arkansas	2,969	6.8	23
California	40,123	11.0	11
Colorado	5,049	8.2	21
Connecticut	3,635	3.6	37
Delaware	927	9.9	17
Florida	21,204	19.2	3
Georgia	10,231	12.8	7
Hawaii	1,386	8.7	20
Idaho	1,630	14.1	6
Illinois	13,097	2.6	42
Indiana	6,518	3.9	35
Iowa	3,026	2.0	45
Kansas	2,853	3.9	34
Kentucky	4,351	4.3	33
Louisiana	4,674	3.3	38
Maine	1,389	5.1	30
Maryland	6,208	10.9	12
Massachusetts	6,759	5.6	29
Michigan	10,599	4.7	31
Minnesota	5,668	10.4	14
Mississippi	3,014	3.2	40
Missouri	6,070	4.6	32
Montana	999	6.8	24
Nebraska	1,789	1.7	46
Nevada	3,058	26.6	1
New Hampshire	1,457	11.2	10
New Jersey	9,256	6.2	26
New Mexico	2,042	5.9	28
New York	19,547	1.5	47
North Carolina	10,011	15.3	5
North Dakota	635	-0.2	50
Ohio	11,635	1.5	48
Oklahoma	3,662	3.2	39
Oregon	4,013	10.2	16
Pennsylvania	12,711	2.3	44
Rhode Island	1,140	5.9	27
South Carolina	4,642	9.1	18
South Dakota	797	2.7	41
Tennessee	6,502	9.0	19
Texas	26,586	16.3	4
Utah	2,783	12.7	8
Vermont	673	8.0	22
Virginia	8,467	11.9	9
Washington	6,951	10.5	13
West Virginia	1,823	0.3	49
Wisconsin	5,883	6.3	25
Wyoming	528	3.7	36
50 States	321,859	8.8	
DC	506	-8.0	
United States *	322,366	8.8	

Due to rounding or data sources, the 50-state total plus D.C. may not equal the U.S. total. Please see introduction.

Rank in order by percentage change

1	Nevada
2	Arizona
3	Florida
4	Texas
5	North Carolina
6	Idaho
7	Georgia
8	Utah
9	Virginia
10	New Hampshire
11	California
12	Maryland
13	Washington
14	Minnesota
15	Alaska
16	Oregon
17	Delaware
18	South Carolina
19	Tennessee
20	Hawaii
21	Colorado
22	Vermont
23	Arkansas
24	Montana
25	Wisconsin
26	New Jersey
27	Rhode Island
28	New Mexico
29	Massachusetts
30	Maine
31	Michigan
32	Missouri
33	Kentucky
34	Kansas
35	Indiana
36	Wyoming
37	Connecticut
38	Louisiana
39	Oklahoma
40	Mississippi
41	South Dakota
42	Illinois
43	Alabama
44	Pennsylvania
45	Iowa
46	Nebraska
47	New York
48	Ohio
49	West Virginia
50	North Dakota

Note: Numbers that appear to be identical are rounded and vary slightly in actual value. The rankings reflect the actual values before rounding. See the introduction for more details.

A-6 Projected Population for the Year 2025

State	Estimated 2025 population (in thousands)	Rank
Alabama	4,800	24
Alaska	821	46
Arizona	9,532	12
Arkansas	3,151	32
California	44,305	1
Colorado	5,523	22
Connecticut	3,691	30
Delaware	991	45
Florida	25,912	3
Georgia	11,439	9
Hawaii	1,439	41
Idaho	1,853	37
Illinois	13,341	5
Indiana	6,721	18
Iowa	2,993	34
Kansas	2,919	35
Kentucky	4,490	27
Louisiana	4,762	25
Maine	1,414	42
Maryland	6,763	17
Massachusetts	6,939	16
Michigan	10,714	10
Minnesota	6,109	20
Mississippi	3,069	33
Missouri	6,315	19
Montana	1,037	44
Nebraska	1,813	38
Nevada	3,863	28
New Hampshire	1,586	40
New Jersey	9,637	11
New Mexico	2,107	36
New York	19,540	4
North Carolina	11,449	8
North Dakota	621	49
Ohio	11,606	7
Oklahoma	3,821	29
Oregon	4,536	26
Pennsylvania	12,802	6
Rhode Island	1,158	43
South Carolina	4,990	23
South Dakota	802	47
Tennessee	7,073	15
Texas	30,865	2
Utah	3,226	31
Vermont	703	48
Virginia	9,364	13
Washington	7,996	14
West Virginia	1,766	39
Wisconsin	6,088	21
Wyoming	529	50
50 States	348,984	
DC	455	
United States	349,439	

	Rank in order by population
1	California
2	Texas
3	Florida
4	New York
5	Illinois
6	Pennsylvania
7	Ohio
8	North Carolina
9	Georgia
10	Michigan
11	New Jersey
12	Arizona
13	Virginia
14	Washington
15	Tennessee
16	Massachusetts
17	Maryland
18	Indiana
19	Missouri
20	Minnesota
21	Wisconsin
22	Colorado
23	South Carolina
24	Alabama
25	Louisiana
26	Oregon
27	Kentucky
28	Nevada
29	Oklahoma
30	Connecticut
31	Utah
32	Arkansas
33	Mississippi
34	Iowa
35	Kansas
36	New Mexico
37	Idaho
38	Nebraska
39	West Virginia
40	New Hampshire
41	Hawaii
42	Maine
43	Rhode Island
44	Montana
45	Delaware
46	Alaska
47	South Dakota
48	Vermont
49	North Dakota
50	Wyoming

A-7　Population Age 65 and Over, 2005

State	Population 65 and over (in thousands)	Percentage of population 65 and over	Rank by percentage
Alabama	604	13.2	18
Alaska	44	6.6	50
Arizona	758	12.8	26
Arkansas	384	13.8	9
California	3,869	10.7	45
Colorado	465	10.0	46
Connecticut	474	13.5	12
Delaware	112	13.3	16
Florida	2,993	16.8	1
Georgia	870	9.6	48
Hawaii	175	13.7	11
Idaho	164	11.5	41
Illinois	1,530	12.0	38
Indiana	778	12.4	32
Iowa	435	14.7	5
Kansas	357	13.0	23
Kentucky	526	12.6	27
Louisiana	532	11.8	39
Maine	193	14.6	6
Maryland	645	11.5	40
Massachusetts	853	13.3	15
Michigan	1,258	12.4	31
Minnesota	623	12.1	36
Mississippi	358	12.3	33
Missouri	773	13.3	14
Montana	129	13.8	10
Nebraska	234	13.3	17
Nevada	273	11.3	44
New Hampshire	163	12.5	30
New Jersey	1,129	13.0	24
New Mexico	235	12.2	34
New York	2,515	13.1	21
North Carolina	1,054	12.1	37
North Dakota	94	14.7	4
Ohio	1,529	13.3	13
Oklahoma	469	13.2	19
Oregon	470	12.9	25
Pennsylvania	1,893	15.2	3
Rhode Island	150	13.9	8
South Carolina	535	12.6	29
South Dakota	111	14.2	7
Tennessee	750	12.6	28
Texas	2,272	9.9	47
Utah	216	8.7	49
Vermont	82	13.2	20
Virginia	865	11.4	43
Washington	721	11.5	42
West Virginia	278	15.3	2
Wisconsin	722	13.0	22
Wyoming	62	12.2	35
50 States	36,723	12.4	
DC	67	12.2	
United States	36,790	12.4	

Rank in order by percentage

1　Florida
2　West Virginia
3　Pennsylvania
4　North Dakota
5　Iowa
6　Maine
7　South Dakota
8　Rhode Island
9　Arkansas
10　Montana
11　Hawaii
12　Connecticut
13　Ohio
14　Missouri
15　Massachusetts
16　Delaware
17　Nebraska
18　Alabama
19　Oklahoma
20　Vermont
21　New York
22　Wisconsin
23　Kansas
24　New Jersey
25　Oregon
26　Arizona
27　Kentucky
28　Tennessee
29　South Carolina
30　New Hampshire
31　Michigan
32　Indiana
33　Mississippi
34　New Mexico
35　Wyoming
36　Minnesota
37　North Carolina
38　Illinois
39　Louisiana
40　Maryland
41　Idaho
42　Washington
43　Virginia
44　Nevada
45　California
46　Colorado
47　Texas
48　Georgia
49　Utah
50　Alaska

Note: Numbers that appear to be identical are rounded and vary slightly in actual value. The rankings reflect the actual values before rounding. See the introduction for more details.

A-8   Population Age 17 and Under, 2005

State	Population 17 and under (in thousands)	Percentage of population 17 and under	Rank by percentage
Alabama	1,090	23.9	28
Alaska	188	28.4	2
Arizona	1,580	26.6	5
Arkansas	676	24.3	21
California	9,702	26.9	4
Colorado	1,181	25.3	14
Connecticut	835	23.8	29
Delaware	196	23.2	38
Florida	4,068	22.9	40
Georgia	2,363	26.0	7
Hawaii	300	23.5	33
Idaho	374	26.2	6
Illinois	3,241	25.4	11
Indiana	1,603	25.6	10
Iowa	671	22.6	44
Kansas	674	24.6	19
Kentucky	980	23.5	34
Louisiana	1,148	25.4	13
Maine	277	21.0	50
Maryland	1,403	25.1	15
Massachusetts	1,458	22.8	42
Michigan	2,524	24.9	16
Minnesota	1,230	24.0	27
Mississippi	749	25.6	9
Missouri	1,378	23.8	30
Montana	205	21.9	46
Nebraska	432	24.5	20
Nevada	621	25.7	8
New Hampshire	303	23.1	39
New Jersey	2,162	24.8	17
New Mexico	489	25.4	12
New York	4,546	23.6	31
North Carolina	2,141	24.7	18
North Dakota	137	21.4	47
Ohio	2,759	24.1	25
Oklahoma	853	24.1	26
Oregon	850	23.3	36
Pennsylvania	2,817	22.7	43
Rhode Island	245	22.8	41
South Carolina	1,027	24.1	23
South Dakota	188	24.3	22
Tennessee	1,391	23.3	37
Texas	6,326	27.7	3
Utah	743	30.1	1
Vermont	133	21.3	48
Virginia	1,825	24.1	24
Washington	1,484	23.6	32
West Virginia	382	21.1	49
Wisconsin	1,296	23.4	35
Wyoming	114	22.4	45
50 States	73,357	24.8	
DC	113	20.5	
United States	73,470	24.8	

Rank in order by percentage

1 Utah
2 Alaska
3 Texas
4 California
5 Arizona
6 Idaho
7 Georgia
8 Nevada
9 Mississippi
10 Indiana
11 Illinois
12 New Mexico
13 Louisiana
14 Colorado
15 Maryland
16 Michigan
17 New Jersey
18 North Carolina
19 Kansas
20 Nebraska
21 Arkansas
22 South Dakota
23 South Carolina
24 Virginia
25 Ohio
26 Oklahoma
27 Minnesota
28 Alabama
29 Connecticut
30 Missouri
31 New York
32 Washington
33 Hawaii
34 Kentucky
35 Wisconsin
36 Oregon
37 Tennessee
38 Delaware
39 New Hampshire
40 Florida
41 Rhode Island
42 Massachusetts
43 Pennsylvania
44 Iowa
45 Wyoming
46 Montana
47 North Dakota
48 Vermont
49 West Virginia
50 Maine

Note: Numbers that appear to be identical are rounded and vary slightly in actual value. The rankings reflect the actual values before rounding. See the introduction for more details.

State	Median age 2005	Rank
Alabama	37.4	21
Alaska	33.9	48
Arizona	34.5	45
Arkansas	37.0	27
California	34.4	46
Colorado	34.7	43
Connecticut	39.3	8
Delaware	37.9	16
Florida	39.5	6
Georgia	34.3	47
Hawaii	38.5	12
Idaho	34.6	44
Illinois	35.6	39
Indiana	36.1	37
Iowa	38.6	11
Kansas	36.1	37
Kentucky	37.5	19
Louisiana	35.4	41
Maine	41.2	1
Maryland	37.1	25
Massachusetts	38.2	14
Michigan	36.9	30
Minnesota	36.7	31
Mississippi	35.5	40
Missouri	37.4	21
Montana	40.2	4
Nebraska	36.2	34
Nevada	35.2	42
New Hampshire	39.5	6
New Jersey	38.0	15
New Mexico	36.2	34
New York	37.5	19
North Carolina	36.2	34
North Dakota	39.1	9
Ohio	37.6	18
Oklahoma	36.5	33
Oregon	37.0	27
Pennsylvania	39.7	5
Rhode Island	38.4	13
South Carolina	37.1	25
South Dakota	37.0	27
Tennessee	37.3	23
Texas	33.2	49
Utah	28.5	50
Vermont	40.7	2
Virginia	37.2	24
Washington	36.7	31
West Virginia	40.7	2
Wisconsin	37.9	16
Wyoming	39.1	9
50 States	n/a	
DC	35.9	
United States	36.4	

Rank in order by age

1	Maine
2	Vermont
2	West Virginia
4	Montana
5	Pennsylvania
6	Florida
6	New Hampshire
8	Connecticut
9	North Dakota
9	Wyoming
11	Iowa
12	Hawaii
13	Rhode Island
14	Massachusetts
15	New Jersey
16	Delaware
16	Wisconsin
18	Ohio
19	Kentucky
19	New York
21	Alabama
21	Missouri
23	Tennessee
24	Virginia
25	Maryland
25	South Carolina
27	Arkansas
27	Oregon
27	South Dakota
30	Michigan
31	Minnesota
31	Washington
33	Oklahoma
34	Nebraska
34	New Mexico
34	North Carolina
37	Indiana
37	Kansas
39	Illinois
40	Mississippi
41	Louisiana
42	Nevada
43	Colorado
44	Idaho
45	Arizona
46	California
47	Georgia
48	Alaska
49	Texas
50	Utah

Note: Ties in ranking reflect ties in actual values.

A-10 African American Population, 2005

State	African American population (in thousands)	Percentage of total population	Rank by percentage of total population
Alabama	1,203	26.4	6
Alaska	24	3.7	34
Arizona	216	3.6	35
Arkansas	437	15.7	13
California	2,434	6.7	27
Colorado	191	4.1	33
Connecticut	354	10.1	21
Delaware	174	20.7	8
Florida	2,799	15.7	12
Georgia	2,700	29.8	3
Hawaii	30	2.3	40
Idaho	8	0.6	49
Illinois	1,928	15.1	14
Indiana	555	8.8	22
Iowa	69	2.3	39
Kansas	162	5.9	30
Kentucky	313	7.5	25
Louisiana	1,497	33.1	2
Maine	10	0.8	47
Maryland	1,640	29.3	4
Massachusetts	439	6.9	26
Michigan	1,451	14.3	16
Minnesota	218	4.3	32
Mississippi	1,079	36.9	1
Missouri	667	11.5	19
Montana	4	0.4	50
Nebraska	76	4.3	31
Nevada	187	7.7	24
New Hampshire	13	1.0	42
New Jersey	1,262	14.5	15
New Mexico	47	2.4	38
New York	3,347	17.4	10
North Carolina	1,889	21.8	7
North Dakota	5	0.8	46
Ohio	1,368	11.9	17
Oklahoma	275	7.7	23
Oregon	66	1.8	41
Pennsylvania	1,318	10.6	20
Rhode Island	66	6.2	28
South Carolina	1,245	29.2	5
South Dakota	6	0.8	45
Tennessee	1,003	16.8	11
Texas	2,673	11.7	18
Utah	24	1.0	43
Vermont	4	0.6	48
Virginia	1,505	19.9	9
Washington	222	3.5	36
West Virginia	58	3.2	37
Wisconsin	331	6.0	29
Wyoming	4	0.9	44
50 States	37,596	12.7	
DC	314	57.0	
United States	37,909	12.8	

Rank in order by percentage	
1	Mississippi
2	Louisiana
3	Georgia
4	Maryland
5	South Carolina
6	Alabama
7	North Carolina
8	Delaware
9	Virginia
10	New York
11	Tennessee
12	Florida
13	Arkansas
14	Illinois
15	New Jersey
16	Michigan
17	Ohio
18	Texas
19	Missouri
20	Pennsylvania
21	Connecticut
22	Indiana
23	Oklahoma
24	Nevada
25	Kentucky
26	Massachusetts
27	California
28	Rhode Island
29	Wisconsin
30	Kansas
31	Nebraska
32	Minnesota
33	Colorado
34	Alaska
35	Arizona
36	Washington
37	West Virginia
38	New Mexico
39	Iowa
40	Hawaii
41	Oregon
42	New Hampshire
43	Utah
44	Wyoming
45	South Dakota
46	North Dakota
47	Maine
48	Vermont
49	Idaho
50	Montana

Note: Numbers that appear to be identical are rounded and vary slightly in actual value. The rankings reflect the actual values before rounding. See the introduction for more details.

A-11 American Indian Population, 2005

State	American Indian population (in thousands)	Percentage of total population	Rank by percentage
Alabama	22.5	0.5	28
Alaska	106.1	16.0	1
Arizona	300.2	5.1	7
Arkansas	19.4	0.7	21
California	422.4	1.2	15
Colorado	52.2	1.1	17
Connecticut	12.0	0.3	36
Delaware	3.4	0.4	32
Florida	76.4	0.4	31
Georgia	27.4	0.3	42
Hawaii	4.4	0.3	35
Idaho	20.1	1.4	11
Illinois	38.9	0.3	41
Indiana	16.9	0.3	45
Iowa	9.9	0.3	37
Kansas	25.8	0.9	19
Kentucky	8.5	0.2	48
Louisiana	26.8	0.6	24
Maine	7.3	0.6	26
Maryland	17.9	0.3	38
Massachusetts	18.3	0.3	43
Michigan	59.7	0.6	25
Minnesota	60.0	1.2	16
Mississippi	13.1	0.4	29
Missouri	25.7	0.4	30
Montana	60.4	6.5	5
Nebraska	16.6	0.9	18
Nevada	34.4	1.4	10
New Hampshire	3.1	0.2	46
New Jersey	27.0	0.3	40
New Mexico	196.6	10.2	2
New York	104.0	0.5	27
North Carolina	111.7	1.3	14
North Dakota	33.8	5.3	6
Ohio	25.3	0.2	47
Oklahoma	288.7	8.1	4
Oregon	49.9	1.4	12
Pennsylvania	21.9	0.2	50
Rhode Island	6.4	0.6	23
South Carolina	15.6	0.4	33
South Dakota	67.9	8.8	3
Tennessee	16.5	0.3	44
Texas	155.4	0.7	22
Utah	32.9	1.3	13
Vermont	2.2	0.4	34
Virginia	23.8	0.3	39
Washington	104.1	1.7	9
West Virginia	3.3	0.2	49
Wisconsin	52.0	0.9	20
Wyoming	12.1	2.4	8
50 States	2,861.1	1.0	
DC	1.9	0.3	
United States	2,863.0	1.0	

Rank in order by percentage

1. Alaska
2. New Mexico
3. South Dakota
4. Oklahoma
5. Montana
6. North Dakota
7. Arizona
8. Wyoming
9. Washington
10. Nevada
11. Idaho
12. Oregon
13. Utah
14. North Carolina
15. California
16. Minnesota
17. Colorado
18. Nebraska
19. Kansas
20. Wisconsin
21. Arkansas
22. Texas
23. Rhode Island
24. Louisiana
25. Michigan
26. Maine
27. New York
28. Alabama
29. Mississippi
30. Missouri
31. Florida
32. Delaware
33. South Carolina
34. Vermont
35. Hawaii
36. Connecticut
37. Iowa
38. Maryland
39. Virginia
40. New Jersey
41. Illinois
42. Georgia
43. Massachusetts
44. Tennessee
45. Indiana
46. New Hampshire
47. Ohio
48. Kentucky
49. West Virginia
50. Pennsylvania

Note: Numbers that appear to be identical are rounded and vary slightly in actual value. The rankings reflect the actual values before rounding. See the introduction for more details.

A-12 Asian American Population, 2005

State	Asian American population (in thousands)	Percentage of total population	Rank by percentage
Alabama	37.8	0.8	43
Alaska	30.3	4.6	9
Arizona	132.3	2.2	21
Arkansas	27.1	1.0	41
California	4,423.6	12.2	2
Colorado	119.8	2.6	19
Connecticut	112.4	3.2	15
Delaware	22.5	2.7	18
Florida	371.9	2.1	24
Georgia	243.9	2.7	17
Hawaii	529.2	41.5	1
Idaho	14.6	1.0	40
Illinois	518.7	4.1	11
Indiana	75.0	1.2	37
Iowa	43.0	1.4	31
Kansas	57.8	2.1	23
Kentucky	38.0	0.9	42
Louisiana	62.5	1.4	33
Maine	10.9	0.8	44
Maryland	267.2	4.8	7
Massachusetts	301.9	4.7	8
Michigan	226.1	2.2	20
Minnesota	176.6	3.4	13
Mississippi	21.6	0.7	45
Missouri	77.0	1.3	34
Montana	4.9	0.5	50
Nebraska	27.3	1.6	29
Nevada	138.1	5.7	6
New Hampshire	22.9	1.7	28
New Jersey	629.5	7.2	3
New Mexico	24.5	1.3	35
New York	1,281.4	6.7	4
North Carolina	155.1	1.8	27
North Dakota	4.2	0.7	47
Ohio	163.7	1.4	32
Oklahoma	54.6	1.5	30
Oregon	125.6	3.4	12
Pennsylvania	275.9	2.2	22
Rhode Island	29.0	2.7	16
South Carolina	46.0	1.1	38
South Dakota	5.2	0.7	46
Tennessee	74.0	1.2	36
Texas	745.6	3.3	14
Utah	46.5	1.9	26
Vermont	6.4	1.0	39
Virginia	345.5	4.6	10
Washington	401.7	6.4	5
West Virginia	10.1	0.6	49
Wisconsin	108.0	2.0	25
Wyoming	3.2	0.6	48
50 States	12,670.4	4.3	
DC	17.0	3.1	
United States	12,687.5	4.3	

Rank in order by percentage

1. Hawaii
2. California
3. New Jersey
4. New York
5. Washington
6. Nevada
7. Maryland
8. Massachusetts
9. Alaska
10. Virginia
11. Illinois
12. Oregon
13. Minnesota
14. Texas
15. Connecticut
16. Rhode Island
17. Georgia
18. Delaware
19. Colorado
20. Michigan
21. Arizona
22. Pennsylvania
23. Kansas
24. Florida
25. Wisconsin
26. Utah
27. North Carolina
28. New Hampshire
29. Nebraska
30. Oklahoma
31. Iowa
32. Ohio
33. Louisiana
34. Missouri
35. New Mexico
36. Tennessee
37. Indiana
38. South Carolina
39. Vermont
40. Idaho
41. Arkansas
42. Kentucky
43. Alabama
44. Maine
45. Mississippi
46. South Dakota
47. North Dakota
48. Wyoming
49. West Virginia
50. Montana

Note: Numbers that appear to be identical are rounded and vary slightly in actual value. The rankings reflect the actual values before rounding. See the introduction for more details.

A-13 Hispanic Population, 2005

State	Hispanic population (in thousands)	Percentage of total population	Rank by percentage
Alabama	105.0	2.3	41
Alaska	33.8	5.1	28
Arizona	1,692.9	28.5	4
Arkansas	130.8	4.7	29
California	12,723.0	35.2	2
Colorado	907.8	19.5	7
Connecticut	382.1	10.9	11
Delaware	50.8	6.0	25
Florida	3,467.5	19.5	6
Georgia	646.6	7.1	20
Hawaii	101.9	8.0	18
Idaho	129.9	9.1	15
Illinois	1,826.3	14.3	10
Indiana	284.9	4.5	30
Iowa	109.0	3.7	34
Kansas	228.3	8.3	17
Kentucky	81.8	2.0	45
Louisiana	128.3	2.8	38
Maine	13.0	1.0	49
Maryland	319.3	5.7	27
Massachusetts	506.4	7.9	19
Michigan	385.3	3.8	33
Minnesota	186.9	3.6	35
Mississippi	50.9	1.7	46
Missouri	155.5	2.7	39
Montana	22.8	2.4	40
Nebraska	124.7	7.1	21
Nevada	568.4	23.5	5
New Hampshire	29.1	2.2	43
New Jersey	1,327.4	15.2	9
New Mexico	837.4	43.4	1
New York	3,101.6	16.1	8
North Carolina	553.1	6.4	24
North Dakota	10.2	1.6	47
Ohio	260.7	2.3	42
Oklahoma	234.2	6.6	23
Oregon	359.8	9.9	14
Pennsylvania	506.1	4.1	32
Rhode Island	115.3	10.7	13
South Carolina	139.8	3.3	36
South Dakota	16.0	2.1	44
Tennessee	180.6	3.0	37
Texas	8,029.8	35.1	3
Utah	268.2	10.9	12
Vermont	6.8	1.1	48
Virginia	452.5	6.0	26
Washington	551.4	8.8	16
West Virginia	15.5	0.9	50
Wisconsin	246.6	4.5	31
Wyoming	34.3	6.7	22
50 States	42,640.0	14.4	
DC	47.3	8.6	
United States	42,687.2	14.4	

Rank in order by percentage

1 New Mexico
2 California
3 Texas
4 Arizona
5 Nevada
6 Florida
7 Colorado
8 New York
9 New Jersey
10 Illinois
11 Connecticut
12 Utah
13 Rhode Island
14 Oregon
15 Idaho
16 Washington
17 Kansas
18 Hawaii
19 Massachusetts
20 Georgia
21 Nebraska
22 Wyoming
23 Oklahoma
24 North Carolina
25 Delaware
26 Virginia
27 Maryland
28 Alaska
29 Arkansas
30 Indiana
31 Wisconsin
32 Pennsylvania
33 Michigan
34 Iowa
35 Minnesota
36 South Carolina
37 Tennessee
38 Louisiana
39 Missouri
40 Montana
41 Alabama
42 Ohio
43 New Hampshire
44 South Dakota
45 Kentucky
46 Mississippi
47 North Dakota
48 Vermont
49 Maine
50 West Virginia

Note: Numbers that appear to be identical are rounded and vary slightly in actual value. The rankings reflect the actual values before rounding. See the introduction for more details.

A-14 White (Non-Hispanic) Population, 2005

State	White population (in thousands)	Percentage of total population	Rank by percentage
Alabama	3,159	69.3	32
Alaska	441	66.5	35
Arizona	3,589	60.4	42
Arkansas	2,139	77.0	27
California	15,829	43.8	48
Colorado	3,363	72.1	30
Connecticut	2,646	75.4	28
Delaware	587	69.6	31
Florida	11,052	62.1	39
Georgia	5,411	59.6	45
Hawaii	299	23.5	50
Idaho	1,243	87.0	10
Illinois	8,393	65.8	36
Indiana	5,289	84.3	15
Iowa	2,715	91.5	5
Kansas	2,239	81.6	20
Kentucky	3,698	88.6	8
Louisiana	2,786	61.6	40
Maine	1,269	96.0	1
Maryland	3,313	59.2	46
Massachusetts	5,139	80.3	22
Michigan	7,884	77.9	24
Minnesota	4,431	86.3	12
Mississippi	1,745	59.7	44
Missouri	4,811	82.9	18
Montana	833	89.0	7
Nebraska	1,502	85.4	14
Nevada	1,450	60.0	43
New Hampshire	1,232	94.1	4
New Jersey	5,510	63.2	38
New Mexico	832	43.1	49
New York	11,717	60.9	41
North Carolina	5,929	68.3	33
North Dakota	578	90.8	6
Ohio	9,530	83.1	17
Oklahoma	2,573	72.5	29
Oregon	2,970	81.6	21
Pennsylvania	10,262	82.6	19
Rhode Island	861	80.0	23
South Carolina	2,787	65.5	37
South Dakota	673	86.8	11
Tennessee	4,645	77.9	25
Texas	11,243	49.2	47
Utah	2,063	83.5	16
Vermont	598	95.9	2
Virginia	5,164	68.2	34
Washington	4,845	77.1	26
West Virginia	1,716	94.4	3
Wisconsin	4,759	86.0	13
Wyoming	451	88.6	9
50 States	198,195	67.0	
DC	171	31.1	
United States	198,366	66.9	

Rank in order by percentage	
1	Maine
2	Vermont
3	West Virginia
4	New Hampshire
5	Iowa
6	North Dakota
7	Montana
8	Kentucky
9	Wyoming
10	Idaho
11	South Dakota
12	Minnesota
13	Wisconsin
14	Nebraska
15	Indiana
16	Utah
17	Ohio
18	Missouri
19	Pennsylvania
20	Kansas
21	Oregon
22	Massachusetts
23	Rhode Island
24	Michigan
25	Tennessee
26	Washington
27	Arkansas
28	Connecticut
29	Oklahoma
30	Colorado
31	Delaware
32	Alabama
33	North Carolina
34	Virginia
35	Alaska
36	Illinois
37	South Carolina
38	New Jersey
39	Florida
40	Louisiana
41	New York
42	Arizona
43	Nevada
44	Mississippi
45	Georgia
46	Maryland
47	Texas
48	California
49	New Mexico
50	Hawaii

Note: Numbers that appear to be identical are rounded and vary slightly in actual value. The rankings reflect the actual values before rounding. See the introduction for more details.

A-15 Mixed-Race Population, 2005

State	Mixed-race population (in thousands)	Percentage of total population	Rank by percentage
Alabama	40.2	0.9	46
Alaska	31.2	4.7	2
Arizona	91.2	1.5	11
Arkansas	32.7	1.2	30
California	877.8	2.4	6
Colorado	85.0	1.8	8
Connecticut	47.6	1.4	19
Delaware	11.4	1.4	20
Florida	220.2	1.2	27
Georgia	93.8	1.0	36
Hawaii	255.8	20.1	1
Idaho	19.2	1.3	21
Illinois	139.3	1.1	32
Indiana	68.2	1.1	33
Iowa	26.7	0.9	45
Kansas	45.1	1.6	9
Kentucky	40.5	1.0	39
Louisiana	37.3	0.8	49
Maine	12.1	0.9	44
Maryland	84.7	1.5	13
Massachusetts	85.4	1.3	22
Michigan	149.4	1.5	16
Minnesota	74.2	1.4	18
Mississippi	18.2	0.6	50
Missouri	74.6	1.3	25
Montana	13.9	1.5	15
Nebraska	19.4	1.1	31
Nevada	61.9	2.6	5
New Hampshire	12.5	1.0	43
New Jersey	112.4	1.3	24
New Mexico	28.4	1.5	17
New York	287.0	1.5	14
North Carolina	87.1	1.0	38
North Dakota	6.1	1.0	41
Ohio	143.8	1.3	26
Oklahoma	142.3	4.0	3
Oregon	85.5	2.3	7
Pennsylvania	120.1	1.0	40
Rhode Island	16.4	1.5	12
South Carolina	36.1	0.8	47
South Dakota	9.2	1.2	29
Tennessee	57.1	1.0	42
Texas	243.8	1.1	34
Utah	32.4	1.3	23
Vermont	6.6	1.1	35
Virginia	120.6	1.6	10
Washington	187.6	3.0	4
West Virginia	15.1	0.8	48
Wisconsin	57.2	1.0	37
Wyoming	6.1	1.2	28
50 States	4,570.5	1.5	
DC	8.5	1.6	
United States	4,579.0	1.5	

Rank in order by percentage

1 Hawaii
2 Alaska
3 Oklahoma
4 Washington
5 Nevada
6 California
7 Oregon
8 Colorado
9 Kansas
10 Virginia
11 Arizona
12 Rhode Island
13 Maryland
14 New York
15 Montana
16 Michigan
17 New Mexico
18 Minnesota
19 Connecticut
20 Delaware
21 Idaho
22 Massachusetts
23 Utah
24 New Jersey
25 Missouri
26 Ohio
27 Florida
28 Wyoming
29 South Dakota
30 Arkansas
31 Nebraska
32 Illinois
33 Indiana
34 Texas
35 Vermont
36 Georgia
37 Wisconsin
38 North Carolina
39 Kentucky
40 Pennsylvania
41 North Dakota
42 Tennessee
43 New Hampshire
44 Maine
45 Iowa
46 Alabama
47 South Carolina
48 West Virginia
49 Louisiana
50 Mississippi

Note: Numbers that appear to be identical are rounded and vary slightly in actual value. The rankings reflect the actual values before rounding. See the introduction for more details.

A-16 Population in Poverty, 2005

State	Population in poverty (in thousands)	Percentage of population in poverty	Rank by percentage
Alabama	750	16.7	4
Alaska	66	10.0	38
Arizona	917	15.2	8
Arkansas	382	13.9	14
California	4,716	13.2	16
Colorado	530	11.4	28
Connecticut	326	9.4	42
Delaware	78	9.3	43
Florida	1,975	11.1	32
Georgia	1,298	14.4	13
Hawaii	110	8.6	46
Idaho	143	9.9	39
Illinois	1,441	11.5	27
Indiana	774	12.6	19
Iowa	327	11.3	29
Kansas	337	12.5	20
Kentucky	599	14.8	11
Louisiana	748	18.3	2
Maine	166	12.6	18
Maryland	542	9.7	40
Massachusetts	641	10.1	37
Michigan	1,196	12.0	24
Minnesota	412	8.1	47
Mississippi	571	20.1	1
Missouri	659	11.6	26
Montana	128	13.8	15
Nebraska	167	9.5	41
Nevada	260	10.6	33
New Hampshire	73	5.6	50
New Jersey	592	6.8	49
New Mexico	347	17.9	3
New York	2,760	14.5	12
North Carolina	1,115	13.1	17
North Dakota	70	11.2	31
Ohio	1,392	12.3	21
Oklahoma	543	15.6	6
Oregon	436	12.0	23
Pennsylvania	1,372	11.2	30
Rhode Island	127	12.1	22
South Carolina	626	15.0	9
South Dakota	90	11.8	25
Tennessee	872	14.9	10
Texas	3,681	16.2	5
Utah	232	9.2	44
Vermont	47	7.6	48
Virginia	684	9.2	45
Washington	636	10.2	35
West Virginia	276	15.4	7
Wisconsin	553	10.2	36
Wyoming	54	10.6	34
50 States	36,837	12.6	
DC	115	21.3	
United States*	36,950	12.6	

Due to rounding or data sources, the 50-state total plus D.C. may not equal the U.S. total. Please see introduction.

Rank in order by percentage

1	Mississippi
2	Louisiana
3	New Mexico
4	Alabama
5	Texas
6	Oklahoma
7	West Virginia
8	Arizona
9	South Carolina
10	Tennessee
11	Kentucky
12	New York
13	Georgia
14	Arkansas
15	Montana
16	California
17	North Carolina
18	Maine
19	Indiana
20	Kansas
21	Ohio
22	Rhode Island
23	Oregon
24	Michigan
25	South Dakota
26	Missouri
27	Illinois
28	Colorado
29	Iowa
30	Pennsylvania
31	North Dakota
32	Florida
33	Nevada
34	Wyoming
35	Washington
36	Wisconsin
37	Massachusetts
38	Alaska
39	Idaho
40	Maryland
41	Nebraska
42	Connecticut
43	Delaware
44	Utah
45	Virginia
46	Hawaii
47	Minnesota
48	Vermont
49	New Jersey
50	New Hampshire

Note: Numbers that appear to be identical are rounded and vary slightly in actual value. The rankings reflect the actual values before rounding. See the introduction for more details.

A-17 Number and Rate of Children in Poverty, 2005

State	Number of persons under 18 in poverty (in thousands)	Percentage in poverty	Rank by percentage
Alabama	262	24.7	3
Alaska	22	11.9	43
Arizona	347	21.6	6
Arkansas	125	18.7	15
California	1,781	18.5	17
Colorado	172	14.6	31
Connecticut	103	12.4	41
Delaware	28	14.4	33
Florida	630	15.8	27
Georgia	497	21.2	9
Hawaii	30	9.9	47
Idaho	49	12.5	39
Illinois	506	15.6	29
Indiana	298	18.6	16
Iowa	98	14.5	32
Kansas	123	17.8	20
Kentucky	210	21.3	8
Louisiana	262	24.7	4
Maine	43	15.8	28
Maryland	183	13.3	38
Massachusetts	173	11.6	45
Michigan	415	16.4	25
Minnesota	122	10.0	46
Mississippi	228	30.6	1
Missouri	243	17.7	21
Montana	42	19.8	12
Nebraska	53	12.2	42
Nevada	87	13.4	37
New Hampshire	16	5.4	50
New Jersey	188	8.8	48
New Mexico	122	24.7	2
New York	923	20.5	11
North Carolina	400	18.3	18
North Dakota	19	13.5	36
Ohio	470	17.4	23
Oklahoma	176	20.8	10
Oregon	154	17.7	22
Pennsylvania	470	16.9	24
Rhode Island	45	18.1	19
South Carolina	194	19.4	14
South Dakota	30	16.2	26
Tennessee	271	19.5	13
Texas	1,419	22.1	5
Utah	90	11.8	44
Vermont	10	7.6	49
Virginia	226	12.4	40
Washington	226	15.0	30
West Virginia	82	21.4	7
Wisconsin	177	13.7	35
Wyoming	16	13.8	34
50 States	12,856	17.6	
DC	43	38.7	
United States*	12,896	17.6	

Due to rounding or data sources, the 50-state total plus D.C. may not equal the U.S. total. Please see introduction.

Rank in order by percentage

1. Mississippi
2. New Mexico
3. Alabama
4. Louisiana
5. Texas
6. Arizona
7. West Virginia
8. Kentucky
9. Georgia
10. Oklahoma
11. New York
12. Montana
13. Tennessee
14. South Carolina
15. Arkansas
16. Indiana
17. California
18. North Carolina
19. Rhode Island
20. Kansas
21. Missouri
22. Oregon
23. Ohio
24. Pennsylvania
25. Michigan
26. South Dakota
27. Florida
28. Maine
29. Illinois
30. Washington
31. Colorado
32. Iowa
33. Delaware
34. Wyoming
35. Wisconsin
36. North Dakota
37. Nevada
38. Maryland
39. Idaho
40. Virginia
41. Connecticut
42. Nebraska
43. Alaska
44. Utah
45. Massachusetts
46. Minnesota
47. Hawaii
48. New Jersey
49. Vermont
50. New Hampshire

Note: Numbers that appear to be identical are rounded and vary slightly in actual value. The rankings reflect the actual values before rounding. See the introduction for more details.

A-18 Female and Male Populations, 2005

State	Female population (in thousands)	Male population (in thousands)	Female population as a percentage of total population	Rank by percentage female
Alabama	2,346	2,212	51.5	6
Alaska	320	343	48.3	50
Arizona	2,966	2,973	49.9	44
Arkansas	1,416	1,363	51.0	18
California	18,087	18,045	50.1	43
Colorado	2,310	2,356	49.5	48
Connecticut	1,805	1,705	51.4	8
Delaware	432	411	51.2	13
Florida	9,065	8,725	51.0	19
Georgia	4,585	4,488	50.5	32
Hawaii	639	636	50.1	39
Idaho	712	717	49.8	45
Illinois	6,492	6,271	50.9	21
Indiana	3,184	3,088	50.8	26
Iowa	1,506	1,461	50.8	27
Kansas	1,381	1,364	50.3	35
Kentucky	2,123	2,050	50.9	20
Louisiana	2,324	2,200	51.4	9
Maine	676	646	51.1	14
Maryland	2,887	2,713	51.6	3
Massachusetts	3,298	3,101	51.5	4
Michigan	5,145	4,976	50.8	22
Minnesota	2,584	2,548	50.4	34
Mississippi	1,502	1,419	51.4	7
Missouri	2,964	2,836	51.1	15
Montana	469	467	50.1	40
Nebraska	889	870	50.5	31
Nevada	1,185	1,229	49.1	49
New Hampshire	664	646	50.7	29
New Jersey	4,469	4,249	51.3	10
New Mexico	980	948	50.8	23
New York	9,928	9,327	51.6	2
North Carolina	4,412	4,272	50.8	24
North Dakota	319	318	50.1	41
Ohio	5,876	5,588	51.3	11
Oklahoma	1,795	1,753	50.6	30
Oregon	1,830	1,811	50.3	37
Pennsylvania	6,399	6,030	51.5	5
Rhode Island	556	520	51.7	1
South Carolina	2,181	2,074	51.3	12
South Dakota	390	386	50.3	36
Tennessee	3,042	2,921	51.0	17
Texas	11,472	11,388	50.2	38
Utah	1,229	1,240	49.8	46
Vermont	316	307	50.7	28
Virginia	3,844	3,723	50.8	25
Washington	3,149	3,139	50.1	42
West Virginia	928	889	51.1	16
Wisconsin	2,794	2,742	50.5	33
Wyoming	253	257	49.6	47
50 States	150,121	145,739	50.7	
DC	289	261	52.6	
United States	150,411	146,000	50.7	

Rank in order by percentage female

1 Rhode Island
2 New York
3 Maryland
4 Massachusetts
5 Pennsylvania
6 Alabama
7 Mississippi
8 Connecticut
9 Louisiana
10 New Jersey
11 Ohio
12 South Carolina
13 Delaware
14 Maine
15 Missouri
16 West Virginia
17 Tennessee
18 Arkansas
19 Florida
20 Kentucky
21 Illinois
22 Michigan
23 New Mexico
24 North Carolina
25 Virginia
26 Indiana
27 Iowa
28 Vermont
29 New Hampshire
30 Oklahoma
31 Nebraska
32 Georgia
33 Wisconsin
34 Minnesota
35 Kansas
36 South Dakota
37 Oregon
38 Texas
39 Hawaii
40 Montana
41 North Dakota
42 Washington
43 California
44 Arizona
45 Idaho
46 Utah
47 Wyoming
48 Colorado
49 Nevada
50 Alaska

Note: Numbers that appear to be identical are rounded and vary slightly in actual value. The rankings reflect the actual values before rounding. See the introduction for more details.

A-19 Birth Rates, 2004

State	Births per 1,000 population	Rank
Alabama	13.1	33
Alaska	15.8	5
Arizona	16.3	3
Arkansas	14.0	19
California	15.2	7
Colorado	14.9	10
Connecticut	12.0	44
Delaware	13.7	24
Florida	12.5	41
Georgia	15.7	6
Hawaii	14.5	15
Idaho	16.2	4
Illinois	14.2	18
Indiana	14.0	19
Iowa	13.0	34
Kansas	14.5	15
Kentucky	13.4	28
Louisiana	14.5	15
Maine	10.6	49
Maryland	13.4	28
Massachusetts	12.2	43
Michigan	12.8	38
Minnesota	13.8	23
Mississippi	14.8	12
Missouri	13.5	25
Montana	12.4	42
Nebraska	15.1	8
Nevada	15.1	8
New Hampshire	11.2	48
New Jersey	13.2	31
New Mexico	14.9	10
New York	13.0	34
North Carolina	14.0	19
North Dakota	12.9	37
Ohio	13.0	34
Oklahoma	14.6	14
Oregon	12.7	39
Pennsylvania	11.7	46
Rhode Island	11.8	45
South Carolina	13.5	25
South Dakota	14.7	13
Tennessee	13.5	25
Texas	17.0	2
Utah	21.2	1
Vermont	10.6	49
Virginia	13.9	22
Washington	13.2	31
West Virginia	11.5	47
Wisconsin	12.7	39
Wyoming	13.4	28
50 States	n/a	
DC	14.3	
United States	14.0	

Rank in order by rate	
1	Utah
2	Texas
3	Arizona
4	Idaho
5	Alaska
6	Georgia
7	California
8	Nebraska
8	Nevada
10	Colorado
10	New Mexico
12	Mississippi
13	South Dakota
14	Oklahoma
15	Hawaii
15	Kansas
15	Louisiana
18	Illinois
19	Arkansas
19	Indiana
19	North Carolina
22	Virginia
23	Minnesota
24	Delaware
25	Missouri
25	South Carolina
25	Tennessee
28	Kentucky
28	Maryland
28	Wyoming
31	New Jersey
31	Washington
33	Alabama
34	Iowa
34	New York
34	Ohio
37	North Dakota
38	Michigan
39	Oregon
39	Wisconsin
41	Florida
42	Montana
43	Massachusetts
44	Connecticut
45	Rhode Island
46	Pennsylvania
47	West Virginia
48	New Hampshire
49	Maine
49	Vermont

Note: Ties in ranking reflect ties in actual values.

A-20 Death Rates (age-adjusted), 2004

State	Deaths per 100,000 population	Rank
Alabama	992.3	2
Alaska	749.5	37
Arizona	757.6	33
Arkansas	925.2	8
California	754.3	35
Colorado	736.5	43
Connecticut	705.6	47
Delaware	824.7	18
Florida	763.3	30
Georgia	925.2	8
Hawaii	623.6	50
Idaho	754.7	34
Illinois	834.5	17
Indiana	850.3	14
Iowa	728.9	46
Kansas	793.5	25
Kentucky	935.4	7
Louisiana	988.1	3
Maine	803.6	23
Maryland	805.8	22
Massachusetts	741.1	40
Michigan	812.6	20
Minnesota	692.0	49
Mississippi	998.2	1
Missouri	871.7	13
Montana	778.8	27
Nebraska	746.4	39
Nevada	877.9	11
New Hampshire	761.0	31
New Jersey	794.8	24
New Mexico	778.5	28
New York	733.7	44
North Carolina	874.9	12
North Dakota	697.6	48
Ohio	848.5	15
Oklahoma	947.5	6
Oregon	778.1	29
Pennsylvania	814.5	19
Rhode Island	740.9	41
South Carolina	898.2	10
South Dakota	747.1	38
Tennessee	954.1	5
Texas	836.5	16
Utah	760.3	32
Vermont	730.9	45
Virginia	809.2	21
Washington	739.1	42
West Virginia	966.1	4
Wisconsin	749.9	36
Wyoming	788.5	26
50 States	n/a	
DC	970.2	
United States	801.0	

Rank in order by rate	
1	Mississippi
2	Alabama
3	Louisiana
4	West Virginia
5	Tennessee
6	Oklahoma
7	Kentucky
8	Arkansas
8	Georgia
10	South Carolina
11	Nevada
12	North Carolina
13	Missouri
14	Indiana
15	Ohio
16	Texas
17	Illinois
18	Delaware
19	Pennsylvania
20	Michigan
21	Virginia
22	Maryland
23	Maine
24	New Jersey
25	Kansas
26	Wyoming
27	Montana
28	New Mexico
29	Oregon
30	Florida
31	New Hampshire
32	Utah
33	Arizona
34	Idaho
35	California
36	Wisconsin
37	Alaska
38	South Dakota
39	Nebraska
40	Massachusetts
41	Rhode Island
42	Washington
43	Colorado
44	New York
45	Vermont
46	Iowa
47	Connecticut
48	North Dakota
49	Minnesota
50	Hawaii

Note: Ties in ranking reflect ties in actual values.

A-21 Population Density, 2005

State	Persons per square mile	Rank
Alabama	90	26
Alaska	1	50
Arizona	52	35
Arkansas	53	33
California	232	11
Colorado	45	37
Connecticut	724	4
Delaware	432	6
Florida	330	8
Georgia	157	18
Hawaii	199	13
Idaho	17	44
Illinois	230	12
Indiana	175	17
Iowa	53	34
Kansas	34	40
Kentucky	105	22
Louisiana	104	23
Maine	43	38
Maryland	573	5
Massachusetts	816	3
Michigan	178	16
Minnesota	64	31
Mississippi	62	32
Missouri	84	28
Montana	6	48
Nebraska	23	42
Nevada	22	43
New Hampshire	146	19
New Jersey	1,175	1
New Mexico	16	45
New York	408	7
North Carolina	178	15
North Dakota	9	47
Ohio	280	9
Oklahoma	52	36
Oregon	38	39
Pennsylvania	277	10
Rhode Island	1,030	2
South Carolina	141	21
South Dakota	10	46
Tennessee	145	20
Texas	87	27
Utah	30	41
Vermont	67	30
Virginia	191	14
Washington	94	25
West Virginia	75	29
Wisconsin	102	24
Wyoming	5	49
50 States	84	
DC	9,025	
United States	84	

Rank in order by density

1 New Jersey
2 Rhode Island
3 Massachusetts
4 Connecticut
5 Maryland
6 Delaware
7 New York
8 Florida
9 Ohio
10 Pennsylvania
11 California
12 Illinois
13 Hawaii
14 Virginia
15 North Carolina
16 Michigan
17 Indiana
18 Georgia
19 New Hampshire
20 Tennessee
21 South Carolina
22 Kentucky
23 Louisiana
24 Wisconsin
25 Washington
26 Alabama
27 Texas
28 Missouri
29 West Virginia
30 Vermont
31 Minnesota
32 Mississippi
33 Arkansas
34 Iowa
35 Arizona
36 Oklahoma
37 Colorado
38 Maine
39 Oregon
40 Kansas
41 Utah
42 Nebraska
43 Nevada
44 Idaho
45 New Mexico
46 South Dakota
47 North Dakota
48 Montana
49 Wyoming
50 Alaska

Note: Numbers that appear to be identical are rounded and vary slightly in actual value. The rankings reflect the actual values before rounding. See the introduction for more details.

A-22 Legal Immigrants Admitted, FY 2005

State	Legal immigrants admitted	Percentage of total legal immigrants admitted	Rank by number of legal immigrants
Alabama	4,200	0.4	33
Alaska	1,525	0.1	44
Arizona	18,988	1.7	14
Arkansas	2,698	0.2	41
California	232,023	20.7	1
Colorado	11,977	1.1	19
Connecticut	15,335	1.4	18
Delaware	2,992	0.3	39
Florida	122,918	11.0	3
Georgia	31,535	2.8	8
Hawaii	6,480	0.6	26
Idaho	2,768	0.2	40
Illinois	52,419	4.7	6
Indiana	6,915	0.6	25
Iowa	4,536	0.4	31
Kansas	4,514	0.4	32
Kentucky	5,267	0.5	27
Louisiana	3,777	0.3	35
Maine	1,908	0.2	42
Maryland	22,870	2.0	13
Massachusetts	34,236	3.1	7
Michigan	23,597	2.1	12
Minnesota	15,456	1.4	17
Mississippi	1,831	0.2	43
Missouri	8,744	0.8	23
Montana	589	0.1	49
Nebraska	2,997	0.3	38
Nevada	9,823	0.9	20
New Hampshire	3,298	0.3	37
New Jersey	56,180	5.0	5
New Mexico	3,513	0.3	36
New York	136,828	12.2	2
North Carolina	16,715	1.5	16
North Dakota	864	0.1	47
Ohio	16,897	1.5	15
Oklahoma	4,702	0.4	30
Oregon	9,623	0.9	21
Pennsylvania	28,908	2.6	9
Rhode Island	3,852	0.3	34
South Carolina	5,029	0.4	29
South Dakota	881	0.1	46
Tennessee	8,962	0.8	22
Texas	95,958	8.5	4
Utah	5,082	0.5	28
Vermont	1,042	0.1	45
Virginia	27,100	2.4	10
Washington	26,482	2.4	11
West Virginia	847	0.1	48
Wisconsin	7,909	0.7	24
Wyoming	321	0.0	50
50 States	1,113,911	99.2	
DC	2,457	0.2	
United States*	1,122,373	100.0	

Rank in order by number	
1	California
2	New York
3	Florida
4	Texas
5	New Jersey
6	Illinois
7	Massachusetts
8	Georgia
9	Pennsylvania
10	Virginia
11	Washington
12	Michigan
13	Maryland
14	Arizona
15	Ohio
16	North Carolina
17	Minnesota
18	Connecticut
19	Colorado
20	Nevada
21	Oregon
22	Tennessee
23	Missouri
24	Wisconsin
25	Indiana
26	Hawaii
27	Kentucky
28	Utah
29	South Carolina
30	Oklahoma
31	Iowa
32	Kansas
33	Alabama
34	Rhode Island
35	Louisiana
36	New Mexico
37	New Hampshire
38	Nebraska
39	Delaware
40	Idaho
41	Arkansas
42	Maine
43	Mississippi
44	Alaska
45	Vermont
46	South Dakota
47	North Dakota
48	West Virginia
49	Montana
50	Wyoming

Due to rounding or data sources, the 50-state total plus D.C. may not equal the U.S. total. Please see introduction.

A-23 Unauthorized Immigrant Population, 2005

State	Unauthorized immigrant population (in thousands)	Rank
Alabama	30–50	34
Alaska	<10	43
Arizona	400–450	5
Arkansas	30–50	34
California	2,500–2,750	1
Colorado	225–275	11
Connecticut	70–100	24
Delaware	15–35	41
Florida	800–950	3
Georgia	350–450	7
Hawaii	20–35	40
Idaho	25–45	37
Illinois	375–425	6
Indiana	55–85	25
Iowa	55–85	25
Kansas	40–70	29
Kentucky	30–60	33
Louisiana	25–45	37
Maine	<10	43
Maryland	225–275	11
Massachusetts	150–250	14
Michigan	100–150	18
Minnesota	75–100	22
Mississippi	30–50	34
Missouri	35–65	31
Montana	<10	43
Nebraska	35–55	32
Nevada	150–200	15
New Hampshire	10–30	42
New Jersey	350–425	8
New Mexico	50–75	27
New York	550–650	4
North Carolina	300–400	9
North Dakota	<10	43
Ohio	75–150	20
Oklahoma	50–75	27
Oregon	125–175	16
Pennsylvania	125–175	16
Rhode Island	20–40	39
South Carolina	35–75	30
South Dakota	<10	43
Tennessee	100–150	18
Texas	1,400–1,600	2
Utah	75–100	22
Vermont	<10	43
Virginia	250–300	10
Washington	200–250	13
West Virginia	<10	43
Wisconsin	75–115	21
Wyoming	<10	43
50 States	10,685-11,470	
DC	15–30	
United States	10,700–11,500	

Rank in order by number	
1	California
2	Texas
3	Florida
4	New York
5	Arizona
6	Illinois
7	Georgia
8	New Jersey
9	North Carolina
10	Virginia
11	Maryland
11	Colorado
13	Washington
14	Massachusetts
15	Nevada
16	Pennsylvania
16	Oregon
18	Tennessee
18	Michigan
20	Ohio
21	Wisconsin
22	Minnesota
22	Utah
24	Connecticut
25	Indiana
25	Iowa
27	Oklahoma
27	New Mexico
29	Kansas
30	South Carolina
31	Missouri
32	Nebraska
33	Kentucky
34	Alabama
34	Mississippi
34	Arkansas
37	Louisiana
37	Idaho
39	Rhode Island
40	Hawaii
41	Delaware
42	New Hampshire
43	Alaska
43	Wyoming
43	South Dakota
43	Maine
43	Vermont
43	North Dakota
43	Montana
43	West Virginia

Note: Ties in ranking reflect ties in actual values.

Source Notes for Population (Section A)

A-1 Population and Percentage Distribution, 2006: The U.S. population is counted once every decade in years ending in zero. The last such count was in 2000. For all other years, the U.S. Census Bureau prepares estimates for July 1 of each year. The 2006 estimates were released on December 22, 2006 as Table NST-EST2006-01-Annual Estimates of the Population: April 1, 2000 to July 1, 2006 and are available on the bureau's Web site (www.census.gov). Outside experts and the Census Bureau agree that the census undercounts the nation's population and that this undercount tends to be concentrated in low-income areas in major cities. The understatement of population is greatest for these communities and the states that contain them. Because population estimates are used to determine representation in Congress and how much state and local governments get from federal aid programs, some states and cities have gone to court seeking to force the federal government to use more correct estimates. In the past, the Census Bureau successfully resisted these challenges because, while it agrees the official count is inaccurate, it does not know what data might be substituted for that count.

A-2 Population and Percentage Distribution, 2005: This data is similar to the data in Table A-1 but reflects state population estimates in 2005. The numbers were released on the U.S. Census Bureau Web site (www.census.gov) on December 21, 2005 as NST-EST2005-01-Annual Estimates of the Population: April 1, 2000 to July 1, 2005.

A-3 Percentage Change in Population, 2004-2005: From the same source as Table A-2, this table shows population change over one year.

A-4 Percentage Change in Population, 1995-2005: The 1995 population data shown on this table are from intercensal state population estimates released by the U.S. Census Bureau on April 11, 2002. Comparing these numbers to 2005 estimates shows population shifts over a decade.

A-5 Projected Population, 2015, and Population Change, 2005-2015: The population projections for 2015 were made by the U.S. Census Bureau and are available on its Web site (www.census.gov). See Table A-2 for the 2005 population numbers used to calculate the projected change over time. Many private market research and economic forecasting firms also make population projections. The projections reflect recent trends, so western states are predicted to gain population rapidly while the slowest growth appears in the Northeast and the Midwest. Generally, projections for short periods are quite reliable because they are based on events that are predictable for large groups, such as the percentage of persons who will die each year and the percentage of women of childbearing age who will have babies. Over longer periods, more guesswork is involved. Major economic shifts can be caused by changes in defense spending, fluctuations in oil and gas prices, and success or failure of particular firms or industries. Those shifts affect migration of workers and ultimately where they have children and die.

A-6 Projected Population for the Year 2025: See notes to Table A-4.

A-7 Population Age 65 and Over and as a Percentage of Population, 2005: This U.S. Census Bureau estimate is available on the bureau's Web site (www.census.gov). Two kinds of states have the largest percentage of elderly citizens. First, there are states, like Florida and Arkansas, that draw large numbers of retirees from other states. Second, there are states with slow population growth, such as Pennsylvania, that lose many of their working-age younger people through migration to other states.

A-8 Population Age 17 and Under and as a Percentage of Population, 2005: This count, from the same source as Table A-7, shows the flip side of the high concentrations of elderly citizens shown in Table A-7. The highest-ranking states, typified by Utah, have a large percentage of adults of childbearing age and high birth rates.

A-9 Median Age, 2005: In each state, half the population was older than the age shown, while half was younger. This statistic, available on the U.S. Census Bureau's Web site (www.census.gov) captures age differences among states in a single number for each state.

A-10 African American Population and as a Percentage of Population, 2005: The U.S. Census Bureau identifies six race categories: White; Black or African American; American Indian and Alaska Native; Asian; Native Hawaiian and other Pacific Islander; and "some other race" (write-in answer). "Hispanic" is not considered a race by the bureau, so Hispanics are asked to classify themselves using the above six race categories, and also separately as "of Hispanic or Latino origin."

The 2000 census marked the first year respondents were able to check one or more boxes identifying race. This *State Fact Finder* table presents the number of people who classify themselves as African American or Black only. These data are from the bureau's Web site (www.census.gov). The "undercount" (see notes to Table A-1) means that statistics probably undercount African Americans and Hispanics.

A-11 American Indian Population and as a Percentage of Population, 2005: From the same source as Table A-10, this table shows the number of people who classify themselves as American Indian (including Alaska Native).

A-12 Asian American Population and as a Percentage of Population, 2005: From the same source as Table A-10, this table shows the number of people who classify themselves as Asian American.

A-13 Hispanic Population and as a Percentage of Population, 2005: See notes to Tables A-10. While the census theoretically accounts for every resident in the country, illegal immigrants (many of whom are Hispanic) have an understandable fear of being identified by any government agency. Therefore, the count of this group is probably not very accurate. The data come from the U.S. Census Bureau Web site (www.census.gov).

A-14 White (Non-Hispanic) Population and as a Percentage of Population, 2005: This data, available on the U.S. Census Bureau Web site (www.census.gov) presents the number of people who identify themselves as non-Hispanic White.

A-15 Mixed-Race Population and as a Percentage of Population, 2005: Since the 2000 census, respondents now have the option of checking two or more boxes categorizing race. This table shows the number of people who classify themselves as being of two or more races. It is from the same source as Table A-10.

A-16 Population in Poverty, 2005: The federal government has a uniform definition of the income families need to avoid poverty. The amount considered necessary varies with family size but not with rural or urban location or from state to state. The income used to calculate whether households are living in poverty does not include the value of non-cash benefits, such as medical care, provided to the poor under government programs. The estimates shown are from the U.S. Census Bureau Web site (www.census.gov). They are based in part on monthly household surveys of a small sample of the nation's population, not a full count. They reflect possible sampling errors, particularly for less populous states.

A-17 Number and Rate of Children in Poverty, 2005: These statistics are available on the U.S. Census Bureau Web site (www.census.gov) and are subject to the same caveats as similar data for persons of all ages in Table A-16. The percentage of children in poverty exceeds the percentage of all persons in poverty because households with children are often headed by a parent or parents in their early earning years, and the income needed to avoid the poverty standard is higher for families with children than for adults without children.

A-18 Female and Male Populations, 2005: More than half of newly born children are male, but women tend to outlive men. The result is about equal numbers of each in the population as a whole, but disproportionate numbers of women in states with more aged population (see Table A-7). These data come from the same source as Table A-1.

A-19 Birth Rates, 2004: These data show that 14 children are born each year for every 1,000 people. The birth rate is nearly 66.3 per 1,000 when only women of childbearing age are considered. The data come from the National Center for Health Statistics publication, *National Vital Statistics Report* (vol. 55, no. 1, September 29, 2006) available on the Centers for Disease Control Web site (www.cdc.gov). See notes to Table A-20 below.

A-20 Death Rates (age-adjusted), 2004: Raw death rates, like raw birth rates (births related to population), are highly sensitive to the age distribution of a state's population. A state with large numbers of older persons will tend to have lower raw birth rates and higher death rates. The National Center for Health Statistics makes special calculations adjusting deaths for age and births for the numbers of women of childbearing age (called fertility rates).

State Fact Finder illustrates both approaches by using raw rates for births (Table A-19) and adjusted rates for deaths. Data showing raw rates for deaths are, like the age-adjusted death rates shown, available from the National Center for Health Statistics publication, *National Vital Statistics Report* (vol. 54, no. 19, June 28, 2006). This source also provides technical notes indicating exactly how adjustments are made. The notes also explain how a changed population standard makes these rates not directly comparable to those before data year 2000.

A-21 Population Density, 2005: This table is calculated by taking the land area estimate from the 2000 census (see Table C-1) and relating it to the 2005 population. The result is a rough measure of urban-rural characteristics of each state and is often cited as a proxy for possible crowding. However, in many states much of the land area is unusable for settlement because of lack of water, extraordinarily low or high elevation, and other factors. Consequently, much of the population of a low-density state may in fact be densely packed in a few small areas.

A-22 Legal Immigrants Admitted, FY 2005: These statistics, showing immigrants admitted by state of intended residence, are from the *2005 Statistical Yearbook of Immigration Statistics* (www.dhs.gov).

A-23 Unauthorized Immigrant Population, 2005: Counting illegal immigrants, many of whom fear being counted, is inherently difficult. These estimates are from the Pew Hispanic Center (pewhispanic.org) based on data from the 2005 Current Population Survey. Included in this estimate of the unauthorized population are some persons who have temporary permission to reside in the U.S., or whose immigration status is unresolved. While the estimates may not be accurate, they are useful in illustrating the large differences among states.

Economies

U.S. Unemployment Rate by Region, November 2005 and November 2006		
Region	**Rate**	
	2005	**2006**
Midwest	5.3	4.8
New England	4.8	4.5
South	5	4.4
West	4.9	4.4

Source: U.S. Department of Labor, Bureau of Labor Statistics

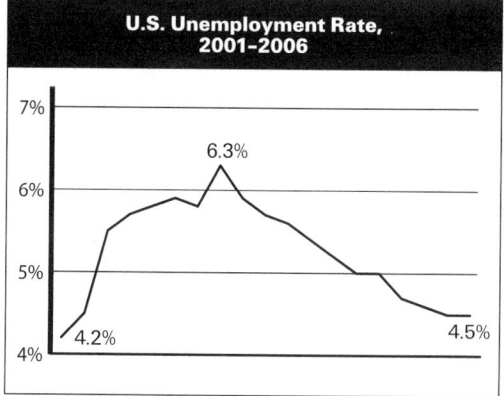

U.S. Unemployment Rate, 2001–2006

Source: U.S. Department of Labor, Bureau of Labor Statistics

One-Year Percent Change in U.S. Housing Prices by Region, 2005–2006		
Region		**Percent**
West	Pacific	11.31
	Mountain	11.20
Northeast	Middle Atlantic	8.07
	New England	3.57
South	South Atlantic	9.52
	East South Central	7.38
	West South Central	7.73
Midwest	East North Central	2.80
	West North Central	3.90
United States		7.73

Source: Office of Federal Housing Enterprise Oversight

B-1   Personal Income, 2005

State	Personal income $ (in millions)	Rank
Alabama	135,018	24
Alaska	23,515	47
Arizona	179,114	21
Arkansas	74,040	33
California	1,332,919	1
Colorado	174,754	22
Connecticut	166,807	23
Delaware	31,281	44
Florida	606,612	4
Georgia	282,979	11
Hawaii	43,953	40
Idaho	40,584	42
Illinois	462,857	5
Indiana	195,372	16
Iowa	94,316	30
Kansas	90,433	31
Kentucky	118,180	26
Louisiana	111,201	28
Maine	40,714	41
Maryland	235,196	14
Massachusetts	279,635	12
Michigan	331,304	9
Minnesota	191,568	17
Mississippi	72,809	34
Missouri	181,542	20
Montana	27,046	45
Nebraska	58,019	36
Nevada	86,403	32
New Hampshire	49,561	38
New Jersey	382,041	7
New Mexico	53,826	37
New York	771,568	2
North Carolina	269,435	13
North Dakota	19,883	49
Ohio	365,319	8
Oklahoma	106,111	29
Oregon	117,149	27
Pennsylvania	433,146	6
Rhode Island	37,903	43
South Carolina	120,043	25
South Dakota	25,328	46
Tennessee	184,566	18
Texas	745,329	3
Utah	67,906	35
Vermont	20,393	48
Virginia	284,174	10
Washington	221,540	15
West Virginia	47,290	39
Wisconsin	184,087	19
Wyoming	18,982	50
50 States	10,193,751	
DC	31,010	
United States	10,224,761	

Rank in order by $

1 California
2 New York
3 Texas
4 Florida
5 Illinois
6 Pennsylvania
7 New Jersey
8 Ohio
9 Michigan
10 Virginia
11 Georgia
12 Massachusetts
13 North Carolina
14 Maryland
15 Washington
16 Indiana
17 Minnesota
18 Tennessee
19 Wisconsin
20 Missouri
21 Arizona
22 Colorado
23 Connecticut
24 Alabama
25 South Carolina
26 Kentucky
27 Oregon
28 Louisiana
29 Oklahoma
30 Iowa
31 Kansas
32 Nevada
33 Arkansas
34 Mississippi
35 Utah
36 Nebraska
37 New Mexico
38 New Hampshire
39 West Virginia
40 Hawaii
41 Maine
42 Idaho
43 Rhode Island
44 Delaware
45 Montana
46 South Dakota
47 Alaska
48 Vermont
49 North Dakota
50 Wyoming

B-2　Gross State Product, Total and Per Capita, 2005

State	Gross state product $ (in millions)	Per capita $	Rank per capita
Alabama	132,213	29,008	45
Alaska	29,878	45,020	5
Arizona	197,774	33,299	35
Arkansas	76,918	27,677	47
California	1,471,045	40,713	10
Colorado	192,639	41,293	8
Connecticut	173,058	49,300	2
Delaware	47,615	56,448	1
Florida	595,846	33,494	34
Georgia	327,451	36,092	20
Hawaii	46,806	36,705	19
Idaho	43,539	30,466	40
Illinois	499,456	39,132	13
Indiana	214,093	34,135	29
Iowa	101,543	34,232	28
Kansas	92,685	33,769	33
Kentucky	124,534	29,840	43
Louisiana	135,362	29,923	42
Maine	39,741	30,073	41
Maryland	216,186	38,602	15
Massachusetts	299,992	46,883	3
Michigan	342,656	33,856	32
Minnesota	209,929	40,900	9
Mississippi	69,672	23,851	50
Missouri	192,241	33,143	36
Montana	25,480	27,232	48
Nebraska	61,786	35,130	25
Nevada	96,585	39,997	12
New Hampshire	50,675	38,685	14
New Jersey	385,494	44,219	6
New Mexico	59,865	31,044	39
New York	867,070	45,032	4
North Carolina	308,402	35,517	23
North Dakota	20,879	32,794	37
Ohio	394,927	34,449	27
Oklahoma	100,791	28,409	46
Oregon	136,619	37,522	17
Pennsylvania	430,310	34,620	26
Rhode Island	38,554	35,825	21
South Carolina	124,343	29,222	44
South Dakota	27,670	35,660	22
Tennessee	203,089	34,058	30
Texas	845,512	36,987	18
Utah	79,169	32,058	38
Vermont	21,103	33,870	31
Virginia	314,085	41,505	7
Washington	239,281	38,055	16
West Virginia	45,701	25,154	49
Wisconsin	194,489	35,130	24
Wyoming	20,655	40,556	11
50 States	10,965,406	37,063	
DC	70,347	127,783	
United States*	11,035,627	37,231	

Rank in order per capita

1	Delaware
2	Connecticut
3	Massachusetts
4	New York
5	Alaska
6	New Jersey
7	Virginia
8	Colorado
9	Minnesota
10	California
11	Wyoming
12	Nevada
13	Illinois
14	New Hampshire
15	Maryland
16	Washington
17	Oregon
18	Texas
19	Hawaii
20	Georgia
21	Rhode Island
22	South Dakota
23	North Carolina
24	Wisconsin
25	Nebraska
26	Pennsylvania
27	Ohio
28	Iowa
29	Indiana
30	Tennessee
31	Vermont
32	Michigan
33	Kansas
34	Florida
35	Arizona
36	Missouri
37	North Dakota
38	Utah
39	New Mexico
40	Idaho
41	Maine
42	Louisiana
43	Kentucky
44	South Carolina
45	Alabama
46	Oklahoma
47	Arkansas
48	Montana
49	West Virginia
50	Mississippi

Note: Numbers that appear to be identical are rounded and vary slightly in actual value. The rankings reflect the actual values before rounding. See the introduction for more details.

Due to rounding or data sources, the 50-state total plus D.C. may not equal the U.S. total. Please see introduction.

B-3   Per Capita Personal Income, 2005

State	Per capita personal income $	Rank
Alabama	29,623	40
Alaska	35,433	15
Arizona	30,157	38
Arkansas	26,641	47
California	36,890	12
Colorado	37,459	8
Connecticut	47,519	1
Delaware	37,084	11
Florida	34,099	20
Georgia	31,191	33
Hawaii	34,468	19
Idaho	28,398	42
Illinois	36,264	13
Indiana	31,150	34
Iowa	31,795	30
Kansas	32,948	23
Kentucky	28,317	43
Louisiana	24,582	50
Maine	30,808	37
Maryland	41,996	4
Massachusetts	43,702	3
Michigan	32,735	24
Minnesota	37,322	9
Mississippi	24,925	49
Missouri	31,299	31
Montana	28,906	41
Nebraska	32,988	22
Nevada	35,780	14
New Hampshire	37,835	6
New Jersey	43,822	2
New Mexico	27,912	45
New York	40,072	5
North Carolina	31,029	35
North Dakota	31,230	32
Ohio	31,867	29
Oklahoma	29,908	39
Oregon	32,174	28
Pennsylvania	34,848	18
Rhode Island	35,219	17
South Carolina	28,212	44
South Dakota	32,642	26
Tennessee	30,952	36
Texas	32,604	27
Utah	27,497	46
Vermont	32,731	25
Virginia	37,552	7
Washington	35,234	16
West Virginia	26,029	48
Wisconsin	33,251	21
Wyoming	37,270	10
50 States	34,455	
DC	56,329	
United States	34,495	

Rank in order per capita

1	Connecticut
2	New Jersey
3	Massachusetts
4	Maryland
5	New York
6	New Hampshire
7	Virginia
8	Colorado
9	Minnesota
10	Wyoming
11	Delaware
12	California
13	Illinois
14	Nevada
15	Alaska
16	Washington
17	Rhode Island
18	Pennsylvania
19	Hawaii
20	Florida
21	Wisconsin
22	Nebraska
23	Kansas
24	Michigan
25	Vermont
26	South Dakota
27	Texas
28	Oregon
29	Ohio
30	Iowa
31	Missouri
32	North Dakota
33	Georgia
34	Indiana
35	North Carolina
36	Tennessee
37	Maine
38	Arizona
39	Oklahoma
40	Alabama
41	Montana
42	Idaho
43	Kentucky
44	South Carolina
45	New Mexico
46	Utah
47	Arkansas
48	West Virginia
49	Mississippi
50	Louisiana

B-4   Personal Income from Wages and Salaries, 2005

State	Wages and salaries $ (in millions)	As percentage of personal income	Rank by percentage
Alabama	69,887	51.8	38
Alaska	13,707	58.3	8
Arizona	99,743	55.7	16
Arkansas	38,272	51.7	39
California	736,560	55.3	21
Colorado	97,263	55.7	17
Connecticut	90,475	54.2	28
Delaware	19,702	63.0	1
Florida	302,397	49.9	44
Georgia	164,162	58.0	9
Hawaii	25,291	57.5	11
Idaho	20,364	50.2	43
Illinois	263,799	57.0	12
Indiana	106,505	54.5	27
Iowa	50,502	53.5	31
Kansas	47,666	52.7	36
Kentucky	64,574	54.6	25
Louisiana	66,307	59.6	2
Maine	20,613	50.6	41
Maryland	118,821	50.5	42
Massachusetts	164,963	59.0	4
Michigan	183,652	55.4	19
Minnesota	112,880	58.9	5
Mississippi	35,824	49.2	45
Missouri	101,725	56.0	15
Montana	13,078	48.4	48
Nebraska	31,740	54.7	24
Nevada	49,973	57.8	10
New Hampshire	26,180	52.8	34
New Jersey	201,643	52.8	35
New Mexico	28,145	52.3	37
New York	452,608	58.7	6
North Carolina	149,327	55.4	20
North Dakota	10,900	54.8	23
Ohio	206,577	56.5	14
Oklahoma	50,079	47.2	49
Oregon	63,383	54.1	29
Pennsylvania	230,427	53.2	32
Rhode Island	19,474	51.4	40
South Carolina	64,430	53.7	30
South Dakota	11,917	47.1	50
Tennessee	101,221	54.8	22
Texas	407,206	54.6	26
Utah	40,152	59.1	3
Vermont	10,828	53.1	33
Virginia	166,170	58.5	7
Washington	125,736	56.8	13
West Virginia	23,002	48.6	46
Wisconsin	102,088	55.5	18
Wyoming	9,189	48.4	47
50 States	5,611,129	55.0	
DC	48,167	155.3	
United States	5,659,296	55.3	

Rank in order by percentage

1	Delaware
2	Louisiana
3	Utah
4	Massachusetts
5	Minnesota
6	New York
7	Virginia
8	Alaska
9	Georgia
10	Nevada
11	Hawaii
12	Illinois
13	Washington
14	Ohio
15	Missouri
16	Arizona
17	Colorado
18	Wisconsin
19	Michigan
20	North Carolina
21	California
22	Tennessee
23	North Dakota
24	Nebraska
25	Kentucky
26	Texas
27	Indiana
28	Connecticut
29	Oregon
30	South Carolina
31	Iowa
32	Pennsylvania
33	Vermont
34	New Hampshire
35	New Jersey
36	Kansas
37	New Mexico
38	Alabama
39	Arkansas
40	Rhode Island
41	Maine
42	Maryland
43	Idaho
44	Florida
45	Mississippi
46	West Virginia
47	Wyoming
48	Montana
49	Oklahoma
50	South Dakota

Note: Numbers that appear to be identical are rounded and vary slightly in actual value. The rankings reflect the actual values before rounding. See the introduction for more details.

B-5 Average Annual Pay, 2005

State	Average annual pay $	Rank
Alabama	34,594	31
Alaska	40,199	15
Arizona	38,154	21
Arkansas	31,260	45
California	46,195	5
Colorado	41,599	10
Connecticut	52,963	1
Delaware	44,655	6
Florida	36,765	23
Georgia	39,089	18
Hawaii	36,355	25
Idaho	30,831	46
Illinois	43,740	8
Indiana	35,433	30
Iowa	33,063	37
Kansas	33,850	34
Kentucky	33,960	33
Louisiana	33,537	35
Maine	32,705	40
Maryland	44,371	7
Massachusetts	50,087	3
Michigan	41,228	11
Minnesota	40,805	12
Mississippi	29,762	48
Missouri	35,945	26
Montana	29,150	49
Nebraska	32,424	42
Nevada	38,760	19
New Hampshire	40,550	14
New Jersey	49,464	4
New Mexico	32,606	41
New York	51,940	2
North Carolina	35,919	27
North Dakota	29,955	47
Ohio	37,331	22
Oklahoma	31,722	43
Oregon	36,585	24
Pennsylvania	39,649	17
Rhode Island	38,746	20
South Carolina	32,916	39
South Dakota	29,149	50
Tennessee	35,841	28
Texas	40,156	16
Utah	33,330	36
Vermont	34,198	32
Virginia	42,289	9
Washington	40,721	13
West Virginia	31,347	44
Wisconsin	35,463	29
Wyoming	33,031	38
50 States	n/a	
DC	66,677	
United States	40,671	

Rank in order by $	
1	Connecticut
2	New York
3	Massachusetts
4	New Jersey
5	California
6	Delaware
7	Maryland
8	Illinois
9	Virginia
10	Colorado
11	Michigan
12	Minnesota
13	Washington
14	New Hampshire
15	Alaska
16	Texas
17	Pennsylvania
18	Georgia
19	Nevada
20	Rhode Island
21	Arizona
22	Ohio
23	Florida
24	Oregon
25	Hawaii
26	Missouri
27	North Carolina
28	Tennessee
29	Wisconsin
30	Indiana
31	Alabama
32	Vermont
33	Kentucky
34	Kansas
35	Louisiana
36	Utah
37	Iowa
38	Wyoming
39	South Carolina
40	Maine
41	New Mexico
42	Nebraska
43	Oklahoma
44	West Virginia
45	Arkansas
46	Idaho
47	North Dakota
48	Mississippi
49	Montana
50	South Dakota

B-6   Average Hourly Earnings, 2006

State	Average hourly earnings $	Rank
Alabama	15.53	33
Alaska	15.91	27
Arizona	15.88	29
Arkansas	13.30	50
California	15.96	26
Colorado	16.80	20
Connecticut	19.85	3
Delaware	18.03	9
Florida	14.61	40
Georgia	14.61	41
Hawaii	15.78	31
Idaho	17.51	14
Illinois	16.08	25
Indiana	18.42	6
Iowa	16.18	24
Kansas	17.68	13
Kentucky	16.85	18
Louisiana	17.24	16
Maine	19.02	5
Maryland	17.89	12
Massachusetts	18.41	7
Michigan	21.95	1
Minnesota	17.02	17
Mississippi	13.68	48
Missouri	17.36	15
Montana	15.90	28
Nebraska	15.11	37
Nevada	15.31	35
New Hampshire	16.83	19
New Jersey	16.49	22
New Mexico	14.03	45
New York	18.27	8
North Carolina	14.52	43
North Dakota	14.77	39
Ohio	19.17	4
Oklahoma	14.61	41
Oregon	15.59	32
Pennsylvania	15.33	34
Rhode Island	13.43	49
South Carolina	14.98	38
South Dakota	13.80	47
Tennessee	14.14	44
Texas	13.98	46
Utah	15.31	35
Vermont	15.86	30
Virginia	16.68	21
Washington	20.91	2
West Virginia	17.93	11
Wisconsin	16.32	23
Wyoming	17.97	10
50 States	n/a	
DC	n/a	
United States	16.81	

Rank in order by $	
1	Michigan
2	Washington
3	Connecticut
4	Ohio
5	Maine
6	Indiana
7	Massachusetts
8	New York
9	Delaware
10	Wyoming
11	West Virginia
12	Maryland
13	Kansas
14	Idaho
15	Missouri
16	Louisiana
17	Minnesota
18	Kentucky
19	New Hampshire
20	Colorado
21	Virginia
22	New Jersey
23	Wisconsin
24	Iowa
25	Illinois
26	California
27	Alaska
28	Montana
29	Arizona
30	Vermont
31	Hawaii
32	Oregon
33	Alabama
34	Pennsylvania
35	Nevada
35	Utah
37	Nebraska
38	South Carolina
39	North Dakota
40	Florida
41	Georgia
41	Oklahoma
43	North Carolina
44	Tennessee
45	New Mexico
46	Texas
47	South Dakota
48	Mississippi
49	Rhode Island
50	Arkansas

Note: Ties in ranking reflect ties in actual values.

B-7　Value Added in Manufacturing, 2004

State	Value added $ (in millions)	Per capita $	Rank per capita		Rank in order per capita	
Alabama	34,002	7,514	21		1	Indiana
Alaska	1,736	2,640	46		2	Iowa
Arizona	24,096	4,198	42		3	Wisconsin
Arkansas	25,655	9,329	9		4	North Carolina
California	202,312	5,645	36		5	Ohio
Colorado	16,965	3,687	43		6	Tennessee
Connecticut	28,745	8,215	15		7	Louisiana
Delaware	7,660	9,229	11		8	Oregon
Florida	44,926	2,584	47		9	Arkansas
Georgia	59,477	6,669	26		10	Michigan
Hawaii	1,489	1,180	50		11	Delaware
Idaho	9,605	6,884	24		12	Kentucky
Illinois	102,971	8,100	16		13	Minnesota
Indiana	86,549	13,900	1		14	South Carolina
Iowa	36,688	12,424	2		15	Connecticut
Kansas	22,108	8,087	17		16	Illinois
Kentucky	36,519	8,817	12		17	Kansas
Louisiana	43,393	9,629	7		18	Vermont
Maine	7,248	5,512	37		19	Missouri
Maryland	19,131	3,440	44		20	Pennsylvania
Massachusetts	45,010	7,025	23		21	Alabama
Michigan	93,659	9,269	10		22	Nebraska
Minnesota	43,707	8,576	13		23	Massachusetts
Mississippi	18,201	6,275	29		24	Idaho
Missouri	44,783	7,775	19		25	Texas
Montana	2,386	2,575	48		26	Georgia
Nebraska	12,477	7,139	22		27	Virginia
Nevada	5,251	2,251	49		28	New Hampshire
New Hampshire	8,466	6,516	28		29	Mississippi
New Jersey	49,127	5,656	35		30	New Mexico
New Mexico	11,708	6,152	30		31	Washington
New York	83,146	4,312	41		32	Rhode Island
North Carolina	90,231	10,565	4		33	South Dakota
North Dakota	2,913	4,579	40		34	Utah
Ohio	117,751	10,284	5		35	New Jersey
Oklahoma	17,933	5,090	38		36	California
Oregon	33,773	9,404	8		37	Maine
Pennsylvania	96,329	7,772	20		38	Oklahoma
Rhode Island	6,322	5,854	32		39	West Virginia
South Carolina	35,663	8,495	14		40	North Dakota
South Dakota	4,500	5,839	33		41	New York
Tennessee	58,678	9,957	6		42	Arizona
Texas	150,698	6,706	25		43	Colorado
Utah	14,015	5,789	34		44	Maryland
Vermont	5,019	8,079	18		45	Wyoming
Virginia	49,715	6,645	27		46	Alaska
Washington	36,834	5,934	31		47	Florida
West Virginia	8,846	4,880	39		48	Montana
Wisconsin	65,693	11,937	3		49	Nevada
Wyoming	1,684	3,328	45		50	Hawaii
50 States	2,025,793	6,912				
DC	164	296				
United States *	2,025,957	6,899				

B-8　Cost of Living, 2006

State	Cost of living index	Rank by index
Alabama	91.6	40
Alaska	123.7	8
Arizona	104.4	14
Arkansas	88.6	48
California	134.7	2
Colorado	101.5	19
Connecticut	127.3	5
Delaware	100.3	23
Florida	103.6	16
Georgia	92.1	39
Hawaii	161.3	1
Idaho	94.5	31
Illinois	95.6	27
Indiana	92.9	38
Iowa	93.1	37
Kansas	90.6	43
Kentucky	94.2	32
Louisiana	94.6	30
Maine	108.6	11
Maryland	126.5	6
Massachusetts	122.7	9
Michigan	101.3	20
Minnesota	97.1	25
Mississippi	89.4	46
Missouri	90.0	45
Montana	99.3	24
Nebraska	90.2	44
Nevada	107.4	12
New Hampshire	n/a	n/a
New Jersey	131.7	3
New Mexico	103.1	18
New York	130.4	4
North Carolina	94.0	35
North Dakota	93.8	36
Ohio	95.4	28
Oklahoma	88.5	49
Oregon	105.8	13
Pennsylvania	100.9	21
Rhode Island	124.4	7
South Carolina	94.2	32
South Dakota	91.1	41
Tennessee	90.8	42
Texas	88.9	47
Utah	96.1	26
Vermont	122.3	10
Virginia	103.5	17
Washington	104.4	14
West Virginia	95.3	29
Wisconsin	94.2	32
Wyoming	100.9	21
50 States	n/a	
DC	140.9	
United States	100.0	

Rank in order by index

1　Hawaii
2　California
3　New Jersey
4　New York
5　Connecticut
6　Maryland
7　Rhode Island
8　Alaska
9　Massachusetts
10　Vermont
11　Maine
12　Nevada
13　Oregon
14　Arizona
14　Washington
16　Florida
17　Virginia
18　New Mexico
19　Colorado
20　Michigan
21　Pennsylvania
21　Wyoming
23　Delaware
24　Montana
25　Minnesota
26　Utah
27　Illinois
28　Ohio
29　West Virginia
30　Louisiana
31　Idaho
32　Kentucky
32　South Carolina
32　Wisconsin
35　North Carolina
36　North Dakota
37　Iowa
38　Indiana
39　Georgia
40　Alabama
41　South Dakota
42　Tennessee
43　Kansas
44　Nebraska
45　Missouri
46　Mississippi
47　Texas
48　Arkansas
49　Oklahoma

Note: Ties in ranking reflect ties in actual values.

B-9   Average Annual Pay in Manufacturing, 2005

State	Average annual pay in manufacturing $	Rank
Alabama	40,654	39
Alaska	35,763	46
Arizona	54,617	7
Arkansas	34,211	49
California	59,744	4
Colorado	53,686	10
Connecticut	63,035	1
Delaware	52,519	11
Florida	43,419	28
Georgia	42,217	35
Hawaii	33,869	50
Idaho	42,843	31
Illinois	50,413	14
Indiana	48,229	17
Iowa	43,058	29
Kansas	44,084	23
Kentucky	44,033	24
Louisiana	49,412	15
Maine	42,110	36
Maryland	54,530	8
Massachusetts	62,475	2
Michigan	56,681	5
Minnesota	48,911	16
Mississippi	34,557	47
Missouri	43,906	25
Montana	36,950	43
Nebraska	36,571	44
Nevada	43,495	27
New Hampshire	52,097	12
New Jersey	60,953	3
New Mexico	41,839	37
New York	51,940	13
North Carolina	42,714	33
North Dakota	36,375	45
Ohio	48,221	18
Oklahoma	39,485	42
Oregon	48,199	19
Pennsylvania	47,290	20
Rhode Island	41,745	38
South Carolina	42,232	34
South Dakota	34,393	48
Tennessee	42,804	32
Texas	54,409	9
Utah	39,874	41
Vermont	46,316	21
Virginia	43,711	26
Washington	54,975	6
West Virginia	43,033	30
Wisconsin	44,455	22
Wyoming	40,594	40
50 States	n/a	
DC	75,822	
United States	49,286	

Rank in order by $	
1	Connecticut
2	Massachusetts
3	New Jersey
4	California
5	Michigan
6	Washington
7	Arizona
8	Maryland
9	Texas
10	Colorado
11	Delaware
12	New Hampshire
13	New York
14	Illinois
15	Louisiana
16	Minnesota
17	Indiana
18	Ohio
19	Oregon
20	Pennsylvania
21	Vermont
22	Wisconsin
23	Kansas
24	Kentucky
25	Missouri
26	Virginia
27	Nevada
28	Florida
29	Iowa
30	West Virginia
31	Idaho
32	Tennessee
33	North Carolina
34	South Carolina
35	Georgia
36	Maine
37	New Mexico
38	Rhode Island
39	Alabama
40	Wyoming
41	Utah
42	Oklahoma
43	Montana
44	Nebraska
45	North Dakota
46	Alaska
47	Mississippi
48	South Dakota
49	Arkansas
50	Hawaii

B-10　Average Annual Pay in Retailing, 2005

State	Average annual pay in retailing $	Rank
Alabama	22,520	33
Alaska	25,781	12
Arizona	27,479	5
Arkansas	20,072	49
California	29,387	1
Colorado	25,394	14
Connecticut	28,751	2
Delaware	24,362	20
Florida	25,821	11
Georgia	24,587	18
Hawaii	25,037	15
Idaho	23,927	23
Illinois	24,739	17
Indiana	21,791	36
Iowa	20,479	44
Kansas	21,299	39
Kentucky	21,253	40
Louisiana	21,482	37
Maine	22,086	34
Maryland	26,566	9
Massachusetts	27,478	6
Michigan	23,786	24
Minnesota	22,743	32
Mississippi	20,442	45
Missouri	22,040	35
Montana	21,158	41
Nebraska	20,345	46
Nevada	28,038	4
New Hampshire	26,035	10
New Jersey	28,608	3
New Mexico	23,041	28
New York	27,242	8
North Carolina	23,123	26
North Dakota	20,204	47
Ohio	22,844	30
Oklahoma	21,157	42
Oregon	24,475	19
Pennsylvania	23,097	27
Rhode Island	24,903	16
South Carolina	22,812	31
South Dakota	20,188	48
Tennessee	24,260	21
Texas	25,566	13
Utah	23,022	29
Vermont	23,748	25
Virginia	23,929	22
Washington	27,432	7
West Virginia	19,838	50
Wisconsin	21,062	43
Wyoming	21,480	38
50 States	n/a	
DC	28,573	
United States	24,930	

Rank in order by $	
1	California
2	Connecticut
3	New Jersey
4	Nevada
5	Arizona
6	Massachusetts
7	Washington
8	New York
9	Maryland
10	New Hampshire
11	Florida
12	Alaska
13	Texas
14	Colorado
15	Hawaii
16	Rhode Island
17	Illinois
18	Georgia
19	Oregon
20	Delaware
21	Tennessee
22	Virginia
23	Idaho
24	Michigan
25	Vermont
26	North Carolina
27	Pennsylvania
28	New Mexico
29	Utah
30	Ohio
31	South Carolina
32	Minnesota
33	Alabama
34	Maine
35	Missouri
36	Indiana
37	Louisiana
38	Wyoming
39	Kansas
40	Kentucky
41	Montana
42	Oklahoma
43	Wisconsin
44	Iowa
45	Mississippi
46	Nebraska
47	North Dakota
48	South Dakota
49	Arkansas
50	West Virginia

B-11 Labor Force, 2006

State	Labor force (in thousands)	Labor force as percentage of population	Rank by percentage
Alabama	2,204	48.3	47
Alaska	348	52.5	25
Arizona	2,969	50.0	39
Arkansas	1,383	49.8	42
California	17,801	49.3	44
Colorado	2,647	56.7	6
Connecticut	1,852	52.8	24
Delaware	447	53.0	21
Florida	9,043	50.8	34
Georgia	4,708	51.9	30
Hawaii	659	51.7	31
Idaho	763	53.4	17
Illinois	6,637	52.0	28
Indiana	3,262	52.0	27
Iowa	1,702	57.4	4
Kansas	1,481	54.0	12
Kentucky	2,035	48.8	46
Louisiana	1,859	41.1	50
Maine	719	54.4	11
Maryland	3,011	53.8	16
Massachusetts	3,387	52.9	22
Michigan	5,112	50.5	36
Minnesota	2,956	57.6	2
Mississippi	1,324	45.3	49
Missouri	3,069	52.9	23
Montana	504	53.9	14
Nebraska	990	56.3	8
Nevada	1,301	53.9	13
New Hampshire	741	56.6	7
New Jersey	4,477	51.4	33
New Mexico	954	49.5	43
New York	9,447	49.1	45
North Carolina	4,467	51.4	32
North Dakota	365	57.3	5
Ohio	5,971	52.1	26
Oklahoma	1,767	49.8	41
Oregon	1,892	52.0	29
Pennsylvania	6,290	50.6	35
Rhode Island	579	53.8	15
South Carolina	2,125	49.9	40
South Dakota	436	56.2	9
Tennessee	2,991	50.2	38
Texas	11,542	50.5	37
Utah	1,316	53.3	18
Vermont	366	58.8	1
Virginia	4,023	53.2	19
Washington	3,337	53.1	20
West Virginia	823	45.3	48
Wisconsin	3,090	55.8	10
Wyoming	293	57.5	3
50 States	151,461	51.2	
DC	289	52.5	
United States	151,750	51.2	

Rank in order by percentage

1 Vermont
2 Minnesota
3 Wyoming
4 Iowa
5 North Dakota
6 Colorado
7 New Hampshire
8 Nebraska
9 South Dakota
10 Wisconsin
11 Maine
12 Kansas
13 Nevada
14 Montana
15 Rhode Island
16 Maryland
17 Idaho
18 Utah
19 Virginia
20 Washington
21 Delaware
22 Massachusetts
23 Missouri
24 Connecticut
25 Alaska
26 Ohio
27 Indiana
28 Illinois
29 Oregon
30 Georgia
31 Hawaii
32 North Carolina
33 New Jersey
34 Florida
35 Pennsylvania
36 Michigan
37 Texas
38 Tennessee
39 Arizona
40 South Carolina
41 Oklahoma
42 Arkansas
43 New Mexico
44 California
45 New York
46 Kentucky
47 Alabama
48 West Virginia
49 Mississippi
50 Louisiana

Note: Numbers that appear to be identical are rounded and vary slightly in actual value. The rankings reflect the actual values before rounding. See the introduction for more details.

B-12 Unemployed and Unemployment Rate, 2006

State	Unemployed (in thousands)	Unemployment rate (percentage of labor force unemployed)	Rank by rate
Alabama	73.7	3.3	41
Alaska	23.0	6.6	3
Arizona	110.6	3.7	34
Arkansas	71.7	5.2	11
California	858.4	4.8	17
Colorado	116.6	4.4	26
Connecticut	86.5	4.7	20
Delaware	16.5	3.7	35
Florida	289.2	3.2	45
Georgia	212.5	4.5	24
Hawaii	16.2	2.5	50
Idaho	25.5	3.3	42
Illinois	294.2	4.4	25
Indiana	165.9	5.1	13
Iowa	57.9	3.4	40
Kansas	64.3	4.3	28
Kentucky	107.1	5.3	9
Louisiana	68.6	3.7	36
Maine	34.1	4.7	19
Maryland	119.5	4.0	32
Massachusetts	171.5	5.1	14
Michigan	363.7	7.1	2
Minnesota	111.9	3.8	33
Mississippi	94.7	7.2	1
Missouri	154.3	5.0	15
Montana	18.0	3.6	39
Nebraska	30.8	3.1	48
Nevada	52.7	4.1	30
New Hampshire	24.0	3.2	43
New Jersey	230.7	5.2	12
New Mexico	39.6	4.1	29
New York	411.0	4.4	27
North Carolina	217.5	4.9	16
North Dakota	11.5	3.2	47
Ohio	316.0	5.3	8
Oklahoma	70.2	4.0	31
Oregon	101.7	5.4	6
Pennsylvania	290.4	4.6	22
Rhode Island	30.2	5.2	10
South Carolina	135.7	6.4	4
South Dakota	14.0	3.2	44
Tennessee	137.8	4.6	23
Texas	548.4	4.8	18
Utah	36.6	2.8	49
Vermont	13.5	3.7	37
Virginia	127.4	3.2	46
Washington	177.1	5.3	7
West Virginia	44.8	5.4	5
Wisconsin	144.3	4.7	21
Wyoming	10.6	3.6	38
50 States	6,942.6	4.6	
DC	17.2	6.0	
United States	6,959.8	4.6	

Rank in order by rate	
1	Mississippi
2	Michigan
3	Alaska
4	South Carolina
5	West Virginia
6	Oregon
7	Washington
8	Ohio
9	Kentucky
10	Rhode Island
11	Arkansas
12	New Jersey
13	Indiana
14	Massachusetts
15	Missouri
16	North Carolina
17	California
18	Texas
19	Maine
20	Connecticut
21	Wisconsin
22	Pennsylvania
23	Tennessee
24	Georgia
25	Illinois
26	Colorado
27	New York
28	Kansas
29	New Mexico
30	Nevada
31	Oklahoma
32	Maryland
33	Minnesota
34	Arizona
35	Delaware
36	Louisiana
37	Vermont
38	Wyoming
39	Montana
40	Iowa
41	Alabama
42	Idaho
43	New Hampshire
44	South Dakota
45	Florida
46	Virginia
47	North Dakota
48	Nebraska
49	Utah
50	Hawaii

Note: Numbers that appear to be identical are rounded and vary slightly in actual value. The rankings reflect the actual values before rounding. See the introduction for more details.

B-13   Employment and Employment Rate, 2006

State	Employed (in thousands)	Employment rate (percentage of labor force employed)	Rank by rate
Alabama	2,130	96.7	10
Alaska	325	93.4	48
Arizona	2,858	96.3	17
Arkansas	1,312	94.8	40
California	16,943	95.2	34
Colorado	2,531	95.6	25
Connecticut	1,765	95.3	31
Delaware	430	96.3	16
Florida	8,754	96.8	6
Georgia	4,495	95.5	27
Hawaii	643	97.5	1
Idaho	737	96.7	9
Illinois	6,342	95.6	26
Indiana	3,096	94.9	38
Iowa	1,644	96.6	11
Kansas	1,417	95.7	23
Kentucky	1,928	94.7	42
Louisiana	1,791	96.3	15
Maine	685	95.3	32
Maryland	2,891	96.0	19
Massachusetts	3,216	94.9	37
Michigan	4,748	92.9	49
Minnesota	2,844	96.2	18
Mississippi	1,229	92.8	50
Missouri	2,914	95.0	36
Montana	486	96.4	12
Nebraska	959	96.9	3
Nevada	1,248	95.9	21
New Hampshire	717	96.8	8
New Jersey	4,246	94.8	39
New Mexico	915	95.9	22
New York	9,036	95.6	24
North Carolina	4,249	95.1	35
North Dakota	353	96.8	4
Ohio	5,655	94.7	43
Oklahoma	1,696	96.0	20
Oregon	1,791	94.6	45
Pennsylvania	6,000	95.4	29
Rhode Island	549	94.8	41
South Carolina	1,989	93.6	47
South Dakota	422	96.8	7
Tennessee	2,854	95.4	28
Texas	10,993	95.2	33
Utah	1,279	97.2	2
Vermont	353	96.3	14
Virginia	3,895	96.8	5
Washington	3,160	94.7	44
West Virginia	779	94.6	46
Wisconsin	2,946	95.3	30
Wyoming	282	96.4	13
50 States	144,518	95.4	
DC	272	94.0	
United States	144,790	95.4	

Rank in order by rate	
1	Hawaii
2	Utah
3	Nebraska
4	North Dakota
5	Virginia
6	Florida
7	South Dakota
8	New Hampshire
9	Idaho
10	Alabama
11	Iowa
12	Montana
13	Wyoming
14	Vermont
15	Louisiana
16	Delaware
17	Arizona
18	Minnesota
19	Maryland
20	Oklahoma
21	Nevada
22	New Mexico
23	Kansas
24	New York
25	Colorado
26	Illinois
27	Georgia
28	Tennessee
29	Pennsylvania
30	Wisconsin
31	Connecticut
32	Maine
33	Texas
34	California
35	North Carolina
36	Missouri
37	Massachusetts
38	Indiana
39	New Jersey
40	Arkansas
41	Rhode Island
42	Kentucky
43	Ohio
44	Washington
45	Oregon
46	West Virginia
47	South Carolina
48	Alaska
49	Michigan
50	Mississippi

Note: Numbers that appear to be identical are rounded and vary slightly in actual value. The rankings reflect the actual values before rounding. See the introduction for more details.

B-14 Government Employment, 2006

State	Government employment (in thousands)	Percentage of total employment	Rank by percentage
Alabama	367	18.5	13
Alaska	82	25.9	1
Arizona	416	15.7	35
Arkansas	207	17.3	23
California	2,459	16.3	30
Colorado	372	16.3	31
Connecticut	246	14.7	39
Delaware	60	13.7	45
Florida	1,104	13.6	46
Georgia	667	16.3	32
Hawaii	124	19.8	9
Idaho	117	18.2	15
Illinois	850	14.3	42
Indiana	427	14.3	41
Iowa	250	16.5	29
Kansas	258	19.3	10
Kentucky	318	17.2	24
Louisiana	365	20.4	7
Maine	107	17.4	22
Maryland	470	18.1	16
Massachusetts	411	12.7	49
Michigan	667	15.3	36
Minnesota	421	15.2	37
Mississippi	247	21.6	5
Missouri	436	15.8	34
Montana	87	19.8	8
Nebraska	166	17.5	19
Nevada	150	11.5	50
New Hampshire	88	13.7	44
New Jersey	648	15.9	33
New Mexico	206	24.5	2
New York	1,498	17.4	21
North Carolina	684	17.1	26
North Dakota	77	21.7	4
Ohio	801	14.7	40
Oklahoma	322	20.9	6
Oregon	293	17.0	28
Pennsylvania	746	12.9	48
Rhode Island	65	13.1	47
South Carolina	343	17.9	18
South Dakota	75	18.7	12
Tennessee	419	15.1	38
Texas	1,715	17.1	25
Utah	207	17.0	27
Vermont	54	17.4	20
Virginia	678	18.1	17
Washington	532	18.5	14
West Virginia	144	19.0	11
Wisconsin	402	14.0	43
Wyoming	66	23.8	3
50 States	21,911	16.2	
DC	231	33.5	
United States	22,142	16.3	

Rank in order by percentage	
1	Alaska
2	New Mexico
3	Wyoming
4	North Dakota
5	Mississippi
6	Oklahoma
7	Louisiana
8	Montana
9	Hawaii
10	Kansas
11	West Virginia
12	South Dakota
13	Alabama
14	Washington
15	Idaho
16	Maryland
17	Virginia
18	South Carolina
19	Nebraska
20	Vermont
21	New York
22	Maine
23	Arkansas
24	Kentucky
25	Texas
26	North Carolina
27	Utah
28	Oregon
29	Iowa
30	California
31	Colorado
32	Georgia
33	New Jersey
34	Missouri
35	Arizona
36	Michigan
37	Minnesota
38	Tennessee
39	Connecticut
40	Ohio
41	Indiana
42	Illinois
43	Wisconsin
44	New Hampshire
45	Delaware
46	Florida
47	Rhode Island
48	Pennsylvania
49	Massachusetts
50	Nevada

Note: Numbers that appear to be identical are rounded and vary slightly in actual value. The rankings reflect the actual values before rounding. See the introduction for more details.

B-15 Manufacturing Employment, 2006

State	Manufacturing employment (in thousands)	Percentage of total employment	Rank by percentage
Alabama	300	15.1	6
Alaska	15	4.5	47
Arizona	183	6.9	40
Arkansas	196	16.3	3
California	1,529	10.2	26
Colorado	151	6.6	41
Connecticut	193	11.5	19
Delaware	34	7.6	38
Florida	399	4.9	44
Georgia	451	11.0	21
Hawaii	15	2.5	50
Idaho	65	10.0	29
Illinois	679	11.3	20
Indiana	572	19.0	1
Iowa	236	15.5	4
Kansas	181	13.4	12
Kentucky	258	13.9	10
Louisiana	147	8.2	34
Maine	59	9.4	32
Maryland	138	5.3	43
Massachusetts	306	9.4	31
Michigan	647	14.7	7
Minnesota	349	12.5	14
Mississippi	175	15.2	5
Missouri	301	10.9	22
Montana	20	4.5	46
Nebraska	103	10.8	23
Nevada	50	3.8	48
New Hampshire	76	11.8	16
New Jersey	316	7.8	37
New Mexico	39	4.6	45
New York	563	6.5	42
North Carolina	558	13.9	11
North Dakota	27	7.4	39
Ohio	805	14.7	8
Oklahoma	148	9.6	30
Oregon	214	12.4	15
Pennsylvania	668	11.5	18
Rhode Island	53	10.7	24
South Carolina	253	13.2	13
South Dakota	43	10.5	25
Tennessee	405	14.5	9
Texas	912	9.1	33
Utah	123	10.0	27
Vermont	37	11.7	17
Virginia	296	7.9	36
Washington	289	10.0	28
West Virginia	62	8.1	35
Wisconsin	512	17.7	2
Wyoming	10	3.7	49
50 States	14,158	10.4	
DC	2	0.3	
United States	14,160	10.4	

Rank in order by percentage

1 Indiana
2 Wisconsin
3 Arkansas
4 Iowa
5 Mississippi
6 Alabama
7 Michigan
8 Ohio
9 Tennessee
10 Kentucky
11 North Carolina
12 Kansas
13 South Carolina
14 Minnesota
15 Oregon
16 New Hampshire
17 Vermont
18 Pennsylvania
19 Connecticut
20 Illinois
21 Georgia
22 Missouri
23 Nebraska
24 Rhode Island
25 South Dakota
26 California
27 Utah
28 Washington
29 Idaho
30 Oklahoma
31 Massachusetts
32 Maine
33 Texas
34 Louisiana
35 West Virginia
36 Virginia
37 New Jersey
38 Delaware
39 North Dakota
40 Arizona
41 Colorado
42 New York
43 Maryland
44 Florida
45 New Mexico
46 Montana
47 Alaska
48 Nevada
49 Wyoming
50 Hawaii

Note: Numbers that appear to be identical are rounded and vary slightly in actual value. The rankings reflect the actual values before rounding. See the introduction for more details.

B-16 Construction Employment, 2006

State	Construction employment (in thousands)	Percentage of total population	Rank by percentage
Alabama	110	5.5	23
Alaska	18	5.8	20
Arizona	248	9.3	2
Arkansas	56	4.7	39
California	916	6.1	16
Colorado	168	7.3	7
Connecticut	64	3.8	50
Delaware	30	6.7	13
Florida	620	7.6	6
Georgia	218	5.3	25
Hawaii	36	5.8	22
Idaho	54	8.4	4
Illinois	276	4.6	41
Indiana	151	5.1	29
Iowa	77	5.1	28
Kansas	65	4.8	34
Kentucky	87	4.7	38
Louisiana	112	6.3	15
Maine	31	5.1	30
Maryland	187	7.2	8
Massachusetts	142	4.4	45
Michigan	193	4.4	44
Minnesota	130	4.7	37
Mississippi	57	5.0	31
Missouri	144	5.2	27
Montana	30	6.9	11
Nebraska	46	4.8	35
Nevada	152	11.7	1
New Hampshire	31	4.9	33
New Jersey	172	4.2	48
New Mexico	60	7.1	9
New York	332	3.8	49
North Carolina	243	6.1	18
North Dakota	17	4.9	32
Ohio	237	4.3	47
Oklahoma	68	4.4	46
Oregon	102	5.9	19
Pennsylvania	259	4.5	42
Rhode Island	23	4.7	40
South Carolina	126	6.6	14
South Dakota	22	5.4	24
Tennessee	124	4.5	43
Texas	610	6.1	17
Utah	99	8.1	5
Vermont	18	5.8	21
Virginia	262	7.0	10
Washington	195	6.8	12
West Virginia	40	5.2	26
Wisconsin	136	4.8	36
Wyoming	23	8.4	3
50 States	7,619	5.6	
DC	13	1.9	
United States	7,632	5.6	

Rank in order by percentage	
1	Nevada
2	Arizona
3	Wyoming
4	Idaho
5	Utah
6	Florida
7	Colorado
8	Maryland
9	New Mexico
10	Virginia
11	Montana
12	Washington
13	Delaware
14	South Carolina
15	Louisiana
16	California
17	Texas
18	North Carolina
19	Oregon
20	Alaska
21	Vermont
22	Hawaii
23	Alabama
24	South Dakota
25	Georgia
26	West Virginia
27	Missouri
28	Iowa
29	Indiana
30	Maine
31	Mississippi
32	North Dakota
33	New Hampshire
34	Kansas
35	Nebraska
36	Wisconsin
37	Minnesota
38	Kentucky
39	Arkansas
40	Rhode Island
41	Illinois
42	Pennsylvania
43	Tennessee
44	Michigan
45	Massachusetts
46	Oklahoma
47	Ohio
48	New Jersey
49	New York
50	Connecticut

Note: Numbers that appear to be identical are rounded and vary slightly in actual value. The rankings reflect the actual values before rounding. See the introduction for more details.

B-17 *Fortune* 500 Companies, 2006

State	Number of *Fortune* 500 companies	*Fortune* 500 companies per million population	Rank per million
Alabama	8	1.8	35
Alaska	0	n/a	n/a
Arizona	13	2.2	28
Arkansas	7	2.5	22
California	110	3.0	20
Colorado	17	3.6	14
Connecticut	29	8.3	1
Delaware	2	2.4	24
Florida	31	1.7	36
Georgia	31	3.4	16
Hawaii	2	1.6	38
Idaho	3	2.1	30
Illinois	62	4.9	5
Indiana	14	2.2	27
Iowa	7	2.4	25
Kansas	5	1.8	34
Kentucky	8	1.9	33
Louisiana	5	1.1	39
Maine	1	0.8	43
Maryland	12	2.1	29
Massachusetts	21	3.3	19
Michigan	34	3.4	17
Minnesota	36	7.0	2
Mississippi	0	n/a	n/a
Missouri	28	4.8	6
Montana	0	n/a	n/a
Nebraska	8	4.5	8
Nevada	8	3.3	18
New Hampshire	3	2.3	26
New Jersey	37	4.2	11
New Mexico	2	1.0	41
New York	92	4.8	7
North Carolina	25	2.9	21
North Dakota	1	1.6	37
Ohio	62	5.4	4
Oklahoma	7	2.0	32
Oregon	4	1.1	40
Pennsylvania	49	3.9	13
Rhode Island	7	6.5	3
South Carolina	4	0.9	42
South Dakota	0	n/a	n/a
Tennessee	21	3.5	15
Texas	102	4.5	10
Utah	5	2.0	31
Vermont	0	n/a	n/a
Virginia	30	4.0	12
Washington	15	2.4	23
West Virginia	1	0.6	44
Wisconsin	25	4.5	9
Wyoming	0	n/a	n/a
50 States	995	3.4	
DC	5	9.1	
United States	1,000	3.4	

Rank in order per million	
1	Connecticut
2	Minnesota
3	Rhode Island
4	Ohio
5	Illinois
6	Missouri
7	New York
8	Nebraska
9	Wisconsin
10	Texas
11	New Jersey
12	Virginia
13	Pennsylvania
14	Colorado
15	Tennessee
16	Georgia
17	Michigan
18	Nevada
19	Massachusetts
20	California
21	North Carolina
22	Arkansas
23	Washington
24	Delaware
25	Iowa
26	New Hampshire
27	Indiana
28	Arizona
29	Maryland
30	Idaho
31	Utah
32	Oklahoma
33	Kentucky
34	Kansas
35	Alabama
36	Florida
37	North Dakota
38	Hawaii
39	Louisiana
40	Oregon
41	New Mexico
42	South Carolina
43	Maine
44	West Virginia

Note: Numbers that appear to be identical are rounded and vary slightly in actual value. The rankings reflect the actual values before rounding. See the introduction for more details.

B-18 Tourism Spending, 2004

State	Tourism spending $ (in millions)	Percentage of U.S. total	Per capita $	Rank per capita
Alabama	5,969	1.1	1,319	44
Alaska	1,470	0.3	2,234	8
Arizona	9,974	1.9	1,738	23
Arkansas	4,281	0.8	1,557	35
California	65,700	12.3	1,833	19
Colorado	9,965	1.9	2,166	10
Connecticut	7,132	1.3	2,038	14
Delaware	1,181	0.2	1,422	39
Florida	46,672	8.8	2,685	4
Georgia	15,390	2.9	1,726	24
Hawaii	8,032	1.5	6,364	2
Idaho	2,404	0.5	1,723	25
Illinois	23,010	4.3	1,810	21
Indiana	7,143	1.3	1,147	49
Iowa	5,014	0.9	1,698	28
Kansas	4,172	0.8	1,526	37
Kentucky	5,868	1.1	1,417	40
Louisiana	9,539	1.8	2,117	12
Maine	2,085	0.4	1,586	33
Maryland	9,734	1.8	1,750	22
Massachusetts	10,975	2.1	1,713	26
Michigan	12,751	2.4	1,262	47
Minnesota	8,494	1.6	1,667	29
Mississippi	5,697	1.1	1,964	16
Missouri	9,465	1.8	1,643	31
Montana	2,184	0.4	2,357	5
Nebraska	2,982	0.6	1,706	27
Nevada	26,250	4.9	11,252	1
New Hampshire	2,860	0.5	2,201	9
New Jersey	15,733	3.0	1,811	20
New Mexico	4,348	0.8	2,285	7
New York	30,458	5.7	1,580	34
North Carolina	13,253	2.5	1,552	36
North Dakota	1,340	0.3	2,105	13
Ohio	13,171	2.5	1,150	48
Oklahoma	4,456	0.8	1,265	46
Oregon	5,835	1.1	1,625	32
Pennsylvania	16,175	3.0	1,305	45
Rhode Island	1,510	0.3	1,398	41
South Carolina	7,764	1.5	1,849	18
South Dakota	1,663	0.3	2,157	11
Tennessee	11,164	2.1	1,894	17
Texas	33,818	6.4	1,505	38
Utah	4,030	0.8	1,665	30
Vermont	1,446	0.3	2,327	6
Virginia	15,041	2.8	2,011	15
Washington	8,594	1.6	1,385	42
West Virginia	1,966	0.4	1,085	50
Wisconsin	7,581	1.4	1,377	43
Wyoming	1,842	0.3	3,640	3
50 States	527,579	99.1	1,800	
DC	4,776	0.9	8,617	
United States	532,355	100.0	1,813	

Rank in order per capita

1	Nevada
2	Hawaii
3	Wyoming
4	Florida
5	Montana
6	Vermont
7	New Mexico
8	Alaska
9	New Hampshire
10	Colorado
11	South Dakota
12	Louisiana
13	North Dakota
14	Connecticut
15	Virginia
16	Mississippi
17	Tennessee
18	South Carolina
19	California
20	New Jersey
21	Illinois
22	Maryland
23	Arizona
24	Georgia
25	Idaho
26	Massachusetts
27	Nebraska
28	Iowa
29	Minnesota
30	Utah
31	Missouri
32	Oregon
33	Maine
34	New York
35	Arkansas
36	North Carolina
37	Kansas
38	Texas
39	Delaware
40	Kentucky
41	Rhode Island
42	Washington
43	Wisconsin
44	Alabama
45	Pennsylvania
46	Oklahoma
47	Michigan
48	Ohio
49	Indiana
50	West Virginia

Note: Numbers that appear to be identical are rounded and vary slightly in actual value. The rankings reflect the actual values before rounding. See the introduction for more details.

B-19 Exports, 2006

State	Exports $ (millions)	Exports per capita $	Rank per capita
Alabama	6,941	1,523	23
Alaska	767	1,156	33
Arizona	8,769	1,476	24
Arkansas	2,223	800	42
California	75,229	2,082	13
Colorado	5,147	1,103	36
Connecticut	9,394	2,676	5
Delaware	1,966	2,330	8
Florida	20,257	1,139	34
Georgia	11,485	1,266	30
Hawaii	201	158	50
Idaho	2,086	1,460	25
Illinois	29,488	2,310	9
Indiana	12,372	1,973	16
Iowa	3,632	1,224	31
Kansas	5,600	2,040	14
Kentucky	9,310	2,231	11
Louisiana	7,162	1,583	22
Maine	1,050	795	44
Maryland	4,126	737	45
Massachusetts	14,472	2,262	10
Michigan	33,302	3,290	3
Minnesota	12,764	2,487	6
Mississippi	2,404	823	41
Missouri	7,497	1,292	29
Montana	461	493	48
Nebraska	1,803	1,025	37
Nevada	2,707	1,121	35
New Hampshire	1,756	1,341	27
New Jersey	18,596	2,133	12
New Mexico	1,782	924	40
New York	34,150	1,774	20
North Carolina	12,013	1,383	26
North Dakota	778	1,222	32
Ohio	21,438	1,870	18
Oklahoma	2,480	699	46
Oregon	8,881	2,439	7
Pennsylvania	16,498	1,327	28
Rhode Island	857	796	43
South Carolina	7,599	1,786	19
South Dakota	451	582	47
Tennessee	11,916	1,998	15
Texas	66,872	2,925	4
Utah	3,966	1,606	21
Vermont	2,132	3,422	2
Virginia	7,518	993	38
Washington	29,571	4,703	1
West Virginia	1,759	968	39
Wisconsin	10,462	1,890	17
Wyoming	178	349	49
50 States	554,265	1,873	
DC	1,725	3,133	
United States*	586,577	1,979	

Due to rounding or data sources, the 50-state total plus D.C. may not equal the U.S. total. Please see introduction.

Rank in order per capita	
1	Washington
2	Vermont
3	Michigan
4	Texas
5	Connecticut
6	Minnesota
7	Oregon
8	Delaware
9	Illinois
10	Massachusetts
11	Kentucky
12	New Jersey
13	California
14	Kansas
15	Tennessee
16	Indiana
17	Wisconsin
18	Ohio
19	South Carolina
20	New York
21	Utah
22	Louisiana
23	Alabama
24	Arizona
25	Idaho
26	North Carolina
27	New Hampshire
28	Pennsylvania
29	Missouri
30	Georgia
31	Iowa
32	North Dakota
33	Alaska
34	Florida
35	Nevada
36	Colorado
37	Nebraska
38	Virginia
39	West Virginia
40	New Mexico
41	Mississippi
42	Arkansas
43	Rhode Island
44	Maine
45	Maryland
46	Oklahoma
47	South Dakota
48	Montana
49	Wyoming
50	Hawaii

B-20 Housing Permits, 2005

State	Housing permits	Permits per 10,000 population	Rank per 10,000
Alabama	30,612	67.2	22
Alaska	2,885	43.5	43
Arizona	90,851	153.0	3
Arkansas	17,932	64.5	23
California	205,020	56.7	29
Colorado	45,891	98.4	9
Connecticut	11,885	33.9	47
Delaware	8,195	97.2	10
Florida	287,250	161.5	2
Georgia	109,336	120.5	6
Hawaii	9,828	77.1	17
Idaho	21,578	151.0	4
Illinois	66,942	52.4	33
Indiana	38,476	61.3	26
Iowa	16,766	56.5	30
Kansas	14,048	51.2	36
Kentucky	21,159	50.7	37
Louisiana	22,811	50.4	38
Maine	8,969	67.9	21
Maryland	30,180	53.9	32
Massachusetts	24,549	38.4	45
Michigan	45,328	44.8	41
Minnesota	36,509	71.1	20
Mississippi	13,396	45.9	40
Missouri	33,114	57.1	28
Montana	4,803	51.3	35
Nebraska	9,929	56.5	31
Nevada	47,728	197.6	1
New Hampshire	7,586	57.9	27
New Jersey	38,588	44.3	42
New Mexico	14,180	73.5	18
New York	61,949	32.2	49
North Carolina	97,910	112.8	7
North Dakota	4,038	63.4	25
Ohio	47,727	41.6	44
Oklahoma	18,362	51.8	34
Oregon	31,024	85.2	12
Pennsylvania	44,525	35.8	46
Rhode Island	2,836	26.4	50
South Carolina	54,157	127.3	5
South Dakota	5,685	73.3	19
Tennessee	46,615	78.2	16
Texas	210,611	92.1	11
Utah	27,799	112.6	8
Vermont	2,917	46.8	39
Virginia	61,518	81.3	14
Washington	52,988	84.3	13
West Virginia	6,140	33.8	48
Wisconsin	35,334	63.8	24
Wyoming	3,997	78.5	15
50 States	2,152,456	72.8	
DC	2,860	52.0	
United States	2,155,316	72.7	

Rank in order per 10,000 population

1	Nevada
2	Florida
3	Arizona
4	Idaho
5	South Carolina
6	Georgia
7	North Carolina
8	Utah
9	Colorado
10	Delaware
11	Texas
12	Oregon
13	Washington
14	Virginia
15	Wyoming
16	Tennessee
17	Hawaii
18	New Mexico
19	South Dakota
20	Minnesota
21	Maine
22	Alabama
23	Arkansas
24	Wisconsin
25	North Dakota
26	Indiana
27	New Hampshire
28	Missouri
29	California
30	Iowa
31	Nebraska
32	Maryland
33	Illinois
34	Oklahoma
35	Montana
36	Kansas
37	Kentucky
38	Louisiana
39	Vermont
40	Mississippi
41	Michigan
42	New Jersey
43	Alaska
44	Ohio
45	Massachusetts
46	Pennsylvania
47	Connecticut
48	West Virginia
49	New York
50	Rhode Island

Note: Numbers that appear to be identical are rounded and vary slightly in actual value. The rankings reflect the actual values before rounding. See the introduction for more details.

B-21 Percentage Change in Home Prices, 2001–2006

State	Percentage change in price	Rank
Alabama	30.18	36
Alaska	53.01	23
Arizona	96.71	6
Arkansas	32.31	33
California	111.93	2
Colorado	23.68	44
Connecticut	62.98	14
Delaware	70.75	11
Florida	112.59	1
Georgia	28.02	39
Hawaii	111.21	3
Idaho	55.27	22
Illinois	42.76	26
Indiana	17.00	50
Iowa	23.61	45
Kansas	24.10	43
Kentucky	24.94	42
Louisiana	37.92	28
Maine	61.74	15
Maryland	102.68	5
Massachusetts	56.98	18
Michigan	18.95	48
Minnesota	46.61	25
Mississippi	27.62	40
Missouri	33.29	32
Montana	55.84	19
Nebraska	21.57	47
Nevada	104.77	4
New Hampshire	61.03	16
New Jersey	84.98	8
New Mexico	50.30	24
New York	72.76	10
North Carolina	28.41	37
North Dakota	39.64	27
Ohio	18.40	49
Oklahoma	26.75	41
Oregon	63.79	13
Pennsylvania	55.57	21
Rhode Island	94.00	7
South Carolina	31.48	34
South Dakota	31.18	35
Tennessee	28.06	38
Texas	22.64	46
Utah	33.39	31
Vermont	65.97	12
Virginia	83.38	9
Washington	60.21	17
West Virginia	34.73	30
Wisconsin	36.00	29
Wyoming	55.61	20
50 States	n/a	
DC	119.97	
United States	56.49	

	Rank in order by percentage
1	Florida
2	California
3	Hawaii
4	Nevada
5	Maryland
6	Arizona
7	Rhode Island
8	New Jersey
9	Virginia
10	New York
11	Delaware
12	Vermont
13	Oregon
14	Connecticut
15	Maine
16	New Hampshire
17	Washington
18	Massachusetts
19	Montana
20	Wyoming
21	Pennsylvania
22	Idaho
23	Alaska
24	New Mexico
25	Minnesota
26	Illinois
27	North Dakota
28	Louisiana
29	Wisconsin
30	West Virginia
31	Utah
32	Missouri
33	Arkansas
34	South Carolina
35	South Dakota
36	Alabama
37	North Carolina
38	Tennessee
39	Georgia
40	Mississippi
41	Oklahoma
42	Kentucky
43	Kansas
44	Colorado
45	Iowa
46	Texas
47	Nebraska
48	Michigan
49	Ohio
50	Indiana

B-22 Net Farm Income, 2005

State	Net farm income $ (in thousands)	Net farm income per capita $	Rank by total income
Alabama	1,923,818	422	12
Alaska	7,529	11	50
Arizona	1,123,157	189	25
Arkansas	1,902,834	685	13
California	9,118,219	252	1
Colorado	1,216,043	261	23
Connecticut	188,551	54	42
Delaware	490,206	581	37
Florida	3,217,376	181	5
Georgia	2,536,329	280	8
Hawaii	103,292	81	46
Idaho	1,125,387	787	24
Illinois	1,064,580	83	27
Indiana	1,390,139	222	20
Iowa	3,446,081	1,162	4
Kansas	2,525,807	920	9
Kentucky	2,082,389	499	10
Louisiana	662,830	147	36
Maine	179,332	136	43
Maryland	744,737	133	33
Massachusetts	130,597	20	44
Michigan	1,337,332	132	21
Minnesota	3,058,691	596	6
Mississippi	1,837,398	629	14
Missouri	1,547,565	267	17
Montana	702,817	751	35
Nebraska	2,699,540	1,535	7
Nevada	122,491	51	45
New Hampshire	58,493	45	47
New Jersey	277,579	32	40
New Mexico	759,588	394	32
New York	1,111,018	58	26
North Carolina	3,616,434	416	3
North Dakota	1,280,048	2,011	22
Ohio	1,452,142	127	18
Oklahoma	1,439,161	406	19
Oregon	1,052,917	289	28
Pennsylvania	1,729,989	139	16
Rhode Island	31,268	29	49
South Carolina	731,905	172	34
South Dakota	1,926,441	2,483	11
Tennessee	894,190	150	31
Texas	6,295,953	275	2
Utah	328,644	133	38
Vermont	213,358	342	41
Virginia	1,004,936	133	30
Washington	1,048,347	167	29
West Virginia	55,000	30	48
Wisconsin	1,741,579	315	15
Wyoming	299,836	589	39
50 States	73,833,892	250	
DC	n/a	n/a	
United States*	73,833,886	249	

Rank in order by total income	
1	California
2	Texas
3	North Carolina
4	Iowa
5	Florida
6	Minnesota
7	Nebraska
8	Georgia
9	Kansas
10	Kentucky
11	South Dakota
12	Alabama
13	Arkansas
14	Mississippi
15	Wisconsin
16	Pennsylvania
17	Missouri
18	Ohio
19	Oklahoma
20	Indiana
21	Michigan
22	North Dakota
23	Colorado
24	Idaho
25	Arizona
26	New York
27	Illinois
28	Oregon
29	Washington
30	Virginia
31	Tennessee
32	New Mexico
33	Maryland
34	South Carolina
35	Montana
36	Louisiana
37	Delaware
38	Utah
39	Wyoming
40	New Jersey
41	Vermont
42	Connecticut
43	Maine
44	Massachusetts
45	Nevada
46	Hawaii
47	New Hampshire
48	West Virginia
49	Rhode Island
50	Alaska

Due to rounding or data sources, the 50-state total plus D.C. may not equal the U.S. total. Please see introduction.

B-23 Financial Institution Assets, 2005

State	Total assets $ (in millions)	Per capita assets $	Rank per capita
Alabama	220,172	48,307	8
Alaska	4,102	6,181	49
Arizona	81,250	13,680	35
Arkansas	44,364	15,963	32
California	656,285	18,163	23
Colorado	43,915	9,413	43
Connecticut	65,829	18,753	22
Delaware	470,876	558,225	2
Florida	142,112	7,988	47
Georgia	274,467	30,252	13
Hawaii	36,239	28,418	15
Idaho	6,476	4,532	50
Illinois	377,154	29,550	14
Indiana	101,738	16,221	30
Iowa	53,749	18,120	24
Kansas	60,548	22,060	19
Kentucky	52,604	12,605	38
Louisiana	72,622	16,054	31
Maine	47,696	36,092	10
Maryland	50,731	9,058	45
Massachusetts	231,132	36,121	9
Michigan	212,187	20,965	20
Minnesota	66,457	12,948	37
Mississippi	47,941	16,412	29
Missouri	98,091	16,911	28
Montana	15,916	17,010	27
Nebraska	36,843	20,948	21
Nevada	391,998	162,331	4
New Hampshire	19,396	14,807	33
New Jersey	157,809	18,102	25
New Mexico	16,731	8,676	46
New York	1,198,703	62,255	7
North Carolina	1,707,833	196,681	3
North Dakota	16,718	26,258	17
Ohio	1,633,926	142,526	5
Oklahoma	62,078	17,497	26
Oregon	25,927	7,121	48
Pennsylvania	383,699	30,870	12
Rhode Island	29,756	27,649	16
South Carolina	48,727	11,451	41
South Dakota	471,238	607,318	1
Tennessee	82,371	13,814	34
Texas	237,631	10,395	42
Utah	224,534	90,920	6
Vermont	8,295	13,314	36
Virginia	269,406	35,601	11
Washington	57,829	9,197	44
West Virginia	21,019	11,569	40
Wisconsin	128,291	23,173	18
Wyoming	6,185	12,144	39
50 States	10,771,596	36,408	
DC	1,094	1,987	
United States*	10,877,075	36,696	

Due to rounding or data sources, the 50-state total plus D.C. may not equal the U.S. total. Please see introduction.

Rank in order per capita	
1	South Dakota
2	Delaware
3	North Carolina
4	Nevada
5	Ohio
6	Utah
7	New York
8	Alabama
9	Massachusetts
10	Maine
11	Virginia
12	Pennsylvania
13	Georgia
14	Illinois
15	Hawaii
16	Rhode Island
17	North Dakota
18	Wisconsin
19	Kansas
20	Michigan
21	Nebraska
22	Connecticut
23	California
24	Iowa
25	New Jersey
26	Oklahoma
27	Montana
28	Missouri
29	Mississippi
30	Indiana
31	Louisiana
32	Arkansas
33	New Hampshire
34	Tennessee
35	Arizona
36	Vermont
37	Minnesota
38	Kentucky
39	Wyoming
40	West Virginia
41	South Carolina
42	Texas
43	Colorado
44	Washington
45	Maryland
46	New Mexico
47	Florida
48	Oregon
49	Alaska
50	Idaho

B-24 Bankruptcy Filings by Individuals and Businesses, 2006

State	Bankruptcy petitions	Petitions per 1,000 residents	Rank per 1,000
Alabama	34,839	7.64	6
Alaska	1,748	2.63	48
Arizona	26,655	4.49	26
Arkansas	21,467	7.72	5
California	117,622	3.26	44
Colorado	31,120	6.67	10
Connecticut	11,468	3.27	43
Delaware	3,252	3.86	36
Florida	73,499	4.13	31
Georgia	61,265	6.75	9
Hawaii	3,195	2.51	50
Idaho	8,189	5.73	17
Illinois	76,570	6.00	15
Indiana	59,969	9.56	1
Iowa	12,767	4.30	29
Kansas	16,272	5.93	16
Kentucky	29,994	7.19	7
Louisiana	25,286	5.59	19
Maine	4,612	3.49	42
Maryland	24,643	4.40	28
Massachusetts	19,559	3.06	47
Michigan	67,197	6.64	13
Minnesota	18,548	3.61	41
Mississippi	16,235	5.56	20
Missouri	38,635	6.66	11
Montana	4,323	4.62	24
Nebraska	8,659	4.92	22
Nevada	17,235	7.14	8
New Hampshire	4,245	3.24	45
New Jersey	34,184	3.92	34
New Mexico	8,164	4.23	30
New York	77,398	4.02	33
North Carolina	31,584	3.64	40
North Dakota	2,471	3.88	35
Ohio	98,775	8.62	2
Oklahoma	27,691	7.80	4
Oregon	22,944	6.30	14
Pennsylvania	56,448	4.54	25
Rhode Island	4,043	3.76	39
South Carolina	10,857	2.55	49
South Dakota	2,969	3.83	37
Tennessee	49,169	8.25	3
Texas	86,794	3.80	38
Utah	13,966	5.66	18
Vermont	1,953	3.13	46
Virginia	30,939	4.09	32
Washington	32,337	5.14	21
West Virginia	12,086	6.65	12
Wisconsin	27,181	4.91	23
Wyoming	2,242	4.40	27
50 States	1,473,263	4.98	
DC	1,670	3.03	
United States*	1,484,570	5.01	

Rank in order per 1,000 residents

1	Indiana
2	Ohio
3	Tennessee
4	Oklahoma
5	Arkansas
6	Alabama
7	Kentucky
8	Nevada
9	Georgia
10	Colorado
11	Missouri
12	West Virginia
13	Michigan
14	Oregon
15	Illinois
16	Kansas
17	Idaho
18	Utah
19	Louisiana
20	Mississippi
21	Washington
22	Nebraska
23	Wisconsin
24	Montana
25	Pennsylvania
26	Arizona
27	Wyoming
28	Maryland
29	Iowa
30	New Mexico
31	Florida
32	Virginia
33	New York
34	New Jersey
35	North Dakota
36	Delaware
37	South Dakota
38	Texas
39	Rhode Island
40	North Carolina
41	Minnesota
42	Maine
43	Connecticut
44	California
45	New Hampshire
46	Vermont
47	Massachusetts
48	Alaska
49	South Carolina
50	Hawaii

Note: Numbers that appear to be identical are rounded and vary slightly in actual value. The rankings reflect the actual values before rounding. See the introduction for more details.

*Due to rounding or data sources, the 50-state total plus D.C. may not equal the U.S. total. Please see introduction.

B-25 Patents Issued, FY 2005

State	Patents issued	Patents per 100,000 population	Rank per 100,000
Alabama	364	8.0	44
Alaska	33	5.0	49
Arizona	1,635	27.5	18
Arkansas	149	5.4	47
California	19,928	55.2	3
Colorado	2,044	43.8	9
Connecticut	1,716	48.9	7
Delaware	386	45.8	8
Florida	2,744	15.4	30
Georgia	1,383	15.2	31
Hawaii	64	5.0	48
Idaho	1,646	115.2	1
Illinois	3,352	26.3	19
Indiana	1,303	20.8	26
Iowa	650	21.9	24
Kansas	509	18.5	28
Kentucky	408	9.8	43
Louisiana	308	6.8	45
Maine	143	10.8	41
Maryland	1,306	23.3	22
Massachusetts	3,443	53.8	4
Michigan	3,907	38.6	12
Minnesota	2,659	51.8	5
Mississippi	138	4.7	50
Missouri	791	13.6	34
Montana	130	13.9	32
Nebraska	222	12.6	38
Nevada	461	19.1	27
New Hampshire	569	43.4	10
New Jersey	2,978	34.2	13
New Mexico	308	16.0	29
New York	5,631	29.2	16
North Carolina	1,882	21.7	25
North Dakota	84	13.2	35
Ohio	2,892	25.2	20
Oklahoma	430	12.1	39
Oregon	1,843	50.6	6
Pennsylvania	2,735	22.0	23
Rhode Island	333	30.9	15
South Carolina	553	13.0	36
South Dakota	78	10.1	42
Tennessee	754	12.6	37
Texas	5,660	24.8	21
Utah	688	27.9	17
Vermont	439	70.5	2
Virginia	1,045	13.8	33
Washington	2,446	38.9	11
West Virginia	106	5.8	46
Wisconsin	1,812	32.7	14
Wyoming	60	11.8	40
50 States	85,148	28.8	
DC	60	10.9	
United States*	85,238	28.8	

Due to rounding or data sources, the 50-state total plus D.C. may not equal the U.S. total. Please see introduction.

Rank in order per 100,000 population	
1	Idaho
2	Vermont
3	California
4	Massachusetts
5	Minnesota
6	Oregon
7	Connecticut
8	Delaware
9	Colorado
10	New Hampshire
11	Washington
12	Michigan
13	New Jersey
14	Wisconsin
15	Rhode Island
16	New York
17	Utah
18	Arizona
19	Illinois
20	Ohio
21	Texas
22	Maryland
23	Pennsylvania
24	Iowa
25	North Carolina
26	Indiana
27	Nevada
28	Kansas
29	New Mexico
30	Florida
31	Georgia
32	Montana
33	Virginia
34	Missouri
35	North Dakota
36	South Carolina
37	Tennessee
38	Nebraska
39	Oklahoma
40	Wyoming
41	Maine
42	South Dakota
43	Kentucky
44	Alabama
45	Louisiana
46	West Virginia
47	Arkansas
48	Hawaii
49	Alaska
50	Mississippi

Note: Numbers that appear to be identical are rounded and vary slightly in actual value. The rankings reflect the actual values before rounding. See the introduction for more details.

B-26 Workers' Compensation Temporary Disability Payments, 2006

State	Maximum weekly benefit $	Rank
Alabama	629.00	27
Alaska	875.00	9
Arizona	374.01	49
Arkansas	488.00	44
California	840.00	10
Colorado	697.20	21
Connecticut	1,005.00	4
Delaware	543.53	38
Florida	683.00	25
Georgia	450.00	47
Hawaii	622.00	28
Idaho	488.77	43
Illinois	1,034.56	3
Indiana	588.00	34
Iowa	1,173.00	1
Kansas	467.00	45
Kentucky	631.22	26
Louisiana	454.00	46
Maine	542.40	39
Maryland	801.00	11
Massachusetts	958.58	5
Michigan	706.00	19
Minnesota	750.00	14
Mississippi	351.14	50
Missouri	696.97	22
Montana	520.00	42
Nebraska	600.00	31
Nevada	690.83	24
New Hampshire	1,123.50	2
New Jersey	691.00	23
New Mexico	585.89	35
New York	400.00	48
North Carolina	730.00	17
North Dakota	604.00	30
Ohio	704.00	20
Oklahoma	577.00	36
Oregon	948.24	7
Pennsylvania	745.00	15
Rhode Island	785.00	12
South Carolina	592.56	32
South Dakota	533.00	41
Tennessee	729.00	18
Texas	540.00	40
Utah	589.00	33
Vermont	950.00	6
Virginia	773.00	13
Washington	905.17	8
West Virginia	568.78	37
Wisconsin	744.00	16
Wyoming	606.32	29
50 States	n/a	
DC	1,022.00	
United States	n/a	

Rank in order by $	
1	Iowa
2	New Hampshire
3	Illinois
4	Connecticut
5	Massachusetts
6	Vermont
7	Oregon
8	Washington
9	Alaska
10	California
11	Maryland
12	Rhode Island
13	Virginia
14	Minnesota
15	Pennsylvania
16	Wisconsin
17	North Carolina
18	Tennessee
19	Michigan
20	Ohio
21	Colorado
22	Missouri
23	New Jersey
24	Nevada
25	Florida
26	Kentucky
27	Alabama
28	Hawaii
29	Wyoming
30	North Dakota
31	Nebraska
32	South Carolina
33	Utah
34	Indiana
35	New Mexico
36	Oklahoma
37	West Virginia
38	Delaware
39	Maine
40	Texas
41	South Dakota
42	Montana
43	Idaho
44	Arkansas
45	Kansas
46	Louisiana
47	Georgia
48	New York
49	Arizona
50	Mississippi

B-27   Average Unemployment Compensation Benefit, 2006

State	Average weekly unemployment compensation benefit $	Rank
Alabama	183.33	49
Alaska	198.70	46
Arizona	194.28	48
Arkansas	241.63	34
California	290.91	9
Colorado	313.20	7
Connecticut	284.14	12
Delaware	247.38	30
Florida	228.74	40
Georgia	252.21	28
Hawaii	362.97	1
Idaho	231.24	37
Illinois	277.80	14
Indiana	276.71	15
Iowa	274.07	18
Kansas	282.11	13
Kentucky	274.72	17
Louisiana	195.49	47
Maine	245.08	31
Maryland	272.20	19
Massachusetts	358.76	2
Michigan	292.63	8
Minnesota	317.78	6
Mississippi	173.68	50
Missouri	209.02	44
Montana	238.64	35
Nebraska	226.35	41
Nevada	271.64	20
New Hampshire	249.11	29
New Jersey	324.80	3
New Mexico	242.82	33
New York	271.53	21
North Carolina	268.24	23
North Dakota	230.96	39
Ohio	287.71	10
Oklahoma	235.04	36
Oregon	266.95	24
Pennsylvania	285.07	11
Rhode Island	321.03	5
South Carolina	224.73	42
South Dakota	208.96	45
Tennessee	213.79	43
Texas	269.18	22
Utah	275.66	16
Vermont	259.44	25
Virginia	255.61	26
Washington	323.74	4
West Virginia	231.20	38
Wisconsin	243.81	32
Wyoming	254.52	27
50 States	n/a	
DC	278.51	
United States	271.21	

Rank in order by $	
1	Hawaii
2	Massachusetts
3	New Jersey
4	Washington
5	Rhode Island
6	Minnesota
7	Colorado
8	Michigan
9	California
10	Ohio
11	Pennsylvania
12	Connecticut
13	Kansas
14	Illinois
15	Indiana
16	Utah
17	Kentucky
18	Iowa
19	Maryland
20	Nevada
21	New York
22	Texas
23	North Carolina
24	Oregon
25	Vermont
26	Virginia
27	Wyoming
28	Georgia
29	New Hampshire
30	Delaware
31	Maine
32	Wisconsin
33	New Mexico
34	Arkansas
35	Montana
36	Oklahoma
37	Idaho
38	West Virginia
39	North Dakota
40	Florida
41	Nebraska
42	South Carolina
43	Tennessee
44	Missouri
45	South Dakota
46	Alaska
47	Louisiana
48	Arizona
49	Alabama
50	Mississippi

B-28 Index of State Economic Momentum, September 2006

State	Index of state economic momentum September 2006	Rank		Rank in order by index
Alabama	0.23	18	1	Arizona
Alaska	-0.57	33	2	Utah
Arizona	3.06	1	3	Nevada
Arkansas	0.12	21	4	Idaho
California	0.27	16	5	Wyoming
Colorado	0.27	17	6	Florida
Connecticut	-0.70	40	7	Texas
Delaware	0.70	10	8	Washington
Florida	1.41	6	9	New Mexico
Georgia	0.60	13	10	Delaware
Hawaii	0.12	20	11	Montana
Idaho	1.97	4	12	Oregon
Illinois	-0.36	31	13	Georgia
Indiana	-0.78	42	14	Oklahoma
Iowa	-0.30	29	15	South Carolina
Kansas	-0.62	35	16	California
Kentucky	-0.67	38	17	Colorado
Louisiana	-4.10	50	18	Alabama
Maine	-1.10	46	19	North Carolina
Maryland	-0.18	26	20	Hawaii
Massachusetts	-0.65	37	21	Arkansas
Michigan	-1.69	49	22	South Dakota
Minnesota	-0.54	32	23	Tennessee
Mississippi	-0.20	27	24	Nebraska
Missouri	-0.21	28	25	Virginia
Montana	0.67	11	26	Maryland
Nebraska	-0.14	24	27	Mississippi
Nevada	2.35	3	28	Missouri
New Hampshire	-0.34	30	29	Iowa
New Jersey	-0.59	34	30	New Hampshire
New Mexico	0.89	9	31	Illinois
New York	-0.73	41	32	Minnesota
North Carolina	0.19	19	33	Alaska
North Dakota	-0.62	36	34	New Jersey
Ohio	-1.25	48	35	Kansas
Oklahoma	0.54	14	36	North Dakota
Oregon	0.64	12	37	Massachusetts
Pennsylvania	-0.83	43	38	Kentucky
Rhode Island	-1.17	47	39	West Virginia
South Carolina	0.45	15	40	Connecticut
South Dakota	-0.04	22	41	New York
Tennessee	-0.13	23	42	Indiana
Texas	1.26	7	43	Pennsylvania
Utah	2.41	2	44	Vermont
Vermont	-0.95	44	45	Wisconsin
Virginia	-0.17	25	46	Maine
Washington	1.08	8	47	Rhode Island
West Virginia	-0.69	39	48	Ohio
Wisconsin	-0.96	45	49	Michigan
Wyoming	1.50	5	50	Louisiana
50 States	-0.00			
DC	-0.70			
United States	-0.00			

Note: Numbers that appear to be identical are rounded and vary slightly in actual value. The rankings reflect the actual values before rounding. See the introduction for more details.

B-29 Employment Change, 2005–2006

State	Change in number of jobs July 2005–2006 (in thousands)	Percentage change in employment	Rank by percentage change
Alabama	32.5	1.68	22
Alaska	4.3	1.29	29
Arizona	117.2	4.75	2
Arkansas	17.2	1.47	25
California	214.0	1.45	26
Colorado	44.5	1.99	17
Connecticut	9.0	0.54	43
Delaware	6.8	1.57	24
Florida	257.0	3.34	6
Georgia	77.2	1.94	18
Hawaii	14.6	2.45	12
Idaho	28.5	4.61	4
Illinois	64.8	1.10	34
Indiana	19.2	0.66	42
Iowa	26.6	1.81	21
Kansas	6.3	0.48	46
Kentucky	21.2	1.17	33
Louisiana	-174.6	-9.00	50
Maine	2.3	0.37	47
Maryland	34.8	1.36	28
Massachusetts	21.9	0.68	41
Michigan	-4.7	-0.11	49
Minnesota	78.9	2.91	11
Mississippi	5.4	0.48	45
Missouri	33.3	1.23	30
Montana	12.5	2.92	10
Nebraska	18.0	1.92	19
Nevada	62.6	5.11	1
New Hampshire	7.6	1.19	32
New Jersey	29.1	0.71	40
New Mexico	25.0	3.11	8
New York	86.0	1.01	36
North Carolina	93.4	2.43	14
North Dakota	5.6	1.65	23
Ohio	26.5	0.49	44
Oklahoma	27.4	1.83	20
Oregon	51.0	3.08	9
Pennsylvania	48.3	0.85	39
Rhode Island	1.6	0.33	48
South Carolina	43.6	2.37	16
South Dakota	9.4	2.39	15
Tennessee	33.5	1.23	31
Texas	236.1	2.44	13
Utah	53.4	4.68	3
Vermont	2.7	0.90	38
Virginia	52.9	1.44	27
Washington	88.1	3.16	7
West Virginia	7.8	1.04	35
Wisconsin	28.8	1.01	37
Wyoming	10.1	3.73	5
50 States	2,019.2	1.52	
DC	11.8	1.72	
United States	2,031.0	1.52	

Rank in order by percentage change

1	Nevada
2	Arizona
3	Utah
4	Idaho
5	Wyoming
6	Florida
7	Washington
8	New Mexico
9	Oregon
10	Montana
11	Minnesota
12	Hawaii
13	Texas
14	North Carolina
15	South Dakota
16	South Carolina
17	Colorado
18	Georgia
19	Nebraska
20	Oklahoma
21	Iowa
22	Alabama
23	North Dakota
24	Delaware
25	Arkansas
26	California
27	Virginia
28	Maryland
29	Alaska
30	Missouri
31	Tennessee
32	New Hampshire
33	Kentucky
34	Illinois
35	West Virginia
36	New York
37	Wisconsin
38	Vermont
39	Pennsylvania
40	New Jersey
41	Massachusetts
42	Indiana
43	Connecticut
44	Ohio
45	Mississippi
46	Kansas
47	Maine
48	Rhode Island
49	Michigan
50	Louisiana

Note: Numbers that appear to be identical are rounded and vary slightly in actual value. The rankings reflect the actual values before rounding. See the introduction for more details.

B-30 Manufacturing Employment Change, 2005–2006

State	Change in number of manufacturing jobs July 2005–2006 (in thousands)	Percentage change in manufacturing employment	Rank by percentage change
Alabama	3.0	1.00	16
Alaska	-0.4	-1.87	42
Arizona	1.5	0.82	18
Arkansas	-2.7	-1.35	39
California	-4.4	-0.29	28
Colorado	-0.8	-0.53	31
Connecticut	-1.2	-0.62	32
Delaware	0.1	0.31	23
Florida	-1.8	-0.45	30
Georgia	0.0	0.00	25
Hawaii	0.2	1.32	13
Idaho	1.3	2.05	9
Illinois	-8.9	-1.29	38
Indiana	5.2	0.92	17
Iowa	4.7	2.03	10
Kansas	-0.3	-0.17	27
Kentucky	-1.0	-0.39	29
Louisiana	-10.3	-6.68	50
Maine	-2.6	-4.25	49
Maryland	-2.1	-1.49	41
Massachusetts	1.9	0.63	20
Michigan	-20.4	-3.16	46
Minnesota	2.5	0.72	19
Mississippi	-2.1	-1.18	37
Missouri	3.7	1.24	14
Montana	0.4	2.02	11
Nebraska	2.6	2.55	7
Nevada	1.7	3.54	4
New Hampshire	-2.8	-3.56	48
New Jersey	-10.8	-3.30	47
New Mexico	1.5	4.13	2
New York	-17.6	-3.04	45
North Carolina	-5.2	-0.92	36
North Dakota	0.3	1.14	15
Ohio	-7.3	-0.90	35
Oklahoma	2.2	1.51	12
Oregon	5.3	2.54	8
Pennsylvania	-13.5	-1.97	43
Rhode Island	-1.1	-2.08	44
South Carolina	-2.2	-0.84	34
South Dakota	2.3	5.71	1
Tennessee	-5.8	-1.43	40
Texas	0.8	0.09	24
Utah	3.6	3.05	6
Vermont	-0.3	-0.81	33
Virginia	1.3	0.44	21
Washington	8.5	3.06	5
West Virginia	-0.1	-0.16	26
Wisconsin	1.9	0.37	22
Wyoming	0.4	4.12	3
50 States	-68.8	-0.48	
DC	0.1	4.76	
United States	-68.7	-0.48	

Rank in order by percentage change

1 South Dakota
2 New Mexico
3 Wyoming
4 Nevada
5 Washington
6 Utah
7 Nebraska
8 Oregon
9 Idaho
10 Iowa
11 Montana
12 Oklahoma
13 Hawaii
14 Missouri
15 North Dakota
16 Alabama
17 Indiana
18 Arizona
19 Minnesota
20 Massachusetts
21 Virginia
22 Wisconsin
23 Delaware
24 Texas
25 Georgia
26 West Virginia
27 Kansas
28 California
29 Kentucky
30 Florida
31 Colorado
32 Connecticut
33 Vermont
34 South Carolina
35 Ohio
36 North Carolina
37 Mississippi
38 Illinois
39 Arkansas
40 Tennessee
41 Maryland
42 Alaska
43 Pennsylvania
44 Rhode Island
45 New York
46 Michigan
47 New Jersey
48 New Hampshire
49 Maine
50 Louisiana

Note: Numbers that appear to be identical are rounded and vary slightly in actual value. The rankings reflect the actual values before rounding. See the introduction for more details.

B-31 Home Ownership, 2005

State	Home ownership rate (as percentage)	Rank
Alabama	76.6	3
Alaska	66.0	43
Arizona	71.1	27
Arkansas	69.2	37
California	59.7	49
Colorado	71.0	29
Connecticut	70.5	32
Delaware	75.8	6
Florida	72.4	20
Georgia	67.9	41
Hawaii	59.8	48
Idaho	74.2	8
Illinois	70.9	30
Indiana	75.0	7
Iowa	73.9	11
Kansas	69.5	36
Kentucky	71.6	23
Louisiana	72.5	19
Maine	73.9	11
Maryland	71.2	25
Massachusetts	63.4	45
Michigan	76.4	5
Minnesota	76.5	4
Mississippi	78.8	2
Missouri	72.3	22
Montana	70.4	33
Nebraska	70.2	34
Nevada	63.4	45
New Hampshire	74.0	10
New Jersey	70.1	35
New Mexico	71.4	24
New York	55.9	50
North Carolina	70.9	30
North Dakota	68.5	38
Ohio	73.3	15
Oklahoma	72.9	17
Oregon	68.2	40
Pennsylvania	73.3	15
Rhode Island	63.1	47
South Carolina	73.9	11
South Dakota	68.4	39
Tennessee	72.4	20
Texas	65.9	44
Utah	73.9	11
Vermont	74.2	8
Virginia	71.2	25
Washington	67.6	42
West Virginia	81.3	1
Wisconsin	71.1	27
Wyoming	72.8	18
50 States	n/a	
DC	45.8	
United States	68.9	

Rank in order by rate

1	West Virginia
2	Mississippi
3	Alabama
4	Minnesota
5	Michigan
6	Delaware
7	Indiana
8	Idaho
8	Vermont
10	New Hampshire
11	Iowa
11	Maine
11	South Carolina
11	Utah
15	Ohio
15	Pennsylvania
17	Oklahoma
18	Wyoming
19	Louisiana
20	Florida
20	Tennessee
22	Missouri
23	Kentucky
24	New Mexico
25	Maryland
25	Virginia
27	Arizona
27	Wisconsin
29	Colorado
30	Illinois
30	North Carolina
32	Connecticut
33	Montana
34	Nebraska
35	New Jersey
36	Kansas
37	Arkansas
38	North Dakota
39	South Dakota
40	Oregon
41	Georgia
42	Washington
43	Alaska
44	Texas
45	Massachusetts
45	Nevada
47	Rhode Island
48	Hawaii
49	California
50	New York

Note: Ties in ranking reflect ties in actual values.

B-32 Annual Electricity Use Per Residential Customer, 2004

State	Average annual kwh use per residential customer	Rank
Alabama	14,940	3
Alaska	8,198	39
Arizona	12,804	13
Arkansas	12,574	15
California	6,916	49
Colorado	7,887	41
Connecticut	9,289	34
Delaware	11,774	22
Florida	14,212	7
Georgia	13,610	9
Hawaii	8,110	40
Idaho	12,416	18
Illinois	8,816	35
Indiana	11,738	23
Iowa	9,804	30
Kansas	10,516	27
Kentucky	13,529	10
Louisiana	15,204	2
Maine	6,485	50
Maryland	13,384	12
Massachusetts	7,669	43
Michigan	7,781	42
Minnesota	9,290	33
Mississippi	14,625	5
Missouri	12,206	19
Montana	9,407	32
Nebraska	11,457	24
Nevada	11,417	25
New Hampshire	7,479	44
New Jersey	8,452	38
New Mexico	7,200	45
New York	6,965	48
North Carolina	13,433	11
North Dakota	12,003	20
Ohio	10,402	28
Oklahoma	12,538	16
Oregon	11,786	21
Pennsylvania	9,879	29
Rhode Island	7,085	47
South Carolina	14,728	4
South Dakota	10,710	26
Tennessee	15,211	1
Texas	14,035	8
Utah	8,709	36
Vermont	7,113	46
Virginia	14,239	6
Washington	12,446	17
West Virginia	12,773	14
Wisconsin	8,516	37
Wyoming	9,558	31
50 States	n/a	
DC	9,071	
United States	10,879	

Rank in order by average use	
1	Tennessee
2	Louisiana
3	Alabama
4	South Carolina
5	Mississippi
6	Virginia
7	Florida
8	Texas
9	Georgia
10	Kentucky
11	North Carolina
12	Maryland
13	Arizona
14	West Virginia
15	Arkansas
16	Oklahoma
17	Washington
18	Idaho
19	Missouri
20	North Dakota
21	Oregon
22	Delaware
23	Indiana
24	Nebraska
25	Nevada
26	South Dakota
27	Kansas
28	Ohio
29	Pennsylvania
30	Iowa
31	Wyoming
32	Montana
33	Minnesota
34	Connecticut
35	Illinois
36	Utah
37	Wisconsin
38	New Jersey
39	Alaska
40	Hawaii
41	Colorado
42	Michigan
43	Massachusetts
44	New Hampshire
45	New Mexico
46	Vermont
47	Rhode Island
48	New York
49	California
50	Maine

B-33 Average Cost Per Kilowatt Hour, 2004

State	Average cost for industrial customer (cents per kwh)	Average cost for residential customer (cents per kwh)	Residential cost as percentage of industrial cost	Rank by residential as percentage of industrial
Alabama	4.1	7.6	183.7	9
Alaska	8.3	12.4	149.3	38
Arizona	5.3	8.4	158.0	34
Arkansas	4.1	7.3	177.1	14
California	9.5	12.5	131.4	46
Colorado	5.1	8.4	164.8	25
Connecticut	7.9	11.6	147.4	40
Delaware	6.0	8.8	144.8	41
Florida	5.8	9.0	153.9	36
Georgia	4.4	7.8	177.4	13
Hawaii	13.3	18.0	135.3	44
Idaho	3.8	6.1	159.8	33
Illinois	4.6	8.4	180.2	11
Indiana	4.1	7.3	176.6	15
Iowa	4.3	8.9	206.8	1
Kansas	4.7	7.7	165.1	24
Kentucky	3.3	6.1	183.0	10
Louisiana	5.8	8.0	138.4	43
Maine	6.5	12.1	185.2	6
Maryland	6.0	7.8	130.3	47
Massachusetts	8.5	11.7	138.5	42
Michigan	4.9	8.3	169.3	20
Minnesota	4.6	7.9	171.1	18
Mississippi	4.8	8.2	169.9	19
Missouri	4.6	7.0	150.8	37
Montana	4.1	7.8	189.4	4
Nebraska	4.3	6.9	162.7	29
Nevada	7.2	9.7	133.9	45
New Hampshire	10.0	12.5	124.7	49
New Jersey	9.0	11.2	124.4	50
New Mexico	5.2	8.6	166.0	22
New York	7.0	14.5	206.6	2
North Carolina	4.9	8.4	173.2	16
North Dakota	4.1	6.8	164.5	26
Ohio	4.9	8.4	172.8	17
Oklahoma	4.7	7.7	162.2	32
Oregon	4.4	7.2	162.3	31
Pennsylvania	5.9	9.6	163.1	27
Rhode Island	9.3	12.2	130.0	48
South Carolina	4.1	8.1	196.9	3
South Dakota	4.6	7.6	166.7	21
Tennessee	4.4	6.9	154.7	35
Texas	5.9	9.7	165.8	23
Utah	4.0	7.2	179.8	12
Vermont	7.9	12.9	162.5	30
Virginia	4.3	8.0	187.2	5
Washington	4.3	6.4	148.8	39
West Virginia	3.8	6.2	162.7	28
Wisconsin	4.9	9.0	183.9	8
Wyoming	3.9	7.2	184.6	7
50 States	n/a	n/a	n/a	
DC	4.7	8.0	169.0	
United States	5.3	8.9	170.3	

Rank in order by percentage

1	Iowa
2	New York
3	South Carolina
4	Montana
5	Virginia
6	Maine
7	Wyoming
8	Wisconsin
9	Alabama
10	Kentucky
11	Illinois
12	Utah
13	Georgia
14	Arkansas
15	Indiana
16	North Carolina
17	Ohio
18	Minnesota
19	Mississippi
20	Michigan
21	South Dakota
22	New Mexico
23	Texas
24	Kansas
25	Colorado
26	North Dakota
27	Pennsylvania
28	West Virginia
29	Nebraska
30	Vermont
31	Oregon
32	Oklahoma
33	Idaho
34	Arizona
35	Tennessee
36	Florida
37	Missouri
38	Alaska
39	Washington
40	Connecticut
41	Delaware
42	Massachusetts
43	Louisiana
44	Hawaii
45	Nevada
46	California
47	Maryland
48	Rhode Island
49	New Hampshire
50	New Jersey

Note: Numbers that appear to be identical are rounded and vary slightly in actual value. The rankings reflect the actual values before rounding. See the introduction for more details.

B-34 New Companies, 2005

State	New companies	New companies per 1,000 employees	Rank per 1,000 employees
Alabama	10,575	5.1	39
Alaska	1,982	6.3	24
Arizona	21,339	7.9	10
Arkansas	7,591	5.9	30
California	121,482	7.3	14
Colorado	26,610	11.0	2
Connecticut	9,220	5.3	34
Delaware	3,299	7.9	11
Florida	84,890	10.2	3
Georgia	29,804	6.9	16
Hawaii	3,763	6.1	27
Idaho	9,312	13.1	1
Illinois	30,445	5.0	42
Indiana	14,545	4.8	45
Iowa	6,004	3.8	50
Kansas	7,095	5.1	41
Kentucky	9,617	5.1	38
Louisiana	9,393	4.9	44
Maine	4,251	6.3	23
Maryland	22,083	7.8	12
Massachusetts	19,723	6.2	25
Michigan	24,642	5.2	36
Minnesota	12,555	4.4	48
Mississippi	6,071	4.9	43
Missouri	17,239	6.0	28
Montana	4,768	10.1	4
Nebraska	5,127	5.4	33
Nevada	11,299	9.7	6
New Hampshire	4,758	6.7	18
New Jersey	33,022	7.8	13
New Mexico	5,272	5.9	29
New York	62,045	6.9	15
North Carolina	25,906	6.3	22
North Dakota	1,893	5.5	32
Ohio	22,542	4.1	49
Oklahoma	8,609	5.2	37
Oregon	14,445	8.3	9
Pennsylvania	36,609	6.1	26
Rhode Island	3,677	6.8	17
South Carolina	12,341	6.4	20
South Dakota	2,102	5.1	40
Tennessee	17,484	6.4	21
Texas	55,858	5.3	35
Utah	11,536	9.5	8
Vermont	1,911	5.6	31
Virginia	25,061	6.6	19
Washington	30,353	9.8	5
West Virginia	3,493	4.6	47
Wisconsin	13,656	4.7	46
Wyoming	2,632	9.6	7
50 States	929,929	6.6	
DC	4,316	15.6	
United States*	939,097	6.6	

Rank in order per 1,000 employees

1	Idaho
2	Colorado
3	Florida
4	Montana
5	Washington
6	Nevada
7	Wyoming
8	Utah
9	Oregon
10	Arizona
11	Delaware
12	Maryland
13	New Jersey
14	California
15	New York
16	Georgia
17	Rhode Island
18	New Hampshire
19	Virginia
20	South Carolina
21	Tennessee
22	North Carolina
23	Maine
24	Alaska
25	Massachusetts
26	Pennsylvania
27	Hawaii
28	Missouri
29	New Mexico
30	Arkansas
31	Vermont
32	North Dakota
33	Nebraska
34	Connecticut
35	Texas
36	Michigan
37	Oklahoma
38	Kentucky
39	Alabama
40	South Dakota
41	Kansas
42	Illinois
43	Mississippi
44	Louisiana
45	Indiana
46	Wisconsin
47	West Virginia
48	Minnesota
49	Ohio
50	Iowa

Note: Numbers that appear to be identical are rounded and vary slightly in actual value. The rankings reflect the actual values before rounding. See the introduction for more details.

*Due to rounding or data sources, the 50-state total plus D.C. may not equal the U.S. total. Please see introduction.

Source Notes for Economies (Section B)

B-1 Personal Income, 2005: These data reflect income of residents of each state, including pensions, dividends, interest, and rent as well as amounts received from employers as wages and salaries. These estimates are made by the Department of Commerce's Bureau of Economic Analysis each quarter. The calendar year 2005 estimates were released in September of 2006 and are available on the bureau's Web site (www.bea.doc.gov).

B-2 Gross State Product, Total and Per Capita, 2005: The gross state product is the state counterpart of the gross national product (now called the gross domestic product). This is the single best measure of the size of a state's economy. It is the sum of all the value of production of goods and services. While estimates of national data are released on a current basis, state-by-state estimates are made by the Department of Commerce only with a substantial lag. These 2005 data were released in October 2006 and come from the same source as Table B-1.

B-3 Per Capita Personal Income, 2005: These data, from the same source as Table B-1, reflect personal income in relation to population. They are a common measure of the relative affluence of each state. The data are also used to determine what percentage of each state's Medicaid costs the federal government pays.

B-4 Personal Income from Wages and Salaries, 2005: These data, from the same source as Table B-1, show the portion of personal income that comes from wages and salaries. The percentages, calculated for *State Fact Finder*, indicate relative reliance of states' economies on current work, as distinct from investments and government payments.

B-5 Average Annual Pay, 2005: These data reflect the average pay of workers in each state. They are from the Department of Labor's Quarterly Census of Employment and Wages (www.bls.gov/cew/home.htm).

B-6 Average Hourly Earnings, 2006: These data are often used to compare wage costs of the states. They are prepared monthly by the Department of Labor and released in the publication *Employment and Earnings* and on the department's Web site (www.bls.gov/cew). The August 2006 data shown in this table cover only production workers, excluding service and retailing employees as well as government employees.

B-7 Value Added in Manufacturing, 2004: This table measures the value that is added by manufacturing operations in each state. Value added is calculated by subtracting the value of inputs to production from the value of the outputs. For example, the value of manufacturing a car is the value of the car minus the value of components, such as engines, purchased to manufacture it. These data are from the U.S.

Census Bureau's *2004 Annual Survey of Manufacturers* issued in January of 2006. Value added per worker can be calculated from this report. This per worker statistic is sometimes used to compare the productivity of state work forces but is a misleading statistic because capital investments in machinery make massive contributions to adding values in highly automated operations such as chemical manufacturing.

B-8 Cost of Living, 2006: The federal government has not attempted to produce measures that compare living costs since the 1980s and, even then, provided the data only for selected large metropolitan areas, not states. Some researchers periodically try to produce such indices, but they are of doubtful statistical validity. The one shown is from the Missouri Economic Research and Information Center and is based on voluntary surveys of chambers of commerce taken by ACCRA, a non-profit economic and community development research organization. The data cover the second quarter of calendar year 2006.

B-9 Average Annual Pay in Manufacturing, 2005: This is the manufacturing component of the data described for Table B-5, from the same source. States with many jobs in high-wage industries, like chemical or vehicle manufacturing, rank highest.

B-10 Average Annual Pay in Retailing, 2005: This is the retailing component of the data described for Table B-5, from the same source. Because most retailing jobs are entry-level positions requiring little experience or formal training, these data are a good measure of the costs of obtaining new workers in the states.

B-11 Labor Force, 2006: About 151.8 million people, 51 percent of Americans, are either working or looking for work but not working (unemployed). These two groups make up the labor force. The rest of the population are not in the labor force because they are retired, too young to work, disabled, or have opted not to work. This group includes "discouraged workers" who indicate that they would like to work but have given up hope of finding a job.

The labor force data are available on the Web site of the Bureau of Labor Statistics (www.bls.gov). They are also available in its monthly publication *Regional and State Employment and Unemployment* released on October 20, 2006, with preliminary estimates for September. The data are seasonally adjusted to make month-to-month comparisons possible despite fluctuations associated with time of the year such as hiring by retail stores for the December holiday season and summertime hiring of students.

The 2005 population estimates come from the U.S. Census Bureau (see Table A-1). Labor force as a percentage of population varies among states because of differences in the percentage of population at working-age and the percentage of people who want to work—the labor force participation rate.

B-12 Unemployed and Unemployment Rate, 2006: The estimates of persons unemployed and the unemployment rate (percentage of labor force unemployed) are from the same source as Table B-11.

B-13 Employment and Employment Rate, 2006: The Bureau of Labor Statistics faces a perpetual dilemma in presenting statistics on employment and unemployment. It must make national unemployment estimates based on a survey of households in which people are asked whether they are looking for work. This *household survey* also provides the national estimate of the people who are employed. But the sample is too small to provide reliable estimates of employment for less populous states. To provide estimates for those states, the bureau obtains monthly reports from employers, called the *establishment survey*. The national totals from the two different surveys often diverge by hundreds of thousands of workers. Periodically, the bureau "benchmarks" the totals and revises past estimates to make them consistent.

To make the matter even more complicated, the bureau attempts in various complex ways to use the results of one survey to guide estimating procedures for the other. How this is done is explained in detail in various technical publications available from the bureau. The net effect harmonizes the results of the two approaches better for large states than small ones. For example, the employment in Wyoming implicit in the bureau's estimates is the labor force (Table B-11) minus the unemployed (Table B-12)—282,000— but the employment published in a different table in the report (see notes to Table B-11) is 275,700. For Table B-13 *State Fact Finder* uses the implicit estimate, employment is thus derived by subtracting the number of unemployed from the labor force. The employment rate is the relationship between the employment shown and the labor force on Table B-11.

Because *State Fact Finder* contains many tables relying on employment data for individual states, it uses the best employment estimates available, those from the establishment survey, in Table B-14 and other tables showing state-by-state details of employment.

B-14 Government Employment, 2006: This table, from the same source as Table B-11, uses seasonally adjusted data from the establishment survey (see notes to Table B-13 on differences between the household and establishment surveys) which were made available by the Bureau of Labor Statistics on October 20, 2006, with preliminary estimates for September. The employment reported on this table includes federal, state, and local employees.

These Bureau of Labor Statistics data on government employment covering 2006 are more current than data provided by the U.S. Census Bureau. The latest Census Bureau data, published in 2006, cover information on March 2005 payrolls. But the Census Bureau data are used often in *State Fact Finder* because the Bureau of Labor Statistics data do not include such details as how much employees are paid and the type of service (for example, education, transportation) they provide.

B-15 Manufacturing Employment, 2006: These data are comparable to those shown in Table B-14 but cover manufacturing.

B-16 Construction Employment, 2006: These data are comparable to those shown in B-14 but cover construction.

B-17 *Fortune* 500 Companies, 2006: The major business magazine, *Fortune*, provides annual listings of the largest companies in America. Because large states tend to have the most large companies, the rankings are based on a calculation of the representation of these companies' headquarters in each state in relation to population of that state.

B-18 Tourism Spending, 2004: The travel industry is a major factor in the economies of all states and a dominant factor in a few. However, data on it are elusive. Many trips combine business and pleasure, so separating tourism from business is difficult. Other trips combine an activity, such as coming home for the holidays, with a tourist activity, such as visiting a museum. Restaurants and gift shops do not normally know whether their customers are tourists or local customers. Consequently, estimates of tourism spending have more guesswork than most of the statistics in *State Fact Finder*. The 2004 data shown in the table are the most up-to-date. They are prepared by the Travel Industry Association of America (TIA) and are published in *Tourism Works for America*. The data are based on the Travel Industry Association's Travel Economic Impact Model. The state tourism offices may use a different methodology and the data and results may not be comparable to this TIA table.

B-19 Exports, 2006: National estimates of exports are made quarterly by the Department of Commerce to develop estimates of gross domestic product and balance of payments with other nations. Relatively current estimates by state are also made by the department but are of doubtful reliability because of data-gathering limitations and conceptual problems. For example, does a shipment from a New York port of a product from an Ohio plant of items made from components from Ohio and Mississippi contained in boxes produced in South Carolina constitute an export from New York, Ohio, or somewhere else? The data shown came from the U.S. Census Bureau Web site (www.census.gov).

B-20 Housing Permits, 2005: No state-by-state system exists to report completion of single-family houses and apartment and condominium units, but there are good data on the issuance of permits for such construction. Although some builders obtain permits and then don't build, permits are expensive so most permits are followed by construction. The data shown were compiled by the National Association of Home Builders (NAHB) and are available on its Web site (www.nahb.org). The relationship to population shows which states have rapidly growing populations and which are more stagnant.

B-21 Percentage Change in Home Prices, 2001–2006: Most people are interested in changes in housing prices because of the implications for a specific existing home—usually the one they own. The data often cited in the media, which come from realtors' sales records, come from averages of homes sold. As a result, they include large percentages of new (and typically larger, better equipped, and more expensive) homes in fast-growing states. A preferable way to measure price changes is to examine prices for successive sales of the same homes. This has recently become possible with improvements in computing capacity and the increasing importance of secondary mortgage lenders, who buy massive numbers of mortgages from banks and other lenders. The data in the table reflect this approach.

The information comes from *House Price Index Second Quarter 2006* published by the Office of Federal Housing Enterprise Oversight and available on its Web site (www.ofheo.gov).

B-22 Net Farm Income, 2005: These data reflect the net income derived from farming—the value of farm sales minus the cost of production. They are estimates made by the Department of Agriculture and are available on its Web site (www.ers.usda.gov). The *State Fact Finder* calculation of per capita amounts provides a basis for comparing the importance of agriculture to the economies of each state.

B-23 Financial Institution Assets, 2005: This table shows total assets of banks, trust companies, and savings institutions. These data, from the Federal Deposit Insurance Corporation's *Statistics on Banking: 2005* (www2.fdic.gov), provide a good measure of the importance of banking in each state. However, they provide no indication of the wealth of individuals in a state as deposits flow freely across state lines. States that have successfully tried to draw financial institutions, like South Dakota and Delaware, show large per capita amounts, as do regional banking centers, such as the Boston banks that serve customers throughout New England.

B-24 Bankruptcy Filings by Individuals and Businesses, 2006: These data show how new bankruptcy cases (mostly individuals rather than businesses) were distributed among the states. These data cover the twelve-month period ending June 30, 2006, and come from the Web site of the Administrative Office of the U.S. Courts (www.uscourts.gov).

B-25 Patents Issued, FY 2005: The United States Patent and Trademark Office issued 85,238 new patents in fiscal year 2005 to residents (corporations and individuals) in the states shown. When related to population, this statistic is often used to compare states in the degree to which they are on the forefront of new technology. The data come from the United States Patent and Trademark Office and are available on its Web site (www.uspto.gov) as *Performance and Accountability Report Fiscal Year 2005*. Because patent applications are often made by or for companies, headquarters of companies (for example, DuPont in Delaware and 3M in Minnesota) affect the results.

B-26 Workers' Compensation Temporary Disability Payments, 2006: All states maintain a program that provides compensation for workers who are injured on the job. These programs differ massively from state to state in how much money is paid for certain injuries, how hard it is to prove disability and its relationship to the job, and how employers are forced to pay program costs. These differences, set by state policy, are not captured by aggregate statistics on workers' compensation costs because some industries (like construction and logging) are inherently more hazardous than others (like banking), so state-by-state costs will vary with the mix of industries. This table compares one major dimension of benefit generosity/parsimony, the maximum payment per month to a worker who is temporarily unable to work because of a job-related injury. The data come from the Department of Labor publication dated January 2006, *State Workers' Compensation Laws.*

B-27 Average Unemployment Compensation Benefit, 2006: All states maintain a federally supervised program of unemployment compensation. States have wide discretion in determining how large unemployment compensation payments will be, how long they will last, and how costs are distributed among employers. This table from the Web site of the Department of Labor Employment and Training Administration (www.doleta.gov/unemploy) shows the average weekly benefit paid in each state in September 2006.

B-28 Index of State Economic Momentum, September 2006: Each quarter *State Policy Reports* publishes its Index of State Economic Momentum, a statistic created by State Policy Research to compare the recent economic performance of each state in relation to the national average. A state growing at the national average rate would show an index of 0.0 while one growing roughly 1.0 percent faster would show an index of 1.0. Negative numbers show states lagging behind national average growth. The index combines (with equal weights) the most recent known one-year changes in (1) employment, (2) personal income, and (3) population.

B-29 Employment Change, 2005–2006: This table uses Department of Labor data from July 2005 and July 2006 (not seasonally adjusted) to show the change in the number of jobs in each state. The data, from the Bureau of Labor Statistics Web site (www.bls.gov), are one component of the state economic momentum index shown in Table B-28.

B-30 Manufacturing Employment Change, 2005–2006: This table uses Department of Labor (see source for Table B-29) data from July 2005 to July 2006 (not seasonally adjusted) to show the states experiencing job loss and those experiencing job growth in manufacturing. These data are released monthly and revised often, but differences in state economic performance tend to persist from month to month.

B-31 Home Ownership, 2005: These data show the percentage of households living in homes they own. The data come from the *Housing Vacancy Survey*, available on the U.S. Census Bureau Web site (www.census.gov). Because of the relatively small samples, the margin of error for less populous states is relatively large.

B-32 Annual Electricity Use Per Residential Customer, 2004: These data from the Edison Electric Institute (EEI) show differences in electricity use among the states. The results are heavily influenced by the relative importance of heating and air conditioning and the mix of fuels used for heating. These data are not strictly comparable to earlier EEI data. Since 2001, EEI has included data for retail customers serviced by alternative power suppliers.

B-33 Average Cost Per Kilowatt Hour, 2004: These data also come from the Edison Electric Institute (see source for Table B-32), which maintains additional details on other years, types of consumers, and more. The data have many uses. The cost per kilowatt hour permits comparisons among states of electricity costs for households and businesses. The residential rate as a percentage of industrial rate is a useful indicator of the extent to which state regulatory policy (which controls rates charged by private companies) is tilted toward providing low industrial rates to stimulate economic development or low residential rates to keep prices low for voters/consumers at the potential expense of loss of industry. Based on costs of service, industrial users should pay less because they are cheaper per kilowatt to bill and often agree to have service curtailed when there is a shortage of power. See source for Table B-33 for information to consider when comparing 2001 and later data to Edison Electric Institute data from previous years.

B-34 New Companies, 2005: These data show the number of companies that applied for new account numbers from state employment services. These data were made available to *State Fact Finder* by the Department of Labor Unemployment Insurance Service in an e-mail dated November 14, 2006. *State Fact Finder* then related these numbers to the total number of workers in each state. These employment numbers are annual averages and are available on the Bureau of Labor Statistics Web site (www.bls.gov).

Geography

Percent Change in U.S. Air Quality 1990–2005	
Pollutant	**Percent**
Nitrogen Dioxide (NO2)	-25
Ozone (O3, 1-hour)	-12
Ozone (O3, 8-hour)	-8
Sulfur Dioxide (SO2)	-48
Particulate Matter (PM 10)	-25
Particulate Matter (PM2.5)	-7
Carbon Monoxide (CO)	-60
Lead (Pb)	-38

Note: measure = concentration of pollutants.
Source: U.S. Environmental Protection Agency

Percent Change in U.S. Emissions 1990–2005	
Pollutant	**Percent**
Nitrogen Oxide (NOx)	-25
Volatile Organic Compounds (VOC)	-31
Sulfur Dioxide (SO2)	-35
Particulate Matter (PM 10)	-38
Particulate Matter (PM2.5)	-13
Carbon Monoxide (CO)	-38
Lead (Pb)	-40

Note: measure = emissions from factories, vehicles, and other sources.
Source: U.S. Environmental Protection Agency

Percent Increase in Use of Alternative-Fueled Vehicles by Region, 2001–2003	
Region	**Percent**
Midwest	30.9
Northeast	30.8
West	16.4
South	15.5
United States	20.1

Source: Energy Information Administration

C-1   Total Land Area, 2000

State	Land area (in square miles)	Rank
Alabama	50,744	28
Alaska	571,951	1
Arizona	113,635	6
Arkansas	52,068	27
California	155,959	3
Colorado	103,718	8
Connecticut	4,845	48
Delaware	1,954	49
Florida	53,927	26
Georgia	57,906	21
Hawaii	6,423	47
Idaho	82,747	11
Illinois	55,584	24
Indiana	35,867	38
Iowa	55,869	23
Kansas	81,815	13
Kentucky	39,728	36
Louisiana	43,562	33
Maine	30,862	39
Maryland	9,774	42
Massachusetts	7,840	45
Michigan	56,804	22
Minnesota	79,610	14
Mississippi	46,907	31
Missouri	68,886	18
Montana	145,552	4
Nebraska	76,872	15
Nevada	109,826	7
New Hampshire	8,968	44
New Jersey	7,417	46
New Mexico	121,356	5
New York	47,214	30
North Carolina	48,711	29
North Dakota	68,976	17
Ohio	40,948	35
Oklahoma	68,667	19
Oregon	95,997	10
Pennsylvania	44,817	32
Rhode Island	1,045	50
South Carolina	30,110	40
South Dakota	75,885	16
Tennessee	41,217	34
Texas	261,797	2
Utah	82,144	12
Vermont	9,250	43
Virginia	39,594	37
Washington	66,544	20
West Virginia	24,078	41
Wisconsin	54,310	25
Wyoming	97,100	9
50 States	3,537,380	
DC	61	
United States	3,537,441	

Rank in order by square mile

1	Alaska
2	Texas
3	California
4	Montana
5	New Mexico
6	Arizona
7	Nevada
8	Colorado
9	Wyoming
10	Oregon
11	Idaho
12	Utah
13	Kansas
14	Minnesota
15	Nebraska
16	South Dakota
17	North Dakota
18	Missouri
19	Oklahoma
20	Washington
21	Georgia
22	Michigan
23	Iowa
24	Illinois
25	Wisconsin
26	Florida
27	Arkansas
28	Alabama
29	North Carolina
30	New York
31	Mississippi
32	Pennsylvania
33	Louisiana
34	Tennessee
35	Ohio
36	Kentucky
37	Virginia
38	Indiana
39	Maine
40	South Carolina
41	West Virginia
42	Maryland
43	Vermont
44	New Hampshire
45	Massachusetts
46	New Jersey
47	Hawaii
48	Connecticut
49	Delaware
50	Rhode Island

C-2 Land Owned by Federal Government, 2004

State	Total acres of federally owned land (in thousands)	Percentage of land federally owned	Rank by total acres
Alabama	514	1.6	38
Alaska	252,496	69.1	1
Arizona	34,933	48.1	4
Arkansas	2,408	7.2	20
California	45,393	45.3	3
Colorado	24,355	36.6	11
Connecticut	14	0.4	49
Delaware	26	2.0	48
Florida	2,859	8.2	18
Georgia	1,409	3.8	26
Hawaii	797	19.4	31
Idaho	26,565	50.2	9
Illinois	642	1.8	35
Indiana	463	2.0	39
Iowa	274	0.8	42
Kansas	631	1.2	36
Kentucky	1,379	5.4	27
Louisiana	1,475	5.1	25
Maine	208	1.1	44
Maryland	179	2.8	45
Massachusetts	94	1.9	47
Michigan	3,638	10.0	14
Minnesota	2,874	5.6	17
Mississippi	2,197	7.3	22
Missouri	2,225	5.0	21
Montana	27,910	29.9	8
Nebraska	665	1.4	34
Nevada	59,363	84.5	2
New Hampshire	776	13.5	32
New Jersey	148	3.1	46
New Mexico	32,484	41.8	6
New York	234	0.8	43
North Carolina	3,710	11.8	13
North Dakota	1,186	2.7	28
Ohio	448	1.7	40
Oklahoma	1,586	3.6	24
Oregon	32,716	53.1	5
Pennsylvania	720	2.5	33
Rhode Island	3	0.4	50
South Carolina	561	2.9	37
South Dakota	3,028	6.2	16
Tennessee	866	3.2	30
Texas	3,130	1.9	15
Utah	30,272	57.5	7
Vermont	443	7.5	41
Virginia	2,534	9.9	19
Washington	12,950	30.3	12
West Virginia	1,146	7.4	29
Wisconsin	1,972	5.6	23
Wyoming	26,391	42.3	10
50 States	653,289	28.8	
DC	10	24.7	
United States	653,299	28.8	

Rank in order by total acres	
1	Alaska
2	Nevada
3	California
4	Arizona
5	Oregon
6	New Mexico
7	Utah
8	Montana
9	Idaho
10	Wyoming
11	Colorado
12	Washington
13	North Carolina
14	Michigan
15	Texas
16	South Dakota
17	Minnesota
18	Florida
19	Virginia
20	Arkansas
21	Missouri
22	Mississippi
23	Wisconsin
24	Oklahoma
25	Louisiana
26	Georgia
27	Kentucky
28	North Dakota
29	West Virginia
30	Tennessee
31	Hawaii
32	New Hampshire
33	Pennsylvania
34	Nebraska
35	Illinois
36	Kansas
37	South Carolina
38	Alabama
39	Indiana
40	Ohio
41	Vermont
42	Iowa
43	New York
44	Maine
45	Maryland
46	New Jersey
47	Massachusetts
48	Delaware
49	Connecticut
50	Rhode Island

C-3 State Park Acreage, FY 2006

State	State park acreage	Acreage per 1,000 population	Rank by total acreage
Alabama	48,154	10.6	42
Alaska	3,353,485	5,053.0	1
Arizona	63,623	10.7	38
Arkansas	53,028	19.1	41
California	1,547,968	42.8	3
Colorado	393,258	84.3	8
Connecticut	204,300	58.2	16
Delaware	24,424	29.0	47
Florida	723,852	40.7	4
Georgia	84,197	9.3	32
Hawaii	31,238	24.5	46
Idaho	45,337	31.7	43
Illinois	465,380	36.5	6
Indiana	181,253	28.9	19
Iowa	66,953	22.6	36
Kansas	32,900	12.0	45
Kentucky	58,347	14.0	40
Louisiana	41,311	9.1	44
Maine	99,729	75.5	30
Maryland	268,203	47.9	12
Massachusetts	306,756	47.9	9
Michigan	273,051	27.0	11
Minnesota	237,408	46.3	14
Mississippi	24,287	8.3	48
Missouri	201,375	34.7	17
Montana	61,933	66.2	39
Nebraska	134,681	76.6	24
Nevada	132,531	54.9	26
New Hampshire	232,012	177.1	15
New Jersey	398,676	45.7	7
New Mexico	91,525	47.5	31
New York	1,549,333	80.5	2
North Carolina	183,459	21.1	18
North Dakota	17,401	27.3	49
Ohio	164,548	14.4	21
Oklahoma	72,257	20.4	34
Oregon	101,010	27.7	29
Pennsylvania	291,132	23.4	10
Rhode Island	8,748	8.1	50
South Carolina	80,734	19.0	33
South Dakota	105,916	136.5	28
Tennessee	140,820	23.6	23
Texas	610,319	26.7	5
Utah	149,667	60.6	22
Vermont	68,899	110.6	35
Virginia	64,537	8.5	37
Washington	259,983	41.3	13
West Virginia	177,133	97.5	20
Wisconsin	134,003	24.2	25
Wyoming	119,266	234.2	27
50 States	14,180,340	47.9	
DC	n/a	n/a	
United States	14,180,340	47.8	

Rank in order by total acreage	
1	Alaska
2	New York
3	California
4	Florida
5	Texas
6	Illinois
7	New Jersey
8	Colorado
9	Massachusetts
10	Pennsylvania
11	Michigan
12	Maryland
13	Washington
14	Minnesota
15	New Hampshire
16	Connecticut
17	Missouri
18	North Carolina
19	Indiana
20	West Virginia
21	Ohio
22	Utah
23	Tennessee
24	Nebraska
25	Wisconsin
26	Nevada
27	Wyoming
28	South Dakota
29	Oregon
30	Maine
31	New Mexico
32	Georgia
33	South Carolina
34	Oklahoma
35	Vermont
36	Iowa
37	Virginia
38	Arizona
39	Montana
40	Kentucky
41	Arkansas
42	Alabama
43	Idaho
44	Louisiana
45	Kansas
46	Hawaii
47	Delaware
48	Mississippi
49	North Dakota
50	Rhode Island

C-4   State Park Visitors, FY 2006

State	State park total visitors (in thousands)	Visitors per capita	Rank per capita
Alabama	2,699	0.6	46
Alaska	4,334	6.5	4
Arizona	2,286	0.4	49
Arkansas	10,455	3.8	15
California	77,049	2.1	25
Colorado	11,204	2.4	24
Connecticut	6,814	1.9	30
Delaware	3,471	4.1	14
Florida	17,381	1.0	44
Georgia	11,488	1.3	41
Hawaii	9,221	7.2	3
Idaho	2,782	1.9	29
Illinois	44,358	3.5	17
Indiana	17,050	2.7	22
Iowa	14,129	4.8	11
Kansas	7,623	2.8	21
Kentucky	7,134	1.7	34
Louisiana	2,183	0.5	47
Maine	2,094	1.6	35
Maryland	11,538	2.1	26
Massachusetts	9,785	1.5	38
Michigan	20,447	2.0	27
Minnesota	8,039	1.6	36
Mississippi	2,942	1.0	43
Missouri	17,318	3.0	18
Montana	5,256	5.6	8
Nebraska	10,086	5.7	7
Nevada	4,149	1.7	33
New Hampshire	n/a	n/a	n/a
New Jersey	15,945	1.8	31
New Mexico	3,840	2.0	28
New York	53,605	2.8	20
North Carolina	11,771	1.4	40
North Dakota	966	1.5	39
Ohio	51,440	4.5	12
Oklahoma	12,742	3.6	16
Oregon	44,253	12.2	1
Pennsylvania	35,095	2.8	19
Rhode Island	5,471	5.1	9
South Carolina	6,508	1.5	37
South Dakota	7,148	9.2	2
Tennessee	29,228	4.9	10
Texas	9,654	0.4	48
Utah	4,274	1.7	32
Vermont	694	1.1	42
Virginia	6,543	0.9	45
Washington	40,331	6.4	6
West Virginia	7,969	4.4	13
Wisconsin	14,492	2.6	23
Wyoming	3,316	6.5	5
50 States	708,602	2.4	
DC	n/a	n/a	
United States	708,602	2.4	

Rank in order per capita

1 Oregon
2 South Dakota
3 Hawaii
4 Alaska
5 Wyoming
6 Washington
7 Nebraska
8 Montana
9 Rhode Island
10 Tennessee
11 Iowa
12 Ohio
13 West Virginia
14 Delaware
15 Arkansas
16 Oklahoma
17 Illinois
18 Missouri
19 Pennsylvania
20 New York
21 Kansas
22 Indiana
23 Wisconsin
24 Colorado
25 California
26 Maryland
27 Michigan
28 New Mexico
29 Idaho
30 Connecticut
31 New Jersey
32 Utah
33 Nevada
34 Kentucky
35 Maine
36 Minnesota
37 South Carolina
38 Massachusetts
39 North Dakota
40 North Carolina
41 Georgia
42 Vermont
43 Mississippi
44 Florida
45 Virginia
46 Alabama
47 Louisiana
48 Texas
49 Arizona

Note: Numbers that appear to be identical are rounded and vary slightly in actual value. The rankings reflect the actual values before rounding. See the introduction for more details.

C-5 Percentage of Population Not Physically Active, 2005

State	Percentage reporting not to be physically active	Rank
Alabama	29.7	7
Alaska	21.4	40
Arizona	22.6	32
Arkansas	30.6	5
California	23.9	25
Colorado	17.3	49
Connecticut	21.2	42
Delaware	23.3	27
Florida	26.9	13
Georgia	27.2	11
Hawaii	19.5	43
Idaho	21.6	38
Illinois	25.6	19
Indiana	26.9	13
Iowa	24.7	23
Kansas	24.4	24
Kentucky	31.5	4
Louisiana	33.4	1
Maine	22.3	36
Maryland	22.9	31
Massachusetts	23.3	27
Michigan	22.5	33
Minnesota	16.2	50
Mississippi	32.4	3
Missouri	25.4	22
Montana	22.4	35
Nebraska	23.8	26
Nevada	26.8	15
New Hampshire	21.6	38
New Jersey	29.2	8
New Mexico	23.3	27
New York	27.1	12
North Carolina	25.6	19
North Dakota	23.1	30
Ohio	25.6	19
Oklahoma	30.6	5
Oregon	18.6	46
Pennsylvania	25.8	18
Rhode Island	25.9	17
South Carolina	26.3	16
South Dakota	22.5	33
Tennessee	33.1	2
Texas	27.4	10
Utah	18.5	47
Vermont	19.2	44
Virginia	21.3	41
Washington	17.4	48
West Virginia	28.5	9
Wisconsin	18.7	45
Wyoming	22.0	37
50 States	n/a	
DC	22.5	
United States	23.8	

Rank in order by percentage

1   Louisiana
2   Tennessee
3   Mississippi
4   Kentucky
5   Arkansas
5   Oklahoma
7   Alabama
8   New Jersey
9   West Virginia
10   Texas
11   Georgia
12   New York
13   Florida
13   Indiana
15   Nevada
16   South Carolina
17   Rhode Island
18   Pennsylvania
19   Illinois
19   North Carolina
19   Ohio
22   Missouri
23   Iowa
24   Kansas
25   California
26   Nebraska
27   Delaware
27   Massachusetts
27   New Mexico
30   North Dakota
31   Maryland
32   Arizona
33   Michigan
33   South Dakota
35   Montana
36   Maine
37   Wyoming
38   Idaho
38   New Hampshire
40   Alaska
41   Virginia
42   Connecticut
43   Hawaii
44   Vermont
45   Wisconsin
46   Oregon
47   Utah
48   Washington
49   Colorado
50   Minnesota

Note: Ties in ranking reflect ties in actual values.

C-6   Hunters with Firearms, 2005

State	Hunters with firearms (in thousands)	Percentage of population	Rank by percentage
Alabama	263	5.8	31
Alaska	n/a	n/a	n/a
Arizona	294	5.0	34
Arkansas	595	21.4	2
California	1,106	3.1	42
Colorado	752	16.1	7
Connecticut	29	0.8	48
Delaware	33	3.9	37
Florida	308	1.7	46
Georgia	729	8.0	20
Hawaii	n/a	n/a	n/a
Idaho	259	18.1	6
Illinois	413	3.2	41
Indiana	409	6.5	29
Iowa	431	14.5	8
Kansas	115	4.2	36
Kentucky	364	8.7	17
Louisiana	857	18.9	5
Maine	118	8.9	16
Maryland	194	3.5	39
Massachusetts	113	1.8	45
Michigan	951	9.4	15
Minnesota	724	14.1	9
Mississippi	280	9.6	14
Missouri	491	8.5	18
Montana	183	19.6	4
Nebraska	126	7.2	24
Nevada	183	7.6	22
New Hampshire	33	2.5	44
New Jersey	117	1.3	47
New Mexico	74	3.8	38
New York	1,358	7.1	26
North Carolina	489	5.6	32
North Dakota	190	29.8	1
Ohio	607	5.3	33
Oklahoma	251	7.1	25
Oregon	302	8.3	19
Pennsylvania	1,481	11.9	11
Rhode Island	31	2.9	43
South Carolina	293	6.9	27
South Dakota	158	20.4	3
Tennessee	392	6.6	28
Texas	1,477	6.5	30
Utah	110	4.5	35
Vermont	70	11.2	12
Virginia	551	7.3	23
Washington	210	3.3	40
West Virginia	203	11.2	13
Wisconsin	675	12.2	10
Wyoming	39	7.7	21
50 States	19,392	6.6	
DC	n/a	n/a	
United States*	19,428	6.6	

Due to rounding or data sources, the 50-state total plus D.C. may not equal the U.S. total. Please see introduction.

Rank in order by percentage	
1	North Dakota
2	Arkansas
3	South Dakota
4	Montana
5	Louisiana
6	Idaho
7	Colorado
8	Iowa
9	Minnesota
10	Wisconsin
11	Pennsylvania
12	Vermont
13	West Virginia
14	Mississippi
15	Michigan
16	Maine
17	Kentucky
18	Missouri
19	Oregon
20	Georgia
21	Wyoming
22	Nevada
23	Virginia
24	Nebraska
25	Oklahoma
26	New York
27	South Carolina
28	Tennessee
29	Indiana
30	Texas
31	Alabama
32	North Carolina
33	Ohio
34	Arizona
35	Utah
36	Kansas
37	Delaware
38	New Mexico
39	Maryland
40	Washington
41	Illinois
42	California
43	Rhode Island
44	New Hampshire
45	Massachusetts
46	Florida
47	New Jersey
48	Connecticut

Note: Numbers that appear to be identical are rounded and vary slightly in actual value. The rankings reflect the actual values before rounding. See the introduction for more details.

C-7   Registered Boats, 2004

State	Registered boats	Registered boats per 1,000 population	Rank by total number of boats
Alabama	264,006	58	17
Alaska	49,225	75	45
Arizona	147,294	26	30
Arkansas	205,745	75	26
California	894,884	25	3
Colorado	98,079	21	34
Connecticut	111,992	32	31
Delaware	51,797	62	43
Florida	946,072	54	1
Georgia	322,252	36	14
Hawaii	13,205	10	50
Idaho	83,639	60	36
Illinois	393,856	31	10
Indiana	213,309	34	21
Iowa	228,140	77	20
Kansas	98,512	36	33
Kentucky	174,463	42	28
Louisiana	309,950	69	15
Maine	94,582	72	35
Maryland	206,681	37	24
Massachusetts	150,683	23	29
Michigan	944,800	93	2
Minnesota	853,448	167	4
Mississippi	209,216	72	23
Missouri	326,210	57	13
Montana	59,271	64	40
Nebraska	77,636	44	37
Nevada	57,612	25	41
New Hampshire	101,626	78	32
New Jersey	209,678	24	22
New Mexico	38,439	20	47
New York	519,066	27	7
North Carolina	356,946	42	11
North Dakota	52,961	83	42
Ohio	414,938	36	8
Oklahoma	206,049	58	25
Oregon	190,119	53	27
Pennsylvania	354,079	29	12
Rhode Island	43,671	40	46
South Carolina	397,458	95	9
South Dakota	51,604	67	44
Tennessee	261,465	44	18
Texas	616,779	27	5
Utah	74,293	31	38
Vermont	32,498	52	48
Virginia	242,642	33	19
Washington	266,056	43	16
West Virginia	63,504	35	39
Wisconsin	605,467	110	6
Wyoming	25,897	51	49
50 States	12,711,794	43	
DC	2,908	5	
United States*	12,781,476	44	

Due to rounding or data sources, the 50-state total plus D.C. may not equal the U.S. total. Please see introduction.

Rank in order by total number

1 Florida
2 Michigan
3 California
4 Minnesota
5 Texas
6 Wisconsin
7 New York
8 Ohio
9 South Carolina
10 Illinois
11 North Carolina
12 Pennsylvania
13 Missouri
14 Georgia
15 Louisiana
16 Washington
17 Alabama
18 Tennessee
19 Virginia
20 Iowa
21 Indiana
22 New Jersey
23 Mississippi
24 Maryland
25 Oklahoma
26 Arkansas
27 Oregon
28 Kentucky
29 Massachusetts
30 Arizona
31 Connecticut
32 New Hampshire
33 Kansas
34 Colorado
35 Maine
36 Idaho
37 Nebraska
38 Utah
39 West Virginia
40 Montana
41 Nevada
42 North Dakota
43 Delaware
44 South Dakota
45 Alaska
46 Rhode Island
47 New Mexico
48 Vermont
49 Wyoming
50 Hawaii

C-8 State Spending on State Arts Agencies, FY 2006

State	State spending for the arts $ (in thousands)	Per capita $	Rank per capita
Alabama	3,920	0.86	24
Alaska	540	0.81	26
Arizona	3,636	0.61	32
Arkansas	1,498	0.54	38
California	2,121	0.06	50
Colorado	700	0.15	48
Connecticut	7,084	2.02	6
Delaware	1,781	2.11	5
Florida	29,416	1.65	9
Georgia	3,901	0.43	43
Hawaii	6,838	5.36	1
Idaho	850	0.59	33
Illinois	19,496	1.53	10
Indiana	3,632	0.58	35
Iowa	1,206	0.41	44
Kansas	1,531	0.56	36
Kentucky	4,225	1.01	20
Louisiana	5,013	1.11	17
Maine	769	0.58	34
Maryland	11,280	2.01	7
Massachusetts	9,644	1.51	11
Michigan	9,823	0.97	22
Minnesota	8,593	1.67	8
Mississippi	1,568	0.54	39
Missouri	485	0.08	49
Montana	406	0.43	42
Nebraska	1,368	0.78	29
Nevada	1,711	0.71	31
New Hampshire	718	0.55	37
New Jersey	29,810	3.42	2
New Mexico	1,954	1.01	19
New York	45,333	2.35	4
North Carolina	7,940	0.91	23
North Dakota	500	0.79	28
Ohio	11,238	0.98	21
Oklahoma	4,243	1.20	14
Oregon	634	0.17	47
Pennsylvania	14,500	1.17	15
Rhode Island	3,246	3.02	3
South Carolina	3,567	0.84	25
South Dakota	603	0.78	30
Tennessee	6,616	1.11	16
Texas	4,257	0.19	46
Utah	2,705	1.10	18
Vermont	495	0.79	27
Virginia	3,543	0.47	40
Washington	2,322	0.37	45
West Virginia	2,424	1.33	12
Wisconsin	2,420	0.44	41
Wyoming	647	1.27	13
50 States	292,752	0.99	
DC	8,552	15.53	
United States*	301,304	1.02	

Rank in order per capita	
1	Hawaii
2	New Jersey
3	Rhode Island
4	New York
5	Delaware
6	Connecticut
7	Maryland
8	Minnesota
9	Florida
10	Illinois
11	Massachusetts
12	West Virginia
13	Wyoming
14	Oklahoma
15	Pennsylvania
16	Tennessee
17	Louisiana
18	Utah
19	New Mexico
20	Kentucky
21	Ohio
22	Michigan
23	North Carolina
24	Alabama
25	South Carolina
26	Alaska
27	Vermont
28	North Dakota
29	Nebraska
30	South Dakota
31	Nevada
32	Arizona
33	Idaho
34	Maine
35	Indiana
36	Kansas
37	New Hampshire
38	Arkansas
39	Mississippi
40	Virginia
41	Wisconsin
42	Montana
43	Georgia
44	Iowa
45	Washington
46	Texas
47	Oregon
48	Colorado
49	Missouri
50	California

Note: Numbers that appear to be identical are rounded and vary slightly in actual value. The rankings reflect the actual values before rounding. See the introduction for more details.

*Due to rounding or data sources, the 50-state total plus D.C. may not equal the U.S. total. Please see introduction.

Energy Consumption, Total and Per Capita, 2002

State	Energy consumption (in trillion BTUs)	BTUs per capita	Rank per capita
Alabama	2,023.6	451,682	8
Alaska	737.1	1,150,462	1
Arizona	1,361.4	250,342	44
Arkansas	1,146.9	423,741	10
California	7,984.4	228,203	48
Colorado	1,348.6	299,795	36
Connecticut	849.1	245,519	45
Delaware	307.9	382,120	18
Florida	4,261.0	255,488	43
Georgia	3,035.7	353,740	24
Hawaii	291.8	236,390	47
Idaho	491.5	365,707	20
Illinois	3,938.0	312,866	34
Indiana	2,880.4	467,997	7
Iowa	1,192.7	406,463	14
Kansas	1,073.2	395,656	15
Kentucky	1,989.4	486,583	6
Louisiana	3,689.1	824,379	3
Maine	467.7	360,608	22
Maryland	1,506.8	276,870	40
Massachusetts	1,561.4	243,529	46
Michigan	3,156.8	314,442	33
Minnesota	1,782.2	354,771	23
Mississippi	1,184.7	413,313	13
Missouri	1,841.1	324,078	28
Montana	381.6	419,159	11
Nebraska	641.1	371,275	19
Nevada	640.9	295,636	38
New Hampshire	326.3	255,989	41
New Jersey	2,519.9	293,829	39
New Mexico	673.9	363,210	21
New York	4,123.4	215,155	49
North Carolina	2,633.8	316,838	32
North Dakota	399.0	629,764	4
Ohio	3,959.4	347,174	27
Oklahoma	1,461.3	419,062	12
Oregon	1,076.2	305,535	35
Pennsylvania	3,916.3	317,768	30
Rhode Island	219.6	205,512	50
South Carolina	1,590.7	387,733	17
South Dakota	266.8	350,883	25
Tennessee	2,252.6	389,029	16
Texas	12,489.3	574,950	5
Utah	694.0	297,003	37
Vermont	157.6	255,730	42
Virginia	2,335.7	320,571	29
Washington	1,925.0	317,326	31
West Virginia	777.0	430,583	9
Wisconsin	1,889.4	347,371	26
Wyoming	440.9	883,487	2
50 States	97,894.2	340,596	
DC	187.5	332,079	
United States*	98,142.5	340,791	

Rank in order per capita	
1	Alaska
2	Wyoming
3	Louisiana
4	North Dakota
5	Texas
6	Kentucky
7	Indiana
8	Alabama
9	West Virginia
10	Arkansas
11	Montana
12	Oklahoma
13	Mississippi
14	Iowa
15	Kansas
16	Tennessee
17	South Carolina
18	Delaware
19	Nebraska
20	Idaho
21	New Mexico
22	Maine
23	Minnesota
24	Georgia
25	South Dakota
26	Wisconsin
27	Ohio
28	Missouri
29	Virginia
30	Pennsylvania
31	Washington
32	North Carolina
33	Michigan
34	Illinois
35	Oregon
36	Colorado
37	Utah
38	Nevada
39	New Jersey
40	Maryland
41	New Hampshire
42	Vermont
43	Florida
44	Arizona
45	Connecticut
46	Massachusetts
47	Hawaii
48	California
49	New York
50	Rhode Island

Due to rounding or data sources, the 50-state total plus D.C. may not equal the U.S. total. Please see introduction.

C-10 Toxic Chemical Release, 2004

State	Toxic chemical release in pounds (in thousands)	Per capita release in pounds	Rank per capita
Alabama	122,899	27.2	11
Alaska	512,278	778.8	1
Arizona	56,616	9.9	29
Arkansas	49,459	18.0	19
California	46,578	1.3	48
Colorado	24,293	5.3	40
Connecticut	5,041	1.4	46
Delaware	14,170	17.1	20
Florida	123,355	7.1	37
Georgia	118,689	13.3	23
Hawaii	3,168	2.5	43
Idaho	64,095	45.9	6
Illinois	135,002	10.6	28
Indiana	239,410	38.4	7
Iowa	43,070	14.6	22
Kansas	25,790	9.4	32
Kentucky	95,919	23.2	14
Louisiana	132,936	29.5	10
Maine	10,540	8.0	35
Maryland	43,628	7.8	36
Massachusetts	8,784	1.4	47
Michigan	98,265	9.7	30
Minnesota	26,163	5.1	41
Mississippi	73,743	25.4	13
Missouri	127,955	22.2	15
Montana	61,091	65.9	4
Nebraska	38,815	22.2	16
Nevada	269,304	115.4	2
New Hampshire	5,249	4.0	42
New Jersey	21,281	2.5	44
New Mexico	10,702	5.6	38
New York	42,408	2.2	45
North Carolina	133,458	15.6	21
North Dakota	22,929	36.0	8
Ohio	244,830	21.4	17
Oklahoma	29,553	8.4	33
Oregon	39,748	11.1	27
Pennsylvania	160,612	13.0	24
Rhode Island	599	0.6	50
South Carolina	80,827	19.3	18
South Dakota	8,546	11.1	26
Tennessee	157,770	26.8	12
Texas	277,538	12.4	25
Utah	167,837	69.3	3
Vermont	365	0.6	49
Virginia	71,833	9.6	31
Washington	32,798	5.3	39
West Virginia	91,597	50.5	5
Wisconsin	46,009	8.4	34
Wyoming	16,132	31.9	9
50 States	4,233,682	14.4	
DC	11	0.0	
United States*	4,244,378	14.5	

Due to rounding or data sources, the 50-state total plus D.C. may not equal the U.S. total. Please see introduction.

Rank in order per capita

1	Alaska
2	Nevada
3	Utah
4	Montana
5	West Virginia
6	Idaho
7	Indiana
8	North Dakota
9	Wyoming
10	Louisiana
11	Alabama
12	Tennessee
13	Mississippi
14	Kentucky
15	Missouri
16	Nebraska
17	Ohio
18	South Carolina
19	Arkansas
20	Delaware
21	North Carolina
22	Iowa
23	Georgia
24	Pennsylvania
25	Texas
26	South Dakota
27	Oregon
28	Illinois
29	Arizona
30	Michigan
31	Virginia
32	Kansas
33	Oklahoma
34	Wisconsin
35	Maine
36	Maryland
37	Florida
38	New Mexico
39	Washington
40	Colorado
41	Minnesota
42	New Hampshire
43	Hawaii
44	New Jersey
45	New York
46	Connecticut
47	Massachusetts
48	California
49	Vermont
50	Rhode Island

Note: Numbers that appear to be identical are rounded and vary slightly in actual value. The rankings reflect the actual values before rounding. See the introduction for more details.

C-11   Hazardous Waste Sites, 2006

State	Hazardous waste sites #	Rank
Alabama	13	29
Alaska	5	44
Arizona	8	42
Arkansas	10	38
California	93	3
Colorado	17	20
Connecticut	14	23
Delaware	14	23
Florida	49	6
Georgia	15	22
Hawaii	3	45
Idaho	6	43
Illinois	42	8
Indiana	29	14
Iowa	11	34
Kansas	10	38
Kentucky	14	23
Louisiana	11	34
Maine	12	31
Maryland	17	20
Massachusetts	32	11
Michigan	66	5
Minnesota	24	18
Mississippi	3	45
Missouri	26	16
Montana	14	23
Nebraska	14	23
Nevada	1	49
New Hampshire	20	19
New Jersey	115	1
New Mexico	12	31
New York	86	4
North Carolina	31	12
North Dakota	0	50
Ohio	30	13
Oklahoma	10	38
Oregon	11	34
Pennsylvania	94	2
Rhode Island	12	31
South Carolina	26	16
South Dakota	2	47
Tennessee	13	29
Texas	42	8
Utah	14	23
Vermont	11	34
Virginia	29	14
Washington	47	7
West Virginia	9	41
Wisconsin	37	10
Wyoming	2	47
50 States	1,226	
DC	1	
United States*	1,243	

Due to rounding or data sources, the 50-state total plus D.C. may not equal the U.S. total. Please see introduction.

Rank in order by #	
1	New Jersey
2	Pennsylvania
3	California
4	New York
5	Michigan
6	Florida
7	Washington
8	Illinois
8	Texas
10	Wisconsin
11	Massachusetts
12	North Carolina
13	Ohio
14	Indiana
14	Virginia
16	Missouri
16	South Carolina
18	Minnesota
19	New Hampshire
20	Colorado
20	Maryland
22	Georgia
23	Connecticut
23	Delaware
23	Kentucky
23	Montana
23	Nebraska
23	Utah
29	Alabama
29	Tennessee
31	Maine
31	New Mexico
31	Rhode Island
34	Iowa
34	Louisiana
34	Oregon
34	Vermont
38	Arkansas
38	Kansas
38	Oklahoma
41	West Virginia
42	Arizona
43	Idaho
44	Alaska
45	Hawaii
45	Mississippi
47	South Dakota
47	Wyoming
49	Nevada
50	North Dakota

Note: Ties in ranking reflect ties in actual values.

C-12 Drinking Water Quality, FY 2004

State	Percentage of community water systems with health violations	Rank
Alabama	1.8	49
Alaska	17.0	3
Arizona	13.4	8
Arkansas	13.2	9
California	5.7	37
Colorado	6.7	30
Connecticut	11.6	16
Delaware	10.6	21
Florida	6.2	33
Georgia	2.7	45
Hawaii	2.6	47
Idaho	11.8	14
Illinois	11.3	19
Indiana	11.3	18
Iowa	5.1	39
Kansas	10.6	20
Kentucky	9.6	23
Louisiana	8.9	26
Maine	19.0	2
Maryland	5.0	40
Massachusetts	7.8	28
Michigan	4.8	42
Minnesota	2.2	48
Mississippi	1.6	50
Missouri	12.7	11
Montana	11.5	17
Nebraska	22.1	1
Nevada	9.1	25
New Hampshire	14.5	6
New Jersey	2.6	46
New Mexico	12.7	12
New York	4.1	43
North Carolina	12.1	13
North Dakota	6.9	29
Ohio	6.0	35
Oklahoma	14.2	7
Oregon	15.2	4
Pennsylvania	5.8	36
Rhode Island	6.0	34
South Carolina	10.0	22
South Dakota	9.4	24
Tennessee	3.7	44
Texas	6.2	32
Utah	8.6	27
Vermont	14.7	5
Virginia	12.8	10
Washington	11.6	15
West Virginia	6.3	31
Wisconsin	5.0	41
Wyoming	5.4	38
50 States	8.3	
DC	33.3	
United States	8.3	

Rank in order by percentage

1 Nebraska
2 Maine
3 Alaska
4 Oregon
5 Vermont
6 New Hampshire
7 Oklahoma
8 Arizona
9 Arkansas
10 Virginia
11 Missouri
12 New Mexico
13 North Carolina
14 Idaho
15 Washington
16 Connecticut
17 Montana
18 Indiana
19 Illinois
20 Kansas
21 Delaware
22 South Carolina
23 Kentucky
24 South Dakota
25 Nevada
26 Louisiana
27 Utah
28 Massachusetts
29 North Dakota
30 Colorado
31 West Virginia
32 Texas
33 Florida
34 Rhode Island
35 Ohio
36 Pennsylvania
37 California
38 Wyoming
39 Iowa
40 Maryland
41 Wisconsin
42 Michigan
43 New York
44 Tennessee
45 Georgia
46 New Jersey
47 Hawaii
48 Minnesota
49 Alabama
50 Mississippi

Note: Numbers that appear to be identical are rounded and vary slightly in actual value. The rankings reflect the actual values before rounding. See the introduction for more details.

C-13 Expired Surface Water Pollution Discharge Permits, 2005

State	Percentage of major facilities with expired Clean Water Act permits	Rank
Alabama	8.7	32
Alaska	32.4	8
Arizona	27.3	11
Arkansas	1.8	45
California	16.1	20
Colorado	11.4	26
Connecticut	28.4	10
Delaware	47.6	4
Florida	16.7	19
Georgia	15.9	22
Hawaii	21.1	17
Idaho	57.1	2
Illinois	10.5	30
Indiana	29.5	9
Iowa	25.2	14
Kansas	3.6	43
Kentucky	37.9	7
Louisiana	12.5	25
Maine	8.0	34
Maryland	8.4	33
Massachusetts	25.8	13
Michigan	10.2	31
Minnesota	5.6	38
Mississippi	0.0	46
Missouri	26.4	12
Montana	61.0	1
Nebraska	1.9	44
Nevada	0.0	46
New Hampshire	44.8	6
New Jersey	16.1	20
New Mexico	22.2	16
New York	5.2	39
North Carolina	10.6	28
North Dakota	0.0	46
Ohio	12.6	24
Oklahoma	7.3	35
Oregon	56.6	3
Pennsylvania	7.1	36
Rhode Island	24.0	15
South Carolina	3.8	42
South Dakota	17.2	18
Tennessee	14.1	23
Texas	10.6	28
Utah	0.0	46
Vermont	6.1	37
Virginia	10.8	27
Washington	44.9	5
West Virginia	4.1	41
Wisconsin	4.6	40
Wyoming	0.0	46
50 States	n/a	
DC	0.0	
United States	15.2	

Rank in order by percentage

1 Montana
2 Idaho
3 Oregon
4 Delaware
5 Washington
6 New Hampshire
7 Kentucky
8 Alaska
9 Indiana
10 Connecticut
11 Arizona
12 Missouri
13 Massachusetts
14 Iowa
15 Rhode Island
16 New Mexico
17 Hawaii
18 South Dakota
19 Florida
20 California
20 New Jersey
22 Georgia
23 Tennessee
24 Ohio
25 Louisiana
26 Colorado
27 Virginia
28 North Carolina
28 Texas
30 Illinois
31 Michigan
32 Alabama
33 Maryland
34 Maine
35 Oklahoma
36 Pennsylvania
37 Vermont
38 Minnesota
39 New York
40 Wisconsin
41 West Virginia
42 South Carolina
43 Kansas
44 Nebraska
45 Arkansas
46 Mississippi
46 Nevada
46 North Dakota
46 Utah
46 Wyoming

Note: Ties in ranking reflect ties in actual values.

C-14 Air Pollution Emissions, 2002

State	Emissions in short tons (in thousands)	Per capita	Rank by total emissions
Alabama	4,112	0.9	15
Alaska	577	0.9	46
Arizona	1,983	0.4	34
Arkansas	2,434	0.9	31
California	8,618	0.2	3
Colorado	2,740	0.6	28
Connecticut	1,292	0.4	39
Delaware	470	0.6	48
Florida	9,082	0.5	2
Georgia	6,590	0.8	7
Hawaii	434	0.4	49
Idaho	1,512	1.1	37
Illinois	5,888	0.5	9
Indiana	5,792	0.9	11
Iowa	3,189	1.1	23
Kansas	3,803	1.4	17
Kentucky	3,342	0.8	22
Louisiana	3,394	0.8	21
Maine	1,059	0.8	43
Maryland	2,740	0.5	27
Massachusetts	2,606	0.4	29
Michigan	6,276	0.6	8
Minnesota	3,958	0.8	16
Mississippi	2,529	0.9	30
Missouri	5,131	0.9	12
Montana	1,158	1.3	41
Nebraska	1,914	1.1	35
Nevada	1,148	0.5	42
New Hampshire	786	0.6	45
New Jersey	2,992	0.3	25
New Mexico	2,162	1.2	32
New York	8,614	0.4	4
North Carolina	5,887	0.7	10
North Dakota	1,468	2.3	38
Ohio	7,713	0.7	5
Oklahoma	3,735	1.1	19
Oregon	2,930	0.8	26
Pennsylvania	7,372	0.6	6
Rhode Island	352	0.3	50
South Carolina	3,114	0.8	24
South Dakota	938	1.2	44
Tennessee	4,374	0.8	14
Texas	13,903	0.6	1
Utah	1,673	0.7	36
Vermont	517	0.8	47
Virginia	4,876	0.7	13
Washington	3,589	0.6	20
West Virginia	2,153	1.2	33
Wisconsin	3,788	0.7	18
Wyoming	1,245	2.5	40
50 States	177,952	0.6	
DC	119	0.2	
United States	178,071	0.6	

Rank in order by total emissions

1	Texas
2	Florida
3	California
4	New York
5	Ohio
6	Pennsylvania
7	Georgia
8	Michigan
9	Illinois
10	North Carolina
11	Indiana
12	Missouri
13	Virginia
14	Tennessee
15	Alabama
16	Minnesota
17	Kansas
18	Wisconsin
19	Oklahoma
20	Washington
21	Louisiana
22	Kentucky
23	Iowa
24	South Carolina
25	New Jersey
26	Oregon
27	Maryland
28	Colorado
29	Massachusetts
30	Mississippi
31	Arkansas
32	New Mexico
33	West Virginia
34	Arizona
35	Nebraska
36	Utah
37	Idaho
38	North Dakota
39	Connecticut
40	Wyoming
41	Montana
42	Nevada
43	Maine
44	South Dakota
45	New Hampshire
46	Alaska
47	Vermont
48	Delaware
49	Hawaii
50	Rhode Island

Note: Numbers that appear to be identical are rounded and vary slightly in actual value. The rankings reflect the actual values before rounding. See the introduction for more details.

Source Notes for Geography (Section C)

C-1 Total Land Area, 2000: This statistic comes from the 2000 census and is prepared by the geography division of the U.S. Census Bureau. It can be combined with population statistics to calculate the population "density" of each state (see Table A-21).

C-2 Land Owned by Federal Government, 2004: The federal government owns land for its buildings, military installations, and other facilities in every state, but these holdings are not major factors in the land use patterns of most states. The federal government also owns massive areas as part of the National Park Service and the Forest Service, and public lands managed by the Department of the Interior, primarily arid lands in western states. These federal land holdings, measured in land area—not land usefulness—are more than half of the land in some states. The data are maintained by the individual federal agencies that own the land, and they are compiled in the General Services Administration's (GSA) publication, *Federal Real Property Profile as of January 30, 2004.* The report can be found on the GSA Web site (www.gsa.gov).

C-3 State Park Acreage, FY 2006: These statistics show the acres of state parks and the number of acres of state parks per one thousand people. The data cover the year ending June 30, 2006. They come from the National Association of State Park Directors (www.naspd.org). The ratio was calculated by *State Fact Finder.*

C-4 State Park Visitors, FY 2006: State park agencies make estimates of the number of visitors to state parks maintained by the National Association of State Park Directors (see source for Table C-3). *State Fact Finder* related these visits to population using Census data. The data can be viewed as indicating that the average person visits a state park about 2.5 times a year.

C-5 Percentage of Population Not Physically Active, 2005: There are few reliable data on a state level on the participation of citizens in various forms of recreational activities, as no one maintains records of who hikes, plays tennis, or fishes except when they use facilities requiring admission. These data are from a survey of the Centers for Disease Control and Prevention (CDC). The data reflect the percentage of those surveyed who answered "no" to the question "During the past month, did you participate in any physical activities?" The numbers are available on the CDC Web site (www.cdc.gov) as part of the Behavioral Risk Factor Surveillance System.

C-6 Hunters with Firearms, 2005: These data show the sharp differences among states in the use of firearms for hunting—statistics highly relevant to debates over use and control of firearms. Note that the participant for the state listed is a resident of that state even though they may not

have hunted in that state. That is, a hunter with firearms in Texas is a resident of Texas even though he or she may have hunted in Louisiana. Estimates by state are made by the National Sporting Goods Association (Mt. Prospect, Illinois 60056) for all major recreation activities.

C-7 Registered Boats, 2004: All states require registration of motorboats and some require registration of other boats, such as canoes and sailboats. These data, collected from state authorities by the U.S. Coast Guard, show the number of registered boats and the relationship between the number of boats and population. The data come from the Consumer Affairs and Analysis Branch of the U.S. Coast Guard and were provided to *State Fact Finder* on November 29, 2005.

C-8 State Spending on State Arts Agencies, FY 2006: Each of the fifty states and six jurisdictional governments supports an arts agency as the primary means of funding the arts and encouraging cultural participation. These agencies receive the bulk of their funding from state level legislative appropriations, with additional support from the National Endowment for the Arts and other sources (governmental, private, and earned). This table measures legislative support for state arts agencies in fiscal year 2006. The National Assembly of State Arts Agencies collects and publishes this information and provided it to *State Fact Finder* on October 10, 2006.

C-9 Energy Consumption, Total and Per Capita, 2002: At the time of the "energy crisis" of the 1970s, the federal government established a Department of Energy (DOE) and a vast data collection mechanism covering production and consumption of all forms of energy, including coal, oil, gas, nuclear power, and renewables. This table from the Energy Information Administration (EIA) of the DOE shows total energy consumption and relates it to the population of each state.

These data show consumption by all users, including businesses, by the state where energy is used, not necessarily where it is produced. States with relatively small populations and intensive energy use for mining and petrochemical manufacturing show the largest use. The EIA has detailed data by state on sources of energy and use in categories, such as residential and industrial. The data, which includes renewable energy sources—solar, wind, hydroelectric, geothermal, ethanol, and wood and waste—are published on the EIA Web site (www.eia.doe.gov). The EIA also publishes an annual report, *State Energy Data Report*, with detailed information regarding energy consumption and prices.

C-10 Toxic Chemical Release, 2004: The U.S. Environmental Protection Agency (EPA) requires detailed reporting of what it defines as "toxic" chemical releases into the atmosphere.

These data, from the *2004 Toxics Release Inventory*, available on the EPA Web site (www.epa.gov), are frequently cited by the media as indicators of health risks and air pollution in particular states. They are of limited value for this purpose. The effects of releases in a particular state often are not felt in that state because they are carried to an adjacent state or the oceans.

C-11 Hazardous Waste Sites, 2006: This table shows the number of sites the Environmental Protection Agency (EPA) has designated for cleanup under the Superfund program. The program and the designations are highly controversial, but the data are often cited as indicators of the relative prevalence of hazardous waste problems in particular states. The data are available on the EPA Web site (www.epa.gov).

C-12 Drinking Water Quality, FY 2004: Under the Safe Drinking Water Act (SDWA), each state reports to the Environmental Protection Agency (EPA) on the status of its community water systems. This table shows what percentage of these systems in each state had reported health-based violations in fiscal year 2004.

C-13 Expired Surface Water Pollution Discharge Permits, 2005: Under the Clean Water Act a system of permits was created to regulate and reduce toxic discharges. These permits are issued to factories, utilities, sewage treatment plants, and any other private or public entity that releases pollutants into the nation's waters. Permits come up for renewal at least every five years, at which time new requirements for pollution reduction or better treatment technologies are generally required. This table based on data from the Environmental Protection Agency's National Pollutant Discharge Elimination System (NPDES) and available on its Web site (cfpub.epa.gov/npdes/permitissuance/backlog.cfm) provides a measure of the permit backlog in each state. Environmental groups argue that while permits remain in limbo, a water pollution program cannot be operated effectively. The EPA has put forth the goal of reducing backlog to 10 percent (the amount determined by the EPA to be acceptable). In September of 2005, nineteen states had reached or exceeded this goal.

C-14 Air Pollution Emissions, 2002: Despite many years and millions of dollars put into efforts to measure air pollution on a state-by-state basis, no satisfactory method has been found to develop a summary measure. There are many problems. Air pollution affects people where they breathe, so for some purposes the relevant measure is what's in the ambient air, but there is little interest in measuring air quality in places with few or no people like mountains and deserts. So, such measures focus on metropolitan areas, not states. Within each state, there are dramatic differences in pollution levels associated with such factors as proximity to prevailing winds and pollution sources and elevation.

Air pollution can only be controlled where it originates, so measurement related to enforcement concentrates on place of origin, which is often not the same as the state where people are affected. Airborne pollutants don't recognize state lines, so the relevant concept is airsheds, not states.

State Fact Finder developed this table primarily to lead users to the vast quantities of data available. The table reflects added estimates of short tons of pollution emissions in each state for six pollutants — carbon monoxide, nitrogen oxide, volatile organic compounds, sulfur dioxide, particulate matter, and ammonia. The per capita calculation is provided only as a subject of possible interest. The ranking based on total tons of emissions is not a proxy for the seriousness of air pollution to the residents of the states listed and not a recognized measure of how effectively states control pollution.

The data on each pollutant by state and major causes (for example, transportation, farming, utility operation) come from the Emission Factor and Inventory Group at the Environmental Protection Agency Office of Air Quality Planning and Standards and were released to *State Fact Finder* on March 21, 2006. This office is a good source for other information useful to readers interested in comparing air pollution emissions of the various states.

Government

Voter Turnout for U.S. Midterm Elections, 1962–2006

Year	Overall Turnout (%)
2006	40.4 *
2002	39.7
1998	38.0
1994	40.0
1990	38.5
1986	38.4
1982	42.1
1978	39.0
1974	39.3
1970	47.7
1966	48.9
1962	48.8

Year	Democratic Turnout (%)
2006	17.9*
2002	16.8
1998	16.7
1994	17.5
1990	18.9
1986	19.5
1982	22.1
1978	19.4
1974	21.2
1970	23.2
1966	23.4
1962	24.5

Year	Republican Turnout (%)
2006	16.8 *
2002	19.2
1998	16.9
1994	20.1
1990	16.0
1986	15.8
1982	17.3
1978	16.3
1974	15.0
1970	20.1
1966	22.2
1962	22.6

estimated

Source: Committee for the Study of the American Electorate

D-1 Members of the United States House, 2007

State	Number of House members	Change from 1990 census	Rank
Alabama	7	0	22
Alaska	1	0	44
Arizona	8	+2	18
Arkansas	4	0	31
California	53	+1	1
Colorado	7	+1	22
Connecticut	5	-1	27
Delaware	1	0	44
Florida	25	+2	4
Georgia	13	+2	9
Hawaii	2	0	39
Idaho	2	0	39
Illinois	19	-1	5
Indiana	9	-1	14
Iowa	5	0	27
Kansas	4	0	31
Kentucky	6	0	25
Louisiana	7	0	22
Maine	2	0	39
Maryland	8	0	18
Massachusetts	10	0	13
Michigan	15	-1	8
Minnesota	8	0	18
Mississippi	4	-1	31
Missouri	9	0	14
Montana	1	0	44
Nebraska	3	0	34
Nevada	3	+1	34
New Hampshire	2	0	39
New Jersey	13	0	9
New Mexico	3	0	34
New York	29	-2	3
North Carolina	13	+1	9
North Dakota	1	0	44
Ohio	18	-1	7
Oklahoma	5	-1	27
Oregon	5	0	27
Pennsylvania	19	-2	5
Rhode Island	2	0	39
South Carolina	6	0	25
South Dakota	1	0	44
Tennessee	9	0	14
Texas	32	+2	2
Utah	3	0	34
Vermont	1	0	44
Virginia	11	0	12
Washington	9	0	14
West Virginia	3	0	34
Wisconsin	8	-1	18
Wyoming	1	0	44
50 States	435		
DC	n/a		
United States	435		

Rank in order by #	
1	California
2	Texas
3	New York
4	Florida
5	Illinois
5	Pennsylvania
7	Ohio
8	Michigan
9	Georgia
9	New Jersey
9	North Carolina
12	Virginia
13	Massachusetts
14	Indiana
14	Missouri
14	Tennessee
14	Washington
18	Arizona
18	Maryland
18	Minnesota
18	Wisconsin
22	Alabama
22	Colorado
22	Louisiana
25	Kentucky
25	South Carolina
27	Connecticut
27	Iowa
27	Oklahoma
27	Oregon
31	Arkansas
31	Kansas
31	Mississippi
34	Nebraska
34	Nevada
34	New Mexico
34	Utah
34	West Virginia
39	Hawaii
39	Idaho
39	Maine
39	New Hampshire
39	Rhode Island
44	Alaska
44	Delaware
44	Montana
44	North Dakota
44	South Dakota
44	Vermont
44	Wyoming

Note: Ties in ranking reflect ties in actual values.

D-2 Members of State Legislatures, 2007

State	Senate members	House members	Total members	Rank by total members
Alabama	35	105	140	27
Alaska	20	40	60	49
Arizona	30	60	90	43
Arkansas	35	100	135	30
California	40	80	120	35
Colorado	35	65	100	42
Connecticut	36	151	187	9
Delaware	21	41	62	48
Florida	40	120	160	18
Georgia	56	180	236	3
Hawaii	25	51	76	46
Idaho	35	70	105	39
Illinois	59	118	177	13
Indiana	50	100	150	19
Iowa	50	100	150	19
Kansas	40	125	165	17
Kentucky	38	100	138	29
Louisiana	39	105	144	25
Maine	35	151	186	10
Maryland	47	141	188	8
Massachusetts	40	160	200	6
Michigan	38	110	148	23
Minnesota	67	134	201	5
Mississippi	52	122	174	14
Missouri	34	163	197	7
Montana	50	100	150	19
Nebraska	49	n/a	49	50
Nevada	21	42	63	47
New Hampshire	24	400	424	1
New Jersey	40	80	120	35
New Mexico	42	70	112	38
New York	62	150	212	4
North Carolina	50	120	170	15
North Dakota	47	94	141	26
Ohio	33	99	132	32
Oklahoma	48	101	149	22
Oregon	30	60	90	43
Pennsylvania	50	203	253	2
Rhode Island	38	75	113	37
South Carolina	46	124	170	15
South Dakota	35	70	105	39
Tennessee	33	99	132	32
Texas	31	150	181	11
Utah	29	75	104	41
Vermont	30	150	180	12
Virginia	40	100	140	27
Washington	49	98	147	24
West Virginia	34	100	134	31
Wisconsin	33	99	132	32
Wyoming	30	60	90	43
50 States	1,971	5,411	7,382	
DC	n/a	n/a	n/a	
United States	1,971	5,411	7,382	

Rank in order by total members	
1	New Hampshire
2	Pennsylvania
3	Georgia
4	New York
5	Minnesota
6	Massachusetts
7	Missouri
8	Maryland
9	Connecticut
10	Maine
11	Texas
12	Vermont
13	Illinois
14	Mississippi
15	North Carolina
15	South Carolina
17	Kansas
18	Florida
19	Indiana
19	Iowa
19	Montana
22	Oklahoma
23	Michigan
24	Washington
25	Louisiana
26	North Dakota
27	Alabama
27	Virginia
29	Kentucky
30	Arkansas
31	West Virginia
32	Ohio
32	Tennessee
32	Wisconsin
35	California
35	New Jersey
37	Rhode Island
38	New Mexico
39	Idaho
39	South Dakota
41	Utah
42	Colorado
43	Arizona
43	Oregon
43	Wyoming
46	Hawaii
47	Nevada
48	Delaware
49	Alaska
50	Nebraska

Note: Ties in ranking reflect ties in actual values.

D-3 State Legislators Per Million Population, 2007

State	Legislators per million population	Rank
Alabama	31	29
Alaska	90	9
Arizona	15	42
Arkansas	49	19
California	3	50
Colorado	21	38
Connecticut	53	17
Delaware	74	11
Florida	9	48
Georgia	26	32
Hawaii	60	14
Idaho	73	12
Illinois	14	44
Indiana	24	34
Iowa	51	18
Kansas	60	13
Kentucky	33	26
Louisiana	32	27
Maine	141	6
Maryland	34	25
Massachusetts	31	28
Michigan	15	43
Minnesota	39	23
Mississippi	60	15
Missouri	34	24
Montana	160	5
Nebraska	28	30
Nevada	26	31
New Hampshire	324	1
New Jersey	14	45
New Mexico	58	16
New York	11	47
North Carolina	20	40
North Dakota	221	3
Ohio	12	46
Oklahoma	42	21
Oregon	25	33
Pennsylvania	20	39
Rhode Island	105	8
South Carolina	40	22
South Dakota	135	7
Tennessee	22	37
Texas	8	49
Utah	42	20
Vermont	289	2
Virginia	19	41
Washington	23	36
West Virginia	74	10
Wisconsin	24	35
Wyoming	177	4
50 States	25	
DC	n/a	
United States	25	

Rank in order per million population

1 New Hampshire
2 Vermont
3 North Dakota
4 Wyoming
5 Montana
6 Maine
7 South Dakota
8 Rhode Island
9 Alaska
10 West Virginia
11 Delaware
12 Idaho
13 Kansas
14 Hawaii
15 Mississippi
16 New Mexico
17 Connecticut
18 Iowa
19 Arkansas
20 Utah
21 Oklahoma
22 South Carolina
23 Minnesota
24 Missouri
25 Maryland
26 Kentucky
27 Louisiana
28 Massachusetts
29 Alabama
30 Nebraska
31 Nevada
32 Georgia
33 Oregon
34 Indiana
35 Wisconsin
36 Washington
37 Tennessee
38 Colorado
39 Pennsylvania
40 North Carolina
41 Virginia
42 Arizona
43 Michigan
44 Illinois
45 New Jersey
46 Ohio
47 New York
48 Florida
49 Texas
50 California

Note: Numbers that appear to be identical are rounded and vary slightly in actual value. The rankings reflect the actual values before rounding. See the introduction for more details.

D-4   Units of Government, 2002

State	Number of government units	Units per 10,000 population	Rank per 10,000 population
Alabama	1,172	2.6	31
Alaska	176	2.7	30
Arizona	639	1.2	42
Arkansas	1,589	5.9	13
California	4,410	1.3	41
Colorado	1,929	4.3	20
Connecticut	581	1.7	37
Delaware	340	4.2	21
Florida	1,192	0.7	48
Georgia	1,449	1.7	36
Hawaii	20	0.2	50
Idaho	1,159	8.6	8
Illinois	6,904	5.5	15
Indiana	3,086	5.0	17
Iowa	1,976	6.7	10
Kansas	3,888	14.3	5
Kentucky	1,440	3.5	25
Louisiana	474	1.1	45
Maine	827	6.4	11
Maryland	266	0.5	49
Massachusetts	842	1.3	40
Michigan	2,805	2.8	29
Minnesota	3,483	6.9	9
Mississippi	1,001	3.5	26
Missouri	3,423	6.0	12
Montana	1,128	12.4	6
Nebraska	2,792	16.2	3
Nevada	211	1.0	46
New Hampshire	560	4.4	19
New Jersey	1,413	1.6	38
New Mexico	859	4.6	18
New York	3,421	1.8	34
North Carolina	961	1.2	43
North Dakota	2,736	43.2	1
Ohio	3,637	3.2	27
Oklahoma	1,799	5.2	16
Oregon	1,440	4.1	22
Pennsylvania	5,032	4.1	23
Rhode Island	119	1.1	44
South Carolina	702	1.7	35
South Dakota	1,867	24.6	2
Tennessee	931	1.6	39
Texas	4,785	2.2	33
Utah	606	2.6	32
Vermont	734	11.9	7
Virginia	522	0.7	47
Washington	1,788	2.9	28
West Virginia	687	3.8	24
Wisconsin	3,049	5.6	14
Wyoming	723	14.5	4
50 States	87,573	3.0	
DC	2	0.0	
United States*	87,576	3.0	

Due to rounding or data sources, the 50-state total plus D.C. may not equal the U.S. total. Please see introduction.

	Rank in order per 10,000 population
1	North Dakota
2	South Dakota
3	Nebraska
4	Wyoming
5	Kansas
6	Montana
7	Vermont
8	Idaho
9	Minnesota
10	Iowa
11	Maine
12	Missouri
13	Arkansas
14	Wisconsin
15	Illinois
16	Oklahoma
17	Indiana
18	New Mexico
19	New Hampshire
20	Colorado
21	Delaware
22	Oregon
23	Pennsylvania
24	West Virginia
25	Kentucky
26	Mississippi
27	Ohio
28	Washington
29	Michigan
30	Alaska
31	Alabama
32	Utah
33	Texas
34	New York
35	South Carolina
36	Georgia
37	Connecticut
38	New Jersey
39	Tennessee
40	Massachusetts
41	California
42	Arizona
43	North Carolina
44	Rhode Island
45	Louisiana
46	Nevada
47	Virginia
48	Florida
49	Maryland
50	Hawaii

Note: Numbers that appear to be identical are rounded and vary slightly in actual value. The rankings reflect the actual values before rounding. See the introduction for more details.

D-5 State Legislator Compensation, 2005

State	Salary $	Per diem during session $	Rank by salary
Alabama	1,050	2,280/month	48
Alaska	24,012	156-200/day	20
Arizona	24,000	35-60/day	21
Arkansas	14,067	110/day	31
California	110,880	138/day	1
Colorado	30,000	45-99/day	17
Connecticut	28,000	0	19
Delaware	39,785	0	11
Florida	29,916	117/day	18
Georgia	16,524	128/day	25
Hawaii	34,200	10-80/day	14
Idaho	15,646	38-99/day	28
Illinois	57,619	102/day	5
Indiana	11,600	134/day	36
Iowa	21,381	65-86/day	22
Kansas	8,376	91/day	41
Kentucky	14,464	100/day	30
Louisiana	16,800	113/day	24
Maine	10,020	70/day	39
Maryland	40,500	128-225/day	10
Massachusetts	55,569	10-100/day	7
Michigan	79,650	12,000/year	2
Minnesota	31,140	66/day	16
Mississippi	10,000	91/day	40
Missouri	31,351	77/day	15
Montana	8,371	90/day	42
Nebraska	12,000	31-91/day	35
Nevada	7,800	federal rate	44
New Hampshire	100	0	49
New Jersey	49,000	0	8
New Mexico	0	146/day	50
New York	79,500	varies	3
North Carolina	13,951	104/day	32
North Dakota	13,500	900/month	33
Ohio	56,261	0	6
Oklahoma	38,400	116/day	12
Oregon	16,284	91/day	27
Pennsylvania	69,647	128/day	4
Rhode Island	12,646	0	34
South Carolina	10,400	95/day	38
South Dakota	6,000	110/day	46
Tennessee	16,500	141/day	26
Texas	7,200	128/day	45
Utah	5,400	118/day	47
Vermont	11,023	35-104/day	37
Virginia	18,000	117/day	23
Washington	34,227	90/day	13
West Virginia	15,000	115/day	29
Wisconsin	45,569	88/day	9
Wyoming	7,950	85/day	43
50 States (average)	26,226	n/a	
DC	92,500	0	
United States (average)	27,525	n/a	

Rank in order by salary

1 California
2 Michigan
3 New York
4 Pennsylvania
5 Illinois
6 Ohio
7 Massachusetts
8 New Jersey
9 Wisconsin
10 Maryland
11 Delaware
12 Oklahoma
13 Washington
14 Hawaii
15 Missouri
16 Minnesota
17 Colorado
18 Florida
19 Connecticut
20 Alaska
21 Arizona
22 Iowa
23 Virginia
24 Louisiana
25 Georgia
26 Tennessee
27 Oregon
28 Idaho
29 West Virginia
30 Kentucky
31 Arkansas
32 North Carolina
33 North Dakota
34 Rhode Island
35 Nebraska
36 Indiana
37 Vermont
38 South Carolina
39 Maine
40 Mississippi
41 Kansas
42 Montana
43 Wyoming
44 Nevada
45 Texas
46 South Dakota
47 Utah
48 Alabama
49 New Hampshire
50 New Mexico

D-6   Percentage of Legislators Who Are Female, 2007

State	Percentage of female legislators	Rank
Alabama	12.9	47
Alaska	21.7	27
Arizona	31.1	8
Arkansas	20.7	29
California	27.5	16
Colorado	34.0	4
Connecticut	27.8	15
Delaware	30.6	9
Florida	25.0	19
Georgia	19.1	36
Hawaii	32.9	6
Idaho	22.9	23
Illinois	27.1	17
Indiana	18.7	37
Iowa	22.7	24
Kansas	29.1	13
Kentucky	12.3	49
Louisiana	17.4	39
Maine	30.6	9
Maryland	33.5	5
Massachusetts	24.5	21
Michigan	19.6	31
Minnesota	34.3	3
Mississippi	13.2	46
Missouri	19.3	33
Montana	25.3	18
Nebraska	20.4	30
Nevada	28.6	14
New Hampshire	35.4	2
New Jersey	19.2	34
New Mexico	30.4	11
New York	22.6	26
North Carolina	24.7	20
North Dakota	17.7	38
Ohio	17.4	39
Oklahoma	12.8	48
Oregon	30.0	12
Pennsylvania	13.8	45
Rhode Island	19.5	32
South Carolina	8.8	50
South Dakota	17.1	41
Tennessee	16.7	43
Texas	21.0	28
Utah	19.2	34
Vermont	35.6	1
Virginia	17.1	41
Washington	32.7	7
West Virginia	14.2	44
Wisconsin	22.7	24
Wyoming	23.3	22
50 States	23.3	
DC	n/a	
United States	23.3	

Rank in order by percentage	
1	Vermont
2	New Hampshire
3	Minnesota
4	Colorado
5	Maryland
6	Hawaii
7	Washington
8	Arizona
9	Delaware
9	Maine
11	New Mexico
12	Oregon
13	Kansas
14	Nevada
15	Connecticut
16	California
17	Illinois
18	Montana
19	Florida
20	North Carolina
21	Massachusetts
22	Wyoming
23	Idaho
24	Iowa
24	Wisconsin
26	New York
27	Alaska
28	Texas
29	Arkansas
30	Nebraska
31	Michigan
32	Rhode Island
33	Missouri
34	New Jersey
34	Utah
36	Georgia
37	Indiana
38	North Dakota
39	Louisiana
39	Ohio
41	South Dakota
41	Virginia
43	Tennessee
44	West Virginia
45	Pennsylvania
46	Mississippi
47	Alabama
48	Oklahoma
49	Kentucky
50	South Carolina

Note: Ties in ranking reflect ties in actual values.

D-7   Turnover in Legislatures, 2006

State	Percentage of new legislators	Rank
Alabama	14.3	33
Alaska	15.0	30
Arizona	24.4	13
Arkansas	26.7	6
California	40.8	1
Colorado	27.0	5
Connecticut	10.7	40
Delaware	11.3	39
Florida	24.4	14
Georgia	11.4	37
Hawaii	17.1	23
Idaho	19.0	19
Illinois	5.1	46
Indiana	8.0	45
Iowa	11.3	38
Kansas	12.8	36
Kentucky	9.4	43
Louisiana	n/a	n/a
Maine	24.7	11
Maryland	18.1	20
Massachusetts	8.5	44
Michigan	26.4	8
Minnesota	26.4	7
Mississippi	n/a	n/a
Missouri	16.8	24
Montana	24.7	12
Nebraska	40.8	2
Nevada	17.5	21
New Hampshire	35.6	3
New Jersey	n/a	n/a
New Mexico	17.1	22
New York	10.4	42
North Carolina	10.6	41
North Dakota	14.2	34
Ohio	25.8	9
Oklahoma	24.8	10
Oregon	14.4	32
Pennsylvania	21.7	15
Rhode Island	15.0	29
South Carolina	14.5	31
South Dakota	31.4	4
Tennessee	16.7	25
Texas	16.0	26
Utah	20.2	17
Vermont	20.6	16
Virginia	n/a	n/a
Washington	12.9	35
West Virginia	15.7	28
Wisconsin	15.9	27
Wyoming	20.0	18
50 States	18.7	
DC	n/a	
United States	18.7	

	Rank in order by percentage
1	California
2	Nebraska
3	New Hampshire
4	South Dakota
5	Colorado
6	Arkansas
7	Minnesota
8	Michigan
9	Ohio
10	Oklahoma
11	Maine
12	Montana
13	Arizona
14	Florida
15	Pennsylvania
16	Vermont
17	Utah
18	Wyoming
19	Idaho
20	Maryland
21	Nevada
22	New Mexico
23	Hawaii
24	Missouri
25	Tennessee
26	Texas
27	Wisconsin
28	West Virginia
29	Rhode Island
30	Alaska
31	South Carolina
32	Oregon
33	Alabama
34	North Dakota
35	Washington
36	Kansas
37	Georgia
38	Iowa
39	Delaware
40	Connecticut
41	North Carolina
42	New York
43	Kentucky
44	Massachusetts
45	Indiana
46	Illinois

Note: Numbers that appear to be identical are rounded and vary slightly in actual value. The rankings reflect the actual values before rounding. See the introduction for more details.

D-8   Term Limits (in years), 2007

State	Consecutive term limits Governor	Consecutive term limits House	Consecutive term limits Senate	Rank by House members
Alabama	8	n/a	n/a	n/a
Alaska	8	n/a	n/a	n/a
Arizona	8	8	8	4
Arkansas	8	6	8	13
California	8	6	8	13
Colorado	8	8	8	4
Connecticut	n/a	n/a	n/a	n/a
Delaware	8	n/a	n/a	n/a
Florida	8	8	8	4
Georgia	8	n/a	n/a	n/a
Hawaii	8	n/a	n/a	n/a
Idaho	n/a	n/a	n/a	n/a
Illinois	n/a	n/a	n/a	n/a
Indiana	8	n/a	n/a	n/a
Iowa	n/a	n/a	n/a	n/a
Kansas	8	n/a	n/a	n/a
Kentucky	8	n/a	n/a	n/a
Louisiana	8	12	12	1
Maine	8	8	8	4
Maryland	8	n/a	n/a	n/a
Massachusetts	n/a	n/a	n/a	n/a
Michigan	8	6	8	13
Minnesota	n/a	n/a	n/a	n/a
Mississippi	8	n/a	n/a	n/a
Missouri	8	8	8	4
Montana	8	8	8	4
Nebraska	8	unicameral	8	4
Nevada	8	12	12	1
New Hampshire	n/a	n/a	n/a	n/a
New Jersey	8	n/a	n/a	n/a
New Mexico	8	n/a	n/a	n/a
New York	n/a	n/a	n/a	n/a
North Carolina	8	n/a	n/a	n/a
North Dakota	n/a	n/a	n/a	n/a
Ohio	8	8	8	4
Oklahoma	8	12	12	1
Oregon	n/a	n/a	n/a	n/a
Pennsylvania	8	n/a	n/a	n/a
Rhode Island	8	n/a	n/a	n/a
South Carolina	8	n/a	n/a	n/a
South Dakota	8	8	8	4
Tennessee	8	n/a	n/a	n/a
Texas	n/a	n/a	n/a	n/a
Utah	12	n/a	n/a	n/a
Vermont	n/a	n/a	n/a	n/a
Virginia	4	n/a	n/a	n/a
Washington	n/a	n/a	n/a	n/a
West Virginia	8	n/a	n/a	n/a
Wisconsin	n/a	n/a	n/a	n/a
Wyoming	8	n/a	n/a	n/a
50 States	n/a	n/a	n/a	
DC	n/a	n/a	n/a	
United States	n/a	n/a	n/a	

Rank in order by House members

1	Louisiana
1	Nevada
1	Oklahoma
4	Arizona
4	Colorado
4	Florida
4	Maine
4	Missouri
4	Montana
4	Nebraska
4	Ohio
4	South Dakota
13	Arkansas
13	California
13	Michigan

Note: Ties in ranking reflect ties in actual values.

D-9   Legislative Session Length, 2007

State	Legislative length in calendar days #	Rank
Alabama	154	10
Alaska	121	17
Arizona	104	27
Arkansas	60	37
California	282	1
Colorado	120	18
Connecticut	155	9
Delaware	173	6
Florida	60	37
Georgia	77	32
Hawaii	107	25
Idaho	77	32
Illinois	no limit	n/a
Indiana	112	21
Iowa	111	22
Kansas	108	24
Kentucky	88	30
Louisiana	60	37
Maine	197	2
Maryland	90	28
Massachusetts	no limit	n/a
Michigan	no limit	n/a
Minnesota	139	14
Mississippi	90	28
Missouri	148	12
Montana	115	20
Nebraska	158	8
Nevada	120	18
New Hampshire	180	4
New Jersey	no limit	n/a
New Mexico	61	36
New York	no limit	n/a
North Carolina	167	7
North Dakota	81	31
Ohio	no limit	n/a
Oklahoma	110	23
Oregon	183	3
Pennsylvania	no limit	n/a
Rhode Island	175	5
South Carolina	150	11
South Dakota	76	34
Tennessee	137	15
Texas	140	13
Utah	45	42
Vermont	133	16
Virginia	46	41
Washington	105	26
West Virginia	60	37
Wisconsin	no limit	n/a
Wyoming	65	35
50 States	n/a	
DC	no limit	
United States	n/a	

Rank in order by #	
1	California
2	Maine
3	Oregon
4	New Hampshire
5	Rhode Island
6	Delaware
7	North Carolina
8	Nebraska
9	Connecticut
10	Alabama
11	South Carolina
12	Missouri
13	Texas
14	Minnesota
15	Tennessee
16	Vermont
17	Alaska
18	Colorado
18	Nevada
20	Montana
21	Indiana
22	Iowa
23	Oklahoma
24	Kansas
25	Hawaii
26	Washington
27	Arizona
28	Maryland
28	Mississippi
30	Kentucky
31	North Dakota
32	Georgia
32	Idaho
34	South Dakota
35	Wyoming
36	New Mexico
37	Arkansas
37	Florida
37	Louisiana
37	West Virginia
41	Virginia
42	Utah

Note: Ties in ranking reflect ties in actual values.

D-10 Party Control of State Legislatures, 2007

State	Democrats in legislature	Republicans in legislature	Legislative control	Percentage of members Republican	Rank by percentage Republican
Alabama	85	55	D	39.3	36
Alaska	26	34	R	56.7	12
Arizona	40	50	R	55.6	15
Arkansas	102	33	D	24.4	46
California	73	47	D	39.2	37
Colorado	59	41	D	41.0	32
Connecticut	130	57	D	30.5	43
Delaware	31	31	S	50.0	20
Florida	55	105	R	65.6	5
Georgia	96	140	R	59.3	8
Hawaii	63	13	D	17.1	48
Idaho	26	79	R	75.2	1
Illinois	103	74	D	41.8	27
Indiana	68	82	S	54.7	16
Iowa	84	65	D	43.3	26
Kansas	57	108	R	65.5	6
Kentucky	77	60	S	43.5	25
Louisiana	86	56	D	38.9	38
Maine	107	77	D	41.4	29
Maryland	139	49	D	26.1	45
Massachusetts	176	24	D	12.0	49
Michigan	75	73	S	49.3	22
Minnesota	129	72	D	35.8	40
Mississippi	101	69	D	39.7	35
Missouri	84	113	R	57.4	10
Montana	75	74	S	49.3	21
Nebraska	0	0	n/a	n/a	n/a
Nevada	37	26	S	41.3	30
New Hampshire	253	171	D	40.3	34
New Jersey	71	49	D	40.8	33
New Mexico	66	46	D	41.1	31
New York	133	79	S	37.3	39
North Carolina	99	71	D	41.8	28
North Dakota	54	87	R	61.7	7
Ohio	58	74	R	56.1	13
Oklahoma	68	81	S	54.4	17
Oregon	48	40	D	44.4	24
Pennsylvania	123	130	S	51.4	18
Rhode Island	93	20	D	17.7	47
South Carolina	71	99	R	58.2	9
South Dakota	35	70	R	66.7	4
Tennessee	69	63	S	47.7	23
Texas	80	101	R	55.8	14
Utah	28	76	R	73.1	3
Vermont	116	56	D	31.1	42
Virginia	57	80	R	57.1	11
Washington	95	52	D	35.4	41
West Virginia	95	39	D	29.1	44
Wisconsin	65	67	S	50.8	19
Wyoming	24	66	R	73.3	2
50 States	3,985	3,324	23D, 15R, 11S	45.0	
DC	n/a	n/a	n/a	n/a	
United States	3,985	3,324	23D, 15R, 11S	45.0	

Rank in order by percentage Republican

1 Idaho
2 Wyoming
3 Utah
4 South Dakota
5 Florida
6 Kansas
7 North Dakota
8 Georgia
9 South Carolina
10 Missouri
11 Virginia
12 Alaska
13 Ohio
14 Texas
15 Arizona
16 Indiana
17 Oklahoma
18 Pennsylvania
19 Wisconsin
20 Delaware
21 Montana
22 Michigan
23 Tennessee
24 Oregon
25 Kentucky
26 Iowa
27 Illinois
28 North Carolina
29 Maine
30 Nevada
31 New Mexico
32 Colorado
33 New Jersey
34 New Hampshire
35 Mississippi
36 Alabama
37 California
38 Louisiana
39 New York
40 Minnesota
41 Washington
42 Vermont
43 Connecticut
44 West Virginia
45 Maryland
46 Arkansas
47 Rhode Island
48 Hawaii
49 Massachusetts

D-11   Governors' Institutional Power Rating, 2007

State	Power rating	Rank
Alabama	2.8	47
Alaska	4.1	2
Arizona	3.4	30
Arkansas	3.6	17
California	3.2	36
Colorado	3.9	8
Connecticut	3.6	17
Delaware	3.5	26
Florida	3.6	17
Georgia	3.2	36
Hawaii	3.4	30
Idaho	3.3	33
Illinois	3.8	10
Indiana	2.9	44
Iowa	3.8	10
Kansas	3.3	33
Kentucky	3.3	33
Louisiana	3.4	30
Maine	3.6	17
Maryland	4.1	2
Massachusetts	4.3	1
Michigan	3.6	17
Minnesota	3.6	17
Mississippi	2.9	44
Missouri	3.6	17
Montana	3.5	26
Nebraska	3.8	10
Nevada	3.0	42
New Hampshire	3.2	36
New Jersey	4.1	2
New Mexico	3.7	16
New York	4.1	2
North Carolina	2.9	44
North Dakota	3.9	8
Ohio	3.6	17
Oklahoma	2.8	47
Oregon	3.5	26
Pennsylvania	3.8	10
Rhode Island	2.6	49
South Carolina	3.0	42
South Dakota	3.8	10
Tennessee	3.8	10
Texas	3.2	36
Utah	4.0	7
Vermont	2.5	50
Virginia	3.2	36
Washington	3.6	17
West Virginia	4.1	2
Wisconsin	3.5	26
Wyoming	3.1	41
50 States	3.5	
DC	n/a	
United States	3.5	

Rank in order by rating

Rank	State
1	Massachusetts
2	Alaska
2	Maryland
2	New Jersey
2	New York
2	West Virginia
7	Utah
8	Colorado
8	North Dakota
10	Illinois
10	Iowa
10	Nebraska
10	Pennsylvania
10	South Dakota
10	Tennessee
16	New Mexico
17	Arkansas
17	Connecticut
17	Florida
17	Maine
17	Michigan
17	Minnesota
17	Missouri
17	Ohio
17	Washington
26	Delaware
26	Montana
26	Oregon
26	Wisconsin
30	Arizona
30	Hawaii
30	Louisiana
33	Idaho
33	Kansas
33	Kentucky
36	California
36	Georgia
36	New Hampshire
36	Texas
36	Virginia
41	Wyoming
42	Nevada
42	South Carolina
44	Indiana
44	Mississippi
44	North Carolina
47	Alabama
47	Oklahoma
49	Rhode Island
50	Vermont

Note: Ties in ranking reflect ties in actual values.

D-12 Number of Statewide Elected Officials, 2006

State	Elected officials #	Rank
Alabama	8	10
Alaska	2	45
Arizona	5	34
Arkansas	6	21
California	8	10
Colorado	6	21
Connecticut	6	21
Delaware	6	21
Florida	8	10
Georgia	11	2
Hawaii	2	45
Idaho	8	10
Illinois	6	21
Indiana	9	4
Iowa	7	17
Kansas	6	21
Kentucky	8	10
Louisiana	7	17
Maine	1	48
Maryland	4	41
Massachusetts	6	21
Michigan	4	41
Minnesota	5	34
Mississippi	9	4
Missouri	6	21
Montana	7	17
Nebraska	6	21
Nevada	6	21
New Hampshire	1	48
New Jersey	1	48
New Mexico	7	17
New York	4	41
North Carolina	10	3
North Dakota	12	1
Ohio	9	4
Oklahoma	8	10
Oregon	6	21
Pennsylvania	5	34
Rhode Island	5	34
South Carolina	9	4
South Dakota	8	10
Tennessee	2	45
Texas	5	34
Utah	5	34
Vermont	6	21
Virginia	3	44
Washington	9	4
West Virginia	5	34
Wisconsin	6	21
Wyoming	9	4
50 States	n/a	
DC	n/a	
United States	n/a	

Rank in order by #	
1	North Dakota
2	Georgia
3	North Carolina
4	Indiana
4	Mississippi
4	Ohio
4	South Carolina
4	Washington
4	Wyoming
10	Alabama
10	California
10	Florida
10	Idaho
10	Kentucky
10	Oklahoma
10	South Dakota
17	Iowa
17	Louisiana
17	Montana
17	New Mexico
21	Arkansas
21	Colorado
21	Connecticut
21	Delaware
21	Illinois
21	Kansas
21	Massachusetts
21	Missouri
21	Nebraska
21	Nevada
21	Oregon
21	Vermont
21	Wisconsin
34	Arizona
34	Minnesota
34	Pennsylvania
34	Rhode Island
34	Texas
34	Utah
34	West Virginia
41	Maryland
41	Michigan
41	New York
44	Virginia
45	Alaska
45	Hawaii
45	Tennessee
48	Maine
48	New Hampshire
48	New Jersey

Note: Ties in ranking reflect ties in actual values.

D-13　State and Local Government Employees, 2005

State	Government employees #	Per 10,000 population	Rank per 10,000 population
Alabama	273,673	600	12
Alaska	51,720	779	2
Arizona	281,796	474	46
Arkansas	160,115	576	15
California	1,771,336	490	44
Colorado	250,068	536	32
Connecticut	185,219	528	36
Delaware	47,114	559	22
Florida	843,284	474	47
Georgia	498,781	550	25
Hawaii	68,630	538	31
Idaho	77,171	540	29
Illinois	637,313	499	42
Indiana	332,761	531	33
Iowa	185,874	627	9
Kansas	181,585	662	4
Kentucky	238,421	571	19
Louisiana	283,287	626	10
Maine	76,008	575	17
Maryland	278,497	497	43
Massachusetts	322,262	504	40
Michigan	495,030	489	45
Minnesota	269,273	525	38
Mississippi	188,707	646	6
Missouri	318,372	549	26
Montana	55,489	593	13
Nebraska	111,586	634	7
Nevada	100,408	416	50
New Hampshire	69,186	528	35
New Jersey	501,643	575	16
New Mexico	128,115	664	3
New York	1,184,190	615	11
North Carolina	483,464	557	23
North Dakota	41,213	647	5
Ohio	620,466	541	28
Oklahoma	205,301	579	14
Oregon	182,390	501	41
Pennsylvania	576,511	464	49
Rhode Island	50,060	465	48
South Carolina	244,281	574	18
South Dakota	43,626	562	21
Tennessee	321,954	540	30
Texas	1,290,828	565	20
Utah	127,713	517	39
Vermont	39,421	633	8
Virginia	417,788	552	24
Washington	329,873	525	37
West Virginia	98,422	542	27
Wisconsin	293,712	531	34
Wyoming	43,762	859	1
50 States	15,877,699	537	
DC	45,951	835	
United States	15,923,650	537	

Note: Numbers that appear to be identical are rounded and vary slightly in actual value. The rankings reflect the actual values before rounding. See the introduction for more details.

D-14 Average Salaries of State and Local Government Employees, 2005

State	Average salary $	Rank
Alabama	35,141	42
Alaska	48,601	9
Arizona	41,908	20
Arkansas	33,160	48
California	57,441	1
Colorado	45,206	13
Connecticut	53,493	3
Delaware	44,656	15
Florida	40,479	22
Georgia	37,065	33
Hawaii	44,251	18
Idaho	35,439	38
Illinois	45,097	14
Indiana	38,019	29
Iowa	38,318	27
Kansas	36,242	35
Kentucky	35,160	41
Louisiana	34,139	46
Maine	36,149	36
Maryland	49,989	6
Massachusetts	49,464	7
Michigan	45,633	12
Minnesota	45,699	11
Mississippi	32,629	50
Missouri	35,228	40
Montana	34,546	45
Nebraska	38,530	26
Nevada	48,478	10
New Hampshire	38,293	28
New Jersey	54,507	2
New Mexico	34,618	44
New York	53,347	4
North Carolina	38,594	25
North Dakota	37,425	31
Ohio	41,545	21
Oklahoma	32,682	49
Oregon	43,391	19
Pennsylvania	44,512	16
Rhode Island	51,209	5
South Carolina	35,272	39
South Dakota	34,839	43
Tennessee	35,799	37
Texas	36,947	34
Utah	37,495	30
Vermont	39,226	24
Virginia	40,211	23
Washington	49,050	8
West Virginia	34,042	47
Wisconsin	44,346	17
Wyoming	37,216	32
50 States	43,767	
DC	55,741	
United States	43,801	

Rank in order by $	
1	California
2	New Jersey
3	Connecticut
4	New York
5	Rhode Island
6	Maryland
7	Massachusetts
8	Washington
9	Alaska
10	Nevada
11	Minnesota
12	Michigan
13	Colorado
14	Illinois
15	Delaware
16	Pennsylvania
17	Wisconsin
18	Hawaii
19	Oregon
20	Arizona
21	Ohio
22	Florida
23	Virginia
24	Vermont
25	North Carolina
26	Nebraska
27	Iowa
28	New Hampshire
29	Indiana
30	Utah
31	North Dakota
32	Wyoming
33	Georgia
34	Texas
35	Kansas
36	Maine
37	Tennessee
38	Idaho
39	South Carolina
40	Missouri
41	Kentucky
42	Alabama
43	South Dakota
44	New Mexico
45	Montana
46	Louisiana
47	West Virginia
48	Arkansas
49	Oklahoma
50	Mississippi

D-15 Local Employment, 2005

State	Number of local employees	Local share of state and local employees %	Rank by percentage
Alabama	188,349	68.8	31
Alaska	27,167	52.5	48
Arizona	212,570	75.4	10
Arkansas	105,930	66.2	39
California	1,384,276	78.1	4
Colorado	184,033	73.6	13
Connecticut	125,392	67.7	36
Delaware	22,568	47.9	49
Florida	657,329	77.9	6
Georgia	377,938	75.8	8
Hawaii	14,344	20.9	50
Idaho	54,268	70.3	27
Illinois	504,379	79.1	2
Indiana	239,827	72.1	20
Iowa	132,928	71.5	23
Kansas	137,278	75.6	9
Kentucky	159,190	66.8	38
Louisiana	192,400	67.9	35
Maine	54,868	72.2	19
Maryland	187,955	67.5	37
Massachusetts	233,729	72.5	16
Michigan	363,776	73.5	14
Minnesota	194,995	72.4	17
Mississippi	132,139	70.0	28
Missouri	226,571	71.2	25
Montana	35,946	64.8	40
Nebraska	79,114	70.9	26
Nevada	74,642	74.3	11
New Hampshire	49,709	71.8	22
New Jersey	347,538	69.3	29
New Mexico	77,894	60.8	45
New York	938,753	79.3	1
North Carolina	348,179	72.0	21
North Dakota	23,093	56.0	47
Ohio	484,096	78.0	5
Oklahoma	140,324	68.4	33
Oregon	124,458	68.2	34
Pennsylvania	416,829	72.3	18
Rhode Island	30,118	60.2	46
South Carolina	167,783	68.7	32
South Dakota	30,149	69.1	30
Tennessee	239,168	74.3	12
Texas	1,016,476	78.7	3
Utah	78,549	61.5	44
Vermont	25,068	63.6	42
Virginia	298,240	71.4	24
Washington	212,591	64.4	41
West Virginia	60,712	61.7	43
Wisconsin	223,523	76.1	7
Wyoming	32,026	73.2	15
50 States	11,669,177	73.5	
DC	45,951	100.0	
United States	11,715,128	73.6	

Rank in order by percentage	
1	New York
2	Illinois
3	Texas
4	California
5	Ohio
6	Florida
7	Wisconsin
8	Georgia
9	Kansas
10	Arizona
11	Nevada
12	Tennessee
13	Colorado
14	Michigan
15	Wyoming
16	Massachusetts
17	Minnesota
18	Pennsylvania
19	Maine
20	Indiana
21	North Carolina
22	New Hampshire
23	Iowa
24	Virginia
25	Missouri
26	Nebraska
27	Idaho
28	Mississippi
29	New Jersey
30	South Dakota
31	Alabama
32	South Carolina
33	Oklahoma
34	Oregon
35	Louisiana
36	Connecticut
37	Maryland
38	Kentucky
39	Arkansas
40	Montana
41	Washington
42	Vermont
43	West Virginia
44	Utah
45	New Mexico
46	Rhode Island
47	North Dakota
48	Alaska
49	Delaware
50	Hawaii

Note: Numbers that appear to be identical are rounded and vary slightly in actual value. The rankings reflect the actual values before rounding. See the introduction for more details.

D-16 Local Spending Accountability, FY 2004

State	Percentage of local spending raised by local government	Rank
Alabama	58.5	35
Alaska	61.7	26
Arizona	58.7	33
Arkansas	46.2	48
California	54.5	40
Colorado	68.8	8
Connecticut	68.9	7
Delaware	48.5	46
Florida	69.0	6
Georgia	63.9	18
Hawaii	78.2	1
Idaho	58.7	34
Illinois	63.9	17
Indiana	59.9	32
Iowa	62.8	21
Kansas	69.2	5
Kentucky	53.9	43
Louisiana	61.6	27
Maine	72.3	3
Maryland	75.2	2
Massachusetts	62.5	24
Michigan	46.7	47
Minnesota	49.0	45
Mississippi	54.0	41
Missouri	66.0	15
Montana	57.7	38
Nebraska	71.7	4
Nevada	63.0	19
New Hampshire	64.9	16
New Jersey	66.7	14
New Mexico	43.0	49
New York	67.4	11
North Carolina	60.1	30
North Dakota	60.3	29
Ohio	57.5	39
Oklahoma	59.9	31
Oregon	58.3	36
Pennsylvania	58.3	37
Rhode Island	67.3	12
South Carolina	67.0	13
South Dakota	68.6	10
Tennessee	62.9	20
Texas	68.7	9
Utah	62.7	22
Vermont	42.3	50
Virginia	62.3	25
Washington	61.3	28
West Virginia	54.0	42
Wisconsin	52.6	44
Wyoming	62.6	23
50 States	61.3	
DC	73.4	
United States	61.3	

Rank in order by percentage	
1	Hawaii
2	Maryland
3	Maine
4	Nebraska
5	Kansas
6	Florida
7	Connecticut
8	Colorado
9	Texas
10	South Dakota
11	New York
12	Rhode Island
13	South Carolina
14	New Jersey
15	Missouri
16	New Hampshire
17	Illinois
18	Georgia
19	Nevada
20	Tennessee
21	Iowa
22	Utah
23	Wyoming
24	Massachusetts
25	Virginia
26	Alaska
27	Louisiana
28	Washington
29	North Dakota
30	North Carolina
31	Oklahoma
32	Indiana
33	Arizona
34	Idaho
35	Alabama
36	Oregon
37	Pennsylvania
38	Montana
39	Ohio
40	California
41	Mississippi
42	West Virginia
43	Kentucky
44	Wisconsin
45	Minnesota
46	Delaware
47	Michigan
48	Arkansas
49	New Mexico
50	Vermont

Note: Numbers that appear to be identical are rounded and vary slightly in actual value. The rankings reflect the actual values before rounding. See the introduction for more details.

D-17 Percentage of Eligible Voters Registered, November 2006

State	Percentage of registered voters	Rank
Alabama	70.81	46
Alaska	101.45	1
Arizona	77.78	41
Arkansas	78.82	39
California	75.09	43
Colorado	87.52	20
Connecticut	87.45	21
Delaware	90.54	11
Florida	82.29	32
Georgia	81.00	35
Hawaii	74.30	45
Idaho	74.55	44
Illinois	84.97	26
Indiana	92.59	8
Iowa	93.95	5
Kansas	84.12	30
Kentucky	86.69	24
Louisiana	86.04	25
Maine	n/a	n/a
Maryland	87.10	23
Massachusetts	88.38	17
Michigan	97.43	2
Minnesota	83.67	31
Mississippi	80.79	36
Missouri	93.04	7
Montana	88.81	15
Nebraska	89.47	13
Nevada	75.83	42
New Hampshire	88.37	18
New Jersey	84.85	27
New Mexico	79.89	37
New York	93.34	6
North Carolina	87.30	22
North Dakota	n/a	n/a
Ohio	92.37	9
Oklahoma	78.79	40
Oregon	96.51	3
Pennsylvania	88.29	19
Rhode Island	90.50	12
South Carolina	81.04	34
South Dakota	95.69	4
Tennessee	81.69	33
Texas	89.25	14
Utah	88.65	16
Vermont	90.62	10
Virginia	84.45	29
Washington	84.71	28
West Virginia	79.31	38
Wisconsin	n/a	n/a
Wyoming	67.63	47
50 States	n/a	
DC	n/a	
United States	85.46	

Rank in order by percentage

1 Alaska
2 Michigan
3 Oregon
4 South Dakota
5 Iowa
6 New York
7 Missouri
8 Indiana
9 Ohio
10 Vermont
11 Delaware
12 Rhode Island
13 Nebraska
14 Texas
15 Montana
16 Utah
17 Massachusetts
18 New Hampshire
19 Pennsylvania
20 Colorado
21 Connecticut
22 North Carolina
23 Maryland
24 Kentucky
25 Louisiana
26 Illinois
27 New Jersey
28 Washington
29 Virginia
30 Kansas
31 Minnesota
32 Florida
33 Tennessee
34 South Carolina
35 Georgia
36 Mississippi
37 New Mexico
38 West Virginia
39 Arkansas
40 Oklahoma
41 Arizona
42 Nevada
43 California
44 Idaho
45 Hawaii
46 Alabama
47 Wyoming

Note: Numbers that appear to be identical are rounded and vary slightly in actual value. The rankings reflect the actual values before rounding. See the introduction for more details.

D-18 Percentage of Population Voting, November 2006

State	Percentage voting	Rank
Alabama	35.9	38
Alaska	51.8	8
Arizona	39.0	34
Arkansas	36.8	37
California	41.2	27
Colorado	45.8	20
Connecticut	47.6	14
Delaware	40.9	29
Florida	38.1	36
Georgia	33.5	45
Hawaii	38.6	35
Idaho	43.9	23
Illinois	40.5	30
Indiana	35.9	38
Iowa	47.4	15
Kansas	43.0	25
Kentucky	39.3	32
Louisiana	26.9	50
Maine	55.4	4
Maryland	46.4	18
Massachusetts	49.2	13
Michigan	51.6	9
Minnesota	59.1	1
Mississippi	27.5	49
Missouri	49.4	12
Montana	55.9	3
Nebraska	46.9	17
Nevada	35.9	38
New Hampshire	42.1	26
New Jersey	39.3	32
New Mexico	41.2	27
New York	35.5	41
North Carolina	30.4	47
North Dakota	44.9	21
Ohio	47.0	16
Oklahoma	35.3	42
Oregon	52.0	7
Pennsylvania	44.2	22
Rhode Island	51.2	10
South Carolina	34.1	44
South Dakota	58.0	2
Tennessee	40.1	31
Texas	30.1	48
Utah	34.5	43
Vermont	54.9	5
Virginia	43.9	23
Washington	46.4	18
West Virginia	32.1	46
Wisconsin	52.4	6
Wyoming	49.8	11
50 States	n/a	
DC	31.5	
United States	40.7	

Rank in order by percentage	
1	Minnesota
2	South Dakota
3	Montana
4	Maine
5	Vermont
6	Wisconsin
7	Oregon
8	Alaska
9	Michigan
10	Rhode Island
11	Wyoming
12	Missouri
13	Massachusetts
14	Connecticut
15	Iowa
16	Ohio
17	Nebraska
18	Maryland
18	Washington
20	Colorado
21	North Dakota
22	Pennsylvania
23	Idaho
23	Virginia
25	Kansas
26	New Hampshire
27	California
27	New Mexico
29	Delaware
30	Illinois
31	Tennessee
32	Kentucky
32	New Jersey
34	Arizona
35	Hawaii
36	Florida
37	Arkansas
38	Alabama
38	Indiana
38	Nevada
41	New York
42	Oklahoma
43	Utah
44	South Carolina
45	Georgia
46	West Virginia
47	North Carolina
48	Texas
49	Mississippi
50	Louisiana

Note: Ties in ranking reflect ties in actual values.

D-19 Statewide Initiatives and Popular Referenda, 2006

State	Number of initiatives	Initiatives approved by voters	Rank by number of initiatives
Alabama	0	n/a	n/a
Alaska	5	4	7
Arizona	10	5	1
Arkansas	0	n/a	n/a
California	9	2	3
Colorado	7	3	5
Connecticut	0	n/a	n/a
Delaware	0	n/a	n/a
Florida	1	1	17
Georgia	0	n/a	n/a
Hawaii	0	n/a	n/a
Idaho	2	0	14
Illinois	0	n/a	n/a
Indiana	0	n/a	n/a
Iowa	0	n/a	n/a
Kansas	0	n/a	n/a
Kentucky	0	n/a	n/a
Louisiana	0	n/a	n/a
Maine	1	0	17
Maryland	1	1	17
Massachusetts	3	0	9
Michigan	3	1	9
Minnesota	0	n/a	n/a
Mississippi	0	n/a	n/a
Missouri	3	2	9
Montana	2	2	14
Nebraska	3	2	9
Nevada	6	4	6
New Hampshire	0	n/a	n/a
New Jersey	0	n/a	n/a
New Mexico	0	n/a	n/a
New York	0	n/a	n/a
North Carolina	0	n/a	n/a
North Dakota	2	1	14
Ohio	4	2	8
Oklahoma	1	0	17
Oregon	10	3	1
Pennsylvania	0	n/a	n/a
Rhode Island	0	n/a	n/a
South Carolina	0	n/a	n/a
South Dakota	9	2	3
Tennessee	0	n/a	n/a
Texas	0	n/a	n/a
Utah	0	n/a	n/a
Vermont	0	n/a	n/a
Virginia	0	n/a	n/a
Washington	3	1	9
West Virginia	0	n/a	n/a
Wisconsin	0	n/a	n/a
Wyoming	0	n/a	n/a
50 States	85	36	
DC	n/a	n/a	
United States	85	36	

Rank in order by #	
1	Arizona
1	Oregon
3	California
3	South Dakota
5	Colorado
6	Nevada
7	Alaska
8	Ohio
9	Massachusetts
9	Michigan
9	Missouri
9	Nebraska
9	Washington
14	Idaho
14	Montana
14	North Dakota
17	Florida
17	Maine
17	Maryland
17	Oklahoma

Note: Ties in ranking reflect ties in actual values.

D-20 Campaign Costs Per Vote in Most Recent Gubernatorial Election, 2002, 2003, 2004, or 2005

State	Number of candidates and election year	Winning party and margin of victory %	Partisan shift (yes or no) and type of race (incumbent or open seat)	Total costs $ (in millions)	Cost per vote $	Rank by cost per vote
Alabama	9 in 2002	R-0.3	Y-I*	34.3	25.1	9
Alaska	18 in 2002	R-15	Y-O	5.8	25.6	7
Arizona	17 in 2002	D-1	Y-O	8.3	6.7	35
Arkansas	5 in 2002	R-6	N-I	4.9	6.1	36
California	16 in 2002	D-5	N-1	119.0	15.9	17
Colorado	5 in 2002	R-29	N-1	6.6	4.7	44
Connecticut	2 in 2002	R-12	N-I	8.5	8.4	32
Delaware	5 in 2004	D-5	N-I	2.7	7.5	33
Florida	6 in 2002	R-13	N-1	18.6	3.7	47
Georgia	5 in 2002	R-5	Y-I*	26.3	13.0	24
Hawaii	18 in 2002	R-4	Y-O	10.3	26.9	6
Idaho	8 in 2002	R-14	N-1	2.4	5.9	37
Illinois	7 in 2002	D-8	Y-O	52.9	15.0	20
Indiana	5 in 2004	R-5	Y-I*	33.1	13.5	22
Iowa	6 in 2002	D-8	N-1	14.3	13.9	21
Kansas	7 in 2002	D-8	Y-O	16.6	19.8	14
Kentucky	9 in 2003	R-10	Y-O	12.1	11.2	27
Louisiana	18 in 2003	D-4	Y-O	41.3	29.4	4
Maine	8 in 2002	D-6	Y-O	4.7	9.3	29
Maryland	6 in 2002	R-4	Y-O	5.6	3.3	49
Massachusetts	9 in 2002	R-5	N-O	33.2	15.0	19
Michigan	9 in 2002	D-4	Y-O	17.6	5.6	40
Minnesota	9 in 2002	R-8	Y-O	6.5	2.9	50
Mississippi	11 in 2003	R-7	Y-I*	20.8	23.2	11
Missouri	14 in 2004	R-3	Y-I*	16.1	5.9	37
Montana	8 in 2004	D-4	Y-O	3.9	8.8	31
Nebraska	5 in 2002	R-41	N-I	1.7	3.6	48
Nevada	15 in 2002	R-46	N-I	2.9	5.9	39
New Hampshire	6 in 2004	D-2	Y-I*	5.9	8.9	30
New Jersey	18 in 2005	D-10	N-O	85.0	37.1	1
New Mexico	7 in 2002	D-17	Y-O	10.9	22.5	13
New York	9 in 2002	R-16	N-I	158.7	33.8	2
North Carolina	9 in 2004	D-13	N-I	18.8	5.4	41
North Dakota	3 in 2004	R-44	N-I	1.4	4.7	44
Ohio	5 in 2002	R-20	N-I	15.7	4.9	43
Oklahoma	9 in 2002	D-0.7	Y-O	12.2	11.8	25
Oregon	12 in 2002	D-3	N-O	16.4	13.0	23
Pennsylvania	5 in 2002	D-9	Y-O	70.7	19.8	15
Rhode Island	6 in 2002	R-10	N-O	7.5	22.7	12
South Carolina	8 in 2002	R-6	Y-I*	32.1	29.2	5
South Dakota	9 in 2002	R-15	N-O	10.1	30.1	3
Tennessee	12 in 2002	D-3	Y-O	18.7	11.3	26
Texas	9 in 2002	R-18	N-I	114.6	25.2	8
Utah	5 in 2004	R-16	N-I	6.5	7.1	34
Vermont	6 in 2004	R-21	N-I	1.2	4.0	46
Virginia	4 in 2005	D-6	N-O	47.0	23.7	10
Washington	15 in 2004	D-0.005	N-O	14.8	5.3	42
West Virginia	26 in 2004	D-30	N-O	11.9	16.1	16
Wisconsin	12 in 2002	D-4	Y-I*	18.6	10.5	28
Wyoming	10 in 2002	D-2	Y-O	2.8	15.1	18
50 States (average)	9.3	10.9	n/a	1,156.0	13.5	
DC	n/a	n/a	n/a	n/a	n/a	
United States (average)	9.3	10.9	n/a	1,156.0	13.5	

incumbent did not win

Rank in order by cost per vote	
1	New Jersey
2	New York
3	South Dakota
4	Louisiana
5	South Carolina
6	Hawaii
7	Alaska
8	Texas
9	Alabama
10	Virginia
11	Mississippi
12	Rhode Island
13	New Mexico
14	Kansas
15	Pennsylvania
16	West Virginia
17	California
18	Wyoming
19	Massachusetts
20	Illinois
21	Iowa
22	Indiana
23	Oregon
24	Georgia
25	Oklahoma
26	Tennessee
27	Kentucky
28	Wisconsin
29	Maine
30	New Hampshire
31	Montana
32	Connecticut
33	Delaware
34	Utah
35	Arizona
36	Arkansas
37	Idaho
37	Missouri
39	Nevada
40	Michigan
41	North Carolina
42	Washington
43	Ohio
44	Colorado
44	North Dakota
46	Vermont
47	Florida
48	Nebraska
49	Maryland
50	Minnesota

Note: Ties in ranking reflect ties in actual values.

Source Notes for Government (Section D)

D-1 Members of the United States House, 2007: Each state is allocated two senators and representation in the House of Representatives based on population, as determined by the census, which is taken in every year ending in zero (for example, 2000 and 2010).

The data in the table list the number of representatives as of 2007, based on unadjusted population numbers (see notes to Table A-1) from the 2000 census. Reapportionment of the 435 House seats resulted in gains in some western and southern states and loses in some northeastern and midwestern states. This allocation will prevail until seats are reapportioned based on the results of the 2010 census.

D-2 Members of State Legislatures, 2007: Like the Congress, state legislatures—except Nebraska's one-house legislature—have an upper and lower house, generally called senates and assemblies. These data come from the organization of legislators nationwide, the National Conference of State Legislatures.

D-3 State Legislators Per Million Population, 2007: Some small population states, like New Hampshire, have large legislatures. Some large states, like California, have relatively small ones. This table highlights the differences by relating the number of legislators (see Table D-2) to the most recent population estimates (see Table A-1).

D-4 Units of Government, 2002: There are more than eighty-seven thousand units of government in the United States, including counties, cities, towns, townships, school districts, and special districts that provide water, maintain sewage systems, build and maintain roads, control mosquitoes, and more. There are so many that they are only counted every five years in the U.S. Census Bureau's Census of Governments, the most recent of which was in 2002. The data are available on the Census Bureau Web site (www.census. gov) as *Government Organization* (GC02(1)-1).

D-5 State Legislator Compensation, 2005: These data show the major sources of cash compensation of legislators, annual salaries, and per diem amounts. The data were drawn from the National Conference of State Legislatures Web site (www.ncsl.org).

Comparisons of legislative pay from state to state are nearly impossible. Some states pay their legislators like most employers pay their employees—a regular salary plus reimbursement of employment-related travel expenses while on official business away from the normal place of work. In addition, because most legislators live in their districts, they are paid expenses when staying overnight in the state capitol. Some states compensate legislators at a per diem rate, often adding an expense allowance that can exceed expenses actually incurred. Additionally, some legislatures provide extra pay for committee chairpersons and legislative leaders. Pensions for legislative service are nonexistent or negligible in some states, while pension and other benefits, such as employer-paid health care, are an important part of legislative compensation in other states.

D-6 Percentage of Legislators Who Are Female, 2007: The percentage of legislators who are women passed 20 percent in 1993 from less than 10 percent in the 1970s and less than 5 percent in the 1960s. The percentages for each state were calculated by the National Conference of State Legislatures and are available on its Web site (www.ncsl. org).

D-7 Turnover in Legislatures, 2006: This table, from Tim Storey of the National Conference of State Legislatures, shows the percentage of new state legislators taking office after the 2006 elections.

D-8 Term Limits (in years), 2007: This table, from the same source as Table D-7 shows the maximum number of consecutive years governors and legislators can serve. The states shown with no limits allow elected officials to serve as long as voters approve. The states are ranked, with many ties, somewhat arbitrarily. Those with the longest allowable terms for members of their lower house are ranked highest.

D-9 Legislative Session Length, 2007: Many states have constitutional limits on the length of time the legislature meets in its regular sessions. Those shown in the table are calendar days (for example, a sixty-day limit would be about two months). Many of the states with short sessions exercise the option of having special sessions called by the legislative leadership or governor. These data are available on the Web site of the National Conference of State Legislatures (www.ncsl.org).

It is difficult to compare the varying practices of the states. While most meet annually, some meet biannually, and some meet throughout the year.

D-10 Party Control of State Legislatures, 2007: These data, developed by the National Conference of State Legislatures shortly after the November 2006 election, show the party affiliation of legislators taking office in 2007. The states are ranked by the percentage of Republicans (reading top to bottom) or Democrats (bottom to top) in the combined legislative houses. S represents a split in party control.

D-11 Governors' Institutional Power Rating, 2007: This table presents the results of an update of the on-going study by Dr. Thad Beyle of the University of North Carolina at Chapel Hill, included in *Politics in the American States: A Comparative Analysis* published by CQ Press. The ranking is based on six measures of institutional power—tenure, appointment power, the number of other statewide elected officials, budget power, veto power, and party control. Those interested in more detailed data on this and earlier studies of the governor's powers should visit Dr. Thad Beyle's Web site (www.unc.edu/~beyle).

D-12 Number of Statewide Elected Officials, 2006: The federal pattern of holding nationwide elections for only the chief executive and running mate (president and vice president) is not followed by the states. States often elect the attorneys general, secretaries of state, comptrollers, treasurers, and auditors. The count in the table, using information collected in the Council of State Government's *The Book of the States* (vol. 37, 2006 Edition), excludes judges, who are also elected in many states.

D-13 State and Local Government Employees, 2005: These statistics, from the U.S. Census Bureau's count of public employees available on the bureau's Web site (www.census. gov), express the full-time equivalent of part-time workers plus full-time workers in state and local governments and relate the totals to population.

D-14 Average Salaries of State and Local Government Employees, 2005: These statistics, from the same source as Table D-13, show annual average state and local government salaries, which were obtained by dividing compensation in March 2005 by the number of employees in 2005 and multiplying by twelve.

D-15 Local Employment, 2005: The count of local employees identified is substantially larger than the number of state employees. The table shows the percentage of local employees. See Table D-13 for the source of these data.

D-16 Local Spending Accountability, FY 2004: Since 1970 there has been a massive growth in both federal and state aid to local governments. As a result, local officials finance over one-third of what they spend with money they do not raise by their own local taxes and fees. Critics say this encourages government spending to be excessive because the elected officials who spend the money do not have to account to taxpayers for raising it. The Wisconsin Taxpayers Association has dubbed this difference "the accountability gap." The table shows a measure of this gap, as calculated by State Policy Research using data from the U.S. Census Bureau (see source note to Table F-1 for important details). The numbers reflect the percentage of their spending local officials raised.

D-17 Percentage of Eligible Voters Registered, November 2006: These statistics were compiled from each state's chief election officer by the Committee for the Study of the American Electorate (CSAE), a non-partisan, non-profit research organization based in Washington, D.C. The table shows the best available data on the percentage of persons presumably eligible to vote in each state, based on the voting-age population in relation to the number who have complied with that state's requirements to vote. Presumably the over 100 percent of registered voters in Alaska is a fiction. According to CSAE, "in any given election the official registration figures provided by the states are inaccurate." This is because registration rolls often contain the names of people who have died or have moved. As part of the Motor-Voter law, states are required to maintain those who have moved or died on the registration rolls for at least two federal elections, though the names, if the election administration has knowledge of them, can be moved to an inactive list.

The accuracy of a state's registration count is related to the practices of a state's election administration—specifically, how often and how thorough the state conducts a so-called list cleaning. CSAE estimates represent their "best estimate of what actual registration is likely to be." This is based on final and official registration figures provided by states, and adjustments both for "inactives" and for a 10 percent inflation factor.

Data are not available for North Dakota because the state has no voter registration. Wisconsin has election day registration at the polls. Maine had incomplete registration counts.

D-18 Percentage of Population Voting, November 2006: Not all persons legally old enough to vote actually do so. The table shows the percentage of eligible U.S citizens who voted in the midterm elections of November 2006.

The data come from the Committee for the Study of the American Electorate (CSAE).

D-19 Statewide Initiatives and Popular Referenda, 2006: In most states, voters select candidates to make policy for them as legislators but never vote directly on policy except when changes in the state constitution are being made. Some states allow "direct democracy," including allowing voters to put up a measure for popular vote by collecting a minimum number of signatures (voter initiatives). This tabulation shows the number of such initiatives on state ballots in elections in 2006.

The numbers reflect (1) whether initiatives are permitted in the state; (2) the difficulty of putting measures on the ballot, as affected by the number for signatures required and other factors in the constitutions of each state; and (3) voter interest in making state policy by this direct democracy approach.

These statistics come from a compilation of ballot measure results from the National Conference of State Legislatures (www.ncsl.org).

D-20 Campaign Costs Per Vote in Most Recent Gubernatorial Election, 2002, 2003, 2004, or 2005: This table was created by Dr. Thad Beyle, Department of Political Science, University of North Carolina at Chapel Hill, NC 27599-3265, and Dr. Jennifer M. Jensen, Department of Political Science, Binghamton University at SUNY, Binghamton, NY 13902-

6000. The authors compiled data from the specific agency in each state that regulates elections and campaign finances. The result is a measure of the gubernatorial campaign costs (converted to 2005 dollars) in each state per vote in each state. Variables that have potential effects on these costs are also presented in this table. These variables include (1) the number of candidates seeking office, (2) the election year, (3) the party that won the office, (4) by what margin of victory, (5) whether or not the election resulted in a partisan shift, (6) whether or not an incumbent was seeking reelection, and (7) whether or not the incumbent won. Anyone interested in more detailed data on these elections should visit Dr. Beyle's Web site (www.unc.edu/~beyle).

Federal Impacts

Percentage Change in Federal Outlays, Actual FY 2006–Preliminary FY 2007*	
Major Category	**Percent**
Defense—Military	10.7
Social Security Benefits	6.6
Medicare	22.1
Medicaid	-2.8
Other Programs and Activities	-17.4
Net Interest on the Public Debt	-5.3
Total	0.2

*adjusted
Source: Office of Management and Budget

Components of Federal Spending		
2006	**$ Amount**	**% of Total**
Military and Homeland Security	542	20
Domestic Discretionary	493	18
Social Security	549	20
Medicare	330	12
Medicaid & SCHIP	191	7
Other Mandatory	369	14
Net Interest	219	8
Total	2,693	100
Projected 2011	**$ Amount**	**% of Total**
Military and Homeland Security	510	16
Domestic Discretionary	506	16
Social Security	720	23
Medicare	511	16
Medicaid & SCHIP	264	8
Other Mandatory	389	12
Net Interest	290	9
Total	3,191	100

Source: Office of Management and Budget

Federal Outlays, Preliminary 2007

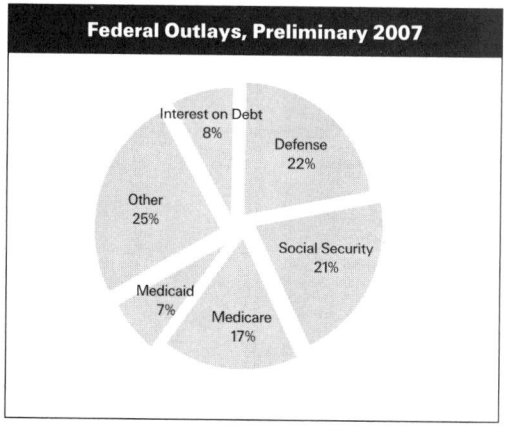

Source: Congressional Budget Office

E-1 Federal Spending, Total and Per Capita, FY 2004

State	Total federal spending $ (in millions)	Per capita federal spending $	Rank per capita
Alabama	39,047	8,619	9
Alaska	8,445	12,885	1
Arizona	41,979	7,309	24
Arkansas	19,489	7,080	28
California	232,387	6,474	34
Colorado	30,060	6,533	33
Connecticut	30,304	8,649	8
Delaware	5,253	6,326	39
Florida	121,934	7,009	29
Georgia	55,153	6,247	41
Hawaii	12,187	9,650	5
Idaho	8,968	6,437	36
Illinois	76,828	6,043	45
Indiana	37,918	6,079	44
Iowa	19,473	6,591	32
Kansas	19,131	6,994	30
Kentucky	31,714	7,649	18
Louisiana	32,954	7,298	25
Maine	10,865	8,248	13
Maryland	64,726	11,645	3
Massachusetts	53,120	8,279	12
Michigan	60,488	5,981	46
Minnesota	28,791	5,644	49
Mississippi	22,338	7,695	17
Missouri	45,730	7,947	15
Montana	7,494	8,085	14
Nebraska	11,795	6,751	31
Nevada	12,769	5,469	50
New Hampshire	7,959	6,125	42
New Jersey	55,264	6,353	38
New Mexico	19,864	10,437	4
New York	143,903	7,484	22
North Carolina	55,233	6,467	35
North Dakota	6,035	9,513	6
Ohio	73,195	6,388	37
Oklahoma	26,644	7,562	21
Oregon	21,871	6,084	43
Pennsylvania	94,900	7,649	19
Rhode Island	8,245	7,630	20
South Carolina	30,051	7,158	27
South Dakota	6,602	8,564	10
Tennessee	45,441	7,701	16
Texas	141,858	6,308	40
Utah	13,684	5,728	47
Vermont	4,633	7,456	23
Virginia	90,638	12,150	2
Washington	44,841	7,228	26
West Virginia	15,183	8,364	11
Wisconsin	31,554	5,728	48
Wyoming	4,393	8,673	7
50 States	2,083,331	7,108	
DC	37,630	67,983	
United States*	2,162,204	7,223	

Due to rounding or data sources, the 50-state total plus D.C. may not equal the U.S. total. Please see introduction.

Rank in order per capita

1 Alaska
2 Virginia
3 Maryland
4 New Mexico
5 Hawaii
6 North Dakota
7 Wyoming
8 Connecticut
9 Alabama
10 South Dakota
11 West Virginia
12 Massachusetts
13 Maine
14 Montana
15 Missouri
16 Tennessee
17 Mississippi
18 Kentucky
19 Pennsylvania
20 Rhode Island
21 Oklahoma
22 New York
23 Vermont
24 Arizona
25 Louisiana
26 Washington
27 South Carolina
28 Arkansas
29 Florida
30 Kansas
31 Nebraska
32 Iowa
33 Colorado
34 California
35 North Carolina
36 Idaho
37 Ohio
38 New Jersey
39 Delaware
40 Texas
41 Georgia
42 New Hampshire
43 Oregon
44 Indiana
45 Illinois
46 Michigan
47 Utah
48 Wisconsin
49 Minnesota
50 Nevada

Note: Numbers that appear to be identical are rounded and vary slightly in actual value. The rankings reflect the actual values before rounding. See the introduction for more details.

Increase in Total Federal Spending, FY 1999–2004

State	Total federal spending FY 1999 $ (in millions)	Percentage increase in federal spending	Rank by percentage increase
Alabama	26,904	45.1	15
Alaska	5,291	59.6	1
Arizona	27,075	55.0	4
Arkansas	13,706	42.2	19
California	168,676	37.8	30
Colorado	21,940	37.0	33
Connecticut	19,644	54.3	5
Delaware	3,816	37.7	31
Florida	87,716	39.0	26
Georgia	39,415	39.9	23
Hawaii	8,660	40.7	21
Idaho	6,207	44.5	16
Illinois	56,646	35.6	38
Indiana	27,013	40.4	22
Iowa	15,708	24.0	49
Kansas	14,520	31.8	47
Kentucky	22,374	41.7	20
Louisiana	24,558	34.2	41
Maine	7,456	45.7	14
Maryland	42,339	52.9	6
Massachusetts	38,820	36.8	34
Michigan	44,128	37.1	32
Minnesota	21,897	31.5	48
Mississippi	16,564	34.9	40
Missouri	33,474	36.6	35
Montana	6,251	19.9	50
Nebraska	8,844	33.4	44
Nevada	8,013	59.4	2
New Hampshire	5,389	47.7	8
New Jersey	41,204	34.1	42
New Mexico	13,616	45.9	13
New York	103,393	39.2	25
North Carolina	37,482	47.4	9
North Dakota	4,578	31.8	46
Ohio	53,772	36.1	37
Oklahoma	19,298	38.1	29
Oregon	15,759	38.8	27
Pennsylvania	69,996	35.6	39
Rhode Island	6,250	31.9	45
South Carolina	20,952	43.4	18
South Dakota	4,943	33.6	43
Tennessee	30,982	46.7	11
Texas	98,488	44.0	17
Utah	9,294	47.2	10
Vermont	3,168	46.2	12
Virginia	58,168	55.8	3
Washington	32,156	39.4	24
West Virginia	11,135	36.4	36
Wisconsin	22,757	38.7	28
Wyoming	2,931	49.9	7
50 States	1,483,366	40.4	
DC	26,232	43.5	
United States*	1,555,651	39.0	

Rank in order by percentage increase	
1	Alaska
2	Nevada
3	Virginia
4	Arizona
5	Connecticut
6	Maryland
7	Wyoming
8	New Hampshire
9	North Carolina
10	Utah
11	Tennessee
12	Vermont
13	New Mexico
14	Maine
15	Alabama
16	Idaho
17	Texas
18	South Carolina
19	Arkansas
20	Kentucky
21	Hawaii
22	Indiana
23	Georgia
24	Washington
25	New York
26	Florida
27	Oregon
28	Wisconsin
29	Oklahoma
30	California
31	Delaware
32	Michigan
33	Colorado
34	Massachusetts
35	Missouri
36	West Virginia
37	Ohio
38	Illinois
39	Pennsylvania
40	Mississippi
41	Louisiana
42	New Jersey
43	South Dakota
44	Nebraska
45	Rhode Island
46	North Dakota
47	Kansas
48	Minnesota
49	Iowa
50	Montana

Note: Numbers that appear to be identical are rounded and vary slightly in actual value. The rankings reflect the actual values before rounding. See the introduction for more details.

Due to rounding or data sources, the 50-state total plus D.C. may not equal the U.S. total. Please see introduction.

E-3 Federal Spending on Grants, Total and Per Capita, FY 2004

State	Federal grants to state and local governments $ (in millions)	Per capita federal grants to state and local government $	Rank per capita
Alabama	7,008	1,547	22
Alaska	3,217	4,908	1
Arizona	8,364	1,456	30
Arkansas	4,683	1,701	16
California	54,534	1,519	23
Colorado	5,643	1,226	46
Connecticut	5,556	1,586	21
Delaware	1,241	1,495	26
Florida	19,610	1,127	48
Georgia	11,759	1,332	39
Hawaii	2,158	1,709	15
Idaho	1,995	1,432	35
Illinois	16,531	1,300	42
Indiana	7,436	1,192	47
Iowa	4,039	1,367	37
Kansas	3,469	1,268	43
Kentucky	6,743	1,626	18
Louisiana	7,787	1,724	14
Maine	2,758	2,094	11
Maryland	8,837	1,590	20
Massachusetts	13,876	2,163	7
Michigan	13,227	1,308	40
Minnesota	7,209	1,413	36
Mississippi	5,379	1,853	13
Missouri	8,734	1,518	24
Montana	1,997	2,155	9
Nebraska	2,531	1,449	31
Nevada	2,322	995	50
New Hampshire	1,879	1,446	32
New Jersey	11,333	1,303	41
New Mexico	4,663	2,450	4
New York	50,009	2,601	3
North Carolina	12,574	1,472	27
North Dakota	1,515	2,388	5
Ohio	16,514	1,441	34
Oklahoma	5,271	1,496	25
Oregon	5,185	1,442	33
Pennsylvania	19,916	1,605	19
Rhode Island	2,329	2,155	8
South Carolina	6,145	1,464	29
South Dakota	1,620	2,101	10
Tennessee	9,863	1,671	17
Texas	27,792	1,236	44
Utah	2,948	1,234	45
Vermont	1,423	2,290	6
Virginia	7,991	1,071	49
Washington	9,083	1,464	28
West Virginia	3,701	2,039	12
Wisconsin	7,484	1,358	38
Wyoming	1,636	3,230	2
50 States	449,517	1,534	
DC	4,205	7,597	
United States*	460,152	1,410	

Rank in order per capita	
1	Alaska
2	Wyoming
3	New York
4	New Mexico
5	North Dakota
6	Vermont
7	Massachusetts
8	Rhode Island
9	Montana
10	South Dakota
11	Maine
12	West Virginia
13	Mississippi
14	Louisiana
15	Hawaii
16	Arkansas
17	Tennessee
18	Kentucky
19	Pennsylvania
20	Maryland
21	Connecticut
22	Alabama
23	California
24	Missouri
25	Oklahoma
26	Delaware
27	North Carolina
28	Washington
29	South Carolina
30	Arizona
31	Nebraska
32	New Hampshire
33	Oregon
34	Ohio
35	Idaho
36	Minnesota
37	Iowa
38	Wisconsin
39	Georgia
40	Michigan
41	New Jersey
42	Illinois
43	Kansas
44	Texas
45	Utah
46	Colorado
47	Indiana
48	Florida
49	Virginia
50	Nevada

Note: Numbers that appear to be identical are rounded and vary slightly in actual value. The rankings reflect the actual values before rounding. See the introduction for more details.

Due to rounding or data sources, the 50-state total plus D.C. may not equal the U.S. total. Please see introduction.

E-4   Federal Spending on Procurement, FY 2004

State	Total spending on procurement $ (in millions)	Per capita procurement spending $	Rank per capita
Alabama	7,600	1,678	7
Alaska	1,700	2,594	5
Arizona	9,797	1,706	6
Arkansas	848	308	50
California	40,254	1,121	15
Colorado	5,747	1,249	13
Connecticut	9,509	2,714	4
Delaware	265	319	49
Florida	11,447	658	33
Georgia	5,813	658	32
Hawaii	2,066	1,636	8
Idaho	1,373	985	19
Illinois	6,583	518	40
Indiana	4,002	642	34
Iowa	1,599	541	39
Kansas	2,242	820	22
Kentucky	4,637	1,118	17
Louisiana	3,418	757	28
Maine	1,711	1,299	12
Maryland	20,804	3,743	2
Massachusetts	9,127	1,422	9
Michigan	4,119	407	46
Minnesota	2,329	457	45
Mississippi	2,372	817	23
Missouri	7,991	1,389	10
Montana	587	633	35
Nebraska	697	399	47
Nevada	1,600	685	31
New Hampshire	985	758	27
New Jersey	6,132	705	30
New Mexico	5,973	3,138	3
New York	8,889	462	43
North Carolina	3,933	460	44
North Dakota	503	793	26
Ohio	6,936	605	36
Oklahoma	2,804	796	24
Oregon	1,283	357	48
Pennsylvania	9,311	751	29
Rhode Island	559	517	41
South Carolina	4,193	999	18
South Dakota	438	568	38
Tennessee	8,118	1,376	11
Texas	26,969	1,199	14
Utah	2,304	964	20
Vermont	541	871	21
Virginia	35,325	4,735	1
Washington	6,946	1,120	16
West Virginia	1,041	573	37
Wisconsin	2,641	479	42
Wyoming	403	796	25
50 States	306,464	1,046	
DC	13,347	24,113	
United States*	339,681	882	

Due to rounding or data sources, the 50-state total plus D.C. may not equal the U.S. total. Please see introduction.

Rank in order per capita	
1	Virginia
2	Maryland
3	New Mexico
4	Connecticut
5	Alaska
6	Arizona
7	Alabama
8	Hawaii
9	Massachusetts
10	Missouri
11	Tennessee
12	Maine
13	Colorado
14	Texas
15	California
16	Washington
17	Kentucky
18	South Carolina
19	Idaho
20	Utah
21	Vermont
22	Kansas
23	Mississippi
24	Oklahoma
25	Wyoming
26	North Dakota
27	New Hampshire
28	Louisiana
29	Pennsylvania
30	New Jersey
31	Nevada
32	Georgia
33	Florida
34	Indiana
35	Montana
36	Ohio
37	West Virginia
38	South Dakota
39	Iowa
40	Illinois
41	Rhode Island
42	Wisconsin
43	New York
44	North Carolina
45	Minnesota
46	Michigan
47	Nebraska
48	Oregon
49	Delaware
50	Arkansas

Note: Numbers that appear to be identical are rounded and vary slightly in actual value. The rankings reflect the actual values before rounding. See the introduction for more details.

E-5   Federal Spending on Payments to Individuals, FY 2004

State	Total federal payments to individuals $ (in millions)	Per capita federal payments to individuals $	Rank per capita
Alabama	20,947	4,624	6
Alaska	1,800	2,746	49
Arizona	20,211	3,519	40
Arkansas	12,449	4,523	7
California	115,570	3,220	45
Colorado	14,213	3,089	48
Connecticut	13,637	3,892	27
Delaware	3,253	3,918	25
Florida	80,482	4,626	5
Georgia	29,257	3,314	44
Hawaii	4,809	3,808	31
Idaho	4,702	3,375	42
Illinois	46,708	3,674	35
Indiana	24,023	3,851	29
Iowa	12,586	4,260	13
Kansas	11,213	4,099	21
Kentucky	17,102	4,125	20
Louisiana	18,931	4,192	14
Maine	5,439	4,129	19
Maryland	24,562	4,419	8
Massachusetts	26,560	4,139	18
Michigan	39,532	3,909	26
Minnesota	16,950	3,323	43
Mississippi	12,493	4,304	11
Missouri	24,963	4,338	10
Montana	4,023	4,340	9
Nebraska	7,269	4,160	16
Nevada	7,501	3,213	47
New Hampshire	4,440	3,417	41
New Jersey	33,471	3,848	30
New Mexico	7,157	3,760	32
New York	75,935	3,949	23
North Carolina	31,529	3,691	34
North Dakota	3,230	5,092	1
Ohio	44,169	3,855	28
Oklahoma	15,107	4,287	12
Oregon	13,500	3,756	33
Pennsylvania	59,064	4,761	4
Rhode Island	4,529	4,191	15
South Carolina	16,558	3,944	24
South Dakota	3,779	4,902	3
Tennessee	23,984	4,064	22
Texas	72,407	3,220	46
Utah	6,281	2,629	50
Vermont	2,264	3,643	37
Virginia	30,979	4,153	17
Washington	22,754	3,668	36
West Virginia	9,084	5,004	2
Wisconsin	19,534	3,546	39
Wyoming	1,833	3,619	38
50 States	1,122,773	3,831	
DC	4,552	8,224	
United States*	1,136,769	3,871	

	Rank in order per capita
1	North Dakota
2	West Virginia
3	South Dakota
4	Pennsylvania
5	Florida
6	Alabama
7	Arkansas
8	Maryland
9	Montana
10	Missouri
11	Mississippi
12	Oklahoma
13	Iowa
14	Louisiana
15	Rhode Island
16	Nebraska
17	Virginia
18	Massachusetts
19	Maine
20	Kentucky
21	Kansas
22	Tennessee
23	New York
24	South Carolina
25	Delaware
26	Michigan
27	Connecticut
28	Ohio
29	Indiana
30	New Jersey
31	Hawaii
32	New Mexico
33	Oregon
34	North Carolina
35	Illinois
36	Washington
37	Vermont
38	Wyoming
39	Wisconsin
40	Arizona
41	New Hampshire
42	Idaho
43	Minnesota
44	Georgia
45	California
46	Texas
47	Nevada
48	Colorado
49	Alaska
50	Utah

Note: Numbers that appear to be identical are rounded and vary slightly in actual value. The rankings reflect the actual values before rounding. See the introduction for more details.

*Due to rounding or data sources, the 50-state total plus D.C. may not equal the U.S. total. Please see introduction.

E-6 Federal Spending on Social Security and Medicare, FY 2004

State	Total Social Security and Medicare spending $ (in millions)	Per capita spending $	Rank per capita
Alabama	14,836	3,275	4
Alaska	895	1,366	50
Arizona	14,313	2,492	36
Arkansas	8,615	3,130	10
California	86,266	2,403	41
Colorado	9,091	1,976	48
Connecticut	11,278	3,219	6
Delaware	2,411	2,903	21
Florida	61,831	3,554	3
Georgia	19,742	2,236	45
Hawaii	3,073	2,433	38
Idaho	3,149	2,260	44
Illinois	35,196	2,768	24
Indiana	17,841	2,860	22
Iowa	8,763	2,966	19
Kansas	7,682	2,808	23
Kentucky	12,709	3,065	14
Louisiana	13,918	3,082	11
Maine	3,925	2,980	18
Maryland	14,100	2,537	35
Massachusetts	20,962	3,267	5
Michigan	31,705	3,135	9
Minnesota	12,314	2,414	39
Mississippi	8,828	3,041	15
Missouri	17,706	3,077	13
Montana	2,490	2,687	29
Nebraska	4,496	2,573	34
Nevada	5,176	2,217	46
New Hampshire	3,350	2,578	33
New Jersey	26,779	3,078	12
New Mexico	4,436	2,331	43
New York	60,875	3,166	8
North Carolina	22,449	2,628	32
North Dakota	1,755	2,767	25
Ohio	34,538	3,014	16
Oklahoma	10,294	2,922	20
Oregon	9,508	2,645	31
Pennsylvania	46,028	3,710	2
Rhode Island	3,455	3,197	7
South Carolina	11,510	2,742	27
South Dakota	2,050	2,660	30
Tennessee	17,615	2,985	17
Texas	48,716	2,166	47
Utah	3,946	1,652	49
Vermont	1,679	2,702	28
Virginia	17,540	2,351	42
Washington	14,951	2,410	40
West Virginia	6,949	3,828	1
Wisconsin	15,160	2,752	26
Wyoming	1,236	2,441	37
50 States	818,131	2,791	
DC	1,637	2,957	
United States*	826,683	2,815	

Rank in order per capita	
1	West Virginia
2	Pennsylvania
3	Florida
4	Alabama
5	Massachusetts
6	Connecticut
7	Rhode Island
8	New York
9	Michigan
10	Arkansas
11	Louisiana
12	New Jersey
13	Missouri
14	Kentucky
15	Mississippi
16	Ohio
17	Tennessee
18	Maine
19	Iowa
20	Oklahoma
21	Delaware
22	Indiana
23	Kansas
24	Illinois
25	North Dakota
26	Wisconsin
27	South Carolina
28	Vermont
29	Montana
30	South Dakota
31	Oregon
32	North Carolina
33	New Hampshire
34	Nebraska
35	Maryland
36	Arizona
37	Wyoming
38	Hawaii
39	Minnesota
40	Washington
41	California
42	Virginia
43	New Mexico
44	Idaho
45	Georgia
46	Nevada
47	Texas
48	Colorado
49	Utah
50	Alaska

Due to rounding or data sources, the 50-state total plus D.C. may not equal the U.S. total. Please see introduction.

E-7   Social Security Benefits Paid, FY 2005

State	Social Security amounts paid $ (in thousands)	Number of recipients	Average monthly benefit $	Rank by average benefit
Alabama	777,620	903,569	861	42
Alaska	56,045	64,843	864	41
Arizona	867,777	922,932	940	16
Arkansas	477,545	566,219	843	48
California	4,115,426	4,463,873	922	26
Colorado	532,857	584,556	912	27
Connecticut	595,943	585,199	1,018	2
Delaware	146,486	150,101	976	4
Florida	3,178,953	3,430,205	927	21
Georgia	1,092,338	1,233,238	886	36
Hawaii	185,730	200,743	925	23
Idaho	203,446	226,250	899	32
Illinois	1,815,500	1,893,055	959	8
Indiana	1,021,925	1,063,854	961	7
Iowa	510,152	552,294	924	24
Kansas	426,598	452,119	944	13
Kentucky	676,681	797,660	848	46
Louisiana	597,785	715,127	836	49
Maine	229,781	270,706	849	45
Maryland	726,689	771,357	942	14
Massachusetts	993,875	1,066,962	931	18
Michigan	1,717,188	1,748,668	982	3
Minnesota	733,954	787,377	932	17
Mississippi	450,024	549,376	819	50
Missouri	958,344	1,063,174	901	31
Montana	149,740	169,375	884	37
Nebraska	265,456	291,980	909	29
Nevada	327,918	346,345	947	12
New Hampshire	209,767	220,796	950	11
New Jersey	1,411,465	1,375,796	1,026	1
New Mexico	263,797	311,468	847	47
New York	2,972,348	3,062,046	971	5
North Carolina	1,357,374	1,509,687	899	33
North Dakota	98,652	114,712	860	43
Ohio	1,815,206	1,960,946	926	22
Oklahoma	560,149	635,619	881	39
Oregon	582,636	618,624	942	15
Pennsylvania	2,299,401	2,419,005	951	10
Rhode Island	179,181	192,829	929	19
South Carolina	697,058	778,480	895	34
South Dakota	120,046	140,773	853	44
Tennessee	960,947	1,089,649	882	38
Texas	2,599,736	2,952,230	881	40
Utah	251,829	273,045	922	25
Vermont	102,177	112,251	910	28
Virginia	1,033,994	1,139,748	907	30
Washington	901,609	937,531	962	6
West Virginia	367,079	414,053	887	35
Wisconsin	908,664	953,581	953	9
Wyoming	75,529	81,495	927	20
50 States	43,600,420	47,165,521	924	
DC	57,223	71,376	802	
United States*	44,351,668	48,434,281	916	

Due to rounding or data sources, the 50-state total plus D.C. may not equal the U.S. total. Please see introduction.

Rank in order by average benefit

1   New Jersey
2   Connecticut
3   Michigan
4   Delaware
5   New York
6   Washington
7   Indiana
8   Illinois
9   Wisconsin
10 Pennsylvania
11 New Hampshire
12 Nevada
13 Kansas
14 Maryland
15 Oregon
16 Arizona
17 Minnesota
18 Massachusetts
19 Rhode Island
20 Wyoming
21 Florida
22 Ohio
23 Hawaii
24 Iowa
25 Utah
26 California
27 Colorado
28 Vermont
29 Nebraska
30 Virginia
31 Missouri
32 Idaho
33 North Carolina
34 South Carolina
35 West Virginia
36 Georgia
37 Montana
38 Tennessee
39 Oklahoma
40 Texas
41 Alaska
42 Alabama
43 North Dakota
44 South Dakota
45 Maine
46 Kentucky
47 New Mexico
48 Arkansas
49 Louisiana
50 Mississippi

Note: Numbers that appear to be identical are rounded and vary slightly in actual value. The rankings reflect the actual values before rounding. See the introduction for more details.

E-8 Federal Spending on Employee Wages and Salaries, FY 2004

State	Total federal spending on wages and salaries $ (in millions)	Per capita spending on wages and salaries $	Rank per capita
Alabama	3,492	771	18
Alaska	1,728	2,636	1
Arizona	3,608	628	29
Arkansas	1,509	548	38
California	22,029	614	31
Colorado	4,457	969	11
Connecticut	1,602	457	45
Delaware	494	595	33
Florida	10,395	598	32
Georgia	8,324	943	13
Hawaii	3,154	2,498	2
Idaho	898	645	28
Illinois	7,007	551	37
Indiana	2,457	394	48
Iowa	1,249	423	47
Kansas	2,208	807	16
Kentucky	3,231	779	17
Louisiana	2,818	624	30
Maine	957	727	23
Maryland	10,523	1,893	4
Massachusetts	3,557	554	36
Michigan	3,610	357	49
Minnesota	2,302	451	46
Mississippi	2,094	721	24
Missouri	4,042	702	25
Montana	886	956	12
Nebraska	1,298	743	22
Nevada	1,347	577	35
New Hampshire	654	503	41
New Jersey	4,328	498	42
New Mexico	2,072	1,089	6
New York	9,070	472	44
North Carolina	7,197	843	15
North Dakota	787	1,241	5
Ohio	5,576	487	43
Oklahoma	3,463	983	9
Oregon	1,903	529	40
Pennsylvania	6,609	533	39
Rhode Island	829	767	19
South Carolina	3,156	752	20
South Dakota	765	992	8
Tennessee	3,476	589	34
Texas	14,690	653	26
Utah	2,150	900	14
Vermont	405	652	27
Virginia	16,342	2,191	3
Washington	6,058	977	10
West Virginia	1,358	748	21
Wisconsin	1,895	344	50
Wyoming	521	1,029	7
50 States	204,580	698	
DC	15,526	28,049	
United States*	225,601	675	

*Due to rounding or data sources, the 50-state total plus D.C. may not equal the U.S. total. Please see introduction.

Rank in order per capita

1	Alaska
2	Hawaii
3	Virginia
4	Maryland
5	North Dakota
6	New Mexico
7	Wyoming
8	South Dakota
9	Oklahoma
10	Washington
11	Colorado
12	Montana
13	Georgia
14	Utah
15	North Carolina
16	Kansas
17	Kentucky
18	Alabama
19	Rhode Island
20	South Carolina
21	West Virginia
22	Nebraska
23	Maine
24	Mississippi
25	Missouri
26	Texas
27	Vermont
28	Idaho
29	Arizona
30	Louisiana
31	California
32	Florida
33	Delaware
34	Tennessee
35	Nevada
36	Massachusetts
37	Illinois
38	Arkansas
39	Pennsylvania
40	Oregon
41	New Hampshire
42	New Jersey
43	Ohio
44	New York
45	Connecticut
46	Minnesota
47	Iowa
48	Indiana
49	Michigan
50	Wisconsin

Note: Numbers that appear to be identical are rounded and vary slightly in actual value. The rankings reflect the actual values before rounding. See the introduction for more details.

E-9   Federal Spending on Defense, FY 2004

<table>
<tr><th>State</th><th>Total spending on defense $ (in millions)</th><th>Per capita defense spending</th><th>Rank per capita</th></tr>
<tr><td>Alabama</td><td>8,725</td><td>1,926</td><td>7</td></tr>
<tr><td>Alaska</td><td>2,522</td><td>3,847</td><td>2</td></tr>
<tr><td>Arizona</td><td>11,135</td><td>1,939</td><td>6</td></tr>
<tr><td>Arkansas</td><td>1,596</td><td>580</td><td>41</td></tr>
<tr><td>California</td><td>42,723</td><td>1,190</td><td>20</td></tr>
<tr><td>Colorado</td><td>6,182</td><td>1,343</td><td>12</td></tr>
<tr><td>Connecticut</td><td>9,735</td><td>2,778</td><td>4</td></tr>
<tr><td>Delaware</td><td>629</td><td>758</td><td>32</td></tr>
<tr><td>Florida</td><td>17,419</td><td>1,001</td><td>26</td></tr>
<tr><td>Georgia</td><td>10,175</td><td>1,152</td><td>22</td></tr>
<tr><td>Hawaii</td><td>4,772</td><td>3,779</td><td>3</td></tr>
<tr><td>Idaho</td><td>744</td><td>534</td><td>42</td></tr>
<tr><td>Illinois</td><td>5,918</td><td>466</td><td>43</td></tr>
<tr><td>Indiana</td><td>4,465</td><td>716</td><td>35</td></tr>
<tr><td>Iowa</td><td>1,262</td><td>427</td><td>45</td></tr>
<tr><td>Kansas</td><td>2,948</td><td>1,078</td><td>23</td></tr>
<tr><td>Kentucky</td><td>5,132</td><td>1,238</td><td>18</td></tr>
<tr><td>Louisiana</td><td>4,433</td><td>982</td><td>27</td></tr>
<tr><td>Maine</td><td>2,297</td><td>1,744</td><td>8</td></tr>
<tr><td>Maryland</td><td>13,796</td><td>2,482</td><td>5</td></tr>
<tr><td>Massachusetts</td><td>8,240</td><td>1,284</td><td>16</td></tr>
<tr><td>Michigan</td><td>3,783</td><td>374</td><td>49</td></tr>
<tr><td>Minnesota</td><td>2,112</td><td>414</td><td>46</td></tr>
<tr><td>Mississippi</td><td>3,624</td><td>1,249</td><td>17</td></tr>
<tr><td>Missouri</td><td>8,585</td><td>1,492</td><td>9</td></tr>
<tr><td>Montana</td><td>658</td><td>710</td><td>36</td></tr>
<tr><td>Nebraska</td><td>1,321</td><td>756</td><td>33</td></tr>
<tr><td>Nevada</td><td>1,612</td><td>690</td><td>37</td></tr>
<tr><td>New Hampshire</td><td>1,125</td><td>866</td><td>29</td></tr>
<tr><td>New Jersey</td><td>5,843</td><td>672</td><td>38</td></tr>
<tr><td>New Mexico</td><td>2,471</td><td>1,298</td><td>15</td></tr>
<tr><td>New York</td><td>7,555</td><td>393</td><td>48</td></tr>
<tr><td>North Carolina</td><td>8,679</td><td>1,016</td><td>24</td></tr>
<tr><td>North Dakota</td><td>833</td><td>1,312</td><td>14</td></tr>
<tr><td>Ohio</td><td>7,539</td><td>658</td><td>39</td></tr>
<tr><td>Oklahoma</td><td>4,279</td><td>1,214</td><td>19</td></tr>
<tr><td>Oregon</td><td>1,311</td><td>365</td><td>50</td></tr>
<tr><td>Pennsylvania</td><td>9,037</td><td>728</td><td>34</td></tr>
<tr><td>Rhode Island</td><td>1,022</td><td>946</td><td>28</td></tr>
<tr><td>South Carolina</td><td>4,881</td><td>1,163</td><td>21</td></tr>
<tr><td>South Dakota</td><td>658</td><td>853</td><td>30</td></tr>
<tr><td>Tennessee</td><td>3,770</td><td>639</td><td>40</td></tr>
<tr><td>Texas</td><td>31,895</td><td>1,418</td><td>10</td></tr>
<tr><td>Utah</td><td>3,305</td><td>1,384</td><td>11</td></tr>
<tr><td>Vermont</td><td>623</td><td>1,003</td><td>25</td></tr>
<tr><td>Virginia</td><td>38,533</td><td>5,165</td><td>1</td></tr>
<tr><td>Washington</td><td>8,321</td><td>1,341</td><td>13</td></tr>
<tr><td>West Virginia</td><td>734</td><td>404</td><td>47</td></tr>
<tr><td>Wisconsin</td><td>2,414</td><td>438</td><td>44</td></tr>
<tr><td>Wyoming</td><td>412</td><td>814</td><td>31</td></tr>
<tr><td>50 States</td><td>331,783</td><td>n/a</td><td></td></tr>
<tr><td>DC</td><td>5,264</td><td>9,509</td><td></td></tr>
<tr><td>United States*</td><td>347,689</td><td>1,148</td><td></td></tr>
</table>

Due to rounding or data sources, the 50-state total plus D.C. may not equal the U.S. total. Please see introduction.

Rank in order per capita

1   Virginia
2   Alaska
3   Hawaii
4   Connecticut
5   Maryland
6   Arizona
7   Alabama
8   Maine
9   Missouri
10 Texas
11 Utah
12 Colorado
13 Washington
14 North Dakota
15 New Mexico
16 Massachusetts
17 Mississippi
18 Kentucky
19 Oklahoma
20 California
21 South Carolina
22 Georgia
23 Kansas
24 North Carolina
25 Vermont
26 Florida
27 Louisiana
28 Rhode Island
29 New Hampshire
30 South Dakota
31 Wyoming
32 Delaware
33 Nebraska
34 Pennsylvania
35 Indiana
36 Montana
37 Nevada
38 New Jersey
39 Ohio
40 Tennessee
41 Arkansas
42 Idaho
43 Illinois
44 Wisconsin
45 Iowa
46 Minnesota
47 West Virginia
48 New York
49 Michigan
50 Oregon

Homeland Security Grants, Total and Per Capita, FY 2006

State	Homeland security grants $ (in thousands)	Per capita	Rank per capita
Alabama	14,649	3.21	45
Alaska	7,829	11.80	6
Arizona	19,242	3.24	44
Arkansas	8,111	2.92	46
California	227,769	6.30	19
Colorado	20,383	4.37	32
Connecticut	13,289	3.79	38
Delaware	10,296	12.21	4
Florida	98,496	5.54	24
Georgia	43,942	4.84	29
Hawaii	12,703	9.96	8
Idaho	11,759	8.23	12
Illinois	90,173	7.06	16
Indiana	20,664	3.29	42
Iowa	13,248	4.47	31
Kansas	13,809	5.03	26
Kentucky	23,654	5.67	23
Louisiana	29,507	6.52	17
Maine	7,785	5.89	21
Maryland	24,059	4.30	34
Massachusetts	40,549	6.34	18
Michigan	46,202	4.57	30
Minnesota	12,931	2.52	48
Mississippi	8,296	2.84	47
Missouri	42,396	7.31	14
Montana	7,930	8.48	10
Nebraska	21,281	12.10	5
Nevada	20,277	8.40	11
New Hampshire	7,654	5.84	22
New Jersey	51,518	5.91	20
New Mexico	8,038	4.17	35
New York	182,512	9.48	9
North Carolina	29,787	3.43	40
North Dakota	10,788	16.94	2
Ohio	39,953	3.49	39
Oklahoma	19,032	5.36	25
Oregon	17,724	4.87	28
Pennsylvania	48,870	3.93	36
Rhode Island	7,605	7.07	15
South Carolina	14,447	3.40	41
South Dakota	7,734	9.97	7
Tennessee	12,833	2.15	49
Texas	86,860	3.80	37
Utah	8,039	3.26	43
Vermont	10,908	17.51	1
Virginia	15,494	2.05	50
Washington	31,525	5.01	27
West Virginia	13,294	7.32	13
Wisconsin	23,966	4.33	33
Wyoming	7,674	15.07	3
50 States	1,567,484	5.30	
DC	54,015	98.12	
United States	1,621,499	5.47	

Rank in order per capita	
1	Vermont
2	North Dakota
3	Wyoming
4	Delaware
5	Nebraska
6	Alaska
7	South Dakota
8	Hawaii
9	New York
10	Montana
11	Nevada
12	Idaho
13	West Virginia
14	Missouri
15	Rhode Island
16	Illinois
17	Louisiana
18	Massachusetts
19	California
20	New Jersey
21	Maine
22	New Hampshire
23	Kentucky
24	Florida
25	Oklahoma
26	Kansas
27	Washington
28	Oregon
29	Georgia
30	Michigan
31	Iowa
32	Colorado
33	Wisconsin
34	Maryland
35	New Mexico
36	Pennsylvania
37	Texas
38	Connecticut
39	Ohio
40	North Carolina
41	South Carolina
42	Indiana
43	Utah
44	Arizona
45	Alabama
46	Arkansas
47	Mississippi
48	Minnesota
49	Tennessee
50	Virginia

Note: Numbers that appear to be identical are rounded and vary slightly in actual value. The rankings reflect the actual values before rounding. See the introduction for more details.

E-11 Federal Grant Spending Per Dollar of State Tax Revenue, FY 2004

State	Federal aid per dollar of state tax revenue $	Rank
Alabama	0.97	10
Alaska	1.80	1
Arizona	0.79	20
Arkansas	0.77	24
California	0.63	36
Colorado	0.74	26
Connecticut	0.44	49
Delaware	0.46	48
Florida	0.63	37
Georgia	0.68	34
Hawaii	0.48	46
Idaho	0.71	30
Illinois	0.68	33
Indiana	0.61	38
Iowa	0.83	18
Kansas	0.59	40
Kentucky	0.74	27
Louisiana	0.98	9
Maine	0.93	12
Maryland	0.59	41
Massachusetts	0.60	39
Michigan	0.67	35
Minnesota	0.49	45
Mississippi	1.10	5
Missouri	0.88	17
Montana	1.16	4
Nebraska	0.70	32
Nevada	0.41	50
New Hampshire	0.78	21
New Jersey	0.47	47
New Mexico	0.95	11
New York	1.00	8
North Carolina	0.71	31
North Dakota	1.07	6
Ohio	0.73	28
Oklahoma	0.75	25
Oregon	0.81	19
Pennsylvania	0.71	29
Rhode Island	0.88	16
South Carolina	0.91	14
South Dakota	1.28	3
Tennessee	1.00	7
Texas	0.90	15
Utah	0.77	23
Vermont	0.77	22
Virginia	0.50	44
Washington	0.56	43
West Virginia	0.92	13
Wisconsin	0.57	42
Wyoming	1.32	2
50 States	0.72	
DC	n/a	
United States	0.72	

Rank in order by $	
1	Alaska
2	Wyoming
3	South Dakota
4	Montana
5	Mississippi
6	North Dakota
7	Tennessee
8	New York
9	Louisiana
10	Alabama
11	New Mexico
12	Maine
13	West Virginia
14	South Carolina
15	Texas
16	Rhode Island
17	Missouri
18	Iowa
19	Oregon
20	Arizona
21	New Hampshire
22	Vermont
23	Utah
24	Arkansas
25	Oklahoma
26	Colorado
27	Kentucky
28	Ohio
29	Pennsylvania
30	Idaho
31	North Carolina
32	Nebraska
33	Illinois
34	Georgia
35	Michigan
36	California
37	Florida
38	Indiana
39	Massachusetts
40	Kansas
41	Maryland
42	Wisconsin
43	Washington
44	Virginia
45	Minnesota
46	Hawaii
47	New Jersey
48	Delaware
49	Connecticut
50	Nevada

Note: Numbers that appear to be identical are rounded and vary slightly in actual value. The rankings reflect the actual values before rounding. See the introduction for more details.

E-12 State and Local General Revenue from Federal Government, FY 2004

State	Total general revenue from federal government $ (in millions)	Percentage of revenue from federal government	Rank by percentage
Alabama	6,819	26.7	16
Alaska	2,421	28.4	11
Arizona	7,587	25.1	19
Arkansas	4,277	29.0	9
California	54,343	21.6	33
Colorado	5,203	18.5	45
Connecticut	4,503	17.4	47
Delaware	1,092	17.5	46
Florida	19,182	18.7	44
Georgia	9,903	20.9	36
Hawaii	1,834	22.3	31
Idaho	1,875	24.2	23
Illinois	15,652	20.5	38
Indiana	7,337	20.6	37
Iowa	4,304	23.4	24
Kansas	3,137	19.3	43
Kentucky	6,242	27.2	15
Louisiana	7,622	27.3	14
Maine	2,677	28.1	12
Maryland	7,262	19.7	41
Massachusetts	10,065	21.3	34
Michigan	15,110	23.1	26
Minnesota	7,161	20.3	40
Mississippi	5,643	33.4	2
Missouri	8,018	25.1	21
Montana	1,880	32.4	3
Nebraska	2,536	21.7	32
Nevada	1,920	14.5	50
New Hampshire	1,572	21.1	35
New Jersey	9,932	16.1	48
New Mexico	3,803	30.5	5
New York	45,695	25.5	17
North Carolina	11,910	24.4	22
North Dakota	1,314	30.2	6
Ohio	16,313	22.6	29
Oklahoma	4,819	25.1	20
Oregon	4,938	22.7	28
Pennsylvania	18,112	23.0	27
Rhode Island	2,124	27.4	13
South Carolina	6,211	25.1	18
South Dakota	1,360	31.0	4
Tennessee	9,524	30.1	7
Texas	27,683	22.3	30
Utah	3,221	23.3	25
Vermont	1,369	30.0	8
Virginia	7,051	16.1	49
Washington	7,738	19.5	42
West Virginia	3,440	28.8	10
Wisconsin	7,262	20.4	39
Wyoming	1,982	35.0	1
50 States	422,977	22.5	
DC	2,706	35.4	
United States	425,683	22.5	

Rank in order by percentage

1	Wyoming
2	Mississippi
3	Montana
4	South Dakota
5	New Mexico
6	North Dakota
7	Tennessee
8	Vermont
9	Arkansas
10	West Virginia
11	Alaska
12	Maine
13	Rhode Island
14	Louisiana
15	Kentucky
16	Alabama
17	New York
18	South Carolina
19	Arizona
20	Oklahoma
21	Missouri
22	North Carolina
23	Idaho
24	Iowa
25	Utah
26	Michigan
27	Pennsylvania
28	Oregon
29	Ohio
30	Texas
31	Hawaii
32	Nebraska
33	California
34	Massachusetts
35	New Hampshire
36	Georgia
37	Indiana
38	Illinois
39	Wisconsin
40	Minnesota
41	Maryland
42	Washington
43	Kansas
44	Florida
45	Colorado
46	Delaware
47	Connecticut
48	New Jersey
49	Virginia
50	Nevada

Note: Numbers that appear to be identical are rounded and vary slightly in actual value. The rankings reflect the actual values before rounding. See the introduction for more details.

E-13   Federal Tax Burden, Total and Per Capita, FY 2004

State	Federal tax burden total $ (in millions)	Federal tax burden per capita $	Rank per capita
Alabama	21,242	4,694	43
Alaska	4,226	6,425	17
Arizona	30,077	5,240	37
Arkansas	12,202	4,437	48
California	251,324	7,012	9
Colorado	32,222	7,002	10
Connecticut	36,984	10,570	1
Delaware	5,696	6,862	13
Florida	109,354	6,290	19
Georgia	51,038	5,723	24
Hawaii	7,049	5,585	29
Idaho	6,482	4,646	45
Illinois	88,971	6,999	11
Indiana	34,171	5,488	31
Iowa	15,706	5,319	35
Kansas	15,295	5,595	28
Kentucky	20,017	4,833	40
Louisiana	20,672	4,587	46
Maine	7,126	5,419	32
Maryland	41,176	7,404	6
Massachusetts	57,128	8,916	3
Michigan	61,070	6,044	20
Minnesota	35,268	6,920	12
Mississippi	11,737	4,046	50
Missouri	32,276	5,604	27
Montana	4,456	4,807	41
Nebraska	9,950	5,693	25
Nevada	15,280	6,550	16
New Hampshire	9,771	7,521	5
New Jersey	78,158	8,999	2
New Mexico	9,376	4,927	39
New York	153,089	7,940	4
North Carolina	45,316	5,306	36
North Dakota	3,266	5,133	38
Ohio	63,754	5,568	30
Oklahoma	16,508	4,685	44
Oregon	20,158	5,613	26
Pennsylvania	78,569	6,339	18
Rhode Island	7,081	6,557	15
South Carolina	20,011	4,767	42
South Dakota	4,129	5,358	33
Tennessee	31,370	5,323	34
Texas	131,256	5,841	23
Utah	10,973	4,533	47
Vermont	3,709	5,971	22
Virginia	50,813	6,792	14
Washington	44,244	7,128	7
West Virginia	7,700	4,248	49
Wisconsin	33,021	6,000	21
Wyoming	3,594	7,105	8
50 States	1,864,065	6,360	
DC	5,432	9,801	
United States*	1,870,300	6,369	

Due to rounding or data sources, the 50-state total plus D.C. may not equal the U.S. total. Please see introduction.

E-14 Federal Spending Per Dollar of Taxes Paid, FY 2004

State	Spending per dollar of taxes paid $	Rank
Alabama	1.71	6
Alaska	1.87	2
Arizona	1.30	18
Arkansas	1.47	12
California	0.79	40
Colorado	0.79	40
Connecticut	0.66	49
Delaware	0.79	40
Florida	1.02	30
Georgia	0.96	35
Hawaii	1.60	8
Idaho	1.28	21
Illinois	0.73	45
Indiana	0.97	33
Iowa	1.11	25
Kansas	1.12	23
Kentucky	1.45	13
Louisiana	1.45	13
Maine	1.40	16
Maryland	1.44	15
Massachusetts	0.77	44
Michigan	0.85	38
Minnesota	0.69	47
Mississippi	1.77	4
Missouri	1.29	20
Montana	1.58	9
Nebraska	1.07	28
Nevada	0.73	45
New Hampshire	0.67	48
New Jersey	0.55	50
New Mexico	2.00	1
New York	0.79	40
North Carolina	1.10	27
North Dakota	1.73	5
Ohio	1.01	32
Oklahoma	1.48	11
Oregon	0.97	33
Pennsylvania	1.06	29
Rhode Island	1.02	30
South Carolina	1.38	17
South Dakota	1.49	10
Tennessee	1.30	18
Texas	0.94	36
Utah	1.14	22
Vermont	1.12	23
Virginia	1.66	7
Washington	0.88	37
West Virginia	1.83	3
Wisconsin	0.82	39
Wyoming	1.11	25
50 States	n/a	
DC	6.64	
United States	1.00	

Rank in order by $

1	New Mexico
2	Alaska
3	West Virginia
4	Mississippi
5	North Dakota
6	Alabama
7	Virginia
8	Hawaii
9	Montana
10	South Dakota
11	Oklahoma
12	Arkansas
13	Kentucky
13	Louisiana
15	Maryland
16	Maine
17	South Carolina
18	Arizona
18	Tennessee
20	Missouri
21	Idaho
22	Utah
23	Kansas
23	Vermont
25	Iowa
25	Wyoming
27	North Carolina
28	Nebraska
29	Pennsylvania
30	Florida
30	Rhode Island
32	Ohio
33	Indiana
33	Oregon
35	Georgia
36	Texas
37	Washington
38	Michigan
39	Wisconsin
40	California
40	Colorado
40	Delaware
40	New York
44	Massachusetts
45	Illinois
45	Nevada
47	Minnesota
48	New Hampshire
49	Connecticut
50	New Jersey

Note: Ties in ranking reflect ties in actual values.

E-15 Highway Charges Returned to States, FY 2005

State	Percentage of charges returned to states	Rank
Alabama	120	17
Alaska	740	1
Arizona	96	46
Arkansas	113	23
California	115	21
Colorado	99	41
Connecticut	166	10
Delaware	194	9
Florida	146	13
Georgia	102	34
Hawaii	212	7
Idaho	157	12
Illinois	93	49
Indiana	93	48
Iowa	100	39
Kansas	118	19
Kentucky	101	37
Louisiana	105	30
Maine	111	24
Maryland	100	38
Massachusetts	110	25
Michigan	101	35
Minnesota	87	50
Mississippi	103	33
Missouri	104	31
Montana	244	4
Nebraska	108	27
Nevada	94	47
New Hampshire	119	18
New Jersey	96	44
New Mexico	117	20
New York	134	14
North Carolina	103	32
North Dakota	260	3
Ohio	105	28
Oklahoma	129	16
Oregon	110	26
Pennsylvania	134	15
Rhode Island	268	2
South Carolina	96	43
South Dakota	222	6
Tennessee	100	40
Texas	96	45
Utah	101	36
Vermont	230	5
Virginia	98	42
Washington	105	29
West Virginia	199	8
Wisconsin	114	22
Wyoming	160	11
50 States	n/a	
DC	497	
United States	114	

Rank in order by percentage	
1	Alaska
2	Rhode Island
3	North Dakota
4	Montana
5	Vermont
6	South Dakota
7	Hawaii
8	West Virginia
9	Delaware
10	Connecticut
11	Wyoming
12	Idaho
13	Florida
14	New York
15	Pennsylvania
16	Oklahoma
17	Alabama
18	New Hampshire
19	Kansas
20	New Mexico
21	California
22	Wisconsin
23	Arkansas
24	Maine
25	Massachusetts
26	Oregon
27	Nebraska
28	Ohio
29	Washington
30	Louisiana
31	Missouri
32	North Carolina
33	Mississippi
34	Georgia
35	Michigan
36	Utah
37	Kentucky
38	Maryland
39	Iowa
40	Tennessee
41	Colorado
42	Virginia
43	South Carolina
44	New Jersey
45	Texas
46	Arizona
47	Nevada
48	Indiana
49	Illinois
50	Minnesota

Note: Numbers that appear to be identical are rounded and vary slightly in actual value. The rankings reflect the actual values before rounding. See the introduction for more details.

E-16 Terms of Trade with the Federal Government, FY 2004

State	Federal grants to state and local governments $ (in millions)	Terms of trade, ratio of federal grants to federal taxes paid	Rank by ratio
Alabama	7,008	1.36	14
Alaska	3,217	3.14	1
Arizona	8,364	1.15	22
Arkansas	4,683	1.58	10
California	54,534	0.89	37
Colorado	5,643	0.72	46
Connecticut	5,556	0.62	49
Delaware	1,241	0.90	35
Florida	19,610	0.74	45
Georgia	11,759	0.95	32
Hawaii	2,158	1.26	21
Idaho	1,995	1.27	19
Illinois	16,531	0.77	44
Indiana	7,436	0.90	36
Iowa	4,039	1.06	28
Kansas	3,469	0.93	33
Kentucky	6,743	1.39	13
Louisiana	7,787	1.55	12
Maine	2,758	1.59	9
Maryland	8,837	0.88	39
Massachusetts	13,876	1.00	31
Michigan	13,227	0.89	38
Minnesota	7,209	0.84	42
Mississippi	5,379	1.89	5
Missouri	8,734	1.11	24
Montana	1,997	1.85	7
Nebraska	2,531	1.05	29
Nevada	2,322	0.63	48
New Hampshire	1,879	0.79	43
New Jersey	11,333	0.60	50
New Mexico	4,663	2.05	2
New York	50,009	1.35	16
North Carolina	12,574	1.14	23
North Dakota	1,515	1.91	4
Ohio	16,514	1.07	26
Oklahoma	5,271	1.32	17
Oregon	5,185	1.06	27
Pennsylvania	19,916	1.04	30
Rhode Island	2,329	1.36	15
South Carolina	6,145	1.27	20
South Dakota	1,620	1.62	8
Tennessee	9,863	1.30	18
Texas	27,792	0.87	40
Utah	2,948	1.11	25
Vermont	1,423	1.58	11
Virginia	7,991	0.65	47
Washington	9,083	0.85	41
West Virginia	3,701	1.98	3
Wisconsin	7,484	0.93	34
Wyoming	1,636	1.88	6
50 States	449,517	0.99	
DC	4,205	3.19	
United States*	460,152	1.00	

Due to rounding or data sources, the 50-state total plus D.C. may not equal the U.S. total. Please see introduction.

Rank in order by ratio	
1	Alaska
2	New Mexico
3	West Virginia
4	North Dakota
5	Mississippi
6	Wyoming
7	Montana
8	South Dakota
9	Maine
10	Arkansas
11	Vermont
12	Louisiana
13	Kentucky
14	Alabama
15	Rhode Island
16	New York
17	Oklahoma
18	Tennessee
19	Idaho
20	South Carolina
21	Hawaii
22	Arizona
23	North Carolina
24	Missouri
25	Utah
26	Ohio
27	Oregon
28	Iowa
29	Nebraska
30	Pennsylvania
31	Massachusetts
32	Georgia
33	Kansas
34	Wisconsin
35	Delaware
36	Indiana
37	California
38	Michigan
39	Maryland
40	Texas
41	Washington
42	Minnesota
43	New Hampshire
44	Illinois
45	Florida
46	Colorado
47	Virginia
48	Nevada
49	Connecticut
50	New Jersey

Note: Numbers that appear to be identical are rounded and vary slightly in actual value. The rankings reflect the actual values before rounding. See the introduction for more details.

E-17 Federal Personal Income Taxes, 2004

State	Federal tax liability $ (in millions)	Federal tax liability per capita $	Rank per capita
Alabama	9.15	2,023	39
Alaska	2.01	3,054	17
Arizona	14.22	2,478	25
Arkansas	4.83	1,758	48
California	121.34	3,385	9
Colorado	14.84	3,225	15
Connecticut	20.30	5,803	1
Delaware	2.72	3,281	12
Florida	57.75	3,322	11
Georgia	22.03	2,470	26
Hawaii	3.31	2,626	22
Idaho	2.67	1,914	45
Illinois	42.66	3,356	10
Indiana	14.67	2,356	30
Iowa	6.38	2,159	37
Kansas	6.59	2,410	29
Kentucky	8.02	1,937	42
Louisiana	8.19	1,818	47
Maine	2.93	2,226	36
Maryland	20.96	3,770	6
Massachusetts	28.39	4,431	3
Michigan	26.26	2,599	23
Minnesota	16.25	3,188	16
Mississippi	4.19	1,445	50
Missouri	13.44	2,333	34
Montana	1.79	1,926	43
Nebraska	4.08	2,334	33
Nevada	8.83	3,785	5
New Hampshire	4.67	3,594	7
New Jersey	39.19	4,512	2
New Mexico	3.55	1,865	46
New York	75.89	3,936	4
North Carolina	19.58	2,292	35
North Dakota	1.37	2,155	38
Ohio	28.19	2,462	27
Oklahoma	6.94	1,969	41
Oregon	8.46	2,356	31
Pennsylvania	35.03	2,826	19
Rhode Island	3.24	3,002	18
South Carolina	8.31	1,980	40
South Dakota	1.81	2,355	32
Tennessee	14.31	2,427	28
Texas	59.94	2,667	20
Utah	4.63	1,914	44
Vermont	1.59	2,559	24
Virginia	25.92	3,465	8
Washington	20.23	3,259	14
West Virginia	2.94	1,621	49
Wisconsin	14.52	2,638	21
Wyoming	1.65	3,270	13
50 States	870.78	2,971	
DC	2.83	5,108	
United States*	879.94	2,996	

*Due to rounding or data sources, the 50-state total plus D.C. may not equal the U.S. total. Please see introduction.

Rank in order per capita

1 Connecticut
2 New Jersey
3 Massachusetts
4 New York
5 Nevada
6 Maryland
7 New Hampshire
8 Virginia
9 California
10 Illinois
11 Florida
12 Delaware
13 Wyoming
14 Washington
15 Colorado
16 Minnesota
17 Alaska
18 Rhode Island
19 Pennsylvania
20 Texas
21 Wisconsin
22 Hawaii
23 Michigan
24 Vermont
25 Arizona
26 Georgia
27 Ohio
28 Tennessee
29 Kansas
30 Indiana
31 Oregon
32 South Dakota
33 Nebraska
34 Missouri
35 North Carolina
36 Maine
37 Iowa
38 North Dakota
39 Alabama
40 South Carolina
41 Oklahoma
42 Kentucky
43 Montana
44 Utah
45 Idaho
46 New Mexico
47 Louisiana
48 Arkansas
49 West Virginia
50 Mississippi

Note: Numbers that appear to be identical are rounded and vary slightly in actual value. The rankings reflect the actual values before rounding. See the introduction for more details.

E-18 Federal Share of Medicaid, FY 2007–2008

State	2007 federal cost-sharing percentages for Medicaid %	2008 federal cost-sharing percentages for Medicaid %	Rank by 2007
Alabama	68.85	67.62	11
Alaska	57.58	52.48	30
Arizona	66.47	66.20	13
Arkansas	73.37	72.94	2
California	50.00	50.00	39
Colorado	50.00	50.00	39
Connecticut	50.00	50.00	39
Delaware	50.00	50.00	39
Florida	58.76	56.83	28
Georgia	61.97	63.10	21
Hawaii	57.55	56.50	31
Idaho	70.36	69.87	5
Illinois	50.00	50.00	39
Indiana	62.61	62.69	19
Iowa	61.98	61.73	20
Kansas	60.25	59.43	25
Kentucky	69.58	69.78	8
Louisiana	69.69	72.47	7
Maine	63.27	63.31	17
Maryland	50.00	50.00	39
Massachusetts	50.00	50.00	39
Michigan	56.38	58.10	33
Minnesota	50.00	50.00	39
Mississippi	75.89	76.29	1
Missouri	61.60	62.42	22
Montana	69.11	68.53	10
Nebraska	57.93	58.02	29
Nevada	53.93	52.64	35
New Hampshire	50.00	50.00	39
New Jersey	50.00	50.00	39
New Mexico	71.93	71.04	4
New York	50.00	50.00	39
North Carolina	64.52	64.05	15
North Dakota	64.72	63.75	14
Ohio	59.66	60.79	26
Oklahoma	68.14	67.10	12
Oregon	61.07	60.86	23
Pennsylvania	54.39	54.08	34
Rhode Island	52.35	52.51	37
South Carolina	69.54	69.79	9
South Dakota	62.92	60.03	18
Tennessee	63.65	63.71	16
Texas	60.78	60.53	24
Utah	70.14	71.63	6
Vermont	58.93	59.03	27
Virginia	50.00	50.00	39
Washington	50.12	51.52	38
West Virginia	72.82	74.25	3
Wisconsin	57.47	57.62	32
Wyoming	52.91	50.00	36
50 States	n/a	n/a	
DC	70.00	70.00	
United States	n/a	n/a	

Rank in order by 2007 percentage

1	Mississippi
2	Arkansas
3	West Virginia
4	New Mexico
5	Idaho
6	Utah
7	Louisiana
8	Kentucky
9	South Carolina
10	Montana
11	Alabama
12	Oklahoma
13	Arizona
14	North Dakota
15	North Carolina
16	Tennessee
17	Maine
18	South Dakota
19	Indiana
20	Iowa
21	Georgia
22	Missouri
23	Oregon
24	Texas
25	Kansas
26	Ohio
27	Vermont
28	Florida
29	Nebraska
30	Alaska
31	Hawaii
32	Wisconsin
33	Michigan
34	Pennsylvania
35	Nevada
36	Wyoming
37	Rhode Island
38	Washington
39	California
39	Colorado
39	Connecticut
39	Delaware
39	Illinois
39	Maryland
39	Massachusetts
39	Minnesota
39	New Hampshire
39	New Jersey
39	New York
39	Virginia

Note: Ties in ranking reflect ties in actual values.

Source Notes for Federal Impacts (Section E)

E-1 Federal Spending, Total and Per Capita, FY 2004: The federal government affects state economies and state finances through its massive spending, accounting for nearly one-quarter of all economic activity in the United States. The primary components of that spending are grants to state and local governments; payments to individuals, such as Social Security; wages and salaries of federal employees; and purchases of goods and services, such as weapons for the Department of Defense.

Details of where these funds are spent are compiled by federal agencies and summarized by the U.S. Census Bureau in *Consolidated Federal Funds Report for Fiscal Year 2004*. Many tables in this section reflect the latest version of this report, covering federal spending in fiscal year 2004, which for the federal government ended in September 2004.

This table reflects total federal spending of $2.2 trillion, along with the results of dividing each state's total by its population to permit meaningful comparisons among states. The federal figures exclude certain forms of federal spending that cannot reasonably be associated with particular states, primarily interest on the federal debt and money spent in other countries.

E-2 Increase in Total Federal Spending, FY 1999–2004: This table uses the U.S. Census Bureau reports for federal fiscal years 1999 and 2004 to show the percentage change in total federal spending in each state over a five-year period. The data come from the federal report described in the notes to Table E-1.

E-3 Federal Spending on Grants, Total and Per Capita, FY 2004: This table reflects the federal spending for grants that help state and local governments finance welfare, Medicaid, highway construction, and other activities. The data come from the federal report described in the notes to Table E-1.

E-4 Federal Spending on Procurement, Total and Per Capita, FY 2004: This table reflects the federal spending for purchases ranging from tanks and space shuttles to gasoline for federal vehicles. The data come from the federal report described in the notes to Table E-1.

E-5 Federal Spending on Payments to Individuals, FY 2004: This table reflects the federal spending for payments to individuals. The primary components are Social Security pensions, Medicare payments to health care providers, pensions for retired federal workers, and food stamps. The data come from the federal report described in the notes to Table E-1.

E-6 Federal Spending on Social Security and Medicare, FY 2004: This table reflects the federal spending for Social Security pensions and Medicare payments to health care providers. This spending is a part of the total covered by

Table E-5. The per capita amounts suggest the massive impact that this flow of funds has among states. While revenues from payroll taxes are concentrated in states that are showing strong economic growth, states with slower growth receive large portions of personal income from these retirement-related federal payments and private pensions. The data come from the federal report described in the notes to Table E-1.

E-7 Social Security Benefits Paid, FY 2005: This table provides another perspective on Social Security payments, using tabulations for December 2005 payments prepared by the Social Security Administration and available on the SSA Web site (www.ssa.gov).

This agency can provide additional details on benefits paid in each state, such as the amounts paid to retired workers, to deceased workers' beneficiaries, and to workers and their families based on disability. Besides the amounts paid and number of recipient households, the table shows the average benefit per household. This amount is appreciably higher in states where salaries have been high (such as in the Northeast) than where they have been low (such as in the South).

E-8 Federal Spending on Employee Wages and Salaries, FY 2004: This table reflects the federal spending on payments for salaries of civilian and military federal employees. The largest amounts are found in states with major federal installations, such as military bases. Because the Postal Service is included and some agencies, such as the Department of Agriculture, which operate in every state, even states without major installations show substantial federal spending. The data come from the federal report described in the notes to Table E-1.

E-9 Federal Spending on Defense, FY 2004: This table reflects federal spending on defense on everything from payroll, to procurement, to military retirees. The data come from the federal report described in the notes to Table E-1.

E-10 Homeland Security Grants, Total and Per Capita, FY 2006: The creation of the Department of Homeland Security (DHS), established to "detect, prepare for, prevent, protect against, respond to, and recover from terrorist attacks," involved a substantial reorganization of the federal government. Many pre-existing public safety programs such as the Federal Emergency Management Agency (FEMA) and the Transportation Security Administration were transferred to the new department. Immigration and Naturalization Services was eliminated and the Bureau of Citizenship and Immigration Services was formed in its place.

The table shows how grants for homeland security were distributed amongst the states in fiscal year 2006. Because there is a generous minimum allocation for each state, less populous areas of the country show high per capita amounts. The data on homeland security grants comes from a special compilation by Federal Funds Information for States (www.ffis.org).

E-11 Federal Grant Spending Per Dollar of State Tax Revenue, FY 2004: Most federal grant spending is now concentrated on state-administered programs, such as welfare and Medicaid. The amounts are substantial when compared with the amount that states raise from state taxes, as shown by the table, which relates the amounts provided by federal grants to the amounts states raised from taxes. The data for fiscal year 2004 are from "Government Finances," available on the U.S. Census Bureau Web site (www.census.gov).

E-12 State and Local General Revenue from Federal Government, FY 2004: These data, covering both state and local government, show the amount of federal aid contributing to "general revenue" as defined by the U.S. Census Bureau in its annual survey of government finances. It excludes certain trust funds, such as unemployment insurance, but includes others, such as those used for highway construction. The data are calculated from the bureau's "State and Local Government Finances: FY 2004" available on the bureau's Web site (www.census.gov).

E-13 Federal Tax Burden, Total and Per Capita, FY 2004: This table shows where the burdens of federal taxes fell in federal fiscal year 2004. The data come from the Tax Foundation's *Special Report* (no. 139, March 2006), which uses formulas to spread the burden of certain taxes, such as the corporate income tax, among states and actual data from federal tax collectors to show the sources of major tax revenues, such as those from personal income and payroll taxes.

E-14 Federal Spending Per Dollar of Taxes Paid, FY 2004: These data relate how much taxpayers in each state pay in federal taxes to the amounts the federal government spends in each state. The information comes from calculations by the Tax Foundation using allocations of tax burdens (see Table E-13) and the U.S. Census Bureau report on federal spending (see Table E-1).

Many states get more than a dollar back in federal spending for every dollar sent to the federal government in taxes. This occurs primarily in states where federal installations and/or purchasing is concentrated. Because a substantial portion of federal spending is financed by borrowing (deficit spending), the nationwide total would show more money returned as spending than paid as taxes, so the Tax Foundation adjusted spending to eliminate the deficit-financed portion.

E-15 Highway Charges Returned to States, FY 2005: Federal spending for highways is financed by special user charges, such as federal taxes on gasoline and diesel fuel. Some states, such as Alaska and Hawaii, receive much more fed-eral highway aid than federal user charges collected in their states. Others, which highway officials call "donor states," can receive less than a dollar of aid from every dollar in federal highway taxes collected within their boundaries. Some states will appear as particularly large "donee states" because of expansive interstate projects underway in a particular period. Which states should "donate" how much is a subject of perpetual controversy in the Congress. The controversy spawns many different ways to measure the federal redistribution of highway revenues.

In fiscal year 2005, federal collections of highway user charges were about $33 billion while allocations of spending authority to states were $38 billion. Federal spending for highways is financed by special "user charges," such as federal taxes on gasoline and diesel fuel.

This table is parallel to Table E-12 but covers only highway spending. It was developed by the Federal Highway Administration and is published in *2005 Highway Statistics.* Data from this book and earlier editions of *Highway Statistics* are available on the FHWA Web site (www.fhwa.dot.gov).

E-16 Terms of Trade with the Federal Government, FY 2004: This table was developed by State Policy Research to show the relationship between amounts paid by taxpayers in each state to the federal grants to state and local government financed by their federal taxes. The table shows federal grants, identical to the amounts shown in Table E-3. Because all grants, even those paid currently out of money the federal government raises by borrowing, are ultimately paid for by taxpayers, the total federal tax revenue to pay for grants was stipulated as equal to the grants for the fifty states and the District of Columbia.

To determine how this tax burden to pay for grants was distributed among states, the total tax burden for grants was allocated based on the percentage of all federal taxes paid by citizens and corporations in each state, using the Tax Foundation's logic (also used to prepare Table E-13). The result is that the sum of grants and of taxes are identical for the fifty states plus the District of Columbia.

However, the amounts are by no means equal for individual states. States with relatively high personal incomes (and thus federal tax liabilities) but low grants will show ratios below one. Conceptually, for example, 0.95 can be considered as getting 95 cents back in grants for every dollar in federal taxes paid, or a 95 percent return. Conversely, states with lower incomes and high grants will show a ratio above one.

E-17 Federal Personal Income Taxes, 2004: This table shows how much households in each state were required to pay in federal income taxes on their income during 2004, as reported in tax returns filed in January through December of 2005. The data were reported in the *SOI Bulletin* (Spring 2005) available on the Web site of the Internal Revenue Service (www.irs.gov).

E-18 Federal Share of Medicaid, FY 2007–2008: The federal grants to states for Medicaid are based on multiplying the total costs of these programs by the federal cost-sharing percentages shown in the table. The formula used to determine each state's share provides the largest federal shares for the states with the lowest per capita incomes. A special rule overrides the calculation for more affluent states, so no state has less than 50 percent of these costs paid by the federal government.

As part of the Jobs and Growth Tax Relief Reconciliation Act of 2003 federal medical assistance percentages were temporarily increased for the last two quarters of fiscal year 2003 and the first three quarters of fiscal year 2004. This fiscal relief ended in fiscal year 2005.

The percentages were published in Federal Funds Information for States' (FFIS) *Issue Brief 06-42*, released September 26, 2006.

Taxes

Percent Change in Quarterly State Tax Revenue, Adjusted for Legislated Tax Changes and Inflation, by Region, Third Quarter 2005–Third Quarter 2006

Region	Percent
New England	-1.3
Mid-Atlantic	1.1
Great Lakes	-2.0
Plains	-1.9
Southeast	1.2
Southwest	5.9
Rocky Mountain	5.5
Far West	1.5
United States	1.1

Source: The Nelson A. Rockefeller Institute of Government

Year-over-Year Change in Quarterly State Tax Revenue, Adjusted for Legislated Tax Changes and Inflation, 2001–2006

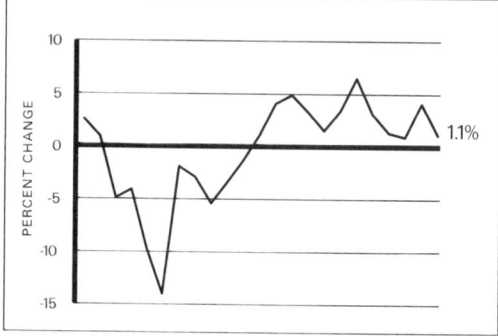

Source: The Nelson A. Rockefeller Institute of Government

Percent Change in Quarterly State Tax Revenue (Unadjusted) Third Quarter 2005–Third Quarter 2006

Type of Tax	Percent
Personal Income	6.6
Corporate Income	10.9
Sales	4.0
Total	4.6

Source: The Nelson A. Rockefeller Institute of Government

F-1   State and Local Tax Revenue, FY 2004

State	State and local taxes $ (in millions)	State and local taxes as a percentage of personal income	Rank by percentage
Alabama	10,535	8.9	50
Alaska	2,376	11.0	20
Arizona	16,481	11.0	22
Arkansas	6,973	10.5	33
California	133,894	11.3	15
Colorado	14,582	9.3	47
Connecticut	17,220	11.4	12
Delaware	2,994	11.0	21
Florida	53,789	10.5	31
Georgia	25,655	10.1	42
Hawaii	4,812	12.5	4
Idaho	3,806	10.9	24
Illinois	45,191	10.8	27
Indiana	18,675	10.5	37
Iowa	9,019	10.8	26
Kansas	9,242	11.5	9
Kentucky	11,460	10.6	30
Louisiana	13,065	11.2	18
Maine	4,983	13.2	3
Maryland	22,331	10.8	25
Massachusetts	27,015	10.7	28
Michigan	33,478	10.6	29
Minnesota	19,424	11.3	16
Mississippi	7,089	10.5	32
Missouri	16,255	9.8	45
Montana	2,431	10.3	39
Nebraska	6,308	12.0	8
Nevada	7,972	11.3	14
New Hampshire	4,070	9.1	48
New Jersey	39,558	11.4	10
New Mexico	5,444	11.4	13
New York	101,426	14.6	1
North Carolina	25,012	10.5	35
North Dakota	1,901	10.5	34
Ohio	39,151	11.4	11
Oklahoma	9,435	10.1	41
Oregon	10,474	10.2	40
Pennsylvania	42,718	10.9	23
Rhode Island	4,202	12.2	5
South Carolina	11,177	10.3	38
South Dakota	2,016	9.3	46
Tennessee	14,947	9.0	49
Texas	64,739	10.1	43
Utah	6,621	11.2	17
Vermont	2,286	12.1	7
Virginia	25,002	10.1	44
Washington	21,425	10.5	36
West Virginia	4,968	11.1	19
Wisconsin	20,441	12.2	6
Wyoming	2,245	13.9	2
50 States	1,006,313	11.0	
DC	3,964	14.9	
United States	1,010,277	11.0	

Rank in order by percentage

1 New York
2 Wyoming
3 Maine
4 Hawaii
5 Rhode Island
6 Wisconsin
7 Vermont
8 Nebraska
9 Kansas
10 New Jersey
11 Ohio
12 Connecticut
13 New Mexico
14 Nevada
15 California
16 Minnesota
17 Utah
18 Louisiana
19 West Virginia
20 Alaska
21 Delaware
22 Arizona
23 Pennsylvania
24 Idaho
25 Maryland
26 Iowa
27 Illinois
28 Massachusetts
29 Michigan
30 Kentucky
31 Florida
32 Mississippi
33 Arkansas
34 North Dakota
35 North Carolina
36 Washington
37 Indiana
38 South Carolina
39 Montana
40 Oregon
41 Oklahoma
42 Georgia
43 Texas
44 Virginia
45 Missouri
46 South Dakota
47 Colorado
48 New Hampshire
49 Tennessee
50 Alabama

Note: Numbers that appear to be identical are rounded and vary slightly in actual value. The rankings reflect the actual values before rounding. See the introduction for more details.

F-2　Per Capita State and Local Tax Revenue, FY 2004

State	State and local taxes per capita $	State taxes per capita $	Local taxes per capita $	Rank by state and local taxes per capita
Alabama	2,326	1,549	776	50
Alaska	3,625	2,049	1,575	14
Arizona	2,869	1,678	1,192	36
Arkansas	2,533	2,027	506	47
California	3,730	2,388	1,342	11
Colorado	3,169	1,532	1,636	25
Connecticut	4,915	2,937	1,978	2
Delaware	3,606	2,861	745	16
Florida	3,092	1,755	1,337	27
Georgia	2,906	1,650	1,255	33
Hawaii	3,811	3,048	763	8
Idaho	2,732	1,900	831	42
Illinois	3,555	1,865	1,690	17
Indiana	2,994	1,917	1,077	30
Iowa	3,053	1,765	1,288	28
Kansas	3,379	1,932	1,447	22
Kentucky	2,764	2,041	723	40
Louisiana	2,893	1,714	1,179	34
Maine	3,783	2,179	1,604	10
Maryland	4,018	2,218	1,800	6
Massachusetts	4,210	2,624	1,586	5
Michigan	3,311	2,240	1,071	24
Minnesota	3,808	2,889	919	9
Mississippi	2,442	1,765	677	49
Missouri	2,825	1,585	1,240	38
Montana	2,623	1,754	869	45
Nebraska	3,610	2,083	1,527	15
Nevada	3,414	2,020	1,394	21
New Hampshire	3,132	1,543	1,589	26
New Jersey	4,548	2,413	2,135	3
New Mexico	2,860	2,103	758	37
New York	5,275	2,383	2,892	1
North Carolina	2,928	1,971	957	31
North Dakota	2,997	1,937	1,060	29
Ohio	3,417	1,961	1,455	20
Oklahoma	2,678	1,824	854	43
Oregon	2,914	1,698	1,216	32
Pennsylvania	3,443	2,043	1,400	19
Rhode Island	3,889	2,229	1,660	7
South Carolina	2,662	1,621	1,042	44
South Dakota	2,615	1,379	1,237	46
Tennessee	2,533	1,615	918	48
Texas	2,879	1,367	1,511	35
Utah	2,772	1,756	1,015	39
Vermont	3,679	2,843	836	13
Virginia	3,352	1,908	1,444	23
Washington	3,454	2,240	1,214	18
West Virginia	2,736	2,065	671	41
Wisconsin	3,710	2,294	1,416	12
Wyoming	4,433	2,971	1,462	4
50 States	3,433	2,014	1,419	
DC	7,161	0	7,161	
United States	3,440	2,011	1,430	

Rank in order by state and local taxes per capita

1　New York
2　Connecticut
3　New Jersey
4　Wyoming
5　Massachusetts
6　Maryland
7　Rhode Island
8　Hawaii
9　Minnesota
10　Maine
11　California
12　Wisconsin
13　Vermont
14　Alaska
15　Nebraska
16　Delaware
17　Illinois
18　Washington
19　Pennsylvania
20　Ohio
21　Nevada
22　Kansas
23　Virginia
24　Michigan
25　Colorado
26　New Hampshire
27　Florida
28　Iowa
29　North Dakota
30　Indiana
31　North Carolina
32　Oregon
33　Georgia
34　Louisiana
35　Texas
36　Arizona
37　New Mexico
38　Missouri
39　Utah
40　Kentucky
41　West Virginia
42　Idaho
43　Oklahoma
44　South Carolina
45　Montana
46　South Dakota
47　Arkansas
48　Tennessee
49　Mississippi
50　Alabama

Note: Numbers that appear to be identical are rounded and vary slightly in actual value. The rankings reflect the actual values before rounding. See the introduction for more details.

F-3   State and Local Tax Effort, FY 2002

State	Tax effort %	Rank
Alabama	85	41
Alaska	82	43
Arizona	93	33
Arkansas	99	19
California	99	19
Colorado	86	40
Connecticut	107	9
Delaware	82	43
Florida	83	42
Georgia	96	25
Hawaii	101	16
Idaho	91	35
Illinois	102	14
Indiana	94	29
Iowa	95	28
Kansas	103	13
Kentucky	89	38
Louisiana	104	12
Maine	118	2
Maryland	114	4
Massachusetts	94	29
Michigan	100	18
Minnesota	107	9
Mississippi	101	16
Missouri	90	37
Montana	78	49
Nebraska	102	14
Nevada	82	43
New Hampshire	75	50
New Jersey	110	7
New Mexico	96	25
New York	134	1
North Carolina	93	33
North Dakota	88	39
Ohio	109	8
Oklahoma	98	23
Oregon	82	43
Pennsylvania	105	11
Rhode Island	115	3
South Carolina	91	35
South Dakota	81	47
Tennessee	81	47
Texas	96	25
Utah	94	29
Vermont	99	19
Virginia	97	24
Washington	99	19
West Virginia	111	6
Wisconsin	113	5
Wyoming	94	29
50 States	n/a	
DC	n/a	
United States	100	

Rank in order by tax effort

1	New York
2	Maine
3	Rhode Island
4	Maryland
5	Wisconsin
6	West Virginia
7	New Jersey
8	Ohio
9	Connecticut
9	Minnesota
11	Pennsylvania
12	Louisiana
13	Kansas
14	Illinois
14	Nebraska
16	Hawaii
16	Mississippi
18	Michigan
19	Arkansas
19	California
19	Vermont
19	Washington
23	Oklahoma
24	Virginia
25	Georgia
25	New Mexico
25	Texas
28	Iowa
29	Indiana
29	Massachusetts
29	Utah
29	Wyoming
33	Arizona
33	North Carolina
35	Idaho
35	South Carolina
37	Missouri
38	Kentucky
39	North Dakota
40	Colorado
41	Alabama
42	Florida
43	Alaska
43	Delaware
43	Nevada
43	Oregon
47	South Dakota
47	Tennessee
49	Montana
50	New Hampshire

Note: Ties in ranking reflect ties in actual values.

F-4　State and Local Tax Capacity, FY 2002

State	Tax capacity %	Rank
Alabama	82	46
Alaska	125	4
Arizona	91	37
Arkansas	76	48
California	110	11
Colorado	115	9
Connecticut	130	1
Delaware	129	2
Florida	104	14
Georgia	93	32
Hawaii	108	13
Idaho	86	43
Illinois	103	16
Indiana	93	32
Iowa	96	23
Kansas	90	38
Kentucky	94	30
Louisiana	83	44
Maine	95	28
Maryland	102	18
Massachusetts	126	3
Michigan	97	22
Minnesota	110	11
Mississippi	72	50
Missouri	94	30
Montana	96	23
Nebraska	96	23
Nevada	117	8
New Hampshire	122	6
New Jersey	118	7
New Mexico	88	41
New York	111	10
North Carolina	93	32
North Dakota	99	21
Ohio	93	32
Oklahoma	82	46
Oregon	100	19
Pennsylvania	92	36
Rhode Island	95	28
South Carolina	83	44
South Dakota	96	23
Tennessee	89	40
Texas	90	38
Utah	88	41
Vermont	103	16
Virginia	100	19
Washington	104	14
West Virginia	74	49
Wisconsin	96	23
Wyoming	123	5
50 States	n/a	
DC	n/a	
United States	100	

Rank in order by tax capacity	
1	Connecticut
2	Delaware
3	Massachusetts
4	Alaska
5	Wyoming
6	New Hampshire
7	New Jersey
8	Nevada
9	Colorado
10	New York
11	California
11	Minnesota
13	Hawaii
14	Florida
14	Washington
16	Illinois
16	Vermont
18	Maryland
19	Oregon
19	Virginia
21	North Dakota
22	Michigan
23	Iowa
23	Montana
23	Nebraska
23	South Dakota
23	Wisconsin
28	Maine
28	Rhode Island
30	Kentucky
30	Missouri
32	Georgia
32	Indiana
32	North Carolina
32	Ohio
36	Pennsylvania
37	Arizona
38	Kansas
38	Texas
40	Tennessee
41	New Mexico
41	Utah
43	Idaho
44	Louisiana
44	South Carolina
46	Alabama
46	Oklahoma
48	Arkansas
49	West Virginia
50	Mississippi

Note: Ties in ranking reflect ties in actual values.

F-5 Change in State and Local Taxes, FY 1999–2004

State	Percentage change in state and local taxes	Percentage change per capita	Change as a percentage of personal income	Rank by percentage change in state and local taxes
Alabama	20.1	15.9	-2.2	34
Alaska	34.9	27.6	7.3	5
Arizona	34.7	12.0	0.9	6
Arkansas	14.7	6.3	-6.5	47
California	27.5	17.8	-0.5	13
Colorado	20.3	6.1	-9.2	33
Connecticut	15.7	8.3	-6.0	46
Delaware	21.1	10.0	-2.1	31
Florida	33.7	16.1	5.2	7
Georgia	19.3	5.2	-6.3	36
Hawaii	23.0	15.4	1.7	22
Idaho	25.2	12.5	-3.3	17
Illinois	19.0	13.5	2.5	38
Indiana	19.9	14.2	-0.0	35
Iowa	17.5	14.1	-0.1	40
Kansas	26.7	23.0	6.8	15
Kentucky	17.4	12.2	-4.8	41
Louisiana	24.0	20.1	3.3	18
Maine	22.1	16.1	-5.2	24
Maryland	34.9	25.5	3.5	4
Massachusetts	21.3	16.7	-1.8	29
Michigan	11.9	9.2	-6.3	50
Minnesota	13.0	5.8	-8.5	49
Mississippi	16.5	11.1	-4.7	43
Missouri	15.9	10.1	-3.6	45
Montana	19.1	13.5	-5.6	37
Nebraska	36.4	30.1	11.1	3
Nevada	50.7	16.7	11.0	2
New Hampshire	30.9	20.9	3.1	10
New Jersey	25.3	17.3	0.7	16
New Mexico	21.8	11.4	-6.5	26
New York	23.5	16.8	3.8	19
North Carolina	23.4	10.6	-0.4	20
North Dakota	13.9	13.9	-8.5	48
Ohio	21.2	19.1	4.0	30
Oklahoma	21.5	15.8	-3.5	27
Oregon	22.7	13.2	2.0	23
Pennsylvania	21.4	17.3	1.7	28
Rhode Island	31.4	20.5	5.8	9
South Carolina	23.3	14.1	-1.6	21
South Dakota	21.9	16.0	-1.9	25
Tennessee	27.2	18.2	1.8	14
Texas	31.5	17.2	4.0	8
Utah	21.1	7.9	-4.4	32
Vermont	28.1	22.5	-0.7	11
Virginia	27.8	17.8	-1.0	12
Washington	18.3	9.7	-5.6	39
West Virginia	16.1	15.6	-4.7	44
Wisconsin	17.4	11.8	-4.3	42
Wyoming	65.4	56.8	22.5	1
50 States	23.8	15.0	-0.1	
DC	33.3	25.0	-1.6	
United States	23.8	15.0	-0.0	

Rank in order by percentage change

1	Wyoming
2	Nevada
3	Nebraska
4	Maryland
5	Alaska
6	Arizona
7	Florida
8	Texas
9	Rhode Island
10	New Hampshire
11	Vermont
12	Virginia
13	California
14	Tennessee
15	Kansas
16	New Jersey
17	Idaho
18	Louisiana
19	New York
20	North Carolina
21	South Carolina
22	Hawaii
23	Oregon
24	Maine
25	South Dakota
26	New Mexico
27	Oklahoma
28	Pennsylvania
29	Massachusetts
30	Ohio
31	Delaware
32	Utah
33	Colorado
34	Alabama
35	Indiana
36	Georgia
37	Montana
38	Illinois
39	Washington
40	Iowa
41	Kentucky
42	Wisconsin
43	Mississippi
44	West Virginia
45	Missouri
46	Connecticut
47	Arkansas
48	North Dakota
49	Minnesota
50	Michigan

Note: Numbers that appear to be identical are rounded and vary slightly in actual value. The rankings reflect the actual values before rounding. See the introduction for more details.

F-6　Property Taxes, FY 2004

State	Property taxes $ (in millions)	Property taxes as a percentage of personal income	Rank by percentage
Alabama	1,662	1.41	50
Alaska	859	3.98	14
Arizona	4,868	3.24	25
Arkansas	1,101	1.66	49
California	34,499	2.91	35
Colorado	4,722	3.01	33
Connecticut	6,802	4.51	7
Delaware	453	1.66	48
Florida	18,500	3.63	19
Georgia	7,845	3.09	31
Hawaii	721	1.87	45
Idaho	1,084	3.10	30
Illinois	17,889	4.26	10
Indiana	6,074	3.40	21
Iowa	3,189	3.81	16
Kansas	3,247	4.03	13
Kentucky	2,136	1.97	43
Louisiana	2,263	1.93	44
Maine	2,099	5.56	2
Maryland	6,019	2.92	34
Massachusetts	9,814	3.87	15
Michigan	11,979	3.81	17
Minnesota	4,920	2.86	36
Mississippi	1,860	2.77	38
Missouri	4,304	2.59	39
Montana	959	4.05	12
Nebraska	2,007	3.80	18
Nevada	2,147	3.04	32
New Hampshire	2,520	5.64	1
New Jersey	18,229	5.28	3
New Mexico	840	1.76	46
New York	32,334	4.64	6
North Carolina	6,093	2.56	40
North Dakota	585	3.23	26
Ohio	11,233	3.28	23
Oklahoma	1,637	1.76	47
Oregon	3,459	3.37	22
Pennsylvania	12,518	3.19	27
Rhode Island	1,759	5.12	4
South Carolina	3,704	3.42	20
South Dakota	705	3.26	24
Tennessee	3,585	2.15	42
Texas	28,176	4.38	9
Utah	1,669	2.81	37
Vermont	950	5.03	5
Virginia	7,715	3.10	29
Washington	6,386	3.13	28
West Virginia	979	2.19	41
Wisconsin	7,429	4.42	8
Wyoming	684	4.23	11
50 States	317,214	3.48	
DC	1,028	3.86	
United States	318,242	3.48	

Rank in order by percentage	
1	New Hampshire
2	Maine
3	New Jersey
4	Rhode Island
5	Vermont
6	New York
7	Connecticut
8	Wisconsin
9	Texas
10	Illinois
11	Wyoming
12	Montana
13	Kansas
14	Alaska
15	Massachusetts
16	Iowa
17	Michigan
18	Nebraska
19	Florida
20	South Carolina
21	Indiana
22	Oregon
23	Ohio
24	South Dakota
25	Arizona
26	North Dakota
27	Pennsylvania
28	Washington
29	Virginia
30	Idaho
31	Georgia
32	Nevada
33	Colorado
34	Maryland
35	California
36	Minnesota
37	Utah
38	Mississippi
39	Missouri
40	North Carolina
41	West Virginia
42	Tennessee
43	Kentucky
44	Louisiana
45	Hawaii
46	New Mexico
47	Oklahoma
48	Delaware
49	Arkansas
50	Alabama

Note: Numbers that appear to be identical are rounded and vary slightly in actual value. The rankings reflect the actual values before rounding. See the introduction for more details.

F-7 Property Taxes Per Capita, FY 2004

State	Property tax per capita $	Rank
Alabama	367	50
Alaska	1,311	12
Arizona	848	35
Arkansas	400	49
California	961	29
Colorado	1,026	23
Connecticut	1,941	2
Delaware	546	43
Florida	1,063	19
Georgia	888	33
Hawaii	571	42
Idaho	778	36
Illinois	1,407	9
Indiana	974	26
Iowa	1,079	18
Kansas	1,187	14
Kentucky	515	45
Louisiana	501	46
Maine	1,594	6
Maryland	1,083	17
Massachusetts	1,530	8
Michigan	1,185	15
Minnesota	965	27
Mississippi	641	40
Missouri	748	37
Montana	1,034	20
Nebraska	1,149	16
Nevada	920	31
New Hampshire	1,939	3
New Jersey	2,096	1
New Mexico	441	48
New York	1,682	4
North Carolina	713	38
North Dakota	922	30
Ohio	980	25
Oklahoma	465	47
Oregon	962	28
Pennsylvania	1,009	24
Rhode Island	1,628	5
South Carolina	882	34
South Dakota	915	32
Tennessee	608	41
Texas	1,253	13
Utah	699	39
Vermont	1,530	7
Virginia	1,034	21
Washington	1,029	22
West Virginia	539	44
Wisconsin	1,349	11
Wyoming	1,350	10
50 States	1,082	
DC	1,857	
United States	1,084	

Note: Numbers that appear to be identical are rounded and vary slightly in actual value. The rankings reflect the actual values before rounding. See the introduction for more details.

F-8 Property Tax Revenue as a Percentage of Three-Tax Revenue, FY 2004

State	Property tax as a percentage of three-tax revenue	Rank
Alabama	18.0	48
Alaska	70.6	2
Arizona	32.1	30
Arkansas	16.9	49
California	29.7	35
Colorado	34.9	26
Connecticut	42.5	11
Delaware	27.0	41
Florida	40.3	13
Georgia	32.6	29
Hawaii	16.0	50
Idaho	31.7	32
Illinois	44.2	10
Indiana	35.1	24
Iowa	38.8	18
Kansas	37.8	20
Kentucky	21.2	45
Louisiana	19.4	46
Maine	45.7	8
Maryland	30.5	34
Massachusetts	40.2	14
Michigan	40.7	12
Minnesota	28.6	38
Mississippi	29.1	36
Missouri	28.6	37
Montana	47.8	6
Nebraska	35.9	22
Nevada	32.0	31
New Hampshire	77.6	1
New Jersey	51.5	3
New Mexico	18.8	47
New York	35.7	23
North Carolina	27.0	42
North Dakota	37.9	19
Ohio	31.4	33
Oklahoma	21.6	44
Oregon	39.1	17
Pennsylvania	35.0	25
Rhode Island	44.3	9
South Carolina	36.5	21
South Dakota	39.7	16
Tennessee	28.5	39
Texas	48.7	4
Utah	27.2	40
Vermont	45.8	7
Virginia	34.5	27
Washington	32.9	28
West Virginia	23.3	43
Wisconsin	40.0	15
Wyoming	48.2	5
50 States	35.6	
DC	31.8	
United States	35.6	

Rank in order by percentage	
1	New Hampshire
2	Alaska
3	New Jersey
4	Texas
5	Wyoming
6	Montana
7	Vermont
8	Maine
9	Rhode Island
10	Illinois
11	Connecticut
12	Michigan
13	Florida
14	Massachusetts
15	Wisconsin
16	South Dakota
17	Oregon
18	Iowa
19	North Dakota
20	Kansas
21	South Carolina
22	Nebraska
23	New York
24	Indiana
25	Pennsylvania
26	Colorado
27	Virginia
28	Washington
29	Georgia
30	Arizona
31	Nevada
32	Idaho
33	Ohio
34	Maryland
35	California
36	Mississippi
37	Missouri
38	Minnesota
39	Tennessee
40	Utah
41	Delaware
42	North Carolina
43	West Virginia
44	Oklahoma
45	Kentucky
46	Louisiana
47	New Mexico
48	Alabama
49	Arkansas
50	Hawaii

Note: Numbers that appear to be identical are rounded and vary slightly in actual value. The rankings reflect the actual values before rounding. See the introduction for more details.

State	State and local sales taxes $ (in millions)	State and local taxes as a percentage of personal income	Rank by percentage
Alabama	5,217	4.41	17
Alaska	358	1.66	47
Arizona	7,989	5.32	8
Arkansas	3,714	5.61	5
California	45,193	3.81	27
Colorado	5,390	3.43	39
Connecticut	4,900	3.25	41
Delaware	394	1.45	49
Florida	27,408	5.37	7
Georgia	9,423	3.71	30
Hawaii	2,606	6.77	1
Idaho	1,427	4.08	20
Illinois	15,344	3.65	33
Indiana	6,992	3.92	24
Iowa	3,012	3.60	34
Kansas	3,427	4.26	18
Kentucky	4,313	3.97	22
Louisiana	7,239	6.18	4
Maine	1,337	3.54	36
Maryland	5,456	2.65	44
Massachusetts	5,740	2.26	45
Michigan	11,066	3.52	37
Minnesota	6,564	3.81	28
Mississippi	3,459	5.14	10
Missouri	6,695	4.03	21
Montana	440	1.86	46
Nebraska	2,334	4.42	16
Nevada	4,568	6.47	2
New Hampshire	674	1.51	48
New Jersey	9,780	2.83	43
New Mexico	2,628	5.50	6
New York	27,397	3.93	23
North Carolina	8,951	3.76	29
North Dakota	742	4.11	19
Ohio	12,318	3.60	35
Oklahoma	3,639	3.90	25
Oregon	1,014	0.99	50
Pennsylvania	12,918	3.29	40
Rhode Island	1,311	3.81	26
South Carolina	4,012	3.70	31
South Dakota	1,071	4.95	11
Tennessee	8,846	5.30	9
Texas	29,656	4.61	14
Utah	2,770	4.67	13
Vermont	693	3.67	32
Virginia	7,249	2.92	42
Washington	12,999	6.37	3
West Virginia	2,150	4.81	12
Wisconsin	5,915	3.52	38
Wyoming	734	4.54	15
50 States	359,476	3.94	
DC	1,153	4.33	
United States	360,629	3.94	

Rank in order by percentage	
1	Hawaii
2	Nevada
3	Washington
4	Louisiana
5	Arkansas
6	New Mexico
7	Florida
8	Arizona
9	Tennessee
10	Mississippi
11	South Dakota
12	West Virginia
13	Utah
14	Texas
15	Wyoming
16	Nebraska
17	Alabama
18	Kansas
19	North Dakota
20	Idaho
21	Missouri
22	Kentucky
23	New York
24	Indiana
25	Oklahoma
26	Rhode Island
27	California
28	Minnesota
29	North Carolina
30	Georgia
31	South Carolina
32	Vermont
33	Illinois
34	Iowa
35	Ohio
36	Maine
37	Michigan
38	Wisconsin
39	Colorado
40	Pennsylvania
41	Connecticut
42	Virginia
43	New Jersey
44	Maryland
45	Massachusetts
46	Montana
47	Alaska
48	New Hampshire
49	Delaware
50	Oregon

Note: Numbers that appear to be identical are rounded and vary slightly in actual value. The rankings reflect the actual values before rounding. See the introduction for more details.

F-10   Sales Taxes Per Capita, FY 2004

State	Sales taxes per capita $	Rank per capita
Alabama	1,152	27
Alaska	546	46
Arizona	1,391	10
Arkansas	1,349	13
California	1,259	17
Colorado	1,171	23
Connecticut	1,399	9
Delaware	475	49
Florida	1,575	5
Georgia	1,067	34
Hawaii	2,063	2
Idaho	1,024	39
Illinois	1,207	20
Indiana	1,121	29
Iowa	1,019	40
Kansas	1,253	18
Kentucky	1,040	37
Louisiana	1,603	4
Maine	1,015	41
Maryland	982	42
Massachusetts	895	45
Michigan	1,094	31
Minnesota	1,287	16
Mississippi	1,191	21
Missouri	1,163	25
Montana	475	48
Nebraska	1,336	14
Nevada	1,957	3
New Hampshire	519	47
New Jersey	1,124	28
New Mexico	1,381	12
New York	1,425	8
North Carolina	1,048	35
North Dakota	1,170	24
Ohio	1,075	32
Oklahoma	1,033	38
Oregon	282	50
Pennsylvania	1,041	36
Rhode Island	1,213	19
South Carolina	956	44
South Dakota	1,389	11
Tennessee	1,499	6
Texas	1,319	15
Utah	1,160	26
Vermont	1,116	30
Virginia	972	43
Washington	2,095	1
West Virginia	1,184	22
Wisconsin	1,074	33
Wyoming	1,449	7
50 States	1,226	
DC	2,083	
United States	1,228	

Rank in order per capita	
1	Washington
2	Hawaii
3	Nevada
4	Louisiana
5	Florida
6	Tennessee
7	Wyoming
8	New York
9	Connecticut
10	Arizona
11	South Dakota
12	New Mexico
13	Arkansas
14	Nebraska
15	Texas
16	Minnesota
17	California
18	Kansas
19	Rhode Island
20	Illinois
21	Mississippi
22	West Virginia
23	Colorado
24	North Dakota
25	Missouri
26	Utah
27	Alabama
28	New Jersey
29	Indiana
30	Vermont
31	Michigan
32	Ohio
33	Wisconsin
34	Georgia
35	North Carolina
36	Pennsylvania
37	Kentucky
38	Oklahoma
39	Idaho
40	Iowa
41	Maine
42	Maryland
43	Virginia
44	South Carolina
45	Massachusetts
46	Alaska
47	New Hampshire
48	Montana
49	Delaware
50	Oregon

Note: Numbers that appear to be identical are rounded and vary slightly in actual value. The rankings reflect the actual values before rounding. See the introduction for more details.

F-11 Sales Tax Revenue as a Percentage of Three-Tax Revenue, FY 2004

State	Sales taxes as a percentage of three-tax revenue	Rank
Alabama	56.6	10
Alaska	29.4	42
Arizona	52.7	12
Arkansas	57.1	9
California	38.9	29
Colorado	39.8	25
Connecticut	30.6	40
Delaware	23.5	47
Florida	59.7	6
Georgia	39.1	28
Hawaii	58.0	8
Idaho	41.7	22
Illinois	37.9	31
Indiana	40.4	23
Iowa	36.7	33
Kansas	39.9	24
Kentucky	42.8	20
Louisiana	61.9	4
Maine	29.1	43
Maryland	27.6	45
Massachusetts	23.5	46
Michigan	37.6	32
Minnesota	38.2	30
Mississippi	54.2	11
Missouri	44.5	19
Montana	22.0	48
Nebraska	41.8	21
Nevada	68.0	2
New Hampshire	20.8	49
New Jersey	27.6	44
New Mexico	58.7	7
New York	30.3	41
North Carolina	39.7	26
North Dakota	48.2	16
Ohio	34.5	35
Oklahoma	47.9	17
Oregon	11.5	50
Pennsylvania	36.1	34
Rhode Island	33.0	37
South Carolina	39.5	27
South Dakota	60.3	5
Tennessee	70.4	1
Texas	51.3	14
Utah	45.2	18
Vermont	33.4	36
Virginia	32.4	38
Washington	67.1	3
West Virginia	51.2	15
Wisconsin	31.8	39
Wyoming	51.8	13
50 States	40.4	
DC	35.7	
United States	40.3	

Rank in order by percentage

1 Tennessee
2 Nevada
3 Washington
4 Louisiana
5 South Dakota
6 Florida
7 New Mexico
8 Hawaii
9 Arkansas
10 Alabama
11 Mississippi
12 Arizona
13 Wyoming
14 Texas
15 West Virginia
16 North Dakota
17 Oklahoma
18 Utah
19 Missouri
20 Kentucky
21 Nebraska
22 Idaho
23 Indiana
24 Kansas
25 Colorado
26 North Carolina
27 South Carolina
28 Georgia
29 California
30 Minnesota
31 Illinois
32 Michigan
33 Iowa
34 Pennsylvania
35 Ohio
36 Vermont
37 Rhode Island
38 Virginia
39 Wisconsin
40 Connecticut
41 New York
42 Alaska
43 Maine
44 New Jersey
45 Maryland
46 Massachusetts
47 Delaware
48 Montana
49 New Hampshire
50 Oregon

Note: Numbers that appear to be identical are rounded and vary slightly in actual value. The rankings reflect the actual values before rounding. See the introduction for more details.

F-12 Sales Tax Rates and Reach, 2007

State	State sales tax rate 2007 %	Number of services subject to sales tax 2004	Rank by sales tax rate
Alabama	4.00	37	37
Alaska	n/a	1	n/a
Arizona	5.60	58	20
Arkansas	6.00	72	10
California	6.25	23	7
Colorado	2.90	14	45
Connecticut	6.00	80	10
Delaware	n/a	143	n/a
Florida	6.00	64	10
Georgia	4.00	36	37
Hawaii	4.00	160	37
Idaho	5.00	30	24
Illinois	6.25	17	7
Indiana	6.00	23	10
Iowa	5.00	94	24
Kansas	5.30	71	23
Kentucky	6.00	29	10
Louisiana	4.00	55	37
Maine	5.00	24	24
Maryland	5.00	39	24
Massachusetts	5.00	19	24
Michigan	6.00	26	10
Minnesota	6.50	67	4
Mississippi	7.00	74	1
Missouri	4.23	28	36
Montana	n/a	19	n/a
Nebraska	5.50	76	21
Nevada	6.50	15	4
New Hampshire	n/a	11	n/a
New Jersey	6.00	55	10
New Mexico	5.00	156	24
New York	4.00	56	37
North Carolina	4.50	30	34
North Dakota	5.00	27	24
Ohio	5.50	68	21
Oklahoma	4.50	32	34
Oregon	n/a	0	n/a
Pennsylvania	6.00	55	10
Rhode Island	7.00	29	1
South Carolina	5.00	34	24
South Dakota	4.00	146	37
Tennessee	7.00	67	1
Texas	6.25	81	7
Utah	4.75	57	33
Vermont	6.00	29	10
Virginia	4.00	18	37
Washington	6.50	157	4
West Virginia	6.00	110	10
Wisconsin	5.00	74	24
Wyoming	4.00	62	37
50 States	n/a	n/a	
DC	5.75	70	
United States	5.60	168	

Rank in order by rate	
1	Mississippi
1	Rhode Island
1	Tennessee
4	Minnesota
4	Nevada
4	Washington
7	California
7	Illinois
7	Texas
10	Arkansas
10	Connecticut
10	Florida
10	Indiana
10	Kentucky
10	Michigan
10	New Jersey
10	Pennsylvania
10	Vermont
10	West Virginia
20	Arizona
21	Nebraska
21	Ohio
23	Kansas
24	Idaho
24	Iowa
24	Maine
24	Maryland
24	Massachusetts
24	New Mexico
24	North Dakota
24	South Carolina
24	Wisconsin
33	Utah
34	North Carolina
34	Oklahoma
36	Missouri
37	Alabama
37	Georgia
37	Hawaii
37	Louisiana
37	New York
37	South Dakota
37	Virginia
37	Wyoming
45	Colorado

Note: Ties in ranking reflect ties in actual values.

F-13   Individual Income Taxes, FY 2004

State	Individual income tax $ (in millions)	Income tax as a percentage of personal income	Rank by percentage
Alabama	2,344	1.98	36
Alaska	0	n/a	n/a
Arizona	2,316	1.54	40
Arkansas	1,688	2.55	22
California	36,399	3.07	11
Colorado	3,414	2.17	32
Connecticut	4,320	2.86	15
Delaware	828	3.04	12
Florida	0	n/a	n/a
Georgia	6,830	2.69	17
Hawaii	1,169	3.04	13
Idaho	908	2.60	20
Illinois	7,218	1.72	38
Indiana	4,232	2.37	28
Iowa	2,011	2.40	25
Kansas	1,916	2.38	27
Kentucky	3,629	3.34	6
Louisiana	2,192	1.87	37
Maine	1,160	3.07	10
Maryland	8,287	4.02	3
Massachusetts	8,830	3.48	5
Michigan	6,362	2.02	35
Minnesota	5,710	3.32	7
Mississippi	1,062	1.58	39
Missouri	4,033	2.43	24
Montana	606	2.56	21
Nebraska	1,243	2.36	29
Nevada	0	n/a	n/a
New Hampshire	55	0.12	42
New Jersey	7,401	2.14	33
New Mexico	1,007	2.11	34
New York	30,745	4.41	1
North Carolina	7,511	3.16	8
North Dakota	214	1.18	41
Ohio	12,183	3.56	4
Oklahoma	2,319	2.49	23
Oregon	4,371	4.26	2
Pennsylvania	10,311	2.63	18
Rhode Island	900	2.62	19
South Carolina	2,439	2.25	31
South Dakota	0	n/a	n/a
Tennessee	140	0.08	43
Texas	0	n/a	n/a
Utah	1,692	2.85	16
Vermont	430	2.27	30
Virginia	7,422	2.99	14
Washington	0	n/a	n/a
West Virginia	1,068	2.39	26
Wisconsin	5,251	3.12	9
Wyoming	0	n/a	n/a
50 States	214,166	2.35	
DC	1,049	3.94	
United States	215,215	2.35	

Rank in order by percentage	
1	New York
2	Oregon
3	Maryland
4	Ohio
5	Massachusetts
6	Kentucky
7	Minnesota
8	North Carolina
9	Wisconsin
10	Maine
11	California
12	Delaware
13	Hawaii
14	Virginia
15	Connecticut
16	Utah
17	Georgia
18	Pennsylvania
19	Rhode Island
20	Idaho
21	Montana
22	Arkansas
23	Oklahoma
24	Missouri
25	Iowa
26	West Virginia
27	Kansas
28	Indiana
29	Nebraska
30	Vermont
31	South Carolina
32	Colorado
33	New Jersey
34	New Mexico
35	Michigan
36	Alabama
37	Louisiana
38	Illinois
39	Mississippi
40	Arizona
41	North Dakota
42	New Hampshire
43	Tennessee

Note: Numbers that appear to be identical are rounded and vary slightly in actual value. The rankings reflect the actual values before rounding. See the introduction for more details.

F-14 Individual Income Taxes Per Capita, FY 2004

State	Income taxes per capita $	Rank per capita
Alabama	517	37
Alaska	0	n/a
Arizona	403	39
Arkansas	613	32
California	1,014	8
Colorado	742	20
Connecticut	1,233	4
Delaware	997	9
Florida	0	n/a
Georgia	774	19
Hawaii	926	12
Idaho	652	30
Illinois	568	35
Indiana	678	27
Iowa	681	26
Kansas	700	24
Kentucky	875	15
Louisiana	485	38
Maine	881	13
Maryland	1,491	2
Massachusetts	1,376	3
Michigan	629	31
Minnesota	1,119	6
Mississippi	366	40
Missouri	701	23
Montana	653	29
Nebraska	711	21
Nevada	0	n/a
New Hampshire	42	42
New Jersey	851	16
New Mexico	529	36
New York	1,599	1
North Carolina	879	14
North Dakota	337	41
Ohio	1,063	7
Oklahoma	658	28
Oregon	1,216	5
Pennsylvania	831	18
Rhode Island	833	17
South Carolina	581	34
South Dakota	0	n/a
Tennessee	24	43
Texas	0	n/a
Utah	708	22
Vermont	692	25
Virginia	995	10
Washington	0	n/a
West Virginia	588	33
Wisconsin	953	11
Wyoming	0	n/a
50 States	731	
DC	1,896	
United States	733	

Rank in order per capita	
1	New York
2	Maryland
3	Massachusetts
4	Connecticut
5	Oregon
6	Minnesota
7	Ohio
8	California
9	Delaware
10	Virginia
11	Wisconsin
12	Hawaii
13	Maine
14	North Carolina
15	Kentucky
16	New Jersey
17	Rhode Island
18	Pennsylvania
19	Georgia
20	Colorado
21	Nebraska
22	Utah
23	Missouri
24	Kansas
25	Vermont
26	Iowa
27	Indiana
28	Oklahoma
29	Montana
30	Idaho
31	Michigan
32	Arkansas
33	West Virginia
34	South Carolina
35	Illinois
36	New Mexico
37	Alabama
38	Louisiana
39	Arizona
40	Mississippi
41	North Dakota
42	New Hampshire
43	Tennessee

F-15 Individual Income Tax Revenue as a Percentage of Three-Tax Revenue, FY 2004

State	Income tax as a percentage of three-tax revenue	Rank
Alabama	25.4	24
Alaska	n/a	n/a
Arizona	15.3	40
Arkansas	26.0	22
California	31.4	11
Colorado	25.2	26
Connecticut	27.0	18
Delaware	49.4	2
Florida	n/a	n/a
Georgia	28.3	15
Hawaii	26.0	21
Idaho	26.6	20
Illinois	17.8	38
Indiana	24.5	28
Iowa	24.5	27
Kansas	22.3	32
Kentucky	36.0	5
Louisiana	18.7	37
Maine	25.2	25
Maryland	41.9	3
Massachusetts	36.2	4
Michigan	21.6	34
Minnesota	33.2	9
Mississippi	16.6	39
Missouri	26.8	19
Montana	30.2	13
Nebraska	22.3	33
Nevada	n/a	n/a
New Hampshire	1.7	42
New Jersey	20.9	35
New Mexico	22.5	31
New York	34.0	7
North Carolina	33.3	8
North Dakota	13.9	41
Ohio	34.1	6
Oklahoma	30.5	12
Oregon	49.4	1
Pennsylvania	28.8	14
Rhode Island	22.7	30
South Carolina	24.0	29
South Dakota	n/a	n/a
Tennessee	1.1	43
Texas	n/a	n/a
Utah	27.6	17
Vermont	20.7	36
Virginia	33.2	10
Washington	n/a	n/a
West Virginia	25.5	23
Wisconsin	28.2	16
Wyoming	n/a	n/a
50 States	24.0	
DC	32.5	
United States	24.1	

Rank in order by percentage	
1	Oregon
2	Delaware
3	Maryland
4	Massachusetts
5	Kentucky
6	Ohio
7	New York
8	North Carolina
9	Minnesota
10	Virginia
11	California
12	Oklahoma
13	Montana
14	Pennsylvania
15	Georgia
16	Wisconsin
17	Utah
18	Connecticut
19	Missouri
20	Idaho
21	Hawaii
22	Arkansas
23	West Virginia
24	Alabama
25	Maine
26	Colorado
27	Iowa
28	Indiana
29	South Carolina
30	Rhode Island
31	New Mexico
32	Kansas
33	Nebraska
34	Michigan
35	New Jersey
36	Vermont
37	Louisiana
38	Illinois
39	Mississippi
40	Arizona
41	North Dakota
42	New Hampshire
43	Tennessee

Note: Numbers that appear to be identical are rounded and vary slightly in actual value. The rankings reflect the actual values before rounding. See the introduction for more details.

F-16 Highest Personal Income Tax Rate, 2006

State	Highest rate %	Rank
Alabama	3.25	39
Alaska	no tax	n/a
Arizona	4.54	32
Arkansas	7.00	11
California	9.30	2
Colorado	4.63	31
Connecticut	5.00	28
Delaware	5.95	21
Florida	no tax	n/a
Georgia	6.00	19
Hawaii	8.25	7
Idaho	7.80	10
Illinois	3.00	41
Indiana	3.40	38
Iowa	5.84	22
Kansas	6.45	18
Kentucky	6.00	19
Louisiana	3.90	35
Maine	8.50	6
Maryland	4.75	30
Massachusetts	5.30	26
Michigan	3.90	35
Minnesota	7.85	9
Mississippi	5.00	28
Missouri	3.90	35
Montana	4.49	33
Nebraska	6.84	15
Nevada	no tax	n/a
New Hampshire	no tax	n/a
New Jersey	8.97	4
New Mexico	5.30	26
New York	6.85	14
North Carolina	8.25	7
North Dakota	5.54	25
Ohio	6.87	13
Oklahoma	4.06	34
Oregon	9.00	3
Pennsylvania	3.07	40
Rhode Island	8.75	5
South Carolina	7.00	11
South Dakota	no tax	n/a
Tennessee	no tax	n/a
Texas	no tax	n/a
Utah	5.78	23
Vermont	9.50	1
Virginia	5.75	24
Washington	no tax	n/a
West Virginia	6.50	17
Wisconsin	6.75	16
Wyoming	no tax	n/a
50 States	n/a	
DC	8.70	
United States	n/a	

Rank in order by percentage

1	Vermont
2	California
3	Oregon
4	New Jersey
5	Rhode Island
6	Maine
7	Hawaii
7	North Carolina
9	Minnesota
10	Idaho
11	Arkansas
11	South Carolina
13	Ohio
14	New York
15	Nebraska
16	Wisconsin
17	West Virginia
18	Kansas
19	Georgia
19	Kentucky
21	Delaware
22	Iowa
23	Utah
24	Virginia
25	North Dakota
26	Massachusetts
26	New Mexico
28	Connecticut
28	Mississippi
30	Maryland
31	Colorado
32	Arizona
33	Montana
34	Oklahoma
35	Louisiana
35	Michigan
35	Missouri
38	Indiana
39	Alabama
40	Pennsylvania
41	Illinois

Note: Ties in ranking reflect ties in actual values.

F-17 Corporate Income Taxes, Total and Per Capita, FY 2004

State	Corporate income taxes $ (in millions)	Corporate income taxes per capita $	Rank per capita
Alabama	292	64	33
Alaska	340	518	1
Arizona	526	92	23
Arkansas	182	66	32
California	6,926	193	7
Colorado	240	52	41
Connecticut	380	108	13
Delaware	218	262	4
Florida	1,441	83	27
Georgia	495	56	39
Hawaii	58	46	43
Idaho	104	74	29
Illinois	1,279	101	16
Indiana	645	103	14
Iowa	90	30	46
Kansas	167	61	36
Kentucky	382	92	22
Louisiana	237	52	40
Maine	112	85	25
Maryland	570	102	15
Massachusetts	1,301	203	6
Michigan	1,841	182	8
Minnesota	637	125	10
Mississippi	244	84	26
Missouri	224	39	44
Montana	68	73	30
Nebraska	167	96	20
Nevada	0	n/a	n/a
New Hampshire	408	314	2
New Jersey	1,897	218	5
New Mexico	138	73	31
New York	5,363	279	3
North Carolina	837	98	19
North Dakota	50	79	28
Ohio	1,061	93	21
Oklahoma	133	38	45
Oregon	320	89	24
Pennsylvania	1,678	135	9
Rhode Island	69	64	34
South Carolina	197	47	42
South Dakota	47	61	35
Tennessee	695	118	12
Texas	0	n/a	n/a
Utah	145	61	37
Vermont	62	100	17
Virginia	422	57	38
Washington	0	n/a	n/a
West Virginia	182	100	18
Wisconsin	682	124	11
Wyoming	0	n/a	n/a
50 States	33,548	114	
DC	168	304	
United States	33,716	115	

Rank in order per capita

1 Alaska
2 New Hampshire
3 New York
4 Delaware
5 New Jersey
6 Massachusetts
7 California
8 Michigan
9 Pennsylvania
10 Minnesota
11 Wisconsin
12 Tennessee
13 Connecticut
14 Indiana
15 Maryland
16 Illinois
17 Vermont
18 West Virginia
19 North Carolina
20 Nebraska
21 Ohio
22 Kentucky
23 Arizona
24 Oregon
25 Maine
26 Mississippi
27 Florida
28 North Dakota
29 Idaho
30 Montana
31 New Mexico
32 Arkansas
33 Alabama
34 Rhode Island
35 South Dakota
36 Kansas
37 Utah
38 Virginia
39 Georgia
40 Louisiana
41 Colorado
42 South Carolina
43 Hawaii
44 Missouri
45 Oklahoma
46 Iowa

Note: Numbers that appear to be identical are rounded and vary slightly in actual value. The rankings reflect the actual values before rounding. See the introduction for more details.

F-18 Motor Fuel Taxes

State	Gasoline tax 2006 cents/gallons	Motor fuel taxes FY 2004 $ (in millions)	Fuel taxes as a percentage of personal income	Rank by gas tax
Alabama	18.00	583	0.49	37
Alaska	8.00	41	0.19	50
Arizona	18.00	672	0.45	37
Arkansas	21.50	453	0.68	23
California	18.00	3,325	0.28	37
Colorado	22.00	598	0.38	21
Connecticut	25.00	457	0.30	11
Delaware	23.00	112	0.41	19
Florida	14.90	2,688	0.53	47
Georgia	15.30	756	0.30	46
Hawaii	16.00	158	0.41	44
Idaho	25.00	218	0.62	11
Illinois	20.10	1,596	0.38	27
Indiana	18.00	802	0.45	37
Iowa	20.70	429	0.51	26
Kansas	24.00	434	0.54	15
Kentucky	18.50	477	0.44	35
Louisiana	20.00	561	0.48	28
Maine	25.90	220	0.58	10
Maryland	23.50	746	0.36	18
Massachusetts	21.00	684	0.27	25
Michigan	19.00	1,081	0.34	33
Minnesota	20.00	648	0.38	28
Mississippi	18.40	469	0.70	36
Missouri	17.55	728	0.44	41
Montana	27.00	198	0.84	7
Nebraska	27.00	303	0.57	7
Nevada	24.80	441	0.62	13
New Hampshire	19.63	130	0.29	32
New Jersey	14.50	547	0.16	48
New Mexico	18.90	211	0.44	34
New York	23.90	519	0.07	17
North Carolina	30.15	1,273	0.53	5
North Dakota	23.00	119	0.66	19
Ohio	28.00	1,548	0.45	6
Oklahoma	17.00	415	0.45	43
Oregon	24.00	414	0.40	15
Pennsylvania	31.20	1,785	0.46	3
Rhode Island	31.00	133	0.39	4
South Carolina	16.00	489	0.45	44
South Dakota	22.00	126	0.58	21
Tennessee	21.40	832	0.50	24
Texas	20.00	2,919	0.45	28
Utah	24.50	342	0.58	14
Vermont	20.00	86	0.45	28
Virginia	17.50	909	0.37	42
Washington	34.00	926	0.45	1
West Virginia	27.00	309	0.69	7
Wisconsin	32.90	936	0.56	2
Wyoming	14.00	70	0.43	49
50 States	n/a	34,917	0.38	
DC	22.50	27	0.10	
United States	n/a	34,944	0.38	

Rank in order by gas tax

1	Washington
2	Wisconsin
3	Pennsylvania
4	Rhode Island
5	North Carolina
6	Ohio
7	Montana
7	Nebraska
7	West Virginia
10	Maine
11	Connecticut
11	Idaho
13	Nevada
14	Utah
15	Kansas
15	Oregon
17	New York
18	Maryland
19	Delaware
19	North Dakota
21	Colorado
21	South Dakota
23	Arkansas
24	Tennessee
25	Massachusetts
26	Iowa
27	Illinois
28	Louisiana
28	Minnesota
28	Texas
28	Vermont
32	New Hampshire
33	Michigan
34	New Mexico
35	Kentucky
36	Mississippi
37	Alabama
37	Arizona
37	California
37	Indiana
41	Missouri
42	Virginia
43	Oklahoma
44	Hawaii
44	South Carolina
46	Georgia
47	Florida
48	New Jersey
49	Wyoming
50	Alaska

Note: Ties in ranking reflect ties in actual values.

F-19 Motor Vehicle Fees and Taxes, 2006

State	Motor vehicle registration fees $	Motor vehicle sales and excise taxes %	Rank by registration fees
Alabama	23.00	2.00	36
Alaska	50.00	n/a	10
Arizona	8.00	5.60	49
Arkansas	25.00	6.00	31
California	30.00	6.00	24
Colorado	28.74	2.90	28
Connecticut	35.00	6.00	19
Delaware	20.00	2.75	40
Florida	32.50	6.00	22
Georgia	20.00	4.00	40
Hawaii	46.42	4.00	12
Idaho	48.00	5.00	11
Illinois	78.00	6.25	6
Indiana	12.00	5.00	46
Iowa	93.00	5.00	2
Kansas	25.00	4.90	31
Kentucky	12.00	6.00	46
Louisiana	26.50	4.00	30
Maine	25.00	5.00	31
Maryland	64.00	5.00	7
Massachusetts	25.00	5.00	31
Michigan	n/a	6.00	n/a
Minnesota	108.75	6.50	1
Mississippi	15.00	5.00	43
Missouri	39.00	4.23	17
Montana	22.00	n/a	38
Nebraska	15.00	5.50	43
Nevada	33.00	6.50	21
New Hampshire	31.20	n/a	23
New Jersey	81.00	6.00	4
New Mexico	42.00	3.00	14
New York	22.50	4.00	37
North Carolina	20.00	3.00	40
North Dakota	79.00	5.00	5
Ohio	39.50	6.00	16
Oklahoma	93.00	3.25	2
Oregon	27.00	n/a	29
Pennsylvania	36.00	6.00	18
Rhode Island	30.00	7.00	24
South Carolina	12.00	5.00	46
South Dakota	42.00	3.00	14
Tennessee	21.50	7.00	39
Texas	59.80	6.25	8
Utah	24.50	4.75	35
Vermont	43.00	6.00	13
Virginia	29.50	3.00	27
Washington	33.75	6.80	20
West Virginia	30.00	5.00	24
Wisconsin	55.00	5.00	9
Wyoming	15.00	3.00	43
50 States	n/a	n/a	
DC	115.00	6.00	
United States	n/a	n/a	

Rank in order by $	
1	Minnesota
2	Iowa
2	Oklahoma
4	New Jersey
5	North Dakota
6	Illinois
7	Maryland
8	Texas
9	Wisconsin
10	Alaska
11	Idaho
12	Hawaii
13	Vermont
14	New Mexico
14	South Dakota
16	Ohio
17	Missouri
18	Pennsylvania
19	Connecticut
20	Washington
21	Nevada
22	Florida
23	New Hampshire
24	California
24	Rhode Island
24	West Virginia
27	Virginia
28	Colorado
29	Oregon
30	Louisiana
31	Arkansas
31	Kansas
31	Maine
31	Massachusetts
35	Utah
36	Alabama
37	New York
38	Montana
39	Tennessee
40	Delaware
40	Georgia
40	North Carolina
43	Mississippi
43	Nebraska
43	Wyoming
46	Indiana
46	Kentucky
46	South Carolina
49	Arizona

Note: Ties in ranking reflect ties in actual values.

F-20 Tobacco Taxes

State	Cigarette tax rate 2006 cents/pack	Tobacco taxes FY 2004 $ (in millions)	Tobacco taxes as a percentage of personal income	Rank by tax rate
Alabama	42.5	110.4	0.09	38
Alaska	160.0	48.8	0.23	7
Arizona	118.0	274.7	0.18	16
Arkansas	59.0	146.5	0.22	31
California	87.0	1,081.6	0.09	22
Colorado	84.0	65.1	0.04	23
Connecticut	151.0	277.3	0.18	8
Delaware	55.0	75.5	0.28	34
Florida	33.9	449.4	0.09	43
Georgia	37.0	227.3	0.09	40
Hawaii	140.0	79.4	0.21	11
Idaho	57.0	52.3	0.15	32
Illinois	98.0	815.4	0.19	20
Indiana	55.5	338.7	0.19	33
Iowa	36.0	94.3	0.11	41
Kansas	79.0	124.6	0.15	26
Kentucky	30.0	20.6	0.02	44
Louisiana	36.0	101.0	0.09	41
Maine	200.0	92.6	0.25	4
Maryland	100.0	272.1	0.13	19
Massachusetts	151.0	425.4	0.17	8
Michigan	200.0	998.9	0.32	4
Minnesota	123.0	190.1	0.11	14
Mississippi	18.0	55.6	0.08	48
Missouri	17.0	125.7	0.08	49
Montana	170.0	45.2	0.19	6
Nebraska	64.0	71.2	0.14	29
Nevada	80.0	129.1	0.18	24
New Hampshire	80.0	100.0	0.22	24
New Jersey	240.0	777.5	0.23	2
New Mexico	91.0	52.7	0.11	21
New York	150.0	1,148.4	0.16	10
North Carolina	30.0	43.7	0.02	44
North Dakota	44.0	21.2	0.12	37
Ohio	125.0	561.9	0.16	13
Oklahoma	103.0	63.4	0.07	18
Oregon	118.0	265.3	0.26	16
Pennsylvania	135.0	981.3	0.25	12
Rhode Island	246.0	115.5	0.34	1
South Carolina	7.0	29.7	0.03	50
South Dakota	53.0	27.6	0.13	36
Tennessee	20.0	119.5	0.07	47
Texas	41.0	534.6	0.08	39
Utah	69.5	61.7	0.10	28
Vermont	119.0	51.2	0.27	15
Virginia	30.0	74.7	0.03	44
Washington	202.5	352.5	0.17	3
West Virginia	55.0	107.6	0.24	34
Wisconsin	77.0	307.4	0.18	27
Wyoming	60.0	18.6	0.11	30
50 States	n/a	12,605.0	0.14	
DC	100.0	20.8	0.08	
United States	n/a	12,625.8	0.14	

Rank in order by tax rate

1	Rhode Island
2	New Jersey
3	Washington
4	Maine
4	Michigan
6	Montana
7	Alaska
8	Connecticut
8	Massachusetts
10	New York
11	Hawaii
12	Pennsylvania
13	Ohio
14	Minnesota
15	Vermont
16	Arizona
16	Oregon
18	Oklahoma
19	Maryland
20	Illinois
21	New Mexico
22	California
23	Colorado
24	Nevada
24	New Hampshire
26	Kansas
27	Wisconsin
28	Utah
29	Nebraska
30	Wyoming
31	Arkansas
32	Idaho
33	Indiana
34	Delaware
34	West Virginia
36	South Dakota
37	North Dakota
38	Alabama
39	Texas
40	Georgia
41	Iowa
41	Louisiana
43	Florida
44	Kentucky
44	North Carolina
44	Virginia
47	Tennessee
48	Mississippi
49	Missouri
50	South Carolina

Note: Ties in ranking reflect ties in actual values.

F-21 State and Local Taxes on High-Income Families, 2005

State	Taxes for family with $150,000/year income $	Percentage of income	Rank by $
Alabama	11,185	7.5	35
Alaska	4,274	2.8	50
Arizona	9,953	6.6	40
Arkansas	13,358	8.9	23
California	14,895	9.9	11
Colorado	10,379	6.9	39
Connecticut	19,754	13.2	1
Delaware	11,754	7.8	32
Florida	5,749	3.8	48
Georgia	14,328	9.6	17
Hawaii	10,583	7.1	37
Idaho	13,866	9.2	21
Illinois	11,623	7.7	33
Indiana	14,517	9.7	14
Iowa	16,083	10.7	5
Kansas	12,218	8.1	29
Kentucky	14,907	9.9	10
Louisiana	11,482	7.7	34
Maine	15,555	10.4	6
Maryland	15,129	10.1	7
Massachusetts	13,143	8.8	25
Michigan	14,714	9.8	12
Minnesota	13,926	9.3	20
Mississippi	13,633	9.1	22
Missouri	14,077	9.4	18
Montana	10,428	7.0	38
Nebraska	14,484	9.7	15
Nevada	5,994	4.0	47
New Hampshire	9,903	6.6	41
New Jersey	12,735	8.5	27
New Mexico	11,103	7.4	36
New York	17,911	11.9	2
North Carolina	13,953	9.3	19
North Dakota	9,445	6.3	42
Ohio	15,052	10.0	9
Oklahoma	12,428	8.3	28
Oregon	15,060	10.0	8
Pennsylvania	16,645	11.1	3
Rhode Island	16,614	11.1	4
South Carolina	13,331	8.9	24
South Dakota	7,153	4.8	45
Tennessee	6,685	4.5	46
Texas	7,222	4.8	44
Utah	12,038	8.0	30
Vermont	14,693	9.8	13
Virginia	11,788	7.9	31
Washington	7,707	5.1	43
West Virginia	13,008	8.7	26
Wisconsin	14,345	9.6	16
Wyoming	4,983	3.3	49
50 States	n/a	n/a	
DC	15,649	10.4	
United States	12,381	8.3	

Rank in order by $	
1	Connecticut
2	New York
3	Pennsylvania
4	Rhode Island
5	Iowa
6	Maine
7	Maryland
8	Oregon
9	Ohio
10	Kentucky
11	California
12	Michigan
13	Vermont
14	Indiana
15	Nebraska
16	Wisconsin
17	Georgia
18	Missouri
19	North Carolina
20	Minnesota
21	Idaho
22	Mississippi
23	Arkansas
24	South Carolina
25	Massachusetts
26	West Virginia
27	New Jersey
28	Oklahoma
29	Kansas
30	Utah
31	Virginia
32	Delaware
33	Illinois
34	Louisiana
35	Alabama
36	New Mexico
37	Hawaii
38	Montana
39	Colorado
40	Arizona
41	New Hampshire
42	North Dakota
43	Washington
44	Texas
45	South Dakota
46	Tennessee
47	Nevada
48	Florida
49	Wyoming
50	Alaska

F-22 State and Local Taxes in the Largest City in Each State, 2005

State	Taxes for family with $50,000/year income $	Percentage of income	Rank by $
Alabama	3,598	7.2	34
Alaska	2,525	5.0	47
Arizona	3,690	7.4	33
Arkansas	3,815	7.6	31
California	4,955	9.9	14
Colorado	3,455	6.9	38
Connecticut	11,327	22.7	1
Delaware	3,782	7.6	32
Florida	2,344	4.7	48
Georgia	4,465	8.9	22
Hawaii	2,177	4.4	50
Idaho	3,848	7.7	28
Illinois	5,277	10.6	10
Indiana	6,113	12.2	6
Iowa	5,001	10.0	13
Kansas	3,181	6.4	43
Kentucky	4,750	9.5	17
Louisiana	3,511	7.0	36
Maine	4,627	9.3	19
Maryland	5,020	10.0	12
Massachusetts	5,878	11.8	7
Michigan	5,571	11.1	8
Minnesota	4,646	9.3	18
Mississippi	4,416	8.8	23
Missouri	4,488	9.0	21
Montana	2,917	5.8	46
Nebraska	4,385	8.8	24
Nevada	3,116	6.2	44
New Hampshire	6,399	12.8	5
New Jersey	6,425	12.9	4
New Mexico	3,506	7.0	37
New York	4,751	9.5	16
North Carolina	4,235	8.5	26
North Dakota	3,300	6.6	40
Ohio	4,793	9.6	15
Oklahoma	3,561	7.1	35
Oregon	4,317	8.6	25
Pennsylvania	6,838	13.7	2
Rhode Island	6,438	12.9	3
South Carolina	3,234	6.5	42
South Dakota	3,311	6.6	39
Tennessee	3,095	6.2	45
Texas	3,277	6.6	41
Utah	3,842	7.7	30
Vermont	5,463	10.9	9
Virginia	3,843	7.7	29
Washington	4,495	9.0	20
West Virginia	3,906	7.8	27
Wisconsin	5,127	10.3	11
Wyoming	2,208	4.4	49
50 States	n/a	n/a	
DC	4,076	8.2	
United States	4,379	8.8	

Rank in order by $	
1	Connecticut
2	Pennsylvania
3	Rhode Island
4	New Jersey
5	New Hampshire
6	Indiana
7	Massachusetts
8	Michigan
9	Vermont
10	Illinois
11	Wisconsin
12	Maryland
13	Iowa
14	California
15	Ohio
16	New York
17	Kentucky
18	Minnesota
19	Maine
20	Washington
21	Missouri
22	Georgia
23	Mississippi
24	Nebraska
25	Oregon
26	North Carolina
27	West Virginia
28	Idaho
29	Virginia
30	Utah
31	Arkansas
32	Delaware
33	Arizona
34	Alabama
35	Oklahoma
36	Louisiana
37	New Mexico
38	Colorado
39	South Dakota
40	North Dakota
41	Texas
42	South Carolina
43	Kansas
44	Nevada
45	Tennessee
46	Montana
47	Alaska
48	Florida
49	Wyoming
50	Hawaii

F-23 Progressivity of Major State and Local Taxes, 2005

State	Progressivity index %	Rank by most progressive to least
Alabama	174.5	42
Alaska	312.5	50
Arizona	174.0	41
Arkansas	139.4	29
California	109.4	12
Colorado	166.8	38
Connecticut	77.1	1
Delaware	132.1	24
Florida	255.1	48
Georgia	135.6	27
Hawaii	174.0	40
Idaho	101.6	9
Illinois	168.8	39
Indiana	127.6	19
Iowa	96.7	5
Kansas	119.3	13
Kentucky	130.9	21
Louisiana	145.2	33
Maine	94.2	3
Maryland	88.3	2
Massachusetts	142.9	32
Michigan	140.5	30
Minnesota	131.9	23
Mississippi	120.8	14
Missouri	132.1	25
Montana	105.5	10
Nebraska	109.3	11
Nevada	248.0	46
New Hampshire	141.4	31
New Jersey	125.5	18
New Mexico	133.3	26
New York	97.7	6
North Carolina	130.5	20
North Dakota	131.6	22
Ohio	124.9	17
Oklahoma	146.5	34
Oregon	121.8	15
Pennsylvania	148.9	35
Rhode Island	99.7	8
South Carolina	123.5	16
South Dakota	195.1	43
Tennessee	250.2	47
Texas	205.2	44
Utah	151.4	36
Vermont	94.3	4
Virginia	152.9	37
Washington	220.6	45
West Virginia	138.3	28
Wisconsin	98.0	7
Wyoming	281.4	49
50 States	n/a	
DC	120.8	
United States	146.8	

	Rank in order by percentage
1	Connecticut
2	Maryland
3	Maine
4	Vermont
5	Iowa
6	New York
7	Wisconsin
8	Rhode Island
9	Idaho
10	Montana
11	Nebraska
12	California
13	Kansas
14	Mississippi
15	Oregon
16	South Carolina
17	Ohio
18	New Jersey
19	Indiana
20	North Carolina
21	Kentucky
22	North Dakota
23	Minnesota
24	Delaware
25	Missouri
26	New Mexico
27	Georgia
28	West Virginia
29	Arkansas
30	Michigan
31	New Hampshire
32	Massachusetts
33	Louisiana
34	Oklahoma
35	Pennsylvania
36	Utah
37	Virginia
38	Colorado
39	Illinois
40	Hawaii
41	Arizona
42	Alabama
43	South Dakota
44	Texas
45	Washington
46	Nevada
47	Tennessee
48	Florida
49	Wyoming
50	Alaska

Note: Numbers that appear to be identical are rounded and vary slightly in actual value. The rankings reflect the actual values before rounding. See the introduction for more details.

F-24 State Estate Taxes, 2006

State	Type of state estate tax 2006	Estate, inheritance, and gift taxes as a percentage of total tax revenues 2005	Rank by percentage
Alabama	Phased out	0.19	43
Alaska	Phased out	0.08	48
Arizona	Phased out	0.30	31
Arkansas	Phased out	0.21	41
California	Phased out	0.22	39
Colorado	Phased out	0.30	31
Connecticut	Inheritance/Estate	2.29	2
Delaware	Phased out	0.23	38
Florida	Phased out	0.87	15
Georgia	Phased out	0.27	35
Hawaii	Phased out	0.29	34
Idaho	Phased out	0.30	31
Illinois	Decoupled	1.14	9
Indiana	Inheritance/Estate	1.12	10
Iowa	Inheritance/Estate	1.34	7
Kansas	Inheritance/Estate	0.93	14
Kentucky	Inheritance/Estate	0.69	21
Louisiana	Phased out	0.35	29
Maine	Decoupled	1.05	12
Maryland	Decoupled	1.36	6
Massachusetts	Decoupled	1.42	5
Michigan	Phased out	0.43	23
Minnesota	Decoupled	0.43	23
Mississippi	Phased out	0.21	41
Missouri	Phased out	0.41	25
Montana	Phased out	0.22	39
Nebraska	Decoupled	0.36	28
Nevada	Phased out	0.41	25
New Hampshire	Phased out	0.56	22
New Jersey	Decoupled	2.27	3
New Mexico	Phased out	0.11	46
New York	Decoupled	1.79	4
North Carolina	Decoupled	0.83	20
North Dakota	Phased out	0.15	45
Ohio	Inheritance/Estate	0.25	37
Oklahoma	Inheritance/Estate	1.10	11
Oregon	Decoupled	0.87	15
Pennsylvania	Inheritance/Estate	2.55	1
Rhode Island	Decoupled	1.23	8
South Carolina	Phased out	0.26	36
South Dakota	Phased out	0.40	27
Tennessee	Inheritance/Estate	0.86	17
Texas	Phased out	0.31	30
Utah	Phased out	0.06	49
Vermont	Decoupled	0.84	18
Virginia	Decoupled	0.94	13
Washington	Inheritance/Estate	0.00	50
West Virginia	Phased out	0.11	46
Wisconsin	Decoupled	0.84	18
Wyoming	Phased out	0.18	44
50 States	n/a	n/a	
DC	Decoupled	n/a	
United States	n/a	0.68	

Rank in order by percentage	
1	Pennsylvania
2	Connecticut
3	New Jersey
4	New York
5	Massachusetts
6	Maryland
7	Iowa
8	Rhode Island
9	Illinois
10	Indiana
11	Oklahoma
12	Maine
13	Virginia
14	Kansas
15	Florida
15	Oregon
17	Tennessee
18	Vermont
18	Wisconsin
20	North Carolina
21	Kentucky
22	New Hampshire
23	Michigan
23	Minnesota
25	Missouri
25	Nevada
27	South Dakota
28	Nebraska
29	Louisiana
30	Texas
31	Arizona
31	Colorado
31	Idaho
34	Hawaii
35	Georgia
36	South Carolina
37	Ohio
38	Delaware
39	California
39	Montana
41	Arkansas
41	Mississippi
43	Alabama
44	Wyoming
45	North Dakota
46	New Mexico
46	West Virginia
48	Alaska
49	Utah
50	Washington

Note: Ties in ranking reflect ties in actual values.

State	Exclusion for state and local pension $	Exclusion for federal civilian pension $	Exclusion for military pension $	Exclusion for Social Security $	Exclusion for private pension $
Alabama	full	full	full	full	varies
Alaska	n/a	n/a	n/a	n/a	n/a
Arizona	2,500	2,500	2,500	full	none
Arkansas	6,000	6,000	6,000	full	6,000
California	none	none	none	full	none
Colorado	20,000–24,000	20,000–24,000	20,000–24,000	20,000–24,000	20,000–24,000
Connecticut	none	none	none	income threshold	none
Delaware	2,000–12,500	2,000–12,500	2,000–12,500	full	2,000–12,500
Florida	n/a	n/a	n/a	n/a	n/a
Georgia	25,000	255,000	25,000	full	25,000
Hawaii	full	full	full	full	varies
Idaho	none–21,900*	none–21,900*	none–21,900*	full	none
Illinois	full	full	full	full	varies
Indiana	none	2,000*	2,000	full	none
Iowa	6,000	6,000	6,000	income threshold	6,000
Kansas	full	full	full	taxed at fed level	none
Kentucky	up to 41,110	up to 41,410	up to 41,410	income threshold	up to 41,410
Louisiana	full	full	full	full	6,000
Maine	6,000*	6,000*	6,000*	full	6,000*
Maryland	21,500*	21,500*	21,500*	full	21,500*
Massachusetts	full	full	full	full	none
Michigan	full	full	full	full	38,550
Minnesota	none	none	none	taxed at fed level	none
Mississippi	full	full	full	full	varies
Missouri	6,000 or under	6,000 or under	6,000 or under	taxed at fed level	4,000
Montana	up to 3,600	up to 3,600	up to 3,600	income threshold	up to 3,600
Nebraska	none	none	none	taxed at fed level	none
Nevada	n/a	n/a	n/a	n/a	n/a
New Hampshire	n/a	n/a	n/a	n/a	n/a
New Jersey	15,000	15,000	full	full	15,000
New Mexico	none–10,000	none–10,000	none–10,000	none–10,000	none–10,000
New York	full	full	full	full	20,000
North Carolina	4,000	4,000	4,000	full	2,000
North Dakota	none–5,000*	5,000*	5,000*	taxed at fed level	none
Ohio	200 credit	200 credit	200 credit	full	200 credit
Oklahoma	50% or 10,000	50% or 10,000	50% or 10,000	full	50% or 10,000
Oregon	9% credit	9% credit	9% credit	full	9% credit
Pennsylvania	full	full	full	full	full
Rhode Island	none	none	none	taxed at fed level	none
South Carolina	3,000–10,000	3,000–10,000	3,000–10,000	full	3,000–10,000
South Dakota	n/a	n/a	n/a	n/a	n/a
Tennessee	n/a	n/a	n/a	n/a	n/a
Texas	n/a	n/a	n/a	n/a	n/a
Utah	4,800–7,500	4,800–7,500	4,800–7,500	4,800–7,500	4,800–7,500
Vermont	none	none	none	taxed at fed level	none
Virginia	12,000	12,000	12,000	full	12,000
Washington	n/a	n/a	n/a	n/a	n/a
West Virginia	2,000–full	2,000	22,000	taxed at fed level	none
Wisconsin	none	none	full	50% exempt	none
Wyoming	n/a	n/a	n/a	n/a	n/a
50 States	n/a	n/a	n/a	n/a	n/a
DC	3,000	3,000	3,000	full	none
United States	n/a	n/a	n/a	n/a	n/a

reduced by the amount of Social Security received

Source Notes for Taxes (Section F)

F-1 State and Local Tax Revenue, Total and as a Percentage of Personal Income, FY 2004: This is the most common definition of the tax burdens of state and local governments. It is the tax component of "general revenue" used by the U.S. Census Bureau in its annual survey of government finances. It excludes taxes used to finance certain trust funds, such as unemployment insurance taxes, but includes other earmarked revenues, such as gasoline tax revenues for highway construction. Tax revenues are related to personal income as a common proxy for tax base or "ability to pay."

For decades, state officials, media, scholars, taxpayer groups, and others have been comparing tax burdens and spending patterns of states using data published by the U.S. Census Bureau in its annual volume *Governmental Finances*. These data were also republished in many secondary sources such as *Significant Features of Fiscal Federalism*, published by the Advisory Commission on Intergovernmental Relations; *Statistical Abstract of the United States*, published by the U.S. Census Bureau and U.S. Government Printing Office; and other secondary sources.

The bureau and other federal statistical agencies have been responding to tight budgets by limiting the number of their printed publications and analyses, both statistical and narrative, of the data they produce. This has allowed them to concentrate their resources on what only they can do—collecting and refining the underlying data. Beginning with the data for 1993, the bureau has stopped publishing state and local fiscal data in printed reports such as *Governmental Finances*, making them available only electronically. Also the bureau has discontinued making popular analytical calculations such as those comparing taxes and spending with personal income and population. This change and budget restrictions have eliminated some secondary sources, such as *Significant Features*.

Anyone with access to the Internet, computer capability, and the ability to unzip and download the Census data can make calculations such as taxes as a percentage of personal income and per capita spending on particular state and/or local functions. However, not everyone has these capabilities, and those that do can produce different data unless they are careful to follow particular complex conventions covering such matters as which concepts of taxing and spending to use, which revision of often-revised government data to use, and which years of population and personal income estimates to use.

No government agency, including the U.S. Census Bureau, will certify the resulting differing numbers as the appropriate ones or vouch for their accuracy in applying past concepts for calculating them. However, many users will demand that comparative numbers be consistent from user to user, from year to year, and from state to state. As a result, some publications are becoming more authoritative than others. Congressional Quarterly Inc., in conjunction with State Policy Research, is committed to publishing these comparative data annually in such widely used publications as *State Fact Finder, State Policy Reports*, and *Governing* magazine. It is likely that these sources, which are using identical data, will become the standard sources for most users.

All of the tables in *State Fact Finder* that rely on U.S. Census Bureau data covering government finances in 2004 use the same conventions, based on past practices of the bureau. The underlying data on tax revenues and spending come from the bureau Web site (www.census.gov). These data reflect fiscal information for varying government fiscal years ending in 2004, which for most states is a fiscal year ending on June 30, 2004, and for many local governments is a fiscal year ending on December 31, 2004.

Following the historical practice of the bureau not to use revised personal income and population numbers, the personal income numbers used for comparison with these fiscal data are calendar year data for 2003 representing the original 2001 estimates released by the Bureau of Economic Analysis. The population data used to calculate per capita amounts are estimates for July 1, 2004, as originally released by the bureau in 2005.

The data on tax burdens and spending in relation to personal income and per capita are comparable with those of prior years, as published by the U.S. Census Bureau and secondary sources, to exactly the degree that bureau data for earlier years have been comparable. Data for any year are not recalculated. While underlying data on government revenues and spending are not normally revised, the U.S. Census Bureau and Bureau of Economic Analysis do re-estimate historical estimates of population and personal income.

F-2 Per Capita State and Local Tax Revenue, FY 2004: This table relates total tax revenue to population, providing another measure of relative tax burdens (see Table F-1). It also shows the division of tax revenues between state and local governments in each state.

F-3 State and Local Tax Effort, FY 2002: The revenue-raising ability of states and their local governments varies markedly among the states. For example, Alaska and Texas get massive revenues by taxing oil and gas, and Nevada gets large revenues from taxing casino gambling, but most states get no revenue from these sources. What states will collect from particular tax rates applied to property, sales, and income is higher in states with more affluent citizens. Because of these differences, the revenue collected (see Tables F-1 and F-2) is not a good indicator of how high tax rates are in each state.

A more appropriate way to compare the relative burden of state and local taxes, or what is often called "tax effort," is to consider what each state would raise if it and its local governments applied national average tax rates to their own tax bases. Unfortunately, this methodology, known as the "representative tax system," is tedious and expensive to apply. The Advisory Commission on Intergovernmental Relations historically did this work but stopped with the 1991 calculations. The commission was phased out in 1996, and no one had stepped forward to do the work until recently, when a report, based on the fiscal year 1994 U.S. Census Bureau data on state and local finances, was issued by the Federal Reserve Bank of Boston. Robert Tannenwald, the author of that report and assistant vice president and economist at the Federal Reserve Bank of Boston, has published subsequent updates. The latest, created in partnership with the Tax Policy Center, covers fiscal year 2002. *Measuring Fiscal Disparities across the U.S. States: A Representative Revenue System/Representative Expenditure System Approach Fiscal Year 2002* is the source for the tax effort statistics shown in this table.

The values reflect differences in tax effort. For example, New York state and local governments have taxes that raise 34 percent more than would be raised if tax rates in that state were equal to the national average.

While the best available data on tax effort and tax capacity are those appearing in Tables F-3 and F-4, they must be used with caution. For states which are quite close to the national average and to each other, the results are not what statisticians call "robust." The measurements of tax base and tax revenues are quite reliable, but not so reliable that they prevent a point or two difference in the index from potentially being explained by errors. Also the differences in tax rates associated with small differences in tax effort are likely to be too small to affect decisions of households and businesses. Finally, the data are for fiscal year 2002, while decisions made today are in fiscal year 2007. The relevant data, which are unavailable, would reflect changes already made and others already underway.

So, for example, the differences between Kansas (103) and Illinois (102) and among Arkansas (99), Oklahoma (98), and Virginia (97) cannot appropriately be used as an argument for changing public policy in those states. This being said, large differences among the states and extreme differences from the national average permit substantial conclusions about differing state policies and their effects.

F-4 State and Local Tax Capacity, FY 2002: The representative tax system (see notes to Table F-3) also permits a comparison of the tax base, or fiscal capacity, of individual states. This is presented in what can be viewed either as percentages of the national average or as index numbers. Either way, the table indicates, for example, that if it applied national average tax rates, Alabama would raise only 82 percent of the amount that those same rates would in the average state. For reasons indicated in the notes to Table F-3, these data are not available for any year more recent than 2002.

F-5 Change in State and Local Taxes, FY 1999–2004: In the five years covered by the table, the U.S. Census Bureau reports for each year indicate that state and local tax revenues have increased by just under 24 percent. However, growth has been much faster in some states than others. See Table F-1 for the source for 2004 figures; 1999 numbers come from *State Fact Finder 2002*.

The table shows increases in state and local taxes as would be expected because the nation's population has been growing and prices have increased due to inflation. Predictably, the increases tend to be largest in states where population and government workloads, such as children in public schools, have grown most rapidly, such as Nevada. However, on average, tax burdens (taxes in relation to personal income) have declined.

F-6 Property Taxes, Total and as a Percentage of Personal Income, FY 2004: This and subsequent tables deal with the total revenues raised by particular state and local taxes. They start with the revenues from those taxes as indicated by U.S. Census Bureau data (see notes to Table F-1). Those revenues are then related to both population and personal income to provide the two most common measures of the levels, or burdens, of those taxes in each state.

F-7 Property Taxes Per Capita, FY 2004: See notes to Table F-6.

F-8 Property Tax Revenue as a Percentage of Three-Tax Revenue, FY 2004: Some people feel that their total state and local taxes are too high, while others may not be sure about total tax burdens but feel that a particular revenue source, such as property taxes, is too heavily used in their state. This table, using Census data (see notes to Table F-1), relates the amount raised from taxing property with the amounts raised from the other two major tax bases—sales and income.

F-9 Sales Taxes, Total and as a Percentage of Personal Income, FY 2004: All states, including those which do not have state sales taxes, show some sales tax revenues. The U.S. Census Bureau counts as sales tax revenues both revenues from sales taxes levied on sales of most goods and special excise taxes on particular goods, such as tobacco and alcoholic beverages. See notes to Table F-6.

F-10 Sales Taxes Per Capita, FY 2004: See notes to Tables F-6 and F-9.

F-11 Sales Tax Revenue as a Percentage of Three-Tax Revenue, FY 2004: See notes to Tables F-8 and F-9.

F-12 Sales Tax Rates and Reach, 2007: Many of the "goods" of today's economy are beyond the reach of the sales tax as it is currently structured. For instance, cars and clothing are taxed, but services such as barbering and landscaping generally are not. Neither are out-of-state mail order or e-commerce purchases. Because of the limited reach of the sales tax, without rate hikes sales tax collections would fall.

Many experts suggest that the sales tax would be fairer and a more productive revenue source if it applied equally to both goods *and* services; bricks-and-mortar *and* Internet shopping. A current debate centers around how to extend the reach of the sales tax, if indeed it should be extended at all. This table provides two elements relevant to that debate. The first column of information shows each state's statewide sales tax rate at the beginning of 2007 (localities may levy additional taxes). The second column shows the number of services covered in 2004 by the sales tax in each state. The table includes states, such as New Hampshire, that have no general sales tax and ones, such as Alaska, that may have special excise taxes on a few services. This count, along with the sales tax rates, was compiled by the Federation of Tax Administrators (FTA) and is available on its Web site (www.taxadmin.org).

For general information on the efforts of some states to simplify and unify the sales tax consult the Streamlined Sales Tax Project (www.streamlinedsalestax.org).

F-13 Individual Income Taxes, Total and as a Percentage of Personal Income, FY 2004: Some states that do not tax personal income from wages and salaries do have taxes based on income from other sources, such as dividends, interest, rent, and capital gains. Revenues from all these taxes appear in the table. For the source, see notes to Table F-6.

F-14 Individual Income Taxes Per Capita, FY 2004: See notes to Tables F-6 and F-13.

F-15 Individual Income Tax Revenue as a Percentage of Three-Tax Revenue, FY 2004: See notes to Tables F-8 and F-13.

F-16 Highest Personal Income Tax Rate, 2006: While some states have no income tax at all, the rates paid by high-income households in a few other states can go as high as 9 percent. This table, developed by State Policy Research from compilations of state tax laws published by CCH, Inc., shows the highest state personal income tax rates. A few states use low flat-rate income taxes with few deductions and exemptions, so the same rate is applicable to all taxable income. Most states use a graduated rate schedule. In most of the states showing the highest rates in the table, this "marginal" or "top bracket" rate is paid only on income exceeding a threshold of $100,000 or more.

The rates shown were those in effect in December 2006 on income earned in 2006, to be reported on tax returns filed in early 2007.

F-17 Corporate Income Taxes, Total and Per Capita, FY 2004: See notes to Table F-6. This table is now the best of many unsatisfactory ways of comparing corporate income taxes in the fifty states. However, since 2004 states have made more changes in corporate income taxes (tax base, tax rates, tax credits) than in any other single tax affecting business.

Because of the widespread use of special tax credits for investment, research and development, job expansion, and other purposes and because of differences among states in how much income of multistate corporations is attributed to the taxing state, comparisons of corporate income tax rates are not particularly meaningful.

The most appropriate way to compare corporate income taxes of states is to make calculations of tax liability for individual hypothetical corporations. Such calculations reflect the different state definitions of the tax base, different tax rates, and different tax credits as well as different characteristics of firms in particular industries which affect tax liability. These calculations are complex because taxes levied by one state depend in part on taxes levied by other states. Such calculations have been made in special studies prepared for individual states, but they are typically made only for those ten to twenty states that the requesting state considers to be its major competitors in economic development.

F-18 Motor Fuel Taxes: States tax motor fuels, such as gasoline and diesel fuel, mostly to provide funds for road construction and maintenance. The table shows the tax rate on gasoline from a special compilation prepared by the Federation of Tax Administrators (FTA), covering rates in effect January 1, 2006. This statistic is available on the FTA Web site (www.taxadmin.org). The table also includes total state and local revenues from motor fuel taxes in fiscal year 2004, compiled by the U.S. Census Bureau and available on its Web site (see notes to Table F-1). *State Fact Finder* related those revenues to personal income.

F-19 Motor Vehicle Fees and Taxes, 2006: States assess vehicle registration fees annually. The amounts shown in this table are those that would be assessed on a 4-door, 6-passenger, 8-cylinder automobile, bought new at $7,900 and weighing 3,522 pounds. In most states, vehicle sales or excise taxes are also assessed on vehicles at the point of sale or titling. The table shows the percentage of fair market value assessed in each state. In some states the tax is capped at a dollar amount.

F-20 Tobacco Taxes: These data come from the same sources as those of Table F-18 but cover cigarette and related tobacco taxes. Over the last three years more than half of the states increased cigarette excise taxes. The rates shown on the table were in effect January 2006.

F-21 State and Local Taxes on High-Income Families, 2005:
The amounts shown are the liability to be faced by a hypothetical family with an adjusted yearly gross income of $150,000. The estimates are based on taxes incurred in the largest city in each state, as calculated by the District of Columbia Department of Finance and Revenue in *Tax Rates and Tax Burdens in the District of Columbia: A Nationwide Comparison.* The calculations for each state's largest city are not necessarily representative of statewide averages.

F-22 State and Local Taxes in the Largest City in Each State, 2005: These data show the costs of state and local taxes in the largest city in each state to typical families with incomes of $50,000. The calculations for each state's largest city are not necessarily representative of statewide averages. For the source of the data see the notes to Table F-21.

F-23 Progressivity of Major State and Local Taxes, 2005: These data compare the tax burdens as a percentage of income on households of two income levels ($25,000 and $150,000), using data from the analysis described in the notes to Table F-21. Low numbers indicate that the percentage paid by higher-income households is significantly higher than the percentage paid by low-income households, making the state and local tax structure "progressive." States with no personal income tax and high reliance on sales and property taxes, such as Nevada, have tax systems that can be called regressive. Their progressivity percentages over one hundred indicate that poorer households pay a larger percentage of their income on state and local taxes than do higher-income households.

F-24 State Estate Taxes, 2006: In 2001, the federal government passed legislation to repeal the federal estate tax. The Economic Growth and Tax Relief Reconciliation Act (EGTRRA) phases out the federal tax by 2010, but only for one year. Prior to EGTRRA, states collected a portion of federal estate taxes. By "picking-up" a share of the federal revenues, states could levy taxes up to the amount of the federal credit without making taxpayers pay more. The "pick-up" tax limited interstate competition for wealthy retirees. With the passage of EGTRRA, the federal credit was repealed over four years, ending in 2005. To avoid the automatic loss of revenues from the pick-up tax some states acted to protect their own tax code from the changes made to the federal tax code. These "decoupled" states remain tied to the federal tax code as it existed prior to the adoption of EGTRRA. Other states already had or recently enacted a stand-alone estate or inheritance tax. The remaining states—nearly half— have not, or not yet, acted.

The table shows which states, as of January 2007, have decoupled, which have stand-alone taxes, and which have expired "pick-up" taxes. The table also shows the percentage of total state tax revenue that came from estate, inheritance and gift taxes in 2005. States in which the tax has expired still show collections because of the lag between the year of death and the filing of estate or inheritance tax returns. The data on 2005 tax receipts come from the Tax Policy Center, a joint venture of the Urban Institute and the Brookings Institution (www.taxpolicycenter.org).

F-25 State Taxes on Retirement Income, 2006: Many of the forty-one states that levy a broad-based personal income tax exempt some or all retirement income. Generally, the purpose is to aid those no longer earning income through engagement in work, and to attract, or retain, retired people.

The table shows how retirement income is treated by the fifty states and the District of Columbia. The exclusions shown are based on a taxpayer filing as an individual for income received in 2006. Ranges, such as that shown for Colorado ($20,000–$24,000) reflect either differences based on the age or the total income of the taxpayer, and, in a few cases, the type of job from which the taxpayer retired.

Four states tax Social Security benefits above a specific income threshold. Seven tax this income at the same level it is taxed by the federal government.

The table shows that states tend to be more generous in their tax treatment of public pensions and Social Security benefits than in their treatment of private pensions. Pennsylvania is the only state to fully exempt income from private pension plans. The table shows that the exclusion for private plans "varies" in four states. Each of these states has particular calculations based on the type of retirement plan. Alabama, for example, excludes income from defined benefit plans. Hawaii does this for contributory plans, while Illinois and Mississippi exempt income from "qualified" retirement plans. There are many details associated with each state's taxation policy on retirement income, both public and private. See the National Conference of State Legislature's "State Personal Income Taxes on Pensions and Retirement Income: Tax Year 2005 (Updated for Legislative Enactments in 2006)" for more detailed information.

Revenues and Finances

Continuum of State Fiscal Stress

All Systems Go

Alabama	Nevada
Arizona	New Jersey
Colorado	New York
Connecticut	North Carolina
Georgia	North Dakota
Hawaii	Ohio
Idaho	Oklahoma
Iowa	Oregon
Kansas	South Carolina
Kentucky	Texas
Maryland	Utah
Massachusetts	Virginia
Missouri	Washington
Montana	West Virginia
Nebraska	Wyoming

Trending Up

Alaska	Minnesota
Arkansas	New Hampshire
California	New Mexico
Delaware	Pennsylvania
Florida	South Dakota
Illinois	Tennessee
Indiana	Vermont
Louisiana	Wisconsin
Maine	

Could Be Better, Could Be Worse

Michigan	Rhode Island
Mississippi	

Source: State Policy Reports, Volume 24, no. 23-24, *based on the National Association of State Budget Officers'* Fiscal Survey of the States: December 2006

G-1 State and Local Total Revenue, FY 2004

State	Total revenue $ (in millions)	Per capita total revenue $	Total revenue as a percentage of personal income	Rank per capita
Alabama	32,065	7,078	27.1	39
Alaska	11,038	16,841	51.2	1
Arizona	38,388	6,683	25.5	46
Arkansas	18,027	6,549	27.2	49
California	358,673	9,993	30.3	5
Colorado	38,744	8,420	24.7	18
Connecticut	29,295	8,361	19.4	19
Delaware	7,102	8,553	26.1	14
Florida	129,687	7,454	25.4	31
Georgia	57,902	6,558	22.8	48
Hawaii	9,983	7,905	25.9	24
Idaho	9,754	7,001	27.9	40
Illinois	100,247	7,885	23.9	25
Indiana	40,977	6,569	23.0	47
Iowa	22,545	7,631	27.0	29
Kansas	18,550	6,781	23.1	44
Kentucky	26,834	6,472	24.7	50
Louisiana	34,107	7,553	29.1	30
Maine	11,131	8,450	29.5	16
Maryland	44,288	7,968	21.5	21
Massachusetts	60,795	9,475	24.0	6
Michigan	80,185	7,929	25.5	22
Minnesota	42,956	8,421	24.9	17
Mississippi	20,670	7,120	30.7	38
Missouri	40,033	6,957	24.1	41
Montana	7,088	7,647	30.0	28
Nebraska	15,479	8,859	29.3	10
Nevada	16,888	7,233	23.9	36
New Hampshire	8,703	6,697	19.5	45
New Jersey	75,083	8,631	21.7	13
New Mexico	14,918	7,838	31.2	26
New York	224,429	11,673	32.2	3
North Carolina	63,458	7,430	26.7	32
North Dakota	6,524	10,285	36.1	4
Ohio	105,382	9,196	30.8	8
Oklahoma	23,954	6,798	25.7	43
Oregon	33,734	9,385	32.9	7
Pennsylvania	102,238	8,241	26.1	20
Rhode Island	9,665	8,944	28.1	9
South Carolina	30,547	7,276	28.2	33
South Dakota	5,593	7,255	25.9	35
Tennessee	42,125	7,139	25.2	37
Texas	153,761	6,837	23.9	42
Utah	18,917	7,918	31.9	23
Vermont	5,266	8,474	27.9	15
Virginia	54,162	7,260	21.8	34
Washington	54,738	8,823	26.8	12
West Virginia	14,117	7,776	31.6	27
Wisconsin	48,698	8,840	29.0	11
Wyoming	6,816	13,457	42.2	2
50 States	2,426,255	8,278	26.6	
DC	8,829	15,950	33.1	
United States	2,435,084	8,292	26.6	

Rank in order per capita	
1	Alaska
2	Wyoming
3	New York
4	North Dakota
5	California
6	Massachusetts
7	Oregon
8	Ohio
9	Rhode Island
10	Nebraska
11	Wisconsin
12	Washington
13	New Jersey
14	Delaware
15	Vermont
16	Maine
17	Minnesota
18	Colorado
19	Connecticut
20	Pennsylvania
21	Maryland
22	Michigan
23	Utah
24	Hawaii
25	Illinois
26	New Mexico
27	West Virginia
28	Montana
29	Iowa
30	Louisiana
31	Florida
32	North Carolina
33	South Carolina
34	Virginia
35	South Dakota
36	Nevada
37	Tennessee
38	Mississippi
39	Alabama
40	Idaho
41	Missouri
42	Texas
43	Oklahoma
44	Kansas
45	New Hampshire
46	Arizona
47	Indiana
48	Georgia
49	Arkansas
50	Kentucky

G-2   State and Local General Revenue, FY 2004

State	General revenue $ (in millions)	Per capita general revenue $	General revenue as a percentage of personal income	Rank per capita
Alabama	25,535	5,637	21.6	41
Alaska	8,529	13,013	39.5	1
Arizona	30,195	5,257	20.1	50
Arkansas	14,745	5,357	22.3	49
California	251,889	7,018	21.3	11
Colorado	28,128	6,113	17.9	27
Connecticut	25,887	7,389	17.2	5
Delaware	6,249	7,526	22.9	4
Florida	102,725	5,905	20.1	31
Georgia	47,336	5,361	18.6	48
Hawaii	8,221	6,510	21.4	18
Idaho	7,758	5,568	22.2	42
Illinois	76,266	5,999	18.2	29
Indiana	35,696	5,723	20.0	37
Iowa	18,396	6,227	22.0	25
Kansas	16,276	5,950	20.2	30
Kentucky	22,982	5,543	21.2	44
Louisiana	27,905	6,179	23.8	26
Maine	9,517	7,225	25.2	8
Maryland	36,777	6,617	17.8	15
Massachusetts	47,172	7,352	18.6	7
Michigan	65,501	6,477	20.8	19
Minnesota	35,230	6,906	20.5	12
Mississippi	16,914	5,827	25.1	34
Missouri	31,982	5,558	19.3	43
Montana	5,796	6,253	24.5	24
Nebraska	11,669	6,679	22.1	14
Nevada	13,267	5,682	18.8	40
New Hampshire	7,440	5,725	16.7	36
New Jersey	61,593	7,081	17.8	10
New Mexico	12,477	6,555	26.1	17
New York	179,380	9,330	25.8	3
North Carolina	48,768	5,710	20.5	38
North Dakota	4,348	6,854	24.1	13
Ohio	72,264	6,306	21.1	23
Oklahoma	19,215	5,453	20.6	46
Oregon	21,770	6,056	21.2	28
Pennsylvania	78,632	6,338	20.1	22
Rhode Island	7,761	7,182	22.6	9
South Carolina	24,714	5,887	22.8	32
South Dakota	4,383	5,685	20.3	39
Tennessee	31,661	5,365	19.0	47
Texas	124,042	5,515	19.3	45
Utah	13,834	5,790	23.3	35
Vermont	4,569	7,352	24.2	6
Virginia	43,829	5,875	17.6	33
Washington	39,758	6,409	19.5	21
West Virginia	11,926	6,570	26.7	16
Wisconsin	35,528	6,449	21.1	20
Wyoming	5,663	11,181	35.1	2
50 States	1,882,101	6,421	20.6	
DC	7,640	13,803	28.7	
United States	1,889,741	6,435	20.7	

Rank in order per capita

1	Alaska
2	Wyoming
3	New York
4	Delaware
5	Connecticut
6	Vermont
7	Massachusetts
8	Maine
9	Rhode Island
10	New Jersey
11	California
12	Minnesota
13	North Dakota
14	Nebraska
15	Maryland
16	West Virginia
17	New Mexico
18	Hawaii
19	Michigan
20	Wisconsin
21	Washington
22	Pennsylvania
23	Ohio
24	Montana
25	Iowa
26	Louisiana
27	Colorado
28	Oregon
29	Illinois
30	Kansas
31	Florida
32	South Carolina
33	Virginia
34	Mississippi
35	Utah
36	New Hampshire
37	Indiana
38	North Carolina
39	South Dakota
40	Nevada
41	Alabama
42	Idaho
43	Missouri
44	Kentucky
45	Texas
46	Oklahoma
47	Tennessee
48	Georgia
49	Arkansas
50	Arizona

G-3 State and Local "Own-Source" General Revenue, FY 2004

State	"Own-source" general revenue $ (in millions)	Per capita "own-source" general revenue $	"Own-source" general revenue as a percentage of personal income	Rank per capita
Alabama	18,716	4,131	15.8	43
Alaska	6,109	9,320	28.3	1
Arizona	22,608	3,936	15.0	46
Arkansas	10,468	3,803	15.8	49
California	197,545	5,504	16.7	8
Colorado	22,925	4,982	14.6	19
Connecticut	21,384	6,104	14.2	5
Delaware	5,157	6,211	18.9	4
Florida	83,543	4,802	16.4	25
Georgia	37,433	4,240	14.7	39
Hawaii	6,387	5,057	16.6	17
Idaho	5,883	4,222	16.8	41
Illinois	60,614	4,768	14.4	28
Indiana	28,360	4,547	15.9	32
Iowa	14,092	4,770	16.9	27
Kansas	13,140	4,803	16.3	24
Kentucky	16,741	4,038	15.4	45
Louisiana	20,282	4,491	17.3	34
Maine	6,841	5,193	18.1	13
Maryland	29,515	5,310	14.3	10
Massachusetts	37,107	5,783	14.6	7
Michigan	50,391	4,983	16.0	18
Minnesota	28,069	5,503	16.3	9
Mississippi	11,272	3,883	16.8	48
Missouri	23,964	4,164	14.4	42
Montana	3,915	4,224	16.6	40
Nebraska	9,133	5,227	17.3	11
Nevada	11,348	4,860	16.1	23
New Hampshire	5,868	4,516	13.1	33
New Jersey	51,661	5,939	15.0	6
New Mexico	8,674	4,557	18.1	31
New York	133,686	6,953	19.2	3
North Carolina	36,858	4,315	15.5	37
North Dakota	3,034	4,783	16.8	26
Ohio	55,951	4,883	16.3	21
Oklahoma	14,396	4,086	15.4	44
Oregon	16,831	4,682	16.4	29
Pennsylvania	60,520	4,878	15.4	22
Rhode Island	5,637	5,217	16.4	12
South Carolina	18,503	4,408	17.1	36
South Dakota	3,023	3,921	14.0	47
Tennessee	22,138	3,752	13.3	50
Texas	96,359	4,285	15.0	38
Utah	10,612	4,442	17.9	35
Vermont	3,200	5,150	16.9	15
Virginia	36,779	4,930	14.8	20
Washington	32,020	5,161	15.7	14
West Virginia	8,486	4,674	19.0	30
Wisconsin	28,266	5,131	16.8	16
Wyoming	3,682	7,269	22.8	2
50 States	1,459,124	4,978	16.0	
DC	4,934	8,913	18.5	
United States	1,464,058	4,986	16.0	

Rank in order per capita	
1	Alaska
2	Wyoming
3	New York
4	Delaware
5	Connecticut
6	New Jersey
7	Massachusetts
8	California
9	Minnesota
10	Maryland
11	Nebraska
12	Rhode Island
13	Maine
14	Washington
15	Vermont
16	Wisconsin
17	Hawaii
18	Michigan
19	Colorado
20	Virginia
21	Ohio
22	Pennsylvania
23	Nevada
24	Kansas
25	Florida
26	North Dakota
27	Iowa
28	Illinois
29	Oregon
30	West Virginia
31	New Mexico
32	Indiana
33	New Hampshire
34	Louisiana
35	Utah
36	South Carolina
37	North Carolina
38	Texas
39	Georgia
40	Montana
41	Idaho
42	Missouri
43	Alabama
44	Oklahoma
45	Kentucky
46	Arizona
47	South Dakota
48	Mississippi
49	Arkansas
50	Tennessee

G-4   State and Local Non-Tax "Own-Source" Revenue, FY 2004

State	Non-tax "own-source" revenue $ (in millions)	Per capita non-tax "own-source" revenue $	Non-tax "own-source" revenue as a percentage of personal income	Rank per capita
Alabama	8,180	1,806	6.9	6
Alaska	3,733	5,696	17.3	1
Arizona	6,126	1,067	4.1	50
Arkansas	3,495	1,270	5.3	45
California	63,652	1,773	5.4	8
Colorado	8,344	1,813	5.3	5
Connecticut	4,164	1,189	2.8	49
Delaware	2,163	2,605	7.9	3
Florida	29,754	1,710	5.8	12
Georgia	11,778	1,334	4.6	40
Hawaii	1,575	1,247	4.1	46
Idaho	2,077	1,491	5.9	25
Illinois	15,423	1,213	3.7	48
Indiana	9,685	1,553	5.4	24
Iowa	5,073	1,717	6.1	11
Kansas	3,898	1,425	4.8	31
Kentucky	5,280	1,274	4.9	44
Louisiana	7,217	1,598	6.2	21
Maine	1,858	1,410	4.9	33
Maryland	7,184	1,292	3.5	43
Massachusetts	10,092	1,573	4.0	23
Michigan	16,913	1,672	5.4	17
Minnesota	8,645	1,695	5.0	15
Mississippi	4,183	1,441	6.2	29
Missouri	7,709	1,340	4.6	39
Montana	1,484	1,601	6.3	20
Nebraska	2,825	1,617	5.4	19
Nevada	3,376	1,446	4.8	28
New Hampshire	1,798	1,384	4.0	38
New Jersey	12,103	1,391	3.5	36
New Mexico	3,230	1,697	6.8	14
New York	32,259	1,678	4.6	16
North Carolina	11,846	1,387	5.0	37
North Dakota	1,133	1,786	6.3	7
Ohio	16,800	1,466	4.9	27
Oklahoma	4,961	1,408	5.3	34
Oregon	6,357	1,769	6.2	9
Pennsylvania	17,802	1,435	4.5	30
Rhode Island	1,435	1,328	4.2	41
South Carolina	7,327	1,745	6.8	10
South Dakota	1,007	1,306	4.7	42
Tennessee	7,191	1,219	4.3	47
Texas	31,620	1,406	4.9	35
Utah	3,991	1,671	6.7	18
Vermont	914	1,471	4.8	26
Virginia	11,776	1,579	4.7	22
Washington	10,595	1,708	5.2	13
West Virginia	3,518	1,938	7.9	4
Wisconsin	7,825	1,420	4.7	32
Wyoming	1,437	2,836	8.9	2
50 States	452,811	1,545	5.0	
DC	970	1,753	3.6	
United States	453,781	1,545	5.0	

Rank in order per capita

1	Alaska
2	Wyoming
3	Delaware
4	West Virginia
5	Colorado
6	Alabama
7	North Dakota
8	California
9	Oregon
10	South Carolina
11	Iowa
12	Florida
13	Washington
14	New Mexico
15	Minnesota
16	New York
17	Michigan
18	Utah
19	Nebraska
20	Montana
21	Louisiana
22	Virginia
23	Massachusetts
24	Indiana
25	Idaho
26	Vermont
27	Ohio
28	Nevada
29	Mississippi
30	Pennsylvania
31	Kansas
32	Wisconsin
33	Maine
34	Oklahoma
35	Texas
36	New Jersey
37	North Carolina
38	New Hampshire
39	Missouri
40	Georgia
41	Rhode Island
42	South Dakota
43	Maryland
44	Kentucky
45	Arkansas
46	Hawaii
47	Tennessee
48	Illinois
49	Connecticut
50	Arizona

G-5   State and Local Total Expenditures, FY 2004

State	Total expenditures $ (in millions)	Per capita total expenditures $	Total expenditures as a percentage of personal income	Rank per capita
Alabama	31,268	6,902	26.4	31
Alaska	10,019	15,286	46.4	1
Arizona	36,072	6,280	24.0	45
Arkansas	16,323	5,930	24.6	49
California	328,029	9,139	27.7	4
Colorado	34,395	7,475	21.9	22
Connecticut	28,837	8,231	19.1	11
Delaware	6,922	8,336	25.4	8
Florida	115,547	6,642	22.7	37
Georgia	58,435	6,618	23.0	39
Hawaii	9,870	7,815	25.7	15
Idaho	8,426	6,048	24.1	47
Illinois	95,421	7,505	22.7	21
Indiana	39,333	6,306	22.0	44
Iowa	20,634	6,984	24.7	28
Kansas	18,361	6,712	22.8	34
Kentucky	26,871	6,481	24.8	40
Louisiana	31,089	6,885	26.6	32
Maine	10,031	7,615	26.5	20
Maryland	38,540	6,934	18.7	29
Massachusetts	58,208	9,072	23.0	5
Michigan	77,621	7,676	24.7	18
Minnesota	42,144	8,262	24.5	10
Mississippi	19,450	6,700	28.9	35
Missouri	35,571	6,181	21.4	46
Montana	6,198	6,688	26.2	36
Nebraska	14,075	8,056	26.7	12
Nevada	16,182	6,931	22.9	30
New Hampshire	8,346	6,422	18.7	42
New Jersey	72,660	8,353	21.0	7
New Mexico	14,068	7,392	29.4	23
New York	219,325	11,407	31.5	2
North Carolina	56,543	6,620	23.8	38
North Dakota	4,486	7,072	24.8	26
Ohio	89,598	7,819	26.2	14
Oklahoma	20,879	5,926	22.4	50
Oregon	28,215	7,849	27.5	13
Pennsylvania	94,598	7,625	24.1	19
Rhode Island	8,937	8,270	26.0	9
South Carolina	30,451	7,253	28.1	24
South Dakota	4,612	5,983	21.3	48
Tennessee	41,760	7,077	25.0	25
Texas	144,880	6,442	22.5	41
Utah	16,707	6,993	28.2	27
Vermont	4,812	7,744	25.5	16
Virginia	47,801	6,408	19.2	43
Washington	54,317	8,756	26.6	6
West Virginia	12,201	6,721	27.3	33
Wisconsin	42,410	7,698	25.2	17
Wyoming	5,080	10,029	31.4	3
50 States	2,256,558	7,699	24.7	
DC	8,493	15,343	31.9	
United States	2,265,051	7,713	24.8	

Rank in order per capita

1	Alaska
2	New York
3	Wyoming
4	California
5	Massachusetts
6	Washington
7	New Jersey
8	Delaware
9	Rhode Island
10	Minnesota
11	Connecticut
12	Nebraska
13	Oregon
14	Ohio
15	Hawaii
16	Vermont
17	Wisconsin
18	Michigan
19	Pennsylvania
20	Maine
21	Illinois
22	Colorado
23	New Mexico
24	South Carolina
25	Tennessee
26	North Dakota
27	Utah
28	Iowa
29	Maryland
30	Nevada
31	Alabama
32	Louisiana
33	West Virginia
34	Kansas
35	Mississippi
36	Montana
37	Florida
38	North Carolina
39	Georgia
40	Kentucky
41	Texas
42	New Hampshire
43	Virginia
44	Indiana
45	Arizona
46	Missouri
47	Idaho
48	South Dakota
49	Arkansas
50	Oklahoma

G-6 State and Local General Expenditures, FY 2004

State	General expenditures $ (in millions)	General expenditures as a percentage of personal income	Rank by percentage
Alabama	27,089	22.9	14
Alaska	8,496	39.4	1
Arizona	30,075	20.0	33
Arkansas	14,577	22.0	19
California	260,960	22.0	18
Colorado	28,424	18.1	45
Connecticut	25,018	16.6	49
Delaware	6,191	22.7	15
Florida	100,771	19.8	36
Georgia	50,211	19.8	35
Hawaii	8,673	22.5	16
Idaho	7,540	21.6	24
Illinois	79,495	18.9	43
Indiana	35,540	19.9	34
Iowa	18,396	22.0	20
Kansas	16,284	20.2	32
Kentucky	23,342	21.5	26
Louisiana	27,251	23.3	11
Maine	9,282	24.6	6
Maryland	34,111	16.5	50
Massachusetts	48,446	19.1	40
Michigan	67,643	21.5	25
Minnesota	36,637	21.3	27
Mississippi	17,282	25.7	4
Missouri	31,020	18.7	44
Montana	5,547	23.5	9
Nebraska	10,776	20.4	30
Nevada	13,619	19.3	38
New Hampshire	7,549	16.9	48
New Jersey	61,224	17.7	46
New Mexico	12,616	26.4	3
New York	175,803	25.2	5
North Carolina	48,490	20.4	31
North Dakota	4,157	23.0	13
Ohio	74,445	21.7	23
Oklahoma	18,148	19.5	37
Oregon	22,309	21.8	22
Pennsylvania	80,339	20.5	29
Rhode Island	7,643	22.2	17
South Carolina	25,591	23.6	8
South Dakota	4,132	19.1	41
Tennessee	31,581	18.9	42
Texas	124,057	19.3	39
Utah	13,906	23.4	10
Vermont	4,398	23.3	12
Virginia	42,955	17.3	47
Washington	42,579	20.9	28
West Virginia	10,604	23.7	7
Wisconsin	36,714	21.8	21
Wyoming	4,535	28.1	2
50 States	1,896,471	20.8	
DC	6,723	25.2	
United States	1,903,194	20.8	

Rank in order by percentage	
1	Alaska
2	Wyoming
3	New Mexico
4	Mississippi
5	New York
6	Maine
7	West Virginia
8	South Carolina
9	Montana
10	Utah
11	Louisiana
12	Vermont
13	North Dakota
14	Alabama
15	Delaware
16	Hawaii
17	Rhode Island
18	California
19	Arkansas
20	Iowa
21	Wisconsin
22	Oregon
23	Ohio
24	Idaho
25	Michigan
26	Kentucky
27	Minnesota
28	Washington
29	Pennsylvania
30	Nebraska
31	North Carolina
32	Kansas
33	Arizona
34	Indiana
35	Georgia
36	Florida
37	Oklahoma
38	Nevada
39	Texas
40	Massachusetts
41	South Dakota
42	Tennessee
43	Illinois
44	Missouri
45	Colorado
46	New Jersey
47	Virginia
48	New Hampshire
49	Connecticut
50	Maryland

Note: Numbers that appear to be identical are rounded and vary slightly in actual value. The rankings reflect the actual values before rounding. See the introduction for more details.

G-7   State and Local General Expenditures Per Capita, FY 2004

State	State and local general expenditure per capita $	State general expenditure per capita $	Local general expenditure per capita $	Rank by state and local general expenditure per capita
Alabama	5,980	2,971	3,009	30
Alaska	12,962	8,826	4,136	1
Arizona	5,236	2,089	3,147	49
Arkansas	5,296	3,070	2,226	48
California	7,270	2,534	4,737	6
Colorado	6,177	2,211	3,966	24
Connecticut	7,141	3,788	3,352	8
Delaware	7,456	4,807	2,648	5
Florida	5,792	2,161	3,632	37
Georgia	5,687	2,439	3,248	40
Hawaii	6,868	5,501	1,367	13
Idaho	5,412	2,581	2,831	44
Illinois	6,253	2,557	3,696	21
Indiana	5,698	2,498	3,200	39
Iowa	6,227	2,877	3,349	22
Kansas	5,953	2,641	3,312	32
Kentucky	5,630	3,323	2,307	42
Louisiana	6,035	3,011	3,023	28
Maine	7,046	4,268	2,778	11
Maryland	6,137	2,999	3,139	26
Massachusetts	7,550	4,277	3,273	4
Michigan	6,689	2,717	3,972	15
Minnesota	7,182	3,087	4,096	7
Mississippi	5,953	3,084	2,869	31
Missouri	5,390	2,472	2,918	45
Montana	5,984	3,414	2,570	29
Nebraska	6,167	2,833	3,334	25
Nevada	5,833	1,973	3,860	34
New Hampshire	5,809	2,819	2,990	36
New Jersey	7,038	3,018	4,020	12
New Mexico	6,629	3,668	2,960	17
New York	9,144	3,336	5,808	2
North Carolina	5,677	2,656	3,022	41
North Dakota	6,553	3,722	2,831	18
Ohio	6,497	2,687	3,809	19
Oklahoma	5,150	2,657	2,493	50
Oregon	6,206	2,761	3,446	23
Pennsylvania	6,476	2,909	3,567	20
Rhode Island	7,073	4,166	2,906	10
South Carolina	6,096	3,287	2,808	27
South Dakota	5,360	2,796	2,564	46
Tennessee	5,352	2,591	2,760	47
Texas	5,516	2,251	3,265	43
Utah	5,821	3,198	2,623	35
Vermont	7,077	4,337	2,740	9
Virginia	5,758	2,520	3,238	38
Washington	6,863	3,240	3,624	14
West Virginia	5,841	3,643	2,198	33
Wisconsin	6,664	2,814	3,850	16
Wyoming	8,952	3,912	5,040	3
50 States	6,470	2,797	3,674	
DC	12,145	n/a	12,145	
United States	6,481	2,791	3,690	

Rank in order by state and local per capita	
1	Alaska
2	New York
3	Wyoming
4	Massachusetts
5	Delaware
6	California
7	Minnesota
8	Connecticut
9	Vermont
10	Rhode Island
11	Maine
12	New Jersey
13	Hawaii
14	Washington
15	Michigan
16	Wisconsin
17	New Mexico
18	North Dakota
19	Ohio
20	Pennsylvania
21	Illinois
22	Iowa
23	Oregon
24	Colorado
25	Nebraska
26	Maryland
27	South Carolina
28	Louisiana
29	Montana
30	Alabama
31	Mississippi
32	Kansas
33	West Virginia
34	Nevada
35	Utah
36	New Hampshire
37	Florida
38	Virginia
39	Indiana
40	Georgia
41	North Carolina
42	Kentucky
43	Texas
44	Idaho
45	Missouri
46	South Dakota
47	Tennessee
48	Arkansas
49	Arizona
50	Oklahoma

Note: Numbers that appear to be identical are rounded and vary slightly in actual value. The rankings reflect the actual values before rounding. See the introduction for more details.

G-8 Percentage Change in State and Local Expenditures, FY 1999–2004

State	Percentage change	Rank
Alabama	32.2	23
Alaska	12.1	50
Arizona	44.1	3
Arkansas	29.6	32
California	35.6	14
Colorado	33.1	19
Connecticut	20.4	46
Delaware	28.3	38
Florida	41.4	4
Georgia	28.4	37
Hawaii	19.5	48
Idaho	35.8	13
Illinois	26.4	39
Indiana	28.4	36
Iowa	28.5	35
Kansas	31.9	24
Kentucky	25.1	42
Louisiana	29.0	34
Maine	36.6	11
Maryland	39.7	7
Massachusetts	31.2	26
Michigan	25.1	43
Minnesota	22.1	45
Mississippi	33.0	20
Missouri	29.6	33
Montana	30.0	29
Nebraska	40.5	5
Nevada	52.0	2
New Hampshire	36.0	12
New Jersey	25.7	41
New Mexico	33.7	17
New York	30.8	28
North Carolina	29.9	30
North Dakota	20.1	47
Ohio	31.5	25
Oklahoma	33.0	21
Oregon	17.6	49
Pennsylvania	29.6	31
Rhode Island	39.8	6
South Carolina	34.3	16
South Dakota	30.9	27
Tennessee	35.5	15
Texas	37.3	10
Utah	32.5	22
Vermont	39.3	9
Virginia	33.6	18
Washington	26.0	40
West Virginia	39.6	8
Wisconsin	24.9	44
Wyoming	64.4	1
50 States	31.7	
DC	40.1	
United States	31.7	

Rank in order by percentage	
1	Wyoming
2	Nevada
3	Arizona
4	Florida
5	Nebraska
6	Rhode Island
7	Maryland
8	West Virginia
9	Vermont
10	Texas
11	Maine
12	New Hampshire
13	Idaho
14	California
15	Tennessee
16	South Carolina
17	New Mexico
18	Virginia
19	Colorado
20	Mississippi
21	Oklahoma
22	Utah
23	Alabama
24	Kansas
25	Ohio
26	Massachusetts
27	South Dakota
28	New York
29	Montana
30	North Carolina
31	Pennsylvania
32	Arkansas
33	Missouri
34	Louisiana
35	Iowa
36	Indiana
37	Georgia
38	Delaware
39	Illinois
40	Washington
41	New Jersey
42	Kentucky
43	Michigan
44	Wisconsin
45	Minnesota
46	Connecticut
47	North Dakota
48	Hawaii
49	Oregon
50	Alaska

Note: Numbers that appear to be identical are rounded and vary slightly in actual value. The rankings reflect the actual values before rounding. See the introduction for more details.

State	State government general revenue $ (in millions)	State government general revenue per capita $	Rank per capita
Alabama	17,616	3,893	32
Alaska	6,630	10,076	1
Arizona	18,980	3,307	45
Arkansas	11,680	4,247	20
California	154,485	4,310	19
Colorado	14,957	3,250	47
Connecticut	17,423	4,979	13
Delaware	5,144	6,198	3
Florida	56,673	3,260	46
Georgia	28,205	3,163	49
Hawaii	6,675	5,290	7
Idaho	5,310	3,806	37
Illinois	44,042	3,465	44
Indiana	23,465	3,768	39
Iowa	11,916	4,035	28
Kansas	9,869	3,610	41
Kentucky	17,498	4,224	21
Louisiana	18,867	4,186	24
Maine	6,769	5,147	11
Maryland	22,855	4,110	25
Massachusetts	32,980	5,147	10
Michigan	45,366	4,490	16
Minnesota	24,217	4,751	14
Mississippi	12,196	4,204	22
Missouri	20,287	3,522	43
Montana	4,245	4,580	15
Nebraska	7,338	4,198	23
Nevada	7,296	3,127	50
New Hampshire	5,024	3,868	34
New Jersey	37,909	4,365	17
New Mexico	9,798	5,149	9
New York	106,300	5,513	5
North Carolina	32,951	3,858	35
North Dakota	3,172	4,987	12
Ohio	45,732	3,994	30
Oklahoma	13,700	3,888	33
Oregon	13,766	3,834	36
Pennsylvania	50,029	4,037	27
Rhode Island	5,619	5,203	8
South Carolina	16,836	4,011	29
South Dakota	2,907	3,770	38
Tennessee	20,901	3,547	42
Texas	71,568	3,185	48
Utah	9,560	3,949	31
Vermont	3,795	6,111	4
Virginia	27,972	3,739	40
Washington	25,202	4,060	26
West Virginia	9,638	5,316	6
Wisconsin	23,934	4,348	18
Wyoming	4,061	8,026	2
50 States	1,193,359	4,074	
DC	n/a	n/a	
United States	1,194,056	4,074	

Rank in order per capita	
1	Alaska
2	Wyoming
3	Delaware
4	Vermont
5	New York
6	West Virginia
7	Hawaii
8	Rhode Island
9	New Mexico
10	Massachusetts
11	Maine
12	North Dakota
13	Connecticut
14	Minnesota
15	Montana
16	Michigan
17	New Jersey
18	Wisconsin
19	California
20	Arkansas
21	Kentucky
22	Mississippi
23	Nebraska
24	Louisiana
25	Maryland
26	Washington
27	Pennsylvania
28	Iowa
29	South Carolina
30	Ohio
31	Utah
32	Alabama
33	Oklahoma
34	New Hampshire
35	North Carolina
36	Oregon
37	Idaho
38	South Dakota
39	Indiana
40	Virginia
41	Kansas
42	Tennessee
43	Missouri
44	Illinois
45	Arizona
46	Florida
47	Colorado
48	Texas
49	Georgia
50	Nevada

Note: Numbers that appear to be identical are rounded and vary slightly in actual value. The rankings reflect the actual values before rounding. See the introduction for more details.

G-10   State Government General Spending, FY 2004

State	State government general spending $ (in millions)	State government general spending per capita	Rank per capita
Alabama	17,622	3,894	31
Alaska	6,835	10,387	1
Arizona	19,541	3,404	45
Arkansas	11,683	4,248	23
California	171,079	4,773	12
Colorado	15,035	3,267	47
Connecticut	16,669	4,764	13
Delaware	4,915	5,921	3
Florida	54,064	3,110	49
Georgia	30,869	3,461	44
Hawaii	7,081	5,611	6
Idaho	5,093	3,651	40
Illinois	45,809	3,604	41
Indiana	23,543	3,781	36
Iowa	12,031	4,074	25
Kansas	10,103	3,695	38
Kentucky	17,746	4,284	21
Louisiana	18,008	3,996	30
Maine	6,671	5,073	9
Maryland	22,299	4,010	29
Massachusetts	33,647	5,252	8
Michigan	46,507	4,603	16
Minnesota	25,384	4,980	10
Mississippi	12,833	4,424	19
Missouri	19,487	3,383	46
Montana	4,120	4,444	18
Nebraska	6,646	3,802	35
Nevada	7,556	3,239	48
New Hampshire	4,942	3,805	34
New Jersey	36,064	4,153	24
New Mexico	10,013	5,262	7
New York	108,248	5,614	5
North Carolina	33,009	3,865	33
North Dakota	2,975	4,677	15
Ohio	46,524	4,063	26
Oklahoma	13,078	3,711	37
Oregon	14,560	4,055	27
Pennsylvania	48,243	3,892	32
Rhode Island	5,371	4,973	11
South Carolina	17,961	4,278	22
South Dakota	2,732	3,543	42
Tennessee	20,594	3,495	43
Texas	67,661	3,011	50
Utah	9,753	4,028	28
Vermont	3,676	5,920	4
Virginia	27,618	3,692	39
Washington	27,010	4,352	20
West Virginia	8,555	4,719	14
Wisconsin	24,789	4,504	17
Wyoming	3,186	6,295	2
50 States	1,209,436	4,126	
DC	n/a	n/a	
United States	1,209,436	4,126	

Rank in order per capita	
1	Alaska
2	Wyoming
3	Delaware
4	Vermont
5	New York
6	Hawaii
7	New Mexico
8	Massachusetts
9	Maine
10	Minnesota
11	Rhode Island
12	California
13	Connecticut
14	West Virginia
15	North Dakota
16	Michigan
17	Wisconsin
18	Montana
19	Mississippi
20	Washington
21	Kentucky
22	South Carolina
23	Arkansas
24	New Jersey
25	Iowa
26	Ohio
27	Oregon
28	Utah
29	Maryland
30	Louisiana
31	Alabama
32	Pennsylvania
33	North Carolina
34	New Hampshire
35	Nebraska
36	Indiana
37	Oklahoma
38	Kansas
39	Virginia
40	Idaho
41	Illinois
42	South Dakota
43	Tennessee
44	Georgia
45	Arizona
46	Missouri
47	Colorado
48	Nevada
49	Florida
50	Texas

G-11 State Government General Fund Spending, FY 2005

State	State government general fund spending $ (in millions)	As a percentage of personal income	Rank by percentage
Alabama	17,406	12.9	27
Alaska	8,689	37.0	2
Arizona	22,808	12.7	30
Arkansas	14,290	19.3	7
California	159,713	12.0	35
Colorado	14,218	8.1	50
Connecticut	21,169	12.7	31
Delaware	6,197	19.8	5
Florida	58,332	9.6	44
Georgia	29,184	10.3	43
Hawaii	8,753	19.9	4
Idaho	4,801	11.8	37
Illinois	41,864	9.0	46
Indiana	25,467	13.0	25
Iowa	12,358	13.1	23
Kansas	10,585	11.7	38
Kentucky	19,333	16.4	13
Louisiana	15,236	13.7	19
Maine	6,754	16.6	11
Maryland	24,708	10.5	42
Massachusetts	26,322	9.4	45
Michigan	40,571	12.2	34
Minnesota	24,554	12.8	29
Mississippi	11,947	16.4	12
Missouri	19,110	10.5	41
Montana	3,954	14.6	17
Nebraska	7,472	12.9	28
Nevada	7,055	8.2	49
New Hampshire	4,420	8.9	47
New Jersey	41,503	10.9	40
New Mexico	10,422	19.4	6
New York	100,668	13.0	24
North Carolina	35,558	13.2	22
North Dakota	3,182	16.0	14
Ohio	50,665	13.9	18
Oklahoma	14,027	13.2	21
Oregon	19,791	16.9	10
Pennsylvania	51,321	11.8	36
Rhode Island	6,038	15.9	15
South Carolina	17,992	15.0	16
South Dakota	3,403	13.4	20
Tennessee	24,019	13.0	26
Texas	64,964	8.7	48
Utah	8,493	12.5	32
Vermont	3,670	18.0	8
Virginia	31,712	11.2	39
Washington	27,498	12.4	33
West Virginia	17,738	37.5	1
Wisconsin	31,868	17.3	9
Wyoming	5,556	29.3	3
50 States	1,237,358	12.1	
DC	n/a	n/a	
United States	1,237,358	12.1	

Rank in order by percentage	
1	West Virginia
2	Alaska
3	Wyoming
4	Hawaii
5	Delaware
6	New Mexico
7	Arkansas
8	Vermont
9	Wisconsin
10	Oregon
11	Maine
12	Mississippi
13	Kentucky
14	North Dakota
15	Rhode Island
16	South Carolina
17	Montana
18	Ohio
19	Louisiana
20	South Dakota
21	Oklahoma
22	North Carolina
23	Iowa
24	New York
25	Indiana
26	Tennessee
27	Alabama
28	Nebraska
29	Minnesota
30	Arizona
31	Connecticut
32	Utah
33	Washington
34	Michigan
35	California
36	Pennsylvania
37	Idaho
38	Kansas
39	Virginia
40	New Jersey
41	Missouri
42	Maryland
43	Georgia
44	Florida
45	Massachusetts
46	Illinois
47	New Hampshire
48	Texas
49	Nevada
50	Colorado

Note: Numbers that appear to be identical are rounded and vary slightly in actual value. The rankings reflect the actual values before rounding. See the introduction for more details.

G-12 State and Local Debt, FY 2004

State	State and local debt $ (in millions)	State and local debt per capita $	State and local debt as a percentage of personal income	Rank per capita
Alabama	21,629	4,774	18.3	38
Alaska	8,626	13,160	40.0	1
Arizona	29,844	5,196	19.9	30
Arkansas	10,409	3,782	15.7	46
California	269,935	7,520	22.8	10
Colorado	33,841	7,355	21.5	12
Connecticut	30,516	8,710	20.2	4
Delaware	6,053	7,289	22.2	13
Florida	108,764	6,252	21.3	21
Georgia	34,848	3,947	13.7	44
Hawaii	9,027	7,148	23.5	14
Idaho	4,021	2,886	11.5	50
Illinois	102,304	8,047	24.3	6
Indiana	29,583	4,743	16.6	39
Iowa	11,335	3,837	13.6	45
Kansas	16,122	5,894	20.0	24
Kentucky	29,143	7,029	26.9	15
Louisiana	22,165	4,908	18.9	37
Maine	6,919	5,253	18.3	29
Maryland	27,795	5,001	13.5	34
Massachusetts	72,898	11,361	28.8	3
Michigan	57,609	5,697	18.3	25
Minnesota	33,670	6,601	19.6	17
Mississippi	10,189	3,510	15.1	49
Missouri	30,408	5,284	18.3	28
Montana	4,297	4,636	18.2	40
Nebraska	8,829	5,053	16.7	32
Nevada	17,851	7,646	25.3	8
New Hampshire	8,135	6,260	18.2	20
New Jersey	64,272	7,389	18.6	11
New Mexico	9,724	5,109	20.3	31
New York	219,358	11,409	31.5	2
North Carolina	37,973	4,446	16.0	42
North Dakota	3,143	4,954	17.4	36
Ohio	57,898	5,053	16.9	33
Oklahoma	13,265	3,765	14.2	47
Oregon	24,753	6,886	24.1	16
Pennsylvania	96,374	7,768	24.6	7
Rhode Island	8,237	7,622	24.0	9
South Carolina	25,940	6,179	23.9	22
South Dakota	3,849	4,992	17.8	35
Tennessee	24,320	4,121	14.6	43
Texas	146,009	6,492	22.7	18
Utah	14,265	5,971	24.0	23
Vermont	3,327	5,354	17.6	27
Virginia	40,006	5,363	16.1	26
Washington	50,370	8,119	24.7	5
West Virginia	8,214	4,525	18.4	41
Wisconsin	35,272	6,403	21.0	19
Wyoming	1,835	3,623	11.4	48
50 States	1,945,171	6,637	21.3	
DC	6,490	11,725	24.4	
United States	1,951,661	6,646	21.3	

	Rank in order per capita
1	Alaska
2	New York
3	Massachusetts
4	Connecticut
5	Washington
6	Illinois
7	Pennsylvania
8	Nevada
9	Rhode Island
10	California
11	New Jersey
12	Colorado
13	Delaware
14	Hawaii
15	Kentucky
16	Oregon
17	Minnesota
18	Texas
19	Wisconsin
20	New Hampshire
21	Florida
22	South Carolina
23	Utah
24	Kansas
25	Michigan
26	Virginia
27	Vermont
28	Missouri
29	Maine
30	Arizona
31	New Mexico
32	Nebraska
33	Ohio
34	Maryland
35	South Dakota
36	North Dakota
37	Louisiana
38	Alabama
39	Indiana
40	Montana
41	West Virginia
42	North Carolina
43	Tennessee
44	Georgia
45	Iowa
46	Arkansas
47	Oklahoma
48	Wyoming
49	Mississippi
50	Idaho

G-13 State and Local Debt Related to Revenue, FY 2004

State	State and local debt as a percentage of general revenue	Rank
Alabama	67.5	31
Alaska	78.1	20
Arizona	77.7	21
Arkansas	57.7	41
California	75.3	24
Colorado	87.3	12
Connecticut	104.2	4
Delaware	85.2	15
Florida	83.9	18
Georgia	60.2	38
Hawaii	90.4	11
Idaho	41.2	49
Illinois	102.1	5
Indiana	72.2	28
Iowa	50.3	46
Kansas	86.9	13
Kentucky	108.6	2
Louisiana	65.0	33
Maine	62.2	36
Maryland	62.8	35
Massachusetts	119.9	1
Michigan	71.8	29
Minnesota	78.4	19
Mississippi	49.3	47
Missouri	76.0	22
Montana	60.6	37
Nebraska	57.0	43
Nevada	105.7	3
New Hampshire	93.5	9
New Jersey	85.6	14
New Mexico	65.2	32
New York	97.7	6
North Carolina	59.8	39
North Dakota	48.2	48
Ohio	54.9	45
Oklahoma	55.4	44
Oregon	73.4	26
Pennsylvania	94.3	8
Rhode Island	85.2	16
South Carolina	84.9	17
South Dakota	68.8	30
Tennessee	57.7	42
Texas	95.0	7
Utah	75.4	23
Vermont	63.2	34
Virginia	73.9	25
Washington	92.0	10
West Virginia	58.2	40
Wisconsin	72.4	27
Wyoming	26.9	50
50 States	80.2	
DC	73.5	
United States	80.1	

Rank in order by percentage	
1	Massachusetts
2	Kentucky
3	Nevada
4	Connecticut
5	Illinois
6	New York
7	Texas
8	Pennsylvania
9	New Hampshire
10	Washington
11	Hawaii
12	Colorado
13	Kansas
14	New Jersey
15	Delaware
16	Rhode Island
17	South Carolina
18	Florida
19	Minnesota
20	Alaska
21	Arizona
22	Missouri
23	Utah
24	California
25	Virginia
26	Oregon
27	Wisconsin
28	Indiana
29	Michigan
30	South Dakota
31	Alabama
32	New Mexico
33	Louisiana
34	Vermont
35	Maryland
36	Maine
37	Montana
38	Georgia
39	North Carolina
40	West Virginia
41	Arkansas
42	Tennessee
43	Nebraska
44	Oklahoma
45	Ohio
46	Iowa
47	Mississippi
48	North Dakota
49	Idaho
50	Wyoming

Note: Numbers that appear to be identical are rounded and vary slightly in actual value. The rankings reflect the actual values before rounding. See the introduction for more details.

G-14 State and Local Full Faith and Credit Debt, FY 2004

State	Full faith and credit debt $ (in millions)	Per capita $	As a percentage of personal income	Rank per capita
Alabama	7,972	1,760	6.7	31
Alaska	2,881	4,395	13.4	6
Arizona	10,340	1,800	6.9	30
Arkansas	3,372	1,225	5.1	40
California	103,878	2,894	8.8	13
Colorado	9,041	1,965	5.8	24
Connecticut	19,192	5,478	12.7	1
Delaware	2,162	2,604	7.9	14
Florida	19,764	1,136	3.9	41
Georgia	16,213	1,836	6.4	27
Hawaii	6,451	5,108	16.8	4
Idaho	1,006	722	2.9	45
Illinois	60,510	4,759	14.4	5
Indiana	4,071	653	2.3	48
Iowa	4,069	1,377	4.9	37
Kansas	5,451	1,993	6.8	22
Kentucky	4,594	1,108	4.2	42
Louisiana	6,774	1,500	5.8	36
Maine	2,091	1,587	5.5	32
Maryland	11,882	2,138	5.8	19
Massachusetts	33,394	5,204	13.2	3
Michigan	24,326	2,405	7.7	18
Minnesota	16,404	3,216	9.5	11
Mississippi	5,878	2,025	8.7	20
Missouri	7,074	1,229	4.3	39
Montana	609	657	2.6	47
Nebraska	2,312	1,324	4.4	38
Nevada	12,309	5,272	17.4	2
New Hampshire	2,540	1,954	5.7	25
New Jersey	21,421	2,463	6.2	17
New Mexico	3,449	1,812	7.2	29
New York	81,404	4,234	11.7	7
North Carolina	16,088	1,884	6.8	26
North Dakota	576	908	3.2	43
Ohio	22,972	2,005	6.7	21
Oklahoma	2,200	624	2.4	49
Oregon	12,703	3,534	12.4	9
Pennsylvania	39,217	3,161	10.0	12
Rhode Island	2,134	1,975	6.2	23
South Carolina	10,881	2,592	10.0	15
South Dakota	695	902	3.2	44
Tennessee	10,705	1,814	6.4	28
Texas	56,283	2,503	8.8	16
Utah	3,722	1,558	6.3	34
Vermont	986	1,587	5.2	33
Virginia	11,569	1,551	4.7	35
Washington	22,604	3,644	11.1	8
West Virginia	1,306	719	2.9	46
Wisconsin	18,790	3,411	11.2	10
Wyoming	146	288	0.9	50
50 States	746,411	2,547	8.2	
DC	4,624	8,354	17.4	
United States	751,035	2,558	8.2	

Rank in order per capita

1 Connecticut
2 Nevada
3 Massachusetts
4 Hawaii
5 Illinois
6 Alaska
7 New York
8 Washington
9 Oregon
10 Wisconsin
11 Minnesota
12 Pennsylvania
13 California
14 Delaware
15 South Carolina
16 Texas
17 New Jersey
18 Michigan
19 Maryland
20 Mississippi
21 Ohio
22 Kansas
23 Rhode Island
24 Colorado
25 New Hampshire
26 North Carolina
27 Georgia
28 Tennessee
29 New Mexico
30 Arizona
31 Alabama
32 Maine
33 Vermont
34 Utah
35 Virginia
36 Louisiana
37 Iowa
38 Nebraska
39 Missouri
40 Arkansas
41 Florida
42 Kentucky
43 North Dakota
44 South Dakota
45 Idaho
46 West Virginia
47 Montana
48 Indiana
49 Oklahoma
50 Wyoming

Note: Numbers that appear to be identical are rounded and vary slightly in actual value. The rankings reflect the actual values before rounding. See the introduction for more details.

G-15 State Government Bond Ratings, 2006

State	State bond ratings	Rank
Alabama	Aa2	3
Alaska	Aa2	3
Arizona	no general obligation debt	n/a
Arkansas	Aa2	3
California	A1	5
Colorado	no general obligation debt	n/a
Connecticut	Aa3	4
Delaware	Aaa	1
Florida	Aa1	2
Georgia	Aaa	1
Hawaii	Aa2	3
Idaho	no general obligation debt	n/a
Illinois	Aa3	4
Indiana	no general obligation debt	n/a
Iowa	no general obligation debt	n/a
Kansas	no general obligation debt	n/a
Kentucky	no general obligation debt	n/a
Louisiana	A2	6
Maine	Aa3	4
Maryland	Aaa	1
Massachusetts	Aa2	3
Michigan	Aa2	3
Minnesota	Aa1	2
Mississippi	Aa3	4
Missouri	Aaa	1
Montana	Aa3	4
Nebraska	no general obligation debt	n/a
Nevada	Aa1	2
New Hampshire	Aa2	3
New Jersey	Aa3	4
New Mexico	Aa1	2
New York	Aa3	4
North Carolina	Aa1	2
North Dakota	no general obligation debt	n/a
Ohio	Aa1	2
Oklahoma	Aa3	4
Oregon	Aa3	4
Pennsylvania	Aa2	3
Rhode Island	Aa3	4
South Carolina	Aaa	1
South Dakota	no general obligation debt	n/a
Tennessee	Aa2	3
Texas	Aa1	2
Utah	Aaa	1
Vermont	Aa1	2
Virginia	Aaa	1
Washington	Aa1	2
West Virginia	Aa3	4
Wisconsin	Aa3	4
Wyoming	no general obligation debt	n/a
50 States	n/a	
DC	A2	
United States	n/a	

Rank in order by rating

1	Delaware
1	Georgia
1	Maryland
1	Missouri
1	South Carolina
1	Utah
1	Virginia
2	Florida
2	Minnesota
2	Nevada
2	New Mexico
2	North Carolina
2	Ohio
2	Texas
2	Vermont
2	Washington
3	Alabama
3	Alaska
3	Arkansas
3	Hawaii
3	Massachusetts
3	Michigan
3	New Hampshire
3	Pennsylvania
3	Tennessee
4	Connecticut
4	Illinois
4	Maine
4	Mississippi
4	Montana
4	New Jersey
4	New York
4	Oklahoma
4	Oregon
4	Rhode Island
4	West Virginia
4	Wisconsin
5	California
6	Louisiana

Note: Ties in ranking reflect ties in actual values.

G-16 State Solvency Index, 2004

State	State solvency index	Rank by index
Alabama	-697	20
Alaska	38,677	1
Arizona	-477	16
Arkansas	-557	18
California	-1,479	32
Colorado	-1,642	34
Connecticut	-5,507	50
Delaware	231	10
Florida	1,897	5
Georgia	-326	15
Hawaii	-4,542	47
Idaho	19	12
Illinois	-4,594	48
Indiana	-845	23
Iowa	-246	14
Kansas	-1,855	36
Kentucky	-1,420	29
Louisiana	-1,733	35
Maine	-1,446	30
Maryland	-1,474	31
Massachusetts	-5,486	49
Michigan	-1,355	26
Minnesota	-1,532	33
Mississippi	-2,553	43
Missouri	-1,050	25
Montana	110	11
Nebraska	351	9
Nevada	-2,212	39
New Hampshire	-1,384	27
New Jersey	-594	19
New Mexico	3,210	3
New York	-3,317	45
North Carolina	1,050	8
North Dakota	2,218	4
Ohio	-2,590	44
Oklahoma	-2,098	38
Oregon	-988	24
Pennsylvania	-831	22
Rhode Island	-4,354	46
South Carolina	-2,304	40
South Dakota	1,508	6
Tennessee	6	13
Texas	1,108	7
Utah	-1,415	28
Vermont	-703	21
Virginia	-503	17
Washington	-2,052	37
West Virginia	-2,326	41
Wisconsin	-2,361	42
Wyoming	7,517	2
50 States	-1,134	
DC	n/a	
United States	-1,132	

Rank in order by index	
1	Alaska
2	Wyoming
3	New Mexico
4	North Dakota
5	Florida
6	South Dakota
7	Texas
8	North Carolina
9	Nebraska
10	Delaware
11	Montana
12	Idaho
13	Tennessee
14	Iowa
15	Georgia
16	Arizona
17	Virginia
18	Arkansas
19	New Jersey
20	Alabama
21	Vermont
22	Pennsylvania
23	Indiana
24	Oregon
25	Missouri
26	Michigan
27	New Hampshire
28	Utah
29	Kentucky
30	Maine
31	Maryland
32	California
33	Minnesota
34	Colorado
35	Louisiana
36	Kansas
37	Washington
38	Oklahoma
39	Nevada
40	South Carolina
41	West Virginia
42	Wisconsin
43	Mississippi
44	Ohio
45	New York
46	Rhode Island
47	Hawaii
48	Illinois
49	Massachusetts
50	Connecticut

G-17 Assets of State-Administered Pension Plans, FY 2005

State	Total assets $ (in millions)	Total membership #	Average assets per member	Rank by average
Alabama	26,749	255,562	104,669	37
Alaska	11,356	69,425	163,573	12
Arizona	32,140	406,037	79,154	48
Arkansas	16,024	140,579	113,989	32
California	513,089	2,145,116	239,189	3
Colorado	40,941	330,627	123,828	25
Connecticut	25,507	140,012	182,180	6
Delaware	6,411	43,277	148,143	16
Florida	129,848	764,886	169,761	11
Georgia	64,870	556,429	116,583	30
Hawaii	9,326	67,948	137,250	18
Idaho	8,546	72,913	117,212	29
Illinois	114,889	914,519	125,627	23
Indiana	23,477	279,418	84,020	45
Iowa	21,550	231,513	93,085	40
Kansas	12,380	191,357	64,696	50
Kentucky	28,422	302,577	93,932	38
Louisiana	32,230	258,247	124,801	24
Maine	8,821	49,107	179,637	8
Maryland	43,772	278,924	156,933	14
Massachusetts	52,039	371,910	139,924	17
Michigan	73,641	474,053	155,344	15
Minnesota	47,160	502,921	93,772	39
Mississippi	20,267	282,286	71,795	49
Missouri	49,380	313,855	157,333	13
Montana	6,521	73,607	88,590	43
Nebraska	8,280	78,990	104,830	36
Nevada	19,874	103,253	192,475	4
New Hampshire	4,914	53,346	92,122	41
New Jersey	59,117	526,872	112,204	34
New Mexico	18,980	155,868	121,772	26
New York	311,670	1,286,501	242,262	2
North Carolina	64,963	537,774	120,800	27
North Dakota	3,185	35,006	90,975	42
Ohio	136,819	1,178,882	116,058	31
Oklahoma	20,318	172,322	117,906	28
Oregon	50,696	199,579	254,016	1
Pennsylvania	91,871	540,371	170,014	10
Rhode Island	8,507	46,923	181,290	7
South Carolina	29,638	372,147	79,640	47
South Dakota	6,906	50,352	137,154	19
Tennessee	34,199	251,487	135,989	22
Texas	152,494	1,338,073	113,965	33
Utah	16,941	124,020	136,596	20
Vermont	2,832	33,188	85,331	44
Virginia	53,254	489,724	108,743	35
Washington	52,304	301,468	173,496	9
West Virginia	5,704	68,463	83,319	46
Wisconsin	75,722	414,885	182,514	5
Wyoming	5,871	43,170	136,001	21
50 States	2,654,416	17,919,769	148,128	
DC	3,110	11,803	263,512	
United States	2,657,526	17,931,572	148,204	

Rank in order by average	
1	Oregon
2	New York
3	California
4	Nevada
5	Wisconsin
6	Connecticut
7	Rhode Island
8	Maine
9	Washington
10	Pennsylvania
11	Florida
12	Alaska
13	Missouri
14	Maryland
15	Michigan
16	Delaware
17	Massachusetts
18	Hawaii
19	South Dakota
20	Utah
21	Wyoming
22	Tennessee
23	Illinois
24	Louisiana
25	Colorado
26	New Mexico
27	North Carolina
28	Oklahoma
29	Idaho
30	Georgia
31	Ohio
32	Arkansas
33	Texas
34	New Jersey
35	Virginia
36	Nebraska
37	Alabama
38	Kentucky
39	Minnesota
40	Iowa
41	New Hampshire
42	North Dakota
43	Montana
44	Vermont
45	Indiana
46	West Virginia
47	South Carolina
48	Arizona
49	Mississippi
50	Kansas

G-18 State Reserves at the End of FY 2006

State	Balances as a percentage of expenditures	Rank
Alabama	7.9	24
Alaska	59.2	2
Arizona	14.7	8
Arkansas	0.0	50
California	7.8	25
Colorado	5.7	32
Connecticut	6.7	30
Delaware	17.6	5
Florida	16.8	6
Georgia	7.1	27
Hawaii	12.3	10
Idaho	7.0	28
Illinois	2.9	43
Indiana	3.9	38
Iowa	12.1	11
Kansas	9.2	21
Kentucky	7.7	26
Louisiana	10.0	19
Maine	1.9	46
Maryland	15.9	7
Massachusetts	10.2	18
Michigan	0.9	47
Minnesota	5.6	33
Mississippi	0.7	48
Missouri	8.9	22
Montana	13.8	9
Nebraska	20.1	4
Nevada	6.3	31
New Hampshire	3.5	39
New Jersey	3.0	42
New Mexico	9.5	20
New York	7.0	28
North Carolina	2.5	44
North Dakota	23.8	3
Ohio	4.0	37
Oklahoma	11.1	14
Oregon	8.6	23
Pennsylvania	2.5	44
Rhode Island	3.5	39
South Carolina	11.9	12
South Dakota	10.4	16
Tennessee	5.6	33
Texas	10.9	15
Utah	4.4	36
Vermont	4.8	35
Virginia	11.5	13
Washington	10.3	17
West Virginia	3.2	41
Wisconsin	0.1	49
Wyoming	72.6	1
50 States	n/a	
DC	n/a	
United States	7.9	

Rank in order by percentage

1	Wyoming
2	Alaska
3	North Dakota
4	Nebraska
5	Delaware
6	Florida
7	Maryland
8	Arizona
9	Montana
10	Hawaii
11	Iowa
12	South Carolina
13	Virginia
14	Oklahoma
15	Texas
16	South Dakota
17	Washington
18	Massachusetts
19	Louisiana
20	New Mexico
21	Kansas
22	Missouri
23	Oregon
24	Alabama
25	California
26	Kentucky
27	Georgia
28	Idaho
28	New York
30	Connecticut
31	Nevada
32	Colorado
33	Minnesota
33	Tennessee
35	Vermont
36	Utah
37	Ohio
38	Indiana
39	New Hampshire
39	Rhode Island
41	West Virginia
42	New Jersey
43	Illinois
44	North Carolina
44	Pennsylvania
46	Maine
47	Michigan
48	Mississippi
49	Wisconsin
50	Arkansas

Note: Ties in ranking reflect ties in actual values.

G-19 State and Local Capital Outlays and Interest, FY 2004

State	Outlays and interest per capita $	Capital outlays per capita $	Interest per capita $	Rank by outlays and interest per capita
Alabama	1,029	800	229	34
Alaska	2,760	2,096	664	1
Arizona	1,246	994	252	16
Arkansas	844	670	174	44
California	1,366	1,021	344	10
Colorado	1,612	1,254	358	7
Connecticut	1,125	667	458	23
Delaware	1,376	995	381	9
Florida	1,348	1,026	322	11
Georgia	1,166	971	195	19
Hawaii	1,121	738	383	24
Idaho	931	776	155	39
Illinois	1,279	863	415	13
Indiana	905	692	212	42
Iowa	1,099	938	161	25
Kansas	1,127	852	276	22
Kentucky	1,081	695	385	27
Louisiana	1,053	755	298	29
Maine	947	661	286	38
Maryland	918	638	280	41
Massachusetts	1,636	1,096	540	5
Michigan	1,031	747	284	33
Minnesota	1,323	987	336	12
Mississippi	812	626	186	47
Missouri	974	743	231	36
Montana	1,032	820	212	32
Nebraska	1,541	1,309	232	8
Nevada	1,630	1,263	367	6
New Hampshire	902	585	316	43
New Jersey	1,145	859	285	21
New Mexico	928	727	201	40
New York	1,929	1,419	510	2
North Carolina	983	783	200	35
North Dakota	1,178	925	253	18
Ohio	1,070	805	265	28
Oklahoma	791	589	202	48
Oregon	1,040	757	284	31
Pennsylvania	1,046	654	392	30
Rhode Island	820	517	303	46
South Carolina	1,192	863	329	17
South Dakota	1,147	938	209	20
Tennessee	791	610	181	49
Texas	1,278	970	308	14
Utah	1,269	982	286	15
Vermont	788	496	292	50
Virginia	964	704	260	37
Washington	1,747	1,364	383	4
West Virginia	837	605	232	45
Wisconsin	1,086	789	297	26
Wyoming	1,779	1,571	208	3
50 States	1,235	916	318	
DC	2,975	2,449	526	
United States	1,238	919	318	

Rank in order per capita	
1	Alaska
2	New York
3	Wyoming
4	Washington
5	Massachusetts
6	Nevada
7	Colorado
8	Nebraska
9	Delaware
10	California
11	Florida
12	Minnesota
13	Illinois
14	Texas
15	Utah
16	Arizona
17	South Carolina
18	North Dakota
19	Georgia
20	South Dakota
21	New Jersey
22	Kansas
23	Connecticut
24	Hawaii
25	Iowa
26	Wisconsin
27	Kentucky
28	Ohio
29	Louisiana
30	Pennsylvania
31	Oregon
32	Montana
33	Michigan
34	Alabama
35	North Carolina
36	Missouri
37	Virginia
38	Maine
39	Idaho
40	New Mexico
41	Maryland
42	Indiana
43	New Hampshire
44	Arkansas
45	West Virginia
46	Rhode Island
47	Mississippi
48	Oklahoma
49	Tennessee
50	Vermont

G-20 Index of State Budget Process Quality, 2002

State	Index of state budget process quality	Rank
Alabama	56.9	40
Alaska	49.0	45
Arizona	48.6	46
Arkansas	52.0	42
California	60.5	35
Colorado	73.7	14
Connecticut	72.4	15
Delaware	67.0	21
Florida	76.0	13
Georgia	93.0	1
Hawaii	77.0	12
Idaho	37.9	47
Illinois	81.2	3
Indiana	29.9	49
Iowa	72.2	16
Kansas	59.0	39
Kentucky	65.5	26
Louisiana	80.5	6
Maine	62.0	31
Maryland	77.1	11
Massachusetts	79.2	7
Michigan	81.4	2
Minnesota	80.8	5
Mississippi	60.3	37
Missouri	70.9	18
Montana	66.0	24
Nebraska	64.0	28
Nevada	71.0	17
New Hampshire	27.5	50
New Jersey	77.5	9
New Mexico	78.0	8
New York	68.4	20
North Carolina	53.0	41
North Dakota	60.4	36
Ohio	60.6	34
Oklahoma	69.0	19
Oregon	66.8	22
Pennsylvania	65.7	25
Rhode Island	77.3	10
South Carolina	62.7	29
South Dakota	66.4	23
Tennessee	61.5	32
Texas	62.7	29
Utah	81.2	3
Vermont	37.7	48
Virginia	52.0	42
Washington	61.1	33
West Virginia	59.6	38
Wisconsin	51.9	44
Wyoming	64.2	27
50 States	64.6	
DC	n/a	
United States	64.6	

Rank in order by index

1 Georgia
2 Michigan
3 Illinois
3 Utah
5 Minnesota
6 Louisiana
7 Massachusetts
8 New Mexico
9 New Jersey
10 Rhode Island
11 Maryland
12 Hawaii
13 Florida
14 Colorado
15 Connecticut
16 Iowa
17 Nevada
18 Missouri
19 Oklahoma
20 New York
21 Delaware
22 Oregon
23 South Dakota
24 Montana
25 Pennsylvania
26 Kentucky
27 Wyoming
28 Nebraska
29 South Carolina
29 Texas
31 Maine
32 Tennessee
33 Washington
34 Ohio
35 California
36 North Dakota
37 Mississippi
38 West Virginia
39 Kansas
40 Alabama
41 North Carolina
42 Arkansas
42 Virginia
44 Wisconsin
45 Alaska
46 Arizona
47 Idaho
48 Vermont
49 Indiana
50 New Hampshire

Note: Ties in ranking reflect ties in actual values.

G-21 Relative State Spending "Needs," FY 2002

State	Additional spending needed to meet national average %	Rank by least "need" to most
Alabama	8	46
Alaska	0	30
Arizona	2	33
Arkansas	9	48
California	3	37
Colorado	-7	7
Connecticut	-4	18
Delaware	-7	7
Florida	-6	14
Georgia	5	43
Hawaii	-13	1
Idaho	-2	27
Illinois	2	33
Indiana	-2	27
Iowa	-9	3
Kansas	-3	22
Kentucky	2	33
Louisiana	10	49
Maine	-7	7
Maryland	-5	16
Massachusetts	-5	16
Michigan	4	39
Minnesota	-8	6
Mississippi	13	50
Missouri	-3	22
Montana	-3	22
Nebraska	-6	14
Nevada	-9	3
New Hampshire	-12	2
New Jersey	-3	22
New Mexico	8	46
New York	1	31
North Carolina	2	33
North Dakota	4	39
Ohio	-3	22
Oklahoma	1	31
Oregon	-7	7
Pennsylvania	-7	7
Rhode Island	-7	7
South Carolina	5	43
South Dakota	-4	18
Tennessee	4	39
Texas	7	45
Utah	3	37
Vermont	-9	3
Virginia	-4	18
Washington	-4	18
West Virginia	4	39
Wisconsin	-7	7
Wyoming	-2	27
50 States	n/a	
DC	n/a	
United States	0	

Rank in order by percentage

1	Hawaii
2	New Hampshire
3	Iowa
3	Nevada
3	Vermont
6	Minnesota
7	Colorado
7	Delaware
7	Maine
7	Oregon
7	Pennsylvania
7	Rhode Island
7	Wisconsin
14	Florida
14	Nebraska
16	Maryland
16	Massachusetts
18	Connecticut
18	South Dakota
18	Virginia
18	Washington
22	Kansas
22	Missouri
22	Montana
22	New Jersey
22	Ohio
27	Idaho
27	Indiana
27	Wyoming
30	Alaska
31	New York
31	Oklahoma
33	Arizona
33	Illinois
33	Kentucky
33	North Carolina
37	California
37	Utah
39	Michigan
39	North Dakota
39	Tennessee
39	West Virginia
43	Georgia
43	South Carolina
45	Texas
46	Alabama
46	New Mexico
48	Arkansas
49	Louisiana
50	Mississippi

Note: Ties in ranking reflect ties in actual values.

G-22 Structural Deficits

State	Projected state and local surplus or shortfall in 2013 as a percentage of baseline revenues	Rank
Alabama	-10.7	49
Alaska	-5.7	28
Arizona	-5.1	22
Arkansas	-4.2	13
California	-6.2	33
Colorado	-4.4	17
Connecticut	-3.8	11
Delaware	-1.0	2
Florida	-6.8	37
Georgia	-5.2	23
Hawaii	-5.3	25
Idaho	-6.9	38
Illinois	-5.6	26
Indiana	-6.5	35
Iowa	-6.3	34
Kansas	-3.9	12
Kentucky	-4.8	19
Louisiana	-10.5	48
Maine	-1.6	4
Maryland	-2.1	5
Massachusetts	-2.3	6
Michigan	-4.8	19
Minnesota	-4.4	17
Mississippi	-9.8	47
Missouri	-7.4	41
Montana	-5.8	30
Nebraska	-4.3	15
Nevada	-9.3	45
New Hampshire	-0.5	1
New Jersey	-1.0	2
New Mexico	-5.9	32
New York	-5.2	23
North Carolina	-6.7	36
North Dakota	-3.3	10
Ohio	-3.0	9
Oklahoma	-4.3	15
Oregon	-8.2	43
Pennsylvania	-5.6	26
Rhode Island	-5.7	28
South Carolina	-7.0	39
South Dakota	-7.0	39
Tennessee	-9.3	45
Texas	-8.9	44
Utah	-5.8	30
Vermont	-2.9	8
Virginia	-4.2	13
Washington	-8.0	42
West Virginia	-4.8	19
Wisconsin	-2.8	7
Wyoming	-12.9	50
50 States	n/a	
DC	n/a	
United States	-5.7	

Rank in order by percentage	
1	New Hampshire
2	Delaware
2	New Jersey
4	Maine
5	Maryland
6	Massachusetts
7	Wisconsin
8	Vermont
9	Ohio
10	North Dakota
11	Connecticut
12	Kansas
13	Arkansas
13	Virginia
15	Nebraska
15	Oklahoma
17	Colorado
17	Minnesota
19	Kentucky
19	Michigan
19	West Virginia
22	Arizona
23	Georgia
23	New York
25	Hawaii
26	Illinois
26	Pennsylvania
28	Alaska
28	Rhode Island
30	Montana
30	Utah
32	New Mexico
33	California
34	Iowa
35	Indiana
36	North Carolina
37	Florida
38	Idaho
39	South Carolina
39	South Dakota
41	Missouri
42	Washington
43	Oregon
44	Texas
45	Nevada
45	Tennessee
47	Mississippi
48	Louisiana
49	Alabama
50	Wyoming

Note: Ties in ranking reflect ties in actual values.

Source Notes for Revenues and Finances (Section G)

G-1 State and Local Total Revenue, FY 2004: This table and many others in this section of *State Fact Finder* rely on analysis of data collected by the U.S. Census Bureau for fiscal year 2004. For sources of the fiscal data and the population and personal income estimates used to build the tables, see the extensive note associated with Table F-1.

Total revenue, shown in this table, is the most inclusive definition of the financial size of state and local governments used by the bureau in its annual survey of government finances. It includes utilities run by state and local governments and many categories of trust funds. Such funds typically collect revenues, such as unemployment insurance taxes, for a particular purpose, such as paying unemployment compensation benefits, and are not commingled with other public funds. The revenues included come from state and local taxes, fees such as hospital charges and university tuition, and from the federal government.

G-2 State and Local General Revenue, FY 2004: From the same source as Table F-1, this table relates general revenue to population and personal income in each state. Because general revenue eliminates difficult to compare proprietary functions, such as utility and trust fund revenues, it allows for more appropriate state-by-state comparisons.

G-3 State and Local "Own-Source" General Revenue, FY 2004: These data reflect the concept often used to measure the fiscal burdens associated with state and local activity. Revenues from federal aid are excluded, along with the revenues of trust funds and utilities. For source see the notes to Table F-1.

G-4 State and Local Non-Tax "Own-Source" Revenue, FY 2004: The principal sources of non-tax revenues are (1) fees related to use of state facilities and services, such as those charged by public hospitals and universities, and (2) interest earned on money held by governments in anticipation of spending. For source see the notes to Table F-1.

G-5 State and Local Total Expenditures, FY 2004: This is the spending counterpart of the revenues shown on Table G-1. For source see the notes to Table F-1.

G-6 State and Local General Expenditures, FY 2004: This concept of "general" spending (see notes to Table G-2) is the most appropriate for comparing spending among states. For source see the notes to Table F-1.

G-7 State and Local General Expenditures Per Capita, FY 2004: This table relates general expenditures to population with separate totals for state governments and local governments. State aid to local governments is included only when local officials spend the resources, to avoid double counting. For source see the notes to Table F-1.

G-8 Percentage Change in State and Local Expenditures, FY 1999–2004: This statistic shows the differences among states in the five-year growth of state and local spending. The changes shown are not adjusted for factors that might account for some of the differences in growth rates, such as growth in population and other factors affecting needs for government services. Fiscal year 1997 data are from the U.S. Census Bureau and are published in *State Fact Finder 2002*. For fiscal year 2004 data, see source for Table F-1.

G-9 State Government General Revenue, FY 2004: Unlike Tables G-1 through G-8, these data deal with state governments alone, not state and local governments combined. They are from the 2004 version of "State Government Finances," available on the U.S. Census Bureau Web site (www.census.gov).

For most purposes, comparisons of finances among states need to include state and local revenues and spending because of major differences in the division of state and local responsibilities between states. For example, New York local governments pay nearly half of all state and local welfare costs, but local governments in most other states have almost no responsibility for paying these costs. Comparisons of states alone would make New York spending look artificially small. In Hawaii, the state alone pays for schools, while in other states local governments pay half these costs. Comparisons of states alone would make Hawaii's spending look artificially large.

However, comparisons of state governments alone are useful for those attempting to evaluate state officeholders and aspirants and for discussions of state government spending priorities and tax burdens.

This table and Table G-10 show "general" revenues and expenditures, a less inclusive measure than "total" expenditures. The difference is primarily associated with enterprises run by some state governments and not others, particularly liquor sales monopolies run by about a third of the states and the electric power marketing operations run by a few states. State impacts on utility services and liquor prices and sales are similar from state to state but some states achieve them by directly managing these functions. Because huge amounts of money are involved, inclusion of these operations in state comparisons would artificially distort the spending comparisons, so the concepts of general expenditures and general revenues exclude them.

G-10 State Government General Spending, FY 2004: See notes to Table G-9.

G-11 State Government General Fund Spending, FY 2005: These data reflect other estimates of state government spending. They come from a survey of state executive branch budget offices reported in the *2005 State Expenditure Report* by the National Association of State Budget Officers (NASBO). They reflect state fiscal year 2005 definitions. The year ended on June 30, 2005, for forty-six states, while one state ended the fiscal year in the spring and three ended in the fall.

The NASBO report differs from the U.S. Census Bureau reports in many ways. The bureau reports include all funds, while the NASBO report covers primarily funds subject to appropriation by legislatures and therefore for most states excludes funds of quasi-independent entities such as toll highway authorities. The bureau does not distinguish among funds within state government, while the NASBO report presents data separately for state general funds, federal funds, and other state funds. The data shown in the table reflect the total of all reported funds. The NASBO data use different definitions of spending categories than do the U.S. Census Bureau data. See the notes for Table G-9 on the hazards of considering state spending without also considering local spending.

G-12 State and Local Debt, FY 2004: These data, from the U.S. Census Bureau (see notes to Table F-1), reflect the total debt of all state and local governments at the end of fiscal year 2002, including debt of special authorities.

G-13 State and Local Debt Related to Revenue, FY 2004: This table relates total debt (see Table G-12) to total revenue (see Table G-1). Consequently, it offers a measure of how state and local budgets are strained by the costs of paying principal and interest on past obligations.

G-14 State and Local Full Faith and Credit Debt, FY 2004: These data reflect the component of total debt (see Table G-12) that is backed by the "full faith and credit" of the governments that issued the debt. This debt, commonly known as "general obligation" debt, is backed by all revenue sources of the issuing government. The debt not included in these totals, often known as revenue bonds, is backed only by specified revenues, not general taxes.

G-15 State Government Bond Ratings, 2006: Because thousands of individual state and local governments issue bonds, purchasers such as individuals and mutual funds find it difficult to analyze the risks associated with each individual issue. As a result, three rating agencies (Fitch, Moody's, and Standard & Poor's) evaluate the quality of individual bond issues. The ratings of revenue bonds are unique to the bonds and the revenue sources that back them. The ratings of general obligation bonds shown in this table are reflections of the fiscal soundness of state governments overall. As a result, they affect perceptions of fiscal soundness of states by voters as well as by potential bond purchasers.

The ratings shown come from Moody's and are dated May 26, 2006. Ratings from the other two agencies would show about the same ranking of states. Moody's system considers Aaa highest, followed by Aa1, Aa2, Aa3, A1, A2,

and so on, down to lower ratings, which are awarded to some local governments but no states, which are generally considered good credit risks. Some states have so little general obligation debt that they have no recent ratings and therefore are not ranked in this table. While there is no clearly appropriate way to insert them in the rankings, many of these states have strong credit and would rank above many of the states shown in the rankings.

G-16 State Solvency Index, 2004: While state financial reports and U.S. Census Bureau data provide substantial detail about state finances, they do not provide answers to some common sense questions about state financial status. One of these questions is equivalent to "net worth," a fundamental concept in viewing the finances of individuals and companies. This table reflects a special study created by State Policy Research using data from a variety of dates as close to late 2004 as possible. See *State Policy Reports* (vol. 20, no. 20) for more on the Solvency Index.

Conceptually, the number shown is an answer to the question: If each state were to cease operations tomorrow and pay off all debts (including pension promises to employees), how much money would be left over? For some states, the answer is that nothing would be left. Instead, they would have to levy a special assessment on each citizen (the amounts shown as negative numbers) in order to cease operations. Some states, particularly Alaska with its large reserves built from oil revenues, would have money left over that could be distributed to taxpayers. The calculations exclude the value of physical assets, such as state park lands, trucks, and computers.

G-17 Assets of State-Administered Pension Plans, FY 2005: States run pension plans for their own employees and, in most states, for teachers, city workers, and other local employees as well. To be considered actuarially sound, these plans must have built up enough assets from contributions of employees and their government employers to be able to cover the amounts needed to pay retired workers plus current workers when they retire. How much this amounts to depends on many factors, such as the exact benefits promised and the life expectancy of workers. There is no substitute for actuarial studies of each plan for determining the right amount each plan should have to cover future obligations. This table shows the assets of state-administered plans and the persons who are considered members of these plans—retirees and active workers accruing retirement benefits. Dividing these two numbers produces average assets per member, which is a rough measure of the relative solvency of the public pension plans in each state. The data come from the U.S. Census Bureau Web site (www. census.gov).

G-18 State Reserves at the End of FY 2006: These data reflect the projected cash reserves of state governments as they finished fiscal year 2006, generally in the summer of 2006. These reserves come in two primary forms—balances (equivalent to the balances people show in their checkbooks) and "rainy day" or stabilization funds (formal reserves, somewhat akin to the savings accounts maintained by individuals). The data come from a survey of state budget officers by the National Association of State Budget Officers (NASBO) published in June 2006, titled *The Fiscal Survey of States*, and available on the NASBO Web site (www.nasbo.org).

Relating balances to spending provides a basis for comparisons among states of different sizes and financial responsibilities. Nationwide, this table indicates that states have enough in reserve to pay their normal bills for about 7.9 percent of their fiscal years, or roughly twenty-nine days, with no additional revenue coming in.

G-19 State and Local Capital Outlays and Interest, FY 2004:
This table, from the same source as Table F-1, shows per capita amounts of spending in fiscal year 2002 for interest and capital outlays. The outlays reflect the pace of activity in financing new facilities, such as roads and schools. The interest reflects the extent to which taxpayers of each state are seeing their tax funds used to pay interest on past spending, normally borrowing to finance capital outlays.

G-20 Index of State Budget Process Quality, 2002:
Experts in public administration and budgeting generally agree on criteria of best budgeting practices, such as considering the impacts of spending and tax decisions over a longer period than one year. The numbers shown in the table are scores, with a perfect score being 100, developed by State Policy Research by comparing these criteria with actual state budget practices, as reported by the National Association of State Budget Officers (NASBO) in its special report *Budget Processes in the States* (January 2002).

G-21 Relative State Spending "Needs," FY 2002:
Individual states have quite different population characteristics, as shown by many of the tables in *State Fact Finder*. For example, school-age children are an extraordinarily large proportion of the population of Utah, but a smaller-than-average proportion of Pennsylvania's population. As a result, some states would have higher per capita spending than others, even if all states spent identical amounts per pupil, had identical welfare payments, and identical levels of other services. These differences are important to consider in viewing differences in per capita spending among states.

Robert Tannenwald of the Federal Reserve Bank of Boston partnered with the Tax Policy Center to create this table. It can be found in the Center's publication, *Measuring Fiscal Disparities Across the U.S. States*. Tannenwald and his co-authors calculated what state and local governments in each state would have to spend if they applied national average spending (for example, spending per pupil) to their own particular mix of population using government services. For example, to match national average spending patterns, Mississippi would have to spend 13 percent more than the national average. Why? Because the state has extra burdens associated with large percentages of welfare recipients and school-age children.

These data are conceptually similar to concepts of tax capacity shown in Table F-4. Together, these data reflect a consistent pattern of strains that circumstances put on taxpayers and decision makers of individual states. More affluent states, such as Connecticut, often combine above-average tax bases with below-average spending needs while less affluent states, like Mississippi, show the reverse.

G-22 Structural Deficits:
Though current fiscal conditions are relatively sanguine, many state officials worry about *structural* deficits—long-term shortfalls because revenues from current taxes will be insufficient to cover the spending needed to maintain current programs. If such deficits exist, they would be obscured by extraordinary performance of the economy and tax collections, but would be magnified by *cyclical* deficits during any economic downturn.

This table shows the result of subtracting projected spending from projected revenues eight years from 2005. A budget gap or structural deficit is indicated by all the negative results. A value of zero indicates that state and local governments could cover the future costs of their current policies, including adjustments for inflation and workload changes, with revenues from their current tax system, with no change in tax rates or the definition of bases. A positive value means covering costs with money left.

The methodology used to derive this table was created by State Policy Research. An explanation of the methodology and the original calculations are published in *The Outlook for State and Local Finances*, National Education Association. The update that appears in this table was created by the National Center for Public Policy and Higher Education (www.highereducation.org).

Education

Percent Scoring Below Basic on NAEP Reading Test

	4th Grade	8th Grade
1998	40	27
2005	36	27

Percent Scoring Below Basic on NAEP Mathematics Test

	4th Grade	8th Grade
1996	37	39
2005	20	31

Percent Scoring Below Basic on NAEP Science Test

	4th Grade	8th Grade	12th Grade
1996	37	40	46
2005	32	41	43

Percent Scoring Below Basic on NAEP Writing Test

	4th Grade	8th Grade	12th Grade
1998	16	16	22
2002	14	15	26

Source: National Assessment of Educational Progress

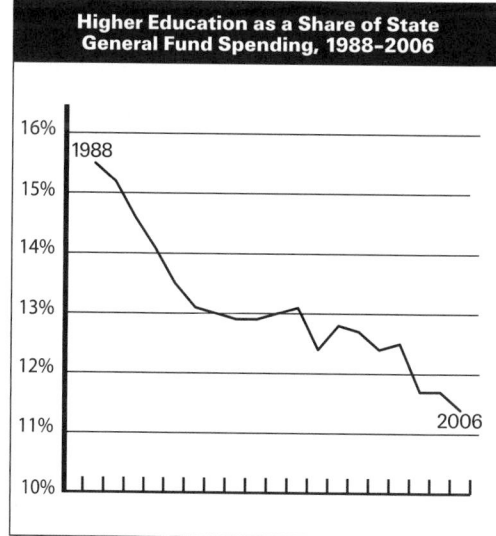

Higher Education as a Share of State General Fund Spending, 1988–2006

Source: National Association of State Budget Officers

H-1 Average Proficiency in Math, Eighth Grade, 2005

State	Average math score	Percent at or above basic	Rank by score
Alabama	262	53	49
Alaska	279	69	29
Arizona	274	64	35
Arkansas	272	64	38
California	269	57	44
Colorado	281	70	20
Connecticut	281	70	20
Delaware	281	72	20
Florida	274	65	35
Georgia	272	62	38
Hawaii	266	56	47
Idaho	281	73	20
Illinois	278	68	31
Indiana	282	74	16
Iowa	284	75	10
Kansas	284	77	10
Kentucky	274	64	35
Louisiana	268	59	46
Maine	281	74	20
Maryland	278	66	31
Massachusetts	292	80	1
Michigan	277	68	33
Minnesota	290	79	2
Mississippi	262	52	49
Missouri	276	68	34
Montana	286	80	6
Nebraska	284	75	10
Nevada	270	60	43
New Hampshire	285	77	7
New Jersey	284	74	10
New Mexico	263	53	48
New York	280	70	28
North Carolina	282	72	16
North Dakota	287	81	3
Ohio	283	74	15
Oklahoma	271	63	41
Oregon	282	72	16
Pennsylvania	281	72	20
Rhode Island	272	63	38
South Carolina	281	71	20
South Dakota	287	80	3
Tennessee	271	61	41
Texas	281	72	20
Utah	279	71	29
Vermont	287	78	3
Virginia	284	75	10
Washington	285	75	7
West Virginia	269	60	44
Wisconsin	285	76	7
Wyoming	282	76	16
50 States	n/a	n/a	
DC	245	31	
United States	278	68	

Rank in order by score	
1	Massachusetts
2	Minnesota
3	North Dakota
3	South Dakota
3	Vermont
6	Montana
7	New Hampshire
7	Washington
7	Wisconsin
10	Iowa
10	Kansas
10	Nebraska
10	New Jersey
10	Virginia
15	Ohio
16	Indiana
16	North Carolina
16	Oregon
16	Wyoming
20	Colorado
20	Connecticut
20	Delaware
20	Idaho
20	Maine
20	Pennsylvania
20	South Carolina
20	Texas
28	New York
29	Alaska
29	Utah
31	Illinois
31	Maryland
33	Michigan
34	Missouri
35	Arizona
35	Florida
35	Kentucky
38	Arkansas
38	Georgia
38	Rhode Island
41	Oklahoma
41	Tennessee
43	Nevada
44	California
44	West Virginia
46	Louisiana
47	Hawaii
48	New Mexico
49	Alabama
49	Mississippi

Note: Ties in ranking reflect ties in actual values.

H-2 Average Proficiency in Reading, Eighth Grade, 2005

State	Reading score	Percent at or above basic	Rank by score
Alabama	252	63	46
Alaska	259	70	34
Arizona	255	65	42
Arkansas	258	69	36
California	250	60	49
Colorado	265	75	19
Connecticut	264	74	23
Delaware	266	80	17
Florida	256	66	41
Georgia	257	67	39
Hawaii	249	58	50
Idaho	264	76	23
Illinois	264	75	23
Indiana	261	73	29
Iowa	267	79	12
Kansas	267	78	12
Kentucky	264	75	23
Louisiana	253	64	44
Maine	270	81	2
Maryland	261	69	29
Massachusetts	274	83	1
Michigan	261	73	29
Minnesota	268	80	9
Mississippi	251	60	47
Missouri	265	76	19
Montana	269	82	5
Nebraska	267	80	12
Nevada	253	63	44
New Hampshire	270	80	2
New Jersey	269	80	5
New Mexico	251	62	47
New York	265	75	19
North Carolina	258	69	36
North Dakota	270	83	2
Ohio	267	78	12
Oklahoma	260	72	33
Oregon	263	74	27
Pennsylvania	267	77	12
Rhode Island	261	71	29
South Carolina	257	67	39
South Dakota	269	82	5
Tennessee	259	71	34
Texas	258	69	36
Utah	262	73	28
Vermont	269	79	5
Virginia	268	78	9
Washington	265	75	19
West Virginia	255	67	42
Wisconsin	266	77	17
Wyoming	268	81	9
50 States	n/a	n/a	
DC	238	45	
United States	260	71	

	Rank in order by score
1	Massachusetts
2	Maine
2	New Hampshire
2	North Dakota
5	Montana
5	New Jersey
5	South Dakota
5	Vermont
9	Minnesota
9	Virginia
9	Wyoming
12	Iowa
12	Kansas
12	Nebraska
12	Ohio
12	Pennsylvania
17	Delaware
17	Wisconsin
19	Colorado
19	Missouri
19	New York
19	Washington
23	Connecticut
23	Idaho
23	Illinois
23	Kentucky
27	Oregon
28	Utah
29	Indiana
29	Maryland
29	Michigan
29	Rhode Island
33	Oklahoma
34	Alaska
34	Tennessee
36	Arkansas
36	North Carolina
36	Texas
39	Georgia
39	South Carolina
41	Florida
42	Arizona
42	West Virginia
44	Louisiana
44	Nevada
46	Alabama
47	Mississippi
47	New Mexico
49	California
50	Hawaii

Note: Ties in ranking reflect ties in actual values.

Armed Forces Qualification Test Ranks, FY 2004

State	AFQT rank	Rank
Alabama	60.1	45
Alaska	66.9	1
Arizona	63.4	24
Arkansas	60.4	43
California	61.4	37
Colorado	65.7	6
Connecticut	63.2	25
Delaware	62.2	33
Florida	61.5	36
Georgia	60.2	44
Hawaii	58.8	48
Idaho	65.7	6
Illinois	62.5	31
Indiana	65.5	9
Iowa	65.3	10
Kansas	65.1	15
Kentucky	60.8	41
Louisiana	58.0	49
Maine	65.1	15
Maryland	62.7	28
Massachusetts	64.2	18
Michigan	63.5	23
Minnesota	66.1	5
Mississippi	57.3	50
Missouri	62.2	33
Montana	65.3	10
Nebraska	65.2	12
Nevada	62.8	27
New Hampshire	66.7	2
New Jersey	61.0	40
New Mexico	59.8	47
New York	62.0	35
North Carolina	61.1	38
North Dakota	65.1	15
Ohio	64.0	19
Oklahoma	61.1	38
Oregon	66.3	4
Pennsylvania	63.8	21
Rhode Island	63.0	26
South Carolina	60.1	45
South Dakota	63.7	22
Tennessee	62.6	30
Texas	62.4	32
Utah	65.2	12
Vermont	63.9	20
Virginia	62.7	28
Washington	66.7	2
West Virginia	60.6	42
Wisconsin	65.7	6
Wyoming	65.2	12
50 States	n/a	
DC	58.6	
United States	62.5	

	Rank in order by rank
1	Alaska
2	New Hampshire
2	Washington
4	Oregon
5	Minnesota
6	Colorado
6	Idaho
6	Wisconsin
9	Indiana
10	Iowa
10	Montana
12	Nebraska
12	Utah
12	Wyoming
15	Kansas
15	Maine
15	North Dakota
18	Massachusetts
19	Ohio
20	Vermont
21	Pennsylvania
22	South Dakota
23	Michigan
24	Arizona
25	Connecticut
26	Rhode Island
27	Nevada
28	Maryland
28	Virginia
30	Tennessee
31	Illinois
32	Texas
33	Delaware
33	Missouri
35	New York
36	Florida
37	California
38	North Carolina
38	Oklahoma
40	New Jersey
41	Kentucky
42	West Virginia
43	Arkansas
44	Georgia
45	Alabama
45	South Carolina
47	New Mexico
48	Hawaii
49	Louisiana
50	Mississippi

Note: Ties in ranking reflect ties in actual values.

H-4 SAT Scores, 2006

State	Average SAT score	Percentage of graduates tested	Rank by score
Alabama	n/a	n/a	n/a
Alaska	1,034	51	6
Arizona	1,049	32	3
Arkansas	n/a	n/a	n/a
California	1,019	49	10
Colorado	n/a	n/a	n/a
Connecticut	1,028	84	8
Delaware	995	73	20
Florida	993	65	21
Georgia	990	70	24
Hawaii	991	60	23
Idaho	n/a	n/a	n/a
Illinois	n/a	n/a	n/a
Indiana	1,007	62	14
Iowa	n/a	n/a	n/a
Kansas	n/a	n/a	n/a
Kentucky	n/a	n/a	n/a
Louisiana	n/a	n/a	n/a
Maine	1,002	73	17
Maryland	1,012	70	11
Massachusetts	1,037	85	5
Michigan	n/a	n/a	n/a
Minnesota	n/a	n/a	n/a
Mississippi	n/a	n/a	n/a
Missouri	n/a	n/a	n/a
Montana	n/a	n/a	n/a
Nebraska	n/a	n/a	n/a
Nevada	1,006	40	15
New Hampshire	1,044	82	4
New Jersey	1,011	82	12
New Mexico	n/a	n/a	n/a
New York	1,003	88	16
North Carolina	1,008	71	13
North Dakota	n/a	n/a	n/a
Ohio	n/a	n/a	n/a
Oklahoma	n/a	n/a	n/a
Oregon	1,052	55	2
Pennsylvania	993	74	21
Rhode Island	997	69	18
South Carolina	985	62	25
South Dakota	n/a	n/a	n/a
Tennessee	n/a	n/a	n/a
Texas	997	52	18
Utah	n/a	n/a	n/a
Vermont	1,032	67	7
Virginia	1,025	73	9
Washington	1,059	54	1
West Virginia	n/a	n/a	n/a
Wisconsin	n/a	n/a	n/a
Wyoming	n/a	n/a	n/a
50 States	n/a	n/a	
DC	959	78	
United States	1,021	48	

Rank in order by score

1. Washington
2. Oregon
3. Arizona
4. New Hampshire
5. Massachusetts
6. Alaska
7. Vermont
8. Connecticut
9. Virginia
10. California
11. Maryland
12. New Jersey
13. North Carolina
14. Indiana
15. Nevada
16. New York
17. Maine
18. Rhode Island
18. Texas
20. Delaware
21. Florida
21. Pennsylvania
23. Hawaii
24. Georgia
25. South Carolina

Note: Ties in ranking reflect ties in actual values.

H-5   ACT Scores, 2006

State	ACT composite scores	Percentage of graduates tested	Rank by score
Alabama	20.2	79	22
Alaska	n/a	n/a	n/a
Arizona	n/a	n/a	n/a
Arkansas	20.6	75	16
California	n/a	n/a	n/a
Colorado	20.3	100	21
Connecticut	n/a	n/a	n/a
Delaware	n/a	n/a	n/a
Florida	n/a	n/a	n/a
Georgia	n/a	n/a	n/a
Hawaii	n/a	n/a	n/a
Idaho	21.4	57	13
Illinois	20.5	100	19
Indiana	n/a	n/a	n/a
Iowa	22.1	65	3
Kansas	21.8	75	6
Kentucky	20.6	76	16
Louisiana	20.1	74	23
Maine	n/a	n/a	n/a
Maryland	n/a	n/a	n/a
Massachusetts	n/a	n/a	n/a
Michigan	21.5	67	11
Minnesota	22.3	67	1
Mississippi	18.8	93	25
Missouri	21.6	70	9
Montana	21.9	57	4
Nebraska	21.9	76	4
Nevada	n/a	n/a	n/a
New Hampshire	n/a	n/a	n/a
New Jersey	n/a	n/a	n/a
New Mexico	20.1	60	23
New York	n/a	n/a	n/a
North Carolina	n/a	n/a	n/a
North Dakota	21.4	80	13
Ohio	21.5	66	11
Oklahoma	20.5	72	19
Oregon	n/a	n/a	n/a
Pennsylvania	n/a	n/a	n/a
Rhode Island	n/a	n/a	n/a
South Carolina	n/a	n/a	n/a
South Dakota	21.8	75	6
Tennessee	20.7	93	15
Texas	n/a	n/a	n/a
Utah	21.7	69	8
Vermont	n/a	n/a	n/a
Virginia	n/a	n/a	n/a
Washington	n/a	n/a	n/a
West Virginia	20.6	64	16
Wisconsin	22.2	68	2
Wyoming	21.6	71	9
50 States	n/a	n/a	
DC	n/a	n/a	
United States	21.1	40	

Rank in order by score	
1	Minnesota
2	Wisconsin
3	Iowa
4	Montana
4	Nebraska
6	Kansas
6	South Dakota
8	Utah
9	Missouri
9	Wyoming
11	Michigan
11	Ohio
13	Idaho
13	North Dakota
15	Tennessee
16	Arkansas
16	Kentucky
16	West Virginia
19	Illinois
19	Oklahoma
21	Colorado
22	Alabama
23	Louisiana
23	New Mexico
25	Mississippi

Note: Ties in ranking reflect ties in actual values.

H-6 Percentage of Population Over 25 with a High School Diploma, 2005

State	High school graduates %	Rank by percentage
Alabama	80.9	45
Alaska	91.7	5
Arizona	85.8	33
Arkansas	81.4	43
California	80.4	46
Colorado	89.3	15
Connecticut	90.0	10
Delaware	86.9	26
Florida	86.8	29
Georgia	85.7	34
Hawaii	87.2	22
Idaho	89.1	16
Illinois	87.2	22
Indiana	87.2	22
Iowa	89.8	13
Kansas	91.4	7
Kentucky	78.9	49
Louisiana	80.2	47
Maine	87.2	22
Maryland	86.9	26
Massachusetts	87.5	21
Michigan	88.6	17
Minnesota	92.7	1
Mississippi	79.8	48
Missouri	85.5	36
Montana	92.1	3
Nebraska	89.8	13
Nevada	86.6	30
New Hampshire	91.9	4
New Jersey	86.9	26
New Mexico	81.2	44
New York	85.7	34
North Carolina	84.0	38
North Dakota	90.0	10
Ohio	87.9	20
Oklahoma	85.2	37
Oregon	88.6	17
Pennsylvania	86.3	31
Rhode Island	83.9	39
South Carolina	83.0	40
South Dakota	88.4	19
Tennessee	81.8	42
Texas	78.2	50
Utah	92.5	2
Vermont	90.0	10
Virginia	86.0	32
Washington	91.5	6
West Virginia	82.5	41
Wisconsin	90.4	9
Wyoming	90.9	8
50 States	n/a	
DC	84.1	
United States	85.2	

Rank in order by percentage

1	Minnesota
2	Utah
3	Montana
4	New Hampshire
5	Alaska
6	Washington
7	Kansas
8	Wyoming
9	Wisconsin
10	Connecticut
10	North Dakota
10	Vermont
13	Iowa
13	Nebraska
15	Colorado
16	Idaho
17	Michigan
17	Oregon
19	South Dakota
20	Ohio
21	Massachusetts
22	Hawaii
22	Illinois
22	Indiana
22	Maine
26	Delaware
26	Maryland
26	New Jersey
29	Florida
30	Nevada
31	Pennsylvania
32	Virginia
33	Arizona
34	Georgia
34	New York
36	Missouri
37	Oklahoma
38	North Carolina
39	Rhode Island
40	South Carolina
41	West Virginia
42	Tennessee
43	Arkansas
44	New Mexico
45	Alabama
46	California
47	Louisiana
48	Mississippi
49	Kentucky
50	Texas

Note: Ties in ranking reflect ties in actual values.

H-7 Students in Private Schools, 2003–2004

State	Private school enrollment	Percentage of total enrollment	Rank by percentage
Alabama	73,105	9.9	21
Alaska	6,177	4.4	46
Arizona	46,366	4.6	44
Arkansas	27,500	5.7	40
California	623,105	9.0	25
Colorado	50,123	6.2	38
Connecticut	74,430	11.4	15
Delaware	25,576	17.8	1
Florida	323,766	11.1	16
Georgia	120,697	7.3	34
Hawaii	37,228	16.9	2
Idaho	10,994	4.2	47
Illinois	270,490	11.5	14
Indiana	109,101	9.7	22
Iowa	45,309	8.6	27
Kansas	41,762	8.2	29
Kentucky	71,067	10.1	19
Louisiana	140,492	16.2	3
Maine	20,696	9.3	23
Maryland	149,253	14.7	6
Massachusetts	134,708	12.1	11
Michigan	160,049	8.5	28
Minnesota	93,935	10.0	20
Mississippi	49,729	9.3	24
Missouri	119,812	11.8	12
Montana	8,924	5.7	41
Nebraska	39,454	12.2	10
Nevada	18,219	4.5	45
New Hampshire	23,692	10.3	18
New Jersey	204,732	12.9	9
New Mexico	22,416	6.5	37
New York	458,079	13.9	7
North Carolina	102,642	7.0	36
North Dakota	6,209	5.8	39
Ohio	239,323	11.6	13
Oklahoma	27,603	4.2	48
Oregon	46,968	7.8	33
Pennsylvania	316,337	14.9	5
Rhode Island	28,119	15.0	4
South Carolina	58,005	7.9	32
South Dakota	10,817	8.0	31
Tennessee	87,055	8.6	26
Texas	220,206	4.9	43
Utah	15,907	3.2	49
Vermont	12,218	11.1	17
Virginia	104,304	8.0	30
Washington	78,746	7.2	35
West Virginia	14,397	4.9	42
Wisconsin	134,474	13.3	8
Wyoming	2,079	2.4	50
50 States	5,106,395	9.6	
DC	16,376	20.1	
United States*	5,122,772	9.6	

Due to rounding or data sources, the 50-state total plus D.C. may not equal the U.S. total. Please see introduction.

Rank in order by percentage	
1	Delaware
2	Hawaii
3	Louisiana
4	Rhode Island
5	Pennsylvania
6	Maryland
7	New York
8	Wisconsin
9	New Jersey
10	Nebraska
11	Massachusetts
12	Missouri
13	Ohio
14	Illinois
15	Connecticut
16	Florida
17	Vermont
18	New Hampshire
19	Kentucky
20	Minnesota
21	Alabama
22	Indiana
23	Maine
24	Mississippi
25	California
26	Tennessee
27	Iowa
28	Michigan
29	Kansas
30	Virginia
31	South Dakota
32	South Carolina
33	Oregon
34	Georgia
35	Washington
36	North Carolina
37	New Mexico
38	Colorado
39	North Dakota
40	Arkansas
41	Montana
42	West Virginia
43	Texas
44	Arizona
45	Nevada
46	Alaska
47	Idaho
48	Oklahoma
49	Utah
50	Wyoming

Note: Numbers that appear to be identical are rounded and vary slightly in actual value. The rankings reflect the actual values before rounding. See the introduction for more details.

H-8   High School Dropout Rates, 2002

State	Dropout rates %	Rank
Alabama	3.7	29
Alaska	8.1	2
Arizona	10.5	1
Arkansas	5.3	12
California	n/a	n/a
Colorado	n/a	n/a
Connecticut	2.6	41
Delaware	6.2	9
Florida	3.7	29
Georgia	6.5	6
Hawaii	5.1	14
Idaho	3.9	22
Illinois	6.4	7
Indiana	2.3	44
Iowa	2.4	43
Kansas	3.1	36
Kentucky	4.0	19
Louisiana	7.0	5
Maine	2.8	39
Maryland	3.9	22
Massachusetts	n/a	n/a
Michigan	n/a	n/a
Minnesota	3.8	26
Mississippi	3.9	22
Missouri	3.6	33
Montana	3.9	22
Nebraska	4.2	18
Nevada	6.4	7
New Hampshire	4.0	19
New Jersey	2.5	42
New Mexico	5.2	13
New York	7.1	3
North Carolina	5.7	11
North Dakota	2.0	45
Ohio	3.1	36
Oklahoma	4.4	16
Oregon	4.9	15
Pennsylvania	3.3	34
Rhode Island	4.3	17
South Carolina	3.3	34
South Dakota	2.8	39
Tennessee	3.8	26
Texas	3.8	26
Utah	3.7	29
Vermont	4.0	19
Virginia	2.9	38
Washington	7.1	3
West Virginia	3.7	29
Wisconsin	1.9	46
Wyoming	5.8	10
50 States	n/a	
DC	n/a	
United States	3.6	

Rank in order by percentage

1	Arizona
2	Alaska
3	New York
3	Washington
5	Louisiana
6	Georgia
7	Illinois
7	Nevada
9	Delaware
10	Wyoming
11	North Carolina
12	Arkansas
13	New Mexico
14	Hawaii
15	Oregon
16	Oklahoma
17	Rhode Island
18	Nebraska
19	Kentucky
19	New Hampshire
19	Vermont
22	Idaho
22	Maryland
22	Mississippi
22	Montana
26	Minnesota
26	Tennessee
26	Texas
29	Alabama
29	Florida
29	Utah
29	West Virginia
33	Missouri
34	Pennsylvania
34	South Carolina
36	Kansas
36	Ohio
38	Virginia
39	Maine
39	South Dakota
41	Connecticut
42	New Jersey
43	Iowa
44	Indiana
45	North Dakota
46	Wisconsin

Note: Ties in ranking reflect ties in actual values.

H-9　Pupil-Teacher Ratio, 2004–2005

State	Pupils per teacher in public K-12 schools	Rank by ratio
Alabama	15.7	19
Alaska	16.8	11
Arizona	21.5	2
Arkansas	13.8	36
California	19.9	3
Colorado	17.0	9
Connecticut	13.3	41
Delaware	14.9	25
Florida	16.6	12
Georgia	14.8	27
Hawaii	16.1	14
Idaho	17.6	8
Illinois	15.9	16
Indiana	16.9	10
Iowa	13.8	36
Kansas	14.3	33
Kentucky	15.9	16
Louisiana	14.8	27
Maine	11.9	47
Maryland	15.4	22
Massachusetts	14.6	31
Michigan	17.8	7
Minnesota	16.0	15
Mississippi	15.8	18
Missouri	13.3	41
Montana	14.3	33
Nebraska	13.8	36
Nevada	19.4	5
New Hampshire	13.5	40
New Jersey	12.7	44
New Mexico	15.0	23
New York	12.7	44
North Carolina	14.8	27
North Dakota	12.9	43
Ohio	16.2	13
Oklahoma	15.6	20
Oregon	19.8	4
Pennsylvania	15.0	23
Rhode Island	11.3	49
South Carolina	14.6	31
South Dakota	13.6	39
Tennessee	15.6	20
Texas	14.9	25
Utah	22.6	1
Vermont	10.9	50
Virginia	11.8	48
Washington	19.3	6
West Virginia	14.1	35
Wisconsin	14.7	30
Wyoming	12.6	46
50 States	n/a	
DC	12.4	
United States	15.6	

Rank in order by ratio	
1	Utah
2	Arizona
3	California
4	Oregon
5	Nevada
6	Washington
7	Michigan
8	Idaho
9	Colorado
10	Indiana
11	Alaska
12	Florida
13	Ohio
14	Hawaii
15	Minnesota
16	Illinois
16	Kentucky
18	Mississippi
19	Alabama
20	Oklahoma
20	Tennessee
22	Maryland
23	New Mexico
23	Pennsylvania
25	Delaware
25	Texas
27	Georgia
27	Louisiana
27	North Carolina
30	Wisconsin
31	Massachusetts
31	South Carolina
33	Kansas
33	Montana
35	West Virginia
36	Arkansas
36	Iowa
36	Nebraska
39	South Dakota
40	New Hampshire
41	Connecticut
41	Missouri
43	North Dakota
44	New Jersey
44	New York
46	Wyoming
47	Maine
48	Virginia
49	Rhode Island
50	Vermont

Note: Ties in ranking reflect ties in actual values.

H-10 Public School Enrollment, 2005–2006

State	Enrollment (in thousands)	Percentage of total population	Rank by percentage
Alabama	738	16.3	24
Alaska	133	20.4	1
Arizona	1,010	17.6	9
Arkansas	453	16.5	18
California	6,424	17.9	7
Colorado	781	17.0	13
Connecticut	577	16.5	19
Delaware	121	14.6	48
Florida	2,670	15.3	40
Georgia	1,598	18.1	4
Hawaii	183	14.5	50
Idaho	251	18.0	5
Illinois	2,033	16.0	29
Indiana	1,034	16.6	16
Iowa	483	16.4	21
Kansas	467	17.1	12
Kentucky	638	15.4	38
Louisiana	654	14.5	49
Maine	199	15.1	44
Maryland	873	15.7	33
Massachusetts	972	15.1	43
Michigan	1,742	17.2	10
Minnesota	836	16.4	20
Mississippi	482	16.6	15
Missouri	898	15.6	36
Montana	145	15.7	34
Nebraska	286	16.3	22
Nevada	413	17.7	8
New Hampshire	206	15.8	32
New Jersey	1,395	16.0	28
New Mexico	327	17.2	11
New York	2,816	14.6	46
North Carolina	1,383	16.2	27
North Dakota	97	15.3	41
Ohio	1,863	16.3	26
Oklahoma	634	18.0	6
Oregon	553	15.4	39
Pennsylvania	1,813	14.6	47
Rhode Island	161	14.9	45
South Carolina	686	16.3	23
South Dakota	121	15.7	35
Tennessee	935	15.8	31
Texas	4,506	20.0	3
Utah	485	20.3	2
Vermont	95	15.2	42
Virginia	1,215	16.3	25
Washington	1,033	16.7	14
West Virginia	280	15.4	37
Wisconsin	875	15.9	30
Wyoming	84	16.5	17
50 States	48,658	16.6	
DC	61	11.1	
United States	48,719	16.6	

Rank in order by percentage

1. Alaska
2. Utah
3. Texas
4. Georgia
5. Idaho
6. Oklahoma
7. California
8. Nevada
9. Arizona
10. Michigan
11. New Mexico
12. Kansas
13. Colorado
14. Washington
15. Mississippi
16. Indiana
17. Wyoming
18. Arkansas
19. Connecticut
20. Minnesota
21. Iowa
22. Nebraska
23. South Carolina
24. Alabama
25. Virginia
26. Ohio
27. North Carolina
28. New Jersey
29. Illinois
30. Wisconsin
31. Tennessee
32. New Hampshire
33. Maryland
34. Montana
35. South Dakota
36. Missouri
37. West Virginia
38. Kentucky
39. Oregon
40. Florida
41. North Dakota
42. Vermont
43. Massachusetts
44. Maine
45. Rhode Island
46. New York
47. Pennsylvania
48. Delaware
49. Louisiana
50. Hawaii

Note: Numbers that appear to be identical are rounded and vary slightly in actual value. The rankings reflect the actual values before rounding. See the introduction for more details.

H-11 Public Library Holdings Per Capita, FY 2004

State	Holdings per capita	Rank per capita
Alabama	2.0	41
Alaska	3.4	20
Arizona	1.8	48
Arkansas	2.1	38
California	2.2	37
Colorado	2.6	30
Connecticut	4.2	9
Delaware	2.1	38
Florida	1.9	45
Georgia	1.8	48
Hawaii	2.5	34
Idaho	3.1	23
Illinois	3.8	16
Indiana	4.2	9
Iowa	4.1	13
Kansas	4.7	6
Kentucky	2.0	41
Louisiana	2.6	30
Maine	5.3	2
Maryland	2.7	27
Massachusetts	4.9	4
Michigan	3.4	20
Minnesota	3.2	22
Mississippi	2.0	41
Missouri	3.6	18
Montana	3.0	24
Nebraska	4.6	7
Nevada	1.7	50
New Hampshire	4.6	7
New Jersey	3.7	17
New Mexico	2.6	30
New York	3.9	14
North Carolina	1.9	45
North Dakota	4.2	9
Ohio	4.2	9
Oklahoma	2.4	35
Oregon	2.8	26
Pennsylvania	2.4	35
Rhode Island	3.9	14
South Carolina	2.1	38
South Dakota	5.5	1
Tennessee	1.9	45
Texas	2.0	41
Utah	2.7	27
Vermont	5.0	3
Virginia	2.6	30
Washington	2.9	25
West Virginia	2.7	27
Wisconsin	3.5	19
Wyoming	4.8	5
50 States	n/a	
DC	4.4	
United States	2.8	

Rank in order per capita	
1	South Dakota
2	Maine
3	Vermont
4	Massachusetts
5	Wyoming
6	Kansas
7	Nebraska
7	New Hampshire
9	Connecticut
9	Indiana
9	North Dakota
9	Ohio
13	Iowa
14	New York
14	Rhode Island
16	Illinois
17	New Jersey
18	Missouri
19	Wisconsin
20	Alaska
20	Michigan
22	Minnesota
23	Idaho
24	Montana
25	Washington
26	Oregon
27	Maryland
27	Utah
27	West Virginia
30	Colorado
30	Louisiana
30	New Mexico
30	Virginia
34	Hawaii
35	Oklahoma
35	Pennsylvania
37	California
38	Arkansas
38	Delaware
38	South Carolina
41	Alabama
41	Kentucky
41	Mississippi
41	Texas
45	Florida
45	North Carolina
45	Tennessee
48	Arizona
48	Georgia
50	Nevada

Note: Ties in ranking reflect ties in actual values.

H-12 Children with Disabilities, 2005

State	Children with disabilities #	Percentage of public school enrollment	Rank by percentage
Alabama	92,635	12.7	39
Alaska	17,997	13.5	34
Arizona	124,504	12.6	40
Arkansas	67,314	14.9	21
California	676,318	10.7	50
Colorado	83,498	10.9	49
Connecticut	71,968	12.5	42
Delaware	18,857	15.8	14
Florida	398,916	15.2	19
Georgia	197,596	12.7	38
Hawaii	21,963	12.0	45
Idaho	29,021	11.6	47
Illinois	323,444	15.4	16
Indiana	177,826	17.4	5
Iowa	72,457	15.1	20
Kansas	65,595	14.0	31
Kentucky	108,798	17.1	6
Louisiana	90,453	12.5	41
Maine	36,522	18.3	2
Maryland	110,959	12.8	37
Massachusetts	162,654	16.7	7
Michigan	243,607	14.1	28
Minnesota	116,511	13.9	33
Mississippi	68,099	14.0	29
Missouri	143,204	16.1	10
Montana	19,259	13.1	35
Nebraska	45,239	15.9	12
Nevada	47,794	11.9	46
New Hampshire	31,782	15.4	17
New Jersey	249,385	17.9	3
New Mexico	50,322	15.5	15
New York	447,422	15.9	13
North Carolina	192,820	14.3	27
North Dakota	13,883	14.0	32
Ohio	266,447	14.4	26
Oklahoma	96,601	15.4	18
Oregon	77,376	14.0	30
Pennsylvania	288,733	15.9	11
Rhode Island	30,681	19.1	1
South Carolina	110,219	16.4	8
South Dakota	17,631	14.5	24
Tennessee	120,122	12.9	36
Texas	507,405	11.6	48
Utah	60,526	12.2	43
Vermont	13,917	14.6	23
Virginia	174,640	14.5	25
Washington	124,498	12.2	44
West Virginia	49,677	17.8	4
Wisconsin	130,076	14.8	22
Wyoming	13,696	16.4	9
50 States	6,700,867	13.9	
DC	11,738	18.8	
United States*	6,813,656	14.1	

Due to rounding or data sources, the 50-state total plus D.C. may not equal the U.S. total. Please see introduction.

Rank in order by percentage	
1	Rhode Island
2	Maine
3	New Jersey
4	West Virginia
5	Indiana
6	Kentucky
7	Massachusetts
8	South Carolina
9	Wyoming
10	Missouri
11	Pennsylvania
12	Nebraska
13	New York
14	Delaware
15	New Mexico
16	Illinois
17	New Hampshire
18	Oklahoma
19	Florida
20	Iowa
21	Arkansas
22	Wisconsin
23	Vermont
24	South Dakota
25	Virginia
26	Ohio
27	North Carolina
28	Michigan
29	Mississippi
30	Oregon
31	Kansas
32	North Dakota
33	Minnesota
34	Alaska
35	Montana
36	Tennessee
37	Maryland
38	Georgia
39	Alabama
40	Arizona
41	Louisiana
42	Connecticut
43	Utah
44	Washington
45	Hawaii
46	Nevada
47	Idaho
48	Texas
49	Colorado
50	California

Note: Numbers that appear to be identical are rounded and vary slightly in actual value. The rankings reflect the actual values before rounding. See the introduction for more details.

H-13 State and Local Education Spending, FY 2004

State	Education spending $ (in millions)	Education spending per capita	Education spending as a percentage of personal income	Rank per capita
Alabama	9,437	2,083	8.0	35
Alaska	2,299	3,508	10.7	1
Arizona	10,074	1,754	6.7	48
Arkansas	5,429	1,972	8.2	38
California	84,395	2,351	7.1	13
Colorado	9,702	2,109	6.2	32
Connecticut	8,753	2,498	5.8	8
Delaware	2,191	2,639	8.0	7
Florida	29,396	1,690	5.8	49
Georgia	19,239	2,179	7.6	27
Hawaii	2,488	1,970	6.5	39
Idaho	2,636	1,892	7.5	43
Illinois	28,621	2,251	6.8	24
Indiana	13,616	2,183	7.6	26
Iowa	7,020	2,376	8.4	12
Kansas	6,205	2,268	7.7	21
Kentucky	7,748	1,869	7.1	45
Louisiana	8,616	1,908	7.4	42
Maine	2,863	2,173	7.6	28
Maryland	12,519	2,252	6.1	23
Massachusetts	14,654	2,284	5.8	19
Michigan	26,974	2,667	8.6	6
Minnesota	11,951	2,343	6.9	14
Mississippi	5,611	1,933	8.3	41
Missouri	10,836	1,883	6.5	44
Montana	1,935	2,087	8.2	34
Nebraska	4,041	2,313	7.7	16
Nevada	4,157	1,781	5.9	47
New Hampshire	2,753	2,119	6.2	31
New Jersey	24,712	2,841	7.2	2
New Mexico	4,657	2,447	9.7	9
New York	51,655	2,687	7.4	5
North Carolina	17,240	2,018	7.2	37
North Dakota	1,525	2,405	8.4	11
Ohio	26,472	2,310	7.7	17
Oklahoma	6,921	1,964	7.4	40
Oregon	7,553	2,101	7.4	33
Pennsylvania	28,703	2,314	7.3	15
Rhode Island	2,441	2,259	7.1	22
South Carolina	8,999	2,144	8.3	30
South Dakota	1,422	1,845	6.6	46
Tennessee	9,756	1,653	5.8	50
Texas	49,707	2,210	7.7	25
Utah	5,434	2,275	9.2	20
Vermont	1,761	2,834	9.3	4
Virginia	16,107	2,159	6.5	29
Washington	14,228	2,294	7.0	18
West Virginia	3,738	2,059	8.4	36
Wisconsin	13,366	2,426	8.0	10
Wyoming	1,437	2,837	8.9	3
50 States	653,992	2,231	7.2	
DC	1,369	2,473	5.1	
United States	655,361	2,232	7.2	

Rank in order per capita	
1	Alaska
2	New Jersey
3	Wyoming
4	Vermont
5	New York
6	Michigan
7	Delaware
8	Connecticut
9	New Mexico
10	Wisconsin
11	North Dakota
12	Iowa
13	California
14	Minnesota
15	Pennsylvania
16	Nebraska
17	Ohio
18	Washington
19	Massachusetts
20	Utah
21	Kansas
22	Rhode Island
23	Maryland
24	Illinois
25	Texas
26	Indiana
27	Georgia
28	Maine
29	Virginia
30	South Carolina
31	New Hampshire
32	Colorado
33	Oregon
34	Montana
35	Alabama
36	West Virginia
37	North Carolina
38	Arkansas
39	Hawaii
40	Oklahoma
41	Mississippi
42	Louisiana
43	Idaho
44	Missouri
45	Kentucky
46	South Dakota
47	Nevada
48	Arizona
49	Florida
50	Tennessee

Note: Numbers that appear to be identical are rounded and vary slightly in actual value. The rankings reflect the actual values before rounding. See the introduction for more details.

H-14 State and Local Education Spending as a Percentage of General Spending, FY 2004

State	Education spending as a percentage of general spending	Rank by percentage
Alabama	34.8	30
Alaska	27.1	50
Arizona	33.5	34
Arkansas	37.2	13
California	32.3	39
Colorado	34.1	32
Connecticut	35.0	26
Delaware	35.4	23
Florida	29.2	48
Georgia	38.3	6
Hawaii	28.7	49
Idaho	35.0	27
Illinois	36.0	19
Indiana	38.3	7
Iowa	38.2	8
Kansas	38.1	10
Kentucky	33.2	36
Louisiana	31.6	42
Maine	30.8	44
Maryland	36.7	15
Massachusetts	30.2	46
Michigan	39.9	4
Minnesota	32.6	37
Mississippi	32.5	38
Missouri	34.9	28
Montana	34.9	29
Nebraska	37.5	11
Nevada	30.5	45
New Hampshire	36.5	17
New Jersey	40.4	1
New Mexico	36.9	14
New York	29.4	47
North Carolina	35.6	22
North Dakota	36.7	16
Ohio	35.6	21
Oklahoma	38.1	9
Oregon	33.9	33
Pennsylvania	35.7	20
Rhode Island	31.9	40
South Carolina	35.2	25
South Dakota	34.4	31
Tennessee	30.9	43
Texas	40.1	2
Utah	39.1	5
Vermont	40.0	3
Virginia	37.5	12
Washington	33.4	35
West Virginia	35.2	24
Wisconsin	36.4	18
Wyoming	31.7	41
50 States	34.5	
DC	20.4	
United States	34.4	

Rank in order by percentage

1	New Jersey
2	Texas
3	Vermont
4	Michigan
5	Utah
6	Georgia
7	Indiana
8	Iowa
9	Oklahoma
10	Kansas
11	Nebraska
12	Virginia
13	Arkansas
14	New Mexico
15	Maryland
16	North Dakota
17	New Hampshire
18	Wisconsin
19	Illinois
20	Pennsylvania
21	Ohio
22	North Carolina
23	Delaware
24	West Virginia
25	South Carolina
26	Connecticut
27	Idaho
28	Missouri
29	Montana
30	Alabama
31	South Dakota
32	Colorado
33	Oregon
34	Arizona
35	Washington
36	Kentucky
37	Minnesota
38	Mississippi
39	California
40	Rhode Island
41	Wyoming
42	Louisiana
43	Tennessee
44	Maine
45	Nevada
46	Massachusetts
47	New York
48	Florida
49	Hawaii
50	Alaska

Note: Numbers that appear to be identical are rounded and vary slightly in actual value. The rankings reflect the actual values before rounding. See the introduction for more details.

H-15 Spending Per Pupil, 2005–2006

State	Spending per pupil $	Rank		Rank in order by $
Alabama	7,303	42	1	New Jersey
Alaska	10,171	12	2	New York
Arizona	5,585	49	3	Connecticut
Arkansas	6,309	48	4	Vermont
California	8,205	29	5	Massachusetts
Colorado	8,277	28	6	Wyoming
Connecticut	12,436	3	7	Delaware
Delaware	11,423	7	8	Maine
Florida	7,650	39	9	Rhode Island
Georgia	9,147	21	10	Illinois
Hawaii	8,745	24	11	New Hampshire
Idaho	6,966	45	12	Alaska
Illinois	10,271	10	13	Wisconsin
Indiana	8,978	22	14	Michigan
Iowa	7,807	36	15	Pennsylvania
Kansas	8,178	31	16	Ohio
Kentucky	8,195	30	17	West Virginia
Louisiana	8,812	23	18	Minnesota
Maine	11,285	8	19	Maryland
Maryland	9,622	19	20	Virginia
Massachusetts	12,276	5	21	Georgia
Michigan	10,069	14	22	Indiana
Minnesota	9,675	18	23	Louisiana
Mississippi	6,763	46	24	Hawaii
Missouri	7,680	38	25	New Mexico
Montana	8,361	27	26	South Carolina
Nebraska	7,980	34	27	Montana
Nevada	7,085	43	28	Colorado
New Hampshire	10,206	11	29	California
New Jersey	13,781	1	30	Kentucky
New Mexico	8,629	25	31	Kansas
New York	13,551	2	32	Washington
North Carolina	7,465	40	33	Oregon
North Dakota	7,760	37	34	Nebraska
Ohio	10,034	16	35	South Dakota
Oklahoma	6,745	47	36	Iowa
Oregon	8,141	33	37	North Dakota
Pennsylvania	10,052	15	38	Missouri
Rhode Island	11,089	9	39	Florida
South Carolina	8,531	26	40	North Carolina
South Dakota	7,911	35	41	Texas
Tennessee	7,079	44	42	Alabama
Texas	7,397	41	43	Nevada
Utah	5,347	50	44	Tennessee
Vermont	12,326	4	45	Idaho
Virginia	9,275	20	46	Mississippi
Washington	8,166	32	47	Oklahoma
West Virginia	9,790	17	48	Arkansas
Wisconsin	10,072	13	49	Arizona
Wyoming	11,971	6	50	Utah
50 States	n/a			
DC	15,864			
United States	9,022			

H-16 Average Teacher Salary, 2005–2006

State	Average teacher salary $	Rank
Alabama	40,347	41
Alaska	53,553	12
Arizona	44,672	24
Arkansas	42,093	33
California	59,345	2
Colorado	45,616	22
Connecticut	59,499	1
Delaware	54,264	10
Florida	43,302	29
Georgia	48,300	17
Hawaii	51,599	13
Idaho	43,390	28
Illinois	57,819	4
Indiana	47,255	18
Iowa	40,877	39
Kansas	41,369	37
Kentucky	41,903	34
Louisiana	40,253	43
Maine	40,737	40
Maryland	54,486	9
Massachusetts	56,587	7
Michigan	58,482	3
Minnesota	48,489	16
Mississippi	37,924	48
Missouri	39,922	44
Montana	39,832	45
Nebraska	41,026	38
Nevada	44,426	25
New Hampshire	45,263	23
New Jersey	57,707	5
New Mexico	41,637	36
New York	57,354	6
North Carolina	43,922	26
North Dakota	37,773	49
Ohio	50,314	14
Oklahoma	38,772	46
Oregon	48,981	15
Pennsylvania	54,027	11
Rhode Island	54,730	8
South Carolina	43,242	31
South Dakota	34,709	50
Tennessee	42,537	32
Texas	41,744	35
Utah	40,316	42
Vermont	46,622	19
Virginia	43,823	27
Washington	46,326	21
West Virginia	38,284	47
Wisconsin	46,390	20
Wyoming	43,255	30
50 States	n/a	
DC	61,195	
United States	49,109	

Rank in order by $	
1	Connecticut
2	California
3	Michigan
4	Illinois
5	New Jersey
6	New York
7	Massachusetts
8	Rhode Island
9	Maryland
10	Delaware
11	Pennsylvania
12	Alaska
13	Hawaii
14	Ohio
15	Oregon
16	Minnesota
17	Georgia
18	Indiana
19	Vermont
20	Wisconsin
21	Washington
22	Colorado
23	New Hampshire
24	Arizona
25	Nevada
26	North Carolina
27	Virginia
28	Idaho
29	Florida
30	Wyoming
31	South Carolina
32	Tennessee
33	Arkansas
34	Kentucky
35	Texas
36	New Mexico
37	Kansas
38	Nebraska
39	Iowa
40	Maine
41	Alabama
42	Utah
43	Louisiana
44	Missouri
45	Montana
46	Oklahoma
47	West Virginia
48	Mississippi
49	North Dakota
50	South Dakota

H-17 Sources of School Funds, 2004–2005

State	Percentage from federal	Percentage from state	Percentage from local	Rank by percentage local
Alabama	11.8	57.4	30.8	36
Alaska	12.5	63.5	23.9	46
Arizona	7.7	51.2	41.0	27
Arkansas	11.3	51.8	36.9	33
California	10.8	63.7	25.5	44
Colorado	7.0	43.3	49.7	14
Connecticut	6.0	39.2	54.8	9
Delaware	10.0	63.0	27.0	43
Florida	10.8	42.7	46.6	19
Georgia	9.1	45.2	45.7	21
Hawaii	10.5	87.2	2.3	50
Idaho	9.6	60.1	30.4	38
Illinois	8.5	29.2	62.3	1
Indiana	6.8	50.3	42.9	23
Iowa	7.3	46.2	46.4	20
Kansas	8.1	52.8	39.2	30
Kentucky	11.8	58.5	29.7	39
Louisiana	13.5	48.6	37.8	32
Maine	9.6	40.8	49.7	15
Maryland	7.2	37.3	55.5	7
Massachusetts	6.2	41.1	52.7	11
Michigan	7.4	64.0	28.7	41
Minnesota	6.8	69.5	23.7	47
Mississippi	15.1	54.2	30.7	37
Missouri	9.1	32.4	58.5	5
Montana	12.2	47.1	40.7	29
Nebraska	7.4	37.8	54.8	8
Nevada	7.6	31.6	60.8	2
New Hampshire	6.2	51.8	41.9	25
New Jersey	3.3	37.7	59.0	4
New Mexico	18.0	69.7	12.3	48
New York	6.6	45.3	48.1	17
North Carolina	11.6	63.6	24.8	45
North Dakota	14.2	35.7	50.0	13
Ohio	6.3	46.0	47.8	18
Oklahoma	13.1	53.6	33.2	34
Oregon	10.1	49.1	40.8	28
Pennsylvania	8.3	35.6	56.1	6
Rhode Island	3.4	36.7	59.9	3
South Carolina	11.5	44.8	43.7	22
South Dakota	16.4	34.4	49.2	16
Tennessee	12.1	45.8	42.1	24
Texas	11.6	37.3	51.1	12
Utah	9.5	57.7	32.9	35
Vermont	8.0	85.9	6.1	49
Virginia	7.3	38.2	54.5	10
Washington	10.3	61.6	28.1	42
West Virginia	11.9	59.3	28.8	40
Wisconsin	6.8	52.0	41.2	26
Wyoming	9.5	51.4	39.0	31
50 States	n/a	n/a	n/a	
DC	14.8	0.0	85.2	
United States	8.9	48.3	42.7	

Rank in order by percentage local

1. Illinois
2. Nevada
3. Rhode Island
4. New Jersey
5. Missouri
6. Pennsylvania
7. Maryland
8. Nebraska
9. Connecticut
10. Virginia
11. Massachusetts
12. Texas
13. North Dakota
14. Colorado
15. Maine
16. South Dakota
17. New York
18. Ohio
19. Florida
20. Iowa
21. Georgia
22. South Carolina
23. Indiana
24. Tennessee
25. New Hampshire
26. Wisconsin
27. Arizona
28. Oregon
29. Montana
30. Kansas
31. Wyoming
32. Louisiana
33. Arkansas
34. Oklahoma
35. Utah
36. Alabama
37. Mississippi
38. Idaho
39. Kentucky
40. West Virginia
41. Michigan
42. Washington
43. Delaware
44. California
45. North Carolina
46. Alaska
47. Minnesota
48. New Mexico
49. Vermont
50. Hawaii

Note: Numbers that appear to be identical are rounded and vary slightly in actual value. The rankings reflect the actual values before rounding. See the introduction for more details.

H-18 State Aid Per Pupil in Average Daily Attendance, 2005–2006

State	State aid per pupil $ (in thousands)	Rank
Alabama	4,673	29
Alaska	7,274	7
Arizona	4,224	38
Arkansas	4,956	26
California	6,418	10
Colorado	4,046	41
Connecticut	5,639	18
Delaware	8,344	4
Florida	4,061	39
Georgia	4,429	34
Hawaii	11,606	2
Idaho	4,358	35
Illinois	3,058	49
Indiana	5,547	19
Iowa	4,721	28
Kansas	6,301	14
Kentucky	5,690	17
Louisiana	4,469	33
Maine	5,121	22
Maryland	4,841	27
Massachusetts	6,338	13
Michigan	8,211	5
Minnesota	8,368	3
Mississippi	4,522	31
Missouri	3,491	45
Montana	4,999	25
Nebraska	3,461	46
Nevada	2,515	50
New Hampshire	5,064	24
New Jersey	5,218	21
New Mexico	7,478	6
New York	6,533	9
North Carolina	5,091	23
North Dakota	3,506	44
Ohio	5,800	16
Oklahoma	4,244	37
Oregon	5,399	20
Pennsylvania	4,250	36
Rhode Island	3,789	42
South Carolina	4,532	30
South Dakota	3,188	48
Tennessee	3,622	43
Texas	3,259	47
Utah	4,056	40
Vermont	14,396	1
Virginia	4,500	32
Washington	6,250	15
West Virginia	6,416	11
Wisconsin	6,370	12
Wyoming	6,889	8
50 States	5,170	
DC	n/a	
United States	5,164	

Rank in order by $	
1	Vermont
2	Hawaii
3	Minnesota
4	Delaware
5	Michigan
6	New Mexico
7	Alaska
8	Wyoming
9	New York
10	California
11	West Virginia
12	Wisconsin
13	Massachusetts
14	Kansas
15	Washington
16	Ohio
17	Kentucky
18	Connecticut
19	Indiana
20	Oregon
21	New Jersey
22	Maine
23	North Carolina
24	New Hampshire
25	Montana
26	Arkansas
27	Maryland
28	Iowa
29	Alabama
30	South Carolina
31	Mississippi
32	Virginia
33	Louisiana
34	Georgia
35	Idaho
36	Pennsylvania
37	Oklahoma
38	Arizona
39	Florida
40	Utah
41	Colorado
42	Rhode Island
43	Tennessee
44	North Dakota
45	Missouri
46	Nebraska
47	Texas
48	South Dakota
49	Illinois
50	Nevada

H-19 State and Local Spending for Higher Education (Census Definition), FY 2004

State	Higher education spending $ (in millions)	Per capita $	Percentage of personal income	Rank per capita
Alabama	3,375	745	2.9	14
Alaska	581	887	2.7	3
Arizona	3,128	545	2.1	35
Arkansas	1,664	604	2.5	27
California	22,054	614	1.9	24
Colorado	2,878	625	1.8	22
Connecticut	1,836	524	1.2	36
Delaware	695	837	2.6	4
Florida	6,757	388	1.3	50
Georgia	4,479	507	1.8	39
Hawaii	770	610	2.0	25
Idaho	826	593	2.4	29
Illinois	7,655	602	1.8	28
Indiana	3,992	640	2.2	20
Iowa	2,467	835	3.0	5
Kansas	2,213	809	2.7	9
Kentucky	2,520	608	2.3	26
Louisiana	2,291	507	2.0	38
Maine	657	498	1.7	42
Maryland	3,684	663	1.8	17
Massachusetts	2,707	422	1.1	49
Michigan	7,939	785	2.5	11
Minnesota	3,010	590	1.7	30
Mississippi	1,912	659	2.8	18
Missouri	2,724	473	1.6	43
Montana	593	639	2.5	21
Nebraska	1,307	748	2.5	13
Nevada	995	426	1.4	48
New Hampshire	613	471	1.4	44
New Jersey	4,389	505	1.3	41
New Mexico	1,572	826	3.3	8
New York	8,847	460	1.3	45
North Carolina	6,745	790	2.8	10
North Dakota	570	898	3.2	2
Ohio	6,331	552	1.8	33
Oklahoma	2,283	648	2.4	19
Oregon	2,622	729	2.6	15
Pennsylvania	6,341	511	1.6	37
Rhode Island	494	457	1.4	46
South Carolina	2,313	551	2.1	34
South Dakota	391	507	1.8	40
Tennessee	2,675	453	1.6	47
Texas	13,973	621	2.2	23
Utah	2,231	934	3.8	1
Vermont	519	835	2.7	6
Virginia	4,311	578	1.7	31
Washington	4,384	707	2.1	16
West Virginia	1,029	567	2.3	32
Wisconsin	4,222	766	2.5	12
Wyoming	422	834	2.6	7
50 States	172,984	590	1.9	
DC	102	183	0.4	
United States	173,086	589	1.9	

Rank in order per capita	
1	Utah
2	North Dakota
3	Alaska
4	Delaware
5	Iowa
6	Vermont
7	Wyoming
8	New Mexico
9	Kansas
10	North Carolina
11	Michigan
12	Wisconsin
13	Nebraska
14	Alabama
15	Oregon
16	Washington
17	Maryland
18	Mississippi
19	Oklahoma
20	Indiana
21	Montana
22	Colorado
23	Texas
24	California
25	Hawaii
26	Kentucky
27	Arkansas
28	Illinois
29	Idaho
30	Minnesota
31	Virginia
32	West Virginia
33	Ohio
34	South Carolina
35	Arizona
36	Connecticut
37	Pennsylvania
38	Louisiana
39	Georgia
40	South Dakota
41	New Jersey
42	Maine
43	Missouri
44	New Hampshire
45	New York
46	Rhode Island
47	Tennessee
48	Nevada
49	Massachusetts
50	Florida

Note: Numbers that appear to be identical are rounded and vary slightly in actual value. The rankings reflect the actual values before rounding. See the introduction for more details.

H-20 State and Local Spending for Higher Education as a Percentage of General Spending, FY 2004

State	Higher education spending as a percentage of general spending	Rank
Alabama	12.5	8
Alaska	6.8	46
Arizona	10.4	23
Arkansas	11.4	14
California	8.5	37
Colorado	10.1	25
Connecticut	7.3	42
Delaware	11.2	17
Florida	6.7	47
Georgia	8.9	32
Hawaii	8.9	33
Idaho	11.0	19
Illinois	9.6	28
Indiana	11.2	16
Iowa	13.4	5
Kansas	13.6	4
Kentucky	10.8	21
Louisiana	8.4	38
Maine	7.1	45
Maryland	10.8	20
Massachusetts	5.6	49
Michigan	11.7	12
Minnesota	8.2	39
Mississippi	11.1	18
Missouri	8.8	34
Montana	10.7	22
Nebraska	12.1	9
Nevada	7.3	43
New Hampshire	8.1	40
New Jersey	7.2	44
New Mexico	12.5	7
New York	5.0	50
North Carolina	13.9	2
North Dakota	13.7	3
Ohio	8.5	35
Oklahoma	12.6	6
Oregon	11.8	11
Pennsylvania	7.9	41
Rhode Island	6.5	48
South Carolina	9.0	31
South Dakota	9.5	29
Tennessee	8.5	36
Texas	11.3	15
Utah	16.0	1
Vermont	11.8	10
Virginia	10.0	26
Washington	10.3	24
West Virginia	9.7	27
Wisconsin	11.5	13
Wyoming	9.3	30
50 States	9.1	
DC	1.5	
United States	9.1	

Rank in order by percentage	
1	Utah
2	North Carolina
3	North Dakota
4	Kansas
5	Iowa
6	Oklahoma
7	New Mexico
8	Alabama
9	Nebraska
10	Vermont
11	Oregon
12	Michigan
13	Wisconsin
14	Arkansas
15	Texas
16	Indiana
17	Delaware
18	Mississippi
19	Idaho
20	Maryland
21	Kentucky
22	Montana
23	Arizona
24	Washington
25	Colorado
26	Virginia
27	West Virginia
28	Illinois
29	South Dakota
30	Wyoming
31	South Carolina
32	Georgia
33	Hawaii
34	Missouri
35	Ohio
36	Tennessee
37	California
38	Louisiana
39	Minnesota
40	New Hampshire
41	Pennsylvania
42	Connecticut
43	Nevada
44	New Jersey
45	Maine
46	Alaska
47	Florida
48	Rhode Island
49	Massachusetts
50	New York

Note: Numbers that appear to be identical are rounded and vary slightly in actual value. The rankings reflect the actual values before rounding. See the introduction for more details.

Public Higher Education Enrollment, 2004

	Rank in order by percentage
1	North Dakota
2	New Mexico
3	Kansas
4	Wyoming
5	Utah
6	Arizona
7	California
8	Colorado
9	Oklahoma
10	Nebraska
11	Iowa
12	Alabama
13	Michigan
14	South Dakota
15	Wisconsin
16	Kentucky
17	Texas
18	Mississippi
19	Minnesota
20	Washington
21	West Virginia
22	Maryland
23	Louisiana
24	Delaware
25	Oregon
26	Virginia
27	Montana
28	North Carolina
29	Alaska
30	Arkansas
31	Illinois
32	Idaho
33	Indiana
34	Nevada
35	South Carolina
36	Ohio
37	Hawaii
38	Florida
39	Georgia
40	Missouri
41	Vermont
42	Rhode Island
43	Maine
44	Tennessee
45	New Jersey
46	New York
47	Connecticut
48	New Hampshire
49	Pennsylvania
50	Massachusetts

State	Higher education enrollment #	Percentage of total population	Rank
Alabama	226,989	5.0	12
Alaska	29,899	4.5	29
Arizona	320,554	5.6	6
Arkansas	124,742	4.5	30
California	1,998,125	5.6	7
Colorado	251,853	5.5	8
Connecticut	111,348	3.2	47
Delaware	38,243	4.6	24
Florida	677,283	3.9	38
Georgia	336,066	3.8	39
Hawaii	50,569	4.0	37
Idaho	60,695	4.4	32
Illinois	563,808	4.4	31
Indiana	267,073	4.3	33
Iowa	149,776	5.1	11
Kansas	172,484	6.3	3
Kentucky	197,991	4.8	16
Louisiana	211,241	4.7	23
Maine	47,284	3.6	43
Maryland	260,931	4.7	22
Massachusetts	188,246	2.9	50
Michigan	501,169	5.0	13
Minnesota	241,406	4.7	19
Mississippi	137,543	4.7	18
Missouri	216,176	3.8	40
Montana	42,289	4.6	27
Nebraska	93,195	5.3	10
Nevada	96,773	4.1	34
New Hampshire	40,642	3.1	48
New Jersey	306,365	3.5	45
New Mexico	121,339	6.4	2
New York	632,058	3.3	46
North Carolina	389,278	4.6	28
North Dakota	43,275	6.8	1
Ohio	463,555	4.0	36
Oklahoma	190,671	5.4	9
Oregon	165,375	4.6	25
Pennsylvania	387,115	3.1	49
Rhode Island	39,920	3.7	42
South Carolina	172,412	4.1	35
South Dakota	37,598	4.9	14
Tennessee	208,889	3.5	44
Texas	1,072,401	4.8	17
Utah	146,623	6.1	5
Vermont	22,998	3.7	41
Virginia	344,147	4.6	26
Washington	293,562	4.7	20
West Virginia	85,513	4.7	21
Wisconsin	266,884	4.8	15
Wyoming	31,599	6.2	4
50 States	13,075,970	4.5	
DC	5,388	1.0	
United States	13,081,358	4.5	

Note: Numbers that appear to be identical are rounded and vary slightly in actual value. The rankings reflect the actual values before rounding. See the introduction for more details.

H-22 Per Pupil State Support of Higher Education, FY 2006

State	Per pupil support $	Rank
Alabama	6,124	10
Alaska	8,354	2
Arizona	3,039	48
Arkansas	5,876	13
California	4,818	30
Colorado	2,361	50
Connecticut	7,423	4
Delaware	5,659	17
Florida	4,865	29
Georgia	6,187	9
Hawaii	9,733	1
Idaho	5,519	19
Illinois	4,639	32
Indiana	5,356	21
Iowa	5,207	25
Kansas	4,375	40
Kentucky	6,098	11
Louisiana	6,259	8
Maine	5,244	23
Maryland	4,802	31
Massachusetts	4,877	28
Michigan	4,026	43
Minnesota	5,656	18
Mississippi	5,689	16
Missouri	3,960	44
Montana	4,085	42
Nebraska	5,820	14
Nevada	5,783	15
New Hampshire	2,883	49
New Jersey	6,610	7
New Mexico	5,917	12
New York	6,901	6
North Carolina	7,514	3
North Dakota	4,975	26
Ohio	4,556	36
Oklahoma	4,385	39
Oregon	3,706	46
Pennsylvania	5,288	22
Rhode Island	4,568	35
South Carolina	4,450	37
South Dakota	4,399	38
Tennessee	5,376	20
Texas	4,889	27
Utah	4,586	34
Vermont	3,567	47
Virginia	4,633	33
Washington	5,220	24
West Virginia	3,732	45
Wisconsin	4,240	41
Wyoming	6,994	5
50 States	5,097	
DC	n/a	
United States	5,094	

Rank in order by $	
1	Hawaii
2	Alaska
3	North Carolina
4	Connecticut
5	Wyoming
6	New York
7	New Jersey
8	Louisiana
9	Georgia
10	Alabama
11	Kentucky
12	New Mexico
13	Arkansas
14	Nebraska
15	Nevada
16	Mississippi
17	Delaware
18	Minnesota
19	Idaho
20	Tennessee
21	Indiana
22	Pennsylvania
23	Maine
24	Washington
25	Iowa
26	North Dakota
27	Texas
28	Massachusetts
29	Florida
30	California
31	Maryland
32	Illinois
33	Virginia
34	Utah
35	Rhode Island
36	Ohio
37	South Carolina
38	South Dakota
39	Oklahoma
40	Kansas
41	Wisconsin
42	Montana
43	Michigan
44	Missouri
45	West Virginia
46	Oregon
47	Vermont
48	Arizona
49	New Hampshire
50	Colorado

H-23   Average In-State Tuition and Fees at Public Universities, 2005–2006

State	Average in-state tuition and fees $	Rank
Alabama	4,773	32
Alaska	3,808	41
Arizona	4,429	35
Arkansas	4,888	30
California	4,543	34
Colorado	4,200	37
Connecticut	6,573	13
Delaware	7,050	9
Florida	3,213	48
Georgia	3,760	42
Hawaii	3,697	44
Idaho	3,922	39
Illinois	7,214	8
Indiana	6,170	16
Iowa	5,619	20
Kansas	4,826	31
Kentucky	5,124	25
Louisiana	3,734	43
Maine	6,000	18
Maryland	6,767	12
Massachusetts	7,403	7
Michigan	7,031	10
Minnesota	6,981	11
Mississippi	4,232	36
Missouri	6,361	15
Montana	5,088	26
Nebraska	5,455	21
Nevada	3,060	49
New Hampshire	8,656	4
New Jersey	8,601	5
New Mexico	2,854	50
New York	5,031	28
North Carolina	3,674	45
North Dakota	5,074	27
Ohio	9,047	2
Oklahoma	3,924	38
Oregon	5,430	22
Pennsylvania	8,700	3
Rhode Island	6,439	14
South Carolina	7,416	6
South Dakota	4,911	29
Tennessee	4,773	32
Texas	5,414	23
Utah	3,583	46
Vermont	9,494	1
Virginia	6,034	17
Washington	5,252	24
West Virginia	3,860	40
Wisconsin	5,656	19
Wyoming	3,429	47
50 States	n/a	
DC	2,520	
United States	5,489	

Rank in order by $	
1	Vermont
2	Ohio
3	Pennsylvania
4	New Hampshire
5	New Jersey
6	South Carolina
7	Massachusetts
8	Illinois
9	Delaware
10	Michigan
11	Minnesota
12	Maryland
13	Connecticut
14	Rhode Island
15	Missouri
16	Indiana
17	Virginia
18	Maine
19	Wisconsin
20	Iowa
21	Nebraska
22	Oregon
23	Texas
24	Washington
25	Kentucky
26	Montana
27	North Dakota
28	New York
29	South Dakota
30	Arkansas
31	Kansas
32	Alabama
32	Tennessee
34	California
35	Arizona
36	Mississippi
37	Colorado
38	Oklahoma
39	Idaho
40	West Virginia
41	Alaska
42	Georgia
43	Louisiana
44	Hawaii
45	North Carolina
46	Utah
47	Wyoming
48	Florida
49	Nevada
50	New Mexico

Note: Ties in ranking reflect ties in actual values.

H-24 Average Out-of-State Tuition and Fees at Public Universities, 2005–2006

State	Average out-of-state tuition and fees $	Rank
Alabama	13,516	34
Alaska	11,724	46
Arizona	13,671	33
Arkansas	13,222	37
California	25,254	2
Colorado	22,826	5
Connecticut	20,416	9
Delaware	17,474	20
Florida	16,610	27
Georgia	16,848	24
Hawaii	10,177	47
Idaho	12,738	41
Illinois	22,720	6
Indiana	19,558	15
Iowa	16,998	23
Kansas	13,866	32
Kentucky	12,884	39
Louisiana	12,689	42
Maine	17,050	22
Maryland	20,145	12
Massachusetts	18,397	19
Michigan	27,601	1
Minnesota	20,252	11
Mississippi	9,744	50
Missouri	17,192	21
Montana	13,883	31
Nebraska	14,436	30
Nevada	12,943	38
New Hampshire	21,498	8
New Jersey	16,835	25
New Mexico	13,437	35
New York	12,328	44
North Carolina	18,411	18
North Dakota	12,659	43
Ohio	19,018	16
Oklahoma	12,301	45
Oregon	16,569	28
Pennsylvania	21,744	7
Rhode Island	19,934	13
South Carolina	18,956	17
South Dakota	9,816	48
Tennessee	16,360	29
Texas	16,636	26
Utah	13,371	36
Vermont	24,934	3
Virginia	24,100	4
Washington	19,802	14
West Virginia	12,874	40
Wisconsin	20,280	10
Wyoming	9,816	48
50 States	n/a	
DC	n/a	
United States	16,730	

Rank in order by $	
1	Michigan
2	California
3	Vermont
4	Virginia
5	Colorado
6	Illinois
7	Pennsylvania
8	New Hampshire
9	Connecticut
10	Wisconsin
11	Minnesota
12	Maryland
13	Rhode Island
14	Washington
15	Indiana
16	Ohio
17	South Carolina
18	North Carolina
19	Massachusetts
20	Delaware
21	Missouri
22	Maine
23	Iowa
24	Georgia
25	New Jersey
26	Texas
27	Florida
28	Oregon
29	Tennessee
30	Nebraska
31	Montana
32	Kansas
33	Arizona
34	Alabama
35	New Mexico
36	Utah
37	Arkansas
38	Nevada
39	Kentucky
40	West Virginia
41	Idaho
42	Louisiana
43	North Dakota
44	New York
45	Oklahoma
46	Alaska
47	Hawaii
48	South Dakota
48	Wyoming
50	Mississippi

Note: Ties in ranking reflect ties in actual values.

H-25 Percentage Change in Tuition and Fees at Public Universities, 2005–2006

State	Average in-state tuition and fees $	Average out-of-state tuition and fees $	Rank by in-state $
Alabama	6.1	6.7	28
Alaska	8.0	10.8	18
Arizona	8.6	4.6	15
Arkansas	6.2	6.4	26
California	6.6	10.2	23
Colorado	17.2	5.3	1
Connecticut	4.5	5.7	41
Delaware	6.4	5	25
Florida	5.4	6	36
Georgia	6.9	8.1	21
Hawaii	3.2	1.2	44
Idaho	8.0	9.3	18
Illinois	11.9	8.9	8
Indiana	5.3	8.1	37
Iowa	3.9	5.9	43
Kansas	14.7	9.3	2
Kentucky	14.6	7.2	3
Louisiana	2.5	14.4	46
Maine	6.2	8	26
Maryland	5.3	7.6	37
Massachusetts	4.9	3	40
Michigan	13.6	6	5
Minnesota	5.8	3	33
Mississippi	5.8	5.2	33
Missouri	5.9	3.9	31
Montana	14.4	8.6	4
Nebraska	13.4	7.1	6
Nevada	7.4	10.5	20
New Hampshire	5.9	6.1	31
New Jersey	6.1	7.9	28
New Mexico	-9.2	8	50
New York	-0.1	0.7	49
North Carolina	0.6	4.9	48
North Dakota	10.2	9.9	10
Ohio	8.2	5.5	17
Oklahoma	2.9	5.5	45
Oregon	6.1	26.8	28
Pennsylvania	2.0	4.6	47
Rhode Island	8.6	8.7	15
South Carolina	11.6	12.9	9
South Dakota	9.0	5.6	13
Tennessee	10.1	12.6	11
Texas	6.7	22	22
Utah	9.7	7.7	12
Vermont	5.1	4.5	39
Virginia	8.7	6.2	14
Washington	6.6	11.2	23
West Virginia	4.3	6.7	42
Wisconsin	12.0	2.1	7
Wyoming	5.7	5.9	35
50 States	n/a	n/a	
DC	n/a	n/a	
United States	6.7	7.4	

Rank in order by in-state $	
1	Colorado
2	Kansas
3	Kentucky
4	Montana
5	Michigan
6	Nebraska
7	Wisconsin
8	Illinois
9	South Carolina
10	North Dakota
11	Tennessee
12	Utah
13	South Dakota
14	Virginia
15	Arizona
15	Rhode Island
17	Ohio
18	Alaska
18	Idaho
20	Nevada
21	Georgia
22	Texas
23	California
23	Washington
25	Delaware
26	Arkansas
26	Maine
28	Alabama
28	New Jersey
28	Oregon
31	Missouri
31	New Hampshire
33	Minnesota
33	Mississippi
35	Wyoming
36	Florida
37	Indiana
37	Maryland
39	Vermont
40	Massachusetts
41	Connecticut
42	West Virginia
43	Iowa
44	Hawaii
45	Oklahoma
46	Louisiana
47	Pennsylvania
48	North Carolina
49	New York
50	New Mexico

Note: Ties in ranking reflect ties in actual values.

H-26 Higher Education Affordability Index, 2006

State	Affordability index (100=most affordable)	Rank
Alabama	43	42
Alaska	50	29
Arizona	47	36
Arkansas	54	17
California	71	1
Colorado	55	15
Connecticut	50	29
Delaware	54	17
Florida	49	34
Georgia	51	26
Hawaii	65	3
Idaho	64	4
Illinois	59	8
Indiana	57	10
Iowa	50	29
Kansas	54	17
Kentucky	51	26
Louisiana	50	29
Maine	42	45
Maryland	53	22
Massachusetts	47	36
Michigan	51	26
Minnesota	64	4
Mississippi	50	29
Missouri	47	36
Montana	39	49
Nebraska	53	22
Nevada	49	34
New Hampshire	39	49
New Jersey	63	6
New Mexico	57	10
New York	54	17
North Carolina	57	10
North Dakota	47	36
Ohio	42	45
Oklahoma	55	15
Oregon	42	45
Pennsylvania	54	17
Rhode Island	40	48
South Carolina	43	42
South Dakota	43	42
Tennessee	47	36
Texas	57	10
Utah	71	1
Vermont	52	24
Virginia	57	10
Washington	60	7
West Virginia	46	41
Wisconsin	58	9
Wyoming	52	24
50 States	n/a	
DC	n/a	
United States	n/a	

Rank in order by index	
1	California
1	Utah
3	Hawaii
4	Idaho
4	Minnesota
6	New Jersey
7	Washington
8	Illinois
9	Wisconsin
10	Indiana
10	New Mexico
10	North Carolina
10	Texas
10	Virginia
15	Colorado
15	Oklahoma
17	Arkansas
17	Delaware
17	Kansas
17	New York
17	Pennsylvania
22	Maryland
22	Nebraska
24	Vermont
24	Wyoming
26	Georgia
26	Kentucky
26	Michigan
29	Alaska
29	Connecticut
29	Iowa
29	Louisiana
29	Mississippi
34	Florida
34	Nevada
36	Arizona
36	Massachusetts
36	Missouri
36	North Dakota
36	Tennessee
41	West Virginia
42	Alabama
42	South Carolina
42	South Dakota
45	Maine
45	Ohio
45	Oregon
48	Rhode Island
49	Montana
49	New Hampshire

Note: Ties in ranking reflect ties in actual values.

H-27 Average Salary of Associate Professors at "Flagship" State Universities, 2005–2006

State	Associate professor average salary $ (in thousands)	Rank
Alabama	68.0	30
Alaska	61.9	43
Arizona	71.2	23
Arkansas	66.2	36
California	82.0	5
Colorado	74.5	16
Connecticut	82.3	4
Delaware	78.5	8
Florida	71.7	21
Georgia	67.6	31
Hawaii	68.7	27
Idaho	58.3	48
Illinois	77.6	12
Indiana	72.8	20
Iowa	70.9	24
Kansas	68.7	27
Kentucky	67.2	35
Louisiana	63.2	41
Maine	63.3	39
Maryland	80.3	7
Massachusetts	82.5	3
Michigan	83.7	1
Minnesota	75.6	14
Mississippi	63.3	39
Missouri	67.3	32
Montana	55.4	49
Nebraska	69.8	26
Nevada	78.1	9
New Hampshire	74.7	15
New Jersey	80.7	6
New Mexico	61.0	46
New York	51.6	50
North Carolina	77.9	10
North Dakota	61.5	45
Ohio	74.2	17
Oklahoma	64.0	38
Oregon	63.1	42
Pennsylvania	77.7	11
Rhode Island	67.3	32
South Carolina	68.6	29
South Dakota	58.5	47
Tennessee	71.6	22
Texas	72.9	18
Utah	70.6	25
Vermont	67.3	32
Virginia	82.7	2
Washington	72.9	18
West Virginia	61.7	44
Wisconsin	76.5	13
Wyoming	64.4	37
50 States	70.2	
DC	86.0	
United States	70.5	

Rank in order by $	
1	Michigan
2	Virginia
3	Massachusetts
4	Connecticut
5	California
6	New Jersey
7	Maryland
8	Delaware
9	Nevada
10	North Carolina
11	Pennsylvania
12	Illinois
13	Wisconsin
14	Minnesota
15	New Hampshire
16	Colorado
17	Ohio
18	Texas
18	Washington
20	Indiana
21	Florida
22	Tennessee
23	Arizona
24	Iowa
25	Utah
26	Nebraska
27	Hawaii
27	Kansas
29	South Carolina
30	Alabama
31	Georgia
32	Missouri
32	Rhode Island
32	Vermont
35	Kentucky
36	Arkansas
37	Wyoming
38	Oklahoma
39	Maine
39	Mississippi
41	Louisiana
42	Oregon
43	Alaska
44	West Virginia
45	North Dakota
46	New Mexico
47	South Dakota
48	Idaho
49	Montana
50	New York

Note: Ties in ranking reflect ties in actual values.

H-28 State and Local Education Employees, 2005

State	Education employees #	Per 10,000 population	Rank per 10,000 population
Alabama	103,101	226	28
Alaska	20,500	309	3
Arizona	110,817	187	45
Arkansas	72,379	260	10
California	672,004	186	46
Colorado	98,475	211	38
Connecticut	90,371	257	12
Delaware	16,273	193	44
Florida	316,796	178	47
Georgia	231,057	255	16
Hawaii	24,937	196	43
Idaho	30,977	217	35
Illinois	270,979	212	37
Indiana	136,609	218	34
Iowa	77,753	262	8
Kansas	77,684	283	5
Kentucky	109,261	262	9
Louisiana	111,008	245	21
Maine	37,857	286	4
Maryland	111,155	198	41
Massachusetts	150,090	235	24
Michigan	223,837	221	33
Minnesota	115,793	226	30
Mississippi	74,878	256	14
Missouri	134,128	231	26
Montana	23,221	248	19
Nebraska	41,404	235	22
Nevada	39,219	162	49
New Hampshire	34,616	264	7
New Jersey	225,494	259	11
New Mexico	48,297	250	17
New York	472,664	245	20
North Carolina	185,902	214	36
North Dakota	14,833	233	25
Ohio	259,268	226	29
Oklahoma	90,897	256	15
Oregon	64,199	176	48
Pennsylvania	250,246	201	39
Rhode Island	21,234	197	42
South Carolina	100,077	235	23
South Dakota	19,976	257	13
Tennessee	132,049	221	32
Texas	633,934	277	6
Utah	49,333	200	40
Vermont	20,439	328	1
Virginia	188,749	249	18
Washington	100,310	160	50
West Virginia	41,946	231	27
Wisconsin	124,298	225	31
Wyoming	16,449	323	2
50 States	6,617,773	224	
DC	11,862	215	
United States	6,629,635	224	

Rank in order per 10,000 population	
1	Vermont
2	Wyoming
3	Alaska
4	Maine
5	Kansas
6	Texas
7	New Hampshire
8	Iowa
9	Kentucky
10	Arkansas
11	New Jersey
12	Connecticut
13	South Dakota
14	Mississippi
15	Oklahoma
16	Georgia
17	New Mexico
18	Virginia
19	Montana
20	New York
21	Louisiana
22	Nebraska
23	South Carolina
24	Massachusetts
25	North Dakota
26	Missouri
27	West Virginia
28	Alabama
29	Ohio
30	Minnesota
31	Wisconsin
32	Tennessee
33	Michigan
34	Indiana
35	Idaho
36	North Carolina
37	Illinois
38	Colorado
39	Pennsylvania
40	Utah
41	Maryland
42	Rhode Island
43	Hawaii
44	Delaware
45	Arizona
46	California
47	Florida
48	Oregon
49	Nevada
50	Washington

Note: Numbers that appear to be identical are rounded and vary slightly in actual value. The rankings reflect the actual values before rounding. See the introduction for more details.

H-29 Federal Research and Development Spending, FY 2003

State	Federal R&D spending $ (in thousands)	Federal R&D spending per capita $	Rank per capita
Alabama	2,932,910	651	5
Alaska	246,021	379	10
Arizona	1,856,783	333	13
Arkansas	139,716	51	50
California	17,410,257	491	7
Colorado	1,612,002	354	12
Connecticut	2,067,969	593	6
Delaware	91,384	112	39
Florida	2,522,054	148	35
Georgia	1,514,260	175	28
Hawaii	349,644	280	17
Idaho	216,120	158	33
Illinois	1,900,260	150	34
Indiana	561,238	91	43
Iowa	465,249	158	32
Kansas	189,979	70	48
Kentucky	232,097	56	49
Louisiana	441,902	98	42
Maine	144,936	111	40
Maryland	7,804,386	1,416	2
Massachusetts	5,156,530	803	4
Michigan	1,673,200	166	30
Minnesota	861,269	170	29
Mississippi	1,173,860	407	9
Missouri	1,269,896	222	19
Montana	129,548	141	36
Nebraska	146,325	84	44
Nevada	409,308	183	26
New Hampshire	363,118	282	16
New Jersey	1,785,820	207	23
New Mexico	2,850,052	1,517	1
New York	3,972,873	207	22
North Carolina	1,610,868	191	25
North Dakota	101,753	161	31
Ohio	2,396,000	209	21
Oklahoma	274,349	78	46
Oregon	480,234	135	37
Pennsylvania	3,787,926	306	14
Rhode Island	523,349	486	8
South Carolina	411,723	99	41
South Dakota	54,788	72	47
Tennessee	1,039,274	178	27
Texas	4,757,023	215	20
Utah	650,187	276	18
Vermont	181,870	294	15
Virginia	6,212,933	844	3
Washington	2,292,132	374	11
West Virginia	367,393	203	24
Wisconsin	657,170	120	38
Wyoming	41,096	82	45
50 States	88,331,034	304	
DC	2,916,133	5,230	
United States*	91,525,003	315	

*Due to rounding or data sources, the 50-state total plus D.C. may not equal the U.S. total. Please see introduction.

Rank in order per capita	
1	New Mexico
2	Maryland
3	Virginia
4	Massachusetts
5	Alabama
6	Connecticut
7	California
8	Rhode Island
9	Mississippi
10	Alaska
11	Washington
12	Colorado
13	Arizona
14	Pennsylvania
15	Vermont
16	New Hampshire
17	Hawaii
18	Utah
19	Missouri
20	Texas
21	Ohio
22	New York
23	New Jersey
24	West Virginia
25	North Carolina
26	Nevada
27	Tennessee
28	Georgia
29	Minnesota
30	Michigan
31	North Dakota
32	Iowa
33	Idaho
34	Illinois
35	Florida
36	Montana
37	Oregon
38	Wisconsin
39	Delaware
40	Maine
41	South Carolina
42	Louisiana
43	Indiana
44	Nebraska
45	Wyoming
46	Oklahoma
47	South Dakota
48	Kansas
49	Kentucky
50	Arkansas

Note: Numbers that appear to be identical are rounded and vary slightly in actual value. The rankings reflect the actual values before rounding. See the introduction for more details.

H-30 Total Library Operating Expenditures, FY 2004

State	Library spending $ (in thousands)	Library spending per capita	Rank per capita
Alabama	75,972	16.93	45
Alaska	24,568	37.48	12
Arizona	128,596	23.69	34
Arkansas	41,231	15.49	48
California	995,802	27.56	25
Colorado	174,039	39.29	9
Connecticut	146,188	41.97	7
Delaware	19,459	24.83	32
Florida	437,741	25.06	31
Georgia	163,295	19.19	41
Hawaii	27,287	21.70	37
Idaho	28,965	24.00	33
Illinois	528,232	46.43	3
Indiana	256,401	45.16	4
Iowa	78,471	26.85	28
Kansas	85,789	37.34	13
Kentucky	86,409	21.17	39
Louisiana	117,368	25.99	30
Maine	31,320	26.58	29
Maryland	197,076	36.30	14
Massachusetts	211,869	32.97	16
Michigan	331,112	33.42	15
Minnesota	157,053	30.87	20
Mississippi	38,427	13.24	50
Missouri	160,342	31.36	19
Montana	16,212	18.01	43
Nebraska	39,879	28.18	22
Nevada	65,406	27.13	27
New Hampshire	41,104	31.76	18
New Jersey	362,810	43.52	5
New Mexico	35,115	21.33	38
New York	903,665	47.74	2
North Carolina	157,082	18.66	42
North Dakota	9,692	17.58	44
Ohio	608,656	53.12	1
Oklahoma	67,913	23.51	35
Oregon	129,544	40.22	8
Pennsylvania	276,871	23.11	36
Rhode Island	41,200	38.51	10
South Carolina	87,322	21.06	40
South Dakota	16,295	27.89	24
Tennessee	92,845	16.02	47
Texas	343,320	16.93	45
Utah	66,135	27.90	23
Vermont	15,863	27.50	26
Virginia	210,699	28.84	21
Washington	257,391	42.58	6
West Virginia	26,339	14.57	49
Wisconsin	181,531	32.81	17
Wyoming	19,206	38.32	11
50 States	8,615,106	n/a	
DC	27,922	50.44	
United States	8,643,028	30.49	

Rank in order per capita	
1	Ohio
2	New York
3	Illinois
4	Indiana
5	New Jersey
6	Washington
7	Connecticut
8	Oregon
9	Colorado
10	Rhode Island
11	Wyoming
12	Alaska
13	Kansas
14	Maryland
15	Michigan
16	Massachusetts
17	Wisconsin
18	New Hampshire
19	Missouri
20	Minnesota
21	Virginia
22	Nebraska
23	Utah
24	South Dakota
25	California
26	Vermont
27	Nevada
28	Iowa
29	Maine
30	Louisiana
31	Florida
32	Delaware
33	Idaho
34	Arizona
35	Oklahoma
36	Pennsylvania
37	Hawaii
38	New Mexico
39	Kentucky
40	South Carolina
41	Georgia
42	North Carolina
43	Montana
44	North Dakota
45	Alabama
45	Texas
47	Tennessee
48	Arkansas
49	West Virginia
50	Mississippi

Note: Ties in ranking reflect ties in actual values.

H-31 Head Start Enrollment and Funding, 2005

State	Head Start enrollment #	Head Start spending per enrollee $	Rank by $ per enrollee
Alabama	16,374	6,495	44
Alaska	1,725	7,211	19
Arizona	13,215	7,811	10
Arkansas	10,942	5,881	49
California	98,432	8,427	7
Colorado	9,820	6,941	29
Connecticut	7,126	7,264	16
Delaware	2,197	6,008	48
Florida	35,530	7,386	14
Georgia	23,508	7,149	20
Hawaii	3,049	7,486	12
Idaho	2,640	8,619	6
Illinois	39,640	6,812	32
Indiana	14,231	6,742	35
Iowa	7,735	6,647	40
Kansas	7,931	6,404	46
Kentucky	16,071	6,693	38
Louisiana	21,982	6,620	43
Maine	3,955	6,963	27
Maryland	10,347	7,522	11
Massachusetts	12,846	8,412	8
Michigan	35,069	6,670	39
Minnesota	10,332	6,950	28
Mississippi	26,657	6,049	47
Missouri	17,451	6,800	33
Montana	2,939	7,109	21
Nebraska	5,080	7,079	23
Nevada	2,754	8,793	3
New Hampshire	1,632	8,180	9
New Jersey	14,717	8,743	4
New Mexico	7,451	7,000	25
New York	49,127	8,794	2
North Carolina	19,003	7,415	13
North Dakota	2,353	7,280	15
Ohio	38,021	6,476	45
Oklahoma	13,915	5,809	50
Oregon	8,792	6,746	34
Pennsylvania	32,282	7,049	24
Rhode Island	3,150	6,970	26
South Carolina	12,248	6,718	36
South Dakota	2,827	6,641	41
Tennessee	16,445	7,238	17
Texas	67,327	7,091	22
Utah	5,518	6,826	31
Vermont	1,569	8,619	5
Virginia	13,696	7,216	18
Washington	11,102	9,016	1
West Virginia	7,610	6,637	42
Wisconsin	13,538	6,695	37
Wyoming	1,792	6,885	30
50 States	803,693	7,276	
DC	3,403	7,358	
United States*	906,993	7,545	

Due to rounding or data sources, the 50-state total plus D.C. may not equal the U.S. total. Please see introduction.

Rank in order $ per enrollee	
1	Washington
2	New York
3	Nevada
4	New Jersey
5	Vermont
6	Idaho
7	California
8	Massachusetts
9	New Hampshire
10	Arizona
11	Maryland
12	Hawaii
13	North Carolina
14	Florida
15	North Dakota
16	Connecticut
17	Tennessee
18	Virginia
19	Alaska
20	Georgia
21	Montana
22	Texas
23	Nebraska
24	Pennsylvania
25	New Mexico
26	Rhode Island
27	Maine
28	Minnesota
29	Colorado
30	Wyoming
31	Utah
32	Illinois
33	Missouri
34	Oregon
35	Indiana
36	South Carolina
37	Wisconsin
38	Kentucky
39	Michigan
40	Iowa
41	South Dakota
42	West Virginia
43	Louisiana
44	Alabama
45	Ohio
46	Kansas
47	Mississippi
48	Delaware
49	Arkansas
50	Oklahoma

Note: Numbers that appear to be identical are rounded and vary slightly in actual value. The rankings reflect the actual values before rounding. See the introduction for more details.

Source Notes for Education (Section H)

H-1 Average Proficiency in Math, Eighth Grade, 2005: These statistics reflect scores on national tests administered to eighth graders to determine their ability to deal with basic concepts of mathematics. The statistics were developed through the National Assessment of Educational Progress, as administered by the Department of Education. They are available as the *NAEP 2005 Mathematics Report Card* (nces.ed.gov).

Statistics comparing the educational achievements of students in individual states, school districts, and schools are a central component of The No Child Left Behind Act. Supporters of these statistics and tests argue that it is much more appropriate to compare results in education programs than the common statistics that just compare costs, such as how much is spent per pupil. Statistics on test results measure achievement of pupils, not that of teachers or school systems. Experts disagree on the relative influence of factors affecting student achievement, but all agree that it is heavily influenced by such out-of-school factors as early childhood training in the home, children's physical and mental health, and participation of parents in the educational process.

H-2 Average Proficiency in Reading, Eighth Grade, 2005: These data are comparable to those shown in Table H-1, except they cover reading. These statistics come from the *NAEP 2005 Reading Report Card* (nces.ed.gov).

H-3 Armed Forces Qualification Test Ranks, FY 2004: Many employers test potential employees to determine their suitability for work, as indicated by such factors as ability to read and understand instructions and perform simple calculations. One of the most widely used tests is offered nationwide to persons seeking to enlist in the armed forces. These data reflect average scores of test-takers in the period from October 2003 to the end of September 2004. These data are prepared by the Department of Defense and published annually, along with other information about persons in uniform, in *Population Representation in the Military Services.*

The Department of Defense, which does not want to become an arbitrator of which states prepare students best for jobs, tries to discourage the use of these results to rank states. Regardless, the results provide the best single measure of performance of high school graduates being tested by an employer using criteria approximating aptitude for work.

H-4 SAT Scores, 2006: College-bound students are generally required to take an achievement test to gain admission to the college or university of their choice. There are two major tests used for this purpose, the Scholastic Aptitude Test (SAT), which is administered by the College Board (www.collegeboard.com), and the ACT test, which is administered by the American College Testing Program (act.org). Both organizations seek to discourage the use of their test scores as a way to compare education systems of states, but they are commonly used because of the lack of other comparisons indicating how well states and individual school districts and schools compare in meeting these standards for college admissions. The test scores are presented here and in Table H-5, with neither table including all states. Each state's results are given only for the test that is most often taken in that state. Failure to sort in this way would produce highly misleading results. For example, many southern states rely primarily on the ACT, but their students who seek admission to exclusive private universities in the northeast and California must take the SAT. As a result, the SAT is taken by a small fraction of high school graduates, but those who take it score extraordinarily high.

H-5 ACT Scores, 2006: See notes to Table H-4.

H-6 Percentage of Population Over 25 with a High School Diploma, 2005: These data reflect the percentage of the total population over age twenty-five that has a high school diploma. Because each generation of Americans has, on average, attended school longer than its predecessors, the states with the highest ranks tend to be those with the fastest growth and thus youngest population. The source is the U.S. Census Bureau (www.census.gov).

H-7 Students in Private Schools, 2003–2004: Just over five million students in kindergarten through the twelfth grade attend private schools. The private enrollment statistics were released in March 2006 by the Department of Education, National Center for Education Statistics (NCES). The data are posted on the NCES Web site (nces.ed.gov). Private enrollment statistics are gathered every two years as part of the National Education Association's Private School Survey (PSS).

H-8 High School Dropout Rates, 2002: The data printed here are from a U.S. Department of Education, National Center for Education Statistics report titled *Dropout Rates in the United States: 2002 and 2003*, released on the NCES Web site (nces.ed.gov) in June of 2006.

H-9 Pupil-Teacher Ratio, 2004–2005: Small classes are generally believed to be more beneficial to students than large ones, so pupil-teacher ratios are commonly used as a proxy measure of educational quality. The statistic shows a ratio lower than typical class sizes because some specialized teachers, such as those teaching art or special education, are included. These data come from the National Education Association's *Rankings and Estimates, A Report of School Statistics Update* released in fall of 2005 on the NEA Web site (www.nea.org).

For these and other commonly used educational statistics comparing states, there are three primary sources: the Department of Education, the National Education Association

(NEA), and the American Federation of Teachers (which, like the NEA, represents teachers). These organizations produce somewhat different data, using different concepts and different schedules. However, the rankings of states on any particular indicator are about the same regardless of the source used.

H-10 Public School Enrollment, 2005–2006: These statistics show how the nation's 48.7 million public school pupils are distributed among the states. The comparison with each state's population is a rough indicator of the differences among states in the financial burdens of providing free public education. These data come from the National Education Association's *Rankings and Estimates: Rankings of the States 2005* and *Estimates of School Statistics 2006*, released in November of 2006 on the NEA Web site (www.nea.org).

H-11 Public Library Holdings Per Capita, FY 2004: These data, from *Public Libraries Survey, FY 2004* published by the National Center of Educational Statistics, relate the holdings of books (and related materials) to the population of each state. Nationally, public libraries hold about three books for every person. The reports exclude significant sources of reading materials not in public libraries, such as collections of private and university libraries and certain public school systems.

H-12 Children with Disabilities, 2005: A substantial percentage of the nation's public school students are given special financing by state and federal programs because of something unique about them. The table reflects a Department of Education count of students in 2005 classified as disabled or receiving extra school money because of poverty. These data come from the Department of Education, Office of Special Education Programs, Data Analysis System (www.ed.gov).

H-13 State and Local Education Spending, FY 2004: This table relates spending data to population and personal income in each state. The data come from the U.S. Census Bureau's electronic publication "State and Local Government Finance Estimates, by State," available on the bureau's Web site (www.census.gov). Population numbers, also from the Census, are as of July 1, 2004, and personal income numbers are from the Department of Commerce. Based on census historical practices, *State Fact Finder* used calendar year 2003 numbers. See notes to Table F-1 for more extensive information on the source of the data.

H-14 State and Local Education Spending as a Percentage of General Spending, FY 2004: This table, from the same source as Table H-13, shows the relative importance of education spending in state and local budgets. It is derived by comparing this spending with total "general" spending.

General spending includes essentially all other spending, except municipal electric and other utilities and trust funds, such as those for workers' compensation.

H-15 Spending Per Pupil, 2005–2006: This table, from the same source as Table H-10, shows spending in public schools for operations (excluding capital outlays) in relation to the number of pupils enrolled.

H-16 Average Teacher Salary, 2005–2006: These average salary calculations, from the same source as Table H-10, show the average gross wage of teachers, not including special pay for leading student activities or teaching in summer sessions.

H-17 Sources of School Funds, 2004–2005: Federal aid covers just under 9 percent of the costs of educating public school students. State and local governments divide the remainder in proportions that vary considerably from state to state, as shown in the table. The data come from the same source as Table H-9.

H-18 State Aid Per Pupil in Average Daily Attendance, 2005–2006: These data, calculated from statistics in the National Education Association's 2006 release *Rankings and Estimates,* show the amount each state government spends on supporting local public schools, expressed in relation to the number of pupils attending school.

H-19 State and Local Spending for Higher Education (Census Definition), FY 2004: This table relates spending data to population and personal income in each state. For source, see notes to Table H-13. For more statisitics, with slightly different assumptions, on higher education finance see publications from the State Higher Education Executive Officers (www.sheeo.org).

H-20 State and Local Spending for Higher Education as a Percentage of General Spending, FY 2004: This table, from the same source as Table H-13, shows the relative importance of higher education in state and local budgets. It is derived by comparing this spending with total "general" spending. General spending includes essentially all other spending excepting municipal electric and other utilities and trust funds, such as those for workers' compensation.

H-21 Public Higher Education Enrollment, 2004: This table shows the total number of students enrolled in public universities and colleges in fall 2004 and relates this number to the total population of each state. This percentage is an indicator of the relative costs of supporting public higher education in each state. The enrollment data were made available to *State Fact Finder* by the Department of Education, National Center for Education Statistics, Postsecondary Studies Division.

H-22 Per Pupil State Support of Higher Education, FY 2006:
There are a variety of different statistics seeking to measure state outlays for higher education on a per pupil basis. None are totally satisfactory for complex reasons, such as the difficulty in classifying pupils as private or public in institutions that receive public support for some of their programs but are truly private in financing other programs. This table relates state government spending for fiscal year 2006 to the latest available enrollment data for all Title IV institutions of higher education. The amount of state support comes from a survey of fiscal year 2006 state appropriations for higher education conducted by the Center for the Study of Education Policy at Illinois State University (www.grapevine.ilstu.edu).

H-23 Average In-State Tuition and Fees at Public Universities, 2005–2006: These data reflect a composite of average in-state tuition and general fees charged by public four-year institutions of higher education in the 2005–2006 academic year. They are from the *2005–2006 College Board Annual Survey of Colleges* and are printed in *2005–2006 Student Charges and Financial Aid* from the American Association of State Colleges and Universities and the National Association of State Universities and Land-Grant Colleges.

H-24 Average Out-of-State Tuition and Fees at Public Universities, 2005–2006: These data are similar to those in Table H-23, but cover out-of-state tuition. They are printed in *2005–2006 Washington State Tuition and Fee Report* from the Washington Higher Education Coordinating Board.

H-25 Percentage Change in Tuition and Fees at Public Universities, 2005–2006: This table shows one-year increases in public higher education tuition. See notes to Table H-23 for the source of in-state increases and the notes to Table H-24 for out-of-state tuition increases.

H-26 Higher Education Affordability Index, 2006: These affordability scores and rankings were developed by The National Center for Public Policy and Higher Education (www.highereducation.org) and collected in *Measuring Up 2006: The National Report Card on Higher Education.* They reflect a composite of indicators, including the percent of income needed to pay for college expenses for all income groups at public, private, and community colleges; availability of state and Pell grants, and other financial aid; and average loan amount borrowed by undergraduates. In the report, the results are presented in both letter grades and index scores, 100 equalling the most affordable.

H-27 Average Salary of Associate Professors at "Flagship" State Universities, 2005–2006: These statistics were developed for *State Fact Finder* based on detailed salary surveys by the American Association of University Professors as printed in its magazine *Academe* (March/April 2006).

To make the comparisons, the "flagship" university salary for an associate professor was used. Usually the "flagship" is the largest, oldest state university, but in some states several institutions can be considered flagships, such as the University of Michigan and Michigan State. In those cases, *State Fact Finder* generally selected the university originally constituted as the general land-grant institution (for example, the University of Michigan) rather than the one initially designated as an agricultural and mechanical school (for example, Michigan State).

H-28 State and Local Education Employees, 2005: This statistic comes from "Public Employment," a U.S. Census Bureau survey of state and local government employment, available on the Internet (www.census.gov). It covers employees of public schools, from janitors to principals, but it does not include higher education employees.

H-29 Federal Research and Development Spending, FY 2003: The federal government is a major supplier of funds for research and development of new products and processes. This federally supported research provides an important source of income for state and private universities and a base from which state economies can develop in high technology industries. The table shows how federal research and development spending in fiscal year 2003 was distributed among the states and relates that spending to the population of each state. The data were developed by the National Science Foundation.

H-30 Total Library Operating Expenditures, FY 2004: These data are from the same source as Table H-11.

H-31 Head Start Enrollment and Funding, 2005: Head Start is a federally-funded program designed to prepare disadvantaged students for the experience of K-12 school. Grants are awarded directly to local public agencies, private organizations, Indian tribes, and school systems. These data are from the Administration for Children and Families (ACF) Web site (www.acf.hhs.gov).

Health

Percent of U.S. Population Uninsured by Age Group, 2005	
Age Group	**Percent**
Under 18	11.2
18–24	30.6
25–34	26.4
35–44	18.8
45–54	15.2
55–64	13.6
65 and over	1.3

Source: U.S. Census Bureau

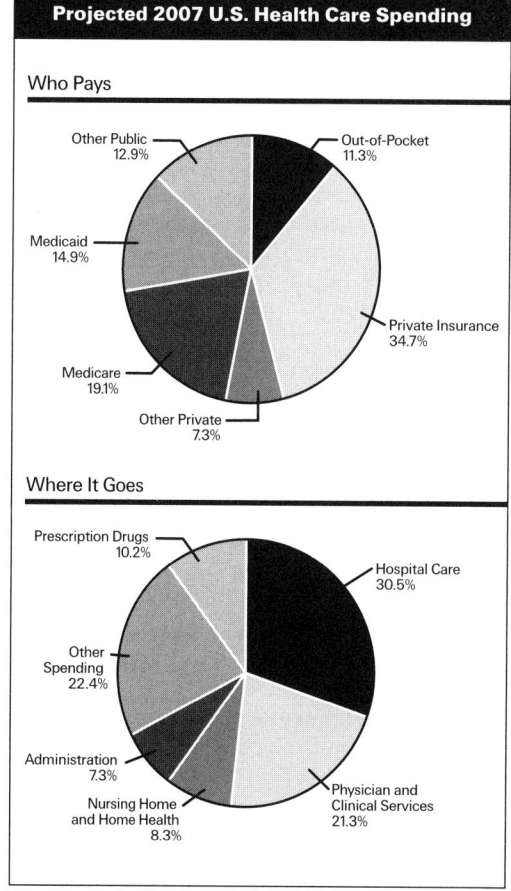

Projected 2007 U.S. Health Care Spending

Who Pays

Other Public 12.9%
Out-of-Pocket 11.3%
Medicaid 14.9%
Private Insurance 34.7%
Medicare 19.1%
Other Private 7.3%

Where It Goes

Prescription Drugs 10.2%
Hospital Care 30.5%
Other Spending 22.4%
Administration 7.3%
Nursing Home and Home Health 8.3%
Physician and Clinical Services 21.3%

Source: Centers for Medicare & Medicaid Services

I-1   Immunization Rates, 2005

State	Vaccination coverage %	Rank
Alabama	86.0	12
Alaska	80.3	39
Arizona	81.5	31
Arkansas	70.3	50
California	80.5	38
Colorado	85.1	18
Connecticut	89.4	3
Delaware	86.7	9
Florida	81.5	31
Georgia	86.2	11
Hawaii	81.4	35
Idaho	79.3	40
Illinois	84.9	22
Indiana	78.9	43
Iowa	85.7	14
Kansas	87.5	8
Kentucky	84.8	23
Louisiana	78.2	45
Maine	88.8	5
Maryland	84.3	27
Massachusetts	95.6	1
Michigan	84.5	24
Minnesota	88.4	6
Mississippi	85.1	18
Missouri	82.2	30
Montana	84.1	28
Nebraska	91.0	2
Nevada	71.2	49
New Hampshire	85.0	20
New Jersey	79.3	40
New Mexico	81.5	31
New York	85.0	20
North Carolina	89.1	4
North Dakota	86.6	10
Ohio	85.4	17
Oklahoma	77.3	46
Oregon	76.1	47
Pennsylvania	84.5	24
Rhode Island	85.7	14
South Carolina	79.2	42
South Dakota	88.4	6
Tennessee	84.4	26
Texas	81.5	31
Utah	75.7	48
Vermont	83.4	29
Virginia	86.0	12
Washington	81.2	36
West Virginia	78.8	44
Wisconsin	85.6	16
Wyoming	80.7	37
50 States	n/a	
DC	81.4	
United States	83.1	

Rank in order by percentage

1	Massachusetts
2	Nebraska
3	Connecticut
4	North Carolina
5	Maine
6	Minnesota
6	South Dakota
8	Kansas
9	Delaware
10	North Dakota
11	Georgia
12	Alabama
12	Virginia
14	Iowa
14	Rhode Island
16	Wisconsin
17	Ohio
18	Colorado
18	Mississippi
20	New Hampshire
20	New York
22	Illinois
23	Kentucky
24	Michigan
24	Pennsylvania
26	Tennessee
27	Maryland
28	Montana
29	Vermont
30	Missouri
31	Arizona
31	Florida
31	New Mexico
31	Texas
35	Hawaii
36	Washington
37	Wyoming
38	California
39	Alaska
40	Idaho
40	New Jersey
42	South Carolina
43	Indiana
44	West Virginia
45	Louisiana
46	Oklahoma
47	Oregon
48	Utah
49	Nevada
50	Arkansas

Note: Ties in ranking reflect ties in actual values.

I-2   Infant Mortality Rates, 2005

State	Infant deaths per 1,000 live births	Rank
Alabama	8.5	7
Alaska	6.3	28
Arizona	6.6	24
Arkansas	8.7	4
California	5.1	43
Colorado	6.6	24
Connecticut	5.6	36
Delaware	6.9	19
Florida	6.9	19
Georgia	7.9	12
Hawaii	4.5	48
Idaho	6.8	22
Illinois	7.1	17
Indiana	8.6	6
Iowa	5.1	43
Kansas	6.5	26
Kentucky	6.7	23
Louisiana	9.6	2
Maine	6.1	31
Maryland	8.1	10
Massachusetts	4.4	50
Michigan	7.4	14
Minnesota	4.9	47
Mississippi	9.3	3
Missouri	7.3	16
Montana	5.6	36
Nebraska	6.3	28
Nevada	6.0	34
New Hampshire	5.2	41
New Jersey	5.0	46
New Mexico	6.2	30
New York	6.1	31
North Carolina	8.2	9
North Dakota	5.4	39
Ohio	7.7	13
Oklahoma	8.0	11
Oregon	5.6	36
Pennsylvania	6.9	19
Rhode Island	5.2	41
South Carolina	8.3	8
South Dakota	7.4	14
Tennessee	8.7	4
Texas	5.9	35
Utah	5.1	43
Vermont	4.5	48
Virginia	7.0	18
Washington	5.3	40
West Virginia	6.4	27
Wisconsin	6.1	31
Wyoming	9.7	1
50 States	n/a	
DC	9.9	
United States	6.6	

Rank in order by rate	
1	Wyoming
2	Louisiana
3	Mississippi
4	Arkansas
4	Tennessee
6	Indiana
7	Alabama
8	South Carolina
9	North Carolina
10	Maryland
11	Oklahoma
12	Georgia
13	Ohio
14	Michigan
14	South Dakota
16	Missouri
17	Illinois
18	Virginia
19	Delaware
19	Florida
19	Pennsylvania
22	Idaho
23	Kentucky
24	Arizona
24	Colorado
26	Kansas
27	West Virginia
28	Alaska
28	Nebraska
30	New Mexico
31	Maine
31	New York
31	Wisconsin
34	Nevada
35	Texas
36	Connecticut
36	Montana
36	Oregon
39	North Dakota
40	Washington
41	New Hampshire
41	Rhode Island
43	California
43	Iowa
43	Utah
46	New Jersey
47	Minnesota
48	Hawaii
48	Vermont
50	Massachusetts

Note: Ties in ranking reflect ties in actual values.

State	State health rankings	Rank
Alabama	-14.8	45
Alaska	-0.8	31
Arizona	-4.0	34
Arkansas	-16.1	46
California	4.7	23
Colorado	8.9	16
Connecticut	17.2	5
Delaware	-0.6	30
Florida	-10.6	41
Georgia	-11.7	42
Hawaii	17.9	4
Idaho	6.5	19
Illinois	3.7	25
Indiana	-3.7	33
Iowa	12.5	11
Kansas	7.9	17
Kentucky	-10.1	39
Louisiana	-20.4	50
Maine	13.7	9
Maryland	-2.7	32
Massachusetts	15.3	7
Michigan	2.3	27
Minnesota	21.2	1
Mississippi	-19.9	49
Missouri	-4.1	35
Montana	4.9	22
Nebraska	12.4	12
Nevada	-8.4	38
New Hampshire	18.9	3
New Jersey	11.0	14
New Mexico	-10.4	40
New York	1.1	29
North Carolina	-4.3	36
North Dakota	15.0	8
Ohio	3.7	25
Oklahoma	-13.1	44
Oregon	6.5	19
Pennsylvania	1.8	28
Rhode Island	11.4	13
South Carolina	-16.4	48
South Dakota	7.5	18
Tennessee	-16.2	47
Texas	-4.7	37
Utah	16.3	6
Vermont	20.5	2
Virginia	5.7	21
Washington	10.2	15
West Virginia	-12.8	43
Wisconsin	13.3	10
Wyoming	4.7	23
50 States	n/a	
DC	n/a	
United States	n/a	

Rank in order by ranking

1	Minnesota
2	Vermont
3	New Hampshire
4	Hawaii
5	Connecticut
6	Utah
7	Massachusetts
8	North Dakota
9	Maine
10	Wisconsin
11	Iowa
12	Nebraska
13	Rhode Island
14	New Jersey
15	Washington
16	Colorado
17	Kansas
18	South Dakota
19	Idaho
19	Oregon
21	Virginia
22	Montana
23	California
23	Wyoming
25	Illinois
25	Ohio
27	Michigan
28	Pennsylvania
29	New York
30	Delaware
31	Alaska
32	Maryland
33	Indiana
34	Arizona
35	Missouri
36	North Carolina
37	Texas
38	Nevada
39	Kentucky
40	New Mexico
41	Florida
42	Georgia
43	West Virginia
44	Oklahoma
45	Alabama
46	Arkansas
47	Tennessee
48	South Carolina
49	Mississippi
50	Louisiana

Note: Ties in ranking reflect ties in actual values.

I-4 Percentage of Non-Elderly Population without Health Insurance, 2005

State	Percentage of non-elderly without health insurance	Rank
Alabama	17.6	21
Alaska	18.8	15
Arizona	22.8	4
Arkansas	20.5	10
California	21.3	6
Colorado	18.6	16
Connecticut	12.9	40
Delaware	14.8	31
Florida	24.4	2
Georgia	20.6	9
Hawaii	10.3	48
Idaho	17.1	22
Illinois	16.1	25
Indiana	15.7	26
Iowa	9.9	49
Kansas	12.2	43
Kentucky	14.4	32
Louisiana	21.5	5
Maine	12.3	42
Maryland	15.7	26
Massachusetts	11.1	47
Michigan	12.7	41
Minnesota	9.6	50
Mississippi	19.7	13
Missouri	13.8	36
Montana	20.1	12
Nebraska	13.2	38
Nevada	19.4	14
New Hampshire	11.8	45
New Jersey	16.9	23
New Mexico	23.4	3
New York	15.3	29
North Carolina	18.1	18
North Dakota	14.1	34
Ohio	14.0	35
Oklahoma	21.2	7
Oregon	18.3	17
Pennsylvania	12.1	44
Rhode Island	13.3	37
South Carolina	20.2	11
South Dakota	14.2	33
Tennessee	16.3	24
Texas	26.9	1
Utah	17.9	20
Vermont	13.1	39
Virginia	14.9	30
Washington	15.4	28
West Virginia	20.9	8
Wisconsin	11.2	46
Wyoming	18.1	18
50 States	n/a	
DC	14.8	
United States	17.9	

Rank in order by percentage	
1	Texas
2	Florida
3	New Mexico
4	Arizona
5	Louisiana
6	California
7	Oklahoma
8	West Virginia
9	Georgia
10	Arkansas
11	South Carolina
12	Montana
13	Mississippi
14	Nevada
15	Alaska
16	Colorado
17	Oregon
18	North Carolina
18	Wyoming
20	Utah
21	Alabama
22	Idaho
23	New Jersey
24	Tennessee
25	Illinois
26	Indiana
26	Maryland
28	Washington
29	New York
30	Virginia
31	Delaware
32	Kentucky
33	South Dakota
34	North Dakota
35	Ohio
36	Missouri
37	Rhode Island
38	Nebraska
39	Vermont
40	Connecticut
41	Michigan
42	Maine
43	Kansas
44	Pennsylvania
45	New Hampshire
46	Wisconsin
47	Massachusetts
48	Hawaii
49	Iowa
50	Minnesota

Note: Ties in ranking reflect ties in actual values.

I-5   Abortions, 2003

State	Abortions #	Per 1,000 births	Rank per 1,000 births
Alabama	10,979	184	26
Alaska	1,806	179	28
Arizona	10,316	113	40
Arkansas	5,408	143	35
California	n/a	n/a	n/a
Colorado	9,852	142	36
Connecticut	12,404	289	8
Delaware	4,178	369	4
Florida	88,247	416	3
Georgia	34,363	253	15
Hawaii	3,608	199	24
Idaho	911	42	46
Illinois	42,247	231	18
Indiana	11,458	133	37
Iowa	5,916	155	31
Kansas	11,600	294	7
Kentucky	3,621	66	45
Louisiana	10,642	164	30
Maine	2,550	184	26
Maryland	11,485	153	33
Massachusetts	25,741	321	5
Michigan	29,540	225	19
Minnesota	14,091	201	23
Mississippi	3,753	89	42
Missouri	8,350	108	41
Montana	2,213	194	25
Nebraska	3,990	154	32
Nevada	9,323	277	10
New Hampshire	n/a	n/a	n/a
New Jersey	32,762	280	9
New Mexico	5,832	210	21
New York	124,957	509	1
North Carolina	31,006	262	12
North Dakota	1,354	170	29
Ohio	35,319	236	17
Oklahoma	6,644	130	38
Oregon	12,622	275	11
Pennsylvania	36,908	253	15
Rhode Island	5,538	419	2
South Carolina	6,573	118	39
South Dakota	819	74	43
Tennessee	17,610	223	20
Texas	79,166	210	21
Utah	3,576	72	44
Vermont	1,679	255	14
Virginia	26,437	261	13
Washington	25,084	312	6
West Virginia	n/a	n/a	n/a
Wisconsin	10,557	151	34
Wyoming	7	n/a	n/a
50 States	843,042	n/a	
DC	5,121	672	
United States	848,163	241	

Rank in order per 1,000 births

1 New York
2 Rhode Island
3 Florida
4 Delaware
5 Massachusetts
6 Washington
7 Kansas
8 Connecticut
9 New Jersey
10 Nevada
11 Oregon
12 North Carolina
13 Virginia
14 Vermont
15 Georgia
15 Pennsylvania
17 Ohio
18 Illinois
19 Michigan
20 Tennessee
21 New Mexico
21 Texas
23 Minnesota
24 Hawaii
25 Montana
26 Alabama
26 Maine
28 Alaska
29 North Dakota
30 Louisiana
31 Iowa
32 Nebraska
33 Maryland
34 Wisconsin
35 Arkansas
36 Colorado
37 Indiana
38 Oklahoma
39 South Carolina
40 Arizona
41 Missouri
42 Mississippi
43 South Dakota
44 Utah
45 Kentucky
46 Idaho

Note: Ties in ranking reflect ties in actual values.

I-6   Alcohol Consumption Per Capita, 2003

State	Per capita consumption in gallons	Rank
Alabama	1.89	45
Alaska	2.43	13
Arizona	2.48	10
Arkansas	1.76	47
California	2.22	28
Colorado	2.60	7
Connecticut	2.22	28
Delaware	3.11	3
Florida	2.63	6
Georgia	2.11	35
Hawaii	2.39	18
Idaho	2.33	24
Illinois	2.34	23
Indiana	1.96	41
Iowa	2.05	37
Kansas	1.88	46
Kentucky	1.74	48
Louisiana	2.39	18
Maine	2.36	20
Maryland	2.11	35
Massachusetts	2.48	10
Michigan	2.13	34
Minnesota	2.41	15
Mississippi	2.14	33
Missouri	2.26	25
Montana	2.59	8
Nebraska	2.23	27
Nevada	3.63	2
New Hampshire	4.03	1
New Jersey	2.24	26
New Mexico	2.40	16
New York	1.93	43
North Carolina	2.00	40
North Dakota	2.56	9
Ohio	2.03	38
Oklahoma	1.93	43
Oregon	2.35	21
Pennsylvania	2.20	30
Rhode Island	2.42	14
South Carolina	2.35	21
South Dakota	2.40	16
Tennessee	1.96	41
Texas	2.19	31
Utah	1.31	50
Vermont	2.47	12
Virginia	2.03	38
Washington	2.19	31
West Virginia	1.71	49
Wisconsin	2.81	5
Wyoming	2.82	4
50 States	n/a	
DC	3.84	
United States	2.22	

Rank in order per capita	
1	New Hampshire
2	Nevada
3	Delaware
4	Wyoming
5	Wisconsin
6	Florida
7	Colorado
8	Montana
9	North Dakota
10	Arizona
10	Massachusetts
12	Vermont
13	Alaska
14	Rhode Island
15	Minnesota
16	New Mexico
16	South Dakota
18	Hawaii
18	Louisiana
20	Maine
21	Oregon
21	South Carolina
23	Illinois
24	Idaho
25	Missouri
26	New Jersey
27	Nebraska
28	California
28	Connecticut
30	Pennsylvania
31	Texas
31	Washington
33	Mississippi
34	Michigan
35	Georgia
35	Maryland
37	Iowa
38	Ohio
38	Virginia
40	North Carolina
41	Indiana
41	Tennessee
43	New York
43	Oklahoma
45	Alabama
46	Kansas
47	Arkansas
48	Kentucky
49	West Virginia
50	Utah

Note: Ties in ranking reflect ties in actual values.

I-7   Percentage of Adult Smokers, 2005

State	Percentage of adult smokers	Rank
Alabama	24.8	7
Alaska	24.9	6
Arizona	20.2	30
Arkansas	23.5	10
California	15.2	49
Colorado	19.8	35
Connecticut	16.5	48
Delaware	20.6	25
Florida	21.7	19
Georgia	22.1	17
Hawaii	17.0	47
Idaho	17.9	44
Illinois	19.9	34
Indiana	27.3	2
Iowa	20.4	28
Kansas	17.8	45
Kentucky	28.7	1
Louisiana	22.6	13
Maine	20.8	23
Maryland	18.9	40
Massachusetts	18.1	42
Michigan	22.0	18
Minnesota	20.0	32
Mississippi	23.6	8
Missouri	23.4	11
Montana	19.2	39
Nebraska	21.3	21
Nevada	23.1	12
New Hampshire	20.4	28
New Jersey	18.0	43
New Mexico	21.5	20
New York	20.5	27
North Carolina	22.6	13
North Dakota	20.1	31
Ohio	22.3	16
Oklahoma	25.1	5
Oregon	18.5	41
Pennsylvania	23.6	8
Rhode Island	19.8	35
South Carolina	22.5	15
South Dakota	19.8	35
Tennessee	26.7	3
Texas	20.0	32
Utah	11.5	50
Vermont	19.3	38
Virginia	20.6	25
Washington	17.6	46
West Virginia	26.7	3
Wisconsin	20.7	24
Wyoming	21.3	21
50 States	n/a	
DC	20.0	
United States	20.6	

Rank in order by percentage	
1	Kentucky
2	Indiana
3	Tennessee
3	West Virginia
5	Oklahoma
6	Alaska
7	Alabama
8	Mississippi
8	Pennsylvania
10	Arkansas
11	Missouri
12	Nevada
13	Louisiana
13	North Carolina
15	South Carolina
16	Ohio
17	Georgia
18	Michigan
19	Florida
20	New Mexico
21	Nebraska
21	Wyoming
23	Maine
24	Wisconsin
25	Delaware
25	Virginia
27	New York
28	Iowa
28	New Hampshire
30	Arizona
31	North Dakota
32	Minnesota
32	Texas
34	Illinois
35	Colorado
35	Rhode Island
35	South Dakota
38	Vermont
39	Montana
40	Maryland
41	Oregon
42	Massachusetts
43	New Jersey
44	Idaho
45	Kansas
46	Washington
47	Hawaii
48	Connecticut
49	California
50	Utah

Note: Ties in ranking reflect ties in actual values.

I-8 Percentage of Population Obese, 2005

State	Percentage of population obese	Rank
Alabama	28.9	5
Alaska	27.4	8
Arizona	21.1	44
Arkansas	28.0	7
California	22.7	36
Colorado	17.8	50
Connecticut	20.1	48
Delaware	23.5	32
Florida	22.8	35
Georgia	26.5	14
Hawaii	19.7	49
Idaho	24.5	24
Illinois	25.1	22
Indiana	27.2	10
Iowa	25.4	19
Kansas	23.9	29
Kentucky	28.6	6
Louisiana	30.8	2
Maine	22.7	36
Maryland	24.4	25
Massachusetts	20.7	46
Michigan	26.2	15
Minnesota	23.7	31
Mississippi	30.9	1
Missouri	26.9	12
Montana	21.3	41
Nebraska	26.0	16
Nevada	21.2	42
New Hampshire	23.1	34
New Jersey	22.1	39
New Mexico	21.7	40
New York	22.2	38
North Carolina	25.9	17
North Dakota	25.4	19
Ohio	24.3	27
Oklahoma	26.8	13
Oregon	23.8	30
Pennsylvania	25.3	21
Rhode Island	21.0	45
South Carolina	29.1	4
South Dakota	25.5	18
Tennessee	27.4	8
Texas	27.0	11
Utah	21.2	42
Vermont	20.2	47
Virginia	25.1	22
Washington	23.3	33
West Virginia	30.6	3
Wisconsin	24.4	25
Wyoming	24.2	28
50 States	n/a	
DC	n/a	
United States	24.4	

Rank in order by percentage	
1	Mississippi
2	Louisiana
3	West Virginia
4	South Carolina
5	Alabama
6	Kentucky
7	Arkansas
8	Alaska
8	Tennessee
10	Indiana
11	Texas
12	Missouri
13	Oklahoma
14	Georgia
15	Michigan
16	Nebraska
17	North Carolina
18	South Dakota
19	Iowa
19	North Dakota
21	Pennsylvania
22	Illinois
22	Virginia
24	Idaho
25	Maryland
25	Wisconsin
27	Ohio
28	Wyoming
29	Kansas
30	Oregon
31	Minnesota
32	Delaware
33	Washington
34	New Hampshire
35	Florida
36	California
36	Maine
38	New York
39	New Jersey
40	New Mexico
41	Montana
42	Nevada
42	Utah
44	Arizona
45	Rhode Island
46	Massachusetts
47	Vermont
48	Connecticut
49	Hawaii
50	Colorado

Note: Ties in ranking reflect ties in actual values.

I-9   AIDS Cases, 2005

State	AIDS cases #	Rate per 100,000 residents	Rank by rate
Alabama	518	11.4	16
Alaska	26	3.9	37
Arizona	642	10.8	19
Arkansas	242	8.7	21
California	4,088	11.3	17
Colorado	359	7.7	27
Connecticut	666	19.0	7
Delaware	176	20.9	6
Florida	4,960	27.9	3
Georgia	2,333	25.7	4
Hawaii	109	8.5	22
Idaho	25	1.7	46
Illinois	1,922	15.1	9
Indiana	409	6.5	32
Iowa	95	3.2	39
Kansas	107	3.9	37
Kentucky	257	6.2	33
Louisiana	961	21.2	5
Maine	21	1.6	47
Maryland	1,595	28.5	2
Massachusetts	692	10.8	19
Michigan	822	8.1	25
Minnesota	225	4.4	35
Mississippi	387	13.2	13
Missouri	386	6.7	31
Montana	20	2.1	45
Nebraska	53	3.0	40
Nevada	296	12.3	14
New Hampshire	34	2.6	41
New Jersey	1,278	14.7	10
New Mexico	136	7.1	29
New York	6,299	32.7	1
North Carolina	945	10.9	18
North Dakota	10	1.6	47
Ohio	784	6.8	30
Oklahoma	282	7.9	26
Oregon	220	6.0	34
Pennsylvania	1,510	12.1	15
Rhode Island	89	8.3	24
South Carolina	668	15.7	8
South Dakota	19	2.4	43
Tennessee	841	14.1	11
Texas	3,113	13.6	12
Utah	65	2.6	41
Vermont	6	1.0	50
Virginia	646	8.5	22
Washington	486	7.7	27
West Virginia	74	4.1	36
Wisconsin	123	2.2	44
Wyoming	6	1.2	49
50 States	40,026	n/a	
DC	707	128.4	
United States	40,733	13.7	

Rank in order by rate	
1	New York
2	Maryland
3	Florida
4	Georgia
5	Louisiana
6	Delaware
7	Connecticut
8	South Carolina
9	Illinois
10	New Jersey
11	Tennessee
12	Texas
13	Mississippi
14	Nevada
15	Pennsylvania
16	Alabama
17	California
18	North Carolina
19	Arizona
19	Massachusetts
21	Arkansas
22	Hawaii
22	Virginia
24	Rhode Island
25	Michigan
26	Oklahoma
27	Colorado
27	Washington
29	New Mexico
30	Ohio
31	Missouri
32	Indiana
33	Kentucky
34	Oregon
35	Minnesota
36	West Virginia
37	Alaska
37	Kansas
39	Iowa
40	Nebraska
41	New Hampshire
41	Utah
43	South Dakota
44	Wisconsin
45	Montana
46	Idaho
47	Maine
47	North Dakota
49	Wyoming
50	Vermont

Note: Ties in ranking reflect ties in actual values.

I-10   Physicians Per 100,000 Population, 2006

State	Physicians per 100,000 population	Rank
Alabama	221	40
Alaska	231	34
Arizona	228	35
Arkansas	210	45
California	260	24
Colorado	267	19
Connecticut	359	5
Delaware	270	16
Florida	256	25
Georgia	223	38
Hawaii	306	9
Idaho	176	50
Illinois	283	13
Indiana	226	37
Iowa	215	43
Kansas	244	29
Kentucky	240	31
Louisiana	197	47
Maine	292	11
Maryland	406	2
Massachusetts	447	1
Michigan	291	12
Minnesota	280	14
Mississippi	185	49
Missouri	268	18
Montana	223	38
Nebraska	252	28
Nevada	199	46
New Hampshire	265	20
New Jersey	330	7
New Mexico	237	32
New York	379	3
North Carolina	254	27
North Dakota	242	30
Ohio	295	10
Oklahoma	211	44
Oregon	262	22
Pennsylvania	327	8
Rhode Island	368	4
South Carolina	236	33
South Dakota	228	35
Tennessee	269	17
Texas	221	40
Utah	218	42
Vermont	346	6
Virginia	273	15
Washington	256	25
West Virginia	263	21
Wisconsin	260	23
Wyoming	191	48
50 States	274	
DC	786	
United States	278	

Rank in order per 100,000 population	
1	Massachusetts
2	Maryland
3	New York
4	Rhode Island
5	Connecticut
6	Vermont
7	New Jersey
8	Pennsylvania
9	Hawaii
10	Ohio
11	Maine
12	Michigan
13	Illinois
14	Minnesota
15	Virginia
16	Delaware
17	Tennessee
18	Missouri
19	Colorado
20	New Hampshire
21	West Virginia
22	Oregon
23	Wisconsin
24	California
25	Florida
25	Washington
27	North Carolina
28	Nebraska
29	Kansas
30	North Dakota
31	Kentucky
32	New Mexico
33	South Carolina
34	Alaska
35	Arizona
35	South Dakota
37	Indiana
38	Georgia
38	Montana
40	Alabama
40	Texas
42	Utah
43	Iowa
44	Oklahoma
45	Arkansas
46	Nevada
47	Louisiana
48	Wyoming
49	Mississippi
50	Idaho

Note: Ties in ranking reflect ties in actual values.

I-11   Hospital Beds Per 1,000 Population, 2005

State	Hospital beds per 1,000 population	Rank
Alabama	3.4	13
Alaska	2.1	41
Arizona	2.0	44
Arkansas	3.4	14
California	1.9	45
Colorado	2.1	42
Connecticut	2.2	37
Delaware	2.3	36
Florida	2.9	21
Georgia	2.8	23
Hawaii	2.4	33
Idaho	2.3	34
Illinois	2.7	24
Indiana	2.8	22
Iowa	3.6	9
Kansas	3.7	8
Kentucky	3.6	10
Louisiana	3.4	12
Maine	2.7	27
Maryland	2.0	43
Massachusetts	2.5	32
Michigan	2.6	29
Minnesota	3.1	18
Mississippi	4.4	4
Missouri	3.3	15
Montana	4.6	3
Nebraska	4.3	5
Nevada	1.9	46
New Hampshire	2.2	40
New Jersey	2.5	31
New Mexico	1.8	48
New York	3.3	16
North Carolina	2.7	26
North Dakota	5.5	2
Ohio	2.9	20
Oklahoma	3.0	19
Oregon	1.8	49
Pennsylvania	3.2	17
Rhode Island	2.2	38
South Carolina	2.7	25
South Dakota	5.6	1
Tennessee	3.5	11
Texas	2.5	30
Utah	1.8	47
Vermont	2.2	39
Virginia	2.3	35
Washington	1.7	50
West Virginia	4.0	7
Wisconsin	2.6	28
Wyoming	4.0	6
50 States	2.7	
DC	6.4	
United States	2.7	

Note: Numbers that appear to be identical are rounded and vary slightly in actual value. The rankings reflect the actual values before rounding. See the introduction for more details.

State	Medicaid recipients # (in thousands)	Percentage of population	Rank by percentage
Alabama	821	18.0	11
Alaska	98	14.7	24
Arizona	997	16.8	12
Arkansas	624	22.5	2
California	6,553	18.1	10
Colorado	410	8.8	46
Connecticut	403	11.5	38
Delaware	140	16.6	14
Florida	2,248	12.6	33
Georgia	1,378	15.2	22
Hawaii	201	15.7	18
Idaho	172	12.0	36
Illinois	1,827	14.3	26
Indiana	811	12.9	31
Iowa	298	10.0	41
Kansas	276	10.0	42
Kentucky	692	16.6	15
Louisiana	964	21.3	6
Maine	266	20.2	8
Maryland	716	12.8	32
Massachusetts	992	15.5	19
Michigan	1,435	14.2	27
Minnesota	573	11.2	40
Mississippi	633	21.7	4
Missouri	949	16.4	16
Montana	84	9.0	44
Nebraska	207	11.8	37
Nevada	175	7.2	50
New Hampshire	100	7.6	49
New Jersey	802	9.2	43
New Mexico	411	21.3	5
New York	4,189	21.8	3
North Carolina	1,138	13.1	29
North Dakota	54	8.5	47
Ohio	1,711	14.9	23
Oklahoma	544	15.3	20
Oregon	411	11.3	39
Pennsylvania	1,698	13.7	28
Rhode Island	180	16.8	13
South Carolina	833	19.6	9
South Dakota	101	13.0	30
Tennessee	1,350	22.6	1
Texas	2,767	12.1	34
Utah	203	8.2	48
Vermont	130	20.9	7
Virginia	674	8.9	45
Washington	963	15.3	21
West Virginia	296	16.3	17
Wisconsin	813	14.7	25
Wyoming	61	12.1	35
50 States	44,374	15.0	
DC	141	25.6	
United States*	45,392	15.3	

Due to rounding or data sources, the 50-state total plus D.C. may not equal the U.S. total. Please see introduction.

Rank in order by percentage	
1	Tennessee
2	Arkansas
3	New York
4	Mississippi
5	New Mexico
6	Louisiana
7	Vermont
8	Maine
9	South Carolina
10	California
11	Alabama
12	Arizona
13	Rhode Island
14	Delaware
15	Kentucky
16	Missouri
17	West Virginia
18	Hawaii
19	Massachusetts
20	Oklahoma
21	Washington
22	Georgia
23	Ohio
24	Alaska
25	Wisconsin
26	Illinois
27	Michigan
28	Pennsylvania
29	North Carolina
30	South Dakota
31	Indiana
32	Maryland
33	Florida
34	Texas
35	Wyoming
36	Idaho
37	Nebraska
38	Connecticut
39	Oregon
40	Minnesota
41	Iowa
42	Kansas
43	New Jersey
44	Montana
45	Virginia
46	Colorado
47	North Dakota
48	Utah
49	New Hampshire
50	Nevada

Note: Numbers that appear to be identical are rounded and vary slightly in actual value. The rankings reflect the actual values before rounding. See the introduction for more details.

I-13 Medicaid Recipients as a Percentage of Poverty Population, Mid-Year 2005

State	Recipients as a percentage of poverty population	Rank
Alabama	109.4	34
Alaska	148.1	10
Arizona	108.8	35
Arkansas	163.4	4
California	138.9	15
Colorado	77.4	46
Connecticut	123.8	23
Delaware	179.7	3
Florida	113.8	30
Georgia	106.1	37
Hawaii	182.3	2
Idaho	120.3	26
Illinois	126.8	21
Indiana	104.7	38
Iowa	91.1	43
Kansas	81.8	45
Kentucky	115.5	29
Louisiana	128.9	20
Maine	160.4	5
Maryland	132.1	19
Massachusetts	154.8	6
Michigan	120.0	27
Minnesota	139.1	14
Mississippi	110.9	33
Missouri	144.1	12
Montana	65.8	50
Nebraska	123.9	22
Nevada	67.3	49
New Hampshire	137.0	16
New Jersey	135.5	17
New Mexico	118.5	28
New York	151.8	8
North Carolina	102.0	39
North Dakota	77.0	47
Ohio	122.9	25
Oklahoma	100.2	40
Oregon	94.4	42
Pennsylvania	123.7	24
Rhode Island	142.1	13
South Carolina	133.1	18
South Dakota	112.1	32
Tennessee	154.8	7
Texas	75.2	48
Utah	87.5	44
Vermont	277.0	1
Virginia	98.5	41
Washington	151.4	9
West Virginia	107.3	36
Wisconsin	147.1	11
Wyoming	113.8	31
50 States	120.5	
DC	122.5	
United States	122.8	

Rank in order by percentage	
1	Vermont
2	Hawaii
3	Delaware
4	Arkansas
5	Maine
6	Massachusetts
7	Tennessee
8	New York
9	Washington
10	Alaska
11	Wisconsin
12	Missouri
13	Rhode Island
14	Minnesota
15	California
16	New Hampshire
17	New Jersey
18	South Carolina
19	Maryland
20	Louisiana
21	Illinois
22	Nebraska
23	Connecticut
24	Pennsylvania
25	Ohio
26	Idaho
27	Michigan
28	New Mexico
29	Kentucky
30	Florida
31	Wyoming
32	South Dakota
33	Mississippi
34	Alabama
35	Arizona
36	West Virginia
37	Georgia
38	Indiana
39	North Carolina
40	Oklahoma
41	Virginia
42	Oregon
43	Iowa
44	Utah
45	Kansas
46	Colorado
47	North Dakota
48	Texas
49	Nevada
50	Montana

Note: Numbers that appear to be identical are rounded and vary slightly in actual value. The rankings reflect the actual values before rounding. See the introduction for more details.

I-14   State and Local Spending for Health and Hospitals, FY 2004

State	Total spending $ (in millions)	Per capita $	Percentage of personal income	Rank per capita
Alabama	4,568	1,008	3.9	2
Alaska	241	368	1.1	40
Arizona	2,010	350	1.3	41
Arkansas	1,075	391	1.6	36
California	24,281	676	2.0	10
Colorado	2,427	527	1.5	17
Connecticut	1,752	500	1.2	21
Delaware	348	420	1.3	31
Florida	8,779	505	1.7	19
Georgia	5,096	577	2.0	13
Hawaii	674	533	1.8	15
Idaho	697	500	2.0	20
Illinois	5,399	425	1.3	27
Indiana	3,324	533	1.9	16
Iowa	2,131	721	2.5	8
Kansas	1,109	405	1.4	35
Kentucky	1,547	373	1.4	38
Louisiana	3,667	812	3.1	4
Maine	579	439	1.5	26
Maryland	1,736	312	0.8	44
Massachusetts	1,927	300	0.8	45
Michigan	6,820	674	2.2	11
Minnesota	2,088	409	1.2	34
Mississippi	2,342	807	3.5	5
Missouri	3,023	525	1.8	18
Montana	355	383	1.5	37
Nebraska	728	417	1.4	32
Nevada	981	420	1.4	30
New Hampshire	178	137	0.4	50
New Jersey	2,810	323	0.8	42
New Mexico	859	451	1.8	25
New York	13,925	724	2.0	7
North Carolina	5,951	697	2.5	9
North Dakota	115	182	0.6	48
Ohio	6,180	539	1.8	14
Oklahoma	1,305	370	1.4	39
Oregon	1,631	454	1.6	24
Pennsylvania	5,265	424	1.3	28
Rhode Island	321	297	0.9	46
South Carolina	3,450	822	3.2	3
South Dakota	188	244	0.9	47
Tennessee	3,723	631	2.2	12
Texas	10,301	458	1.6	23
Utah	1,005	421	1.7	29
Vermont	111	179	0.6	49
Virginia	3,498	469	1.4	22
Washington	4,754	766	2.3	6
West Virginia	570	314	1.3	43
Wisconsin	2,280	414	1.4	33
Wyoming	700	1,383	4.3	1
50 States	158,826	542	1.7	
DC	850	1,535	3.2	
United States	159,676	544	1.7	

Rank in order per capita	
1	Wyoming
2	Alabama
3	South Carolina
4	Louisiana
5	Mississippi
6	Washington
7	New York
8	Iowa
9	North Carolina
10	California
11	Michigan
12	Tennessee
13	Georgia
14	Ohio
15	Hawaii
16	Indiana
17	Colorado
18	Missouri
19	Florida
20	Idaho
21	Connecticut
22	Virginia
23	Texas
24	Oregon
25	New Mexico
26	Maine
27	Illinois
28	Pennsylvania
29	Utah
30	Nevada
31	Delaware
32	Nebraska
33	Wisconsin
34	Minnesota
35	Kansas
36	Arkansas
37	Montana
38	Kentucky
39	Oklahoma
40	Alaska
41	Arizona
42	New Jersey
43	West Virginia
44	Maryland
45	Massachusetts
46	Rhode Island
47	South Dakota
48	North Dakota
49	Vermont
50	New Hampshire

Note: Numbers that appear to be identical are rounded and vary slightly in actual value. The rankings reflect the actual values before rounding. See the introduction for more details.

I-15 State and Local Health and Hospital Spending as a Percentage of General Spending, FY 2004

State	Health and hospital spending as a percentage of general spending	Rank
Alabama	16.9	1
Alaska	2.8	47
Arizona	6.7	33
Arkansas	7.4	23
California	9.3	14
Colorado	8.5	17
Connecticut	7.0	28
Delaware	5.6	40
Florida	8.7	16
Georgia	10.1	10
Hawaii	7.8	22
Idaho	9.2	15
Illinois	6.8	31
Indiana	9.4	13
Iowa	11.6	8
Kansas	6.8	30
Kentucky	6.6	34
Louisiana	13.5	5
Maine	6.2	37
Maryland	5.1	42
Massachusetts	4.0	46
Michigan	10.1	11
Minnesota	5.7	39
Mississippi	13.6	3
Missouri	9.7	12
Montana	6.4	36
Nebraska	6.8	32
Nevada	7.2	26
New Hampshire	2.4	50
New Jersey	4.6	43
New Mexico	6.8	29
New York	7.9	21
North Carolina	12.3	6
North Dakota	2.8	48
Ohio	8.3	19
Oklahoma	7.2	27
Oregon	7.3	24
Pennsylvania	6.6	35
Rhode Island	4.2	45
South Carolina	13.5	4
South Dakota	4.5	44
Tennessee	11.8	7
Texas	8.3	18
Utah	7.2	25
Vermont	2.5	49
Virginia	8.1	20
Washington	11.2	9
West Virginia	5.4	41
Wisconsin	6.2	38
Wyoming	15.4	2
50 States	8.4	
DC	12.6	
United States	8.4	

Note: Numbers that appear to be identical are rounded and vary slightly in actual value. The rankings reflect the actual values before rounding. See the introduction for more details.

I-16   Per Capita Medicaid Spending, FY 2005

State	Per capita Medicaid spending $	Rank
Alabama	848	32
Alaska	1,487	5
Arizona	965	22
Arkansas	1,023	20
California	941	25
Colorado	604	47
Connecticut	1,171	12
Delaware	1,030	18
Florida	752	44
Georgia	862	29
Hawaii	819	34
Idaho	716	46
Illinois	857	31
Indiana	840	33
Iowa	816	35
Kansas	722	45
Kentucky	1,030	19
Louisiana	1,209	11
Maine	1,702	2
Maryland	941	24
Massachusetts	1,518	4
Michigan	861	30
Minnesota	1,093	15
Mississippi	1,155	13
Missouri	1,138	14
Montana	752	43
Nebraska	801	39
Nevada	491	50
New Hampshire	963	23
New Jersey	874	28
New Mexico	1,229	9
New York	2,255	1
North Carolina	1,073	16
North Dakota	809	36
Ohio	1,032	17
Oklahoma	794	40
Oregon	783	42
Pennsylvania	1,277	7
Rhode Island	1,571	3
South Carolina	988	21
South Dakota	793	41
Tennessee	1,275	8
Texas	807	37
Utah	553	49
Vermont	1,394	6
Virginia	591	48
Washington	914	26
West Virginia	1,227	10
Wisconsin	878	27
Wyoming	806	38
50 States	1,028	
DC	2,319	
United States	1,030	

Rank in order per capita	
1	New York
2	Maine
3	Rhode Island
4	Massachusetts
5	Alaska
6	Vermont
7	Pennsylvania
8	Tennessee
9	New Mexico
10	West Virginia
11	Louisiana
12	Connecticut
13	Mississippi
14	Missouri
15	Minnesota
16	North Carolina
17	Ohio
18	Delaware
19	Kentucky
20	Arkansas
21	South Carolina
22	Arizona
23	New Hampshire
24	Maryland
25	California
26	Washington
27	Wisconsin
28	New Jersey
29	Georgia
30	Michigan
31	Illinois
32	Alabama
33	Indiana
34	Hawaii
35	Iowa
36	North Dakota
37	Texas
38	Wyoming
39	Nebraska
40	Oklahoma
41	South Dakota
42	Oregon
43	Montana
44	Florida
45	Kansas
46	Idaho
47	Colorado
48	Virginia
49	Utah
50	Nevada

Note: Numbers that appear to be identical are rounded and vary slightly in actual value. The rankings reflect the actual values before rounding. See the introduction for more details.

I-17 Average Medicaid Spending Per Aged Recipient, FY 2003

State	Average spending per aged recipient $	Rank
Alabama	7,485	44
Alaska	17,921	4
Arizona	7,531	43
Arkansas	9,919	29
California	8,016	39
Colorado	12,290	22
Connecticut	20,158	2
Delaware	14,524	10
Florida	8,986	36
Georgia	7,336	45
Hawaii	10,102	28
Idaho	14,368	12
Illinois	4,749	50
Indiana	12,360	21
Iowa	13,351	18
Kansas	14,027	15
Kentucky	9,526	31
Louisiana	7,671	42
Maine	5,054	48
Maryland	14,345	13
Massachusetts	14,052	14
Michigan	11,601	25
Minnesota	13,977	16
Mississippi	8,142	38
Missouri	11,386	26
Montana	13,591	17
Nebraska	15,166	8
Nevada	7,336	45
New Hampshire	17,442	5
New Jersey	14,893	9
New Mexico	11,701	24
New York	21,903	1
North Carolina	9,478	32
North Dakota	16,966	6
Ohio	19,843	3
Oklahoma	8,847	37
Oregon	9,689	30
Pennsylvania	14,452	11
Rhode Island	16,045	7
South Carolina	4,901	49
South Dakota	12,259	23
Tennessee	7,307	47
Texas	7,842	41
Utah	10,295	27
Vermont	7,849	40
Virginia	9,065	35
Washington	9,347	33
West Virginia	13,001	20
Wisconsin	9,272	34
Wyoming	13,118	19
50 States	n/a	
DC	18,038	
United States	10,799	

Rank in order by $	
1	New York
2	Connecticut
3	Ohio
4	Alaska
5	New Hampshire
6	North Dakota
7	Rhode Island
8	Nebraska
9	New Jersey
10	Delaware
11	Pennsylvania
12	Idaho
13	Maryland
14	Massachusetts
15	Kansas
16	Minnesota
17	Montana
18	Iowa
19	Wyoming
20	West Virginia
21	Indiana
22	Colorado
23	South Dakota
24	New Mexico
25	Michigan
26	Missouri
27	Utah
28	Hawaii
29	Arkansas
30	Oregon
31	Kentucky
32	North Carolina
33	Washington
34	Wisconsin
35	Virginia
36	Florida
37	Oklahoma
38	Mississippi
39	California
40	Vermont
41	Texas
42	Louisiana
43	Arizona
44	Alabama
45	Georgia
45	Nevada
47	Tennessee
48	Maine
49	South Carolina
50	Illinois

Note: Ties in ranking reflect ties in actual values.

I-18 Average Medicaid Spending Per Child, FY 2003

State	Average spending per child $	Rank
Alabama	1,595	20
Alaska	3,504	2
Arizona	1,443	31
Arkansas	1,396	36
California	1,210	44
Colorado	1,603	18
Connecticut	1,920	8
Delaware	1,887	11
Florida	1,160	46
Georgia	1,302	41
Hawaii	1,413	33
Idaho	1,220	43
Illinois	1,372	38
Indiana	1,402	35
Iowa	1,540	25
Kansas	1,499	29
Kentucky	1,844	13
Louisiana	912	50
Maine	3,961	1
Maryland	2,327	3
Massachusetts	1,593	21
Michigan	1,033	49
Minnesota	2,254	5
Mississippi	1,225	42
Missouri	1,552	23
Montana	1,888	10
Nebraska	1,768	15
Nevada	1,409	34
New Hampshire	2,292	4
New Jersey	1,749	16
New Mexico	1,907	9
New York	1,885	12
North Carolina	1,540	25
North Dakota	1,537	27
Ohio	1,357	39
Oklahoma	1,319	40
Oregon	1,598	19
Pennsylvania	1,780	14
Rhode Island	2,175	6
South Carolina	1,421	32
South Dakota	1,688	17
Tennessee	1,163	45
Texas	1,478	30
Utah	1,591	22
Vermont	2,095	7
Virginia	1,393	37
Washington	1,050	48
West Virginia	1,545	24
Wisconsin	1,076	47
Wyoming	1,517	28
50 States	n/a	
DC	2,775	
United States	1,467	

Rank in order by $	
1	Maine
2	Alaska
3	Maryland
4	New Hampshire
5	Minnesota
6	Rhode Island
7	Vermont
8	Connecticut
9	New Mexico
10	Montana
11	Delaware
12	New York
13	Kentucky
14	Pennsylvania
15	Nebraska
16	New Jersey
17	South Dakota
18	Colorado
19	Oregon
20	Alabama
21	Massachusetts
22	Utah
23	Missouri
24	West Virginia
25	Iowa
25	North Carolina
27	North Dakota
28	Wyoming
29	Kansas
30	Texas
31	Arizona
32	South Carolina
33	Hawaii
34	Nevada
35	Indiana
36	Arkansas
37	Virginia
38	Illinois
39	Ohio
40	Oklahoma
41	Georgia
42	Mississippi
43	Idaho
44	California
45	Tennessee
46	Florida
47	Wisconsin
48	Washington
49	Michigan
50	Louisiana

Note: Ties in ranking reflect ties in actual values.

Medicare Payment Per Hospital Day, FY 2004

State	Average payment per hospital day $	Rank
Alabama	4,453	12
Alaska	4,434	14
Arizona	5,620	4
Arkansas	3,388	39
California	7,758	2
Colorado	5,389	5
Connecticut	3,635	29
Delaware	2,849	47
Florida	5,336	6
Georgia	3,810	23
Hawaii	3,765	24
Idaho	3,582	33
Illinois	4,436	13
Indiana	3,385	40
Iowa	3,302	42
Kansas	4,195	15
Kentucky	3,393	38
Louisiana	3,946	21
Maine	3,212	44
Maryland	2,068	50
Massachusetts	3,324	41
Michigan	3,624	30
Minnesota	4,519	10
Mississippi	3,189	46
Missouri	4,009	20
Montana	3,423	37
Nebraska	4,795	9
Nevada	6,565	3
New Hampshire	3,559	35
New Jersey	7,894	1
New Mexico	4,016	19
New York	3,579	34
North Carolina	3,202	45
North Dakota	3,218	43
Ohio	3,752	25
Oklahoma	3,595	32
Oregon	4,095	17
Pennsylvania	5,174	7
Rhode Island	3,611	31
South Carolina	4,106	16
South Dakota	3,670	28
Tennessee	3,687	27
Texas	4,896	8
Utah	4,016	18
Vermont	2,809	48
Virginia	3,726	26
Washington	4,454	11
West Virginia	2,569	49
Wisconsin	3,862	22
Wyoming	3,536	36
50 States	4,464	
DC	4,722	
United States	4,421	

Rank in order by $
1 New Jersey
2 California
3 Nevada
4 Arizona
5 Colorado
6 Florida
7 Pennsylvania
8 Texas
9 Nebraska
10 Minnesota
11 Washington
12 Alabama
13 Illinois
14 Alaska
15 Kansas
16 South Carolina
17 Oregon
18 Utah
19 New Mexico
20 Missouri
21 Louisiana
22 Wisconsin
23 Georgia
24 Hawaii
25 Ohio
26 Virginia
27 Tennessee
28 South Dakota
29 Connecticut
30 Michigan
31 Rhode Island
32 Oklahoma
33 Idaho
34 New York
35 New Hampshire
36 Wyoming
37 Montana
38 Kentucky
39 Arkansas
40 Indiana
41 Massachusetts
42 Iowa
43 North Dakota
44 Maine
45 North Carolina
46 Mississippi
47 Delaware
48 Vermont
49 West Virginia
50 Maryland

Note: Numbers that appear to be identical are rounded and vary slightly in actual value. The rankings reflect the actual values before rounding. See the introduction for more details.

I-20 Hospital Expense Per Inpatient Day, 2005

State	Expense per inpatient day $	Rank
Alabama	2,124	50
Alaska	4,707	2
Arizona	2,769	29
Arkansas	2,271	47
California	3,110	23
Colorado	3,541	11
Connecticut	2,983	27
Delaware	2,952	28
Florida	2,330	45
Georgia	2,709	33
Hawaii	2,602	39
Idaho	3,545	10
Illinois	3,053	25
Indiana	3,258	19
Iowa	3,241	20
Kansas	2,742	32
Kentucky	2,426	44
Louisiana	2,218	48
Maine	3,829	9
Maryland	3,001	26
Massachusetts	3,840	8
Michigan	3,215	21
Minnesota	3,347	14
Mississippi	2,183	49
Missouri	3,109	24
Montana	3,428	13
Nebraska	2,767	30
Nevada	2,469	42
New Hampshire	4,326	3
New Jersey	2,581	40
New Mexico	3,299	16
New York	2,648	36
North Carolina	2,761	31
North Dakota	3,290	18
Ohio	3,291	17
Oklahoma	2,282	46
Oregon	3,984	6
Pennsylvania	2,677	35
Rhode Island	3,343	15
South Carolina	2,449	43
South Dakota	3,205	22
Tennessee	2,509	41
Texas	2,695	34
Utah	3,520	12
Vermont	4,964	1
Virginia	2,612	38
Washington	4,159	4
West Virginia	2,626	37
Wisconsin	3,888	7
Wyoming	3,994	5
50 States	2,872	
DC	2,937	
United States	2,873	

Rank in order by $	
1	Vermont
2	Alaska
3	New Hampshire
4	Washington
5	Wyoming
6	Oregon
7	Wisconsin
8	Massachusetts
9	Maine
10	Idaho
11	Colorado
12	Utah
13	Montana
14	Minnesota
15	Rhode Island
16	New Mexico
17	Ohio
18	North Dakota
19	Indiana
20	Iowa
21	Michigan
22	South Dakota
23	California
24	Missouri
25	Illinois
26	Maryland
27	Connecticut
28	Delaware
29	Arizona
30	Nebraska
31	North Carolina
32	Kansas
33	Georgia
34	Texas
35	Pennsylvania
36	New York
37	West Virginia
38	Virginia
39	Hawaii
40	New Jersey
41	Tennessee
42	Nevada
43	South Carolina
44	Kentucky
45	Florida
46	Oklahoma
47	Arkansas
48	Louisiana
49	Mississippi
50	Alabama

I-21 Percentage of Population in Health Maintenance Organizations, 2005

State	Percentage of population in HMOs	Rank
Alabama	2.8	46
Alaska	0.0	50
Arizona	16.4	25
Arkansas	6.4	43
California	49.1	1
Colorado	25.6	12
Connecticut	36.1	4
Delaware	10.1	37
Florida	26.6	8
Georgia	16.4	25
Hawaii	37.4	2
Idaho	2.9	45
Illinois	15.7	30
Indiana	22.5	19
Iowa	10.9	33
Kansas	16.6	24
Kentucky	10.2	36
Louisiana	10.7	34
Maine	25.9	10
Maryland	28.0	6
Massachusetts	37.4	2
Michigan	26.3	9
Minnesota	25.4	13
Mississippi	0.1	49
Missouri	24.6	16
Montana	8.1	38
Nebraska	5.3	44
Nevada	25.2	14
New Hampshire	21.9	21
New Jersey	25.0	15
New Mexico	24.3	17
New York	24.0	18
North Carolina	10.5	35
North Dakota	0.4	48
Ohio	16.4	25
Oklahoma	7.1	41
Oregon	16.2	28
Pennsylvania	29.8	5
Rhode Island	25.9	10
South Carolina	7.1	41
South Dakota	7.9	40
Tennessee	14.4	31
Texas	11.8	32
Utah	21.3	22
Vermont	16.1	29
Virginia	22.2	20
Washington	18.1	23
West Virginia	8.1	38
Wisconsin	26.8	7
Wyoming	2.1	47
50 States	n/a	
DC	42.2	
United States	n/a	

Rank in order by percentage	
1	California
2	Hawaii
2	Massachusetts
4	Connecticut
5	Pennsylvania
6	Maryland
7	Wisconsin
8	Florida
9	Michigan
10	Maine
10	Rhode Island
12	Colorado
13	Minnesota
14	Nevada
15	New Jersey
16	Missouri
17	New Mexico
18	New York
19	Indiana
20	Virginia
21	New Hampshire
22	Utah
23	Washington
24	Kansas
25	Arizona
25	Georgia
25	Ohio
28	Oregon
29	Vermont
30	Illinois
31	Tennessee
32	Texas
33	Iowa
34	Louisiana
35	North Carolina
36	Kentucky
37	Delaware
38	Montana
38	West Virginia
40	South Dakota
41	Oklahoma
41	South Carolina
43	Arkansas
44	Nebraska
45	Idaho
46	Alabama
47	Wyoming
48	North Dakota
49	Mississippi
50	Alaska

Note: Ties in ranking reflect ties in actual values.

I-22 Prescription Drugs as a Percentage of Health Care Spending, FY 2004

State	Prescription drugs as a percentage of health care spending	Rank
Alabama	15.4	2
Alaska	8.2	49
Arizona	11.2	37
Arkansas	13.0	16
California	10.1	42
Colorado	8.2	49
Connecticut	12.8	18
Delaware	12.8	18
Florida	13.4	13
Georgia	13.6	11
Hawaii	11.6	30
Idaho	12.5	20
Illinois	12.0	24
Indiana	13.4	13
Iowa	11.6	30
Kansas	12.0	24
Kentucky	15.6	1
Louisiana	13.2	15
Maine	11.9	26
Maryland	12.5	20
Massachusetts	10.5	41
Michigan	13.6	11
Minnesota	9.8	43
Mississippi	14.0	9
Missouri	11.7	28
Montana	9.1	46
Nebraska	11.6	30
Nevada	11.5	35
New Hampshire	11.6	30
New Jersey	14.4	5
New Mexico	9.7	44
New York	12.3	23
North Carolina	14.7	4
North Dakota	11.6	30
Ohio	11.7	28
Oklahoma	12.9	17
Oregon	8.5	47
Pennsylvania	12.4	22
Rhode Island	14.1	8
South Carolina	14.3	7
South Dakota	8.4	48
Tennessee	15.1	3
Texas	10.7	39
Utah	11.9	26
Vermont	10.9	38
Virginia	13.8	10
Washington	9.7	44
West Virginia	14.4	5
Wisconsin	10.7	39
Wyoming	11.3	36
50 States	n/a	
DC	5.0	
United States	12.1	

Rank in order by percentage	
1	Kentucky
2	Alabama
3	Tennessee
4	North Carolina
5	New Jersey
5	West Virginia
7	South Carolina
8	Rhode Island
9	Mississippi
10	Virginia
11	Georgia
11	Michigan
13	Florida
13	Indiana
15	Louisiana
16	Arkansas
17	Oklahoma
18	Connecticut
18	Delaware
20	Idaho
20	Maryland
22	Pennsylvania
23	New York
24	Illinois
24	Kansas
26	Maine
26	Utah
28	Missouri
28	Ohio
30	Hawaii
30	Iowa
30	Nebraska
30	New Hampshire
30	North Dakota
35	Nevada
36	Wyoming
37	Arizona
38	Vermont
39	Texas
39	Wisconsin
41	Massachusetts
42	California
43	Minnesota
44	New Mexico
44	Washington
46	Montana
47	Oregon
48	South Dakota
49	Alaska
49	Colorado

Note: Ties in ranking reflect ties in actual values.

I-23   Average Annual Increase in Health Care Spending, 1980–2004

State	Average annual percentage increase in health care spending 1980–2004	Rank
Alabama	8.8	22
Alaska	9.5	12
Arizona	10.0	4
Arkansas	8.8	22
California	8.0	44
Colorado	9.2	18
Connecticut	8.5	31
Delaware	10.0	4
Florida	10.0	4
Georgia	9.6	11
Hawaii	8.3	36
Idaho	9.7	9
Illinois	7.4	49
Indiana	8.6	29
Iowa	7.6	48
Kansas	7.9	46
Kentucky	9.3	15
Louisiana	8.3	36
Maine	9.4	13
Maryland	8.7	26
Massachusetts	8.3	36
Michigan	7.1	50
Minnesota	8.6	29
Mississippi	9.0	21
Missouri	8.3	36
Montana	8.7	26
Nebraska	8.4	35
Nevada	11.2	1
New Hampshire	10.2	3
New Jersey	8.8	22
New Mexico	9.4	13
New York	8.2	40
North Carolina	10.3	2
North Dakota	7.9	46
Ohio	8.1	41
Oklahoma	8.0	44
Oregon	8.7	26
Pennsylvania	8.1	41
Rhode Island	8.5	31
South Carolina	10.0	4
South Dakota	8.8	22
Tennessee	9.2	18
Texas	9.3	15
Utah	9.7	9
Vermont	9.8	8
Virginia	9.2	18
Washington	9.3	15
West Virginia	8.1	41
Wisconsin	8.5	31
Wyoming	8.5	31
50 States	n/a	
DC	6.4	
United States	8.6	

Rank in order by percentage	
1	Nevada
2	North Carolina
3	New Hampshire
4	Arizona
4	Delaware
4	Florida
4	South Carolina
8	Vermont
9	Idaho
9	Utah
11	Georgia
12	Alaska
13	Maine
13	New Mexico
15	Kentucky
15	Texas
15	Washington
18	Colorado
18	Tennessee
18	Virginia
21	Mississippi
22	Alabama
22	Arkansas
22	New Jersey
22	South Dakota
26	Maryland
26	Montana
26	Oregon
29	Indiana
29	Minnesota
31	Connecticut
31	Rhode Island
31	Wisconsin
31	Wyoming
35	Nebraska
36	Hawaii
36	Louisiana
36	Massachusetts
36	Missouri
40	New York
41	Ohio
41	Pennsylvania
41	West Virginia
44	California
44	Oklahoma
46	Kansas
46	North Dakota
48	Iowa
49	Illinois
50	Michigan

Note: Ties in ranking reflect ties in actual values.

Source Notes for Health (Section I)

I-1 Immunization Rates, 2005: Information on immunization is collected by the Centers for Disease Control and Prevention (CDC) as part of their National Immunization Survey and are available on the CDC Web site (www.cdc.gov).

I-2 Infant Mortality Rates, 2005: These data are collected by the Centers for Disease Control and Prevention and are available on the CDC Web site (www.cdc.gov). They cover deaths of all children under one year of age, expressed in relation to each one thousand live births. This statistic is considered one of the best indicators with which to compare health among states and local areas. Higher death rates are associated with poor health of the mother, absence of medical care during pregnancy, and lack of medical treatment for infants.

I-3 State Health Rankings, 2006: These scores and rankings are developed annually for the United Health Foundation. The results are published in *America's Health: State Health Rankings*. They reflect a composite of indicators, including unemployment, health practices (such as smoking), the availability of health services, and outcomes (such as death rates). Probably no two researchers would use identical lists to produce such rankings, but the state rankings would likely be similar. While decisions by states have some impact on health rankings, decisions on health practices by individual citizens have as much, or more, impact.

I-4 Percentage of Non-Elderly Population without Health Insurance, 2005: Most Americans get health insurance coverage through their employers. All Americans over age sixty-four are covered by Medicare. About 13 percent of the non-elderly, including all welfare recipients, get coverage paid for by state and federal governments through Medicaid. Non-elderly citizens who have no health insurance comprise 17.9 percent of the population. These data are part of a compilation titled "Table HI-6" from the Housing and Household Economic Statistics Division of the U.S. Census Bureau.

I-5 Abortions, 2003: This count comes from the Centers for Disease Control and Prevention (CDC) and available on its Web site (www.cdc.gov). The abortion rate compares the number of abortions with the number of live births.

I-6 Alcohol Consumption Per Capita, 2003: Some public health authorities consider high levels of alcoholic beverage consumption an indicator of poor health of a state's population. The data show the number of gallons of pure ethanol (typical liquor is about 43 percent ethanol or ethanol alcohol, wine 14 percent, and beer about 6 percent) consumed per resident age fourteen and over. The data are derived by dividing sales of alcoholic beverages by population. Those shown were developed by the Department of Health and Human Services (National Institute on Alcohol Abuse and Alcoholism) and are published on its Web site (www.niaaa.

nih.gov). They are called "apparent" alcohol consumption because some alcoholic beverages are bought in one state for consumption by residents of another. This raises the apparent consumption of tourist-destination states, like Nevada, and states with low prices, like New Hampshire, which draw purchasers from other states.

I-7 Percentage of Adult Smokers, 2005: These estimates, results of sample surveys, are developed by the Behavioral Surveillance Branch of the Centers for Disease Control and Prevention (CDC) and are available on the CDC Web site (www.cdc.gov). They reflect the percentage of the population who have smoked 100 cigarettes in their lifetime and reported smoking every day or some days.

I-8 Percentage of Population Obese, 2005: These data are part of the Centers for Disease Control and Prevention's (CDC) behavioral risk factor surveillance system. The 2005 statistics are published in United Health Foundation's annual report *America's Health: State Health Rankings*. Different definitions of how high a person's body mass index (BMI) can be without being considered a health risk would produce different percentages for every state, but not appreciably affect the rankings. A person with a BMI of 30 or more is considered *obese*, while a BMI of 25 to 29.9 is considered *overweight*.

I-9 AIDS Cases, 2005: These data are developed by the Centers for Disease Control and Prevention (CDC) and reported in the *HIV/AIDS Surveillance Report* (vol. 17). They cover cases newly reported in calendar year 2005. The rate shown is cases per one hundred thousand residents. Because persons at most risk of contracting AIDS are predominantly found in larger metropolitan areas, states containing those areas typically show the highest rates.

I-10 Physicians Per 100,000 Population, 2006: This table shows the number of physicians in relation to population. Rural states will show below-average numbers in part because intensive medical care, such as that received from major hospitals, is often sought in nearby states with large metropolitan areas. The statistics are based on data from Medical Marketing Service, Inc. (www.mmslists.com).

I-11 Hospital Beds Per 1,000 Population, 2005: This table shows the number of community hospital beds in relation to population. The data come from *Hospital Statistics, 2007 Edition*, a publication of the American Hospital Association. As of 1998, the AHA state data no longer cover all hospitals. Thus, the data shown here reflect only community (non-federal, short-term, general and other special) hospitals.

I-12 Medicaid Recipients, Mid-Year 2005: Over forty-five million people receive health care through the Medicaid program each year. The federal government sets minimum standards for this program and pays about 60 percent of the costs nationwide through a formula that provides 50 percent of the costs in the most affluent states and up to 76 percent in the poorest states. Within federal guidelines, states set the rules for eligibility, the health services covered, and the amount of reimbursements to the providers of care.

The primary recipients are families that receive cash assistance from states through Temporary Assistance for Needy Families (TANF) or from the federal government through Supplemental Security Income (SSI). In 2005, about 25 percent of Medicaid recipients were elderly or disabled. Also covered by Medicare, these so-called "dual-eligibles" received supplemental coverage through the Medicaid program for specific services such as prescription drugs and long-term care. Though these populations made up only a quarter of Medicaid enrollment, they accounted for about 70 percent of Medicaid expenditures. In 2006, some prescription drug costs shifted to Medicare as the new Medicare prescription drug benefit went into effect.

These data, reflecting a count as of June 30, 2005, come from tabulations of the Department of Health and Human Services Centers for Medicare and Medicaid Services (CMS) and are available on its Web site (www.cms.hhs.gov).

I-13 Medicaid Recipients as a Percentage of Poverty Population, Mid-Year 2005: These data, from the same source as Table I-12, relate the number of Medicaid recipients to the number of persons in households with income below federally defined poverty levels (see Table A-16). The differences among states are a good indication of how inclusive are the eligibility criteria set by the individual states.

I-14 State and Local Spending for Health and Hospitals, FY 2004: This table relates spending data to population and personal income in each state. The data come from the U.S. Census Bureau's electronic publication "State and Local Government Finance Estimates, by State," available on the bureau's Web site (www.census.gov). See notes to Table F-1 for more extensive information on the source of the data.

The spending includes public health activities plus the gross outlays of hospitals and nursing homes run by state and local governments, including costs defrayed by the charges hospitals make to patients and their health insurance providers. The largest outlays appear in states that rely heavily on government-owned hospitals.

I-15 State and Local Health and Hospital Spending as a Percentage of General Spending, FY 2004: This table shows the relative importance of health and hospital outlays in state and local budgets. It is derived by comparing this spending (see Table I-14) with total "general" spending. General spending includes essentially all other spending except municipal electric and other utilities and trust funds, such as those for workers' compensation.

I-16 Per Capita Medicaid Spending, FY 2005: These data, from the same source as the number of recipients in Table I-12, reflect the major impact that Medicaid costs are having on government budgets. The amounts shown reflect primarily federal grants spent by states, about 60 percent of the total with differences among the states, and state government matching funds. In a few states, particularly New York, some of the federally required state match is provided by local governments.

I-17 Average Medicaid Spending Per Aged Recipient, FY 2003: These data, from The Urban Institute and Kaiser Commission on Medicaid and the Uninsured, are based on data from Medicaid Statistical Information System (MSIS) reports from the Centers for Medicare and Medicaid Services (CMS). They illustrate differences among the states in this component of Medicaid costs. They relate total spending on all Medicaid recipients age sixty-five and over to the number of recipients. Over half of the nursing home residents in the United States are having their bills paid by Medicaid. States differ in the extent and success of programs designed to encourage people to live at home and with relatives rather than enter nursing homes. Those programs typically provide visiting nurses and homemakers who assist frail elderly persons in their homes, thereby reducing the need for institutionalization.

I-18 Average Medicaid Spending Per Child, FY 2003: These data reflect the same concepts and come from the same source as those shown in Table I-17. Differences among states primarily reflect differences in how much doctors and other providers of health care are compensated for providing services.

I-19 Medicare Payment Per Hospital Day, FY 2004: These data are one way to measure health care cost differences among states. They reflect the cost of a day in short-stay hospitals as reimbursed by the federal Medicare program. The data come from the Centers for Medicare and Medicaid Services and are available on its Web site (www.cms.hhs.gov). These data include both the basic rate for staying in the hospital (see Table I-20) and charges for specific services.

I-20 Hospital Expense Per Inpatient Day, 2005: These data result from a comparison of inpatient days and hospital unit total expenses at community hospitals as reported by the American Hospital Association in the annual publication *Hospital Statistics*. See source for Table I-11.

I-21 Percentage of Population in Health Maintenance Organizations, 2005: Most Americans receive their health care by purchasing it from individual doctors, hospitals, pharmacies, and others. However, a percentage are served by health maintenance organizations that provide complete packages of care for one monthly fee. Many people believe that this approach to buying care will reduce health care costs because the service providers cannot increase their incomes by providing additional services. The statistics, reflecting enrollment in July 2005 as a percentage of population, come from HealthLeaders-InterStudy (Nashville, TN) and are published in *The Competitive Edge, January 2005.*

I-22 Prescription Drugs as a Percentage of Health Care Spending, FY 2004: These data, from the Centers for Medicare and Medicaid Services (www.cms.hhs.gov), show what percentage of health care dollars spent in fiscal year 2004 went toward prescription drugs.

I-23 Average Annual Increase in Health Care Spending, 1980–2004: This table, from the same source as Table I-22, shows the average annual percentage growth in health care spending over more than a two decade period.

Crime and Law Enforcement

Preliminary 2006 U.S. Crime Rates Percent Change by Region

	Northeast	Midwest	South	West
Violent crime	+2.9	+3.9	+3.3	+4.7
Murder	+0.5	-2.0	+3.3	+1.6
Forcible rape	-2.5	+1.0	+1.1	-1.0
Robbery	+5.8	+10.4	+8.0	-14.6
Aggravated assault	+1.7	+1.1	+1.5	+0.6
Property crime	-0.3	+1.7	-3.0	-5.7
Burglary	+4.1	+5.8	+0.9	-2.6
Larceny-theft	-0.6	+0.7	-4.7	-7.2
Motor vehicle theft	-5.6	+0.3	-0.2	-3.9
Arson	+4.3	+6.6	+3.4	+11.5

Source: FBI Uniform Crime Reports

Percent Change in U.S. State and Federal Prison Populations, 1995–2005

Year	Percent
1995	6.7
1996	5.1
1997	5.0
1998	4.7
1999	3.4
2000	1.3
2001	1.1
2002	2.6
2003	2.0
2004	1.9
2005	1.9
Average annual increase 1995–2005	3.1

Source: Bureau of Justice Statistics

Percent Change in Prisoners, by Gender

	Men	Women
Percent change 2004–2005	1.9	2.6
Average annual 1995–2005	3.0	4.6

Source: Bureau of Justice Statistics

J-1   Total Crime Rate, 2005

State	Crime rate (per 100,000 population)	Rank	Rank in order by rate	
Alabama	4,324	17	1	Arizona
Alaska	4,244	20	2	Washington
Arizona	5,351	1	3	South Carolina
Arkansas	4,585	12	4	Hawaii
California	3,849	24	5	Tennessee
Colorado	4,436	16	6	Texas
Connecticut	2,833	41	7	New Mexico
Delaware	3,744	26	8	Nevada
Florida	4,716	9	9	Florida
Georgia	4,621	11	10	Oregon
Hawaii	5,048	4	11	Georgia
Idaho	2,955	36	12	Arkansas
Illinois	3,632	29	13	Oklahoma
Indiana	3,780	25	14	North Carolina
Iowa	3,125	34	15	Missouri
Kansas	4,174	21	16	Colorado
Kentucky	2,797	43	17	Alabama
Louisiana	4,278	18	18	Louisiana
Maine	2,525	46	19	Maryland
Maryland	4,247	19	20	Alaska
Massachusetts	2,821	42	21	Kansas
Michigan	3,643	28	22	Utah
Minnesota	3,381	33	23	Ohio
Mississippi	3,539	30	24	California
Missouri	4,453	15	25	Indiana
Montana	3,424	31	26	Delaware
Nebraska	3,710	27	27	Nebraska
Nevada	4,848	8	28	Michigan
New Hampshire	1,928	50	29	Illinois
New Jersey	2,688	44	30	Mississippi
New Mexico	4,851	7	31	Montana
New York	2,554	45	32	Wyoming
North Carolina	4,543	14	33	Minnesota
North Dakota	2,076	48	34	Iowa
Ohio	4,014	23	35	Rhode Island
Oklahoma	4,551	13	36	Idaho
Oregon	4,687	10	37	Virginia
Pennsylvania	2,842	40	38	Wisconsin
Rhode Island	2,970	35	39	West Virginia
South Carolina	5,101	3	40	Pennsylvania
South Dakota	1,952	49	41	Connecticut
Tennessee	5,028	5	42	Massachusetts
Texas	4,862	6	43	Kentucky
Utah	4,096	22	44	New Jersey
Vermont	2,400	47	45	New York
Virginia	2,921	37	46	Maine
Washington	5,239	2	47	Vermont
West Virginia	2,898	39	48	North Dakota
Wisconsin	2,902	38	49	South Dakota
Wyoming	3,385	32	50	New Hampshire
50 States	n/a			
DC	6,206			
United States	3,899			

J-2 Violent Crime Rate, 2005

State	Violent crime rate (per 100,000 population)	Rank
Alabama	432	22
Alaska	632	7
Arizona	513	16
Arkansas	528	13
California	526	14
Colorado	397	24
Connecticut	275	37
Delaware	632	6
Florida	708	3
Georgia	449	20
Hawaii	255	41
Idaho	257	40
Illinois	552	11
Indiana	324	29
Iowa	291	31
Kansas	387	25
Kentucky	267	39
Louisiana	594	9
Maine	112	49
Maryland	703	4
Massachusetts	457	19
Michigan	552	10
Minnesota	297	30
Mississippi	278	36
Missouri	525	15
Montana	282	35
Nebraska	287	32
Nevada	607	8
New Hampshire	132	47
New Jersey	355	26
New Mexico	702	5
New York	446	21
North Carolina	468	18
North Dakota	98	50
Ohio	351	27
Oklahoma	509	17
Oregon	287	33
Pennsylvania	425	23
Rhode Island	251	42
South Carolina	761	1
South Dakota	176	46
Tennessee	753	2
Texas	530	12
Utah	227	45
Vermont	120	48
Virginia	283	34
Washington	346	28
West Virginia	273	38
Wisconsin	242	43
Wyoming	230	44
50 States	n/a	
DC	1,459	
United States	469	

Rank in order by rate

1	South Carolina
2	Tennessee
3	Florida
4	Maryland
5	New Mexico
6	Delaware
7	Alaska
8	Nevada
9	Louisiana
10	Michigan
11	Illinois
12	Texas
13	Arkansas
14	California
15	Missouri
16	Arizona
17	Oklahoma
18	North Carolina
19	Massachusetts
20	Georgia
21	New York
22	Alabama
23	Pennsylvania
24	Colorado
25	Kansas
26	New Jersey
27	Ohio
28	Washington
29	Indiana
30	Minnesota
31	Iowa
32	Nebraska
33	Oregon
34	Virginia
35	Montana
36	Mississippi
37	Connecticut
38	West Virginia
39	Kentucky
40	Idaho
41	Hawaii
42	Rhode Island
43	Wisconsin
44	Wyoming
45	Utah
46	South Dakota
47	New Hampshire
48	Vermont
49	Maine
50	North Dakota

Note: Numbers that appear to be identical are rounded and vary slightly in actual value. The rankings reflect the actual values before rounding. See the introduction for more details.

Murder and Rape Rates, 2005

State	Murder rate (per 100,000 population)	Rape rate (per 100,000 population)	Rank by murder rate
Alabama	8.2	34.3	4
Alaska	4.8	81.1	24
Arizona	7.5	33.8	5
Arkansas	6.7	42.9	12
California	6.9	26.0	10
Colorado	3.7	43.4	30
Connecticut	2.9	20.0	35
Delaware	4.4	44.7	28
Florida	5.0	37.1	23
Georgia	6.2	23.6	14
Hawaii	1.9	26.9	44
Idaho	2.4	40.4	39
Illinois	6.0	33.7	19
Indiana	5.7	29.6	20
Iowa	1.3	27.9	48
Kansas	3.7	38.4	30
Kentucky	4.6	34.0	26
Louisiana	9.9	31.4	1
Maine	1.4	24.7	46
Maryland	9.9	22.6	1
Massachusetts	2.7	27.1	36
Michigan	6.1	51.3	16
Minnesota	2.2	44.0	42
Mississippi	7.3	39.3	8
Missouri	6.9	28.0	10
Montana	1.9	32.2	44
Nebraska	2.5	32.9	38
Nevada	8.5	42.1	3
New Hampshire	1.4	30.9	46
New Jersey	4.8	13.9	24
New Mexico	7.4	54.1	6
New York	4.5	18.9	27
North Carolina	6.7	26.5	12
North Dakota	1.1	24.2	50
Ohio	5.1	39.8	22
Oklahoma	5.3	41.7	21
Oregon	2.2	34.8	42
Pennsylvania	6.1	28.9	16
Rhode Island	3.2	29.8	34
South Carolina	7.4	42.5	6
South Dakota	2.3	46.7	40
Tennessee	7.2	36.4	9
Texas	6.2	37.2	14
Utah	2.3	37.3	40
Vermont	1.3	23.3	48
Virginia	6.1	22.7	16
Washington	3.3	44.7	33
West Virginia	4.4	17.7	28
Wisconsin	3.5	20.6	32
Wyoming	2.7	24.0	36
50 States	n/a	n/a	
DC	35.4	30.2	
United States	5.6	31.7	

Rank in order by murder rate	
1	Louisiana
1	Maryland
3	Nevada
4	Alabama
5	Arizona
6	New Mexico
6	South Carolina
8	Mississippi
9	Tennessee
10	California
10	Missouri
12	Arkansas
12	North Carolina
14	Georgia
14	Texas
16	Michigan
16	Pennsylvania
16	Virginia
19	Illinois
20	Indiana
21	Oklahoma
22	Ohio
23	Florida
24	Alaska
24	New Jersey
26	Kentucky
27	New York
28	Delaware
28	West Virginia
30	Colorado
30	Kansas
32	Wisconsin
33	Washington
34	Rhode Island
35	Connecticut
36	Massachusetts
36	Wyoming
38	Nebraska
39	Idaho
40	South Dakota
40	Utah
42	Minnesota
42	Oregon
44	Hawaii
44	Montana
46	Maine
46	New Hampshire
48	Iowa
48	Vermont
50	North Dakota

Note: Ties in ranking reflect ties in actual values.

J-4 Property Crime Rate, 2005

State	Property crime rate (per 100,000 population)	Rank
Alabama	3,892	17
Alaska	3,613	22
Arizona	4,838	2
Arkansas	4,058	12
California	3,323	26
Colorado	4,040	14
Connecticut	2,558	40
Delaware	3,111	30
Florida	4,008	15
Georgia	4,172	9
Hawaii	4,793	3
Idaho	2,698	36
Illinois	3,080	33
Indiana	3,456	24
Iowa	2,834	34
Kansas	3,787	19
Kentucky	2,531	41
Louisiana	3,683	20
Maine	2,413	43
Maryland	3,544	23
Massachusetts	2,364	44
Michigan	3,091	31
Minnesota	3,084	32
Mississippi	3,260	27
Missouri	3,928	16
Montana	3,143	29
Nebraska	3,423	25
Nevada	4,242	8
New Hampshire	1,796	49
New Jersey	2,333	45
New Mexico	4,148	10
New York	2,109	47
North Carolina	4,075	11
North Dakota	1,978	48
Ohio	3,663	21
Oklahoma	4,042	13
Oregon	4,400	4
Pennsylvania	2,417	42
Rhode Island	2,719	35
South Carolina	4,339	5
South Dakota	1,776	50
Tennessee	4,276	7
Texas	4,332	6
Utah	3,869	18
Vermont	2,281	46
Virginia	2,638	38
Washington	4,893	1
West Virginia	2,625	39
Wisconsin	2,660	37
Wyoming	3,155	28
50 States	n/a	
DC	4,747	
United States	3,430	

Rank in order by rate	
1	Washington
2	Arizona
3	Hawaii
4	Oregon
5	South Carolina
6	Texas
7	Tennessee
8	Nevada
9	Georgia
10	New Mexico
11	North Carolina
12	Arkansas
13	Oklahoma
14	Colorado
15	Florida
16	Missouri
17	Alabama
18	Utah
19	Kansas
20	Louisiana
21	Ohio
22	Alaska
23	Maryland
24	Indiana
25	Nebraska
26	California
27	Mississippi
28	Wyoming
29	Montana
30	Delaware
31	Michigan
32	Minnesota
33	Illinois
34	Iowa
35	Rhode Island
36	Idaho
37	Wisconsin
38	Virginia
39	West Virginia
40	Connecticut
41	Kentucky
42	Pennsylvania
43	Maine
44	Massachusetts
45	New Jersey
46	Vermont
47	New York
48	North Dakota
49	New Hampshire
50	South Dakota

J-5 Motor Vehicle Theft Rate, 2005

State	Motor vehicle theft rate (per 100,000 population)	Rank
Alabama	288	31
Alaska	391	18
Arizona	924	2
Arkansas	262	34
California	713	5
Colorado	560	7
Connecticut	297	29
Delaware	279	32
Florida	423	12
Georgia	490	9
Hawaii	716	4
Idaho	202	42
Illinois	309	28
Indiana	347	21
Iowa	185	44
Kansas	340	23
Kentucky	211	38
Louisiana	318	25
Maine	102	49
Maryland	608	6
Massachusetts	295	30
Michigan	477	10
Minnesota	278	33
Mississippi	257	35
Missouri	443	11
Montana	211	38
Nebraska	317	27
Nevada	1,115	1
New Hampshire	102	49
New Jersey	318	25
New Mexico	415	14
New York	186	43
North Carolina	328	24
North Dakota	166	45
Ohio	361	20
Oklahoma	392	17
Oregon	529	8
Pennsylvania	237	36
Rhode Island	409	15
South Carolina	384	19
South Dakota	108	47
Tennessee	421	13
Texas	409	15
Utah	344	22
Vermont	103	48
Virginia	211	38
Washington	784	3
West Virginia	210	41
Wisconsin	227	37
Wyoming	145	46
50 States	n/a	
DC	1,402	
United States	417	

Rank in order by rate	
1	Nevada
2	Arizona
3	Washington
4	Hawaii
5	California
6	Maryland
7	Colorado
8	Oregon
9	Georgia
10	Michigan
11	Missouri
12	Florida
13	Tennessee
14	New Mexico
15	Rhode Island
15	Texas
17	Oklahoma
18	Alaska
19	South Carolina
20	Ohio
21	Indiana
22	Utah
23	Kansas
24	North Carolina
25	Louisiana
25	New Jersey
27	Nebraska
28	Illinois
29	Connecticut
30	Massachusetts
31	Alabama
32	Delaware
33	Minnesota
34	Arkansas
35	Mississippi
36	Pennsylvania
37	Wisconsin
38	Virginia
38	Kentucky
38	Montana
41	West Virginia
42	Idaho
43	New York
44	Iowa
45	North Dakota
46	Wyoming
47	South Dakota
48	Vermont
49	New Hampshire
49	Maine

Note: Ties in ranking reflect ties in actual values.

J-6 Violent Crime Rate Change, 2001-2005

State	2001 violent crime rate (per 100,000 population)	Percentage increase in violent crime 2001-2005	Rank by percentage increase
Alabama	439	-1.6	22
Alaska	588	7.4	8
Arizona	540	-5.0	30
Arkansas	453	16.5	2
California	617	-14.7	45
Colorado	351	13.1	5
Connecticut	336	-18.2	46
Delaware	611	3.4	15
Florida	797	-11.2	40
Georgia	497	-9.7	36
Hawaii	255	0.2	18
Idaho	243	5.6	10
Illinois	637	-13.4	42
Indiana	372	-12.9	41
Iowa	269	8.2	7
Kansas	405	-4.3	28
Kentucky	257	3.8	12
Louisiana	687	-13.5	43
Maine	112	0.6	17
Maryland	783	-10.2	38
Massachusetts	480	-4.7	29
Michigan	555	-0.5	20
Minnesota	264	12.3	6
Mississippi	350	-20.5	49
Missouri	541	-2.9	26
Montana	352	-20.1	48
Nebraska	304	-5.7	32
Nevada	587	3.4	14
New Hampshire	170	-22.5	50
New Jersey	390	-9.1	35
New Mexico	781	-10.1	37
New York	516	-13.6	44
North Carolina	494	-5.3	31
North Dakota	80	23.4	1
Ohio	352	-0.2	19
Oklahoma	512	-0.7	21
Oregon	307	-6.5	33
Pennsylvania	410	3.4	13
Rhode Island	310	-18.9	47
South Carolina	720	5.7	9
South Dakota	155	13.5	4
Tennessee	745	1.0	16
Texas	573	-7.5	34
Utah	234	-2.9	27
Vermont	105	14.0	3
Virginia	291	-2.9	25
Washington	355	-2.6	24
West Virginia	279	-2.4	23
Wisconsin	231	4.5	11
Wyoming	257	-10.6	39
50 States	n/a	n/a	
DC	1,737	-16.0	
United States	504	-7.0	

Rank in order by percentage increase

1   North Dakota
2   Arkansas
3   Vermont
4   South Dakota
5   Colorado
6   Minnesota
7   Iowa
8   Alaska
9   South Carolina
10 Idaho
11 Wisconsin
12 Kentucky
13 Pennsylvania
14 Nevada
15 Delaware
16 Tennessee
17 Maine
18 Hawaii
19 Ohio
20 Michigan
21 Oklahoma
22 Alabama
23 West Virginia
24 Washington
25 Virginia
26 Missouri
27 Utah
28 Kansas
29 Massachusetts
30 Arizona
31 North Carolina
32 Nebraska
33 Oregon
34 Texas
35 New Jersey
36 Georgia
37 New Mexico
38 Maryland
39 Wyoming
40 Florida
41 Indiana
42 Illinois
43 Louisiana
44 New York
45 California
46 Connecticut
47 Rhode Island
48 Montana
49 Mississippi
50 New Hampshire

Note: Numbers that appear to be identical are rounded and vary slightly in actual value. The rankings reflect the actual values before rounding. See the introduction for more details.

J-7   Prisoners, 2005

State	Prisoners #	Rank
Alabama	27,888	15
Alaska	4,812	41
Arizona	33,471	13
Arkansas	13,511	28
California	170,676	1
Colorado	21,456	23
Connecticut	19,442	26
Delaware	6,944	35
Florida	89,768	3
Georgia	48,749	6
Hawaii	6,146	39
Idaho	6,818	36
Illinois	44,919	8
Indiana	24,455	19
Iowa	8,737	34
Kansas	9,068	33
Kentucky	19,662	25
Louisiana	36,083	11
Maine	2,023	49
Maryland	22,737	21
Massachusetts	10,701	31
Michigan	49,546	5
Minnesota	9,281	32
Mississippi	20,515	24
Missouri	30,823	14
Montana	3,509	44
Nebraska	4,455	42
Nevada	11,782	30
New Hampshire	2,530	46
New Jersey	27,359	16
New Mexico	6,571	37
New York	62,743	4
North Carolina	36,365	10
North Dakota	1,385	50
Ohio	45,854	7
Oklahoma	24,826	18
Oregon	13,411	29
Pennsylvania	42,380	9
Rhode Island	3,654	43
South Carolina	23,160	20
South Dakota	3,463	45
Tennessee	26,369	17
Texas	169,003	2
Utah	6,373	38
Vermont	2,078	47
Virginia	35,344	12
Washington	17,382	27
West Virginia	5,312	40
Wisconsin	22,720	22
Wyoming	2,047	48
50 States	**1,338,306**	
DC	n/a	
United States	**1,338,306**	

J-8   Average Annual Change in Prisoners, 1995–2005

State	Percentage change in prisoners	Rank
Alabama	3.0	31
Alaska	3.1	30
Arizona	4.5	18
Arkansas	4.6	17
California	2.5	35
Colorado	6.8	6
Connecticut	2.3	38
Delaware	2.8	32
Florida	3.5	29
Georgia	3.6	28
Hawaii	5.5	12
Idaho	7.4	4
Illinois	1.8	42
Indiana	4.3	19
Iowa	4.0	22
Kansas	2.5	35
Kentucky	4.8	14
Louisiana	3.7	25
Maine	3.7	25
Maryland	0.8	46
Massachusetts	-1.4	50
Michigan	1.9	41
Minnesota	6.7	7
Mississippi	4.7	16
Missouri	4.9	13
Montana	5.8	10
Nebraska	3.7	25
Nevada	4.2	20
New Hampshire	2.3	38
New Jersey	0.1	48
New Mexico	4.8	14
New York	-0.9	49
North Carolina	1.2	44
North Dakota	9.3	1
Ohio	0.3	47
Oklahoma	2.5	35
Oregon	7.5	3
Pennsylvania	2.7	33
Rhode Island	1.0	45
South Carolina	1.7	43
South Dakota	6.3	8
Tennessee	5.7	11
Texas	2.2	40
Utah	6.2	9
Vermont	3.9	23
Virginia	2.6	34
Washington	4.1	21
West Virginia	7.9	2
Wisconsin	7.4	4
Wyoming	3.9	23
50 States	n/a	
DC	n/a	
United States	2.6	

Rank in order by percentage

1	North Dakota
2	West Virginia
3	Oregon
4	Idaho
4	Wisconsin
6	Colorado
7	Minnesota
8	South Dakota
9	Utah
10	Montana
11	Tennessee
12	Hawaii
13	Missouri
14	Kentucky
14	New Mexico
16	Mississippi
17	Arkansas
18	Arizona
19	Indiana
20	Nevada
21	Washington
22	Iowa
23	Vermont
23	Wyoming
25	Louisiana
25	Maine
25	Nebraska
28	Georgia
29	Florida
30	Alaska
31	Alabama
32	Delaware
33	Pennsylvania
34	Virginia
35	California
35	Kansas
35	Oklahoma
38	Connecticut
38	New Hampshire
40	Texas
41	Michigan
42	Illinois
43	South Carolina
44	North Carolina
45	Rhode Island
46	Maryland
47	Ohio
48	New Jersey
49	New York
50	Massachusetts

Note: Ties in ranking reflect ties in actual values.

State	Incarceration rate (per 100,000 population)	Rank
Alabama	373	28
Alaska	144	50
Arizona	239	45
Arkansas	192	47
California	313	38
Colorado	326	36
Connecticut	340	33
Delaware	189	48
Florida	247	43
Georgia	351	32
Hawaii	388	26
Idaho	294	39
Illinois	330	34
Indiana	489	11
Iowa	180	49
Kansas	529	7
Kentucky	245	44
Louisiana	208	46
Maine	400	23
Maryland	443	20
Massachusetts	380	27
Michigan	591	5
Minnesota	479	12
Mississippi	467	15
Missouri	499	10
Montana	533	6
Nebraska	459	18
Nevada	797	1
New Hampshire	394	25
New Jersey	660	3
New Mexico	360	31
New York	652	4
North Carolina	525	8
North Dakota	440	21
Ohio	691	2
Oklahoma	464	17
Oregon	291	40
Pennsylvania	414	22
Rhode Island	521	9
South Carolina	466	16
South Dakota	457	19
Tennessee	340	33
Texas	472	14
Utah	373	28
Vermont	474	13
Virginia	323	37
Washington	365	30
West Virginia	252	42
Wisconsin	273	41
Wyoming	400	23
50 States	n/a	
DC	n/a	
United States	435	

Rank in order by rate	
1	Nevada
2	Ohio
3	New Jersey
4	New York
5	Michigan
6	Montana
7	Kansas
8	North Carolina
9	Rhode Island
10	Missouri
11	Indiana
12	Minnesota
13	Vermont
14	Texas
15	Mississippi
16	South Carolina
17	Oklahoma
18	Nebraska
19	South Dakota
20	Maryland
21	North Dakota
22	Pennsylvania
23	Maine
23	Wyoming
25	New Hampshire
26	Hawaii
27	Massachusetts
28	Alabama
28	Utah
30	Washington
31	New Mexico
32	Georgia
33	Connecticut
33	Tennessee
34	Illinois
36	Colorado
37	Virginia
38	California
39	Idaho
40	Oregon
41	Wisconsin
42	West Virginia
43	Florida
44	Kentucky
45	Arizona
46	Louisiana
47	Arkansas
48	Delaware
49	Iowa
50	Alaska

Note: Ties in ranking reflect ties in actual values.

J-10 Juvenile Violent Crime Index, 2003

State	Juvenile crime rate (per 100,000 youths)	Rank
Alabama	126	39
Alaska	243	19
Arizona	223	22
Arkansas	130	38
California	364	7
Colorado	231	20
Connecticut	290	12
Delaware	595	2
Florida	524	3
Georgia	266	15
Hawaii	197	28
Idaho	160	33
Illinois	944	1
Indiana	317	9
Iowa	251	17
Kansas	131	37
Kentucky	229	21
Louisiana	355	8
Maine	78	45
Maryland	505	4
Massachusetts	269	14
Michigan	166	32
Minnesota	176	31
Mississippi	136	36
Missouri	295	11
Montana	202	27
Nebraska	96	42
Nevada	n/a	n/a
New Hampshire	71	46
New Jersey	386	6
New Mexico	220	24
New York	264	16
North Carolina	310	10
North Dakota	45	48
Ohio	150	34
Oklahoma	217	25
Oregon	149	35
Pennsylvania	402	5
Rhode Island	288	13
South Carolina	47	47
South Dakota	108	40
Tennessee	223	22
Texas	185	29
Utah	216	26
Vermont	81	44
Virginia	106	41
Washington	246	18
West Virginia	40	49
Wisconsin	184	30
Wyoming	88	43
50 States	n/a	
DC	n/a	
United States	291	

Rank in order by rate	
n/a	Nevada
1	Illinois
2	Delaware
3	Florida
4	Maryland
5	Pennsylvania
6	New Jersey
7	California
8	Louisiana
9	Indiana
10	North Carolina
11	Missouri
12	Connecticut
13	Rhode Island
14	Massachusetts
15	Georgia
16	New York
17	Iowa
18	Washington
19	Alaska
20	Colorado
21	Kentucky
22	Arizona
22	Tennessee
24	New Mexico
25	Oklahoma
26	Utah
27	Montana
28	Hawaii
29	Texas
30	Wisconsin
31	Minnesota
32	Michigan
33	Idaho
34	Ohio
35	Oregon
36	Mississippi
37	Kansas
38	Arkansas
39	Alabama
40	South Dakota
41	Virginia
42	Nebraska
43	Wyoming
44	Vermont
45	Maine
46	New Hampshire
47	South Carolina
48	North Dakota
49	West Virginia

Note: Ties in ranking reflect ties in actual values.

J-11 State and Local Law Enforcement Employees, 2005

State	Law enforcement employees #	Per 10,000 population #	Rank per 10,000 population
Alabama	13,294	29.2	20
Alaska	1,686	25.4	39
Arizona	19,730	33.2	9
Arkansas	8,091	29.1	21
California	99,567	27.6	32
Colorado	13,112	28.1	29
Connecticut	10,845	30.9	12
Delaware	2,528	30.0	15
Florida	63,815	35.9	7
Georgia	26,193	28.9	23
Hawaii	3,577	28.1	30
Idaho	3,672	25.7	38
Illinois	48,206	37.8	4
Indiana	17,590	28.0	31
Iowa	7,645	25.8	37
Kansas	9,240	33.7	8
Kentucky	10,869	26.0	36
Louisiana	16,639	36.8	5
Maine	2,946	22.3	46
Maryland	16,582	29.6	17
Massachusetts	23,526	36.8	6
Michigan	23,954	23.7	43
Minnesota	10,703	20.9	50
Mississippi	8,687	29.7	16
Missouri	18,439	31.8	10
Montana	2,497	26.7	35
Nebraska	5,071	28.8	24
Nevada	7,082	29.3	19
New Hampshire	3,706	28.3	28
New Jersey	36,285	41.6	2
New Mexico	6,009	31.2	11
New York	85,424	44.4	1
North Carolina	24,780	28.5	27
North Dakota	1,405	22.1	47
Ohio	33,188	28.9	22
Oklahoma	10,866	30.6	13
Oregon	8,870	24.4	41
Pennsylvania	31,138	25.1	40
Rhode Island	3,091	28.7	26
South Carolina	12,795	30.1	14
South Dakota	1,858	23.9	42
Tennessee	17,548	29.4	18
Texas	61,534	26.9	34
Utah	5,722	23.2	44
Vermont	1,358	21.8	48
Virginia	20,664	27.3	33
Washington	14,192	22.6	45
West Virginia	3,943	21.7	49
Wisconsin	15,959	28.8	25
Wyoming	1,967	38.6	3
50 States	898,088	30.4	
DC	4,284	77.8	
United States	902,372	30.4	

Rank in order per 10,000 population

1	New York
2	New Jersey
3	Wyoming
4	Illinois
5	Louisiana
6	Massachusetts
7	Florida
8	Kansas
9	Arizona
10	Missouri
11	New Mexico
12	Connecticut
13	Oklahoma
14	South Carolina
15	Delaware
16	Mississippi
17	Maryland
18	Tennessee
19	Nevada
20	Alabama
21	Arkansas
22	Ohio
23	Georgia
24	Nebraska
25	Wisconsin
26	Rhode Island
27	North Carolina
28	New Hampshire
29	Colorado
30	Hawaii
31	Indiana
32	California
33	Virginia
34	Texas
35	Montana
36	Kentucky
37	Iowa
38	Idaho
39	Alaska
40	Pennsylvania
41	Oregon
42	South Dakota
43	Michigan
44	Utah
45	Washington
46	Maine
47	North Dakota
48	Vermont
49	West Virginia
50	Minnesota

Note: Numbers that appear to be identical are rounded and vary slightly in actual value. The rankings reflect the actual values before rounding. See the introduction for more details.

J-12 State and Local Corrections Employees, 2005

State	Correction employees #	Per 10,000 population #	Rank per 10,000 population
Alabama	7,882	17.3	42
Alaska	1,787	26.9	12
Arizona	15,325	25.8	13
Arkansas	6,311	22.7	23
California	80,080	22.2	25
Colorado	10,254	22.0	28
Connecticut	7,727	22.0	27
Delaware	2,739	32.5	1
Florida	43,587	24.5	15
Georgia	27,788	30.6	3
Hawaii	2,278	17.9	41
Idaho	2,941	20.6	32
Illinois	24,154	18.9	36
Indiana	14,602	23.3	21
Iowa	4,384	14.8	49
Kansas	6,232	22.7	24
Kentucky	7,975	19.1	35
Louisiana	13,675	30.2	6
Maine	2,118	16.0	46
Maryland	15,199	27.1	11
Massachusetts	9,407	14.7	50
Michigan	23,029	22.8	22
Minnesota	8,695	16.9	44
Mississippi	5,526	18.9	37
Missouri	16,280	28.1	9
Montana	1,706	18.2	40
Nebraska	3,669	20.9	31
Nevada	5,887	24.4	16
New Hampshire	1,976	15.1	47
New Jersey	16,858	19.3	34
New Mexico	6,041	31.3	2
New York	58,284	30.3	5
North Carolina	25,422	29.3	8
North Dakota	950	14.9	48
Ohio	25,236	22.0	26
Oklahoma	6,575	18.5	39
Oregon	8,594	23.6	19
Pennsylvania	29,483	23.7	18
Rhode Island	1,739	16.2	45
South Carolina	10,137	23.8	17
South Dakota	1,324	17.1	43
Tennessee	13,884	23.3	20
Texas	68,371	29.9	7
Utah	5,213	21.1	30
Vermont	1,171	18.8	38
Virginia	21,112	27.9	10
Washington	13,721	21.8	29
West Virginia	3,542	19.5	33
Wisconsin	13,732	24.8	14
Wyoming	1,543	30.3	4
50 States	706,145	23.9	
DC	1,221	22.2	
United States	707,366	23.9	

Rank in order per 10,000 population	
1	Delaware
2	New Mexico
3	Georgia
4	Wyoming
5	New York
6	Louisiana
7	Texas
8	North Carolina
9	Missouri
10	Virginia
11	Maryland
12	Alaska
13	Arizona
14	Wisconsin
15	Florida
16	Nevada
17	South Carolina
18	Pennsylvania
19	Oregon
20	Tennessee
21	Indiana
22	Michigan
23	Arkansas
24	Kansas
25	California
26	Ohio
27	Connecticut
28	Colorado
29	Washington
30	Utah
31	Nebraska
32	Idaho
33	West Virginia
34	New Jersey
35	Kentucky
36	Illinois
37	Mississippi
38	Vermont
39	Oklahoma
40	Montana
41	Hawaii
42	Alabama
43	South Dakota
44	Minnesota
45	Rhode Island
46	Maine
47	New Hampshire
48	North Dakota
49	Iowa
50	Massachusetts

Note: Numbers that appear to be identical are rounded and vary slightly in actual value. The rankings reflect the actual values before rounding. See the introduction for more details.

J-13 State Corrections Spending, FY 2005

State	Corrections spending $ (in millions)	Corrections spending per prisoner $	Rank per prisoner
Alabama	378	13,554	49
Alaska	194	40,316	11
Arizona	752	22,467	36
Arkansas	216	15,987	45
California	6,431	37,680	15
Colorado	498	23,210	35
Connecticut	599	30,810	24
Delaware	202	29,090	28
Florida	1,961	21,845	37
Georgia	1,243	25,498	34
Hawaii	165	26,847	32
Idaho	147	21,561	38
Illinois	1,198	26,670	33
Indiana	663	27,111	31
Iowa	274	31,361	22
Kansas	276	30,437	26
Kentucky	407	20,700	39
Louisiana	644	17,848	43
Maine	128	63,272	3
Maryland	923	40,595	10
Massachusetts	994	92,889	1
Michigan	1,890	38,146	14
Minnesota	377	40,621	9
Mississippi	228	11,114	50
Missouri	508	16,481	44
Montana	111	31,633	21
Nebraska	149	33,446	19
Nevada	185	15,702	47
New Hampshire	76	30,040	27
New Jersey	1,337	48,869	4
New Mexico	205	31,198	23
New York	2,396	38,188	13
North Carolina	995	27,361	30
North Dakota	45	32,491	20
Ohio	1,671	36,442	17
Oklahoma	389	15,669	48
Oregon	496	36,985	16
Pennsylvania	1,537	36,267	18
Rhode Island	294	80,460	2
South Carolina	364	15,717	46
South Dakota	67	19,347	42
Tennessee	519	19,682	40
Texas	3,321	19,651	41
Utah	261	40,954	8
Vermont	96	46,198	5
Virginia	1,078	30,500	25
Washington	721	41,480	7
West Virginia	150	28,238	29
Wisconsin	905	39,833	12
Wyoming	91	44,455	6
50 States	38,755	28,958	
DC	n/a	n/a	
United States	38,755	28,958	

Rank in order per prisoner	
1	Massachusetts
2	Rhode Island
3	Maine
4	New Jersey
5	Vermont
6	Wyoming
7	Washington
8	Utah
9	Minnesota
10	Maryland
11	Alaska
12	Wisconsin
13	New York
14	Michigan
15	California
16	Oregon
17	Ohio
18	Pennsylvania
19	Nebraska
20	North Dakota
21	Montana
22	Iowa
23	New Mexico
24	Connecticut
25	Virginia
26	Kansas
27	New Hampshire
28	Delaware
29	West Virginia
30	North Carolina
31	Indiana
32	Hawaii
33	Illinois
34	Georgia
35	Colorado
36	Arizona
37	Florida
38	Idaho
39	Kentucky
40	Tennessee
41	Texas
42	South Dakota
43	Louisiana
44	Missouri
45	Arkansas
46	South Carolina
47	Nevada
48	Oklahoma
49	Alabama
50	Mississippi

J-14 Percentage Increase in State Corrections Spending, FY 2003–2005

State	Percentage increase in state corrections spending	Rank
Alabama	22.3	3
Alaska	2.6	43
Arizona	17.9	11
Arkansas	20.7	7
California	20.3	8
Colorado	9.5	24
Connecticut	5.8	34
Delaware	8.6	28
Florida	21.5	5
Georgia	1.1	44
Hawaii	9.3	26
Idaho	8.9	27
Illinois	3.1	41
Indiana	3.8	40
Iowa	12.8	19
Kansas	4.9	37
Kentucky	9.7	23
Louisiana	9.3	25
Maine	12.3	20
Maryland	18.3	9
Massachusetts	21.1	6
Michigan	10.6	22
Minnesota	-5.5	49
Mississippi	-2.6	47
Missouri	5.6	36
Montana	15.6	15
Nebraska	6.4	31
Nevada	-5.1	48
New Hampshire	2.7	42
New Jersey	14.1	17
New Mexico	-7.7	50
New York	6.0	33
North Carolina	16.2	13
North Dakota	15.4	16
Ohio	4.4	39
Oklahoma	4.6	38
Oregon	7.6	30
Pennsylvania	5.8	35
Rhode Island	116.2	1
South Carolina	-1.6	45
South Dakota	17.5	12
Tennessee	13.1	18
Texas	-1.7	46
Utah	7.9	29
Vermont	21.5	4
Virginia	16.2	14
Washington	10.9	21
West Virginia	29.3	2
Wisconsin	6.1	32
Wyoming	18.2	10
50 States	10.5	
DC	n/a	
United States	10.5	

Rank in order by percentage

1	Rhode Island
2	West Virginia
3	Alabama
4	Vermont
5	Florida
6	Massachusetts
7	Arkansas
8	California
9	Maryland
10	Wyoming
11	Arizona
12	South Dakota
13	North Carolina
14	Virginia
15	Montana
16	North Dakota
17	New Jersey
18	Tennessee
19	Iowa
20	Maine
21	Washington
22	Michigan
23	Kentucky
24	Colorado
25	Louisiana
26	Hawaii
27	Idaho
28	Delaware
29	Utah
30	Oregon
31	Nebraska
32	Wisconsin
33	New York
34	Connecticut
35	Pennsylvania
36	Missouri
37	Kansas
38	Oklahoma
39	Ohio
40	Indiana
41	Illinois
42	New Hampshire
43	Alaska
44	Georgia
45	South Carolina
46	Texas
47	Mississippi
48	Nevada
49	Minnesota
50	New Mexico

Note: Numbers that appear to be identical are rounded and vary slightly in actual value. The rankings reflect the actual values before rounding. See the introduction for more details.

J-15 State and Local Spending for Law Enforcement, FY 2004

State	Law enforcement spending $ (in millions)	Law enforcement spending per capita $	Rank per capita
Alabama	1,364	301	41
Alaska	366	558	3
Arizona	2,592	451	12
Arkansas	899	327	38
California	20,644	575	2
Colorado	1,929	419	15
Connecticut	1,361	389	24
Delaware	404	487	9
Florida	8,565	492	8
Georgia	3,497	396	20
Hawaii	422	334	34
Idaho	483	347	29
Illinois	5,288	416	16
Indiana	1,837	295	43
Iowa	808	274	47
Kansas	949	347	30
Kentucky	1,213	293	44
Louisiana	1,837	407	18
Maine	369	280	46
Maryland	2,741	493	7
Massachusetts	2,499	389	23
Michigan	4,363	431	14
Minnesota	1,840	361	28
Mississippi	871	300	42
Missouri	1,911	332	36
Montana	313	337	32
Nebraska	582	333	35
Nevada	1,251	536	4
New Hampshire	369	284	45
New Jersey	4,502	518	6
New Mexico	868	456	11
New York	11,647	606	1
North Carolina	2,948	345	31
North Dakota	144	228	50
Ohio	4,367	381	25
Oklahoma	1,164	330	37
Oregon	1,582	440	13
Pennsylvania	4,930	397	19
Rhode Island	446	413	17
South Carolina	1,310	312	40
South Dakota	203	264	48
Tennessee	1,888	320	39
Texas	8,376	372	26
Utah	881	369	27
Vermont	208	334	33
Virginia	2,929	393	22
Washington	2,444	394	21
West Virginia	433	238	49
Wisconsin	2,545	462	10
Wyoming	270	533	5
50 States	125,649	429	
DC	579	1,046	
United States	126,228	430	

Rank in order per capita

1	New York
2	California
3	Alaska
4	Nevada
5	Wyoming
6	New Jersey
7	Maryland
8	Florida
9	Delaware
10	Wisconsin
11	New Mexico
12	Arizona
13	Oregon
14	Michigan
15	Colorado
16	Illinois
17	Rhode Island
18	Louisiana
19	Pennsylvania
20	Georgia
21	Washington
22	Virginia
23	Massachusetts
24	Connecticut
25	Ohio
26	Texas
27	Utah
28	Minnesota
29	Idaho
30	Kansas
31	North Carolina
32	Montana
33	Vermont
34	Hawaii
35	Nebraska
36	Missouri
37	Oklahoma
38	Arkansas
39	Tennessee
40	South Carolina
41	Alabama
42	Mississippi
43	Indiana
44	Kentucky
45	New Hampshire
46	Maine
47	Iowa
48	South Dakota
49	West Virginia
50	North Dakota

Note: Numbers that appear to be identical are rounded and vary slightly in actual value. The rankings reflect the actual values before rounding. See the introduction for more details.

J-16 State and Local Law Enforcement Spending as a Percentage of General Spending, FY 2004

State	Law enforcement spending as a percentage of general spending	Rank
Alabama	5.04	40
Alaska	4.30	47
Arizona	8.62	2
Arkansas	6.17	22
California	7.91	5
Colorado	6.79	12
Connecticut	5.44	33
Delaware	6.53	17
Florida	8.50	3
Georgia	6.97	8
Hawaii	4.86	44
Idaho	6.41	20
Illinois	6.65	15
Indiana	5.17	36
Iowa	4.39	46
Kansas	5.82	30
Kentucky	5.20	35
Louisiana	6.74	14
Maine	3.97	49
Maryland	8.03	4
Massachusetts	5.16	37
Michigan	6.45	18
Minnesota	5.02	41
Mississippi	5.04	39
Missouri	6.16	23
Montana	5.63	32
Nebraska	5.40	34
Nevada	9.19	1
New Hampshire	4.89	43
New Jersey	7.35	6
New Mexico	6.88	10
New York	6.63	16
North Carolina	6.08	25
North Dakota	3.47	50
Ohio	5.87	28
Oklahoma	6.41	19
Oregon	7.09	7
Pennsylvania	6.14	24
Rhode Island	5.84	29
South Carolina	5.12	38
South Dakota	4.92	42
Tennessee	5.98	26
Texas	6.75	13
Utah	6.34	21
Vermont	4.72	45
Virginia	6.82	11
Washington	5.74	31
West Virginia	4.08	48
Wisconsin	6.93	9
Wyoming	5.95	27
50 States	6.63	
DC	8.61	
United States	6.63	

Rank in order by percentage

1	Nevada
2	Arizona
3	Florida
4	Maryland
5	California
6	New Jersey
7	Oregon
8	Georgia
9	Wisconsin
10	New Mexico
11	Virginia
12	Colorado
13	Texas
14	Louisiana
15	Illinois
16	New York
17	Delaware
18	Michigan
19	Oklahoma
20	Idaho
21	Utah
22	Arkansas
23	Missouri
24	Pennsylvania
25	North Carolina
26	Tennessee
27	Wyoming
28	Ohio
29	Rhode Island
30	Kansas
31	Washington
32	Montana
33	Connecticut
34	Nebraska
35	Kentucky
36	Indiana
37	Massachusetts
38	South Carolina
39	Mississippi
40	Alabama
41	Minnesota
42	South Dakota
43	New Hampshire
44	Hawaii
45	Vermont
46	Iowa
47	Alaska
48	West Virginia
49	Maine
50	North Dakota

Note: Numbers that appear to be identical are rounded and vary slightly in actual value. The rankings reflect the actual values before rounding. See the introduction for more details.

Source Notes for Crime and Law Enforcement (Section J)

J-1 Total Crime Rate, 2005: This table reflects the total crime rate as derived from the uniform crime reporting system of the Federal Bureau of Investigation (FBI). The reports are compiled by individual law enforcement agencies throughout the nation and summarized in the FBI publication *Crime in the United States, 2005*. This report is available on the FBI Web site (www.fbi.gov).

Since 1960, the FBI has published a "Total Crime Index." The 2005 report (issued in September of 2006) does not contain this aggregate index but does contain the elements necessary to make the calculation. As explained in the summary in *Crime in the United States, 2003*, nearly 60 percent of crimes are classified as larceny-theft. Thus, "the Crime Index was driven upward by the offense with the highest number creating a bias against a jurisdiction with a high number of larceny-thefts, but a low number of other serious crimes such as murder and forcible rape." In light of this potential distortion, the bureau has suspended publication of the Crime Index. Until a more accurate Index is developed, *State Fact Finder* will continue to publish the calculated Crime Index, acknowledging the above caveat.

In addition, the crime rate statistics in Tables J-1 through J-6 inherently cover only crime known to law enforcement agencies, so they are often cited as "crime reported to the police." Certain crimes, such as murder and thefts for which victims seek insurance reimbursement, are almost always reported to police. Victims often fail to report other categories of crime, ranging from rape to thefts of small items. To capture information on crimes actually committed, the Department of Justice does a survey (known as the "victimization survey") of U.S. households. Because that survey is based on nationwide samples, data from it are not available on a state-by-state basis.

The FBI has worked for years to make the statistics reported from different states and cities more comparable. However, some significant differences remain. Some reflect differences among states in their criminal laws and crime reporting systems. Some reflect inherent differences among citizens in reporting crime that are in turn related to differences in perceptions of whether law enforcement authorities will be able to solve the crimes. Small thefts, for example, are often not reported in large cities but are commonly reported in some smaller communities.

J-2 Violent Crime Rate, 2005: Crimes fall into two major classes. Some, such as murder and assault, involve violence or the threat of violence. Others, such as auto theft and burglary, do not. This table, from the same source as Table J-1, shows the rates for all violent crimes combined.

J-3 Murder and Rape Rates, 2005: This table, from the same source as Table J-1, shows the rates for two specific crimes.

J-4 Property Crime Rate, 2005: This table, from the same source as Table J-1, shows the rates for crimes against property, such as burglary and auto theft.

J-5 Motor Vehicle Theft Rate, 2005: This table combines auto theft with theft of other vehicles, such as pickup trucks, using the same source as Table J-1.

J-6 Violent Crime Rate Change, 2001–2005: In the four-year period from 2001 to 2005 there was a nationwide decrease in the crime rate (crimes per one hundred thousand people) of 7.0 percent. The data come from the 2001 and 2005 editions of the Department of Justice's *Crime in the United States.*

J-7 Prisoners, 2005: This table shows the total number of prisoners held in state penal institutions at the end of 2005. These data are developed by the Department of Justice from statistical reports of state and federal corrections agencies. The data shown are available on the department's Web site (www.ojp.usdoj.gov). They reflect state prisoners only. Federal prisoners constitute about 12 percent of all prisoners. The count of total state prisoners covers only those sentenced for more than a year and thus excludes persons who are being held for short periods in local jails.

J-8 Average Annual Change in Prisoners, 1995–2005: This table, from the same source as Table J-7, shows the average annual percentage change in the number of prisoners.

J-9 Incarceration Rate, 2005: This table measures the relationship between state prison populations (see Table J-7) and total population. While the national rate is equivalent to having 0.5 percent of the population in prison, the percentages are much higher for certain age and ethnic groups and for males.

J-10 Juvenile Violent Crime Index, 2003: This table is from the Web site of the Office of Juvenile Justice and Delinquency Prevention of the Department of Justice (www.ojjdp.ncjrs.org). It reflects the number of violent crime arrests during 2003 of youths between the ages of ten and seventeen per one hundred thousand youths in the population of each state.

J-11 State and Local Law Enforcement Employees, 2005: These statistics come from a U.S. Census Bureau survey of state and local government employment, *Public Employment in 2005*. The survey is available only on the bureau's Web site (www.census.gov).

J-12 State and Local Corrections Employees, 2005: This statistic comes from the same source as Table J-11.

J-13 State Corrections Spending, FY 2005: These data provide one way to look at the costs of maintaining prison systems in each state. The total spending shown is the general fund spending reported by state budget offices in the National Association of State Budget Officers' *2005 State Expenditure Report*. These general fund data showing about $38.8 billion for the fifty states exclude about $4.1 billion financed outside state general funds, primarily by bond funds used to finance prison construction. The per-inmate spending is the result of dividing the spending in fiscal year 2005 by the number of inmates in prison at the end of 2005.

The resulting calculation is somewhat arbitrary as it does not separately account for the supervision of inmates on parole, which is another major function of corrections agencies not associated directly with inmates in prison.

J-14 Percentage Increase in State Corrections Spending, FY 2003–2005: These data, from the same source as Table J-13, reflect the major impact that growing prison populations are having on state government budgets. Large deviations from one year to the next are often associated with large one-time expenditures for capital outlays in one of the years being compared. *State Fact Finder* has accounted for this by comparing spending over a two year interval.

J-15 State and Local Spending for Law Enforcement, FY 2004: This table relates spending on police and corrections to population in each state. The data come from the U.S. Census Bureau's electronic publication "State and Local Government Finance Estimates, by State," available on the bureau's Web site (www.census.gov). Population numbers, also from the U.S. Census Bureau, are as of July 1, 2004. See notes to Table F-1 for more extensive information on the source of the data.

J-16 State and Local Law Enforcement Spending as a Percentage of General Spending, FY 2004: This table shows the relative importance of law enforcement outlays in state and local budgets. It is derived by comparing this spending (see Table J-16) with total "general" spending. General spending includes essentially all other spending except municipal electric and other utilities and trust funds, such as those for workers' compensation.

Transportation

Percent Change in State Transportation Expenditures by Region, FY 2004–2005

Region	Percent
New England	-20.7
Mid-Atlantic	7.0
Great Lakes	-0.2
Plains	1.9
Southeast	11.7
Southwest	13.5
Rocky Mountain	10.6
Far West	17.3
United States	7.3

Note: From fiscal year 2003 to fiscal year 2004, New England increased transportation spending by 46.3 percent

Percent Change in State Transportation Expenditures by Region, FY 2005–Estimated FY 2006

Region	Percent
New England	8.7
Mid-Atlantic	8.8
Great Lakes	9.5
Plains	5.0
Southeast	11.1
Southwest	7.2
Rocky Mountain	-2.4
Far West	14.1
United States	9.5

Source: National Association of State Budget Officers

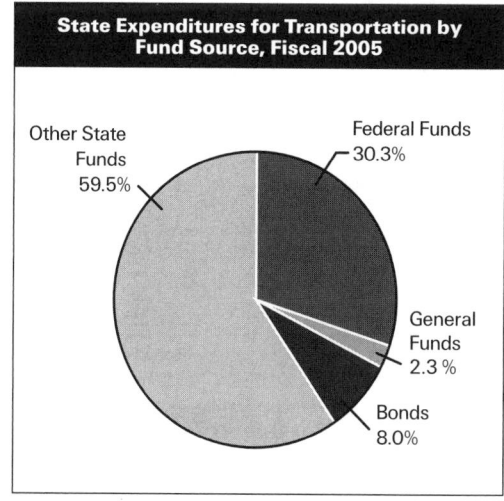

State Expenditures for Transportation by Fund Source, Fiscal 2005

Other State Funds 59.5%
Federal Funds 30.3%
General Funds 2.3%
Bonds 8.0%

Source: National Association of State Budget Officers

K-1 Travel on Interstate Highways, 2005

State	Annual interstate vehicle-miles (in millions)	Percentage of travel on interstates	Rank by percentage
Alabama	13,321	22.3	35
Alaska	1,504	29.9	6
Arizona	13,570	22.7	33
Arkansas	8,073	25.3	23
California	88,898	27.0	18
Colorado	11,780	24.6	25
Connecticut	10,230	32.3	2
Delaware	1,385	14.6	50
Florida	34,416	17.1	48
Georgia	30,372	26.8	20
Hawaii	1,908	18.9	46
Idaho	3,398	22.9	31
Illinois	31,620	29.4	11
Indiana	16,290	22.7	34
Iowa	7,231	23.3	30
Kansas	6,934	23.4	27
Kentucky	12,737	26.8	19
Louisiana	12,597	28.0	14
Maine	3,092	20.7	40
Maryland	16,807	29.8	7
Massachusetts	16,591	29.9	5
Michigan	22,245	21.4	39
Minnesota	12,637	22.2	36
Mississippi	7,103	16.8	49
Missouri	18,245	26.5	21
Montana	2,814	25.3	22
Nebraska	3,984	20.7	41
Nevada	4,854	23.4	29
New Hampshire	2,890	21.5	38
New Jersey	14,922	20.2	43
New Mexico	7,171	29.9	4
New York	26,725	19.4	45
North Carolina	20,087	19.8	44
North Dakota	1,719	22.7	32
Ohio	32,658	29.6	9
Oklahoma	9,620	20.5	42
Oregon	8,892	25.2	24
Pennsylvania	25,661	23.8	26
Rhode Island	2,265	27.3	16
South Carolina	13,436	27.2	17
South Dakota	2,467	29.4	10
Tennessee	20,169	28.5	13
Texas	54,980	23.4	28
Utah	9,114	36.2	1
Vermont	1,662	21.5	37
Virginia	23,834	29.7	8
Washington	15,414	27.8	15
West Virginia	5,868	28.6	12
Wisconsin	10,350	17.2	47
Wyoming	2,855	31.5	3
50 States	727,395	24.4	
DC	465	12.5	
United States	727,860	24.3	

Rank in order by percentage

1 Utah
2 Connecticut
3 Wyoming
4 New Mexico
5 Massachusetts
6 Alaska
7 Maryland
8 Virginia
9 Ohio
10 South Dakota
11 Illinois
12 West Virginia
13 Tennessee
14 Louisiana
15 Washington
16 Rhode Island
17 South Carolina
18 California
19 Kentucky
20 Georgia
21 Missouri
22 Montana
23 Arkansas
24 Oregon
25 Colorado
26 Pennsylvania
27 Kansas
28 Texas
29 Nevada
30 Iowa
31 Idaho
32 North Dakota
33 Arizona
34 Indiana
35 Alabama
36 Minnesota
37 Vermont
38 New Hampshire
39 Michigan
40 Maine
41 Nebraska
42 Oklahoma
43 New Jersey
44 North Carolina
45 New York
46 Hawaii
47 Wisconsin
48 Florida
49 Mississippi
50 Delaware

Note: Numbers that appear to be identical are rounded and vary slightly in actual value. The rankings reflect the actual values before rounding. See the introduction for more details.

K-2 Percentage of Interstate Mileage in "Unacceptable" Condition, 2005

State	Percentage of interstate mileage in "unacceptable" condition	Rank
Alabama	4.4	16
Alaska	16.4	2
Arizona	0.4	41
Arkansas	2.4	25
California	1.6	32
Colorado	2.5	23
Connecticut	2.5	23
Delaware	0.0	48
Florida	0.0	48
Georgia	0.1	46
Hawaii	9.9	4
Idaho	0.5	39
Illinois	4.6	14
Indiana	1.9	29
Iowa	7.1	9
Kansas	0.3	44
Kentucky	0.0	48
Louisiana	7.3	8
Maine	4.5	15
Maryland	0.8	33
Massachusetts	0.8	33
Michigan	3.8	17
Minnesota	0.6	36
Mississippi	2.7	21
Missouri	6.3	11
Montana	0.5	39
Nebraska	7.7	7
Nevada	0.1	46
New Hampshire	6.7	10
New Jersey	9.2	6
New Mexico	0.2	45
New York	11.3	3
North Carolina	3.6	18
North Dakota	3.1	19
Ohio	0.8	33
Oklahoma	5.8	12
Oregon	1.7	30
Pennsylvania	2.7	21
Rhode Island	28.6	1
South Carolina	0.4	41
South Dakota	9.3	5
Tennessee	0.4	41
Texas	0.6	36
Utah	2.4	25
Vermont	5.1	13
Virginia	1.7	30
Washington	2.2	28
West Virginia	2.4	25
Wisconsin	3.0	20
Wyoming	0.6	36
50 States	n/a	
DC	n/a	
United States	2.9	

Rank in order by percentage	
1	Rhode Island
2	Alaska
3	New York
4	Hawaii
5	South Dakota
6	New Jersey
7	Nebraska
8	Louisiana
9	Iowa
10	New Hampshire
11	Missouri
12	Oklahoma
13	Vermont
14	Illinois
15	Maine
16	Alabama
17	Michigan
18	North Carolina
19	North Dakota
20	Wisconsin
21	Pennsylvania
21	Mississippi
23	Colorado
23	Connecticut
25	West Virginia
25	Arkansas
25	Utah
28	Washington
29	Indiana
30	Oregon
30	Virginia
32	California
33	Ohio
33	Maryland
33	Massachusetts
36	Wyoming
36	Minnesota
36	Texas
39	Idaho
39	Montana
41	Arizona
41	South Carolina
41	Tennessee
44	Kansas
45	New Mexico
46	Georgia
46	Nevada
48	Kentucky
48	Delaware
48	Florida

Note: Ties in ranking reflect ties in actual values.

K-3   Deficient Bridges, 2005

State	Total deficient bridges #	Percentage of bridges deficient	Rank by percentage
Alabama	4,488	28.6	18
Alaska	358	30.5	15
Arizona	720	10.0	50
Arkansas	3,019	24.2	30
California	6,531	28.2	19
Colorado	1,404	17.0	44
Connecticut	1,388	33.3	12
Delaware	130	15.3	47
Florida	2,076	18.0	42
Georgia	2,970	20.5	39
Hawaii	514	46.6	3
Idaho	753	18.5	41
Illinois	4,346	16.8	45
Indiana	4,045	22.1	35
Iowa	6,839	27.5	22
Kansas	5,663	22.2	34
Kentucky	4,104	30.4	16
Louisiana	4,200	31.5	14
Maine	822	34.7	9
Maryland	1,403	27.9	20
Massachusetts	2,572	52.3	2
Michigan	3,030	27.9	21
Minnesota	1,586	12.2	48
Mississippi	4,509	26.7	24
Missouri	7,965	33.4	11
Montana	1,018	20.7	38
Nebraska	3,864	25.0	28
Nevada	196	12.0	49
New Hampshire	744	31.5	13
New Jersey	2,341	36.3	7
New Mexico	724	18.9	40
New York	6,510	37.5	5
North Carolina	5,125	29.3	17
North Dakota	1,023	22.9	31
Ohio	7,006	25.0	29
Oklahoma	8,400	35.9	8
Oregon	1,872	25.9	26
Pennsylvania	9,560	42.9	4
Rhode Island	413	55.1	1
South Carolina	2,101	22.8	32
South Dakota	1,575	26.4	25
Tennessee	4,452	22.5	33
Texas	10,264	20.9	36
Utah	502	17.8	43
Vermont	929	34.4	10
Virginia	3,390	25.6	27
Washington	2,080	27.4	23
West Virginia	2,576	37.3	6
Wisconsin	2,262	16.5	46
Wyoming	627	20.7	37
50 States	154,989	26.2	
DC	155	63.3	
United States*	156,177	26.3	

Due to rounding or data sources, the 50-state total plus D.C. may not equal the U.S. total. Please see introduction.

	Rank in order by percentage
1	Rhode Island
2	Massachusetts
3	Hawaii
4	Pennsylvania
5	New York
6	West Virginia
7	New Jersey
8	Oklahoma
9	Maine
10	Vermont
11	Missouri
12	Connecticut
13	New Hampshire
14	Louisiana
15	Alaska
16	Kentucky
17	North Carolina
18	Alabama
19	California
20	Maryland
21	Michigan
22	Iowa
23	Washington
24	Mississippi
25	South Dakota
26	Oregon
27	Virginia
28	Nebraska
29	Ohio
30	Arkansas
31	North Dakota
32	South Carolina
33	Tennessee
34	Kansas
35	Indiana
36	Texas
37	Wyoming
38	Montana
39	Georgia
40	New Mexico
41	Idaho
42	Florida
43	Utah
44	Colorado
45	Illinois
46	Wisconsin
47	Delaware
48	Minnesota
49	Nevada
50	Arizona

Note: Numbers that appear to be identical are rounded and vary slightly in actual value. The rankings reflect the actual values before rounding. See the introduction for more details.

K-4   Traffic Deaths Per 100 Million Vehicle-Miles, 2005

State	Traffic deaths per 100 million vehicle-miles	Rank
Alabama	1.90	11
Alaska	1.43	27
Arizona	1.97	10
Arkansas	2.03	9
California	1.31	32
Colorado	1.26	35
Connecticut	0.87	49
Delaware	1.41	28
Florida	1.76	17
Georgia	1.52	20
Hawaii	1.39	29
Idaho	1.85	13
Illinois	1.26	34
Indiana	1.31	33
Iowa	1.45	24
Kansas	1.44	25
Kentucky	2.08	6
Louisiana	2.12	5
Maine	1.13	40
Maryland	1.09	42
Massachusetts	0.80	50
Michigan	1.09	43
Minnesota	0.98	47
Mississippi	2.21	4
Missouri	1.83	14
Montana	2.26	1
Nebraska	1.43	26
Nevada	2.06	7
New Hampshire	1.24	36
New Jersey	1.01	46
New Mexico	2.04	8
New York	1.04	45
North Carolina	1.51	21
North Dakota	1.62	19
Ohio	1.20	37
Oklahoma	1.71	18
Oregon	1.38	30
Pennsylvania	1.50	22
Rhode Island	1.05	44
South Carolina	2.21	3
South Dakota	2.22	2
Tennessee	1.79	16
Texas	1.49	23
Utah	1.12	41
Vermont	0.95	48
Virginia	1.18	38
Washington	1.17	39
West Virginia	1.82	15
Wisconsin	1.36	31
Wyoming	1.88	12
50 States	1.45	
DC	1.29	
United States	1.45	

Rank in order by rate

1	Montana
2	South Dakota
3	South Carolina
4	Mississippi
5	Louisiana
6	Kentucky
7	Nevada
8	New Mexico
9	Arkansas
10	Arizona
11	Alabama
12	Wyoming
13	Idaho
14	Missouri
15	West Virginia
16	Tennessee
17	Florida
18	Oklahoma
19	North Dakota
20	Georgia
21	North Carolina
22	Pennsylvania
23	Texas
24	Iowa
25	Kansas
26	Nebraska
27	Alaska
28	Delaware
29	Hawaii
30	Oregon
31	Wisconsin
32	California
33	Indiana
34	Illinois
35	Colorado
36	New Hampshire
37	Ohio
38	Virginia
39	Washington
40	Maine
41	Utah
42	Maryland
43	Michigan
44	Rhode Island
45	New York
46	New Jersey
47	Minnesota
48	Vermont
49	Connecticut
50	Massachusetts

Note: Numbers that appear to be identical are rounded and vary slightly in actual value. The rankings reflect the actual values before rounding. See the introduction for more details.

K-5 Percentage of Drivers Using Seat Belts, 2005

State	Percentage of drivers using seat belts	Rank
Alabama	82	23
Alaska	78	32
Arizona	94	4
Arkansas	68	45
California	93	5
Colorado	79	29
Connecticut	82	23
Delaware	84	19
Florida	74	39
Georgia	82	23
Hawaii	95	1
Idaho	76	35
Illinois	86	13
Indiana	81	26
Iowa	86	13
Kansas	69	43
Kentucky	67	46
Louisiana	78	32
Maine	76	35
Maryland	91	8
Massachusetts	65	47
Michigan	93	5
Minnesota	83	20
Mississippi	61	48
Missouri	77	34
Montana	80	27
Nebraska	79	29
Nevada	95	1
New Hampshire	n/a	n/a
New Jersey	86	13
New Mexico	90	9
New York	85	16
North Carolina	87	11
North Dakota	76	35
Ohio	79	29
Oklahoma	83	20
Oregon	93	5
Pennsylvania	83	20
Rhode Island	75	38
South Carolina	70	42
South Dakota	69	43
Tennessee	74	39
Texas	90	9
Utah	87	11
Vermont	85	16
Virginia	80	27
Washington	95	1
West Virginia	85	16
Wisconsin	73	41
Wyoming	n/a	n/a
50 States	n/a	
DC	89	
United States	82	

Rank in order by percentage

1	Hawaii
1	Washington
1	Nevada
4	Arizona
5	Oregon
5	Michigan
5	California
8	Maryland
9	Texas
9	New Mexico
11	Utah
11	North Carolina
13	Illinois
13	New Jersey
13	Iowa
16	New York
16	West Virginia
16	Vermont
19	Delaware
20	Pennsylvania
20	Oklahoma
20	Minnesota
23	Alabama
23	Connecticut
23	Georgia
26	Indiana
27	Virginia
27	Montana
29	Colorado
29	Nebraska
29	Ohio
32	Alaska
32	Louisiana
34	Missouri
35	North Dakota
35	Idaho
35	Maine
38	Rhode Island
39	Tennessee
39	Florida
41	Wisconsin
42	South Carolina
43	Kansas
43	South Dakota
45	Arkansas
46	Kentucky
47	Massachusetts
48	Mississippi

Note: Ties in ranking reflect ties in actual values.

K-6   Vehicle-Miles Traveled Per Capita, 2005

State	Vehicle-miles traveled (in millions)	Vehicle-miles traveled per capita	Rank per capita
Alabama	59,661	13,090	4
Alaska	5,035	7,587	49
Arizona	59,799	10,068	34
Arkansas	31,972	11,504	14
California	329,267	9,113	39
Colorado	47,962	10,281	31
Connecticut	31,675	9,023	40
Delaware	9,508	11,272	20
Florida	201,531	11,328	17
Georgia	113,509	12,511	5
Hawaii	10,083	7,907	47
Idaho	14,866	10,402	28
Illinois	107,706	8,439	46
Indiana	71,799	11,448	15
Iowa	31,060	10,471	27
Kansas	29,621	10,792	25
Kentucky	47,466	11,373	16
Louisiana	44,979	9,943	36
Maine	14,925	11,294	19
Maryland	56,319	10,056	35
Massachusetts	55,458	8,667	43
Michigan	104,052	10,281	30
Minnesota	56,904	11,086	21
Mississippi	42,186	14,442	2
Missouri	68,754	11,854	11
Montana	11,126	11,891	8
Nebraska	19,291	10,968	22
Nevada	20,776	8,604	44
New Hampshire	13,429	10,252	32
New Jersey	73,819	8,467	45
New Mexico	23,966	12,428	6
New York	137,521	7,142	50
North Carolina	101,268	11,662	12
North Dakota	7,570	11,890	9
Ohio	110,491	9,638	38
Oklahoma	47,019	13,253	3
Oregon	35,282	9,690	37
Pennsylvania	108,042	8,692	42
Rhode Island	8,300	7,712	48
South Carolina	49,434	11,618	13
South Dakota	8,397	10,822	24
Tennessee	70,814	11,876	10
Texas	235,170	10,287	29
Utah	25,158	10,187	33
Vermont	7,713	12,379	7
Virginia	80,337	10,616	26
Washington	55,476	8,823	41
West Virginia	20,523	11,296	18
Wisconsin	60,017	10,841	23
Wyoming	9,058	17,785	1
50 States	2,986,094	10,093	
DC	3,713	6,745	
United States	2,989,807	10,087	

Rank in order per capita	
1	Wyoming
2	Mississippi
3	Oklahoma
4	Alabama
5	Georgia
6	New Mexico
7	Vermont
8	Montana
9	North Dakota
10	Tennessee
11	Missouri
12	North Carolina
13	South Carolina
14	Arkansas
15	Indiana
16	Kentucky
17	Florida
18	West Virginia
19	Maine
20	Delaware
21	Minnesota
22	Nebraska
23	Wisconsin
24	South Dakota
25	Kansas
26	Virginia
27	Iowa
28	Idaho
29	Texas
30	Michigan
31	Colorado
32	New Hampshire
33	Utah
34	Arizona
35	Maryland
36	Louisiana
37	Oregon
38	Ohio
39	California
40	Connecticut
41	Washington
42	Pennsylvania
43	Massachusetts
44	Nevada
45	New Jersey
46	Illinois
47	Hawaii
48	Rhode Island
49	Alaska
50	New York

Note: Numbers that appear to be identical are rounded and vary slightly in actual value. The rankings reflect the actual values before rounding. See the introduction for more details.

K-7 Percentage of Workers Using Public Transportation, 2005

State	Percentage of workers using public transportation	Rank
Alabama	0.4	45
Alaska	1.2	28
Arizona	1.9	20
Arkansas	0.3	49
California	4.7	8
Colorado	2.7	15
Connecticut	4.2	10
Delaware	2.2	18
Florida	1.8	22
Georgia	2.2	18
Hawaii	5.7	6
Idaho	0.9	30
Illinois	8.2	4
Indiana	0.9	30
Iowa	0.8	36
Kansas	0.4	45
Kentucky	0.9	30
Louisiana	1.9	20
Maine	0.7	37
Maryland	8.5	3
Massachusetts	8.1	5
Michigan	1.1	29
Minnesota	2.8	14
Mississippi	0.4	45
Missouri	1.3	27
Montana	0.6	42
Nebraska	0.6	42
Nevada	3.0	13
New Hampshire	0.7	37
New Jersey	10.3	2
New Mexico	0.9	30
New York	25.8	1
North Carolina	0.9	30
North Dakota	0.4	45
Ohio	1.7	23
Oklahoma	0.6	42
Oregon	4.1	11
Pennsylvania	5.1	7
Rhode Island	2.7	15
South Carolina	0.7	37
South Dakota	0.3	49
Tennessee	0.7	37
Texas	1.7	23
Utah	2.3	17
Vermont	0.9	30
Virginia	3.7	12
Washington	4.7	8
West Virginia	0.7	37
Wisconsin	1.5	26
Wyoming	1.6	25
50 States	n/a	
DC	37.7	
United States	4.7	

Rank in order by percentage	
1	New York
2	New Jersey
3	Maryland
4	Illinois
5	Massachusetts
6	Hawaii
7	Pennsylvania
8	California
8	Washington
10	Connecticut
11	Oregon
12	Virginia
13	Nevada
14	Minnesota
15	Colorado
15	Rhode Island
17	Utah
18	Delaware
18	Georgia
20	Arizona
20	Louisiana
22	Florida
23	Ohio
23	Texas
25	Wyoming
26	Wisconsin
27	Missouri
28	Alaska
29	Michigan
30	Idaho
30	Indiana
30	Kentucky
30	New Mexico
30	North Carolina
30	Vermont
36	Iowa
37	Maine
37	New Hampshire
37	South Carolina
37	Tennessee
37	West Virginia
42	Montana
42	Nebraska
42	Oklahoma
45	Alabama
45	Kansas
45	Mississippi
45	North Dakota
49	Arkansas
49	South Dakota

Note: Ties in ranking reflect ties in actual values.

K-8 Road and Street Miles, 2005

State	Total road and street miles #	Total miles under state control #	Percentage under state control	Rank by percentage
Alabama	96,045	10,955	11.4	33
Alaska	14,369	5,659	39.4	6
Arizona	59,790	6,800	11.4	34
Arkansas	98,659	16,444	16.7	20
California	169,906	15,213	9.0	43
Colorado	87,598	9,106	10.4	38
Connecticut	21,194	3,717	17.5	18
Delaware	6,094	5,243	86.0	2
Florida	120,557	12,040	10.0	40
Georgia	117,645	17,930	15.2	26
Hawaii	4,321	928	21.5	15
Idaho	47,129	4,957	10.5	37
Illinois	138,833	16,103	11.6	32
Indiana	95,575	11,183	11.7	30
Iowa	113,972	8,895	7.8	48
Kansas	135,462	10,370	7.7	49
Kentucky	78,021	27,510	35.3	8
Louisiana	60,953	16,693	27.4	10
Maine	22,807	8,548	37.5	7
Maryland	30,962	5,140	16.6	21
Massachusetts	35,897	2,849	7.9	47
Michigan	121,456	9,698	8.0	46
Minnesota	132,048	11,871	9.0	42
Mississippi	74,181	10,896	14.7	27
Missouri	125,822	32,464	25.8	12
Montana	69,338	10,789	15.6	23
Nebraska	93,310	9,975	10.7	36
Nevada	34,624	5,399	15.6	22
New Hampshire	15,566	3,975	25.5	13
New Jersey	38,552	2,321	6.0	50
New Mexico	63,758	11,990	18.8	16
New York	113,343	15,033	13.3	29
North Carolina	103,128	79,031	76.6	4
North Dakota	86,793	7,382	8.5	44
Ohio	124,840	19,292	15.5	24
Oklahoma	112,937	12,285	10.9	35
Oregon	64,543	7,532	11.7	31
Pennsylvania	120,668	39,890	33.1	9
Rhode Island	6,491	1,102	17.0	19
South Carolina	66,238	41,391	62.5	5
South Dakota	83,911	7,873	9.4	41
Tennessee	90,451	13,817	15.3	25
Texas	304,171	79,648	26.2	11
Utah	43,575	5,858	13.4	28
Vermont	14,399	2,634	18.3	17
Virginia	71,961	57,860	80.4	3
Washington	83,381	7,045	8.4	45
West Virginia	37,028	33,987	91.8	1
Wisconsin	114,142	11,782	10.3	39
Wyoming	27,700	6,757	24.4	14
50 States	3,994,144	775,860	19.4	
DC	1,500	1,392	92.8	
United States	3,995,644	777,252	19.5	

Rank in order by percentage

1	West Virginia
2	Delaware
3	Virginia
4	North Carolina
5	South Carolina
6	Alaska
7	Maine
8	Kentucky
9	Pennsylvania
10	Louisiana
11	Texas
12	Missouri
13	New Hampshire
14	Wyoming
15	Hawaii
16	New Mexico
17	Vermont
18	Connecticut
19	Rhode Island
20	Arkansas
21	Maryland
22	Nevada
23	Montana
24	Ohio
25	Tennessee
26	Georgia
27	Mississippi
28	Utah
29	New York
30	Indiana
31	Oregon
32	Illinois
33	Alabama
34	Arizona
35	Oklahoma
36	Nebraska
37	Idaho
38	Colorado
39	Wisconsin
40	Florida
41	South Dakota
42	Minnesota
43	California
44	North Dakota
45	Washington
46	Michigan
47	Massachusetts
48	Iowa
49	Kansas
50	New Jersey

Note: Numbers that appear to be identical are rounded and vary slightly in actual value. The rankings reflect the actual values before rounding. See the introduction for more details.

State and Local Highway Employees, 2005

State	Highway employees #	Per 10,000 population	Rank per 10,000 population
Alabama	11,556	25.4	16
Alaska	3,536	53.3	1
Arizona	8,592	14.5	44
Arkansas	7,298	26.3	14
California	41,608	11.5	50
Colorado	9,286	19.9	29
Connecticut	6,445	18.4	33
Delaware	2,158	25.6	15
Florida	22,882	12.9	46
Georgia	14,286	15.7	41
Hawaii	1,623	12.7	47
Idaho	3,385	23.7	19
Illinois	20,023	15.7	42
Indiana	10,852	17.3	37
Iowa	9,601	32.4	11
Kansas	9,273	33.8	8
Kentucky	8,351	20.0	28
Louisiana	10,577	23.4	21
Maine	4,438	33.6	9
Maryland	9,267	16.5	39
Massachusetts	10,619	16.6	38
Michigan	12,551	12.4	49
Minnesota	12,053	23.5	20
Mississippi	8,248	28.2	12
Missouri	14,067	24.3	18
Montana	3,453	36.9	3
Nebraska	5,713	32.5	10
Nevada	3,055	12.7	48
New Hampshire	3,514	26.8	13
New Jersey	18,887	21.7	23
New Mexico	4,080	21.2	25
New York	40,740	21.2	24
North Carolina	15,720	18.1	34
North Dakota	2,209	34.7	4
Ohio	22,043	19.2	31
Oklahoma	8,693	24.5	17
Oregon	7,378	20.3	27
Pennsylvania	24,440	19.7	30
Rhode Island	1,641	15.2	43
South Carolina	7,551	17.7	35
South Dakota	2,627	33.9	7
Tennessee	11,326	19.0	32
Texas	36,605	16.0	40
Utah	3,399	13.8	45
Vermont	2,136	34.3	5
Virginia	13,181	17.4	36
Washington	14,336	22.8	22
West Virginia	6,222	34.2	6
Wisconsin	11,559	20.9	26
Wyoming	2,444	48.0	2
50 States	545,527	18.4	
DC	693	12.6	
United States	546,220	18.4	

Rank in order per 10,000 population

1	Alaska
2	Wyoming
3	Montana
4	North Dakota
5	Vermont
6	West Virginia
7	South Dakota
8	Kansas
9	Maine
10	Nebraska
11	Iowa
12	Mississippi
13	New Hampshire
14	Arkansas
15	Delaware
16	Alabama
17	Oklahoma
18	Missouri
19	Idaho
20	Minnesota
21	Louisiana
22	Washington
23	New Jersey
24	New York
25	New Mexico
26	Wisconsin
27	Oregon
28	Kentucky
29	Colorado
30	Pennsylvania
31	Ohio
32	Tennessee
33	Connecticut
34	North Carolina
35	South Carolina
36	Virginia
37	Indiana
38	Massachusetts
39	Maryland
40	Texas
41	Georgia
42	Illinois
43	Rhode Island
44	Arizona
45	Utah
46	Florida
47	Hawaii
48	Nevada
49	Michigan
50	California

Note: Numbers that appear to be identical are rounded and vary slightly in actual value. The rankings reflect the actual values before rounding. See the introduction for more details.

K-10 State and Local Public Transit Employees, 2005

State	Transit employees #	Per 10,000 population	Rank per 10,000 population
Alabama	236	0.5	45
Alaska	239	3.6	24
Arizona	298	0.5	46
Arkansas	248	0.9	40
California	33,172	9.2	6
Colorado	2,912	6.2	12
Connecticut	563	1.6	33
Delaware	632	7.5	10
Florida	8,061	4.5	19
Georgia	4,997	5.5	17
Hawaii	47	0.4	48
Idaho	36	0.3	50
Illinois	15,946	12.5	3
Indiana	1,669	2.7	27
Iowa	801	2.7	25
Kansas	284	1.0	39
Kentucky	1,009	2.4	30
Louisiana	1,656	3.7	23
Maine	103	0.8	42
Maryland	3,200	5.7	15
Massachusetts	5,805	9.1	7
Michigan	4,002	4.0	21
Minnesota	2,835	5.5	16
Mississippi	132	0.5	47
Missouri	3,375	5.8	13
Montana	176	1.9	31
Nebraska	427	2.4	29
Nevada	254	1.1	38
New Hampshire	112	0.9	41
New Jersey	11,187	12.8	2
New Mexico	718	3.7	22
New York	63,517	33.0	1
North Carolina	1,101	1.3	35
North Dakota	38	0.6	43
Ohio	6,559	5.7	14
Oklahoma	189	0.5	44
Oregon	3,070	8.4	8
Pennsylvania	13,089	10.5	5
Rhode Island	826	7.7	9
South Carolina	455	1.1	37
South Dakota	26	0.3	49
Tennessee	1,032	1.7	32
Texas	10,762	4.7	18
Utah	1,730	7.0	11
Vermont	165	2.6	28
Virginia	1,043	1.4	34
Washington	7,642	12.2	4
West Virginia	485	2.7	26
Wisconsin	2,400	4.3	20
Wyoming	61	1.2	36
50 States	219,322	7.4	
DC	9,886	179.6	
United States	229,208	7.7	

Rank in order per 10,000 population

1	New York
2	New Jersey
3	Illinois
4	Washington
5	Pennsylvania
6	California
7	Massachusetts
8	Oregon
9	Rhode Island
10	Delaware
11	Utah
12	Colorado
13	Missouri
14	Ohio
15	Maryland
16	Minnesota
17	Georgia
18	Texas
19	Florida
20	Wisconsin
21	Michigan
22	New Mexico
23	Louisiana
24	Alaska
25	Iowa
26	West Virginia
27	Indiana
28	Vermont
29	Nebraska
30	Kentucky
31	Montana
32	Tennessee
33	Connecticut
34	Virginia
35	North Carolina
36	Wyoming
37	South Carolina
38	Nevada
39	Kansas
40	Arkansas
41	New Hampshire
42	Maine
43	North Dakota
44	Oklahoma
45	Alabama
46	Arizona
47	Mississippi
48	Hawaii
49	South Dakota
50	Idaho

Note: Numbers that appear to be identical are rounded and vary slightly in actual value. The rankings reflect the actual values before rounding. See the introduction for more details.

K-11 State and Local Spending for Highways, FY 2004

State	Highway spending $ (in millions)	Highway spending per capita $	Highway spending as a percentage of personal income	Rank per capita
Alabama	1,604	354	1.36	44
Alaska	953	1,453	4.42	1
Arizona	2,076	361	1.38	42
Arkansas	1,279	465	1.93	20
California	11,053	308	0.93	47
Colorado	2,439	530	1.55	15
Connecticut	1,281	366	0.85	40
Delaware	498	599	1.83	7
Florida	7,060	406	1.38	28
Georgia	2,436	276	0.96	50
Hawaii	352	279	0.92	49
Idaho	654	469	1.87	19
Illinois	4,969	391	1.18	31
Indiana	2,317	371	1.30	38
Iowa	1,583	536	1.89	14
Kansas	1,576	576	1.96	9
Kentucky	1,977	477	1.82	18
Louisiana	1,684	373	1.44	37
Maine	695	528	1.84	16
Maryland	1,940	349	0.94	45
Massachusetts	3,490	544	1.38	12
Michigan	3,855	381	1.23	33
Minnesota	2,888	566	1.68	10
Mississippi	1,336	460	1.99	21
Missouri	2,568	446	1.55	22
Montana	624	673	2.64	6
Nebraska	1,034	592	1.96	8
Nevada	1,573	674	2.23	5
New Hampshire	525	404	1.17	29
New Jersey	3,260	375	0.94	35
New Mexico	820	431	1.72	23
New York	8,213	427	1.18	25
North Carolina	3,468	406	1.46	27
North Dakota	501	791	2.77	3
Ohio	4,112	359	1.20	43
Oklahoma	1,280	363	1.37	41
Oregon	1,365	380	1.33	34
Pennsylvania	4,855	391	1.24	30
Rhode Island	369	341	1.07	46
South Carolina	1,604	382	1.48	32
South Dakota	605	785	2.80	4
Tennessee	1,791	304	1.07	48
Texas	8,412	374	1.31	36
Utah	995	417	1.68	26
Vermont	333	536	1.76	13
Virginia	2,741	367	1.10	39
Washington	2,655	428	1.30	24
West Virginia	1,013	558	2.27	11
Wisconsin	2,875	522	1.71	17
Wyoming	520	1,027	3.22	2
50 States	118,108	403	1.29	
DC	71	129	0.27	
United States	118,179	402	1.29	

Rank in order per capita

1 Alaska
2 Wyoming
3 North Dakota
4 South Dakota
5 Nevada
6 Montana
7 Delaware
8 Nebraska
9 Kansas
10 Minnesota
11 West Virginia
12 Massachusetts
13 Vermont
14 Iowa
15 Colorado
16 Maine
17 Wisconsin
18 Kentucky
19 Idaho
20 Arkansas
21 Mississippi
22 Missouri
23 New Mexico
24 Washington
25 New York
26 Utah
27 North Carolina
28 Florida
29 New Hampshire
30 Pennsylvania
31 Illinois
32 South Carolina
33 Michigan
34 Oregon
35 New Jersey
36 Texas
37 Louisiana
38 Indiana
39 Virginia
40 Connecticut
41 Oklahoma
42 Arizona
43 Ohio
44 Alabama
45 Maryland
46 Rhode Island
47 California
48 Tennessee
49 Hawaii
50 Georgia

Note: Numbers that appear to be identical are rounded and vary slightly in actual value. The rankings reflect the actual values before rounding. See the introduction for more details.

K-12 State and Local Highway Spending as a Percentage of General Spending, FY 2004

State	Highway spending as a percentage of general spending	Rank
Alabama	5.92	39
Alaska	11.21	6
Arizona	6.90	28
Arkansas	8.78	10
California	4.24	49
Colorado	8.58	13
Connecticut	5.12	45
Delaware	8.04	16
Florida	7.01	26
Georgia	4.85	46
Hawaii	4.06	50
Idaho	8.67	11
Illinois	6.25	34
Indiana	6.52	30
Iowa	8.61	12
Kansas	9.68	7
Kentucky	8.47	14
Louisiana	6.18	36
Maine	7.49	21
Maryland	5.69	41
Massachusetts	7.20	22
Michigan	5.70	40
Minnesota	7.88	17
Mississippi	7.73	19
Missouri	8.28	15
Montana	11.25	5
Nebraska	9.59	8
Nevada	11.55	3
New Hampshire	6.95	27
New Jersey	5.32	44
New Mexico	6.50	31
New York	4.67	48
North Carolina	7.15	24
North Dakota	12.06	2
Ohio	5.52	43
Oklahoma	7.05	25
Oregon	6.12	37
Pennsylvania	6.04	38
Rhode Island	4.82	47
South Carolina	6.27	33
South Dakota	14.64	1
Tennessee	5.67	42
Texas	6.78	29
Utah	7.16	23
Vermont	7.58	20
Virginia	6.38	32
Washington	6.23	35
West Virginia	9.56	9
Wisconsin	7.83	18
Wyoming	11.47	4
50 States	6.23	
DC	1.06	
United States	6.21	

Rank in order by percentage

1	South Dakota
2	North Dakota
3	Nevada
4	Wyoming
5	Montana
6	Alaska
7	Kansas
8	Nebraska
9	West Virginia
10	Arkansas
11	Idaho
12	Iowa
13	Colorado
14	Kentucky
15	Missouri
16	Delaware
17	Minnesota
18	Wisconsin
19	Mississippi
20	Vermont
21	Maine
22	Massachusetts
23	Utah
24	North Carolina
25	Oklahoma
26	Florida
27	New Hampshire
28	Arizona
29	Texas
30	Indiana
31	New Mexico
32	Virginia
33	South Carolina
34	Illinois
35	Washington
36	Louisiana
37	Oregon
38	Pennsylvania
39	Alabama
40	Michigan
41	Maryland
42	Tennessee
43	Ohio
44	New Jersey
45	Connecticut
46	Georgia
47	Rhode Island
48	New York
49	California
50	Hawaii

Source Notes for Transportation (Section K)

K-1 Travel on Interstate Highways, 2005: Use of highways is measured by vehicle-miles (travel by one vehicle for one mile). By this measure, interstate highways account for nearly one-fourth of the nation's highway travel, according to calculations based on the Department of Transportation's *2005 Highway Statistics*. The federal government provides 90 percent of the money used to build interstates, but lower percentages for other highways. Having a large percentage of travel on interstates is good fiscal news as well as an indication of highway quality.

K-2 Percentage of Interstate Mileage in "Unacceptable" Condition, 2005: This table provides one measurement of pavement conditions. It is based on the International Roughness Index (IRI) which is an objective, equipment-based (as opposed to human observation) rating of the smoothness/bumpiness of interstate pavement. The IRI does not measure deterioration of other types. This table shows the percentage of interstate mileage given an IRI rating of 170 or above, the level identified as "unacceptable" in the Federal Highway Administration's *Conditions and Performance Report 1999*. The IRI data are from FHA's *2005 Highway Statistics*.

K-3 Deficient Bridges, 2005: This table shows the total number of deficient bridges on major highways in each state. Details appear in the complete inventory, *The Status of the Nation's Highway Bridges*, published in March 2006 by the Department of Transportation (DOT) and updated biannually. The statistics are also posted on the DOT Web site (wwwcf.fhwa.dot.gov). Bridges can be classified as deficient as a result of deterioration, poor maintenance, or by original design (for example, too narrow for modern traffic).

K-4 Traffic Deaths Per 100 Million Vehicle-Miles, 2005: Relating deaths to total miles traveled is a common way of measuring the safety of highways. Many factors could affect the totals, including weather conditions, highway designs, congestion, and traffic law enforcement by the states. The figures come from the Department of Transportation (see notes to Table K-1).

K-5 Percentage of Drivers Using Seat Belts, 2005: These data come from periodic checks of safety belt usage, as reported by the Department of Transportation, National Highway Traffic Safety Administration in "Safety Belt Use in 2005" (www-nrd.nhtsa.dot.gov).

K-6 Vehicle-Miles Traveled Per Capita, 2005: Vehicle-miles of travel, as reported by the Department of Transportation in *2005 Highway Statistics*, show the intensity of use of state highway systems. Vehicle-miles per capita show that the average American travels 10,088 miles a year. Short distances between homes, stores, and offices plus mass transit make usage lowest in northern urban areas.

K-7 Percentage of Workers Using Public Transportation, 2005: This table shows the percentage of workers who used public transportation systems for their journeys to work in 2005. The estimates come from questions about transportation usage from the Census 2004 American Community Survey.

K-8 Road and Street Miles, 2005: These data, from the same source as Table K-1, reflect total road and street (as distinct from highway) miles. They show the percentage of these miles that are controlled and maintained by state governments. Some states, such as Delaware and Virginia, maintain many local service roads that are controlled and maintained by counties and municipalities in other states.

K-9 State and Local Highway Employees, 2005: This statistic comes from a U.S. Census Bureau survey of state and local government employment, *Public Employment in 2005*. It is available on the Internet at the bureau's Web site (www.census.gov). The data show the higher levels of employees, and thus costs, associated with maintaining highways in rural states.

K-10 State and Local Public Transit Employees, 2005: This statistic, from the same source as Table K-9, shows the higher levels of employees, and thus costs, associated with transit in urbanized states.

K-11 State and Local Spending for Highways, FY 2004: This table relates spending data to population and personal income in each state. The spending data, which cover local streets as well as state highways, come from the U.S. Census Bureau's electronic publication "State and Local Government Finance Estimates, by State," available on the bureau's Web site (www.census.gov). Population numbers, also from the census, are as of July 1, 2004, and personal income numbers are from the Department of Commerce. Based on census historical practices, *State Fact Finder* used calendar year 2003 numbers. See notes to Table F-1 for more extensive information on the source of the data.

K-12 State and Local Highway Spending as a Percentage of General Spending, FY 2004: This table shows the relative importance of highway outlays in state and local budgets. It is derived by comparing highway spending with total "general" spending (see notes to Table K-11). General spending includes essentially all other spending excepting municipal electric and other utilities and trust funds, such as those for workers' compensation.

Welfare

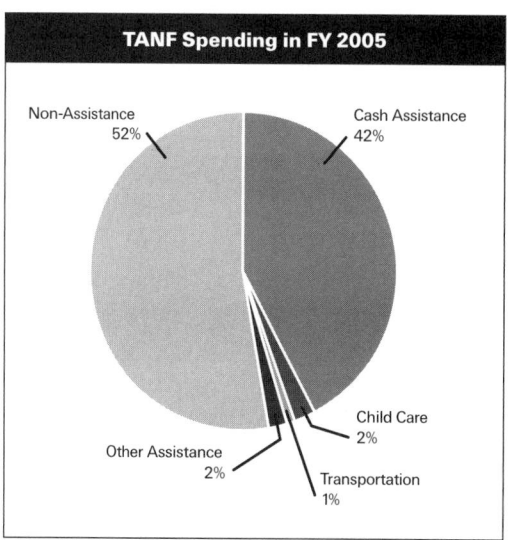

Source: U.S. Department of Health and Human Services, Administration for Children and Families

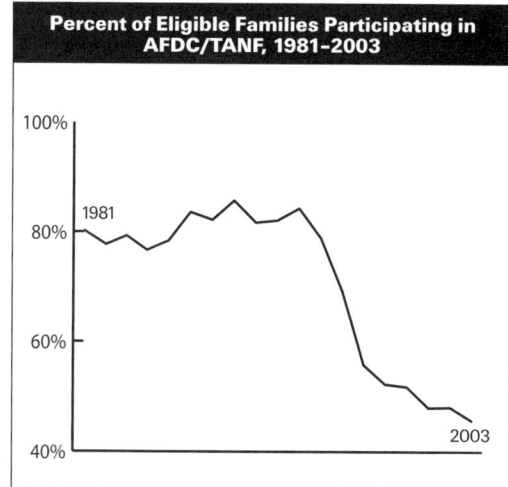

Source: U.S. Department of Health and Human Services, Administration for Children and Families

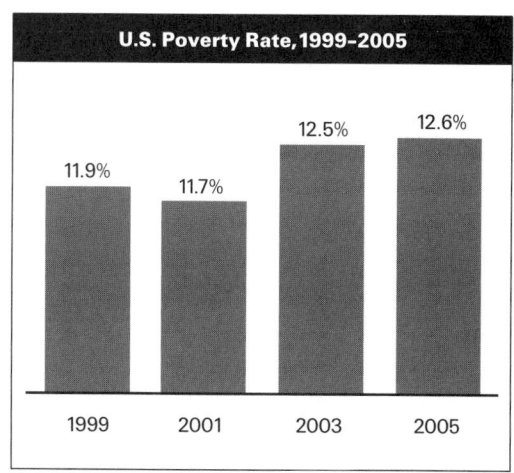

Source: U.S. Census Bureau

L-1 Percentage of Births to Unwed Mothers, 2004

State	Percentage of births to unwed mothers	Rank
Alabama	36.2	20
Alaska	34.6	28
Arizona	42.2	5
Arkansas	38.8	10
California	34.4	29
Colorado	27.5	47
Connecticut	30.6	40
Delaware	42.3	4
Florida	41.4	7
Georgia	39.2	9
Hawaii	33.4	32
Idaho	22.6	49
Illinois	36.3	19
Indiana	38.8	10
Iowa	31.0	38
Kansas	33.0	33
Kentucky	35.0	26
Louisiana	49.1	1
Maine	34.1	31
Maryland	35.7	22
Massachusetts	28.5	46
Michigan	35.7	22
Minnesota	29.0	45
Mississippi	48.3	3
Missouri	37.0	17
Montana	34.3	30
Nebraska	30.2	42
Nevada	39.7	8
New Hampshire	26.4	48
New Jersey	30.1	43
New Mexico	48.8	2
New York	37.8	14
North Carolina	36.9	18
North Dakota	29.9	44
Ohio	37.4	15
Oklahoma	38.4	12
Oregon	32.5	34
Pennsylvania	35.2	24
Rhode Island	37.3	16
South Carolina	41.9	6
South Dakota	35.1	25
Tennessee	38.2	13
Texas	36.0	21
Utah	17.5	50
Vermont	32.3	35
Virginia	31.0	38
Washington	30.4	41
West Virginia	34.8	27
Wisconsin	31.3	37
Wyoming	31.7	36
50 States	n/a	
DC	55.9	
United States	35.8	

Rank in order by percentage

1	Louisiana
2	New Mexico
3	Mississippi
4	Delaware
5	Arizona
6	South Carolina
7	Florida
8	Nevada
9	Georgia
10	Arkansas
10	Indiana
12	Oklahoma
13	Tennessee
14	New York
15	Ohio
16	Rhode Island
17	Missouri
18	North Carolina
19	Illinois
20	Alabama
21	Texas
22	Maryland
22	Michigan
24	Pennsylvania
25	South Dakota
26	Kentucky
27	West Virginia
28	Alaska
29	California
30	Montana
31	Maine
32	Hawaii
33	Kansas
34	Oregon
35	Vermont
36	Wyoming
37	Wisconsin
38	Iowa
38	Virginia
40	Connecticut
41	Washington
42	Nebraska
43	New Jersey
44	North Dakota
45	Minnesota
46	Massachusetts
47	Colorado
48	New Hampshire
49	Idaho
50	Utah

Note: Ties in ranking reflect ties in actual values.

L-2 Temporary Assistance for Needy Families (TANF) Recipients, 2006

State	Average monthly number of recipients	Average monthly number of families	Recipients as a percentage of population	Rank by percentage
Alabama	44,445	18,992	1.0	31
Alaska	10,737	3,883	1.6	13
Arizona	86,493	39,496	1.5	18
Arkansas	17,770	8,194	0.6	44
California	1,055,250	451,961	2.9	2
Colorado	39,195	15,131	0.8	33
Connecticut	36,520	18,236	1.0	30
Delaware	11,980	5,434	1.4	19
Florida	84,309	51,835	0.5	47
Georgia	62,252	31,775	0.7	40
Hawaii	17,407	6,935	1.4	21
Idaho	3,126	1,848	0.2	49
Illinois	91,857	37,019	0.7	38
Indiana	119,732	47,444	1.9	8
Iowa	40,223	16,720	1.4	22
Kansas	44,377	17,052	1.6	14
Kentucky	70,083	33,150	1.7	11
Louisiana	24,307	11,030	0.5	45
Maine	24,619	9,131	1.9	9
Maryland	46,207	20,164	0.8	34
Massachusetts	93,443	46,641	1.5	17
Michigan	215,319	81,326	2.1	5
Minnesota	67,469	27,738	1.3	24
Mississippi	26,939	13,078	0.9	32
Missouri	94,074	38,956	1.6	12
Montana	10,370	3,982	1.1	27
Nebraska	24,517	10,262	1.4	20
Nevada	11,818	5,269	0.5	46
New Hampshire	13,858	6,157	1.1	29
New Jersey	100,906	40,839	1.2	26
New Mexico	42,588	16,815	2.2	4
New York	309,042	135,256	1.6	15
North Carolina	58,320	30,111	0.7	42
North Dakota	6,923	2,720	1.1	28
Ohio	169,045	79,161	1.5	16
Oklahoma	23,492	10,537	0.7	43
Oregon	45,969	20,248	1.3	25
Pennsylvania	247,536	95,555	2.0	7
Rhode Island	23,918	9,683	2.2	3
South Carolina	34,473	15,291	0.8	35
South Dakota	5,934	2,780	0.8	37
Tennessee	180,792	68,381	3.0	1
Texas	154,153	68,742	0.7	41
Utah	18,890	7,745	0.8	36
Vermont	10,895	4,401	1.7	10
Virginia	26,259	9,240	0.3	48
Washington	130,227	55,128	2.1	6
West Virginia	24,040	11,004	1.3	23
Wisconsin	38,841	17,727	0.7	39
Wyoming	539	302	0.1	50
50 States	4,141,478	1,780,505	1.4	
DC	38,506	15,683	7.0	
United States*	4,230,951	1,814,040	1.4	

*Due to rounding or data sources, the 50-state total plus D.C. may not equal the U.S. total. Please see introduction.

Rank in order by percentage

1	Tennessee
2	California
3	Rhode Island
4	New Mexico
5	Michigan
6	Washington
7	Pennsylvania
8	Indiana
9	Maine
10	Vermont
11	Kentucky
12	Missouri
13	Alaska
14	Kansas
15	New York
16	Ohio
17	Massachusetts
18	Arizona
19	Delaware
20	Nebraska
21	Hawaii
22	Iowa
23	West Virginia
24	Minnesota
25	Oregon
26	New Jersey
27	Montana
28	North Dakota
29	New Hampshire
30	Connecticut
31	Alabama
32	Mississippi
33	Colorado
34	Maryland
35	South Carolina
36	Utah
37	South Dakota
38	Illinois
39	Wisconsin
40	Georgia
41	Texas
42	North Carolina
43	Oklahoma
44	Arkansas
45	Louisiana
46	Nevada
47	Florida
48	Virginia
49	Idaho
50	Wyoming

Note: Numbers that appear to be identical are rounded and vary slightly in actual value. The rankings reflect the actual values before rounding. See the introduction for more details.

Change in TANF/AFDC Recipients, FY 1996–2006

State	Average monthly AFDC recipients FY 1996	Percentage decrease FY 1996–2006	Rank by percentage decrease
Alabama	100,662	-55.8	35
Alaska	35,544	-69.8	19
Arizona	169,442	-49.0	43
Arkansas	56,343	-68.5	21
California	2,581,948	-59.1	28
Colorado	95,788	-59.1	29
Connecticut	159,246	-77.1	10
Delaware	23,654	-49.4	42
Florida	533,801	-84.2	5
Georgia	330,302	-81.2	7
Hawaii	66,482	-73.8	15
Idaho	21,780	-85.6	4
Illinois	642,644	-85.7	3
Indiana	142,604	-16.0	50
Iowa	86,146	-53.3	39
Kansas	63,783	-30.4	48
Kentucky	172,193	-59.3	27
Louisiana	228,115	-89.3	2
Maine	53,873	-54.3	37
Maryland	194,127	-76.2	12
Massachusetts	226,030	-58.7	30
Michigan	502,354	-57.1	34
Minnesota	169,744	-60.3	26
Mississippi	123,828	-78.2	8
Missouri	222,820	-57.8	31
Montana	29,130	-64.4	23
Nebraska	39,228	-37.5	47
Nevada	34,261	-65.5	22
New Hampshire	22,937	-39.6	46
New Jersey	275,637	-63.4	24
New Mexico	99,661	-57.3	33
New York	1,143,962	-73.0	17
North Carolina	267,326	-78.2	9
North Dakota	13,146	-47.3	44
Ohio	549,312	-69.2	20
Oklahoma	96,201	-75.6	13
Oregon	78,419	-41.4	45
Pennsylvania	531,059	-53.4	38
Rhode Island	56,560	-57.7	32
South Carolina	114,273	-69.8	18
South Dakota	15,896	-62.7	25
Tennessee	254,818	-29.1	49
Texas	649,018	-76.2	11
Utah	39,073	-51.7	40
Vermont	24,331	-55.2	36
Virginia	152,845	-82.8	6
Washington	268,927	-51.6	41
West Virginia	89,039	-73.0	16
Wisconsin	148,888	-73.9	14
Wyoming	11,398	-95.3	1
50 States	12,008,598	-65.5	
DC	69,292	-44.4	
United States*	12,242,125	-65.4	

Rank in order by percentage decrease

1	Wyoming
2	Louisiana
3	Illinois
4	Idaho
5	Florida
6	Virginia
7	Georgia
8	Mississippi
9	North Carolina
10	Connecticut
11	Texas
12	Maryland
13	Oklahoma
14	Wisconsin
15	Hawaii
16	West Virginia
17	New York
18	South Carolina
19	Alaska
20	Ohio
21	Arkansas
22	Nevada
23	Montana
24	New Jersey
25	South Dakota
26	Minnesota
27	Kentucky
28	California
29	Colorado
30	Massachusetts
31	Missouri
32	Rhode Island
33	New Mexico
34	Michigan
35	Alabama
36	Vermont
37	Maine
38	Pennsylvania
39	Iowa
40	Utah
41	Washington
42	Delaware
43	Arizona
44	North Dakota
45	Oregon
46	New Hampshire
47	Nebraska
48	Kansas
49	Tennessee
50	Indiana

Note: Numbers that appear to be identical are rounded and vary slightly in actual value. The rankings reflect the actual values before rounding. See the introduction for more details.

*Due to rounding or data sources, the 50-state total plus D.C. may not equal the U.S. total. Please see introduction.

L-4   Food Stamp Recipients, FY 2006

State	Food stamp recipients #	Recipients as a percentage of population	Rank by percentage
Alabama	538,517	11.8	12
Alaska	60,184	9.1	22
Arizona	534,186	9.0	23
Arkansas	382,061	13.7	6
California	2,005,494	5.6	42
Colorado	256,486	5.5	43
Connecticut	212,568	6.1	41
Delaware	66,201	7.8	27
Florida	1,232,111	6.9	31
Georgia	932,955	10.3	16
Hawaii	86,251	6.8	35
Idaho	91,032	6.4	40
Illinois	1,233,782	9.7	18
Indiana	575,602	9.2	21
Iowa	229,199	7.7	28
Kansas	180,105	6.6	38
Kentucky	587,274	14.1	3
Louisiana	636,371	14.1	4
Maine	154,415	11.7	13
Maryland	305,595	5.5	44
Massachusetts	434,201	6.8	34
Michigan	1,149,212	11.4	14
Minnesota	268,483	5.2	46
Mississippi	404,165	13.8	5
Missouri	795,963	13.7	7
Montana	81,870	8.7	25
Nebraska	119,836	6.8	33
Nevada	117,221	4.9	47
New Hampshire	56,865	4.3	50
New Jersey	406,670	4.7	49
New Mexico	245,484	12.7	8
New York	1,791,725	9.3	20
North Carolina	855,547	9.9	17
North Dakota	41,542	6.5	39
Ohio	1,074,637	9.4	19
Oklahoma	433,476	12.2	10
Oregon	434,567	11.9	11
Pennsylvania	1,092,193	8.8	24
Rhode Island	73,500	6.8	32
South Carolina	532,491	12.5	9
South Dakota	59,457	7.7	29
Tennessee	868,921	14.6	2
Texas	2,424,937	10.6	15
Utah	130,113	5.3	45
Vermont	47,359	7.6	30
Virginia	506,733	6.7	36
Washington	539,086	8.6	26
West Virginia	265,987	14.6	1
Wisconsin	370,455	6.7	37
Wyoming	23,816	4.7	48
50 States	25,946,901	8.8	
DC	88,517	16.1	
United States*	26,076,409	8.8	

Due to rounding or data sources, the 50-state total plus D.C. may not equal the U.S. total. Please see introduction.

	Rank in order by percentage
1	West Virginia
2	Tennessee
3	Kentucky
4	Louisiana
5	Mississippi
6	Arkansas
7	Missouri
8	New Mexico
9	South Carolina
10	Oklahoma
11	Oregon
12	Alabama
13	Maine
14	Michigan
15	Texas
16	Georgia
17	North Carolina
18	Illinois
19	Ohio
20	New York
21	Indiana
22	Alaska
23	Arizona
24	Pennsylvania
25	Montana
26	Washington
27	Delaware
28	Iowa
29	South Dakota
30	Vermont
31	Florida
32	Rhode Island
33	Nebraska
34	Massachusetts
35	Hawaii
36	Virginia
37	Wisconsin
38	Kansas
39	North Dakota
40	Idaho
41	Connecticut
42	California
43	Colorado
44	Maryland
45	Utah
46	Minnesota
47	Nevada
48	Wyoming
49	New Jersey
50	New Hampshire

Note: Numbers that appear to be identical are rounded and vary slightly in actual value. The rankings reflect the actual values before rounding. See the introduction for more details.

L-5 Supplemental Security Income (SSI) Recipients, 2005

State	SSI recipients #	Recipients as a percentage of population	Rank by percentage
Alabama	163,878	3.6	4
Alaska	11,064	1.7	32
Arizona	97,934	1.6	34
Arkansas	90,968	3.3	8
California	1,209,842	3.3	6
Colorado	55,532	1.2	47
Connecticut	52,260	1.5	40
Delaware	13,767	1.6	35
Florida	423,209	2.4	16
Georgia	203,555	2.2	19
Hawaii	22,754	1.8	28
Idaho	22,261	1.6	39
Illinois	258,634	2.0	25
Indiana	98,614	1.6	38
Iowa	43,373	1.5	41
Kansas	39,162	1.4	42
Kentucky	179,955	4.3	1
Louisiana	152,698	3.4	5
Maine	31,990	2.4	15
Maryland	94,656	1.7	30
Massachusetts	171,137	2.7	12
Michigan	222,053	2.2	21
Minnesota	72,943	1.4	43
Mississippi	124,584	4.3	2
Missouri	117,760	2.0	24
Montana	14,793	1.6	37
Nebraska	22,331	1.3	45
Nevada	33,479	1.4	44
New Hampshire	13,689	1.0	49
New Jersey	152,142	1.7	29
New Mexico	53,865	2.8	10
New York	633,473	3.3	7
North Carolina	199,337	2.3	17
North Dakota	7,907	1.2	46
Ohio	250,364	2.2	22
Oklahoma	79,743	2.2	18
Oregon	60,701	1.7	31
Pennsylvania	317,808	2.6	13
Rhode Island	30,164	2.8	9
South Carolina	105,553	2.5	14
South Dakota	12,542	1.6	36
Tennessee	161,322	2.7	11
Texas	504,082	2.2	20
Utah	22,606	0.9	50
Vermont	13,110	2.1	23
Virginia	137,662	1.8	27
Washington	115,692	1.8	26
West Virginia	76,820	4.2	3
Wisconsin	92,288	1.7	33
Wyoming	5,786	1.1	48
50 States	7,091,842	2.4	
DC	21,108	3.8	
United States*	7,113,879	2.4	

Rank in order by percentage

1 Kentucky
2 Mississippi
3 West Virginia
4 Alabama
5 Louisiana
6 California
7 New York
8 Arkansas
9 Rhode Island
10 New Mexico
11 Tennessee
12 Massachusetts
13 Pennsylvania
14 South Carolina
15 Maine
16 Florida
17 North Carolina
18 Oklahoma
19 Georgia
20 Texas
21 Michigan
22 Ohio
23 Vermont
24 Missouri
25 Illinois
26 Washington
27 Virginia
28 Hawaii
29 New Jersey
30 Maryland
31 Oregon
32 Alaska
33 Wisconsin
34 Arizona
35 Delaware
36 South Dakota
37 Montana
38 Indiana
39 Idaho
40 Connecticut
41 Iowa
42 Kansas
43 Minnesota
44 Nevada
45 Nebraska
46 North Dakota
47 Colorado
48 Wyoming
49 New Hampshire
50 Utah

Note: Numbers that appear to be identical are rounded and vary slightly in actual value. The rankings reflect the actual values before rounding. See the introduction for more details.

Due to rounding or data sources, the 50-state total plus D.C. may not equal the U.S. total. Please see introduction.

L-6 Women, Infants, and Children (WIC) Recipients and Average Monthly Benefit, FY 2005

State	Average monthly WIC recipients #	Average monthly benefit $	Rank by benefit amount
Alabama	118,751	44.52	4
Alaska	26,840	45.80	2
Arizona	177,538	36.90	19
Arkansas	88,463	35.55	25
California	1,309,413	38.47	14
Colorado	84,013	33.58	34
Connecticut	52,059	42.08	7
Delaware	19,361	32.75	38
Florida	371,365	38.54	13
Georgia	267,452	36.78	20
Hawaii	32,586	52.40	1
Idaho	37,850	30.59	47
Illinois	275,094	39.99	12
Indiana	134,706	32.84	37
Iowa	67,823	32.70	40
Kansas	68,218	33.14	36
Kentucky	121,644	38.20	15
Louisiana	143,362	42.50	5
Maine	23,454	27.89	49
Maryland	108,540	31.45	44
Massachusetts	114,161	34.53	29
Michigan	226,601	34.40	31
Minnesota	123,275	34.94	28
Mississippi	101,694	40.50	11
Missouri	132,227	31.91	42
Montana	21,102	35.03	27
Nebraska	40,818	35.17	26
Nevada	48,803	30.99	45
New Hampshire	16,677	30.86	46
New Jersey	146,888	37.76	17
New Mexico	64,216	35.98	23
New York	482,807	44.70	3
North Carolina	225,252	37.96	16
North Dakota	14,248	41.66	8
Ohio	272,632	33.92	33
Oklahoma	119,779	32.65	41
Oregon	102,793	36.42	21
Pennsylvania	240,754	33.25	35
Rhode Island	22,914	35.98	23
South Carolina	108,341	37.20	18
South Dakota	21,580	32.72	39
Tennessee	155,330	42.26	6
Texas	892,195	31.62	43
Utah	68,147	27.36	50
Vermont	16,306	41.46	9
Virginia	138,221	34.53	29
Washington	160,703	40.97	10
West Virginia	49,961	36.02	22
Wisconsin	112,942	34.34	32
Wyoming	12,699	29.23	48
50 States	7,782,598	n/a	
DC	15,923	42.67	
United States*	8,022,615	37.42	

Due to rounding or data sources, the 50-state total plus D.C. may not equal the U.S. total. Please see introduction.

Rank in order by benefit amount	
1	Hawaii
2	Alaska
3	New York
4	Alabama
5	Louisiana
6	Tennessee
7	Connecticut
8	North Dakota
9	Vermont
10	Washington
11	Mississippi
12	Illinois
13	Florida
14	California
15	Kentucky
16	North Carolina
17	New Jersey
18	South Carolina
19	Arizona
20	Georgia
21	Oregon
22	West Virginia
23	New Mexico
23	Rhode Island
25	Arkansas
26	Nebraska
27	Montana
28	Minnesota
29	Massachusetts
29	Virginia
31	Michigan
32	Wisconsin
33	Ohio
34	Colorado
35	Pennsylvania
36	Kansas
37	Indiana
38	Delaware
39	South Dakota
40	Iowa
41	Oklahoma
42	Missouri
43	Texas
44	Maryland
45	Nevada
46	New Hampshire
47	Idaho
48	Wyoming
49	Maine
50	Utah

Note: Ties in ranking reflect ties in actual values.

National School Lunch Program (NSLP) Participants, FY 2006

State	NSLP participants #	Participation rate	Rank by rate
Alabama	566,207	75.4	7
Alaska	53,180	50.8	44
Arizona	603,646	61.0	30
Arkansas	344,449	72.6	11
California	2,884,753	46.8	49
Colorado	345,131	47.6	48
Connecticut	306,936	55.8	37
Delaware	83,309	67.1	16
Florida	1,519,972	56.4	35
Georgia	1,246,093	77.4	4
Hawaii	112,106	61.3	28
Idaho	160,687	69.2	13
Illinois	1,099,246	56.6	34
Indiana	718,779	68.4	14
Iowa	388,469	73.6	9
Kansas	330,390	65.2	20
Kentucky	540,505	75.7	6
Louisiana	567,160	83.3	1
Maine	108,808	55.1	38
Maryland	444,674	50.9	42
Massachusetts	559,073	56.7	33
Michigan	887,069	50.3	45
Minnesota	595,531	67.3	15
Mississippi	402,363	78.3	2
Missouri	632,346	65.2	21
Montana	82,793	56.9	32
Nebraska	231,671	78.2	3
Nevada	180,769	41.2	50
New Hampshire	112,533	54.4	40
New Jersey	639,450	49.8	46
New Mexico	211,944	62.7	25
New York	1,817,930	59.0	31
North Carolina	941,106	65.7	19
North Dakota	78,470	74.9	8
Ohio	1,085,302	48.8	47
Oklahoma	410,524	64.7	22
Oregon	300,858	54.5	39
Pennsylvania	1,135,896	61.4	27
Rhode Island	83,761	53.7	41
South Carolina	489,346	66.3	18
South Dakota	104,403	76.3	5
Tennessee	666,827	73.2	10
Texas	2,992,569	66.3	17
Utah	303,852	61.2	29
Vermont	55,160	56.2	36
Virginia	745,164	63.2	24
Washington	523,707	50.9	43
West Virginia	203,127	69.4	12
Wisconsin	590,559	64.0	23
Wyoming	52,187	62.1	26
50 States	29,540,791	n/a	
DC	45,329	63.2	
United States*	30,003,710	59.8	

Rank in order by rate	
1	Louisiana
2	Mississippi
3	Nebraska
4	Georgia
5	South Dakota
6	Kentucky
7	Alabama
8	North Dakota
9	Iowa
10	Tennessee
11	Arkansas
12	West Virginia
13	Idaho
14	Indiana
15	Minnesota
16	Delaware
17	Texas
18	South Carolina
19	North Carolina
20	Kansas
21	Missouri
22	Oklahoma
23	Wisconsin
24	Virginia
25	New Mexico
26	Wyoming
27	Pennsylvania
28	Hawaii
29	Utah
30	Arizona
31	New York
32	Montana
33	Massachusetts
34	Illinois
35	Florida
36	Vermont
37	Connecticut
38	Maine
39	Oregon
40	New Hampshire
41	Rhode Island
42	Maryland
43	Washington
44	Alaska
45	Michigan
46	New Jersey
47	Ohio
48	Colorado
49	California
50	Nevada

Note: Numbers that appear to be identical are rounded and vary slightly in actual value. The rankings reflect the actual values before rounding. See the introduction for more details.

Due to rounding or data sources, the 50-state total plus D.C. may not equal the U.S. total. Please see introduction.

L-8   Condition of Children Index, 2006

State	Condition of children index "child well-being" ranked from 1 (highest) to 50 (lowest)
Alabama	43
Alaska	35
Arizona	37
Arkansas	45
California	18
Colorado	25
Connecticut	3
Delaware	29
Florida	33
Georgia	44
Hawaii	21
Idaho	20
Illinois	24
Indiana	32
Iowa	5
Kansas	12
Kentucky	42
Louisiana	49
Maine	11
Maryland	23
Massachusetts	10
Michigan	27
Minnesota	4
Mississippi	50
Missouri	30
Montana	34
Nebraska	8
Nevada	36
New Hampshire	1
New Jersey	7
New Mexico	48
New York	22
North Carolina	41
North Dakota	9
Ohio	26
Oklahoma	40
Oregon	15
Pennsylvania	16
Rhode Island	31
South Carolina	47
South Dakota	14
Tennessee	46
Texas	39
Utah	6
Vermont	2
Virginia	19
Washington	17
West Virginia	38
Wisconsin	13
Wyoming	28
50 States	n/a
DC	n/a
United States	n/a

Rank in order by index ranked highest (1) to lowest (50)

1	New Hampshire
2	Vermont
3	Connecticut
4	Minnesota
5	Iowa
6	Utah
7	New Jersey
8	Nebraska
9	North Dakota
10	Massachusetts
11	Maine
12	Kansas
13	Wisconsin
14	South Dakota
15	Oregon
16	Pennsylvania
17	Washington
18	California
19	Virginia
20	Idaho
21	Hawaii
22	New York
23	Maryland
24	Illinois
25	Colorado
26	Ohio
27	Michigan
28	Wyoming
29	Delaware
30	Missouri
31	Rhode Island
32	Indiana
33	Florida
34	Montana
35	Alaska
36	Nevada
37	Arizona
38	West Virginia
39	Texas
40	Oklahoma
41	North Carolina
42	Kentucky
43	Alabama
44	Georgia
45	Arkansas
46	Tennessee
47	South Carolina
48	New Mexico
49	Louisiana
50	Mississippi

L-9 Percentage of Families with Children Headed by a Single Parent, 2004

State	Percentage of families headed by single parent	Rank
Alabama	36	7
Alaska	30	23
Arizona	31	19
Arkansas	38	5
California	29	27
Colorado	26	40
Connecticut	27	36
Delaware	35	9
Florida	36	7
Georgia	35	9
Hawaii	28	32
Idaho	23	48
Illinois	28	32
Indiana	28	32
Iowa	24	44
Kansas	24	44
Kentucky	30	23
Louisiana	44	1
Maine	33	15
Maryland	33	15
Massachusetts	29	27
Michigan	31	19
Minnesota	24	44
Mississippi	42	2
Missouri	31	19
Montana	27	36
Nebraska	23	48
Nevada	31	19
New Hampshire	26	40
New Jersey	25	43
New Mexico	38	5
New York	34	11
North Carolina	34	11
North Dakota	24	44
Ohio	33	15
Oklahoma	34	11
Oregon	29	27
Pennsylvania	30	23
Rhode Island	39	4
South Carolina	40	3
South Dakota	27	36
Tennessee	34	11
Texas	32	18
Utah	17	50
Vermont	26	40
Virginia	29	27
Washington	30	23
West Virginia	29	27
Wisconsin	28	32
Wyoming	27	36
50 States	n/a	
DC	68	
United States	31	

Rank in order by percentage

Rank	State
1	Louisiana
2	Mississippi
3	South Carolina
4	Rhode Island
5	Arkansas
5	New Mexico
7	Alabama
7	Florida
9	Delaware
9	Georgia
11	New York
11	North Carolina
11	Oklahoma
11	Tennessee
15	Maine
15	Maryland
15	Ohio
18	Texas
19	Arizona
19	Michigan
19	Missouri
19	Nevada
23	Alaska
23	Kentucky
23	Pennsylvania
23	Washington
27	California
27	Massachusetts
27	Oregon
27	Virginia
27	West Virginia
32	Hawaii
32	Illinois
32	Indiana
32	Wisconsin
36	Connecticut
36	Montana
36	South Dakota
36	Wyoming
40	Colorado
40	New Hampshire
40	Vermont
43	New Jersey
44	Iowa
44	Kansas
44	Minnesota
44	North Dakota
48	Idaho
48	Nebraska
50	Utah

Note: Ties in ranking reflect ties in actual values.

L-10 Average Monthly TANF Cash Assistance Per Family, FY 2005

State	Average monthly TANF payment $	Rank
Alabama	208	45
Alaska	882	5
Arizona	338	31
Arkansas	188	47
California	646	8
Colorado	414	21
Connecticut	575	11
Delaware	296	38
Florida	296	39
Georgia	308	36
Hawaii	982	3
Idaho	329	33
Illinois	275	40
Indiana	199	46
Iowa	377	26
Kansas	319	35
Kentucky	264	42
Louisiana	388	25
Maine	822	6
Maryland	514	14
Massachusetts	592	10
Michigan	422	19
Minnesota	413	22
Mississippi	171	48
Missouri	267	41
Montana	414	20
Nebraska	438	17
Nevada	524	13
New Hampshire	477	16
New Jersey	900	4
New Mexico	371	27
New York	1,086	2
North Carolina	300	37
North Dakota	342	30
Ohio	333	32
Oklahoma	263	43
Oregon	433	18
Pennsylvania	355	28
Rhode Island	620	9
South Carolina	400	23
South Dakota	349	29
Tennessee	147	49
Texas	220	44
Utah	486	15
Vermont	683	7
Virginia	1,291	1
Washington	396	24
West Virginia	326	34
Wisconsin	543	12
Wyoming	n/a	n/a
50 States	500	
DC	352	
United States	493	

Rank in order by $	
1	Virginia
2	New York
3	Hawaii
4	New Jersey
5	Alaska
6	Maine
7	Vermont
8	California
9	Rhode Island
10	Massachusetts
11	Connecticut
12	Wisconsin
13	Nevada
14	Maryland
15	Utah
16	New Hampshire
17	Nebraska
18	Oregon
19	Michigan
20	Montana
21	Colorado
22	Minnesota
23	South Carolina
24	Washington
25	Louisiana
26	Iowa
27	New Mexico
28	Pennsylvania
29	South Dakota
30	North Dakota
31	Arizona
32	Ohio
33	Idaho
34	West Virginia
35	Kansas
36	Georgia
37	North Carolina
38	Delaware
39	Florida
40	Illinois
41	Missouri
42	Kentucky
43	Oklahoma
44	Texas
45	Alabama
46	Indiana
47	Arkansas
48	Mississippi
49	Tennessee

Note: Numbers that appear to be identical are rounded and vary slightly in actual value. The rankings reflect the actual values before rounding. See the introduction for more details.

L-11 Assistance and Earnings of Three-Person TANF Family as a Percentage of Poverty-Level Income, 2003

State	Estimated assistance and earnings as a percentage of poverty-level income	Rank
Alabama	69.9	45
Alaska	103.2	3
Arizona	75.3	41
Arkansas	81.1	27
California	109.2	2
Colorado	79.4	36
Connecticut	117.8	1
Delaware	90.9	15
Florida	79.8	34
Georgia	73.6	44
Hawaii	102.1	5
Idaho	76.5	38
Illinois	83.5	21
Indiana	79.6	35
Iowa	83.5	21
Kansas	81.7	26
Kentucky	76.0	39
Louisiana	69.9	45
Maine	100.2	7
Maryland	81.1	27
Massachusetts	102.9	4
Michigan	84.3	20
Minnesota	95.2	10
Mississippi	69.9	45
Missouri	69.9	45
Montana	87.6	16
Nebraska	82.6	23
Nevada	69.9	45
New Hampshire	92.0	11
New Jersey	80.9	29
New Mexico	82.4	25
New York	91.9	12
North Carolina	76.0	39
North Dakota	85.2	18
Ohio	85.0	19
Oklahoma	77.0	37
Oregon	91.7	13
Pennsylvania	80.8	30
Rhode Island	97.7	8
South Carolina	74.9	43
South Dakota	80.8	30
Tennessee	80.1	32
Texas	69.9	45
Utah	86.4	17
Vermont	100.8	6
Virginia	91.3	14
Washington	96.9	9
West Virginia	80.1	32
Wisconsin	82.6	23
Wyoming	75.0	42
50 States	n/a	
DC	91.3	
United States	n/a	

Rank in order by percentage

1	Connecticut
2	California
3	Alaska
4	Massachusetts
5	Hawaii
6	Vermont
7	Maine
8	Rhode Island
9	Washington
10	Minnesota
11	New Hampshire
12	New York
13	Oregon
14	Virginia
15	Delaware
16	Montana
17	Utah
18	North Dakota
19	Ohio
20	Michigan
21	Illinois
21	Iowa
23	Nebraska
23	Wisconsin
25	New Mexico
26	Kansas
27	Arkansas
27	Maryland
29	New Jersey
30	Pennsylvania
30	South Dakota
32	Tennessee
32	West Virginia
34	Florida
35	Indiana
36	Colorado
37	Oklahoma
38	Idaho
39	Kentucky
39	North Carolina
41	Arizona
42	Wyoming
43	South Carolina
44	Georgia
45	Alabama
45	Louisiana
45	Mississippi
45	Missouri
45	Nevada
45	Texas

Note: Ties in ranking reflect ties in actual values.

L-12 Supplemental Security Income (SSI) State Supplements, 2005

State	Average monthly SSI state supplements per recipient $	Rank
Alabama	56.40	33
Alaska	277.90	11
Arizona	50.00	38
Arkansas	33.88	44
California	225.55	15
Colorado	219.09	16
Connecticut	433.77	6
Delaware	124.26	19
Florida	116.82	20
Georgia	39.30	43
Hawaii	436.24	5
Idaho	54.03	34
Illinois	79.03	28
Indiana	260.53	13
Iowa	499.18	2
Kansas	66.40	30
Kentucky	376.77	7
Louisiana	49.06	39
Maine	18.89	47
Maryland	268.49	12
Massachusetts	80.83	26
Michigan	160.41	18
Minnesota	191.18	17
Mississippi	60.71	32
Missouri	252.19	14
Montana	79.84	27
Nebraska	93.16	24
Nevada	50.57	37
New Hampshire	51.99	36
New Jersey	44.68	41
New Mexico	100.00	22
New York	74.17	29
North Carolina	457.43	3
North Dakota	449.43	4
Ohio	44.80	40
Oklahoma	40.08	42
Oregon	99.03	23
Pennsylvania	320.91	8
Rhode Island	63.62	31
South Carolina	314.08	9
South Dakota	81.30	25
Tennessee	25.60	45
Texas	4.68	48
Utah	3.00	49
Vermont	53.66	35
Virginia	301.58	10
Washington	513.00	1
West Virginia	n/a	n/a
Wisconsin	101.04	21
Wyoming	20.00	46
50 States	n/a	
DC	187.94	
United States	282.83	

Rank in order by $

1	Washington
2	Iowa
3	North Carolina
4	North Dakota
5	Hawaii
6	Connecticut
7	Kentucky
8	Pennsylvania
9	South Carolina
10	Virginia
11	Alaska
12	Maryland
13	Indiana
14	Missouri
15	California
16	Colorado
17	Minnesota
18	Michigan
19	Delaware
20	Florida
21	Wisconsin
22	New Mexico
23	Oregon
24	Nebraska
25	South Dakota
26	Massachusetts
27	Montana
28	Illinois
29	New York
30	Kansas
31	Rhode Island
32	Mississippi
33	Alabama
34	Idaho
35	Vermont
36	New Hampshire
37	Nevada
38	Arizona
39	Louisiana
40	Ohio
41	New Jersey
42	Oklahoma
43	Georgia
44	Arkansas
45	Tennessee
46	Wyoming
47	Maine
48	Texas
49	Utah

L-13 State Income Tax Liability of Typical Family in Poverty, 2005

State	Income tax liability $	Rank
Alabama	458	1
Alaska	n/a	n/a
Arizona	0	17
Arkansas	126	7
California	0	17
Colorado	0	17
Connecticut	0	17
Delaware	43	14
Florida	n/a	n/a
Georgia	82	10
Hawaii	373	2
Idaho	0	17
Illinois	80	11
Indiana	77	12
Iowa	0	17
Kansas	-549	35
Kentucky	0	17
Louisiana	155	5
Maine	0	17
Maryland	-626	37
Massachusetts	-622	36
Michigan	186	4
Minnesota	-1,100	39
Mississippi	35	15
Missouri	44	13
Montana	143	6
Nebraska	0	17
Nevada	n/a	n/a
New Hampshire	n/a	n/a
New Jersey	-829	38
New Mexico	-70	32
New York	-1,121	40
North Carolina	21	16
North Dakota	0	17
Ohio	90	9
Oklahoma	-17	31
Oregon	117	8
Pennsylvania	0	17
Rhode Island	-104	33
South Carolina	0	17
South Dakota	n/a	n/a
Tennessee	n/a	n/a
Texas	n/a	n/a
Utah	0	17
Vermont	-1,327	41
Virginia	0	17
Washington	n/a	n/a
West Virginia	287	3
Wisconsin	-403	34
Wyoming	n/a	n/a
50 States	n/a	
DC	-1,047	
United States	n/a	

Rank in order by $	
1	Alabama
2	Hawaii
3	West Virginia
4	Michigan
5	Louisiana
6	Montana
7	Arkansas
8	Oregon
9	Ohio
10	Georgia
11	Illinois
12	Indiana
13	Missouri
14	Delaware
15	Mississippi
16	North Carolina
17	Arizona
17	California
17	Colorado
17	Connecticut
17	Idaho
17	Iowa
17	Kentucky
17	Maine
17	Nebraska
17	North Dakota
17	Pennsylvania
17	South Carolina
17	Utah
17	Virginia
31	Oklahoma
32	New Mexico
33	Rhode Island
34	Wisconsin
35	Kansas
36	Massachusetts
37	Maryland
38	New Jersey
39	Minnesota
40	New York
41	Vermont

Note: Ties in ranking reflect ties in actual values.

L-14 Child Support Collections, FY 2005

State	Total collections $ (in thousands)	Per capita collections $	Rank per capita		Rank in order per capita
Alabama	237,315	52.07	42	1	Ohio
Alaska	85,091	128.21	3	2	Michigan
Arizona	266,572	44.88	48	3	Alaska
Arkansas	155,101	55.81	38	4	Pennsylvania
California	2,222,045	61.50	35	5	Minnesota
Colorado	236,265	50.64	44	6	Wisconsin
Connecticut	235,391	67.06	29	7	New Jersey
Delaware	66,482	78.81	19	8	Wyoming
Florida	1,076,686	60.52	36	9	North Dakota
Georgia	498,898	54.99	41	10	Iowa
Hawaii	83,584	65.55	31	11	Washington
Idaho	115,543	80.85	16	12	West Virginia
Illinois	561,788	44.02	49	13	Nebraska
Indiana	481,250	76.73	21	14	Oregon
Iowa	289,928	97.74	10	15	Maryland
Kansas	152,581	55.59	39	16	Idaho
Kentucky	336,566	80.65	17	17	Kentucky
Louisiana	289,311	63.96	33	18	Missouri
Maine	100,777	76.26	22	19	Delaware
Maryland	453,402	80.96	15	20	Texas
Massachusetts	466,045	72.83	24	21	Indiana
Michigan	1,381,522	136.50	2	22	Maine
Minnesota	568,968	110.85	5	23	South Dakota
Mississippi	195,329	66.87	30	24	Massachusetts
Missouri	467,499	80.60	18	25	New York
Montana	46,807	50.03	45	26	Vermont
Nebraska	159,217	90.53	13	27	Tennessee
Nevada	115,524	47.84	47	28	Virginia
New Hampshire	80,795	61.68	34	29	Connecticut
New Jersey	915,476	105.01	7	30	Mississippi
New Mexico	68,448	35.49	50	31	Hawaii
New York	1,400,129	72.72	25	32	North Carolina
North Carolina	565,129	65.08	32	33	Louisiana
North Dakota	62,992	98.94	9	34	New Hampshire
Ohio	1,657,505	144.58	1	35	California
Oklahoma	177,478	50.02	46	36	Florida
Oregon	303,781	83.43	14	37	Utah
Pennsylvania	1,413,913	113.75	4	38	Arkansas
Rhode Island	55,364	51.44	43	39	Kansas
South Carolina	236,178	55.50	40	40	South Carolina
South Dakota	58,450	75.33	23	41	Georgia
Tennessee	414,918	69.58	27	42	Alabama
Texas	1,781,323	77.92	20	43	Rhode Island
Utah	148,672	60.20	37	44	Colorado
Vermont	44,520	71.46	26	45	Montana
Virginia	518,976	68.58	28	46	Oklahoma
Washington	609,073	96.87	11	47	Nevada
West Virginia	171,130	94.19	12	48	Arizona
Wisconsin	601,203	108.59	6	49	Illinois
Wyoming	51,243	100.62	8	50	New Mexico
50 States	22,682,181	76.67			
DC	47,973	87.14			
United States*	23,005,880	77.61			

Due to rounding or data sources, the 50-state total plus D.C. may not equal the U.S. total. Please see introduction.

L-15   Child Support Collections Per Dollar of Administrative Costs, FY 2005

State	Collections per dollar of costs $	Rank
Alabama	4.26	35
Alaska	4.54	32
Arizona	4.73	30
Arkansas	3.68	41
California	2.15	49
Colorado	3.68	41
Connecticut	3.68	41
Delaware	3.10	47
Florida	4.80	25
Georgia	5.20	21
Hawaii	4.39	33
Idaho	5.58	17
Illinois	3.68	41
Indiana	8.53	1
Iowa	5.80	15
Kansas	3.39	46
Kentucky	5.95	12
Louisiana	4.71	31
Maine	4.27	34
Maryland	4.88	24
Massachusetts	5.93	13
Michigan	6.70	6
Minnesota	4.22	36
Mississippi	8.53	1
Missouri	5.41	19
Montana	4.02	38
Nebraska	3.57	45
Nevada	2.98	48
New Hampshire	4.75	27
New Jersey	4.74	28
New Mexico	2.10	50
New York	4.79	26
North Carolina	5.10	22
North Dakota	6.03	11
Ohio	5.66	16
Oklahoma	3.79	40
Oregon	5.93	13
Pennsylvania	6.39	9
Rhode Island	6.45	8
South Carolina	7.07	4
South Dakota	7.76	3
Tennessee	5.44	18
Texas	6.81	5
Utah	4.03	37
Vermont	3.91	39
Virginia	6.52	7
Washington	4.74	28
West Virginia	4.90	23
Wisconsin	5.41	19
Wyoming	6.25	10
50 States	n/a	
DC	2.45	
United States	4.58	

Rank in order by $

1	Indiana
1	Mississippi
3	South Dakota
4	South Carolina
5	Texas
6	Michigan
7	Virginia
8	Rhode Island
9	Pennsylvania
10	Wyoming
11	North Dakota
12	Kentucky
13	Massachusetts
13	Oregon
15	Iowa
16	Ohio
17	Idaho
18	Tennessee
19	Missouri
19	Wisconsin
21	Georgia
22	North Carolina
23	West Virginia
24	Maryland
25	Florida
26	New York
27	New Hampshire
28	New Jersey
28	Washington
30	Arizona
31	Louisiana
32	Alaska
33	Hawaii
34	Maine
35	Alabama
36	Minnesota
37	Utah
38	Montana
39	Vermont
40	Oklahoma
41	Arkansas
41	Colorado
41	Connecticut
41	Illinois
45	Nebraska
46	Kansas
47	Delaware
48	Nevada
49	California
50	New Mexico

Note: Ties in ranking reflect ties in actual values.

L-16   Children in Foster Care, FY 2003

State	Children in foster care #	Children in foster care per 10,000 children #	Rank per 10,000 children
Alabama	6,079	55	37
Alaska	2,040	108	3
Arizona	7,469	49	38
Arkansas	3,000	44	41
California	97,261	103	7
Colorado	8,754	76	24
Connecticut	6,742	81	21
Delaware	814	41	43
Florida	30,677	78	22
Georgia	13,578	59	33
Hawaii	2,967	100	9
Idaho	1,401	38	47
Illinois	21,608	67	29
Indiana	8,899	55	36
Iowa	5,011	72	25
Kansas	5,781	83	18
Kentucky	6,895	69	26
Louisiana	4,541	39	46
Maine	2,999	105	5
Maryland	11,521	84	17
Massachusetts	12,608	85	13
Michigan	21,376	84	16
Minnesota	7,338	59	34
Mississippi	2,812	37	48
Missouri	11,900	85	14
Montana	1,866	86	12
Nebraska	6,091	138	1
Nevada	3,599	62	30
New Hampshire	1,217	40	44
New Jersey	12,801	60	32
New Mexico	2,100	42	42
New York	37,067	82	19
North Carolina	9,534	46	40
North Dakota	1,238	84	15
Ohio	19,323	69	27
Oklahoma	9,194	105	4
Oregon	9,381	110	2
Pennsylvania	21,768	77	23
Rhode Island	2,334	96	10
South Carolina	4,894	48	39
South Dakota	1,580	81	20
Tennessee	9,487	68	28
Texas	22,191	36	49
Utah	2,033	27	50
Vermont	1,409	103	8
Virginia	7,046	39	45
Washington	9,213	62	31
West Virginia	4,069	104	6
Wisconsin	7,824	59	35
Wyoming	1,055	87	11
50 States	512,385	70	
DC	3,092	285	
United States*	523,085	72	

Rank in order per 10,000 children	
1	Nebraska
2	Oregon
3	Alaska
4	Oklahoma
5	Maine
6	West Virginia
7	California
8	Vermont
9	Hawaii
10	Rhode Island
11	Wyoming
12	Montana
13	Massachusetts
14	Missouri
15	North Dakota
16	Michigan
17	Maryland
18	Kansas
19	New York
20	South Dakota
21	Connecticut
22	Florida
23	Pennsylvania
24	Colorado
25	Iowa
26	Kentucky
27	Ohio
28	Tennessee
29	Illinois
30	Nevada
31	Washington
32	New Jersey
33	Georgia
34	Minnesota
35	Wisconsin
36	Indiana
37	Alabama
38	Arizona
39	South Carolina
40	North Carolina
41	Arkansas
42	New Mexico
43	Delaware
44	New Hampshire
45	Virginia
46	Louisiana
47	Idaho
48	Mississippi
49	Texas
50	Utah

Note: Numbers that appear to be identical are rounded and vary slightly in actual value. The rankings reflect the actual values before rounding. See the introduction for more details.

*Due to rounding or data sources, the 50-state total plus D.C. may not equal the U.S. total. Please see introduction.

L-17 State and Local Welfare Spending, FY 2004

State	Welfare spending $ (in millions)	Per capita $	Percentage of personal income	Rank per capita
Alabama	4,624	1,021	3.9	27
Alaska	1,375	2,097	6.4	2
Arizona	4,969	865	3.3	44
Arkansas	3,012	1,094	4.5	23
California	40,209	1,120	3.4	21
Colorado	3,183	692	2.0	49
Connecticut	4,173	1,191	2.8	17
Delaware	1,020	1,229	3.7	16
Florida	16,117	926	3.2	37
Georgia	8,693	985	3.4	34
Hawaii	1,367	1,083	3.6	24
Idaho	1,231	884	3.5	43
Illinois	11,534	907	2.7	41
Indiana	5,741	920	3.2	38
Iowa	3,081	1,043	3.7	26
Kansas	2,499	914	3.1	40
Kentucky	5,268	1,271	4.9	13
Louisiana	4,079	903	3.5	42
Maine	2,308	1,752	6.1	4
Maryland	5,610	1,009	2.7	29
Massachusetts	10,305	1,606	4.1	7
Michigan	10,245	1,013	3.3	28
Minnesota	8,907	1,746	5.2	5
Mississippi	3,866	1,332	5.7	10
Missouri	5,714	993	3.4	33
Montana	776	837	3.3	46
Nebraska	1,943	1,112	3.7	22
Nevada	1,454	623	2.1	50
New Hampshire	1,515	1,166	3.4	19
New Jersey	8,147	937	2.4	36
New Mexico	2,556	1,343	5.3	9
New York	40,518	2,107	5.8	1
North Carolina	8,570	1,003	3.6	30
North Dakota	719	1,133	4.0	20
Ohio	14,592	1,273	4.3	12
Oklahoma	3,527	1,001	3.8	31
Oregon	3,523	980	3.4	35
Pennsylvania	17,650	1,423	4.5	8
Rhode Island	1,939	1,795	5.6	3
South Carolina	4,931	1,175	4.5	18
South Dakota	706	916	3.3	39
Tennessee	7,811	1,324	4.7	11
Texas	18,204	809	2.8	48
Utah	2,007	840	3.4	45
Vermont	1,016	1,634	5.4	6
Virginia	6,215	833	2.5	47
Washington	6,495	1,047	3.2	25
West Virginia	2,262	1,246	5.1	14
Wisconsin	6,858	1,245	4.1	15
Wyoming	506	1,000	3.1	32
50 States	333,571	1,138	3.7	
DC	1,686	3,046	6.3	
United States	335,257	1,142	3.7	

Rank in order per capita	
1	New York
2	Alaska
3	Rhode Island
4	Maine
5	Minnesota
6	Vermont
7	Massachusetts
8	Pennsylvania
9	New Mexico
10	Mississippi
11	Tennessee
12	Ohio
13	Kentucky
14	West Virginia
15	Wisconsin
16	Delaware
17	Connecticut
18	South Carolina
19	New Hampshire
20	North Dakota
21	California
22	Nebraska
23	Arkansas
24	Hawaii
25	Washington
26	Iowa
27	Alabama
28	Michigan
29	Maryland
30	North Carolina
31	Oklahoma
32	Wyoming
33	Missouri
34	Georgia
35	Oregon
36	New Jersey
37	Florida
38	Indiana
39	South Dakota
40	Kansas
41	Illinois
42	Louisiana
43	Idaho
44	Arizona
45	Utah
46	Montana
47	Virginia
48	Texas
49	Colorado
50	Nevada

L-18 State and Local Welfare Spending as a Percentage of General Spending, FY 2004

State	Welfare spending as a percentage of general spending	Rank by percentage
Alabama	17.1	25
Alaska	16.2	32
Arizona	16.5	28
Arkansas	20.7	12
California	15.4	37
Colorado	11.2	48
Connecticut	16.7	27
Delaware	16.5	29
Florida	16.0	34
Georgia	17.3	22
Hawaii	15.8	36
Idaho	16.3	31
Illinois	14.5	43
Indiana	16.2	33
Iowa	16.7	26
Kansas	15.3	38
Kentucky	22.6	7
Louisiana	15.0	41
Maine	24.9	2
Maryland	16.4	30
Massachusetts	21.3	11
Michigan	15.1	40
Minnesota	24.3	4
Mississippi	22.4	8
Missouri	18.4	19
Montana	14.0	46
Nebraska	18.0	20
Nevada	10.7	50
New Hampshire	20.1	14
New Jersey	13.3	47
New Mexico	20.3	13
New York	23.0	6
North Carolina	17.7	21
North Dakota	17.3	23
Ohio	19.6	15
Oklahoma	19.4	16
Oregon	15.8	35
Pennsylvania	22.0	9
Rhode Island	25.4	1
South Carolina	19.3	17
South Dakota	17.1	24
Tennessee	24.7	3
Texas	14.7	42
Utah	14.4	45
Vermont	23.1	5
Virginia	14.5	44
Washington	15.3	39
West Virginia	21.3	10
Wisconsin	18.7	18
Wyoming	11.2	49
50 States	17.6	
DC	25.1	
United States	17.6	

Rank in order by percentage	
1	Rhode Island
2	Maine
3	Tennessee
4	Minnesota
5	Vermont
6	New York
7	Kentucky
8	Mississippi
9	Pennsylvania
10	West Virginia
11	Massachusetts
12	Arkansas
13	New Mexico
14	New Hampshire
15	Ohio
16	Oklahoma
17	South Carolina
18	Wisconsin
19	Missouri
20	Nebraska
21	North Carolina
22	Georgia
23	North Dakota
24	South Dakota
25	Alabama
26	Iowa
27	Connecticut
28	Arizona
29	Delaware
30	Maryland
31	Idaho
32	Alaska
33	Indiana
34	Florida
35	Oregon
36	Hawaii
37	California
38	Kansas
39	Washington
40	Michigan
41	Louisiana
42	Texas
43	Illinois
44	Virginia
45	Utah
46	Montana
47	New Jersey
48	Colorado
49	Wyoming
50	Nevada

Note: Numbers that appear to be identical are rounded and vary slightly in actual value. The rankings reflect the actual values before rounding. See the introduction for more details.

L-19   Average Monthly Administrative Costs Per TANF Case, FY 2005

State	Costs per case $	Rank
Alabama	54.33	39
Alaska	124.51	20
Arizona	81.20	34
Arkansas	78.78	35
California	97.76	28
Colorado	115.97	21
Connecticut	133.72	16
Delaware	88.35	31
Florida	149.45	10
Georgia	49.84	43
Hawaii	144.53	12
Idaho	99.70	27
Illinois	52.11	41
Indiana	71.09	36
Iowa	66.79	38
Kansas	40.92	47
Kentucky	41.68	46
Louisiana	184.05	7
Maine	54.00	40
Maryland	141.07	13
Massachusetts	50.73	42
Michigan	96.86	29
Minnesota	135.72	15
Mississippi	33.96	50
Missouri	43.45	45
Montana	113.10	23
Nebraska	46.72	44
Nevada	262.73	3
New Hampshire	96.46	30
New Jersey	163.05	9
New Mexico	35.70	48
New York	227.67	4
North Carolina	108.24	25
North Dakota	105.02	26
Ohio	139.28	14
Oklahoma	124.85	19
Oregon	110.80	24
Pennsylvania	86.75	33
Rhode Island	125.10	18
South Carolina	114.92	22
South Dakota	86.97	32
Tennessee	34.92	49
Texas	146.73	11
Utah	210.94	5
Vermont	126.54	17
Virginia	419.67	1
Washington	68.56	37
West Virginia	188.98	6
Wisconsin	167.28	8
Wyoming	284.01	2
50 States	108.28	
DC	79.18	
United States	106.96	

Rank in order by $	
1	Virginia
2	Wyoming
3	Nevada
4	New York
5	Utah
6	West Virginia
7	Louisiana
8	Wisconsin
9	New Jersey
10	Florida
11	Texas
12	Hawaii
13	Maryland
14	Ohio
15	Minnesota
16	Connecticut
17	Vermont
18	Rhode Island
19	Oklahoma
20	Alaska
21	Colorado
22	South Carolina
23	Montana
24	Oregon
25	North Carolina
26	North Dakota
27	Idaho
28	California
29	Michigan
30	New Hampshire
31	Delaware
32	South Dakota
33	Pennsylvania
34	Arizona
35	Arkansas
36	Indiana
37	Washington
38	Iowa
39	Alabama
40	Maine
41	Illinois
42	Massachusetts
43	Georgia
44	Nebraska
45	Missouri
46	Kentucky
47	Kansas
48	New Mexico
49	Tennessee
50	Mississippi

Source Notes for Welfare (Section L)

L-1 Percentage of Births to Unwed Mothers, 2004: These data come from state reports summarized by the National Center for Health Statistics in its *National Vital Statistics Report* (vol. 55, no. 1, September 29, 2006). The birth data, which come from hospitals, are highly reliable, but some states report the marital status of mothers somewhat differently.

L-2 TANF Recipients, Total and as a Percentage of Population, 2006: This table, from the Department of Health and Human Services Web site (www.acf.dhhs.gov), shows the total number of recipients and families receiving Temporary Assistance to Needy Families (TANF) as of March 2006. The table also expresses TANF recipients as a percentage of population. Because states set their own eligibility standards, states with high percentages of persons in poverty do not necessarily have a larger-than-average percentage.

L-3 Change in TANF/AFDC Recipients, FY 1996–2006: Under federal welfare reform legislation passed in 1996, states, during 1997 and 1998, made the transition from Aid to Families with Dependent Children (AFDC) to new programs. This table compares the 1996 average monthly number of recipients in each state with the 2006 average to show changes in welfare participation. The data come from the same source as Table L-2.

L-4 Food Stamp Recipients, Total and as a Percentage of Population, FY 2006: Unlike those for Temporary Assistance for Needy Families (TANF), food stamp standards of eligibility are uniform nationwide, so participation in this program tends to resemble closely the percentage of state population in poverty. The data are compiled by the U.S. Department of Agriculture, Food and Nutrition Service and are available on its Web site (www.fns.usda.gov).

L-5 SSI Recipients, Total and as a Percentage of Population, 2005: The Supplemental Security Income (SSI) program provides federal cash payments to persons eligible by reason of a combination of low-income and disability, blindness, or being over age sixty-four. The eligibility standards are uniform nationwide, as are the cash payments, except in about half the states that supplement the federal payments with state money (see Table L-12). The data, reflecting recipients at year-end 2005, were calculated from information posted on the Social Security Administration Web site (www.ssa.gov).

L-6 Women, Infants, and Children (WIC) Recipients and Average Monthly Benefit, FY 2005: WIC targets low-income, nutritionally at risk pregnant or breastfeeding women, infants, and children under age five. The program provides food aid, education, counseling, health screenings, and referrals to other social services. Participation and benefit data come from the same source as Table L-4.

L-7 National School Lunch Program (NSLP) Participants, FY 2006: Schools are required to offer free meals to children of households below 130 percent of the poverty level (reduced price meals are offered to those between 130 and 185 percent of the poverty level). These data, from the same source as Table L-4, show the number of children who participate, and express that number as a percentage of total enrollment in the schools and institutions that offer the program.

L-8 Condition of Children Index, 2006: This is a ranking of states (1 highest, 50 lowest) prepared by the Annie E. Casey Foundation based on ten indicators of health, income, education, and other factors. The details behind the rankings are found in *Kids Count Data Book* for 2006, the foundation's annual comprehensive publication.

L-9 Percentage of Families with Children Headed by a Single Parent, 2004: A large and growing number of American children do not live in households with two parents. These statistics (from *Kids Count*; see notes to Table L-8) include only children in households with a single parent present.

L-10 Average Monthly TANF Cash Assistance Per Family, FY 2005: These data show what a welfare family would receive to cover basic needs in a month. Assistance comes largely in the form of cash payments. Each state sets its own level of benefits. In addition to these cash payments, a typical welfare household might receive food stamps, assistance in paying heating and cooling bills, and free medical care under the Medicaid program. Some households would also receive additional cash as "emergency assistance" and reduced rents under various federal housing subsidy programs. For the source see Table L-2.

L-11 Assistance and Earnings of Three-Person TANF Family as a Percentage of Poverty-Level Income, 2003: These data are from a special compilation of the Congressional Research Service (CRS) and are included in the 2004 "Green Book" of the Ways and Means Committee of the U.S. House of Representatives (waysandmeans.house.gov). These data reflect assumed benefits and earnings for a single parent with two children working half-time at minimum wage in the thirteenth month of work. Assumed earnings from part-time minimum wage employment (approximately $5,000 annually in most states) and an assumed earned income credit are combined with TANF cash payments and food stamps. The total is compared with poverty level income, which, in 2003, was $15,260 for a family of three.

The TANF cash payments are set by the states (see notes to Table L-10). In the six states tied for the lowest rank TANF benefits are exhausted by the thirteenth month of work. Federally determined food stamp values differ from state to state, as greater amounts are provided in states with low cash welfare payments. The poverty level is uniform nationwide. CRS provides two numbers for the states of

California, Michigan, and New York. *State Fact Finder* included the data for Wayne County, Michigan, rather than Washtenaw County (86%), New York City rather than Suffolk County (98.9%), and those for Region 1 in California rather than Region 2 (109.2%).

L-12 SSI State Supplements, 2005: These data compare the extent to which states supplement benefits under the federal Supplemental Security Income (SSI) program. For a description of the program see the notes to Table L-5. The complex rules for determining who receives supplements and how large they are mean that the averages shown are not necessarily indicative of the average supplement received. Some states provide relatively large supplements to some beneficiaries and none to the rest. However, the extreme differences among states show marked differences in their willingness to add to federally funded benefits using their own funds. The data were calculated from information from the Social Security Administration provided to *State Fact Finder* in December, 2006.

L-13 State Income Tax Liability of Typical Family in Poverty, 2005: States have quite different approaches toward taxes on poor working families. The table illustrates these by showing how much state income tax a family of three making the 2005 poverty-level income ($15,577) would have to pay in tax on their 2005 income.

A few states, like the federal government, supplement the income of poverty-level families with a refundable credit indicated by the minus amounts shown in the table. Some states do not have income taxes (n/a on the table) or have a tax but do not make such families pay it (shown as zeros on the table). The others charge the taxes shown. The calculations were performed by the Center on Budget and Policy Priorities and are available on its Web site (www.cbpp.org).

L-14 Child Support Collections, FY 2005: Because large numbers of families on welfare consist of mothers and children who receive little or no child support from fathers, state and federal officials are intensifying efforts to ensure that fathers pay the support amounts they owe. The table provides an indication of the relative significance of the resulting child support payments in each state.

Collections are reported by the Department of Health and Human Services, Office of Child Support Enforcement (www.acf.dhhs.gov). The per capita amounts are those collections divided by each state's population on July 1, 2005. While most differences among states are real, some reflect the different degrees to which individual states enforce child support requirements through centralized systems.

L-15 Child Support Collections Per Dollar of Administrative Costs, FY 2005: Nationwide, it costs about 22 cents to collect every dollar of child support. These data, from the same source as Table L-14, indicate that the effectiveness of collections efforts varies considerably among the states.

L-16 Children in Foster Care, FY 2003: On the last day of fiscal year 2003, 523,062 children were in foster care. Most commonly, these are children who have been removed from their natural parent(s) because of suspected abuse or neglect. The count is from the Department of Health and Human Services, Administration for Children and Families (www.acf.hhs.gov). High rankings are not necessarily good or bad. Having large numbers of children in foster care for long periods is generally viewed as undesirable because the alternatives (adoption, return to natural parents) provide more stability for the child than do temporary homes with strangers. However, having small numbers may indicate that child welfare authorities are leaving abused and neglected children in homes where they should not be left.

L-17 State and Local Welfare Spending, FY 2004: This table relates spending data to population and personal income in each state. The data come from the U.S. Census Bureau's electronic publication "State and Local Government Finance Estimates, by State," available on the bureau's Web site (www.census.gov). Population numbers, also from the Census, are as of July 1, 2004, and personal income numbers are from the Department of Commerce. Based on census historical practices, *State Fact Finder* used calendar year 2003 numbers. See notes to Table F-1 for more extensive information on the source of the data. In addition to cash payments, the bureau's definition of welfare spending includes Medicaid and other payments to vendors, administrative costs, and welfare-related social services.

L-18 State and Local Welfare Spending as a Percentage of General Spending, FY 2004: These data (see notes to Table L-17) show the importance of welfare spending relative to total spending of state and local governments for "general" activities, a category that excludes spending for certain trust funds such as unemployment compensation and municipal utilities.

L-19 Average Monthly Administrative Costs Per TANF Case, FY 2005: In fiscal year 2005 the average monthly costs of administering welfare run about $107 per case, with substantial variation among the states. The information comes from unpublished tabulations by the Department of Health and Human Services, Administration for Children and Families (see notes to Table L-2).

Technology

Use of Broadband in U.S. Homes by Population Group

	% with broadband at home 2006	% increase 2005–2006
Gender		
Male	45	45
Female	38	41
Age		
18–29	55	45
30–49	50	39
50–64	38	41
65+	13	63
Race/Ethnicity		
White (not Hispanic)	42	35
Black (not Hispanic)	31	121
Hispanic (English speaking)	41	46
Educational Attainment		
Less than high school	17	70
High school graduate	31	55
Some college	47	34
College +	62	32
Household Income		
Under $30K	21	40
$30K–$50K	43	59
$50K–$75K	48	37
Over $75K	68	19
Community Type		
Urban	44	42
Suburban	46	39
Rural	25	39
Total	**42**	**40**

Source: Pew Internet & American Life Project

Top 5 States by Numeric High-Tech Employment Growth, 2003–2004

	State	Numeric Growth
1	Virginia	9,103
2	Florida	6,683
3	Maryland	2,834
4	New Hampshire	2,386
5	Arkansas	1,335

Source: AeA

M-1 Percentage of Households with Computers, 2003

State	Percentage with computers	Rank
Alabama	53.9	47
Alaska	73.4	2
Arizona	64.5	19
Arkansas	49.8	49
California	66.3	13
Colorado	70.3	5
Connecticut	69.2	6
Delaware	64.4	20
Florida	61.1	29
Georgia	60.7	30
Hawaii	63.3	24
Idaho	69.1	7
Illinois	60.1	33
Indiana	59.7	37
Iowa	64.6	18
Kansas	63.6	23
Kentucky	58.4	40
Louisiana	52.5	48
Maine	67.9	9
Maryland	66.2	14
Massachusetts	64.2	21
Michigan	59.9	34
Minnesota	68.0	8
Mississippi	48.8	50
Missouri	60.6	31
Montana	59.8	36
Nebraska	66.4	12
Nevada	61.3	28
New Hampshire	71.7	3
New Jersey	65.2	17
New Mexico	54.1	46
New York	59.9	34
North Carolina	57.9	41
North Dakota	61.5	27
Ohio	58.8	39
Oklahoma	55.3	43
Oregon	67.1	10
Pennsylvania	60.2	32
Rhode Island	62.3	25
South Carolina	55.2	44
South Dakota	62.2	26
Tennessee	56.8	42
Texas	59.1	38
Utah	74.1	1
Vermont	65.6	15
Virginia	67.0	11
Washington	71.4	4
West Virginia	54.7	45
Wisconsin	63.8	22
Wyoming	65.5	16
50 States	n/a	
DC	59.5	
United States	61.8	

Rank in order by percentage	
1	Utah
2	Alaska
3	New Hampshire
4	Washington
5	Colorado
6	Connecticut
7	Idaho
8	Minnesota
9	Maine
10	Oregon
11	Virginia
12	Nebraska
13	California
14	Maryland
15	Vermont
16	Wyoming
17	New Jersey
18	Iowa
19	Arizona
20	Delaware
21	Massachusetts
22	Wisconsin
23	Kansas
24	Hawaii
25	Rhode Island
26	South Dakota
27	North Dakota
28	Nevada
29	Florida
30	Georgia
31	Missouri
32	Pennsylvania
33	Illinois
34	Michigan
34	New York
36	Montana
37	Indiana
38	Texas
39	Ohio
40	Kentucky
41	North Carolina
42	Tennessee
43	Oklahoma
44	South Carolina
45	West Virginia
46	New Mexico
47	Alabama
48	Louisiana
49	Arkansas
50	Mississippi

Note: Ties in ranking reflect ties in actual values.

M-2 Percentage of Households with Internet Access, 2003

State	Percentage using Internet	Rank
Alabama	45.8	46
Alaska	68.5	1
Arizona	55.3	24
Arkansas	42.3	49
California	59.6	11
Colorado	63.4	3
Connecticut	62.9	4
Delaware	56.9	19
Florida	55.7	22
Georgia	53.7	29
Hawaii	54.9	26
Idaho	56.4	20
Illinois	51.2	38
Indiana	51.2	38
Iowa	57.0	18
Kansas	54.3	28
Kentucky	49.9	41
Louisiana	44.1	48
Maine	58.1	13
Maryland	59.4	12
Massachusetts	58.1	13
Michigan	52.0	35
Minnesota	61.7	7
Mississippi	39.5	50
Missouri	53.0	33
Montana	50.8	40
Nebraska	55.8	21
Nevada	55.3	24
New Hampshire	65.5	2
New Jersey	60.2	10
New Mexico	44.8	47
New York	53.3	32
North Carolina	51.3	37
North Dakota	53.6	31
Ohio	52.4	34
Oklahoma	48.3	43
Oregon	61.1	8
Pennsylvania	54.7	27
Rhode Island	55.7	22
South Carolina	45.9	45
South Dakota	53.7	29
Tennessee	49.0	42
Texas	51.8	36
Utah	62.6	5
Vermont	58.0	15
Virginia	60.4	9
Washington	62.3	6
West Virginia	47.4	44
Wisconsin	57.5	17
Wyoming	57.9	16
50 States	n/a	
DC	53.2	
United States	54.7	

Rank in order by percentage

1	Alaska
2	New Hampshire
3	Colorado
4	Connecticut
5	Utah
6	Washington
7	Minnesota
8	Oregon
9	Virginia
10	New Jersey
11	California
12	Maryland
13	Maine
13	Massachusetts
15	Vermont
16	Wyoming
17	Wisconsin
18	Iowa
19	Delaware
20	Idaho
21	Nebraska
22	Florida
22	Rhode Island
24	Arizona
24	Nevada
26	Hawaii
27	Pennsylvania
28	Kansas
29	Georgia
29	South Dakota
31	North Dakota
32	New York
33	Missouri
34	Ohio
35	Michigan
36	Texas
37	North Carolina
38	Illinois
38	Indiana
40	Montana
41	Kentucky
42	Tennessee
43	Oklahoma
44	West Virginia
45	South Carolina
46	Alabama
47	New Mexico
48	Louisiana
49	Arkansas
50	Mississippi

Note: Ties in ranking reflect ties in actual values.

M-3 Percentage of Zip Codes with Broadband Telecommunications Service, 2005

State	Percentage of zip codes with at least one subscriber	Number of broadband providers	Rank by percentage
Alabama	100	55	1
Alaska	100	18	1
Arizona	100	51	1
Arkansas	100	35	1
California	100	77	1
Colorado	99	59	26
Connecticut	100	27	1
Delaware	100	18	1
Florida	100	53	1
Georgia	100	63	1
Hawaii	94	10	50
Idaho	98	38	39
Illinois	98	113	39
Indiana	99	80	26
Iowa	99	175	26
Kansas	100	76	1
Kentucky	95	58	48
Louisiana	99	40	26
Maine	97	29	46
Maryland	100	39	1
Massachusetts	100	41	1
Michigan	100	71	1
Minnesota	97	100	46
Mississippi	100	37	1
Missouri	98	81	39
Montana	99	32	26
Nebraska	100	65	1
Nevada	99	30	26
New Hampshire	100	33	1
New Jersey	100	40	1
New Mexico	99	34	26
New York	99	75	26
North Carolina	100	56	1
North Dakota	100	38	1
Ohio	100	69	1
Oklahoma	99	56	26
Oregon	98	57	39
Pennsylvania	98	73	39
Rhode Island	100	19	1
South Carolina	100	39	1
South Dakota	99	39	26
Tennessee	99	52	26
Texas	99	132	26
Utah	98	35	39
Vermont	100	23	1
Virginia	98	59	39
Washington	99	64	26
West Virginia	95	24	48
Wisconsin	100	75	1
Wyoming	100	22	1
50 States	n/a	n/a	
DC	100	24	
United States	99	1,344	

Rank in order by percentage

1	Alabama
1	Alaska
1	Arizona
1	Arkansas
1	California
1	Connecticut
1	Delaware
1	Florida
1	Georgia
1	Kansas
1	Maryland
1	Massachusetts
1	Michigan
1	Mississippi
1	Nebraska
1	New Hampshire
1	New Jersey
1	North Carolina
1	North Dakota
1	Ohio
1	Rhode Island
1	South Carolina
1	Vermont
1	Wisconsin
1	Wyoming
26	Colorado
26	Indiana
26	Iowa
26	Louisiana
26	Montana
26	Nevada
26	New Mexico
26	New York
26	Oklahoma
26	South Dakota
26	Tennessee
26	Texas
26	Washington
39	Idaho
39	Illinois
39	Missouri
39	Oregon
39	Pennsylvania
39	Utah
39	Virginia
46	Maine
46	Minnesota
48	Kentucky
48	West Virginia
50	Hawaii

Note: Ties in ranking reflect ties in actual values.

M-4　High-Tech Jobs, 2004

State	Employment in the high-tech industry	High-tech employment per 1,000 private sector workers	Rank per 1,000 workers
Alabama	69,149	46	23
Alaska	9,089	41	30
Arizona	110,778	56	15
Arkansas	28,433	30	39
California	904,920	72	7
Colorado	159,752	89	1
Connecticut	66,920	48	21
Delaware	18,468	52	17
Florida	265,484	41	29
Georgia	162,348	51	19
Hawaii	13,497	29	42
Idaho	35,012	73	6
Illinois	204,537	42	27
Indiana	68,166	28	44
Iowa	39,359	33	36
Kansas	53,980	51	18
Kentucky	41,581	29	41
Louisiana	37,909	25	48
Maine	15,591	31	37
Maryland	157,779	78	4
Massachusetts	233,234	85	3
Michigan	178,038	49	20
Minnesota	125,227	56	14
Mississippi	19,306	22	50
Missouri	86,531	39	31
Montana	9,922	31	38
Nebraska	30,459	42	28
Nevada	27,527	27	46
New Hampshire	37,467	71	8
New Jersey	197,107	60	11
New Mexico	42,547	73	5
New York	300,683	44	24
North Carolina	134,625	43	25
North Dakota	9,667	37	32
Ohio	151,248	33	34
Oklahoma	38,750	34	33
Oregon	81,650	61	10
Pennsylvania	200,277	42	26
Rhode Island	18,890	46	22
South Carolina	41,628	28	43
South Dakota	9,057	30	40
Tennessee	61,347	27	45
Texas	435,446	57	13
Utah	49,285	56	16
Vermont	14,865	60	12
Virginia	253,316	89	2
Washington	152,025	69	9
West Virginia	13,918	25	47
Wisconsin	77,842	33	35
Wyoming	4,460	24	49
50 States	5,499,096	n/a	
DC	33,831	79	
United States*	5,539,975	51	

*Due to rounding or data sources, the 50-state total plus D.C. may not equal the U.S. total. Please see introduction.

Rank in order per 1,000 workers

1　Colorado
2　Virginia
3　Massachusetts
4　Maryland
5　New Mexico
6　Idaho
7　California
8　New Hampshire
9　Washington
10　Oregon
11　New Jersey
12　Vermont
13　Texas
14　Minnesota
15　Arizona
16　Utah
17　Delaware
18　Kansas
19　Georgia
20　Michigan
21　Connecticut
22　Rhode Island
23　Alabama
24　New York
25　North Carolina
26　Pennsylvania
27　Illinois
28　Nebraska
29　Florida
30　Alaska
31　Missouri
32　North Dakota
33　Oklahoma
34　Ohio
35　Wisconsin
36　Iowa
37　Maine
38　Montana
39　Arkansas
40　South Dakota
41　Kentucky
42　Hawaii
43　South Carolina
44　Indiana
45　Tennessee
46　Nevada
47　West Virginia
48　Louisiana
49　Wyoming
50　Mississippi

Note: Numbers that appear to be identical are rounded and vary slightly in actual value. The rankings reflect the actual values before rounding. See the introduction for more details.

M-5   Percentage Change in High-Tech Employment, 2003–2004

State	Percentage change in high-tech employment	Rank
Alabama	-0.6	24
Alaska	3.1	4
Arizona	1.2	15
Arkansas	4.9	2
California	-1.2	29
Colorado	-1.5	31
Connecticut	-3.3	46
Delaware	-1.4	30
Florida	2.6	6
Georgia	-3.1	43
Hawaii	1.9	9
Idaho	2.8	5
Illinois	-2.9	41
Indiana	0.7	20
Iowa	0.9	16
Kansas	-3.2	45
Kentucky	-3.8	47
Louisiana	1.7	12
Maine	0.1	23
Maryland	1.8	11
Massachusetts	-1.0	27
Michigan	-2.8	39
Minnesota	0.3	21
Mississippi	1.9	9
Missouri	-0.7	25
Montana	-0.8	26
Nebraska	0.9	16
Nevada	-1.9	34
New Hampshire	6.8	1
New Jersey	-2.7	38
New Mexico	-2.9	41
New York	-1.5	31
North Carolina	-1.0	27
North Dakota	1.5	14
Ohio	-4.7	50
Oklahoma	-3.8	47
Oregon	0.3	21
Pennsylvania	-1.7	33
Rhode Island	2.3	7
South Carolina	-2.0	35
South Dakota	-3.1	43
Tennessee	-2.8	39
Texas	-2.4	37
Utah	1.6	13
Vermont	-4.0	49
Virginia	3.7	3
Washington	0.8	18
West Virginia	-2.3	36
Wisconsin	0.8	18
Wyoming	2.2	8
50 States	-0.9	
DC	1.6	
United States	-0.8	

Rank in order by percentage	
1	New Hampshire
2	Arkansas
3	Virginia
4	Alaska
5	Idaho
6	Florida
7	Rhode Island
8	Wyoming
9	Hawaii
9	Mississippi
11	Maryland
12	Louisiana
13	Utah
14	North Dakota
15	Arizona
16	Iowa
16	Nebraska
18	Washington
18	Wisconsin
20	Indiana
21	Minnesota
21	Oregon
23	Maine
24	Alabama
25	Missouri
26	Montana
27	Massachusetts
27	North Carolina
29	California
30	Delaware
31	Colorado
31	New York
33	Pennsylvania
34	Nevada
35	South Carolina
36	West Virginia
37	Texas
38	New Jersey
39	Michigan
39	Tennessee
41	Illinois
41	New Mexico
43	Georgia
43	South Dakota
45	Kansas
46	Connecticut
47	Kentucky
47	Oklahoma
49	Vermont
50	Ohio

Note: Ties in ranking reflect ties in actual values.

M-6 State Government Web Site Ratings, 2006

State	Web site rating	Rank
Alabama	28.4	49
Alaska	28.3	50
Arizona	39.5	35
Arkansas	33.8	45
California	40.8	29
Colorado	36.8	41
Connecticut	41.5	27
Delaware	44.8	15
Florida	41.6	26
Georgia	38.0	38
Hawaii	35.3	43
Idaho	40.8	29
Illinois	46.9	8
Indiana	46.6	9
Iowa	42.0	23
Kansas	42.0	23
Kentucky	42.9	21
Louisiana	40.6	32
Maine	43.8	18
Maryland	39.5	35
Massachusetts	42.5	22
Michigan	48.5	4
Minnesota	44.9	13
Mississippi	33.4	47
Missouri	43.0	20
Montana	47.8	6
Nebraska	43.6	19
Nevada	37.3	39
New Hampshire	40.1	34
New Jersey	51.5	2
New Mexico	34.3	44
New York	47.3	7
North Carolina	41.9	25
North Dakota	44.9	13
Ohio	44.1	16
Oklahoma	37.3	39
Oregon	49.1	3
Pennsylvania	46.4	10
Rhode Island	40.6	32
South Carolina	44.0	17
South Dakota	41.1	28
Tennessee	45.7	11
Texas	51.7	1
Utah	48.1	5
Vermont	38.6	37
Virginia	40.8	29
Washington	45.4	12
West Virginia	33.6	46
Wisconsin	36.5	42
Wyoming	29.0	48
50 States	n/a	
DC	n/a	
United States	n/a	

	Rank in order by rating
1	Texas
2	New Jersey
3	Oregon
4	Michigan
5	Utah
6	Montana
7	New York
8	Illinois
9	Indiana
10	Pennsylvania
11	Tennessee
12	Washington
13	Minnesota
13	North Dakota
15	Delaware
16	Ohio
17	South Carolina
18	Maine
19	Nebraska
20	Missouri
21	Kentucky
22	Massachusetts
23	Iowa
23	Kansas
25	North Carolina
26	Florida
27	Connecticut
28	South Dakota
29	California
29	Idaho
29	Virginia
32	Louisiana
32	Rhode Island
34	New Hampshire
35	Arizona
35	Maryland
37	Vermont
38	Georgia
39	Nevada
39	Oklahoma
41	Colorado
42	Wisconsin
43	Hawaii
44	New Mexico
45	Arkansas
46	West Virginia
47	Mississippi
48	Wyoming
49	Alabama
50	Alaska

Note: Ties in ranking reflect ties in actual values.

M-7 Average Number of Online Services Available on State Government Web Sites, 2006

State	Average number of online services	Rank
Alabama	2.5	47
Alaska	1.9	48
Arizona	3.1	44
Arkansas	2.6	46
California	3.3	43
Colorado	4.1	36
Connecticut	3.0	45
Delaware	5.5	25
Florida	5.3	27
Georgia	4.1	36
Hawaii	4.1	36
Idaho	8.3	10
Illinois	4.2	34
Indiana	5.6	23
Iowa	5.5	25
Kansas	5.7	21
Kentucky	6.6	17
Louisiana	5.0	29
Maine	7.0	15
Maryland	4.6	32
Massachusetts	6.5	18
Michigan	7.6	13
Minnesota	7.1	14
Mississippi	4.3	33
Missouri	4.2	34
Montana	12.7	3
Nebraska	8.3	10
Nevada	5.9	20
New Hampshire	4.7	30
New Jersey	9.2	5
New Mexico	5.2	28
New York	7.0	15
North Carolina	3.9	40
North Dakota	5.7	21
Ohio	7.7	12
Oklahoma	5.6	23
Oregon	13.9	2
Pennsylvania	8.4	8
Rhode Island	10.1	4
South Carolina	8.4	8
South Dakota	3.8	41
Tennessee	8.9	6
Texas	25.3	1
Utah	8.5	7
Vermont	4.1	36
Virginia	4.7	30
Washington	6.2	19
West Virginia	3.7	42
Wisconsin	1.8	49
Wyoming	0.7	50
50 States	n/a	
DC	n/a	
United States	n/a	

Rank in order by number	
1	Texas
2	Oregon
3	Montana
4	Rhode Island
5	New Jersey
6	Tennessee
7	Utah
8	Pennsylvania
8	South Carolina
10	Idaho
10	Nebraska
12	Ohio
13	Michigan
14	Minnesota
15	Maine
15	New York
17	Kentucky
18	Massachusetts
19	Washington
20	Nevada
21	Kansas
21	North Dakota
23	Oklahoma
23	Indiana
25	Delaware
25	Iowa
27	Florida
28	New Mexico
29	Louisiana
30	Virginia
30	New Hampshire
32	Maryland
33	Mississippi
34	Missouri
34	Illinois
36	Georgia
36	Vermont
36	Colorado
36	Hawaii
40	North Carolina
41	South Dakota
42	West Virginia
43	California
44	Arizona
45	Connecticut
46	Arkansas
47	Alabama
48	Alaska
49	Wisconsin
50	Wyoming

Note: Ties in ranking reflect ties in actual values.

M-8   Students Per Computer, 2005

State	Students per instructional computer	Rank
Alabama	4.7	8
Alaska	2.7	45
Arizona	4.5	10
Arkansas	3.6	29
California	5.1	3
Colorado	4.2	14
Connecticut	4.0	16
Delaware	4.5	12
Florida	3.5	36
Georgia	3.8	23
Hawaii	4.9	6
Idaho	3.6	28
Illinois	3.8	21
Indiana	3.4	37
Iowa	3.3	39
Kansas	2.7	46
Kentucky	3.8	22
Louisiana	4.4	13
Maine	1.9	49
Maryland	4.8	7
Massachusetts	3.6	30
Michigan	3.7	25
Minnesota	3.8	24
Mississippi	4.6	9
Missouri	3.5	32
Montana	2.7	47
Nebraska	3.0	43
Nevada	5.0	4
New Hampshire	5.2	2
New Jersey	3.7	27
New Mexico	3.6	31
New York	4.2	15
North Carolina	4.0	17
North Dakota	2.9	44
Ohio	3.5	33
Oklahoma	3.9	20
Oregon	4.5	11
Pennsylvania	3.5	34
Rhode Island	5.0	5
South Carolina	3.7	26
South Dakota	1.8	50
Tennessee	4.0	18
Texas	3.4	38
Utah	5.2	1
Vermont	3.5	35
Virginia	3.1	41
Washington	3.9	19
West Virginia	3.0	42
Wisconsin	3.2	40
Wyoming	2.4	48
50 States	n/a	
DC	3.5	
United States	3.8	

Rank in order by number	
1	Utah
2	New Hampshire
3	California
4	Nevada
5	Rhode Island
6	Hawaii
7	Maryland
8	Alabama
9	Mississippi
10	Arizona
11	Oregon
12	Delaware
13	Louisiana
14	Colorado
15	New York
16	Connecticut
17	North Carolina
18	Tennessee
19	Washington
20	Oklahoma
21	Illinois
22	Kentucky
23	Georgia
24	Minnesota
25	Michigan
26	South Carolina
27	New Jersey
28	Idaho
29	Arkansas
30	Massachusetts
31	New Mexico
32	Missouri
33	Ohio
34	Pennsylvania
35	Vermont
36	Florida
37	Indiana
38	Texas
39	Iowa
40	Wisconsin
41	Virginia
42	West Virginia
43	Nebraska
44	North Dakota
45	Alaska
46	Kansas
47	Montana
48	Wyoming
49	Maine
50	South Dakota

Note: Numbers that appear to be identical are rounded and vary slightly in actual value. The rankings reflect the actual values before rounding. See the introduction for more details.

M-9 Students Per Internet-Connected Computer, 2005

State	Students per Internet-connected instructional computer	Rank
Alabama	4.9	5
Alaska	3.0	44
Arizona	4.6	11
Arkansas	3.7	27
California	5.3	2
Colorado	4.5	13
Connecticut	3.6	30
Delaware	4.9	4
Florida	3.6	31
Georgia	3.9	23
Hawaii	4.8	6
Idaho	3.8	25
Illinois	3.8	24
Indiana	3.5	33
Iowa	3.3	39
Kansas	2.7	47
Kentucky	4.1	16
Louisiana	4.5	12
Maine	2.0	49
Maryland	4.8	7
Massachusetts	4.1	18
Michigan	3.7	28
Minnesota	3.9	21
Mississippi	4.7	10
Missouri	3.3	38
Montana	2.9	45
Nebraska	2.9	46
Nevada	5.2	3
New Hampshire	4.4	14
New Jersey	3.6	29
New Mexico	3.5	32
New York	4.3	15
North Carolina	4.1	17
North Dakota	3.0	43
Ohio	3.5	34
Oklahoma	3.9	20
Oregon	4.8	8
Pennsylvania	3.4	35
Rhode Island	4.7	9
South Carolina	3.7	26
South Dakota	1.8	50
Tennessee	3.9	22
Texas	3.4	36
Utah	5.6	1
Vermont	3.3	40
Virginia	3.0	41
Washington	4.0	19
West Virginia	3.0	42
Wisconsin	3.3	37
Wyoming	2.3	48
50 States	n/a	
DC	3.9	
United States	3.9	

Rank in order by number	
1	Utah
2	California
3	Nevada
4	Delaware
5	Alabama
6	Hawaii
7	Maryland
8	Oregon
9	Rhode Island
10	Mississippi
11	Arizona
12	Louisiana
13	Colorado
14	New Hampshire
15	New York
16	Kentucky
17	North Carolina
18	Massachusetts
19	Washington
20	Oklahoma
21	Minnesota
22	Tennessee
23	Georgia
24	Illinois
25	Idaho
26	South Carolina
27	Arkansas
28	Michigan
29	New Jersey
30	Connecticut
31	Florida
32	New Mexico
33	Indiana
34	Ohio
35	Pennsylvania
36	Texas
37	Wisconsin
38	Missouri
39	Iowa
40	Vermont
41	Virginia
42	West Virginia
43	North Dakota
44	Alaska
45	Montana
46	Nebraska
47	Kansas
48	Wyoming
49	Maine
50	South Dakota

Note: Numbers that appear to be identical are rounded and vary slightly in actual value. The rankings reflect the actual values before rounding. See the introduction for more details.

M-10 Public Library Internet Terminals, FY 2004

State	Internet terminals per 5,000 population	Rank
Alabama	3.8	14
Alaska	4.3	10
Arizona	2.4	44
Arkansas	2.2	46
California	1.9	49
Colorado	3.0	25
Connecticut	3.4	20
Delaware	2.0	48
Florida	2.4	44
Georgia	3.0	25
Hawaii	2.1	47
Idaho	3.3	21
Illinois	3.5	19
Indiana	4.6	7
Iowa	4.8	6
Kansas	5.2	3
Kentucky	2.6	41
Louisiana	2.9	30
Maine	5.0	5
Maryland	2.8	36
Massachusetts	3.3	21
Michigan	3.7	16
Minnesota	3.6	18
Mississippi	2.6	41
Missouri	3.8	14
Montana	3.0	25
Nebraska	5.2	3
Nevada	1.9	49
New Hampshire	4.5	8
New Jersey	2.9	30
New Mexico	3.3	21
New York	2.9	30
North Carolina	2.8	36
North Dakota	3.9	13
Ohio	4.2	11
Oklahoma	3.0	25
Oregon	2.9	30
Pennsylvania	2.9	30
Rhode Island	4.0	12
South Carolina	2.8	36
South Dakota	6.8	1
Tennessee	2.5	43
Texas	3.0	25
Utah	2.9	30
Vermont	6.4	2
Virginia	2.7	39
Washington	3.2	24
West Virginia	2.7	39
Wisconsin	3.7	16
Wyoming	4.4	9
50 States	n/a	
DC	2.2	
United States	3.0	

Rank in order by percentage

1	South Dakota
2	Vermont
3	Kansas
3	Nebraska
5	Maine
6	Iowa
7	Indiana
8	New Hampshire
9	Wyoming
10	Alaska
11	Ohio
12	Rhode Island
13	North Dakota
14	Alabama
14	Missouri
16	Michigan
16	Wisconsin
18	Minnesota
19	Illinois
20	Connecticut
21	Idaho
21	Massachusetts
21	New Mexico
24	Washington
25	Colorado
25	Georgia
25	Montana
25	Oklahoma
25	Texas
30	Louisiana
30	New Jersey
30	New York
30	Oregon
30	Pennsylvania
30	Utah
36	Maryland
36	North Carolina
36	South Carolina
39	Virginia
39	West Virginia
41	Kentucky
41	Mississippi
43	Tennessee
44	Arizona
44	Florida
46	Arkansas
47	Hawaii
48	Delaware
49	California
49	Nevada

Note: Ties in ranking reflect ties in actual values.

Source Notes for Technology (Section M)

M-1 Percentage of Households with Computers, 2003: In 1995, the National Telecommunication and Information Administration (NTIA), an agency of the Department of Commerce, began publishing a series of reports on access to technology in the United States based on data from the U.S. Census Bureau's Current Population Survey. The statistics on computer ownership come from the U.S. Census Bureau interviews with approximately 57,000 sample households. They are available on the bureau's Web site (www.census. gov).

M-2 Percentage of Households with Internet Access, 2003: This table is from the same source as cited in the notes to Table M-1.

M-3 Percentage of Zip Codes with Broadband Telecommunications Service, 2005: High-speed, high-capacity, "always on" broadband telecommunications services allow large amounts of information to be transmitted quickly, providing at least the promise of increased productivity. The majority of these services are supplied by cable lines and digital subscriber lines (DSL), a small percentage come from satellite, wireless, and other technologies. As many who live in rural areas know, broadband service is not yet universally available.

The Federal Communications Commission (FCC) began tracking access to broadband services in 1998. While it does not count individual subscribers, the FCC does keep statistics on the number of broadband providers in each zip code. This information for 2005 is provided in the table. The first column shows the percentage of zip codes in each state that have one or more subscribers to one or more broadband services. According to the FCC report from which the data is culled ("High-Speed Services for Internet Access: Status as of December 31, 2005"), 99 percent of the U.S. population resides in those zip codes. The second column of the table shows the number of companies that supply broadband service within each state, providing some indication of competition in the broadband market.

M-4 High-Tech Jobs, 2004: The recognized authority on employment statistics—the Bureau of Labor Statistics (BLS)—does not currently release "high-tech" industry data for states, but the bureau does assign every category of job an employment code (North American Industrial Classification System, or NAICS code). In order to create this table, the AeA (formerly the American Electronics Association) sifted through these NAICS codes to create its own definition of the high-tech industry. In *Cyberstates 2006* the source of the data in this table, AeA calls their definition "a solid, yet conservative, representation of the core components of today's high-tech industry." It includes high-tech manufacturing, communications services, and software and computer-related services. It does not include the biotechnology industry (due to the difficulty of separating "tech" from "bio" activities), temporary employees, consultants, or freelance workers. High-technology is not an easy industry to isolate. Other groups are bound to develop differing definitions.

Cyberstates 2006 also includes detailed state-level information on high-tech wages, establishments, and payroll, as well as information on trade, venture capital investments, and research and development expenditures.

M-5 Percentage Change in High-Tech Employment, 2003–2004: Overall high-tech employment dropped by less than one percent between 2003 and 2004, reflecting a loss of 44,738 jobs. The total U.S. private sector saw employment grow by 1.32 percent over the same period. For source, see notes to Table M-4.

M-6 State Government Web Site Ratings, 2006: Citing the Internet as an important means for governments to deliver information and services to citizens, Daniel M. West, Director of the Taubman Center for Public Policy at Brown University, has taken on the task of rating "e-government." West's report, "State and Federal E-Government in the United States, 2006," published on www.InsidePolitics. org, analyzes 1,564 government Web sites from a "citizen's perspective." A variety of measures were used to evaluate Web sites. These include the presence of online services, publications and databases, security and privacy measures, handicap accessibility, readability, and other services such as foreign language translation, digital signatures, credit card payments, and comment forms. Each state was given a score out of a possible 100. Texas topped the scale with a score of 51.7.

M-7: Average Number of Online Services Available on State Government Web Sites, 2006: State and federal governments are offering more services online. Some examples of available online services are vehicle registration, driver's license renewal, registering to vote, ordering birth or death certificates, filing consumer complaints, and filing business and payroll taxes. These data, from the same source as Table M-6, show the average number of online services offered on state government Web sites.

M-8: Students Per Computer, 2005: This table is one measure of student access to technology in public schools. The data are from *Education Week's* "Technology Counts 2006" (www. edweek.org), which includes additional information on how computers and the Internet are used in the classroom. For more information on the capacity to use technology see also, the National Center for Education Statistics' report, "Teachers' Tools for the 21st Century: A Report on Teachers' Use of Technology."

M-9: Students Per Internet-Connected Computer, 2005: See notes to Table M-4.

M-10: Public Library Internet Terminals, FY 2004: These data are from the U.S. Department of Education's *Public Libraries Survey, Fiscal Year 2004.* This report once tracked the percentage of public libraries with access to the Internet. As that percentage quickly climbed towards one hundred percent, the report now compares the number of Internet-connected computers in each state's public libraries to the population of that state. In South Dakota there are almost seven Internet terminals per 5,000 population, in Nevada the number is closer to two.

State Rankings

Alabama

"Own-Source" General Revenue	43
Per Capita Non-Tax Revenue	6
Per Capita Total Spending	31
General Spending as a Percentage of Income	14
Per Capita General Spending	30
Change in General Expenditures	23
State Government General Revenue	32
State Government General Spending	31
State Government General Fund Spending	27
State and Local Debt	38
Debt as a Percentage of Revenue	31
Per Capita Full Faith and Credit Debt	31
Bond Ratings	3
State Solvency Index	20
Pension Plan Assets	37
State Reserves	24
Capital Outlays and Interest	34
State Budget Process Quality	40
Relative State Spending "Needs"	46
Structural Deficits	49

Education - Section H

Math Proficiency, Eighth Grade	49
Reading Proficiency, Eighth Grade	46
AFQT Ranks	45
SAT Scores	n/a
ACT Scores	22
Population Over 25 with a High School Diploma	45
Students in Private Schools	21
High School Dropout Rates	29
Pupil-Teacher Ratio	19
Public School Enrollment	24
Library Holdings Per Capita	41
Children with Disabilities	39
Education Spending Per Capita	35
Education Spending as a Percentage of General Spending	30
Spending Per Pupil	42
Average Teacher Salary	41
Sources of School Funds	36
State Aid Per Pupil	29
Per Capita Higher Education Spending	14
Higher Education Spending as a Percentage of General Spending	8
Public Higher Education Enrollment	12
Per Pupil Support of Higher Education	10
In-State Tuition and Fees	32
Out-of-State Tuition and Fees	34
Change in Tuition and Fees	28
Affordability Index	42
Average Professor Salary	30

Education Employees	28
R and D Spending	5
Library Operating Spending	45
Head Start Spending	44

Health - Section I

Immunization Rates	12
Infant Mortality Rates	7
State Health Rankings	45
Population without Health Insurance	21
Abortions	26
Alcohol Consumption	45
Percentage of Adult Smokers	7
Percentage Obese	5
AIDS Cases	16
Physicians Per 100,000 Population	40
Hospital Beds Per 1,000 Population	13
Medicaid Recipients	11
Medicaid Recipients as a Percentage of Poverty Population	34
Health and Hospital Spending	2
Health and Hospital Spending as a Percentage of General Spending	1
Per Capita Medicaid Spending	32
Medicaid Spending Per Aged	44
Medicaid Spending Per Child	20
Medicare Payment Per Hospital Day	12
Hospital Expense Per Inpatient Day	50
Population in HMOs	46
Prescription Drugs as a Percentage of Health Care Spending	2
Average Annual Increase in Health Care Expenditures	22

Crime - Section J

Crime Rate	17
Violent Crime Rate	22
Murder Rate	4
Property Crime Rate	17
Motor Vehicle Theft Rate	31
Violent Crime Rate Change	22
Prisoners	15
Change in Prisoners	31
Incarceration Rate	28
Juvenile Violent Crime Rate	39
Law Enforcement Employees	20
Corrections Employees	42
State Corrections Spending	49
Increase in State Corrections Spending	3
Law Enforcement Spending	41
Law Enforcement Spending as a Percentage of General Spending	40

Transportation - Section K

Travel on Interstates	35
Interstate Mileage in "Unacceptable" Condition	16
Deficient Bridges	18
Traffic Deaths	11
Seat Belt Use	23
Vehicle-Miles Traveled Per Capita	4
Use of Public Transportation	45
Road and Street Miles	33
Highway Employees	16
Public Transit Employees	45
Highway Spending Per Capita	44
Highway Spending as a Percentage of General Spending	39

Welfare - Section L

Births to Unwed Mothers	20
TANF Recipients	31
Change in TANF/AFDC Recipients	35
Food Stamp Recipients	12
SSI Recipients	4
WIC Average Monthly Benefit	4
NSLP Recipients	7
Condition of Children Index	43
Families with Single Parent	7
Average Monthly TANF Payments	45
Welfare as a Percentage of Poverty-Level Income	45
State Supplements of SSI	33
State Income Tax Liability of Typical Family in Poverty	1
Child Support Collections	42
Child Support Collections Per Dollar of Administrative Costs	35
Children in Foster Care	37
Welfare Spending Per Capita	27
Welfare Spending as a Percentage of General Spending	25
Administrative Costs Per TANF Case	39

Technology - Section M

Households with Computers	47
Percentage Using Internet	46
Zip Codes with Broadband Service	1
High-Tech Jobs	23
Change in High-Tech Jobs	24
State Government Web Site Ratings	49
Number of Online Government Services	47
Students Per Computer	8
Students Per Internet-Connected Computer	5
Public Library Internet Terminals	14

Alaska

"Own-Source" General Revenue	1
Per Capita Non-Tax Revenue	1
Per Capita Total Spending	1
General Spending as a Percentage of Income	1
Per Capita General Spending	1
Change in General Expenditures	50
State Government General Revenue	1
State Government General Spending	1
State Government General Fund Spending	2
State and Local Debt	1
Debt as a Percentage of Revenue	20
Per Capita Full Faith and Credit Debt	6
Bond Ratings	3
State Solvency Index	1
Pension Plan Assets	12
State Reserves	2
Capital Outlays and Interest	1
State Budget Process Quality	45
Relative State Spending "Needs"	30
Structural Deficits	28

Education - Section H

Math Proficiency, Eighth Grade	29
Reading Proficiency, Eighth Grade	34
AFQT Ranks	1
SAT Scores	6
ACT Scores	n/a
Population Over 25 with a High School Diploma	5
Students in Private Schools	46
High School Dropout Rates	2
Pupil-Teacher Ratio	11
Public School Enrollment	1
Library Holdings Per Capita	20
Children with Disabilities	34
Education Spending Per Capita	1
Education Spending as a Percentage of General Spending	50
Spending Per Pupil	12
Average Teacher Salary	12
Sources of School Funds	46
State Aid Per Pupil	7
Per Capita Higher Education Spending	3
Higher Education Spending as a Percentage of General Spending	46
Public Higher Education Enrollment	29
Per Pupil Support of Higher Education	2
In-State Tuition and Fees	41
Out-of-State Tuition and Fees	46
Change in Tuition and Fees	18
Affordability Index	29
Average Professor Salary	43

Education Employees	3
R and D Spending	10
Library Operating Spending	12
Head Start Spending	19

Health - Section I

Immunization Rates	39
Infant Mortality Rates	28
State Health Rankings	31
Population without Health Insurance	15
Abortions	28
Alcohol Consumption	13
Percentage of Adult Smokers	6
Percentage Obese	8
AIDS Cases	37
Physicians Per 100,000 Population	34
Hospital Beds Per 1,000 Population	41
Medicaid Recipients	24
Medicaid Recipients as a Percentage of Poverty Population	10
Health and Hospital Spending	40
Health and Hospital Spending as a Percentage of General Spending	47
Per Capita Medicaid Spending	5
Medicaid Spending Per Aged	4
Medicaid Spending Per Child	2
Medicare Payment Per Hospital Day	14
Hospital Expense Per Inpatient Day	2
Population in HMOs	50
Prescription Drugs as a Percentage of Health Care Spending	49
Average Annual Increase in Health Care Expenditures	12

Crime - Section J

Crime Rate	20
Violent Crime Rate	7
Murder Rate	24
Property Crime Rate	22
Motor Vehicle Theft Rate	18
Violent Crime Rate Change	8
Prisoners	41
Change in Prisoners	30
Incarceration Rate	50
Juvenile Violent Crime Rate	19
Law Enforcement Employees	39
Corrections Employees	12
State Corrections Spending	11
Increase in State Corrections Spending	43
Law Enforcement Spending	3
Law Enforcement Spending as a Percentage of General Spending	47

Transportation - Section K

Travel on Interstates	6
Interstate Mileage in "Unacceptable" Condition	2
Deficient Bridges	15
Traffic Deaths	27
Seat Belt Use	32
Vehicle-Miles Traveled Per Capita	49
Use of Public Transportation	28
Road and Street Miles	6
Highway Employees	1
Public Transit Employees	24
Highway Spending Per Capita	1
Highway Spending as a Percentage of General Spending	6

Welfare - Section L

Births to Unwed Mothers	28
TANF Recipients	13
Change in TANF/AFDC Recipients	19
Food Stamp Recipients	22
SSI Recipients	32
WIC Average Monthly Benefit	2
NSLP Recipients	44
Condition of Children Index	35
Families with Single Parent	23
Average Monthly TANF Payments	5
Welfare as a Percentage of Poverty-Level Income	3
State Supplements of SSI	11
State Income Tax Liability of Typical Family in Poverty	n/a
Child Support Collections	3
Child Support Collections Per Dollar of Administrative Costs	32
Children in Foster Care	3
Welfare Spending Per Capita	2
Welfare Spending as a Percentage of General Spending	32
Administrative Costs Per TANF Case	20

Technology - Section M

Households with Computers	2
Percentage Using Internet	1
Zip Codes with Broadband Service	1
High-Tech Jobs	30
Change in High-Tech Jobs	4
State Government Web Site Ratings	50
Number of Online Government Services	48
Students Per Computer	45
Students Per Internet-Connected Computer	44
Public Library Internet Terminals	10

Arizona

Arkansas

California

Colorado

Connecticut

Delaware

Florida

Georgia

Georgia

Hawaii

Idaho

Idaho

Illinois

Indiana

Iowa

Kansas

Kansas

Kentucky

Louisiana

Maine

Maryland

Massachusetts

"Own-Source" General Revenue	7
Per Capita Non-Tax Revenue	23
Per Capita Total Spending	5
General Spending as a Percentage of Income	40
Per Capita General Spending	4
Change in General Expenditures	26
State Government General Revenue	10
State Government General Spending	8
State Government General Fund Spending	45
State and Local Debt	3
Debt as a Percentage of Revenue	1
Per Capita Full Faith and Credit Debt	3
Bond Ratings	3
State Solvency Index	49
Pension Plan Assets	17
State Reserves	18
Capital Outlays and Interest	5
State Budget Process Quality	7
Relative State Spending "Needs"	16
Structural Deficits	6

Education - Section H

Math Proficiency, Eighth Grade	1
Reading Proficiency, Eighth Grade	1
AFQT Ranks	18
SAT Scores	5
ACT Scores	n/a
Population Over 25 with a High School Diploma	21
Students in Private Schools	11
High School Dropout Rates	n/a
Pupil-Teacher Ratio	31
Public School Enrollment	43
Library Holdings Per Capita	4
Children with Disabilities	7
Education Spending Per Capita	19
Education Spending as a Percentage of General Spending	46
Spending Per Pupil	5
Average Teacher Salary	7
Sources of School Funds	11
State Aid Per Pupil	13
Per Capita Higher Education Spending	49
Higher Education Spending as a Percentage of General Spending	49
Public Higher Education Enrollment	50
Per Pupil Support of Higher Education	28
In-State Tuition and Fees	7
Out-of-State Tuition and Fees	19
Change in Tuition and Fees	40
Affordability Index	36
Average Professor Salary	3

Education Employees	24
R and D Spending	4
Library Operating Spending	16
Head Start Spending	8

Health - Section I

Immunization Rates	1
Infant Mortality Rates	50
State Health Rankings	7
Population without Health Insurance	47
Abortions	5
Alcohol Consumption	10
Percentage of Adult Smokers	42
Percentage Obese	46
AIDS Cases	19
Physicians Per 100,000 Population	1
Hospital Beds Per 1,000 Population	32
Medicaid Recipients	19
Medicaid Recipients as a Percentage of Poverty Population	6
Health and Hospital Spending	45
Health and Hospital Spending as a Percentage of General Spending	46
Per Capita Medicaid Spending	4
Medicaid Spending Per Aged	14
Medicaid Spending Per Child	21
Medicare Payment Per Hospital Day	41
Hospital Expense Per Inpatient Day	8
Population in HMOs	2
Prescription Drugs as a Percentage of Health Care Spending	41
Average Annual Increase in Health Care Expenditures	36

Crime - Section J

Crime Rate	42
Violent Crime Rate	19
Murder Rate	36
Property Crime Rate	44
Motor Vehicle Theft Rate	30
Violent Crime Rate Change	29
Prisoners	31
Change in Prisoners	50
Incarceration Rate	27
Juvenile Violent Crime Rate	14
Law Enforcement Employees	6
Corrections Employees	50
State Corrections Spending	1
Increase in State Corrections Spending	6
Law Enforcement Spending	23
Law Enforcement Spending as a Percentage of General Spending	37

Transportation - Section K

Travel on Interstates	5
Interstate Mileage in "Unacceptable" Condition	33
Deficient Bridges	2
Traffic Deaths	50
Seat Belt Use	47
Vehicle-Miles Traveled Per Capita	43
Use of Public Transportation	5
Road and Street Miles	47
Highway Employees	38
Public Transit Employees	7
Highway Spending Per Capita	12
Highway Spending as a Percentage of General Spending	22

Welfare - Section L

Births to Unwed Mothers	46
TANF Recipients	17
Change in TANF/AFDC Recipients	30
Food Stamp Recipients	34
SSI Recipients	12
WIC Average Monthly Benefit	29
NSLP Recipients	33
Condition of Children Index	10
Families with Single Parent	27
Average Monthly TANF Payments	10
Welfare as a Percentage of Poverty-Level Income	4
State Supplements of SSI	26
State Income Tax Liability of Typical Family in Poverty	36
Child Support Collections	24
Child Support Collections Per Dollar of Administrative Costs	13
Children in Foster Care	13
Welfare Spending Per Capita	7
Welfare Spending as a Percentage of General Spending	11
Administrative Costs Per TANF Case	42

Technology - Section M

Households with Computers	21
Percentage Using Internet	13
Zip Codes with Broadband Service	1
High-Tech Jobs	3
Change in High-Tech Jobs	27
State Government Web Site Ratings	22
Number of Online Government Services	18
Students Per Computer	30
Students Per Internet-Connected Computer	18
Public Library Internet Terminals	21

Michigan

Minnesota

"Own-Source" General Revenue	9
Per Capita Non-Tax Revenue	15
Per Capita Total Spending	10
General Spending as a Percentage of Income	27
Per Capita General Spending	7
Change in General Expenditures	45
State Government General Revenue	14
State Government General Spending	10
State Government General Fund Spending	29
State and Local Debt	17
Debt as a Percentage of Revenue	19
Per Capita Full Faith and Credit Debt	11
Bond Ratings	2
State Solvency Index	33
Pension Plan Assets	39
State Reserves	33
Capital Outlays and Interest	12
State Budget Process Quality	5
Relative State Spending "Needs"	6
Structural Deficits	17

Education - Section H

Math Proficiency, Eighth Grade	2
Reading Proficiency, Eighth Grade	9
AFQT Ranks	5
SAT Scores	n/a
ACT Scores	1
Population Over 25 with a High School Diploma	1
Students in Private Schools	20
High School Dropout Rates	26
Pupil-Teacher Ratio	15
Public School Enrollment	20
Library Holdings Per Capita	22
Children with Disabilities	33
Education Spending Per Capita	14
Education Spending as a Percentage of General Spending	37
Spending Per Pupil	18
Average Teacher Salary	16
Sources of School Funds	47
State Aid Per Pupil	3
Per Capita Higher Education Spending	30
Higher Education Spending as a Percentage of General Spending	39
Public Higher Education Enrollment	19
Per Pupil Support of Higher Education	18
In-State Tuition and Fees	11
Out-of-State Tuition and Fees	11
Change in Tuition and Fees	33
Affordability Index	4
Average Professor Salary	14

Education Employees	30
R and D Spending	29
Library Operating Spending	20
Head Start Spending	28

Health - Section I

Immunization Rates	6
Infant Mortality Rates	47
State Health Rankings	1
Population without Health Insurance	50
Abortions	23
Alcohol Consumption	15
Percentage of Adult Smokers	32
Percentage Obese	31
AIDS Cases	35
Physicians Per 100,000 Population	14
Hospital Beds Per 1,000 Population	18
Medicaid Recipients	40
Medicaid Recipients as a Percentage of Poverty Population	14
Health and Hospital Spending	34
Health and Hospital Spending as a Percentage of General Spending	39
Per Capita Medicaid Spending	15
Medicaid Spending Per Aged	16
Medicaid Spending Per Child	5
Medicare Payment Per Hospital Day	10
Hospital Expense Per Inpatient Day	14
Population in HMOs	13
Prescription Drugs as a Percentage of Health Care Spending	43
Average Annual Increase in Health Care Expenditures	29

Crime - Section J

Crime Rate	33
Violent Crime Rate	30
Murder Rate	42
Property Crime Rate	32
Motor Vehicle Theft Rate	33
Violent Crime Rate Change	6
Prisoners	32
Change in Prisoners	7
Incarceration Rate	12
Juvenile Violent Crime Rate	31
Law Enforcement Employees	50
Corrections Employees	44
State Corrections Spending	9
Increase in State Corrections Spending	49
Law Enforcement Spending	28
Law Enforcement Spending as a Percentage of General Spending	41

Transportation - Section K

Travel on Interstates	36
Interstate Mileage in "Unacceptable" Condition	36
Deficient Bridges	48
Traffic Deaths	47
Seat Belt Use	20
Vehicle-Miles Traveled Per Capita	21
Use of Public Transportation	14
Road and Street Miles	42
Highway Employees	20
Public Transit Employees	16
Highway Spending Per Capita	10
Highway Spending as a Percentage of General Spending	17

Welfare - Section L

Births to Unwed Mothers	45
TANF Recipients	24
Change in TANF/AFDC Recipients	26
Food Stamp Recipients	46
SSI Recipients	43
WIC Average Monthly Benefit	28
NSLP Recipients	15
Condition of Children Index	4
Families with Single Parent	44
Average Monthly TANF Payments	22
Welfare as a Percentage of Poverty-Level Income	10
State Supplements of SSI	17
State Income Tax Liability of Typical Family in Poverty	39
Child Support Collections	5
Child Support Collections Per Dollar of Administrative Costs	36
Children in Foster Care	34
Welfare Spending Per Capita	5
Welfare Spending as a Percentage of General Spending	4
Administrative Costs Per TANF Case	15

Technology - Section M

Households with Computers	8
Percentage Using Internet	7
Zip Codes with Broadband Service	46
High-Tech Jobs	14
Change in High-Tech Jobs	21
State Government Web Site Ratings	13
Number of Online Government Services	14
Students Per Computer	24
Students Per Internet-Connected Computer	21
Public Library Internet Terminals	18

Mississippi

Missouri

Montana

Nebraska

Nebraska

Nevada

New Hampshire

"Own-Source" General Revenue	33
Per Capita Non-Tax Revenue	38
Per Capita Total Spending	42
General Spending as a Percentage of Income	48
Per Capita General Spending	36
Change in General Expenditures	12
State Government General Revenue	34
State Government General Spending	34
State Government General Fund Spending	47
State and Local Debt	20
Debt as a Percentage of Revenue	9
Per Capita Full Faith and Credit Debt	25
Bond Ratings	3
State Solvency Index	27
Pension Plan Assets	41
State Reserves	39
Capital Outlays and Interest	43
State Budget Process Quality	50
Relative State Spending "Needs"	2
Structural Deficits	1

Education · Section H

Math Proficiency, Eighth Grade	7
Reading Proficiency, Eighth Grade	2
AFQT Ranks	2
SAT Scores	4
ACT Scores	n/a
Population Over 25 with a High School Diploma	4
Students in Private Schools	18
High School Dropout Rates	19
Pupil-Teacher Ratio	40
Public School Enrollment	32
Library Holdings Per Capita	7
Children with Disabilities	17
Education Spending Per Capita	31
Education Spending as a Percentage of General Spending	17
Spending Per Pupil	11
Average Teacher Salary	23
Sources of School Funds	25
State Aid Per Pupil	24
Per Capita Higher Education Spending	44
Higher Education Spending as a Percentage of General Spending	40
Public Higher Education Enrollment	48
Per Pupil Support of Higher Education	49
In-State Tuition and Fees	4
Out-of-State Tuition and Fees	8
Change in Tuition and Fees	31
Affordability Index	49
Average Professor Salary	15

Education Employees	7
R and D Spending	16
Library Operating Spending	18
Head Start Spending	9

Health · Section I

Immunization Rates	20
Infant Mortality Rates	41
State Health Rankings	3
Population without Health Insurance	45
Abortions	n/a
Alcohol Consumption	1
Percentage of Adult Smokers	28
Percentage Obese	34
AIDS Cases	41
Physicians Per 100,000 Population	20
Hospital Beds Per 1,000 Population	40
Medicaid Recipients	49
Medicaid Recipients as a Percentage of Poverty Population	16
Health and Hospital Spending	50
Health and Hospital Spending as a Percentage of General Spending	50
Per Capita Medicaid Spending	23
Medicaid Spending Per Aged	5
Medicaid Spending Per Child	4
Medicare Payment Per Hospital Day	35
Hospital Expense Per Inpatient Day	3
Population in HMOs	21
Prescription Drugs as a Percentage of Health Care Spending	30
Average Annual Increase in Health Care Expenditures	3

Crime · Section J

Crime Rate	50
Violent Crime Rate	47
Murder Rate	46
Property Crime Rate	49
Motor Vehicle Theft Rate	49
Violent Crime Rate Change	50
Prisoners	46
Change in Prisoners	38
Incarceration Rate	25
Juvenile Violent Crime Rate	46
Law Enforcement Employees	28
Corrections Employees	47
State Corrections Spending	27
Increase in State Corrections Spending	42
Law Enforcement Spending	45
Law Enforcement Spending as a Percentage of General Spending	43

Transportation · Section K

Travel on Interstates	38
Interstate Mileage in "Unacceptable" Condition	10
Deficient Bridges	13
Traffic Deaths	36
Seat Belt Use	n/a
Vehicle-Miles Traveled Per Capita	32
Use of Public Transportation	37
Road and Street Miles	13
Highway Employees	13
Public Transit Employees	41
Highway Spending Per Capita	29
Highway Spending as a Percentage of General Spending	27

Welfare · Section L

Births to Unwed Mothers	48
TANF Recipients	29
Change in TANF/AFDC Recipients	46
Food Stamp Recipients	50
SSI Recipients	49
WIC Average Monthly Benefit	46
NSLP Recipients	40
Condition of Children Index	1
Families with Single Parent	40
Average Monthly TANF Payments	16
Welfare as a Percentage of Poverty-Level Income	11
State Supplements of SSI	36
State Income Tax Liability of Typical Family in Poverty	n/a
Child Support Collections	34
Child Support Collections Per Dollar of Administrative Costs	27
Children in Foster Care	44
Welfare Spending Per Capita	19
Welfare Spending as a Percentage of General Spending	14
Administrative Costs Per TANF Case	30

Technology · Section M

Households with Computers	3
Percentage Using Internet	2
Zip Codes with Broadband Service	1
High-Tech Jobs	8
Change in High-Tech Jobs	1
State Government Web Site Ratings	34
Number of Online Government Services	30
Students Per Computer	2
Students Per Internet-Connected Computer	14
Public Library Internet Terminals	8

New Jersey

New Jersey

New Mexico

"Own-Source" General Revenue	31
Per Capita Non-Tax Revenue	14
Per Capita Total Spending	23
General Spending as a Percentage of Income	3
Per Capita General Spending	17
Change in General Expenditures	17
State Government General Revenue	9
State Government General Spending	7
State Government General Fund Spending	6
State and Local Debt	31
Debt as a Percentage of Revenue	32
Per Capita Full Faith and Credit Debt	29
Bond Ratings	2
State Solvency Index	3
Pension Plan Assets	26
State Reserves	20
Capital Outlays and Interest	40
State Budget Process Quality	8
Relative State Spending "Needs"	46
Structural Deficits	32

Education · Section H

Math Proficiency, Eighth Grade	48
Reading Proficiency, Eighth Grade	47
AFQT Ranks	47
SAT Scores	n/a
ACT Scores	23
Population Over 25 with a High School Diploma	44
Students in Private Schools	37
High School Dropout Rates	13
Pupil-Teacher Ratio	23
Public School Enrollment	11
Library Holdings Per Capita	30
Children with Disabilities	15
Education Spending Per Capita	9
Education Spending as a Percentage of General Spending	14
Spending Per Pupil	25
Average Teacher Salary	36
Sources of School Funds	48
State Aid Per Pupil	6
Per Capita Higher Education Spending	8
Higher Education Spending as a Percentage of General Spending	7
Public Higher Education Enrollment	2
Per Pupil Support of Higher Education	12
In-State Tuition and Fees	50
Out-of-State Tuition and Fees	35
Change in Tuition and Fees	50
Affordability Index	10
Average Professor Salary	46

Education Employees	17
R and D Spending	1
Library Operating Spending	38
Head Start Spending	25

Health · Section I

Immunization Rates	31
Infant Mortality Rates	30
State Health Rankings	40
Population without Health Insurance	3
Abortions	21
Alcohol Consumption	16
Percentage of Adult Smokers	20
Percentage Obese	40
AIDS Cases	29
Physicians Per 100,000 Population	32
Hospital Beds Per 1,000 Population	48
Medicaid Recipients	5
Medicaid Recipients as a Percentage of Poverty Population	28
Health and Hospital Spending	25
Health and Hospital Spending as a Percentage of General Spending	29
Per Capita Medicaid Spending	9
Medicaid Spending Per Aged	24
Medicaid Spending Per Child	9
Medicare Payment Per Hospital Day	19
Hospital Expense Per Inpatient Day	16
Population in HMOs	17
Prescription Drugs as a Percentage of Health Care Spending	44
Average Annual Increase in Health Care Expenditures	13

Crime · Section J

Crime Rate	7
Violent Crime Rate	5
Murder Rate	6
Property Crime Rate	10
Motor Vehicle Theft Rate	14
Violent Crime Rate Change	37
Prisoners	37
Change in Prisoners	14
Incarceration Rate	31
Juvenile Violent Crime Rate	24
Law Enforcement Employees	11
Corrections Employees	2
State Corrections Spending	23
Increase in State Corrections Spending	50
Law Enforcement Spending	11
Law Enforcement Spending as a Percentage of General Spending	10

Transportation · Section K

Travel on Interstates	4
Interstate Mileage in "Unacceptable" Condition	45
Deficient Bridges	40
Traffic Deaths	8
Seat Belt Use	9
Vehicle-Miles Traveled Per Capita	6
Use of Public Transportation	30
Road and Street Miles	16
Highway Employees	25
Public Transit Employees	22
Highway Spending Per Capita	23
Highway Spending as a Percentage of General Spending	31

Welfare · Section L

Births to Unwed Mothers	2
TANF Recipients	4
Change in TANF/AFDC Recipients	33
Food Stamp Recipients	8
SSI Recipients	10
WIC Average Monthly Benefit	23
NSLP Recipients	25
Condition of Children Index	48
Families with Single Parent	5
Average Monthly TANF Payments	27
Welfare as a Percentage of Poverty-Level Income	25
State Supplements of SSI	22
State Income Tax Liability of Typical Family in Poverty	32
Child Support Collections	50
Child Support Collections Per Dollar of Administrative Costs	50
Children in Foster Care	42
Welfare Spending Per Capita	9
Welfare Spending as a Percentage of General Spending	13
Administrative Costs Per TANF Case	48

Technology · Section M

Households with Computers	46
Percentage Using Internet	47
Zip Codes with Broadband Service	26
High-Tech Jobs	5
Change in High-Tech Jobs	41
State Government Web Site Ratings	44
Number of Online Government Services	28
Students Per Computer	31
Students Per Internet-Connected Computer	32
Public Library Internet Terminals	21

New York

North Carolina

"Own-Source" General Revenue	37	Education Employees	36	**Transportation · Section K**	
Per Capita Non-Tax Revenue	37	R and D Spending	25		
Per Capita Total Spending	38	Library Operating Spending	42	Travel on Interstates	44
General Spending as a Percentage of		Head Start Spending	13	Interstate Mileage in	
Income	31			"Unacceptable" Condition	18

North Dakota

"Own-Source" General Revenue	26
Per Capita Non-Tax Revenue	7
Per Capita Total Spending	26
General Spending as a Percentage of Income	13
Per Capita General Spending	18
Change in General Expenditures	47
State Government General Revenue	12
State Government General Spending	15
State Government General Fund Spending	14
State and Local Debt	36
Debt as a Percentage of Revenue	48
Per Capita Full Faith and Credit Debt	43
Bond Ratings	n/a
State Solvency Index	4
Pension Plan Assets	42
State Reserves	3
Capital Outlays and Interest	18
State Budget Process Quality	36
Relative State Spending "Needs"	39
Structural Deficits	10

Education - Section H

Math Proficiency, Eighth Grade	3
Reading Proficiency, Eighth Grade	2
AFQT Ranks	15
SAT Scores	n/a
ACT Scores	13
Population Over 25 with a High School Diploma	10
Students in Private Schools	39
High School Dropout Rates	45
Pupil-Teacher Ratio	43
Public School Enrollment	41
Library Holdings Per Capita	9
Children with Disabilities	32
Education Spending Per Capita	11
Education Spending as a Percentage of General Spending	16
Spending Per Pupil	37
Average Teacher Salary	49
Sources of School Funds	13
State Aid Per Pupil	44
Per Capita Higher Education Spending	2
Higher Education Spending as a Percentage of General Spending	3
Public Higher Education Enrollment	1
Per Pupil Support of Higher Education	26
In-State Tuition and Fees	27
Out-of-State Tuition and Fees	43
Change in Tuition and Fees	10
Affordability Index	36
Average Professor Salary	45

Education Employees	25
R and D Spending	31
Library Operating Spending	44
Head Start Spending	15

Health - Section I

Immunization Rates	10
Infant Mortality Rates	39
State Health Rankings	8
Population without Health Insurance	34
Abortions	29
Alcohol Consumption	9
Percentage of Adult Smokers	31
Percentage Obese	19
AIDS Cases	47
Physicians Per 100,000 Population	30
Hospital Beds Per 1,000 Population	2
Medicaid Recipients	47
Medicaid Recipients as a Percentage of Poverty Population	47
Health and Hospital Spending	48
Health and Hospital Spending as a Percentage of General Spending	48
Per Capita Medicaid Spending	36
Medicaid Spending Per Aged	6
Medicaid Spending Per Child	27
Medicare Payment Per Hospital Day	43
Hospital Expense Per Inpatient Day	18
Population in HMOs	48
Prescription Drugs as a Percentage of Health Care Spending	30
Average Annual Increase in Health Care Expenditures	46

Crime - Section J

Crime Rate	48
Violent Crime Rate	50
Murder Rate	50
Property Crime Rate	48
Motor Vehicle Theft Rate	45
Violent Crime Rate Change	1
Prisoners	50
Change in Prisoners	1
Incarceration Rate	21
Juvenile Violent Crime Rate	48
Law Enforcement Employees	47
Corrections Employees	48
State Corrections Spending	20
Increase in State Corrections Spending	16
Law Enforcement Spending	50
Law Enforcement Spending as a Percentage of General Spending	50

Transportation - Section K

Travel on Interstates	32
Interstate Mileage in "Unacceptable" Condition	19
Deficient Bridges	31
Traffic Deaths	19
Seat Belt Use	35
Vehicle-Miles Traveled Per Capita	9
Use of Public Transportation	45
Road and Street Miles	44
Highway Employees	4
Public Transit Employees	43
Highway Spending Per Capita	3
Highway Spending as a Percentage of General Spending	2

Welfare - Section L

Births to Unwed Mothers	44
TANF Recipients	28
Change in TANF/AFDC Recipients	44
Food Stamp Recipients	39
SSI Recipients	46
WIC Average Monthly Benefit	8
NSLP Recipients	8
Condition of Children Index	9
Families with Single Parent	44
Average Monthly TANF Payments	30
Welfare as a Percentage of Poverty-Level Income	18
State Supplements of SSI	4
State Income Tax Liability of Typical Family in Poverty	17
Child Support Collections	9
Child Support Collections Per Dollar of Administrative Costs	11
Children in Foster Care	15
Welfare Spending Per Capita	20
Welfare Spending as a Percentage of General Spending	23
Administrative Costs Per TANF Case	26

Technology - Section M

Households with Computers	27
Percentage Using Internet	31
Zip Codes with Broadband Service	1
High-Tech Jobs	32
Change in High-Tech Jobs	14
State Government Web Site Ratings	13
Number of Online Government Services	21
Students Per Computer	44
Students Per Internet-Connected Computer	43
Public Library Internet Terminals	13

Ohio

Oklahoma

Oregon

Pennsylvania

Pennsylvania

Rhode Island

Population · Section A

Population 2006	43
Population 2005	43
Population Change 2004–2005	50
Population Change 1995–2005	36
Population Change 2005–2015	27
Population 2025	43
Percentage 65 and Over	8
Percentage 17 and Under	41
Median Age	13
Percentage African American	28
Percentage American Indian	23
Percentage Asian American	16
Percentage Hispanic	13
Percentage White (Non-Hispanic)	23
Percentage Mixed-Race	12
Percentage in Poverty	22
Child Poverty Rate	19
Percentage Female	1
Birth Rates	45
Death Rates	41
Population Density	2
Legal Immigrants FY 2005	34
Unauthorized Immigrants	39

Economies · Section B

Personal Income 2005	43
Gross State Product	21
Per Capita Personal Income	17
Personal Income from Wages and Salaries	40
Average Annual Pay	20
Average Hourly Earnings	49
Value Added in Manufacturing	32
Cost of Living	7
Average Annual Pay in Manufacturing	38
Average Annual Pay in Retailing	16
Labor Force	15
Unemployment Rate	10
Employment Rate	41
Government Employment	47
Manufacturing Employment	24
Construction Employment	40
Fortune 500 Companies	3
Tourism Spending Per Capita	41
Exports Per Capita	43
Housing Permits	50
Percentage Change in Home Prices	7
Net Farm Income	49
Financial Institution Assets	16
Bankruptcy Filings	39
Patents Issued	15
WC Disability Payment	12
Average Weekly UC Benefit	5
Economic Momentum	47

One-year Employment Change	48
Manufacturing Employment Change	44
Home Ownership	47
Annual Electricity Use Per Residential Customer	47
Cost Per Kwh	48
New Companies	17

Geography · Section C

Total Land Area	50
Federally Owned Land	50
State Park Acreage	50
State Park Visitors	9
Population Not Active	17
Hunters with Firearms	43
Registered Boats	46
State Spending for the Arts	3
Energy Consumption Per Capita	50
Toxic Chemical Release Per Capita	50
Hazardous Waste Sites	31
Drinking Water Quality	34
Expired Water Pollution Permits	15
Air Pollution Emissions	50

Government · Section D

Members of United States House	39
State Legislators	37
Legislators Per Million Population	8
Units of Government	44
Legislators Compensation	34
Female Legislators	32
Turnover in Legislatures	29
Term Limits	n/a
Legislative Session Length	5
Republicans in State Legislatures	47
Governors' Power Rating	49
Number of Statewide Elected Officials	34
State and Local Government Employees	48
State and Local Average Salaries	5
Local Employment	46
Local Spending Accountability	12
Registered Voters	12
Percentage of Population Voting	10
Statewide Initiatives	n/a
Campaign Costs Per Vote	12

Federal Impacts · Section E

Per Capita Federal Spending	20
Increase in Federal Spending	45
Per Capita Federal Grant Spending	8
Per Capita Federal Spending on Procurement	41

Per Capita Federal Spending on Payments to Individuals	15
Per Capita Federal Spending on Social Security and Medicare	7
Social Security Benefits	19
Federal Spending on Employee Wages and Salaries	19
Per Capita Federal Defense Spending	28
Per Capita Homeland Security Grants	15
Federal Grant Spending Per Dollar of State Tax Revenue	16
General Revenue from Federal Government	13
Federal Tax Burden Per Capita	15
Federal Spending Per Dollar of Taxes Paid	30
Highway Charges Returned to States	2
Terms of Trade	15
Federal Personal Income Taxes	18
Federal Share of Medicaid	37

Taxes · Section F

Tax Revenue	5
Per Capita Tax Revenue	7
Tax Effort	3
Tax Capacity	28
Percentage Change in Taxes	9
Property Taxes as a Percentage of Income	4
Property Taxes Per Capita	5
Property Tax Revenue as a Percentage of 3-tax Revenue	9
Sales Taxes as a Percentage of Income	26
Sales Taxes Per Capita	19
Sales Tax Revenue as a Percentage of 3-tax Revenue	37
Sales Tax Rate	1
Income Taxes as a Percentage of Income	19
Income Taxes Per Capita	17
Income Tax Revenue as a Percentage of 3-tax Revenue	30
Highest Personal Income Rate	5
Corporate Income Taxes	34
Motor Fuel Taxes	4
Motor Vehicle Fees	24
Tobacco Taxes	1
Taxes on High-Income Families	4
Taxes in the Largest City in Each State	3
Progressivity of Taxes	8
Estate Tax as a Share of Total Revenue	8

Revenues and Finances · Section G

Per Capita Total Revenue	9
Per Capita General Revenue	9

South Carolina

South Dakota

Tennessee

Texas

"Own-Source" General Revenue	38
Per Capita Non-Tax Revenue	35
Per Capita Total Spending	41
General Spending as a Percentage of Income	39
Per Capita General Spending	43
Change in General Expenditures	10
State Government General Revenue	48
State Government General Spending	50
State Government General Fund Spending	48
State and Local Debt	18
Debt as a Percentage of Revenue	7
Per Capita Full Faith and Credit Debt	16
Bond Ratings	2
State Solvency Index	7
Pension Plan Assets	33
State Reserves	15
Capital Outlays and Interest	14
State Budget Process Quality	29
Relative State Spending "Needs"	45
Structural Deficits	44

Education - Section H

Math Proficiency, Eighth Grade	20
Reading Proficiency, Eighth Grade	36
AFQT Ranks	32
SAT Scores	18
ACT Scores	n/a
Population Over 25 with a High School Diploma	50
Students in Private Schools	43
High School Dropout Rates	26
Pupil-Teacher Ratio	25
Public School Enrollment	3
Library Holdings Per Capita	41
Children with Disabilities	48
Education Spending Per Capita	25
Education Spending as a Percentage of General Spending	2
Spending Per Pupil	41
Average Teacher Salary	35
Sources of School Funds	12
State Aid Per Pupil	47
Per Capita Higher Education Spending	23
Higher Education Spending as a Percentage of General Spending	15
Public Higher Education Enrollment	17
Per Pupil Support of Higher Education	27
In-State Tuition and Fees	23
Out-of-State Tuition and Fees	26
Change in Tuition and Fees	22
Affordability Index	10
Average Professor Salary	18

Education Employees	6
R and D Spending	20
Library Operating Spending	45
Head Start Spending	22

Health - Section I

Immunization Rates	31
Infant Mortality Rates	35
State Health Rankings	37
Population without Health Insurance	1
Abortions	21
Alcohol Consumption	31
Percentage of Adult Smokers	32
Percentage Obese	11
AIDS Cases	12
Physicians Per 100,000 Population	40
Hospital Beds Per 1,000 Population	30
Medicaid Recipients	34
Medicaid Recipients as a Percentage of Poverty Population	48
Health and Hospital Spending	23
Health and Hospital Spending as a Percentage of General Spending	18
Per Capita Medicaid Spending	37
Medicaid Spending Per Aged	41
Medicaid Spending Per Child	30
Medicare Payment Per Hospital Day	8
Hospital Expense Per Inpatient Day	34
Population in HMOs	32
Prescription Drugs as a Percentage of Health Care Spending	39
Average Annual Increase in Health Care Expenditures	15

Crime - Section J

Crime Rate	6
Violent Crime Rate	12
Murder Rate	14
Property Crime Rate	6
Motor Vehicle Theft Rate	15
Violent Crime Rate Change	34
Prisoners	2
Change in Prisoners	40
Incarceration Rate	14
Juvenile Violent Crime Rate	29
Law Enforcement Employees	34
Corrections Employees	7
State Corrections Spending	41
Increase in State Corrections Spending	46
Law Enforcement Spending	26
Law Enforcement Spending as a Percentage of General Spending	13

Transportation - Section K

Travel on Interstates	28
Interstate Mileage in "Unacceptable" Condition	36
Deficient Bridges	36
Traffic Deaths	23
Seat Belt Use	9
Vehicle-Miles Traveled Per Capita	29
Use of Public Transportation	23
Road and Street Miles	11
Highway Employees	40
Public Transit Employees	18
Highway Spending Per Capita	36
Highway Spending as a Percentage of General Spending	29

Welfare - Section L

Births to Unwed Mothers	21
TANF Recipients	41
Change in TANF/AFDC Recipients	11
Food Stamp Recipients	15
SSI Recipients	20
WIC Average Monthly Benefit	43
NSLP Recipients	17
Condition of Children Index	39
Families with Single Parent	18
Average Monthly TANF Payments	44
Welfare as a Percentage of Poverty-Level Income	45
State Supplements of SSI	48
State Income Tax Liability of Typical Family in Poverty	n/a
Child Support Collections	20
Child Support Collections Per Dollar of Administrative Costs	5
Children in Foster Care	49
Welfare Spending Per Capita	48
Welfare Spending as a Percentage of General Spending	42
Administrative Costs Per TANF Case	11

Technology - Section M

Households with Computers	38
Percentage Using Internet	36
Zip Codes with Broadband Service	26
High-Tech Jobs	13
Change in High-Tech Jobs	37
State Government Web Site Ratings	1
Number of Online Government Services	1
Students Per Computer	38
Students Per Internet-Connected Computer	36
Public Library Internet Terminals	25

Utah

Vermont

Virginia

Virginia

Washington

West Virginia

Wisconsin

Wisconsin

Wyoming

Index